Second

BEHAVIOR MODIFICATION

Second Edition

BEHAVIOR MODIFICATION
Principles of Behavior Changes

Edward P. Sarafino
College of New Jersey

WAVELAND
PRESS, INC.
Long Grove, Illinois

For information about this book, contact:
Waveland Press, Inc.
4180 IL Route 83, Suite 101
Long Grove, IL 60047-9580
(847) 634-0081
info@waveland.com
www.waveland.com

To Precious

Brief Contents

Contents

Using Reinforcement to Increase Operant Behavior   109

CHAPTER FIVE

Methods to Decrease Operant Behavior   145

PART 3   Methods to Change Emotional Behavior and Associations   179

CHAPTER SIX

Behavioral Methods for Changing Respondent Behavior   179

CHAPTER 7 SEVEN

Covert Behavioral Methods for Changing
Respondent Behavior   207

PART 4 Program Design and Evaluation 231

CHAPTER EIGHT

Putting Techniques Together to Design a Program 231

CHAPTER NINE

Organizing and Using Data 255

Maintaining Behavior Changes   277

Research Methods in Behavior Modification   303

PART 5   Advanced and Specialized Methods in Behavior Modification   333

CHAPTER TWELVE

Token Economies   333

CHAPTER **13** THIRTEEN

Advanced Behavioral Methods for Therapy   355

CHAPTER **14** FOURTEEN

Cognitive-Behavioral Therapies   377

PART 6   Present and Future Issues for Behavior Modification   401

CHAPTER FIFTEEN

Current Concerns and Future Challenges   401

Preface

"Now that's a book I could use" a nonpsychologist friend said when I told him about the book I was writing on techniques for changing behavior. I hope you will respond in the same way as you read what I have written. Psychologists have discovered a great deal of information about human behavior, but not all of the knowledge we have gained can be applied to improve the way people behave and function in their everyday lives. The field of behavior modification is unique in this respect, having developed a rich and varied system of techniques, based on established principles of learning, that have been applied effectively to improve people's behavior. Applications of behavior change techniques have been successful in almost all areas of psychology and in a wide variety of settings.

My goal in writing this text has been to create a clear and engaging teaching instrument that describes the techniques psychologists and other professionals use in helping people change their behavior. I have drawn on research, theory, and my own experiences to explain and provide examples of the concepts and methods of behavior modification. I have endeavored to write a comprehensive text that is appropriate for several courses, especially those in *behavior modification, applied behavior analysis, behavior therapy*, and the *psychology of learning*.

Two general features of the students' backgrounds in these courses shaped my writing. First, the students who use this book are likely to come from a variety of fields, including psychology, education, counseling, social work, nursing, and allied medical areas such as physical and occupational therapy. I have tried to make the material interesting and relevant to all these readers. Second, the students who use this book are likely to vary in ability and level of academic preparation. I aimed to make the content appropriate for upper-division students, especially juniors, but the straightforward writing style also makes the material accessible to most sophomores. Although students will probably benefit from having taken an introductory psychology course, this is not essential for mastering the material.

The field of behavior modification is enormously exciting, partly because of its relevance to the lives of those who study it as well as to the individuals the students know or will work with in the future. The field is also exciting because its knowledge is applied in so many different settings and can be used to change one's own behavior. Creating a book that is comprehensive in its coverage of behavior change principles and up to date in each area of application is a challenge. I consulted thousands of articles and books in the process of writing this text, which cites about 1,000 references. For this edition of the book, I made several structural changes, added some new content, and thoroughly updated the reference materials.

OBJECTIVES AND DISTINCTIVE FEATURES OF THIS BOOK

Several important objectives guided the content and organization of my writing. This text was designed to

- Provide an understanding of the fundamental techniques of behavior modification by presenting its concepts and procedures in a logical sequence and by giving clear definitions and examples of each technique.
- Teach students how to pinpoint and define the behavior to be changed and how a response is determined by its antecedents and consequences.
- Teach usable, practical skills by specifically stating the purpose of each technique, describing how it is carried out, and presenting guidelines and tips to maximize its effectiveness.
- Describe why and how to design a program to change a behavioral deficit or excess by conducting a functional analysis and then selecting and combining techniques that can be directed at the behavior itself and its antecedents and consequences.
- Illustrate why and how to collect and analyze data.
- Provide students with a handbook to help them design and conduct interventions to modify behaviors (a) when they enter professional careers and (b) if they want to carry out a self-management program to improve their own behavior.

I organized the material in this book with two purposes in mind. First, I tried to present the material within and across chapters in an orderly sequence, thereby establishing each conceptual foundation on which to add new information and principles. Second, I sequenced the chapters so that the book presents all of the *basic techniques* by the end of Chapter 7, thereby enabling instructors to require that students design a simple intervention and submit it well before the end of the course. Chapter 8 focuses on putting techniques together to form a behavior change program. The interventions the students design can focus on their own behavior (a self-management program) or on the behavior of other individuals, such as a child they are working with in a field setting. Depending on the length of the course, instructors might also require students to collect and submit baseline data or to carry out their programs for as long as a month. While the students are engaging in these activities, they will be learning about data analysis methods and advanced techniques for changing behaviors in subsequent chapters.

HOW THIS TEXT IS ORGANIZED

The chapters and material within them are organized to build on relatively simple concepts and techniques toward increasingly complex and specialized methods. The book is divided into 15 chapters in the following six parts:

- *Part 1* introduces the student to the behavior modification approach, defines the basic concepts and processes, describes how behavior change principles have been applied effectively with a wide variety of behaviors in diverse settings, and provides some foundation skills for the design of and assessment in behavior change programs.

- *Part 2* deals with modifying operant behavior. It discusses in depth what antecedents and consequences (reinforcement, punishment, and extinction) are and methods to manage events to change operant behavior.

- *Part 3* examines basic respondent concepts and techniques, including overt and covert methods, and describes how to apply them to change emotional behavior and associations.

- *Part 4* focuses on program design and evaluation. It shows how to combine behavior modification techniques to form an effective program for changing behavior and describes ways to maintain behavior improvements and to evaluate a program's effectiveness. Students who are required to conduct a program will be able to use the material in these chapters to start their intervention, evaluate how well it is working, and add techniques to improve its effectiveness and to maintain the behavior when the intervention ends.

- *Part 5* examines specialized or advanced methods for changing behavior, such as token economies and clinical approaches professionals use in behavior therapy.

- *Part 6* consists of a chapter on concerns and future challenges for the field of behavior modification.

LEARNING AIDS

This book contains many pedagogical features. The chapter outline gives the student an overview of the chapter material and is followed by an engaging, relevant vignette. The body of each chapter includes many *figures* and *tables* to clarify concepts or research findings. For example, special figures were created to show how second-order conditioning occurs and how to collect data for a functional analysis. Graphs illustrate the effects of behavior modification methods on performance. *Key terms* are printed in **boldface** type; these terms are defined in the text and again in the *glossary* at the end of the book.

Three types of boxed material are incorporated throughout the text and are identified with signature icons. They are:

Concept Checks, in which students apply concepts or techniques to specific questions or problems to check their basic understanding of the material they have just read. In some cases, a question is followed by a ⇔, which identifies it as a "critical thinking" item for which more than one answer could be correct. These questions are intended to promote students' analytical and creative thinking about the concepts and procedures they've read about.

 Case Studies describe actual cases in which behavior modification techniques were applied. The person's behavior problem and the intervention are presented in rich detail, giving students an appreciation for how the procedures are conducted along with their impact and utility.

 Close-Ups present theoretical or controversial issues, in-depth conceptual topics and procedural steps, or important research.

Each chapter concludes with a *summary* followed by a list of *key terms*, relevant *review questions*, and suggested *related readings*.

INSTRUCTOR'S RESOURCE GUIDE

An instructor's resource guide contains a test bank and information to help instructors organize and present the subject matter effectively and design activities that enrich the classroom experience.

ACKNOWLEDGMENTS

Writing this book was a huge task. I am indebted first of all to the researchers whose important and creative work I have cited. Without such work, there would be no field of behavior modification. I also received a great deal of direct help and encouragement from a number of people whose contributions I gratefully acknowledge.

My heartfelt thanks go to Frank Graham, the acquisitions editor at Mayfield Publishing Company, who saw merit in my plan and signed the book. Other Mayfield staff helped establish my writing schedule, oversaw the review process, coordinated the production process, and generated the marketing plan. I also appreciate the fine work of Deneen Sedlack, Kay Mikel, Jeanne Schreiber, Glenda King, Robin Mouat, and Marty Granahan.

The cover-to-cover review process generated many helpful suggestions that have made this a better book than it would have been otherwise. I thank the reviewers of the present and past editions of the book for reinforcing me for the work I did and prodding me to do still better. Because the new edition retains many features of the earlier one, I continue to be indebted to the following reviewers who contributed to my preparation of the prior edition. These reviewers are: Henry Adams, University of Georgia; Gywneth Hill Beagley, Alma College; D. Wayne Mitchell, Southwest Missouri State University; Joseph Olmi, University of Southern Mississippi; Robert J.

Presbie, SUNY New Paltz; Brian Rabian, University of Southern Mississippi; Donald Schupe, California State Polytechnic University; A. Robert Sherman, University of California–Santa Barbara; Nelson Smith, University of Rhode Island; John Steffen, University of Cincinnati; and Richard Wesp, Elmira College.

The second edition has benefited greatly from the latest thorough review process and the excellent perspectives of Carl D. Cheney, Utah State University; Richard N. Feil, Mansfield University; Iver H. Iverson, University of North Florida; and Kenneth N. Wildman, Ohio Northern University.

Many other individuals helped too. I thank my very good friend and colleague Jim Armstrong, who read and commented on the first edition chapters before they went out for review. The first edition also benefited from the feedback I received from my students, who used a draft of the book as their text, and from the help of assistants who photocopied hundreds of journal articles. For the second edition, I thank my assistant Wataru Utaka and the staff at The College of New Jersey library, who acquired copies of journal articles and other needed materials.

Very personal thanks go to the closest people in my life—family, friends, and colleagues—for encouraging and supporting my efforts to complete this book and tolerating my preoccupation.

To the Student

"I wish I could eat healthier" a student said, deciding to change her own behavior. But what does her statement mean? She might eat healthier in many different ways. She could eat foods that are lower in calories, lower in saturated fats, higher in fiber, or just better balanced. What specifically should she do or not do? One of the first topics we will consider in this book is the importance of identifying and defining the behavior we wish to change. Once we've established how to define a problem behavior exactly, we'll examine the many techniques behavior modification has to offer in helping to improve people's behavior. You will find that these techniques have been used effectively in psychotherapy, education, parenting, business and industry, and health promotion.

As you learn about the principles of behavior change, you'll discover two appealing features: (1) the material is *personally relevant*, and (2) many of the things you learn can actually be *applied* in your everyday life. Although taking a course in behavior modification and reading this book will not make you an expert in changing people's behavior, you will learn skills to use in your own life and you will acquire an understanding of what behavior modification techniques are and how professionals use them. What you learn in this course will lay the foundation for gaining more training in behavior modification so that you may enter a career in which you can apply its techniques to help other people.

THE BOOK

This book was designed for you, the reader. First and foremost, it provides a thorough and up-to-date presentation of the major issues, theories, concepts, and research in behavior modification. The material throughout the book is organized to build on relatively simple concepts and techniques toward increasingly more complex and specialized methods. Because some of the concepts are complex and technical, I have made a special effort to write in a straightforward, clear, and engaging fashion.

To help you master the material and remember it longer, the book includes the following learning aids:

- *Chapter Outline and Vignette*. Each chapter begins with an outline of the major topics in the order in which they are covered. This is followed by a vignette that is relevant to the material ahead and gives an overview of the basic ideas you will read about.

- *Illustrations.* The many figures and tables in each chapter are designed to clarify concepts and research findings and help them stick in your mind.

- *Concept Checks.* Each chapter contains boxed quizzes at appropriate intervals to check your basic understanding of the material you have just read. The symbol ⇔ identifies the question as a "critical thinking" item for which more than one answer could be correct. These questions are intended to get you thinking analytically and creatively about the concepts and procedures you've read about.

- *Summary.* Each chapter has a substantial summary, which presents the most important ideas covered.

- *Key Terms and Review Questions.* Following the summary are two features: a list of the most important terms in the chapter, arranged in order of their appearance, and a set of essay-type review questions.

- *Glossary.* The glossary at the back of the book gives definitions of important terms and concepts. It will be useful when you are studying or reading and are not sure of the exact meaning of a term.

Each type of boxed material—Concept Checks, Case Studies, and Close-Ups—is identified with a special icon, and "Go to" instructions are included in the text. This instruction will prompt you to read the nearby boxed material that has the same icon.

STUDY HINTS

You can use the features of this book in many ways to learn and study well, and you may want to "experiment" to find the best way for you. I will describe one method that works well for many students.

Survey the chapter first. Read the chapter outline and browse through the chapter, examining the figures and tables. Some students also find it useful to read the summary first, even though it contains terms they may not yet understand. Then read the opening vignette. As you begin each new section of the chapter, look at its title and turn it into a *question*. Thus, the heading early in Chapter 1, "Acquiring and Changing Behavior Through Learning," might become "How can learning help us acquire and change behavior?" Doing this helps you focus on your reading. After reading the section, *reflect* on what you have just read. Can you answer the question you asked when you reworded the title?

When you have finished the body of the chapter, *review* what you have read by reading the summary. Next, define the items in the key terms list. If there is an item you do not understand, look it up in the chapter or the glossary. Then develop in your mind an answer for each of the review questions. Lastly, *reread* the chapter at least once, concentrating on the important concepts or ideas. You may find it helpful to underline or highlight selected material now that you have a good idea of what is important. If your exam will consist of "objective" questions, such as multiple choice, using this approach intensively should be effective. If your exam will have essay items, you will probably find it helpful to answer the review questions carefully, completely, and in writing.

I hope you enjoy this book and learn a great deal from it. I also hope you will share my enthusiasm and fascination for behavior modification by the time you finish the course.

Behavior Modification

B. F. Skinner (1904–1990) was a pioneer in and founder of behavior modification.

CHAPTER ONE

What Is Behavior Modification?

W
hat do you think this study was about, Karen?" Joel asked a student who had participated in his psychology experiment. "I don't know—nothing much happened," she replied. Her tone suggested she was very curious to know the answer. Actually something important did happen, but Karen didn't realize it. When she arrived at the laboratory an hour ago, Joel had her sit in a chair and instructed her simply to "say all the words you can think of. Say them individually. Do not use sentences or phrases. Do not count. Please continue until I say stop." Joel sat behind her and said nothing, except the sound "mmm-hmm" occasionally, while she recited words for 50 minutes. (The sound Joel made was pronounced "mmm-HMM," the way an English speaker might simply acknowledge something a person said.)

What happened that was so important? Joel was very careful about when he said "mmm-hmm." He only said it when Karen said a plural noun, such as "chairs" or "books." He never said it when she said anything else. Within just a few minutes, her behavior changed dramatically: she began saying lots of plural nouns and kept on saying them as long as Joel said "mmm-hmm"! But she didn't realize she was doing this or that Joel's behavior was linked in any specific way to what she said.

This story, composed on the basis of a classic experiment by Joel Greenspoon (1955), illustrates that environmental events can modify specific behaviors substantially. This is true for almost all behaviors people perform, not just reciting plural nouns. Our behavior in everyday life occurs in the context of *external* events, such as the behavior of other people in our environment, and *internal* events, such as our thoughts and physiological processes. These are naturally occurring events that influence how we behave, regardless of whether we are aware of their effects. By using organized and systematic methods to regulate these events, we can help people change their behavior.

This chapter introduces the field of *behavior modification*—the well-established and exciting approach to understanding and changing people's behavior. We will first examine what behavior is and how it is acquired. Then we will look at some basic characteristics and techniques of behavior modification, chart the history of the field, and consider some examples of effective applications in changing people's behavior.

BEHAVIOR—WHAT IT IS AND WHAT IT ISN'T

Because this book focuses on ways to change behavior, we need to be very specific about what behavior is and is not. The term **behavior** refers to anything a person does, typically in response to internal or external events. When Karen answered "I don't know" to Joel's question about what the study was about, her verbal behavior was in response to an external event. When you feel hungry and go to the kitchen to eat, you are responding to an internal event: feeling hungry. In each case we can describe the individual's specific *actions* or *responses*. Sometimes the behavior we want to change is fairly simple, such as raising one's hand when a teacher asks a question, and sometimes it involves a sequence of actions, as in making a sandwich.

External and Internal Behaviors

The behaviors we have considered so far have been external or *overt*, open to view or observation. There are two types of overt behaviors, verbal and motor. *Verbal behaviors* are actions that require the use of language. Karen's answering Joel's question and reciting words are examples of verbal behavior. *Motor behaviors* involve body movement, without requiring the use of language. Grasping a doorknob is an example of a motor behavior, and swinging a baseball bat, getting dressed, and walking up a flight of stairs are other examples. Some activities, such as filling out a crossword puzzle, require both verbal and motor components. Overt behaviors have been and continue to be the main focus of behavior modification.

But not all behaviors we can change are overt (Homme, 1965; Scott, Scott, & Howe, 1973). Some behaviors are internal or *covert*, not viewable or openly shown. Suppose you hear a "special" song on the radio, which leads you to think about a romantic date you had with your boyfriend or girlfriend. Thinking about that date is a response to an event, but the response is not viewable. Suppose hearing that song also produces inside you some emotions, such as happiness or sadness, and physiological changes, such as increased heart rate. These responses are also covert. You may show some outward signs—for example, facial or verbal expressions—of what's happening internally, but people's outward signs do not always reflect their covert behaviors accurately. An important difference between overt and covert behaviors is that overt behaviors can be measured directly, whereas covert behaviors must be measured either indirectly, perhaps through self-reports, or with special equipment.

What Is Not Behavior?

If I asked you to describe your best friend's behavior, what would you say? Chances are, you wouldn't describe specific behaviors. You'd probably focus on your friend's prominent *traits*, or broad and stable characteristics. You might answer, for instance, "Oh, Nancy's really nice. She's considerate, friendly, honest, smart, and creative. But she's not very conscientious." We tend to focus on broad characteristics to describe a person's behavior because they provide a convenient and efficient way to communicate a lot of information. Although you may have decided Nancy is smart because of specific behaviors you've observed, "smart" is not a behavior. In fact, none of the adjectives in the answer describe a behavior.

One problem with using broad characteristics as if they were behaviors is that they can be misleading and inconsistent. For example, you may have decided that Nancy is "honest" because you've seen her return money that didn't belong to her and "considerate" because you've heard her lie to protect other people's feelings. Aren't these observations inconsistent? Or are the terms "honest" and "considerate" misleading? Another problem with using broad characteristics is that they are imprecise—they don't tell us specifically what we would need to change to improve a person's behavior. Consider Nancy's lack of conscientiousness. In all likelihood, she's conscientious in some ways, but not in others. Perhaps she almost always keeps promises to friends and gets to her part-time job on time, but she rarely cleans her room and often fails to finish her college assignments and studying on time. If we wanted to help improve her conscientiousness, we would focus on specific behaviors involved in cleaning her room and doing her schoolwork. The more precise we are in describing the behavior to be changed, the more successful we are likely to be in measuring and improving the behavior.

In clinical practice, therapists generally use *diagnoses* to classify clients. One client is diagnosed as severely depressed, and another client is schizophrenic. One child is mentally retarded, and another is autistic. The advantages and problems associated with using diagnoses are similar to those associated with using traits: diagnoses are efficient for communicating, but they can be imprecise, and they do not always indicate what specific behaviors need to be changed. Therapists make diagnoses on the basis of behaviors that are common to individuals who have the condition. For example, children receiving the diagnosis of autism tend to have several of the following behavioral characteristics (Lovaas, 1977):

- Absence of speech or severely impaired speech with unusual patterns, such as echoing the speech of others
- Lack of awareness of salient sounds and objects around them
- Indifference to being liked; little or no affection
- Frequent behaviors that seem to provide only self-stimulation: rocking back and forth incessantly, for example, or fluttering their hands in front of their eyes
- Absence or severe impairment of self-help behaviors, such as grooming and dressing themselves, and inability to protect themselves from physical danger
- Frequent and severe self-injurious behaviors, such as biting their arms

But most autistic children have only some of these characteristics and differ in the severity of the specific deficits they show. Knowing simply that a child is autistic does not tell therapists how to help the child. Therapists must assess and try to improve the child's specific behaviors.

Last, the *outcomes of behavior* are not behaviors. People who apply behavior change techniques to produce an outcome of, say, losing weight or improving grades, often misdirect their focus toward the outcome rather than the behavior change needed to reach the outcome. In the example of losing weight, the behavior involves (1) what and how much people eat and (2) how much physical exercise they get, not how much they weigh, which is the outcome of their behavior. Individuals who focus their efforts toward the outcome often fail to identify and deal effectively with the specific behaviors they need to change.

How Behavior Develops

Human babies come into the world with only a small number of well-formed, inborn behaviors. These inborn behaviors are called *reflexes*. Several reflexes have obvious survival value for infants because they are useful in feeding, maintaining physiological functioning, and protecting the baby against injury (Sarafino & Armstrong, 1986). For example, two reflexes that are important for feeding are the *rooting reflex*, in which the baby turns its head toward an object that lightly touches its cheek, and the *sucking reflex*, in which the baby starts to suck when its lips are touched with any small rounded object, such as a nipple or finger. Inborn reflexive behaviors are inherited.

Virtually all other behaviors develop after birth, and their development depends on two processes: heredity and experience. Heredity affects behavioral development in at least two ways (Sarafino & Armstrong, 1986). First, it charts the course of the individual's *maturation*, or physical growth, including growth of the muscle and nervous systems. In the earliest years, physical growth is fastest in the head and upper trunk of the body; it speeds up later in the lower trunk, arms, and legs. This is why a 3-year-old child's head is large relative to the legs, as compared with the bodies of older children and adults. Growth and coordination of the muscle and nervous systems follow the same pattern, showing the fastest advances in the head and upper body in the earliest years and spreading down the arms and legs later. This is why typical 3-year-olds can put on a pullover sweater but cannot tie their shoelaces. Maturation determines when motor actions become possible. Second, hereditary factors provide the foundation for or tendency toward developing behaviors of certain types. For instance, studies have found that people's inheritance influences the likelihood that they will develop a wide variety of behavioral problems, including stuttering (Scarr & Kidd, 1983), severe anxieties (Torgersen, 1983), autism (Cantwell & Baker, 1984), and alcoholism (Goodwin, 1986). The influence of heredity in developing some behaviors is moderately strong, but it is fairly mild for many other behaviors. Experience plays an important role—and is usually the dominant factor—in the development of almost all human behaviors. This role occurs through the process called *learning*. (Go to ☑ —As described in the

CONCEPT CHECK 1.1

Pause now to check your understanding of the concepts you've just read about. Read these five statements about people. In the space following each statement, write "OB" if it describes an overt behavior, "CB" if it describes a covert behavior, "T" if it describes a trait, or "O" if it describes an outcome of behavior.

1. Elly was a very dependable student. _____
2. Jim laughed at the joke. _____
3. Joe developed strong bicep muscles at the gym. _____
4. Dolores dreamed about a spider last night. _____
5. Tony was a motivated employee. _____

Answers: 1. T, 2. OB, 3. O, 4. CB, 5. T

preface, this instruction means that you should read the nearby boxed material that has the same icon.)

ACQUIRING AND CHANGING BEHAVIOR THROUGH LEARNING

People talk a lot about learning things. They say, for instance, "Ginny learned to brush her teeth a few months ago" or "Morry learned the multiplication tables in school" or "I learned to use my new computer software last week" or "I learned to like Japanese food when I was an exchange student in Tokyo." We decide that individuals have learned things by seeing changes in their behavior—assuming we can rule out other influences on behavior, such as an injury that causes a person to walk differently. But what exactly do we mean by the term "learning"? A definition is difficult to frame because learning is an internal process that applies to such a wide range of behaviors, and people don't always display what they have learned. The definition we will use takes these difficulties into account: **learning** is a relatively permanent change in behavioral tendency as a result of experience.

In the next sections, we'll see how different varieties of experiences lead to relatively permanent changes in behavior. The types of learning we will consider will be discussed briefly here and examined in more detail in later chapters. We'll begin with the type of learning called *respondent* (or "classical") *conditioning*.

Respondent Conditioning

Let's first demonstrate an example of respondent conditioning in your life. Sit back, relax, and concentrate on the *name* of your favorite food. Does the name remind you of

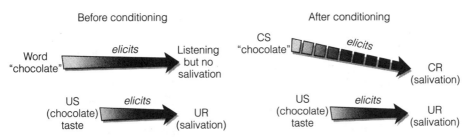

Figure 1.1 The respondent conditioning events. *Before conditioning,* the first couple of times your parents gave you chocolate, their saying, "Here's some chocolate" elicited some listening behavior, but no salivation. You didn't yet associate the word "chocolate" with the US, the taste of chocolate. *After conditioning,* you began to associate the word "chocolate," now a CS, with having the taste in your mouth. The CS could then elicit salivation as a CR. Note that the dashed arrow indicates a learned association. Once conditioning has occurred, the CS can elicit the CR without the US being present, as we showed in our demonstration.

eating that food? If so, fine—you may let your imagination take over. Enjoy how tempting it looks and smells. Savor the delectable taste and allow it to linger in your mouth. . . . Are you salivating more now? If so, this illustrates your learned reaction to the *name* of a food. The flow of saliva is the result of prior respondent conditioning.

This example is a lot like the first laboratory demonstrations of respondent conditioning reported in 1927 by Ivan Pavlov, the Russian Nobel-prize-winning physiologist. Pavlov was studying the role of salivation in dogs' digestive processes when he noticed that the dogs began to salivate before the food was actually in their mouths. From this observation he correctly concluded that the association between the *stimulus,* such as the sight of food, and the salivary *response* must be a learned one. Moreover, he proposed that this learned relationship was formed through its association with the *reflexive,* or automatic, connection between food in the mouth and salivation. Pavlov later showed that virtually any stimulus, such as a light or a tone, regularly associated with this reflexive connection could produce the salivary response.

In our demonstration you salivated in response to the *name* of your favorite food— say, "chocolate." In the past, the name of that food has been frequently associated with eating it: "Oh, that's to-die-for chocolate," you'd think while eating it. The presence of food in one's mouth *elicits* or produces salivation reflexively, or *without prior conditioning.* Thus, food in the mouth is an example of an **unconditioned stimulus** (US)—an event that automatically produces a specific response—and the automatic response to that stimulus is called the **unconditioned response** (UR). Although this reflexive association was not learned, your associating salivation to the *name* of the food was learned through the experience diagrammed in Figure 1.1. We know it was learned because you surely didn't salivate to the word "chocolate" before you had ever eaten any. Because you learned the name–salivation association, the learned stimulus—that is, the food's name—is called the **conditioned stimulus** (CS). And since in our demonstration there was no food in your mouth (that is, there was no US), the salivation elicited by the name of the food is called a **conditioned response** (CR). Notice that the UR and CR are the same behavior. After conditioning has occurred, they are called *respondent behaviors* because they are elicited involuntarily by stimuli.

From this example, we can formulate the following definition: **respondent conditioning** is a learning process in which a stimulus (the CS) gains the ability to elicit a response through repeated association with a stimulus (the US) that already elicits that response. Did you notice how broadly this definition is phrased? Its breadth suggests we can learn many things through respondent conditioning, and we do. For example, at one of Barbra Streisand's concerts in 1967, she forgot the words to three songs in front of a huge audience. She developed severe stage fright from this experience. "I was terrified. It prevented me from performing for all these years," she said in an interview (Seligmann, Namuth, & Miller, 1994). Performing on stage became a CS that began to elicit intense fear as a CR. Emotions, often negative ones, are some of the most important things we learn through respondent conditioning. Negative emotions are not necessarily problematic, and they can be quite beneficial. For instance, a mild fear of heights leads to our being cautious when using a ladder. We probably also learn positive emotions and to like things through respondent conditioning. As an example, by watching comedian Bill Cosby tell funny jokes, you probably learned to like him.

Operant Conditioning

In the story about Karen at the beginning of the chapter, why do you suppose her output of plural nouns increased? It was because of the consequences of her behavior. Each time she said a plural noun, but not other words, Joel said "mmm-hmm." As long as he did this, Karen continued to say lots of plurals. Notice that Joel's saying "mmm-hmm" was *contingent* on—that is, depended on—Karen's saying plural nouns, and her saying plurals was affected by the contingent consequence of that behavior. This story gives an example of operant (or "instrumental") conditioning. **Operant conditioning** is the learning process by which behavior is changed by the *consequences* of that behavior. The responses we acquire through this type of learning are called *operant behaviors*. The term "operant" reflects the view that these behaviors *operate* on the environment, thereby producing consequences.

Consequences in Operant Conditioning   The scientist most prominently associated with operant conditioning is B. F. Skinner, who established the basic techniques and terminology for the study of operant behavior. Skinner (1938, 1953) distinguished between behavioral consequences of two types: reinforcement and punishment. In **reinforcement,** a consequence causes an *increase* in the performance of the behavior on which it is contingent. We saw an example of reinforcement in the story about Karen: her output of plural nouns increased in frequency as a result of Joel's saying "mmm-hmm," which was the consequence of her behavior. Reinforcement typically involves a consequence the person wants or finds pleasant, and perhaps Karen found Joel's "mmm-hmm" pleasant because she may have interpreted it to mean "That's good." In most cases, the consequence in the process of reinforcement is obviously desirable, something people often call a *reward,* such as praise, money, or candy. But our knowing *why* a particular consequence has an effect on behavior may be less important than knowing its results. If performance of a behavior increases when it is followed by a consequence, we can conclude that reinforcement occurred.

In **punishment,** a consequence causes a *decrease* in the performance of the behavior on which it is contingent. In the experiment on which the story about Karen was based, Greenspoon (1955) tested other individuals using exactly the same procedure as we've seen, but the consequence of saying plural nouns was the researcher's saying "huh-uh" (pronounced "huh-UH," in a somewhat noncommittal way). For these individuals, the output of plurals *decreased.* Thus, "huh-uh" served to punish saying plurals. Punishment generally involves a consequence the person does not want or finds unpleasant, and perhaps the people Greenspoon tested interpreted "huh-uh" to mean "That's wrong." (If so, they were unaware of it. They, like the individuals who received "mmm-hmm," didn't realize that their behavior changed or that it was linked to what the researcher had said.) Once again, it isn't necessary to know *why* a particular consequence has an effect on behavior. If performance of a behavior decreases when it is followed by a consequence, we can conclude that punishment occurred. When people try to apply punishment, they generally use events—such as spankings, reprimands, or reducing the person's privileges—they *think* will work, but their thinking is not always correct. The best way to determine whether an event punishes a behavior is to observe the behavior over time: if it decreases when it is followed by the consequence, punishment has occurred.

Antecedents in Operant Conditioning   When you drive a car, traffic lights provide cues that have a strong influence on your behavior. You see the light before you act: if it is red, you depress the brake pedal; if it is green, you depress the gas pedal. Making these distinctions leads to reinforcement and helps you avoid punishment, such as traffic tickets or accidents. Stepping on the gas pedal when the light is red is likely to lead to unpleasant consequences. Clearly, behavior is influenced not only by the consequences that follow it but also by the events and circumstances that precede it. Because these cues precede and set the occasion for your action, they are called **antecedents.** An important learning task in people's lives involves finding and learning cues that help us determine the type of consequence our behavior will bring.

We can now diagram the process of operant conditioning, using the letters A, B, and C to stand for *antecedents, behavior,* and *consequences:*

$$A \rightarrow B \twoheadrightarrow C$$

The boldly printed, thick arrow between the B and C means *produces:* that is, behavior produces consequences. All behaviors we perform produce consequences, regardless of whether we notice them. When you write a word correctly in your notes, the consequence includes being able to move on. You don't really notice this reinforcing event, but it is there. The diagram's thin arrow between the A and B means *sets the occasion for:* that is, antecedents set the occasion for behavior. Whether the behavior occurs depends on many factors, including the strength of the link between the antecedent and the behavior. Being in a place of worship presents a very strong antecedent for certain behaviors, such as whispering rather than talking loudly. At home you have more latitude in how loudly you can talk and what you can say.

Operant conditioning can influence virtually any behavior, regardless of whether the behavior is verbal or motor, overt or covert. In subsequent chapters we will see that programs to alter antecedents and consequences have been applied successfully to change essentially any behavior one can think of in people of all ages and with widely different backgrounds and abilities. (Go to)

CASE STUDY 1.1

Reinstating a Schizophrenic Man's Speech Using Operant Conditioning

This case study involves the use of operant conditioning to reinstate speech in an institutionalized 40-year-old man who had not spoken for the previous 19 years (case described in Isaacs, Thomas, & Goldiamond, 1960). He had been diagnosed as schizophrenic, a condition characterized by major disturbances in thought, emotion, and behavior.

The therapist decided to try using chewing gum as a reward for speaking because of the interest the client had shown toward a package of gum that had fallen out of the therapist's pocket. The procedure progressed through five steps, each lasting a week or two with three meetings a week:

1. The therapist held a stick of gum in front of the client and waited. When the client looked at the gum, the therapist gave it to him. After several of these episodes, the client looked at the gum as soon as it appeared.

2. The therapist held up a stick of gum and waited until the client moved his lips before giving him the gum. After a few of these episodes, the client looked immediately at the gum and moved his lips.

3. The therapist held up the gum and gave it to the client if he made a vocal sound. After a few episodes, the client quickly looked at the gum and vocalized. The client's vocal sounds resembled "a croak."

4. The therapist held up the gum; said, "Say *gum, gum*"; and gave the reward to the client if his vocalizations progressed toward sounding more like "gum."

5. At a session in the sixth week, the therapist said, "Say *gum, gum*," and the client responded, "Gum, please." He also gave his name and age when asked.

At the time this case was written for publication, the client had received very little additional therapy for his speech, which continued to be very limited. Still, this case provides a fascinating demonstration of the utility of operant conditioning.

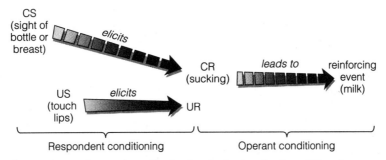

Figure 1.2   Respondent and operant conditioning functioning together in real life, using an example of a newborn infant's feeding experience. *Source:* Adapted from Sarafino & Armstrong, 1986, Figure 4.13.

Relating Respondent and Operant Conditioning

When books or instructors discuss learning, respondent and operant conditioning are usually presented as if they are separate, independent processes. To use looking at photographs as an analogy, you're being told: "Here's respondent conditioning in this picture, and here's operant conditioning in this other picture. See how separate and different they are?" Students often get the idea that respondent and operant conditioning function separately or independently—as discrete units—in real life. Although the two types of conditioning are to some extent separate and different, they almost always happen together in real life, with one flowing into the other (Allan, 1998). In terms of this analogy, real life is more like a videotape than a series of separate pictures. Let's consider a couple of examples of the two types of conditioning occurring together.

The first example is of a newborn baby named Vicki who was being fed. Her behavior involved the UR of sucking on a nipple that provided milk. This was a situation in which respondent conditioning was likely to occur. That is, when the nipple touched Vicki's lips, she would begin to suck reflexively. Stimuli, such as the bottle or breast she noticed at the time her lips were touched (the US), were potential CSs. But the feeding sequence did not stop here. There was an operant component, too, because a baby's sucking behavior is not just a UR, it's also an operant motor behavior. Vicki's sucking produced a consequence, milk, which reinforced that behavior. This sequence is diagrammed in Figure 1.2. In real life, the two components happen together.

Another real life example of the two types of conditioning occurring together has the operant component preceding the respondent component. Ten-year-old Jim was playing with some small firecrackers. He lit one (an operant motor behavior), and it exploded early, burning his hand (punishment for his behavior). For the respondent conditioning part, he was watching the lit fuse (the CS) when he heard and felt the firecracker explosion (the US), which caused him to scream out in fear and pain (the UR). For a few years thereafter, whenever Jim saw a lit fuse (CS), or even a lit match, he felt frightened (CR).

These are just two examples of operant and respondent conditioning happening together. In real life it's unlikely that experiences involving one type of conditioning would not include the other too.

Modeling

Four-year-old Jo watches her father tie his shoelaces and tries to copy his movements. Jo is learning through the process of **modeling,** or learning by watching the behavior of other people. This method of learning involves at least two participants, the *observer* and the *model*. Because of these characteristics, this learning method is frequently called "social," or "observational," or "vicarious" or "imitative" learning. Modeling is a very useful and efficient way to acquire and change behavior because we can learn actions without actually having to perform them. As we are about to see, we can learn both operant and respondent behavior through modeling.

One type of operant behavior people can learn through modeling is aggression, as classic research by Albert Bandura (1965) demonstrated with children as Figure 1.3 illustrates. The children first saw one of three films showing a model performing a series of unusual aggressive acts, such as hitting a Bobo doll with a mallet and shouting "Sockeroo." The consequences the model received for these acts were different in the three films: the model received either punishment, reinforcement, or no consequences for the acts. The children were then taken individually to a room that had a Bobo doll and the other objects they had seen in the film. They were told they could play with the toys in any way they wished, with *no consequences* promised or threatened for their actions. As expected, they copied the model's behavior, but the children who had observed the model being punished for aggression performed fewer of the model's aggressive acts than the other children did. Later, *all* the children were promised very attractive rewards if they would reproduce the aggressive behaviors they had seen the model do. Under this contingency, the children performed the same number of acts, regardless of the consequences they had seen in the film. These results indicate that children learn punished and reinforced aggressive acts equally. Seeing models punished for their acts merely *suppresses* the children's performance of those behaviors. These and other similar findings support the large body of research showing that watching violence on TV increases children's aggressive behavior (Friedrich-Cofer & Huston, 1986).

Modeling is an effective learning method for acquiring and changing a wide variety of operant behaviors, including simple responses, such as pulling a drawer open or shaking a tambourine, and complex behavioral sequences, such as those used in preparing scrambled eggs (Baer, Peterson, & Sherman, 1967; Griffen, Wolery, & Schuster, 1992). Research has also shown that modeling affects the rate at which people drink alcoholic beverages. Individuals increase their drinking rates when others around them are drinking more than they are, and they decrease their drinking rates when others are drinking less (Caudill & Lipscomb, 1980; DeRicco & Niemann, 1980).

People also learn respondent behaviors—such as fears—through modeling. One study had children, with their parents' permission, watch a short film that portrayed a 5-year-old boy screaming and withdrawing when his mother simply showed him a

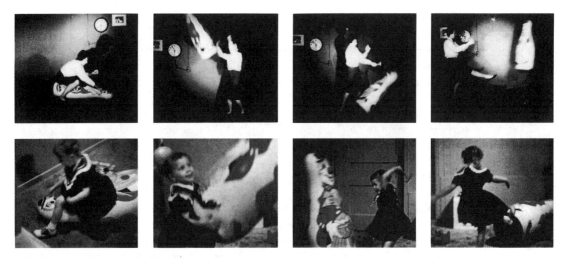

Figure 1.3 These photos show a child in Bandura's research modeling the behaviors she saw the adult in the film perform (see top row).

plastic figure of a cartoon character, Mickey Mouse. But when his mother showed him a plastic figure of Donald Duck, he responded in a calm and undistressed manner (Venn & Short, 1973). After the children watched this film, they participated in a task that involved the Mickey Mouse and Donald Duck figures. At this time they tended to avoid the Mickey Mouse figure (the one feared in the film) in favor of the Donald Duck. What's more, the researchers measured the children's physiological reactions while they watched the film. The children showed greater reactions during the Mickey Mouse (fearful) episode than during the Donald Duck episode. Although initially this fear was pronounced, a day or two later the children showed no avoidance or preference for either figure. Even though these effects were temporary, it is clear that observing fear in other people affects both internal and external behavior.

Cognitive Processes in Learning

The term **cognition** refers to mental activity, particularly thinking and reasoning. In the process of *thinking*, we use mental representations of the knowledge we have learned and stored in memory, mostly in the form of language or images, which are mental pictures. If you see someone perform a behavior you'd like to do, you can "practice" it in your head by describing the actions in words or by forming mental pictures of the actions you would make. In *reasoning*, we apply logic in our thinking processes, usually to make plans, solve problems, and arrive at conclusions. If you take a good photograph, you may think, "Good job," which serves as a reward. If you feel sick, you may try to plan the best course of action to take for your illness. When our thinking and reasoning produce plans, expectations, beliefs, or rules, these ideas are basically statements we make to ourselves that serve as *covert antecedents* to our behavior. If you decide to see your physician for your illness, your plan initiates an action: you call to make an appointment.

Covert antecedents can influence our behavior in very important and broad ways. Let's consider the role of beliefs or expectations, which we learn through our experiences in everyday life. On the basis of this learning, we generate many beliefs about ourselves and our behavior, including beliefs regarding our ability to perform behaviors effectively. **Self-efficacy** refers to a belief regarding our ability to succeed at a specific activity we want to do (Bandura, 1977, 1986). We estimate our chances of success or failure on the basis of our prior experience with similar activities. For example, if you wanted to play the piano but believed you had very poor ability to learn this skill, you would not be likely to try. Thus, these beliefs are covert behaviors that serve as antecedents for other behaviors. Research has shown that self-efficacy does influence people's behavior. Cigarette smokers who believe they cannot kick the habit typically don't try, but smokers who believe they can quit often make the attempt and succeed (DiClemente, Prochaska, & Gilbertini, 1985). Similarly, medical patients with chronic lung diseases who believe they can perform a prescribed program of physical exercise, such as walking certain distances, are more likely to carry out the program than equally ill patients with less self-efficacy (Kaplan, Atkins, & Reinsch, 1984).

To illustrate another kind of belief we generate, consider this example: A friend throws a football while you're not looking, it hits you in the head, and you wonder, "Did he mean to hurt me?" We generate beliefs about other people's actions, motives, and intentions—and we're more likely to respond aggressively to being hit if we think a given act was intentional. Interestingly, individuals who often behave aggressively tend to believe other people's injurious acts are intentional. This was demonstrated in a series of studies with elementary school boys whose behavior was regularly either aggressive or nonaggressive (Dodge & Frame, 1982). In one study, each boy described his beliefs about stories in which he was the victim. An example story had him "sitting at a lunch table and having a peer's milk carton spill milk all over his back." The stories did not indicate why the events happened. The aggressive boys were far more likely than the nonaggressive boys to decide the acts had been intentional and to say they would react aggressively. In another of these studies, the boys were observed playing freely in a large room. Aggressive boys not only initiated more unprovoked aggressive acts than nonaggressive boys but *received* more as well. The finding that aggressive boys received more aggression suggests their tendency to believe others intend to hurt them may be rooted in actual experience. (Go to ☑)

DEFINING BEHAVIOR MODIFICATION

Now that we have seen what behavior is and how people can acquire and change it, we should be able to define what behavior modification is. We will do that, but you should recognize that there is no "official" or fully agreed upon definition. This is because behavior modification has evolved over many years, but not all of the field's experts have seen eye to eye on incorporating each major new idea and method within the

CONCEPT CHECK 1.2

Check your understanding of the preceding concepts. Question 1 is followed by a ⇔, which means that the answer can vary somewhat or take different directions. As explained in the preface, this symbol identifies a "critical-thinking" item—one that encourages you to think analytically and creatively about what you've read and to apply the material to your life. The answers the book gives to critical thinking items are only suggestions; you may come up with different ones that are equally correct.

1. The text mentions that you may have come to like Bill Cosby by watching him tell jokes. What might be the: **a.** US, **b.** UR, **c.** CS, and **d.** CR? ⇔
2. Anita's literature professor announced that a wonderful play was being performed on campus, and students who saw it and wrote a brief review would receive extra credit toward their final grades. Anita went to see the play and wrote a review, and she got the extra credit. Identify the: **a.** antecedent, **b.** behavior, and **c.** consequence.
3. Learning by watching other people's behavior is called _____ .
4. People use thoughts as covert _____ for behavior.

Answers: 1.a. funny joke, b. laugh/feel happy, c. Cosby's face/name, d. feel happy, 2.a. professor's announcement, b. see play and write review, c. extra credit, 3. modeling, 4. antecedents

discipline. Keeping this in mind, we will define **behavior modification** as the field of study that focuses on *using principles of learning and cognition to understand and change people's behavior.*

Behavior modification has several defining characteristics that most experts in the field agree upon and that make its approach unique (Kazdin, 1978; Wixted, Bellack, & Hersen, 1990). These characteristics, which are accepted by most experts, apply when professionals conduct studies of factors that affect behavioral development and use learning principles to modify behavior. We'll begin with the field's focus on behavior.

Focus on Behavior

We have seen that the behavior modification approach focuses on behavior. As a result, professionals who use behavior change techniques place a strong emphasis on: (1) *defining people's current status and progress in terms of behavior* rather than traits or other broad characteristics; (2) being able to *measure the behavior* in some way; and (3) whenever possible, *assessing covert behaviors, such as fear, in terms of overt actions* the person makes so that objective and reliable measurements can be made. The behavior modification approach considers emotional and cognitive events to be accessible to study and change in much the same way as overt behaviors. However, assessing covert behaviors with only subjective measures, such as by having people rate their feelings of fear, provides weak evidence that efforts to change the behavior are succeeding.

Efforts to change a behavior can be directed toward increasing it or decreasing it, depending on whether the problem being addressed involves a deficit or an excess of the behavior. When a **behavioral deficit** exists, the person does *not* perform a specific appropriate behavior often enough, long enough, well enough, or strongly enough. Examples of behavioral deficits include not initiating conversations often enough, not spending enough time studying, and not exercising vigorously enough. When a **behavioral excess** exists, the person performs a particular behavior too frequently, too strongly, or for too long. Examples of behavioral excesses are smoking cigarettes, spending too much time socializing, and experiencing too much fear when taking tests.

Importance of Learning and the Environment

For the most part, human behavior is learned behavior. We discussed earlier that genetic factors can influence behavior and its development, but learning and cognition provide the most substantial and pervasive processes by which people acquire and change almost everything they do. As a result, the application of behavior change techniques assumes behavior is generally malleable and can be modified by providing appropriate new experiences.

The new experiences used in modifying behavior involve altering aspects of the individual's environment, mainly by changing the antecedents and consequences of the behavior. Suppose a teacher wanted to reduce a behavioral excess, such as students being out of their seats too much. If an antecedent condition leading to the behavior was the children's being very far from one another while working on group projects, for instance, the teacher could rearrange the seating. If the consequences of students being out of their seats were more attractive than the consequences of being in their seats, the teacher could introduce rewards for students who stayed in their seats for appropriate amounts of time. The antecedents and consequences addressed in behavior change programs are usually in the person's external environment, but altering covert antecedents and consequences can also be effective in changing behavior.

Although providing new learning experiences has been highly successful in changing behavior, we need to keep four limiting factors in mind. First, the antecedents and consequences altered or introduced must be chosen and applied very carefully. If they are not, the effort to change the behavior will be hampered. Second, the knowledge used in behavior modification is still far from complete and continues to grow. Behavior that is difficult to change now may be easier to change in the future. Third, in some cases, the existing antecedents and consequences for a behavior may be rooted in the person's social or cultural environment. For example, a culture may discourage individuals from working hard or getting an education. Environmental factors like these can exert strong influences on behavior and may be very difficult or impossible to alter substantially or to override. Last, some behaviors are so severely disordered or so strongly determined by physiological processes—for instance, the brain seizures in epilepsy—that behavior modification methods may not be sufficient to change them, at least initially. In these circumstances medication may be prescribed by a physician and used as an adjunct to environmental changes (Wilson & Simpson, 1990), and failing to include medication in the treatment may be unethical. The goal in using principles of behavior change in these cases often includes reducing or eliminating the use of medication over time.

Scientific Orientation

Behavior modification has a strong scientific orientation—its core is the knowledge revealed through the methods of science. The *scientific method* basically involves conducting research by (1) carefully gathering data empirically—that is, by direct observation or measurement—(2) analyzing and interpreting the data, and (3) specifying the precise methods used to gather and analyze the data so that other researchers will know exactly what was done and can repeat the procedures. A hallmark and essential feature of research on and application of principles of behavior change is the careful and precise measurement of behavior. Using the scientific method, researchers have discovered ways by which learning and cognition influence behavior.

Pragmatic and Active Methods to Change Behavior

Behavior modification takes a pragmatic approach in the methods it uses to change behavior (Baer, Wolf, & Risley, 1968). The term *pragmatic* means "practical, rather than theoretical or idealistic." Thus, professionals who use behavior change techniques emphasize finding and using *methods that work* to change behavior, regardless of whether the techniques fit into a particular theory or ideal. By taking this view, the discipline has incorporated and enhanced the effectiveness of many new and creative methods for changing behavior. Behavior modification today includes two broad categories of behavior change techniques: behavioral methods and cognitive methods (Sweet & Loizeaux, 1991). **Behavioral methods** use principles of operant conditioning, respondent conditioning, and modeling, particularly toward changing overt behaviors. **Cognitive methods** focus on changing overt and covert behaviors by modifying people's thought processes—for example, by helping individuals recognize and alter their illogical beliefs. Although these categories appear to be separate and distinct, in practice there is considerable overlap. Some behavior change techniques make use of elements of both, as you would do if you practiced a modeled behavior in your mind. In addition, efforts to change behavior often include techniques from each category. When the methods overlap, the techniques sometimes are called "cognitive-behavioral."

The last characteristic of behavior modification we will consider is that its techniques for changing behavior often require that clients be *active* participants in the process of modifying their behavior. In contrast to other approaches in which clients just talk about their difficulties, behavioral and cognitive methods have clients *do* things to help. Such help may take the form of deciding which techniques to use and how to implement them, by performing the methods under supervision, or by applying some techniques on their own as "homework."

HOW BEHAVIOR MODIFICATION DEVELOPED

Although the discipline of behavior modification was introduced in the mid-1900s, practical applications of behavioral and cognitive methods to influence behavior are by no means new in human history. For instance, psychologists were not the first to realize that rewarding a behavior tends to increase its frequency. What psychologists and other professionals did was to examine these methods, clarify what they are, and determine how to apply them most effectively. In this section, I will outline the highlights in the history of behavior modification. (Go to 🐾)

Theory and Research Leading Toward Behavior Modification

During the first half of the 20th century, the dominant *theories*—or systematic explanations—of why people behave the way they do proposed that behavior resulted from various internal "forces," such as drives, motives, conflicts, and traits. Some of these theories grouped several forces together, with the resulting constellation being called the *personality*. The well-known *psychoanalytic theory* of Sigmund Freud (1933, 1949), for example, views a person's behavior as an expression of his or her personality and its component forces, such as drives and conflicts. According to this theory, each person's personality develops through a maturationally determined series of stages, is profoundly affected by early experiences, and becomes fairly entrenched in childhood. Freud believed changing an individual's problem behavior required that the person talk with a therapist to arrive at a comprehension of the behavior's underlying forces, such as conflicts and unresolved childhood experiences.

A different perspective, called *behaviorism*, began to emerge in the early 1900s, with psychologists John B. Watson (1913, 1930) and B. F. Skinner (1938, 1953) as two of its main proponents. **Behaviorism** is the theoretical orientation that emphasizes the study of observable and measurable behavior and proposes that nearly all behavior is the product of experience. As a result, behavior can be explained by principles of learning, particularly operant and respondent conditioning. This theory developed from two sources: philosophy and science. Certain philosophical views, which had been proposed more than 200 years earlier, had become widely accepted in England and the United States. For instance, the British philosopher John Locke had proposed that a baby's mind has no innate ideas and is essentially a blank tablet (called *tabula rasa* in Latin) on which experience "writes." At the time behaviorism was introduced, psychology was already becoming a separate discipline from philosophy, and the scientific method was seen as the main feature permitting a distinction between the two fields. As a result, early behaviorists rejected philosophy's unobservable concepts, such as mind, consciousness, and soul. Instead, they used the scientific method to examine learning principles. Two lines of research were especially important: Ivan Pavlov (1927) demonstrated the process of respondent conditioning, and Edward Thorndike (1898, 1931) studied how "satisfying" and "annoying" consequences—reinforcement and punishment—affect learning.

CLOSE-UP 1.1

Buddhism and the Principles of Behavior Change

 Buddhism is an Eastern religion with the basic view that people can liberate themselves from life's inevitable suffering by practicing methods of mental and moral self-purification. Many self-purification methods have a lot in common with behavior modification techniques. Buddhism is taught from texts based on anecdotes and teachings passed down from the Buddha's life, about 2,500 years ago. Let's look at some examples Padmal de Silva (1984) described from Buddhist texts.

- **Antecedents:** A monk was having difficulty maintaining a commitment to monastic life: he kept leaving to return to his old life as a farmer. Each time he left, he would plant seed beans—and when they were ripe, he would harvest them and consume all but a pint of beans, which he would save with his spade when he returned to the monastery. At last, "determined to break his attachment to lay life, he threw away what he saw to be the crucial items that lured him" (p. 667). That is, he threw away the seed and spade, which served as antecedents for leaving.
- **Modeling:** The Buddha recognized the influence of social learning on people's behavior when he wrote: "He who has bad men as friends, and does

not make friends with the good, he behaves like bad men" (p. 665).

- **Behavioral Consequences:** When a king who had been overeating regularly and had become lazy asked the Buddha why, he was told: "King, overeating causes problems. Anyone who lives indolently, eats large quantities of food, sleeps all the time, so that he rolls around like a pig fed on grain, such a man is a fool because it is bound to lead to suffering. . . . King, one should observe moderation in eating because that leads to comfort" (pp. 666–667).
- **Rewards:** A father who wanted his unwilling son to learn from the Buddha said, "There is no living being here in the world who may not be influenced by rewards. I shall therefore try to influence my son with rewards" (p. 668). He did so, and it worked—the son listened to the Buddha and was converted!

The approaches in these examples involve behavioral methods. Later in this book we'll see that Buddhist texts also give anecdotes and recommendations that involve cognitive methods that are used in behavior modification.

Two other studies set the stage for applying learning principles to change behavior. In one of these studies, John Watson and Rosalie Rayner (1920) conditioned an 11-month-old boy they called Little Albert to fear a white rat. Albert was not afraid of the rat before conditioning began. On the contrary, his behavior (reaching toward it) suggested he liked it. During conditioning, the researchers presented the rat along with a loud noise (the US) made by striking a steel bar with a hammer, which elicited distress (the UR) in Albert. After several of these episodes in a week's time, the rat (now a CS) elicited distress and efforts to escape. This was an important demonstration: Albert had *learned* to fear the rat through respondent conditioning. Although Watson and Rayner had planned to reverse the conditioning, using methods later shown to be effective in reducing fear, Albert's mother's job change made the child unavailable for this plan. (Note: a study like this one would not be conducted today; the American Psychological Association developed guidelines in 1973 that restrict using potentially harmful procedures in research, as we shall see in Chapter 15.)

A few years later Mary Cover Jones (1924) described how she reduced the fear a toddler named Peter developed in his everyday life. Peter's fear was a lot like Albert's—he was intensely afraid of white furry objects, such as rabbits. The procedure Jones used to reduce the fear involved bringing a rabbit closer and closer while Peter ate favorite foods in the presence of a research assistant whom he liked. After many episodes of this procedure in the course of several weeks, Peter no longer showed signs of fear in the presence of the rabbit and would seek it out, pat it, and play with it. This dramatic change in Peter's fear response demonstrated clearly the potential value of using learning principles to modify behavior.

The next 35 or 40 years witnessed four important historical events (Bandura, 1969; Kazdin, 1978). First, psychology and philosophy became clearly separate disciplines, as illustrated by the humorous poem:

> Alas, poor psychology, sad is her Fate!
> First she lost her Soul, and then she lost her Mind,
> And then she lost Consciousness.
> Now all that's left to her is her Behavior—
> And the less said of that, the better!
> (Anonymous, as cited in Goldiamond, 1974, p. 38)

Second, researchers showed that principles of operant and respondent conditioning could be used effectively in many different settings to change a wide variety of behaviors. The case study we saw earlier of reinstating speech in a mute schizophrenic man is an example. Third, a research area called the *experimental analysis of behavior* developed to study basic theoretical processes in learning, usually without an emphasis on application. Fourth, psychologists became increasingly dissatisfied with the lack of scientific evidence to demonstrate that traditional therapies, such as psychoanalysis, were effective in treating problem behaviors.

Emergence and Growth of Behavior Modification

The 1950s and early 1960s saw the emergence of an academic discipline to study and apply learning principles as an approach for changing people's behavior (Kazdin, 1978). B. F. Skinner continued to have a profound impact on the development of this approach, mainly through his creative descriptions of ways to apply principles of operant conditioning to modify behavior in education, business, government, and therapy. Many other scholars contributed ideas and research findings that furthered the discipline during its emergent years, but two deserve special mention. Joseph Wolpe developed respondent conditioning therapy techniques that were soon shown to be highly effective in helping people reduce strong fears and anxieties. And Hans Eysenck published a series of investigations indicating that patients who received traditional types of psychotherapy, especially psychoanalysis, were no more likely to show improved psychological functioning than individuals who receive no treatment at all. Although Eysenck's conclusions were somewhat exaggerated, they formed the basis for psychotherapists to question the utility of traditional approaches in treating psychosocial problems and to search for new approaches. Some of these new approaches involved the application of behavioral methods.

By the late 1960s, behavior modification had become a formal discipline, journals to publish research articles in the discipline had become established, and an area of research called *applied behavior analysis* had been formed to focus on ways to apply behavioral methods to socially important problems, such as those relating to education, child rearing, crime, and mental illness (Baer, Wolf, & Risley, 1968, 1987; Kazdin, 1978). Also by this time, psychotherapy approaches in clinical psychology included a category called *behavior therapy*, which applies principles of behavior change to treat clients' problems. The treatment techniques used in the early years of behavior therapy were almost entirely based on behavioral methods, but its scope of techniques began to incorporate more and more cognitive methods in the 1970s (Mahoney, 1977; Wixted, Bellack, & Hersen, 1990).

Principles of behavior change are widely applied today. For example, they are used by psychotherapists, teachers in regular and special education classrooms, parents of "normal" children, supervisors in business and industry, personnel in institutions for juvenile delinquents, and personnel working with children with mental retardation and emotional disturbances. A major reason for the wide acceptance of behavioral and cognitive methods is that professionals who use them, in both research and applied settings, measure the behavior they are trying to change and examine these data. Using these data, they can see and show others how well the methods work. (Go to ✔)

EFFECTIVE APPLICATIONS OF
BEHAVIOR MODIFICATION

In this section, we look at some commonly used, effective behavior modification applications. They were conducted by psychologists and other professionals in many settings and have focused on a wide variety of individuals and behaviors. As you read this material, you'll notice three things. First, the potential for applying behavioral and cognitive methods is almost limitless. Second, some details of how applications in this chapter were conducted were left out so you could see an overview of each program. We will examine the details of behavior change programs in later chapters. Third, behavior change techniques have a promising future built on solid research support. The overview begins with a look at how these methods can improve parenting and parent–child relationships.

Parenting and Parent–Child Relationships

Suppose 7-year-old Ken's mother will not buy the junk food he wants while they're shopping, so he sasses her. How will she respond? She may react constructively to dampen his hurtful behavior, or she can aggravate it. She can dampen it by talking with him calmly to explain why she won't buy the food and why his behavior is unacceptable, or she can escalate the encounter by responding in a *coercive*, or dominating, manner—such as by snapping, "You really are a brat today." Coercive acts often fuel a chain reaction of increasingly hostile coercive exchanges by both parties that lead to hitting, yelling, or a nasty tantrum. If this kind of interchange becomes increasingly common, a *coercive pattern* of mutual escalations in hostility may come to characterize family interactions (Patterson, 1982), which can lead to serious outcomes, such as the abuse and neglect of children (Burgess & Richardson, 1984). How can parents acquire the skills they need to promote constructive family environments?

Training in General Parenting Skills   Teaching parents behavioral and cognitive skills can help change their behavior, which, in turn, fosters improvements in their children's behavior. Parents who learn behavioral methods, such as how to use reinforcement and modeling, are often surprised at how effective these techniques can be. Adults tend to overlook the small, appropriate behaviors a child shows, perhaps because we expect them. Research has shown that training parents in behavioral methods is effective in helping them deal with a variety of child-rearing concerns, such as getting their children to do household chores or reduce TV watching (Christophersen et al., 1972; Wolfe, Mendes, & Factor, 1984).

Modeling and discussion are useful in teaching parents general behavioral and cognitive methods to improve their child-rearing practices. Carolyn Webster-Stratton (1982a, 1982b) demonstrated this with mothers and their 3- to 5-year-old children. First she observed each mother and child interact for half an hour in a playroom to examine their positive social behaviors, such as smiling and praising, and negative social behaviors, such as frowning, ridiculing, and slapping. Then the mothers received parent training for 4 weeks, with four 2-hour sessions each week. The training sessions consisted of watching and discussing short videotaped vignettes of parent models who portrayed either positive or negative social behaviors toward children. Assessments through direct observations and surveys soon after the training revealed substantial improvements in mother–child social interactions and in the children's general behavior. Additional assessments a year after each group received the training showed that the gains had persisted.

Correcting a Child's Existing Difficulties   Parents often postpone getting professional help until their child's behavior has become a serious problem. Training parents in behavior change techniques often occurs as part of an effort to correct specific problems that have already developed. This type of parent training is very effective in treating many childhood problems, such as children's oppositional behavior and bed-wetting (TFPDPP, 1993).

Oppositional behavior refers to acting in a hostile and contrary manner, such as a child's frequent ignoring of rules, failure to comply with parents' requests, and habitual fighting or arguing (Wahler & Dumas, 1984). Parents find oppositional behavior very distressing and frustrating. A study by Robert Wahler and his coworkers (1965) was done with three boys with various behavior problems serious enough to motivate their parents to seek professional help. Although parent training helped in all three cases, we'll focus on a 4-year-old named Eddie whose behavior was clearly oppositional. According to Eddie's mother, he generally either ignored her requests at home or did the opposite. She would react with pleas, threats, or spankings, all of which seemed to be ineffective in changing his behavior. Initial observations during 20-minute play sessions confirmed his mother's account of these interactions: Eddie exhibited over 200 oppositional responses and only about 30 cooperative responses per session! What's more, his mother tended to react negatively to oppositional responses but to ignore his cooperative behavior. The researchers trained her to respond enthusiastically and with a smile when Eddie was cooperative and to isolate him in an empty room for a few minutes each time he showed oppositional behavior. When this combination was used in several play sessions, Eddie showed over five times as many cooperative responses as oppositional ones.

Subsequent research has shown that the benefits of training parents to apply principles of behavior change at home appear to be broad and durable. For instance, studies have found that when parents used behavior change methods to reduce disruptive behavior at home the children behaved better in other settings too—such as when shopping, visiting relatives, or in school (McNeil et al., 1991; Sanders & Glynn, 1981). Other findings suggest that the broad benefits of parent training to reduce oppositional behavior can last for many years (Long et al., 1993).

Bed-wetting, technically called *nocturnal enuresis*, is defined as wetting the bed at least twice a month after reaching 5 years of age (Houts, Berman, & Abramson, 1994). About 7% of American 8-year-olds and as many as 3% of adolescents have bed-wetting problems. Normally, people awaken from sleep when bladder tension exceeds a certain

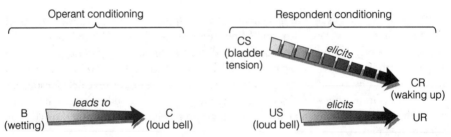

Figure 1.4   Operant and respondent principles applied in a urine alarm apparatus to reduce bed-wetting. In the *operant conditioning* component, wetting the bed leads to the sound of the loud bell, which is an aversive consequence that punishes the release of urine. Parents can also provide praise and other rewards for improvement. In the *respondent conditioning* component, the child learns to wake up (the CR) when the bladder is tense (the CS), but *before* urine is released. Responding to the CS prevents wetting and enables the child to avoid the aversive bell. *Source:* Adapted from Sarafino & Armstrong, 1986, Figure 7.10.

limit. If a physical examination of a bed-wetting child shows nothing organically wrong, the enuresis is usually assumed to result from a failure to learn the response of awakening to the antecedent, bladder tension. Two behavior modification approaches appear to be effective in helping parents eliminate their children's bed-wetting (Doleys, 1977; Houts, Berman, & Abramson, 1994). One approach uses a **urine alarm apparatus** consisting of a liquid-sensitive sheet electrically connected to a loud battery-powered bell or buzzer (Mowrer, 1938). No shock is involved. When urine is released, the bell rings, waking up the child. This technique incorporates both operant and respondent conditioning components, as Figure 1.4 diagrams. Treatment success using this apparatus without any other behavioral methods is fairly high: positive results were reported in about two thirds of treated cases in dozens of studies aimed at stopping bed-wetting (Houts, Berman, & Abramson, 1994).

The second approach for eliminating bed-wetting uses a program of operant conditioning techniques, having the child be an active participant with the parents in the process (Azrin, Hontos, & Besalel-Azrin, 1979; Azrin & Thienes, 1978). The operant program includes having the parents awaken the child periodically in the first few hours of sleep during the first week or two to prevent "accidents." They reward the child for successes but make sure the child remakes the bed and changes pajamas when he or she has an accident. This approach can be quite effective in helping enuretic children stop wetting the bed. There is some evidence that combining operant methods and the urine alarm apparatus may be more successful that using either method alone (Doleys, 1977; Houts, Berman, & Abramson, 1994). (Go to 📷)

Education

Principles of behavior change have been applied effectively in educational settings to improve instructional methods and classroom conduct. Let's see how.

CLOSE-UP 1.2

Are Rewards Bribes?

 Many people think that providing reinforcement for performing appropriate behavior is "bribery." But two arguments can be made against this view. First, dictionary definitions of *bribery* either imply or state that the behavior thus rewarded is unethical or illegal. As psychologists John and Helen Krumboltz (1972) have noted:

> Our language contains many words to represent the exchange of services, products, or money. Wage, salary, commission, honorarium, fee, prize, reward, reparation, bribe, ransom, tip, blackmail, pay, and compensation all refer to the exchange of one valuable for another. However, each different word connotes different circumstances. Only if you wish to pervert the judgment of a child or corrupt the conduct of a child could it be said that you are bribing him by offering him some reinforcer. (p. 26)

Second, the reinforcers we apply are not necessarily material things, such as money, that we usually think of as bribes. They can be praise, smiles, or fun activities, too. The cartoon in Figure 1CU.1 nicely illustrates the distinction between rewards and bribes.

Reprinted with special permission of North America Syndicate.

Figure 1CU.1 The "good grade incentive money" promised to the boy in the striped shirt was intended as a *reward,* probably for studying hard. That boy is proposing to use part of that money as a *bribe* to get Monroe to help him cheat, which is unethical behavior. Note also that the "good grade incentive money" was contingent on reaching *outcome goals* (grades), not on performing the appropriate behavior for achieving good grades (studying). This illustrates why making reinforcers contingent on the behavior you're trying to change is important.

Enhancing Instructional Methods   Angela was sitting at a computer in her kindergarten class and wrote the following story: "I like sprang. Sprang brangs flawers. Berds seng in sprang. I git days off. That is wi I like sprang" (Asbell, 1984). Not a perfect job, but quite remarkable for a 5-year-old! Computers are being used to teach kindergartners language skills, usually by showing them how to spell sounds or syllables, put these together as words, and combine the words into sentences.

The use of computers in classroom instruction has its roots in B. F. Skinner's (1954) concept of **programmed instruction,** a self-teaching process in which students actively learn material presented step by step as a series of discrete items in textbooks or with mechanical devices. Each item presents some information, asks a related question, and gives feedback for the student's answer. The items build toward overall learning goals, such as being able to spell a body of words or to recite multiplication tables. Because students advance at their own pace in small steps, they are unlikely to give wrong answers and are likely to get reinforcement—that is, positive feedback—for their efforts. A more advanced form of programmed instruction, called **computer-assisted instruction** (CAI), uses a computer to coach students through a series of lessons, much as a human tutor might do. CAI programs explain concepts, give examples, ask questions, give feedback for students' answers, and provide additional explanations if needed. Newer forms of computerized training use CD-ROM and Internet technologies to present material in a highly *interactive* manner. Studies have shown that these teaching methods are very effective, especially when computerized training requires students to be very active participants rather than only moderately active or passive participants (Kritch & Bostow, 1998; Ormrod, 1990).

Psychologist Fred Keller (1968) applied behavior modification principles to develop an alternative approach to teaching students at the college level. This approach, called the **personalized system of instruction** (PSI, sometimes called the Keller Plan), divides the course content into units called "modules," has students independently study the modules presented in textbooks and guides, tests students on each unit when they feel ready, and gives immediate feedback on test performance. Students must master each module, getting a high score—such as 80% correct—on the test. If they score lower, they must restudy and take another test on the same material. Advanced student "proctors" provide tutoring, administer tests, and give feedback, under supervision. Because students advance at their own pace, they may complete the course before the end of the semester.

Using students as tutors is an important innovation of the PSI approach that has been effective in primary and secondary school classrooms (Kohler & Strain, 1990). Evidence indicates that peer tutoring is a practical way to give extra help to specific students, individualize the focus of instruction, and enhance the academic and social skills of both the tutee and tutor (Greenwood, Carta, & Kamps, 1990; Greer & Polirstok, 1982).

Improving Classroom Conduct   Children do all sorts of things in school that disrupt the class and upset the teacher. Conduct problems include students being out of their seats without permission, making noises, fighting, name calling, swearing, refusing to follow a teacher's request, and daydreaming. What can a teacher do about conduct problems? The answer can be seen in the operant sequence of antecedent, behavior, and consequence.

Patricia Krantz and Todd Risley (1977) examined the role of antecedents on kindergartners' on-task behavior at a preschool during story reading and demonstration activities. "On-task behavior" was essentially paying attention to the activities and not being disruptive. Two antecedent conditions were studied: the amount of activity the

CONCEPT CHECK 1.4

Check your understanding of the preceding concepts by answering the following fill-in-the-blank questions. Remember that the symbol ⇔ means various answers can be correct.

1. When it becomes usual for a family to deal with an unpleasant behavior by saying or doing increasingly hostile things to each other, a _____ pattern exists.
2. An example of a child's oppositional behavior is _____ . ⇔
3. Before Eddie's mother was trained in behavioral methods, she almost completely ignored his _____ behavior in play sessions.
4. The urine alarm apparatus uses _____ conditioning to stop children's bed-wetting.
5. A behavior modification instructional approach that divides class material into small units and gives immediate feedback on test performance is called _____ . ⇔

Answers: 1. coercive, 2. disobeying rules, 3. cooperative, 4. operant and respondent, 5. programmed instruction, CAI, or PSI

children showed in the periods preceding the activities and the degree of crowding in the seating arrangements during the activities. The researchers found that on-task behavior was far lower when the activities followed a vigorous play period rather than a rest period and when seating during the activities was crowded rather than uncrowded. Antecedents are not always obvious events that appear suddenly before the behavior. Teachers need to watch carefully for antecedents in the classroom that lead to off-task and disruptive behavior so that they can try to alter those antecedents.

Consequences also have strong effects on behavior, and teachers can deploy them quite effectively. One consequence that teachers can employ easily is social attention to students. Early studies of behavior change techniques in classroom settings found that teachers could increase students' on-task behavior by praising or paying attention to it, and they could decrease disruptive behavior by not giving it the attention it had received in the past (Becker et al., 1972; Madsen, Becker, & Thomas, 1968). Another kind of reward teachers can use effectively to improve classroom conduct is the opportunity to engage in free-choice activities, such as playing with toys or crafts (Wasik, 1970).

Using principles of behavior change to reduce classroom misconduct enhances the school environment and has additional positive side effects. Teachers who use behavioral methods come to provide more reinforcement and less punishment than other teachers do, and their students show greater gains in academic achievement (Rollins et al., 1974). Also, students with conduct problems who participate in a behavior modification program to improve their conduct continue in school longer than those who do not (Heaton & Safer, 1982). (Go to ✔)

Health and Sports

Since the late 1970s, psychologists have become increasingly involved in efforts to promote health, treat illness, and improve athletic performance. Let's look at the basis for this involvement and some methods that help.

Health Psychology   If you became really sick, what would you do to get better? One thing you'd probably do is see your physician—that certainly would be a good idea. We typically think of illness as an affliction of the body that results from injury, biochemical imbalances, or bacterial or viral infection that physicians can treat.

In recent years we have become aware that psychological and behavioral circumstances can also affect whether we get sick and how quickly we recover from an illness. For instance, we know that our health can be harmed if we experience long-term intense stress, smoke cigarettes, have a physically inactive lifestyle, eat foods high in fat and low in fiber, have unsafe sex, drive when intoxicated, or fail to carry out the treatment a physician prescribes. As these examples show, health and illness result from the interplay of biological, psychological, and social aspects of life. This perspective is called the *biopsychosocial model* of health and illness (Engel, 1977, 1980). The idea that medicine and psychology are linked led to the field of **health psychology,** which examines the causes of illness and ways to promote and maintain health, prevent and treat illness, and improve health care systems (Sarafino, 1998). Two similar fields are called *behavioral medicine* and *psychosomatic medicine*.

Promoting Health   Principles of behavior change have been applied effectively to promote health and prevent illness or injury in an enormous variety of ways, and we'll look at two. First, we all know that smoking can harm our health, but did you know that a pregnant woman's smoking may harm her baby's health? Babies of mothers who smoke tend to have low birth weight compared with other babies (Cook, Petersen, & Moore, 1990). Thomas Burling and his coworkers (1991) used health warnings as antecedents to reduce pregnant women's smoking. Of the pregnant smokers attending a clinic for prenatal care, half received special antismoking materials. These materials included a letter stating that blood tests had revealed "abnormalities in the chemistry of your blood [that] indicate you are probably a cigarette smoker" and urging them to stop for their own health and that of their babies. Although most of the women who received these materials did not quit smoking, they were more than twice as likely to quit during pregnancy than those who did not receive the materials.

The second application we will consider is a behavior change program to reduce the risk of being infected with the AIDS human immunodeficiency virus (HIV) among gay men whose sexual practices placed them at relatively high risk of infection (Kelly et al., 1989). The program had several components. For instance, it provided the men with information and trained them to identify and alter antecedents for high-risk behaviors, such as their moods when these behaviors occurred in the past, the places at which these behaviors tended to occur, or the intoxicating substances the men had used. Compared with similar men who were waiting to receive the same program, these men dramatically decreased their frequency of high-risk behaviors, especially with regard to having anal intercourse without using a condom. Another AIDS prevention program produced an enormous increase in nurses' use of protective gloves in high-risk hospital situations (DeVries, Burnette, & Redmon, 1991). The program involved showing the nurses data regarding when they had and had not worn the gloves in the previous 2 weeks, praising them for glove use, and urging them to use gloves more often.

Many other behavior modification interventions for health promotion have also been successful—for example, by helping many people improve their diets, exercise more, use seat belts, and reduce stress in their lives (Sarafino, 1998).

Enhancing Medical Treatment   Not only can behavior change techniques help in promoting health when people are well, they also can enhance the medical treatments patients receive when they are ill. For instance, many patients do not adhere to their physicians' recommendations as closely as they should, and behavioral methods have been applied effectively to increase patients' *adherence* to, or *compliance* with, their medical treatment (Sarafino, 1998). Some of these methods involve altering the behavior's antecedents. For example, patients are more likely to take their medication if they have reminders or cues, such as an alarm, to do it and if taking medicine coincides with their habits and rituals, as when pills are taken at meals. Adherence to treatment also improves when rewards are contingent on performing the behavior. Behavioral methods have improved treatment adherence in patients with many different medical conditions, including asthma (Sarafino, 1997), diabetes (Lowe & Lutzker, 1979), kidney disease (Mosley et al., 1993), and severe burns (Hegel et al., 1986).

Principles of behavior change can also enhance medical treatment by reducing the anxiety of hospitalized patients who are awaiting surgery; those with high anxiety tend to stay in the hospital longer and use more medication for pain during recovery than patients with less preoperative anxiety (Anderson & Masur, 1983). A study demonstrated the benefits of modeling techniques for children who were awaiting surgeries that were not life threatening (Melamed & Siegel, 1975). One group of children saw a film that showed the experiences of a hospitalized boy, and the other group saw a film about a boy going on a trip to the country. The children who saw the film about the hospitalized boy experienced less anxiety before and after surgery than those who saw the other film. Other research has shown that children who receive this kind of intervention before surgery recover more quickly than children who do not (Pinto & Hollandsworth, 1989).

Sport Psychology   Researcher Brent Rushall (1993) described the case of a champion female rower who was training to enter an upcoming international competition. To be eligible to compete, she had to take fitness tests twice a month and report the results to the governing body to show that she was maintaining her fitness and motivation for the sport. Even though she was training harder, this athlete had become very concerned because her fitness scores were showing a declining trend and she had started to feel weak and a little ill for a couple of days prior to her testing dates. Cognitive methods were applied to help her overcome her problem: she received training to concentrate her thoughts during fitness testing on each segment of the motor actions she needed to make and to distract her thoughts from her pain and effort. This approach worked. Her fitness scores improved markedly, and her confidence was restored.

Behavior change techniques are also useful in helping less-accomplished athletes improve their sports skills, using modeling and reinforcement for progress in performing the skills (Donahue, Gillis, & King, 1980; Scott, Scott, & Howe, 1998; Whelan, Mahoney, & Meyers, 1991). Technological advances in video and computer equipment can make these methods more precise (Franks & Maile, 1991). Athletes can watch the action performed well on a video monitor, try to copy the action while being videotaped, and then make moment-by-moment comparisons between their actions and the model's.

Employment Settings

Edward Feeney (1972) was working for an air freight business as a vice president when he introduced some behavioral methods into the company's operations. By using behavioral methods, such as praise and other types of reinforcement for good performance, the company saved millions of dollars. Applying behavior modification principles at work sites, such as business and industrial firms and human service agencies, is called **organizational behavior management** (Frederiksen & Lovett, 1980).

Organizational behavior management focuses on changing behavior by altering its antecedents and consequences and by teaching new actions through instructions and modeling (P. L. Brown, 1982; Luthans & Kreitner, 1985). These methods can be effective in achieving many different goals. One frequent outcome goal is to save money, either by reducing losses or by increasing productivity. For example, a large grocery store used behavioral methods to reduce thefts (Carter et al., 1988), a consulting firm reduced the miles employees drove their cars on workdays (Foxx & Schaeffer, 1981), and factories reduced tardiness (Hermann et al., 1973) and absenteeism (Pedalino & Gamboa, 1974). Improving worker safety is another common goal organizational behavior management has addressed successfully by modifying employee behavior to decrease accidents and exposure to toxic chemicals (Hopkins et al., 1986; Komaki, Barwick, & Scott, 1978).

Self-Management: Changing Our Own Behavior

Do you wish you could study more or eat a healthier diet or stop biting your nails or stop complaining so much? If you have tried to change these or other behaviors in the past and failed, you probably lacked the skills to help you succeed. People can learn behavior change skills. Applying these skills to modify one's own behavior is called **self-management,** or *self-modification*. By learning self-management techniques, people can strengthen two general abilities:

- **Self-control** is the ability to *exercise restraint* over our emotions, impulses, or desires. People with self-control can resist temptation or delay gratification when they want something. Young children typically have poor self-control and want things, such as a toy, "right now." Adults often can persevere for months or years to obtain some objectives.

CONCEPT CHECK 1.5

1. As a field of study that joins medicine and psychology, health psychology uses a perspective called the _____ model of health and illness.
2. The text discusses how principles of behavior change can increase patients' adherence to doctor-prescribed behaviors, such as taking medicine and exercising. A prescribed behavior not discussed in the text that you think might respond to behavioral methods is _____ . ⇔
3. Applying behavior modification principles in business and industry is called _____ .
4. A 16-year-old's behavior that would be an example of self-control is _____ . ⇔
5. True or false: The great majority of students' self-management projects succeed in changing their behavior. _____

Answers: 1. biopsychosocial, 2. reducing dietary fat, 3. organizational behavior management, 4. refusing to have sex, particularly without using a condom, 5. true

■ **Self-regulation** is the ability to *direct* and *modulate* our own actions and behave appropriately even when our actions are not being monitored by someone else.

Chances are you called your lack of these abilities "no willpower" when you didn't succeed in changing your behavior in the past. These two abilities often overlap, with self-regulation involving a broader set of skills that may require the person to have strong skills in self-control. Sometimes books use the terms *self-control, self-regulation,* and *self-management* interchangeably, but they really have somewhat different meanings (Brigham, 1982).

Self-management has been applied extensively with considerable success. When this approach is used in behavior therapy, the therapist and client work together to design a self-management program that the client then carries out under supervision. In two very different examples, self-management helped a man to decrease his sulking and bickering behaviors (Goldiamond, 1965) and helped several men to reduce their hard-driving, *type* A behavior and increase the time they spent relaxing after dinner (Nakano, 1990). Self-management seems to be more effective if it is supervised by someone with training in behavior modification—even for just a few minutes a week by phone (Marshall, Presse, & Andrews, 1976; Zeiss, 1978).

What's more, students have learned and applied behavior change techniques successfully in college courses for many years. The vast majority of students meet their preestablished goals of the self-management projects (Hamilton, 1980) and are satisfied with the behavioral changes they achieve (Barrera & Glasgow, 1976). The behaviors people can change in self-management projects are quite diverse. Researchers have reported that self-management programs can markedly increase exercising (Kau & Fischer, 1974) and reduce tooth grinding (Pawlicki & Galotti, 1978). (Go to ✓)

SUMMARY

Behavior is anything people do, usually in response to internal or external events. Behaviors can be overt actions that are open to view or covert activities that are not openly shown. People's traits—broad and stable characteristics—are not behaviors, nor are psychological diagnoses or the outcomes of behavior, such as becoming more physically fit. Both heredity and experience affect behavioral development.

Experience affects behavior through learning. We acquire and change behaviors through respondent conditioning, operant conditioning, modeling, and cognition. In respondent conditioning, a potential conditioned stimulus (CS) gains the ability to elicit a conditioned response (CR) by being associated repeatedly with an unconditioned stimulus (US) that already elicits an unconditioned response (UR). The UR and CR are the same behavior. In operant conditioning, behavior is affected by the consequences it produces and the antecedents that set the occasion for it. There are two broad types of consequences: reinforcement increases performance of a behavior and punishment decreases its performance. Respondent and operant conditioning occur together in everyday life.

Modeling is the process of learning by observing other people's behavior. We can learn both operant and respondent behaviors in this way. Cognition is mental activity, especially thinking and reasoning, by which we generate plans, ideas, expectations, beliefs, and rules that serve as covert antecedents to our behavior. Self-efficacy is our belief concerning our ability to succeed at a particular activity.

Behavior modification is a discipline that uses principles of learning and cognition to understand and change behavior. The discipline has four defining characteristics: (1) it focuses on behavior, trying to modify behavioral deficits and excesses; (2) it considers learning and the environment to be the main sources by which behaviors can be changed; (3) it has a strong scientific orientation; and (4) its approach to changing behavior is pragmatic and active, using both behavioral and cognitive methods.

Although the principles of behavior change developed from the perspective called behaviorism and associated research, the roots of these methods go back at least to the beginnings of Buddhism. These techniques are widely accepted and used today, partly because professionals who have studied and applied them collected data and conducted research showing their utility. Behavioral and cognitive methods are highly effective in changing people's behavior and can be applied to change one's own behavior.

Behavior modification principles can be applied effectively to improve behavior in many spheres of everyday life. For instance, parents can be trained in behavioral and cognitive methods to improve their parenting skills, thereby enhancing their relationships with their children and preventing coercive patterns from developing in their family interactions. Parents can also learn and apply skills to reduce problems their children may have, by altering antecedents and consequences to reduce children's oppositional behavior, for example, or by using a urine alarm apparatus and operant conditioning techniques to decrease children's bed-wetting.

In educational settings, behavioral methods can make instruction more effective through the techniques of programmed instruction, computer-assisted instruction (CAI), and the personalized system of instruction (PSI). These educational approaches divide course material into small units and provide immediate feedback on test performance. To a large degree, they allow each student to progress at his or her own pace. Behavioral methods are also useful in helping teachers decrease class disruptions and increase students' attention to class activities.

After it became clear that physical health and illness result from the interplay of biological, psychological, and social factors in people's lives, the disciplines of medicine and psychology were joined to form the field of health psychology. Professionals from this field, as well as behavioral medicine and psychosomatic medicine, have begun to apply behavioral and cognitive methods to successfully promote human health by helping people stop smoking, fostering their use of safer-sex methods, and enhancing medical treatment. In other effective behavior change applications, athletes have used behavioral and cognitive methods to improve their performance and skills, and employers have used behavioral methods to improve workers' productivity and safety in organizational behavior management programs. People can apply behavioral and cognitive methods in a self-management program to change their own behavior and improve their self-control and self-regulation.

KEY TERMS

behavior	modeling	computer-assisted instruction
learning	cognition	personalized system of instruction
unconditioned stimulus	self-efficacy	health psychology
unconditioned response	behavior modification	organizational behavior management
conditioned stimulus	behavioral deficit	self-management
conditioned response	behavioral excess	self-control
respondent conditioning	behavioral methods	self-regulation
operant conditioning	cognitive methods	
reinforcement	behaviorism	
punishment	urine alarm apparatus	
antecedents	programmed instruction	

REVIEW QUESTIONS

1. Describe the research by Greenspoon (1955) on modifying verbal behavior and why its results are important.
2. What is behavior? Give three examples each of overt and covert behaviors.

3. Why are traits, diagnoses, and outcomes of behavior not behaviors?

4. How is heredity involved in behavioral development?

5. Describe the structure of how respondent conditioning occurs and give an example from your own life.

6. Define the terms *reinforcement* and *punishment* and give two examples of each from your own life.

7. What are antecedents? Give two examples from your life.

8. How was reinforcement used in the case study to reinstate speech in a schizophrenic man?

9. Describe the research and findings of Bandura (1965) on the role of consequences on modeling.

10. Give two examples each of modeling and cognition affecting your behavior.

11. Describe the four defining characteristics of behavior modification.

12. What are behavioral deficits and excesses? Give two examples of each in people you know.

13. Define behavioral methods and cognitive methods.

14. Define the terms *applied behavior analysis* and *behavior therapy*.

15. In the study (Wahler et al., 1965) on oppositional behavior, Eddie performed about seven times more oppositional than cooperative responses when playing with his mother. In terms of operant conditioning, why did he do this?

16. In terms of operant and respondent conditioning, how does the urine alarm apparatus reduce bed-wetting?

17. Describe the process and characteristics of programmed instruction.

18. Describe three types of reminders or cues, other than alarms, patients could use as antecedents to improve adherence in taking medication.

RELATED READINGS

Baum, W. M. (1994). *Understanding behaviorism*. New York: HarperCollins.

Karoly, P., & Kanfer, F. H. (Eds.). (1982). *Self-management and behavior change: From theory to practice*. New York: Pergamon.

Kazdin, A. E. (1978). *History of behavior modification: Experimental foundations of contemporary research*. Baltimore: University Park Press.

Krumboltz, J. D., & Krumboltz, H. B. (1972). *Changing children's behavior*. Englewood Cliffs, NJ: Prentice-Hall.

Luthans, F., & Kreitner, R. (1985). *Organizational behavior modification and beyond: An operant and social learning approach*. Glenview, IL: Scott, Foresman.

Sarafino, E. P. (1998). *Health psychology: Biopsychosocial interactions* (3rd ed.). New York: Wiley.

Skinner, B. F. (1974). *About behaviorism*. New York: Knopf.

Sulzer-Azaroff, B., Drabman, R. M., Greer, R. D., Hall, R. V., Iwata, B. A., & O'Leary, S. G. (Eds.). (1988). *Behavior analysis in education*. Lawrence, KS: Society for the Experimental Analysis of Behavior.

Smoking is a target behavior that is easy to define and assess.

2

Specifying and Assessing What We Want to Change

T he year was 1980: school counselors in junior high and high schools in a medium-sized U.S. city became justifiably alarmed when they realized that drug use among their students had skyrocketed in the last decade and was approaching the levels seen in larger cities. The counselors felt they must do something about this increasing problem. They decided to design a drug prevention *intervention*—a program of behavior change methods—and to request permission from their superintendent of schools to implement it.

Through many hours of meetings, the counselors decided that the way to prevent drug use was to attack two problems: (1) the students' lack of knowledge about the negative effects of using drugs and (2) the students' low levels of self-esteem, which made them vulnerable to the appeal of drugs. The counselors then designed a program to address these two problems. They identified lots of readings and videos that describe how various drugs can cause health problems or even death, lead to addiction, destroy a user's motivation, lead to other criminal behavior, and ruin the user's life. They also contacted former drug users who agreed to come to the schools and give testimonials, confirming these negative effects. To deal with the self-esteem problem, the counselors decided to have discussion groups in which the students could talk about themselves and things that were bothering them. The counselors believed these groups would serve to increase students' self-esteem by helping them dispel negative ideas about themselves and having them share their feelings with one another. Because drug use in their community almost never began before ninth grade, the counselors decided to administer their prevention program to eighth-graders.

The superintendent liked the program and decided to conduct it in half of the city's junior high schools in the fall semester and the remaining schools in the spring. This allowed the counselors to use personnel more efficiently and to make comparisons between students who received the program in the fall and those who would receive it later. When the program was completed, the counselors and the superintendent were elated by the results. The counselors compared students who had participated in the program with those who had not and made before and after comparisons of students who completed the program. These comparisons revealed consistent outcomes: after participating in the program, students reported higher levels of self-esteem, scored much higher on knowledge about drugs, and reported much more negative attitudes toward drugs, drug use, and drug abusers. A news release concluded that the program "was a complete success and accomplished everything the school officials had hoped for."

Was that conclusion correct? We'll answer this question in this chapter, and we'll learn how to specify and assess behaviors we want to change in other individuals and in ourselves. In this book, a person whose behavior is the target for change will often be referred to as "the person" or, if it is not otherwise clear, "the target person," "the target child," or "the client." We saw in Chapter 1 that behavior change programs focus on behavior and use data about the person's responses to decide whether it has changed. The first steps in this process include identifying and defining the goals and behaviors to focus on in the program.

GOALS AND TARGET BEHAVIORS

Suppose you are a personnel expert working in a large organization and a supervisor comes to you for help in dealing with a problem employee. The first thing you ask is "What's the problem?" The supervisor answers, "Well, Al's lazy, he doesn't have much initiative, and he's so negative all the time. He just doesn't seem to care about his work." This sounds bad, but this description doesn't help you decide what to do about the problem. Why? So far all you have are broad characteristics of Al's behavior. As we saw in Chapter 1, broad characteristics don't specify the behaviors that need to change. The behaviors to be changed in a behavior modification program are called **target behaviors.** Some examples of target behaviors people might want to change are anxiety, biting nails, drinking alcohol, smoking, playing socially, exercising, and doing chores.

Without knowing what the specific problem behaviors are, you can't identify the goals the program should have. You also can't determine what the behavior's antecedents and consequences are or devise ways to alter them. You need to get the supervisor to be more specific—to pinpoint the behaviors. **Pinpointing** is the process of converting broad characteristics into specific, objective, and measurable actions (Brown, 1982). There are several ways to pinpoint the behaviors. For instance, you can observe

Al's performance directly, or you can prod the supervisor to describe examples of Al's behavior. Here are some examples:

- When I talk to Al about a new project, he almost always complains about his workload and looks only for difficulties in doing the project rather than trying to find solutions to these difficulties.
- He has come to work late in the mornings and been late after lunch several times this month and acts like I shouldn't think it's a problem when I call him on it.
- He turned in several reports late—2 or 3 days late—this month, and they were poorly prepared. One of them, for instance, contained data for the wrong month.
- When we have staff meetings, Al rarely contributes ideas that help move a project along. Instead, he verbally abuses the others, calling their ideas "stupid" or "silly," and distracts our work with jokes or irrelevant comments.

Now we can see what some of the target behaviors need to be: some involve *behavioral deficits*, such as in his late and poorly prepared reports, and some involve *behavioral excesses*, such as his joking at staff meetings.

Pinpointing is a critical process in all behavior change programs. Once the target behaviors are clear, we can identify and define the behavioral goals of any program we design.

Identifying and Defining Behavioral Goals

The goals we might want to achieve by applying a behavior change program can be of two types: outcome goals and behavioral goals. **Outcome goals** are the broad or abstracted results we want to achieve. In Al's case, the outcome goals might be to help him be a more conscientious, cooperative, and productive employee.

Outcome goals in behavior modification programs are usually very obvious and straightforward, relating directly to the broad characteristics we've noticed about the person. And the need for or value in achieving these goals is usually clear and not widely disputed, as in Al's case and in these examples:

- Improving parent–child relationships
- Improving students' grades in school
- Enabling children with autism to do self-help skills
- Preventing substance abuse
- Preventing the spread of AIDS
- Losing weight

But sometimes the goals or the behaviors targeted to achieve the goals are strongly disputed, as often happens in education. For instance, some parents disagree with schools' goals of having children learn about sex or moral values. And although most educators agree that students should learn to think critically about information they encounter, they sometimes disagree on which specific behaviors or skills should be taught to achieve this goal. Disputes about goals and target behaviors typically are

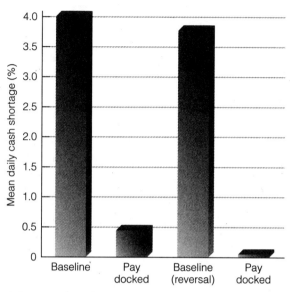

Figure 2.1 Mean daily percentage of cash shortages as compared against cash-register records during baseline (no docking of pay in this period) and intervention (pay docked) phases. *Source:* Data from Marholin & Gray, 1976.

based on differences in values or beliefs. For now, we will defer discussing appropriate goals of behavior change programs until later chapters, especially Chapter 15.

The program's **behavioral goal** is the *level of the target behavior* we hope to achieve. For example, for the target behavior of jogging, the behavioral goal might be to increase jogging to three 1-hour sessions each week. Sometimes outcome and behavioral goals are the same; this can happen when both goals simply involve quitting a particular behavior, such as twirling one's hair. Very often, a program's outcome and behavioral goals are different, with outcome goals being broader or less directly tied to the specific behaviors. Losing weight might be an outcome goal for a dietary target behavior, and the behavioral goal might be to reduce snacking to two servings per day. Another example of the difference between these types of goals comes from an application of behavior change techniques to reduce cash-register shortages in a small restaurant (Marholin & Gray, 1976). The outcome goal was to have the cash in the register equal the register-tape totals at the end of each day, and the consequences introduced to change behavior were contingent on the cashiers' meeting that goal. If a shortage existed that was greater than 1% of daily sales, the cashiers' salaries were docked to cover the loss. Although the program succeeded in achieving the goal, as Figure 2.1 shows, no target behavior or behavioral goal was identified. Is this OK? Maybe not, because the cashiers could meet the goal in many different ways, including shortchanging customers and under-ringing sales on the register. To change behavior in a particular way, such as making cashier transactions more precise, we must identify the target behavior and the behavioral goal, and then change the behavior's consequences.

People who try to lose weight often focus on the outcome goal—losing weight— rather than on the behaviors that enable them to meet the goal. Most people know that the "best" way to lose weight combines two behaviors: eating fewer calories and exercising. But there are many other ways to lose or control weight, some of which are dangerous. For example, bulimia nervosa is an eating disorder characterized by recurrent episodes of binge eating, followed quickly with purging by self-induced vomiting, laxative use, or other means to prevent the food from being digested. Individuals who develop this disorder usually start out dieting normally and then begin to use more extreme methods (Killen et al., 1994; Polivy & Thomsen, 1988). Because people who diet are frequently so focused on the outcome goal, the behaviors that enable them to lose weight may begin to diverge across individuals, with some people trying increasingly desperate methods and becoming convinced that these methods help them meet the goal. Somewhere in this process, they lose the ability to resist tempting foods (self-control) and to direct and modulate their eating behavior (self-regulation). The development of bulimia nervosa is much more complex than this, but it may well include these events.

Once we have identified behavioral goals for a behavior modification program, we need to define them very clearly. In trying to change Al's work performance, it wouldn't be enough to say, for instance, "By the end of the program, Al will come late to work much less than in the past." This goal is too vague. How will we know he achieved it? We must specify the level we want exactly, for example: "By the end of the program, Al should reduce his coming to work late from about 10 instances to fewer than 3 per month, with each lateness being less than 10 minutes." It's a good idea to indicate the starting level, "about 10 instances," in stating the behavioral goal.

Another good idea in defining behavioral goals is to identify **behavioral subgoals**— intermediate levels of the behavior to be achieved during the program. So, if we were to allocate 3 months for Al's program, we might set the following subgoals for his lateness behavior: fewer than 7 latenesses in the first month, 5 in the second, and 3 in the third. Setting subgoals will make the program seem reasonable, and as Al achieves each subgoal, he will gain self-efficacy and motivation for reaching the behavioral goal.

To modify behaviors effectively, we must *define the behaviors clearly, completely, and in measurable terms*. If we fail to do this, we will sometimes think the behavior occurred when it actually didn't, or we won't realize it occurred when it actually did. As a result, our data will be inaccurate and the techniques we apply to change the behavior will frequently be directed toward the wrong actions. These circumstances obviously are not desirable, and they will make the task of changing the target behavior harder and less successful. Decisions about whether a behavior change program has succeeded must be based on whether the behavioral goals have been met. (Go to)

Defining Operant Target Behaviors

To illustrate the importance of defining target behaviors clearly, completely, and in measurable terms, let's suppose you decided to change your own diet, stating your target behavior as "to eat healthy." Some of my students begin in this manner. In prodding

CLOSE-UP 2.1

Deciding Whether a Program to Prevent Substance Abuse Worked

 At the beginning of this chapter we looked at a program school counselors designed and administered to prevent drug abuse, and we asked whether the program was a success. Let's see why we asked this question.

The program focused on preventing substance abuse through drug education. This approach has been widely used in schools, and dozens of studies have been done to assess its effectiveness. In 1988, Robert Bangert-Drowns published an evaluation of these studies' findings, using a research technique called *meta-analysis*, which pools the results of prior research to create an integrated overview of the findings. Meta-analyses are useful in clarifying research results and arriving at an overall conclusion when the effects found in some studies have been different from those in others, as has occurred in the field of substance abuse education. Bangert-Drowns's meta-analysis revealed that "typical substance abuse education had its most positive effects on knowledge and attitudes, but was *unsuccessful in changing the drug-using behaviors* of students" (p. 243, italics added).

Did the counselors' program work? Probably not, because its purpose was to reduce drug use—the target behavior—but they didn't measure this, and indeed, most similar programs have failed to reduce drug use. As in most other programs, the counselors documented desirable changes only in the students' knowledge and attitudes about drugs. To tell whether a program to change behavior worked, we need to measure the target behavior and compare it against a specified behavioral goal.

them to be more precise, I ask, "What does 'eat healthy' mean? Does it mean you'll now eat three meals a day, or eat more vegetables and less fat, or chew your food to a certain consistency, or consume fewer calories?" Eating is an operant behavior, and to change it, you'll need to alter its antecedents and consequences. If you define a target behavior vaguely, you'll be uncertain when, where, and how to introduce appropriate antecedents and consequences.

How much detail your definition of the target behavior must have depends on exactly what you're trying to achieve—the definition must match the goal. If your behavioral goal states or implies certain details of the behavior, such as the specific snacks you will or will not eat, your definition of the target behavior must reflect those details. For instance, some evidence indicates that obese individuals who lose the most weight in a behavior change program chew each bite of food slower than those who are less successful in losing weight (Spiegel, Wadden, & Foster, 1991). If you wanted to modify how fast you chew each bite of food, you'd need to define "bite" and "slower."

Overt and Covert Behaviors In Chapter 1, we saw that behaviors can be overt or covert and that applications and research on principles of behavior change tend to focus on overt behavior. This is because we can usually define external behaviors more clearly and measure them more objectively than internal behaviors.

Think about the overt behavior of playing a guitar. You could define and measure its occurrence very accurately, couldn't you? Although you may have to work a little harder to define some other external behaviors, such as whining and bickering, it can be done. In a program to improve children's behaviors at home, Edward Christophersen and his coworkers (1972) defined "whining" as a "verbal complaint conducted in a sing-song (wavering) manner in a pitch above that of the normal speaking voice" and "bickering" as a "verbal argument between any two or all three of the children conducted in a degree of loudness above the normal speaking voice." Having these definitions makes it easier to recognize the behaviors when they occur.

The tasks of defining and measuring covert behaviors—thoughts, feelings, and physiological changes—are more problematic, but still possible. Suppose you were a therapist and wanted to help a client reduce her negative thoughts about herself. The two of you probably could generate useful definitions of these covert behaviors, perhaps including some typical words or phrases she uses in her thoughts, such as "dumb" or "fat." This would help her recognize negative thoughts when they occur. Only she can know for sure when a negative thought occurs, however, so measuring the behavior will be a very subjective process. Without some independent way of substantiating her self-reports, any progress she makes will be unclear (Baer, Wolf, & Risley, 1968). This situation is less than ideal, but we will see later that there are ways to make evidence from self-reports more convincing.

Defining and measuring internal changes in physiology, such as increases in blood pressure or the secretion of adrenaline, often require special apparatus or biochemical analyses. Professionals in research or therapy may be able to make these assessments. One physiological measure you can make easily and fairly accurately is heart rate: when you take your pulse, you are counting heartbeats.

Task Analyses of Complex Behaviors Sometimes the operant target behavior we want to teach or improve involves a complex set of responses. If so, it is useful to determine what these responses are and whether they need to be performed in a certain sequence, as when we put on a pair of slacks or brush our teeth. A motor activity that consists of a sequence of responses is called a **chain,** and the responses that make up the chain are called *links* (Gagné, 1985). For instance, putting on a shirt with buttons consists of this sequence:

1. Holding the shirt upright with one hand, with the front facing you.
2. Inserting the free arm in the corresponding sleeve.
3. Reaching the other arm behind the back to locate the corresponding sleeve hole.
4. Inserting that arm in the corresponding sleeve.
5. Pulling the front of the shirt together.
6. Inserting the first button into its buttonhole.
7. Inserting the next button, and so on.

To perform a chain correctly, the links must be done pretty much in a particular order. Learning to perform a chain or other complex set of responses can be very difficult, especially if the task is extremely complicated or the person's learning abilities are very limited, as they are if the learner is a young child or has a learning disorder. Once the component responses of a complex task are identified, a program can be designed to train the person to perform each component and to put all the links together.

The process of identifying the responses and any required sequences that make up a complex set of behaviors is called **task analysis.** Stephen Fawcett and L. Keith Miller (1975) conducted a task analysis of public speaking behavior to design and carry out a program to train this complex skill. Their task analysis broke the skill down into two types of behavior: (1) *eye contact* and *gesturing,* which should occur continuously during a speech, and (2) a series of *speaking behaviors* that should occur. The speaker should start by standing in an appropriate position, next scanning the audience briefly while smiling, thanking the host for the introduction, greeting the audience with a statement while smiling, and introducing the topic of the speech. The final speaking behaviors should include a final eye sweep of the audience while smiling and a request for questions. The trainees received feedback on each behavior for each of several speeches, and they improved quickly and dramatically during training. A very different complex skill is cardiopulmonary resuscitation (CPR), which individuals can learn and apply to save heart attack victims' lives. Table 2.1 presents parts of a task analysis of this skill. CPR is a very intricate skill to use and should be learned with formal instruction, practiced often, and maintained by taking refresher courses (AMA, 1989).

Response Generalization   Suppose a boy behaves very aggressively toward classmates in school, and his teacher begins introducing consequences to reduce the target behavior of hitting. Do you think he would decrease making other aggressive behaviors, such as pushing or kicking, too? Chances are, he would. The effects of efforts to modify a target behavior frequently *generalize,* or spread, *to other behaviors* that the intervention did not specifically address (Carr, 1988). **Response generalization** is a phenomenon in which altering one behavior leads to similar changes in another, unaddressed response—usually one that is similar or related to the target behavior. This is an important phenomenon because it can enhance the efficiency of behavior modification programs. If we design a program for someone with many behavioral deficits or excesses, we may be able to produce desirable changes in many behaviors even though the program focuses on only a few target behaviors.

This potential efficiency sounds very helpful—and often it is—but we can't always predict if and to what degree response generalization will occur. Some evidence indicates that generalization occurs more readily to responses that are similar or related to the target behavior (Carr, 1988; Kimble, 1961). For instance, the aggressive behaviors of hitting and pushing are *similar* in that they both use the hands to apply force against another person, and they are *related* in that they often occur together and can be used to get the same rewards, such as getting to use a toy another child will not give up. But response generalization sometimes occurs among behaviors that are not similar or clearly related, as you will see in the following examples of response generalization. The addressed and unaddressed behaviors that changed tend to show more similarity or relatedness in the examples at the beginning of the list than in the ones toward the end:

Table 2.1 Analysis of some tasks and subtasks a trained single-rescuer (SR) would use in performing cardiopulmonary resuscitation (CPR)

Before starting the CPR procedure, the SR determines that the victim is unresponsive by shaking and calling to the person by name if known ("Jan, Jan, are you okay? Can you hear me?"). If no response, the SR calls for help immediately. The CPR procedure follows a sequence: **A** (airway, open), **B** (breathing, start), and **C** (circulation-compression).

A. *Open the victim's airway.* The SR performs three actions to clear the airway and check for breathing:

1. Place hand nearest victim's head on forehead and hand nearest feet around back of neck near base of skull.
2. Elevate neck gently while pushing forehead downward (chin should point nearly straight upward). This should move the tongue from blocking the throat opening.
3. Place ear over victim's mouth while looking at the chest for movement; listen for air exchange and feel for air movement.

B. *Start the breathing process.* If the victim is not breathing, the SR seals his or her lips around the victim's mouth and gives two strong breaths while maintaining the opened airway and pinching the nostrils closed.

C. *Check circulation and use compression.* The SR checks blood circulation by feeling for a pulse in the carotid artery in the neck (to the side of the Adam's apple). If no pulse is felt within a few seconds, the SR conducts compressions with these actions:

1. Bare victim's chest; use middle and index fingers of hand nearest victim's feet to trace edge of ribs up to the notch where ribs meet the sternum in the center of the chest. Place middle finger in notch with index finger on top of the sternum.
2. Place heel of other hand on victim's sternum, just next to and touching the index finger.
3. Remove middle and index fingers (on sternum's tip) and place that hand on the back of the hand that is on sternum. Interlace fingers.
4. With shoulders directly above sternum, elbows locked, and fingers off victim's chest, depress sternum downward (1.5 to 2 inches) by bending from the hips. Without bouncing or losing hand contact with sternum, count 15 compressions as follows: "1&2&3&4&**5**," and "1&2&3&4&**10**," and "1&2 . . . **15**."

The SR then gives two breaths, as in step B. The series of 15 compressions and 2 breaths comprise a "cycle." The SR does three more cycles and checks for pulse and breathing.

Sources: Learn Free (2000); Seaman, Greene, & Watson-Perczel (1986).

- Three 4-year-old girls who were rewarded for changing the forms they made out of blocks in a preschool began to construct forms they never made before (Goetz & Baer, 1973).
- A 5-year-old boy whose oppositional behavior at home was reduced with behavioral methods showed a corresponding reduction in bed-wetting (Nordquist, 1971).
- Pizza delivery drivers who participated in a program to increase their use of seat belts also improved their use of turn signals (Ludwig & Geller, 1991).
- Four 3- to 5-year-olds with mental retardation who were rewarded for complying with therapists' simple requests—for instance, "Touch your nose" and "Open the

door"—increased their compliance. At the same time, the children decreased certain inappropriate behaviors, such as being aggressive toward the therapist, disrupting training sessions, and destroying property (Parrish et al., 1986).

- A 7-year-old boy with mental retardation whose excessive talking with his teacher was reduced by having the teacher stop rewarding it with her attention showed associated increases in disruptive behavior and in talking and playing with other children (Sajwaj, Twardosz, & Burke, 1972).

What's more, a study by Robert Wahler (1975) found that the behaviors that are related to each other and that change together can differ from one individual to the next.

Although we don't yet know all of the factors that affect response generalization and can't always predict when and how much it will occur, we have enough knowledge to use the phenomenon to increase the efficiency of some program designs. For instance, if a client has many behavioral deficits or excesses, we can focus the program on target behaviors we think are similar or related to unaddressed problem behaviors, monitor for changes in these unaddressed behaviors, and revise the program later to address those problem behaviors that do not show response generalization.

Defining Respondent Target Behaviors

We saw in Chapter 1 that respondent behaviors include unconditioned and conditioned responses. People learn through respondent conditioning to associate two previously unrelated events—a conditioned stimulus (CS) and a conditioned response (CR)—so that the CS gains the ability to elicit the CR. Because CRs are learned behaviors, they often are targets of behavior change programs. Emotions, feelings, and likes and dislikes are CRs that are common respondent target behaviors.

Like operant behaviors, respondent behaviors can be internal or external. Often they are both. For example, when we are anxious or afraid, we may show overt signs of fear, such as in facial expressions or efforts to escape the situation, and experience covert behaviors, such as negative thoughts and increased physiological arousal. When designing a program to change a respondent behavior, we need to define the behavior in terms of its internal or external responses, or both. Some programs may need a dual focus to be fully successful. For instance, in behavior change programs to reduce fear of public speaking, successfully reducing people's subjective feelings of fear while giving a speech does not necessarily generalize to such overt signs of fear as frequently moistening their lips or pacing (Marshall, Presse, & Andrews, 1976). To reduce these overt signs of fear, programs probably need to include training in public speaking skills too.

From the example on public speaking, you may be wondering whether response generalization occurs with respondent behaviors. There is evidence that it can (Kimble, 1961), but, as in the case of operant behavior, we do not have enough knowledge yet to predict accurately how much, if any, generalization will occur when respondent behaviors are modified. It's possible that programs to reduce one type of fear, such as of snakes, may help people to cope better with other fears that were not addressed in the intervention. An adult whose fear of snakes was reduced in a behavior modification program reported that the greatest benefit of the "treatment was the feeling that if I could lick [my fear of] snakes, I could lick anything. It gave me the confidence to tackle, also successfully, some personal stuff" (Bandura, Jeffery, & Gajdos, 1975, p. 150).

Alternative or Competing Responses

Can you feel anxious and calm at the same time? Can you bite your fingernails if you put your hands in your pockets? Probably not. Each of these situations involves two incompatible or interfering behaviors, making them difficult to do at the same time. Actions that interfere or are incompatible with other behaviors are called **alternative responses,** or *competing responses*. A useful technique for reducing a target behavior is to encourage the person to replace it with an alternative response. One way to encourage someone to make an alternative response is to reward it. So, if you want to reduce a child's oppositional behavior, you might reinforce cooperative behavior. If we choose to use alternative responses in a program, we should define them, just as we would define target behaviors.

Alternative responses can involve operant or respondent behaviors and can be overt or covert behaviors. Here are some other examples of alternative responses:

- Praising people instead of criticizing them
- Thinking "I can do it" instead of "I'll never do well at this"
- Smiling instead of frowning
- Saying "darn" instead of "#@*$%"
- Exercising instead of lying on the sofa
- Taking a deep breath and "counting to 10" instead of getting angry

As you look at these examples, note that there may be several possible alternative responses for each undesirable behavior.

SPECIAL POPULATIONS: INDIVIDUALS WITH DEVELOPMENTAL DISABILITIES

Young people who are classified as mentally retarded or autistic have disorders that impair essentially all of their developmental processes, making them very unlikely to develop into well-functioning adults. As a result, professionals often classify them as people with *developmental disabilities*. People with mental retardation and autism share many characteristics, particularly a great difficulty in learning almost all skills—motor, cognitive, language, and social. These characteristics greatly influence the choice of target behaviors and behavioral goals, and these individuals need highly structured and well-planned training regimens to learn even simple tasks. Beginning in the 1960s, behavioral methods have provided this kind of training for people of all ages with mental retardation and autism. Behavior modification is currently the only psychological approach with well-established success for treating individuals with these disorders (Didden, Duker, & Korzilius, 1997; TFPDPP, 1993).

Working With People With Mental Retardation

The American Association of Mental Retardation defines mental retardation on the basis of two major characteristics: subaverage general intelligence and deficiencies in adaptive behavior. In actual practice, people are most often classified as retarded on the basis of intelligence quotient (IQ) scores and clinical judgment because there are no adequate tests of adaptive behavior (Davison & Neale, 1994; Hamilton & Matson, 1992). People's IQ scores are determined by their performance on standardized intelligence tests, usually either the *Wechsler Intelligence Scale for Children* or the *Stanford-Binet Intelligence Scale*. The average IQ score is 100.

About 2.5% of individuals in the United States population are mentally retarded, and each of them is classified in one of the following four levels of retardation:

- *Mild* (IQ from about 53 to 69): This category includes the vast majority (about 85%) of retarded individuals. They are labeled "educable" because they can benefit greatly from special education programs and are usually able to function at about a sixth-grade academic level in adulthood and maintain unskilled jobs.
- *Moderate* (IQ from about 38 to 52): These individuals make up about 10% of people with mental retardation and are described as "trainable." They often have poor motor coordination and are unlikely to advance beyond the second-grade academic level by adulthood.
- *Severe* (IQ from about 22 to 37): People with severe retardation can learn only very simple tasks and often have serious physical handicaps too. Although they are likely to remain very dependent on the help of others throughout life, many acquire habits of personal cleanliness and perform simple self-help skills.
- *Profound* (IQ below about 22): These individuals usually have severe physical deformities as well; they require lifelong care and have short life spans.

Many factors can lead to mental retardation. The more serious levels of retardation often stem from abnormal brain development due to genetic disorders, prenatal damage, or diseases. At the less serious levels, particularly among the mildly retarded, there is no detectable brain damage. Their intellectual problems usually become apparent after they enter school, encounter academic difficulties, and do poorly on an IQ test. Individuals with mild retardation frequently come from culturally alienated, poverty-stricken families with neglectful and socially immature parents, and their retardation may result mainly from environmental deprivation.

Training the mentally retarded requires intensive effort, particularly at the more serious levels of retardation. The teacher must break down tasks into small steps, introduce the antecedents and monitor each student's performance carefully, and provide rewards for correct responding. Using these behavioral methods, individuals can learn tasks appropriate to their age and level of ability (Hamilton & Matson, 1992). For example, children who are profoundly retarded can be toilet trained (Azrin & Foxx, 1971), and the severely retarded can learn how to pluralize nouns (Guess et al., 1968) and perform simple social behaviors (Whitman, Mercurio, & Caponigri, 1970). Adult mothers who are mildly retarded can learn basic child-care skills, such as bathing their babies, cleaning baby bottles, and treating diaper rash (Feldman et al., 1992). (Go to)

CASE STUDY 2.1

Sam—An Autistic Child

Sam was born in 1974 to middle-class parents, and his first couple of years seemed fairly normal (case described in Oltmanns, Neale, & Davison, 1991). But by his second birthday, his parents were becoming concerned for several reasons. For instance, Sam's motor development was slow (his sister's had been more rapid), and it

> seemed uneven. He would crawl normally for a few days and then not crawl at all for awhile. Although he made babbling sounds, he had not developed any speech and did not even seem to understand anything his parents said to him. Simple commands such as "Get the ball," "Come," or "Do you want a cookie?" elicited no response. (p. 248)

At first Sam's parents thought he might be deaf. They consulted his pediatrician, who suggested mental retardation as a possibility. When Sam was nearly 3 years old, his

> parents also began to notice him engaging in more and more behavior that seemed strange and puzzling. Most obvious were his repetitive hand movements. Many times each day he would suddenly flap his hands for several minutes. Other times he rolled his eyes around in their sockets. He still did not speak, but he made smacking sounds and sometimes he would burst out into laughing for no apparent reason. (pp. 248–249)

Sam's social and play behavior were also worrisome to his parents. For instance, he would let them hug him, but he acted indifferent to their attention and wouldn't look at them. He didn't play with his sister, and his solitary play also seemed deviant. If he had a toy car, for example, he wouldn't pretend to drive it around, as other children do. He'd turn it over and spin its wheels incessantly.

After a physical and neurological examination revealed no detectable defect, a psychiatrist examined Sam, diagnosed him as autistic, and recommended that he attend a special school for treatment. Like many schools for children with severe disorders, the school he attended used principles of behavior change to provide training.

Working With Children With Autism

For children with autism, like Sam in Case Study 2.1, behavior modification training begins with the simplest of tasks and builds from one task to the next (Lovaas, 1977).

CONCEPT CHECK 2.1

1. Converting a trait, such as honesty, into specific target behaviors is called: _____ .
2. A behavioral goal a college student might choose when modifying how much studying he or she does is _____ . ⇔
3. To tell if a behavior change program was successful, we need to assess the target behavior and compare it against a specified _____ .
4. A link in a chain you might perform when starting your car is _____ . ⇔
5. We would do a _____ to break down a complex skill into its component responses.
6. If behavioral methods were used to increase children's keeping their clothes clean, a likely example of response generalization might be their _____ . ⇔
7. If you were trying to reduce eating junk foods and began eating carrot sticks instead, eating carrot sticks would be a(n) _____ response.
8. The _____ level of retardation is described as "trainable."
9. A behavioral deficit and a behavioral excess in the case study of Sam that might have suggested he was autistic are _____ and _____ . ⇔

Answers: 1. pinpointing, 2. studying 20 hours a week, 3. behavioral goal, 4. inserting the key in the ignition, 5. task analysis, 6. washing their hands, 7. alternative, 8. moderate, 9. no speech at all [and] self-stimulation behavior (spinning wheel).

Children with autism learn slowly and with great difficulty. Tasks must be presented many, many times. Individual instruction, a great deal of structure, and immediate feedback with rewards for correct performance are necessary.

In Sam's case, training for his many behavioral deficits started with developing eye contact with the teacher (Oltmanns, Neale, & Davison, 1991). A teacher might have begun by saying, "Look at me," and rewarding a good response. After Sam learned eye contact, his training during his first year involved learning to imitate simple behaviors ("Sam, stretch your arms up like this."), point to named objects in pictures ("This is an orange. Point to the orange."), imitate simple speech sounds ("Say this, *ah*."), use the toilet, and dress and undress himself. Progress with autistic children usually is very slow. By the end of the first year, Sam could point correctly to only 38 named objects when presented in pairs, such as an orange and a cat.

Children with autism also exhibit many behavioral excesses that must be reduced or eliminated to make the children accessible to treatment (Schreibman, Charlop, & Kurtz, 1992). One of these is called *self-stimulation,* which may consist of rocking back and forth, flapping the hands, twirling objects with the fingers, and so forth. The reason for these behaviors is unknown, but one possibility is that they produce internal perceptual stimuli that are reinforcing (Lovaas, Newsom, & Hickman, 1987). Behavioral methods have been successful in reducing self-stimulation in autistic children (Lovaas et al., 1973). (Go to ☑)

HOW TO ASSESS BEHAVIOR

A student of mine named Dave was planning a self-management project to decrease his swearing behavior when he announced in class, "I've got a big problem. All of a sudden, I don't swear much anymore." Although he hadn't yet collected any data, he believed his swearing had declined markedly. We discussed the problem, and he agreed to ask his roommates to help him keep track of his swearing for a few days. As you probably suspect, his roommates' data showed a considerable amount of swearing. Assessing behavior requires that we collect data, and there are several types of data we can use.

Types of Data

The data we collect must measure the target behavior and reflect any progress that has been made toward the behavioral goal. Behavior can change across several different dimensions, including how *often,* how *long,* how *soon,* how *well,* and how *strongly* it occurs. Each type of data reflects a different dimension, and we need to select the type(s) of data that will best reflect the dimension(s) of target behavior we want to change (Dowrick, 1991). For example, if the behavioral goal is to increase the time a student studies per week, the data must involve a measure of time. As this example suggests, we can express data as a *rate*—that is, per unit of time—as in, "the number of hours a student studies *per week.*" Let's look at the different types of data we can use to assess behavior, beginning with how frequently it occurs.

Frequency   Probably the most common type of data collected in behavior modification programs is **frequency**—the number of times a behavior occurred. Frequency is an appropriate measure when (1) the target behavior is *discrete*—that is, each instance has a clear start and end; (2) performing each instance takes a *fairly constant amount of time;* and (3) the *behavioral goal* involves *changing how often* the behavior occurs. Dave's project to reduce his swearing qualified on all three of these criteria, so he assessed this behavior in terms of its frequency.

Collecting frequency data is relatively easy to do, and most target behaviors can be appropriately assessed with frequency data. In one case, the frequency of a boy's oppositional behavior was assessed in a behavior change program to reduce how often that behavior occurred (Nordquist, 1971). In another case, the number of arithmetic problems computed correctly by underachieving fifth-graders was assessed after they participated in a program to increase their arithmetic skills (Pigott, Fantuzzo, & Clement, 1986). Other target behaviors that can be assessed appropriately with frequency data are attending school classes, biting nails, paying bills on time, taking medication on schedule, smoking cigarettes, doing specific rehabilitation exercises, hitting classmates in school, and thinking unpleasant thoughts. We can keep track of response frequencies in several different ways, including marking on a sheet of paper, moving a coin from one pocket to another, or advancing a golf score counter each time the response occurs.

Duration   **Duration** refers to the length of time each instance of the target behavior lasts from beginning to end. This type of data is appropriate for assessing instances of behavior that are *ongoing activities*, that last or continue for *varying periods of time*, and that are subject to a *behavioral goal* that involves either *increasing or decreasing that time*. For instance, the duration of social interaction was assessed in a program to increase the time two severely withdrawn children with mental retardation spent in simple social activities, such as rolling balls to each other (Whitman, Mercurio, & Caponigri, 1970). Other examples of target behaviors that can be assessed in terms of duration are studying, watching television, exercising, sleeping, sitting in one's seat, having a tantrum, talking on the telephone, spending time with one's children, and feeling anxious or "blue."

Magnitude In a program to reduce someone's anxiety, wouldn't it be important to assess *how strong* the anxiety is? This would involve a measure of the behavior's **magnitude**—its intensity, degree, or size. Assessing the target behavior's magnitude is useful if that measure *can or does vary* and the *behavioral goal* involves *changing the intensity, degree, or size*. For example, the magnitude of the speech of a girl with mental retardation was assessed in a behavior change program to increase the loudness with which she spoke, measured with an electronic device (Jackson & Wallace, 1974). Before the program, her speech had been almost inaudible. In another example, college students participated in a program to increase the intensity with which they did aerobic exercise; magnitude was assessed by using charts that took into account the type of activity, such as jogging or swimming, and its duration (Wysocki et al., 1979). Other ways to assess exercise intensity include taking one's pulse or recording the weights of barbells lifted.

Magnitude can be an appropriate measure for many other target behaviors, including increasing the degree of concentration in studying or decreasing the amount or caloric content of foods in a diet. Measuring intensity is usually important when trying to change emotional behaviors, such as overt and covert expressions of anger, jealousy, anxiety or fear, depression, love, and happiness. The most common method for measuring emotion magnitude is to use a *rating scale* with discrete numerical values. In measuring stress, for example, we might use a 10-point scale ranging from 0 to 9, where 0 equals "no stress" and 9 equals "extreme stress." Similar scales can be used to assess the magnitude of other behaviors.

Data of Other Types Several other types of data are also useful in assessing behavior, and we will describe a few of them briefly. One type is *latency*, the amount of time a person takes to respond appropriately to an antecedent. Measuring the quickness with which a child complies with a teacher's or parent's request would be an example of using latency to assess a target behavior. Another example comes from the treatment of insomnia: the effectiveness of a behavior modification program was evaluated on the basis of people's latencies in getting to sleep after going to bed (Puder et al., 1983).

Sometimes a program's behavioral goal involves improving the *quality* of a target behavior, that is, *how well* it is performed. For instance, a behavior change program was used to improve the quality of students' classroom discussions (Smith et al., 1982). After the students were trained to use reasons, examples, and comparisons as discussion skills, their statements in discussions were rated for quality on the basis of the use of these skills. Other target behaviors for which quality may be an appropriate measure include playing a musical instrument, taking photographs, drawing pictures, and performing sport skills.

The last type of data we'll consider for assessing behavior is the *percentage*—the proportion of behaviors, or individuals performing behaviors, that meet some criterion, multiplied by 100. Percentages are especially useful measures when people have *many opportunities to respond* or when the *opportunities to meet a behavioral criterion vary* across time or circumstances. For example, people's driving over the speed limit probably varies with many conditions, such as the weather, time of day, and day of the week. As a result, a good way to evaluate the effectiveness of a program to reduce speeding would be to look for a reduction in the percentage of cars observed speeding, rather than the number of cars speeding. One study found that the percentage of cars speeding was reduced by posting the percentage of cars that did *not* speed during the day before and during the best day to date (Van Houten, Nau, & Marini, 1980).

There are two other issues to keep in mind about collecting data. First, it is often necessary to collect more than one type of data to reflect changes in a target behavior. For instance, in a behavior change program to reduce someone's feelings of depression, the behavioral goal might include reducing the frequency of these feelings as well as their duration and magnitude. If so, three types of data should be collected. Second, it is typically useful to design and record data on carefully structured *data sheets*, like the one presented in Figure 2.2. Other data sheets can be simpler or more detailed. For instance, they can merely provide spaces for tick marks for frequency data, or they can incorporate a lengthy checklist of behaviors to be assessed with two or more types of data. Using data sheets makes recording and evaluating data much easier and faster. When designing a data sheet, it's a good idea to try it out by collecting some sample or "pilot" data so any design flaws can be corrected before using it in a program.

Strategies for Assessing Behavior

All methods for assessing behavior involve some form of *observation*, and we can "observe" behavior in two ways: *directly*, through seeing or hearing the actual behavior, for example, or *indirectly*, with interviews, questionnaires, or other roundabout methods. Observers can be almost anyone—therapists, teachers, coworkers, relatives, or even the person whose behavior is being changed. When individuals assess their own target behaviors, the strategy is called **self-monitoring,** or *self-observation*. Direct observation strategies should be used to collect data whenever feasible. Overt target behaviors almost always can be assessed directly, but covert behaviors often must be assessed indirectly. (Go to 🔳)

CASE STUDY 2.2

Reducing Bob's Self-Talk

An institutionalized 31-year-old schizophrenic man named Bob had a history of talking to himself frequently and at varying levels of loudness (case described in Wong et al.,

		DATA SHEET: _Exercise Behavior_		

Student: _Bonnie_   Observer: _Mr. Armstrong_

Date	Starting Time	Duration (entire session in minutes)	Magnitude (pulse beats/min., while jogging)	Comments
9-7-94	3⁰⁰	30	120	_She hasn't exercised before_
9-9-94	3³⁰	35	125	
9-12-94	3¹⁵	40	130	
9-14-94	3¹⁵	40	130	_Feeling a little achy_
9-16-94	3⁰⁰	45	140	_Feeling better_

Figure 2.2 Data sheet for use in an exercise program at school, with a physical education teacher as the observer. Each session includes general calesthenics and jogging and is assessed with two types of data: _duration_ of the entire session and _magnitude,_ as measured by the student's pulse rate taken for 1 minute during jogging.

1987). Many mental patients exhibit self-talk, which is one of several fixed patterns of speech called _stereotypic vocalizations._ In this case study, Bob's self-talk was defined and measured in the following way:

> Self-talk, defined as any vocalization not directed at another person, excluding sounds associated with physiological functions (e.g., coughing), was the target response for Bob. Stereotypic vocalizations were monitored with a microcassette recorder (Sony model no. M-203) carried in a shirt jacket worn by the patient. The recorder received input from a tie-clip microphone (Radio Shack catalog no. 33-1058) attached to the jacket lapel. Microcassette tapes were later rated by observers who recorded the duration of self-talk with stopwatches. (p. 78)

Bob's therapists reduced his self-talk by about 60% simply by providing recreational activities that would serve as antecedents for alternative behaviors. Because the study's observers heard and scored Bob's actual self-talk from tape recordings, the method they used involved a _direct assessment_ of the target behavior.

Direct Assessment Methods   **Direct assessment methods** measure instances of the actual target behavior in a straightforward manner; the responses of interest are usually seen or heard. For instance, a teacher may assess a student's hand-raising behavior by watching for instances of it and keeping a record of those instances. When using direct assessment methods, observers may measure the behavior (1) while in the same room or setting as the subject; (2) by watching secretly from an adjacent room, perhaps through a one-way mirror; or (3) by recording the behavior on videotape or audiotape and scoring it later (Dowrick, 1991; Foster & Cone, 1986).

Sometimes direct assessments are taken in a *structured test* of the behavior (Bernstein, Borkovec, & Coles, 1986; Wixted, Bellack, & Hersen, 1990). For example, a client who is extremely afraid of snakes might be tested by having a therapist move a caged snake gradually closer. When the client feels uncomfortable, the test ends and the distance between the snake and the client is measured and recorded. In another type of structured test, anxious or assertive behaviors might be tested by having the client role-play being in specified situations, perhaps giving a speech or requesting a refund in a store, while the therapist rates the performance for specific behaviors such as stammering or facial tension.

Direct assessment methods often use devices to measure physical characteristics or dimensions of behavior. Professionals commonly use tape measures to determine how close a target person can get to a feared object, how high an athlete can jump, and so on. In therapy or rehabilitation settings, the devices used can be quite specialized. For instance, medical patients with severe burns on their arms or legs must perform physical therapy exercises to stretch their limbs as far as they can so they will regain their range of motion. The degree of stretching can be measured with a goniometer, which has two arms joined by a pivot—one arm has a pointer and the other has a protractor scale (Hegel et al., 1986). When the limb is stretched, the physical therapist positions the device on the limb and records the angle the limb forms. In behavior therapy for male sexual dysfunctions, the diameter, rigidity, and duration of penile erections can be measured with a small computerized device called the RigiScan (Ackerman et al., 1991, 1993).

Because direct assessment methods provide straightforward data on the actual behavior, *they are the preferred approach for collecting data in behavior modification research and applications*. But these methods have some drawbacks (Wixted, Bellack, & Hersen, 1990). For one thing, they can be very time consuming and expensive to use if it is necessary to train and employ paid observers. Also, these methods sometimes assess only a sample of the target behavior, and that sample may or may not be representative of the person's behavior in everyday life. One purpose of the indirect assessment methods we are about to examine is to document the occurrence of or change in a given behavior in everyday life.

Indirect Assessment Methods   **Indirect assessment methods** use abstract or round-about ways to measure the target behavior: we might ask the person to describe instances of the behavior or how it has changed, for example. Because these methods do not assess the actual behavior directly, they are sometimes inaccurate or misleading. For instance, people may misperceive or misremember details of the behavior or even whether it occurred at all. Not all of these methods rely on people's memories, however.

We will consider four types of indirect assessment methods: interviews, self-report instruments, nonclient ratings of the client's behavior, and physiological measures.

Interviews   Interviews are the most widely used assessment procedure in behavior therapy (Swan & MacDonald, 1978). Therapists use initial interviews with the client and significant people in his or her life, such as relatives, friends, and teachers, to accomplish three things (Ciminero, 1986; Davison & Neale, 1994; Gross, 1984; Turkat, 1986). First, interviews can help identify the client's behavioral deficits and excesses, as well as appropriate alternative responses, existing antecedents and consequences for the problem behaviors, and potential consequences to use in treatment. Second, interviews may also help in assessing related issues, such as important cultural norms that exist in the client's life and persons who will be affected by changes in the client's behavior. Third, therapists try to establish with interviewees a relationship of mutual trust, called *rapport*. People who are interviewed in the therapy process are often under a great deal of stress and may be unwilling to reveal important information about the client.

Interviews can vary in their degree of structure (Davison & Neale, 1994; Turkat, 1986; Wixted, Bellack, & Hersen, 1990). When interviews are highly structured, the therapist asks a set of questions in a specific order, usually with the goal of identifying or diagnosing the client's problem in a prescribed way. When interviews are unstructured, the therapist has considerable leeway in posing questions and must rely on his or her clinical experience and intuition in deciding the direction questions should take and how to interpret the answers. Because interview assessments are retrospective—that is, the target person looks back at behaviors that have already occurred—therapists must watch for inconsistent answers that may reflect errors in memory.

Self-Report Instruments   Clients can report large amounts of clinically important information very efficiently by filling out questionnaires and rating scales (Jensen & Haynes, 1986; Wixted, Bellack, & Hersen, 1990). Some self-report instruments are constructed by individual therapists for their specific purposes, but many others have been developed for general use and are available to therapists through professional sources. Some therapists have clients fill out a packet of instruments prior to the first session to expedite the assessment process.

Some self-report instruments provide information about the client's background, whereas other instruments are designed to help diagnose the problem and identify target behaviors (Jensen & Haynes, 1986). Questionnaires and rating scales are available to help therapists assess many specific behavioral deficits or excesses, including

- Anger (Novaco, 1976).
- Assertiveness (Rathus, 1973).
- Binge eating (Gormally et al., 1982; Hawkins & Clement, 1980).
- Depression (Beck et al., 1961; Carson, 1986).
- Fears and anxieties (Bernstein, Borcovec, & Coles, 1986; Cautela, 1981; Ollendick, 1983).

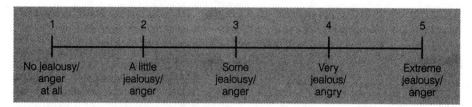

Figure 2.3   A rating scale to measure the magnitude of jealousy/anger experienced in various situations.

- Parent–child conflicts (Cautela, 1981; Frankel, 1993).
- Sexual dysfunctions and skills (Ackerman & Carey, 1995; Malatesta & Adams, 1986).
- Substance abuse (Correa & Sutker, 1986).

When used along with other assessment methods, data from self-report instruments can help guide the selection of target behaviors and treatment approaches.

Nonclient Ratings of the Client's Behavior   Useful information about an individual's behavior can also be obtained by having the target person's teacher, therapist, parents or spouse, friends, or coworkers fill out rating scales or checklists. For instance, Lynn McClannahan and her colleagues (1990) developed a checklist that teacher-therapists can use to assess 20 dimensions of personal appearance and care for children with developmental disabilities. Checklist items include whether a child's nose is clean and his or her socks match. Totaling across dimensions gives an overall rating of the child's appearance. Other ratings scales are very simple and involve only a single class or dimension of behavior, such as in rating how effective psychiatric patients' social skills are (Frederiksen et al., 1976). Figure 2.3 presents a simple rating scale that could be used to measure jealousy/anger.

Physiological Measures   Many different physiological measures can be used to assess internal events, and most of these measures require special equipment or biochemical tests. Taking physiological measures can be useful in behavior change programs under two main circumstances (Bernstein, Borkovec, & Coles, 1986; Kallman & Feuerstein, 1986). First, the target behavior itself may be an internal physiological response, such as high blood pressure. Second, the target behavior may have a consistent physiological component to it, as in the heightened heart rate that accompanies people's feelings of anger or anxiety. In this case, measuring heart rate can be used to confirm clients' self-reports that their feelings have changed.

   Using physiological measures is the only objective approach available to assess covert events, and these assessments can produce data on the frequency, duration, and magnitude of the target behavior. But physiological measures are often expensive to use and don't necessarily give a clearer picture of the current status of a covert behavior, such as anger or fear, than self-reports do (Kallman & Feuerstein, 1986).

Timing and Accuracy in Behavioral Assessments

If you were going to assess a target person's responses, when exactly would you take your measures and how would you try to make sure that the data you collect accurately reflect the status of the behavior? These are the issues we examine next.

Timing Behavioral Assessments   A very common approach to collecting data involves designating a specific period of time—such as a one-hour therapy session, a recess period at school, an entire day at work, or an entire month anywhere—and attempting to assess every instance of the target behavior during that time. The process of assessing and recording all instances of a behavior during a specific time period is called **continuous recording.** This approach can be difficult to use if the behavior occurs at extremely high rates, if assessing each instance requires special equipment or a lot of time, or if the observer must monitor other events, such as other students' classroom activities, at the same time.

Another way to time behavioral assessments is to designate a number of specific observation periods (say, 30 minutes each), divide each period into fairly short intervals of equal length (say, 15 seconds), and record whether the target behavior occurs in each interval. This approach is called **interval recording.** The record for each interval is essentially yes/no, and only one instance of the behavior is recorded for a particular interval even if there were actually many more. Knowing when the intervals start and end is a problem that must be solved, perhaps by having a beeper sound every 15 seconds through an earphone. The data used to evaluate the behavior would be either the number or the percentage of intervals in which the behavior occurred. For example, in a study of children's distracting behavior on shopping trips with their parents, observers followed the family through a store and recorded on audiotape whether distracting behaviors occurred in each 15-second interval (Clark et al., 1977). A program of behavioral methods markedly reduced the percentage of intervals in which distractions occurred.

A third approach for timing assessments, called **time sampling,** involves designating one or more observation periods of equal length, dividing each period into subperiods of equal length (say, 1 minute), and designating a short interval (say, 10 seconds) at the start of each subperiod for collecting data. The type of data that can be collected during these intervals is quite flexible. For instance, researchers in one study assessed the frequency and duration of an employee's in-seat behavior, recording whether she was in her seat for all, part, or none of each interval (Powell, Martindale, & Kulp, 1975). In a study of infant and toddler social behavior, researchers collected a continuous record of nine social behaviors during each interval by jotting down a code for each response (Sarafino, 1985). As in interval recording, the observer using time sampling needs to have a signal for the start and end of each interval. Figure 2.4 gives an example of a data sheet that could be used to make time-sampling assessments of a child's disruptive behavior.

Accuracy and Validity of Behavioral Assessments   Assessments must be reasonably accurate and valid if they are to be useful. What does "valid" mean? Assessments have

DATA SHEET: TIME SAMPLING ASSESSMENT OF DISRUPTIVE BEHAVIOR

Student: _____   Observer: _____

Start time: _____   Day/date: _____ / _____

Intervals

	1	2	3	4	5
First 10 min	A O Y	A O Y	A O Y	A O Y	A O Y
Second 10 min	A O Y	A O Y	A O Y	A O Y	A O Y
Third 10 min	A O Y	A O Y	A O Y	A O Y	A O Y

A = aggression,   O = out of seat,   Y = yelling, making loud noises

Figure 2.4   Data sheet for time-sampling assessment of disruptive behavior of a student in class. In this example, the complete observation period lasts 30 minutes, with fifteen 2-minute subperiods. During the short interval (say, 10 seconds each) at the start of each subperiod, the observer would circle the letter representing any of the three target behaviors that occurred in that interval. In this case, the data would be evaluated in terms of the number or percentage of intervals in which each type of behavior occurred.

validity to the degree that they reflect what they are intended to measure. We will consider the accuracy and validity of direct and indirect assessment methods briefly in this section, and we'll return to these issues again in Chapter 11.

Direct assessment methods generally measure the actual target behavior they are intended to examine. For example, if the target behavior is stuttering, we might count instances of it in a person's speech. How accurate these assessments are depends on how carefully the behavior has been defined, how thoroughly the observers have been trained, and how sensitive or precise the measures are from scales and devices used in assessing the behavior. If the direct assessments are accurate and measure the actual behavior they are intended to examine, these measures usually have a high degree of validity. But direct assessments are sometimes used to infer internal events. For instance, the willingness to approach a feared object might be used to reflect people's fear. In such circumstances, the validity of the measure is not as clear because there may be some other reason for the degree of approach behavior observed. As an example, a child might be feeling intense fear but be willing to get near a big spider if other children are watching.

Indirect assessment methods often involve very subjective estimates and rely on people's memories, as happens when clients are interviewed or fill out self-report instruments. Thus the validity and accuracy may or may not be high. One way to enhance the validity of such measures is to consider the data they produce in the context of data from several assessment approaches—using interviews with or ratings by family members, for example, to corroborate the client's data. Family members' assessments can be fairly accurate if they know exactly what the target behavior is and have opportunities to observe it (McMahon, 1984). If these conditions don't exist—as they will not if parents don't see their child's target behavior, such as truancy—assessments are likely to be inaccurate (Schnelle, 1974). Many other factors can also affect the accuracy of indirect assessment methods. For example, accuracy is enhanced when interview or rating questions are asked and answered clearly and when the person who administers interviews or physiological tests is highly trained.

A phenomenon that can reduce the accuracy and validity of direct and indirect assessment methods is **reactivity**—the process by which people's behavior tends to change when they know they are being observed (Bornstein, Hamilton, & Bornstein, 1986; Monette, Sullivan, & DeJong, 1990). As an example of reactivity, consider trying to assess store customers' everyday stealing behavior if they can see you are watching them intently. If no one steals anything during your observation, their behavior might reflect their reactivity rather than their honesty. Or suppose a third-grade teacher started keeping records on a pad of students' in-seat behavior and announced this new procedure to the class. Chances are the students would stay in their seats longer than usual, at least for a while. Reactivity generally brings people's behavior more in line with their values or their ideas about socially acceptable conduct. The effects of reactivity on behavior can be short-lived if the observee "gets used to" being observed, doesn't want to behave in the new way, and finds that there are no new consequences for behaving that way. Keep in mind that the observee and the observer are the same person when self-monitoring strategies are used. Behavior therapists often have clients use self-monitoring techniques to capitalize on the beneficial effects of reactivity on target behaviors (Bornstein, Hamilton, & Bornstein, 1986).

Developmental and Normative Comparisons

Do people at 2, 10, 30, and 70 years of age behave the same? Of course not, and they're not expected to behave alike. What is "normal" or acceptable behavior changes with age. The strategies we use in assessing behavior and the way we interpret the data must be sensitive to the individual's developmental level (Edelbrock, 1984; Evans & Nelson, 1986; Ollendick & Hersen, 1984). We'll focus on development in childhood because of the rapid and enormous changes that occur in children's motor, cognitive, and social abilities.

The strategies used in assessing children's behavior must be appropriate to the child's abilities, and we'll consider three examples. First, children below 10 years of age or so may have difficulty filling out self-report instruments on their own, especially if a questionnaire or rating scale requires strong verbal or reading abilities. Sometimes we can reduce these problems by using nonverbal symbols, such as happy faces, instead of words. Also, self-report instruments must ask questions that are appropriate to the

✔

CONCEPT CHECK 2.2

1. A behavior not mentioned in the book that qualifies for using frequency data in its assessment is _____ . ⟺
2. Rating the degree of self-esteem is an example of the type of data called _____ .
3. When opportunities to meet a behavioral criterion vary across time, it is useful to convert the data to _____ .
4. Having people assess their own target behavior is called _____ .
5. An example of an indirect assessment method is _____ . ⟺
6. The only objective approach to assess covert events involves using _____ measures.
7. The method of collecting data during a short segment of time at the beginning of each observation subperiod is called _____ .
8. An example of reactivity that students might show when they know they're being observed in school is _____ . ⟺

Answers: 1. saying "like" in your speech, 2. magnitude, 3. percentages, 4. self-monitoring, 5. interviews, 6. physiological, 7. time sampling, 8. studying at their desks

child's age. For instance, it wouldn't make sense to ask a 5-year-old about the stresses of dating. Second, children below the age of 6 or so appear to lack the ability to judge and record the occurrence of a target behavior, making self-monitoring an inappropriate strategy for preschoolers. Third, many young children are fearful or wary of strangers, which may increase the effects of reactivity. This problem usually can be overcome by having observers spend time playing with the children before trying to assess their behavior.

When interpreting assessment data or setting behavioral goals, we must consider what behavioral characteristics are normal for the child's age. We should not expect a child's motor, language, or social abilities to be greater than those of most other children at the same age. We also need to be aware that certain behavior problems are more common at some ages than others. For instance, fears and whining as behavior problems are common in early childhood and decline sharply by adolescence, and certain specific fears, such as fears of animals, are very common at early ages but not later. Truancy and substance use occur very rarely before early adolescence. (Go to ✔)

USING DATA AND DOING RESEARCH IN BEHAVIOR MODIFICATION

Using the data we collect with direct and indirect assessment methods, we can determine whether our efforts to change a behavior worked. You may be thinking, "Sure, it's important to see if our efforts worked. But why do we need to collect and examine data?

If our efforts worked, wouldn't it be obvious?" Occasionally it is, but usually it's not. An example comes from teachers' efforts at a preschool to stop a boy named Davey from pinching adults. They tried at first just to ignore his pinching, but Davey pinched

> hard enough to produce at least an involuntary startle. Teachers next decided to develop a substitute behavior. They selected patting as a logical substitute. Whenever the child reached toward a teacher, she attempted to forestall a pinch by saying, "Pat, Davey," sometimes adding, "Not pinch," and then strongly approving his patting, when it occurred. Patting behavior increased rapidly to a high level. The teachers agreed that they had indeed succeeded in reducing the pinching behavior through substituting patting. Then they were shown the recorded data [which] showed clearly that although patting behavior was indeed high, pinching behavior continued at the previous level. (Harris, Wolf, & Baer, 1964, pp. 16–17)

It may be that the teachers were so focused on the increase in patting that they didn't notice the pinching so much anymore, but whatever the reason, they wrongly evaluated the success of their efforts. Later in this book we'll see that there are other reasons for collecting data that are important too. Anytime behavior modification techniques are used, data must be collected and evaluated.

Using Data

Suppose you were a teacher, had a "Davey" in your class, and decided to try an intervention to stop his pinching. What data would you collect, and what would you look for to decide whether the intervention had worked? You'd probably want to keep track of exactly how often Davey pinched, perhaps by having the people he pinched record each instance on index cards they would carry all day. What would you look for in the data they collect?

At the very least, you'd want to see that the frequency of pinching decreased during the intervention compared to what it was before you tried to change it. This means you'd need to collect "baseline" data *before* starting the intervention. The term **baseline** has two meanings: it can refer to the *data* collected before the intervention begins or to the *period of time* during which those data were collected. If your intervention worked, the frequency of pinching during intervention would decline from its baseline level. You could see this pattern best in a graph, like the one in Figure 2.5. Occasionally, behavior modification data are presented with a *cumulative graph* in which the data are summed from one point to the next. For example, if a mute autistic girl said 2 simple words on the first day of training, 3 words on the second day, and 3 words on the third, a cumulative graph of words spoken would show 5 words for day two and 8 words for day three.

Doing Research

When scientists do research in behavior modification, they try to determine whether certain methods affect behavior and which ones do so most effectively. Typically, the

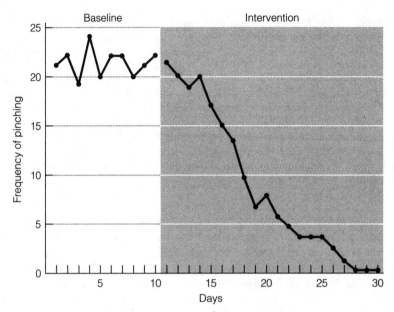

Figure 2.5 How a graph of "Davey's" pinching behavior might look like if the intervention was successful. Although the graph assumes the baseline period lasted 10 days and the intervention lasted 20, the durations of these periods can vary.

research they do can be classified into one of three designs: intrasubject, between-subjects, and within-subjects.

In *intrasubject designs* researchers evaluate behavior and look for changes *within* individual subjects across time while interventions are either in effect or absent, as we did in the Davey example. Because the focus is on one subject, this type of research is often called the "single-subject design." Intrasubject designs usually assess behavior in a sequence of four phases—baseline, intervention, reversal, and intervention—rather than just the first two. In a *reversal phase*, the intervention is withdrawn or altered to see whether the behavior will revert toward baseline levels. Alternating the presence and absence of the intervention allows us to see whether there are corresponding changes in the person's behavior.

Between-subjects designs use many subjects who are separated into two or more groups. Data on their behaviors are combined and compared to see if the groups differ. The researchers usually give the groups different treatments—for instance, if one group receives an intervention, another group might not—and comparisons of their behavior are intended to determine whether any differences found are linked to the treatments administered. The study at the beginning of Chapter 1 of people's saying plural nouns is an example: when subjects in one group said plurals, the researcher said "mmm-hmm"; when subjects in the other group said plurals, the researcher said "huh-uh." The subjects' output of plurals differed depending on which response the researcher made to their words (Greenspoon, 1955).

Within-subjects designs use many subjects and test all of them in more than one treatment condition. In research on the principles of behavior change, these designs usually resemble intrasubject designs, with each subject's behavior being tested in baseline and intervention phases. But instead of focusing on individual subjects, the data are combined. The researcher then evaluates whether the grouped data changed systematically with the presence and absence of the intervention. For our purposes, you may think of within-subjects designs as intrasubject designs with many subjects.

This discussion of using data and doing research was designed to provide only the most basic concepts so that you will be prepared for the material in the next several chapters. More information on collecting data and research methods will appear in other chapters, especially Chapters 9 and 11.

ANALYZING THE FUNCTIONS OF BEHAVIOR

An essential part of designing a program to change behavior is answering the question, "What functions does the behavior serve?" (Groden, 1989; O'Neill et al., 1990). To answer this question, we must know the times and situations in which the behavior does or does not occur and how the person benefits from his or her current pattern of behavior. When people try to change behavior without analyzing its functions, they frequently make the situation worse without realizing they are doing so. Conducting a functional analysis improves the success of behavior change programs (Didden, Duker, & Korzillius, 1997). (Go to ▦)

CASE STUDY **2.3**

The Functions of a Boy's Temper Tantrums

An 11-year-old boy of normal intelligence and with no apparent organic disorder often showed disruptive classroom behavior that was unusual for a child his age (case described in Zimmerman & Zimmerman, 1962). He would speak baby talk, voice irrelevant comments and questions, and have several temper tantrums each week. For instance, when he refused to go to class, attendants would drag him down the hall as he

> screamed and buckled his knees. On several of these occasions, the boy threw himself on the floor in front of the classroom door. A crowd of staff members inevitably gathered around him. The group usually watched and commented as he sat or lay on the floor, kicking and screaming. Some members of the group hypothesized that such behavior seemed to appear after the boy was teased or frustrated in some way. However, the only observable in the situation was the consistent consequence of the behavior in terms of the formation of a group of staff members around the boy. (p. 60)

This description suggests two possible reasons for this boy's tantrums: the *antecedents,* being frustrated or teased, and the *consequences,* receiving attention. The possible role of the tantrums' consequences was based on observing the actual situation. When the staff was instructed not to attend to the boy's tantrums, they disappeared gradually over several weeks. Because the staff hadn't realized that the function of the tantrums was to get their attention, they had been rewarding the behavior unknowingly. Determining the functions of behavior usually requires careful observation.

What Is a Functional Analysis?

A **functional analysis** is an assessment of the connections between a behavior and its antecedents and consequences (Cone, 1997; O'Neill et al., 1990). Functional analyses vary in the rigor and completeness in which they are carried out. They can be highly detailed and exhaustive, as they often are in carefully conducted research (for example, Cooper et al., 1992; Iwata et al., 1982; Johnson et al., 1995; Sasso et al., 1992; Wacker et al., 1990). At the other end of the spectrum, they can be very informal, as they are in our everyday, casual observations of why people behave the way they do (O'Neill et al., 1990). For most behavior change programs, moderately rigorous and complete functional analyses are sufficient and should have three outcomes. They should (1) define the target behavior exactly and clearly, (2) determine which antecedents function to produce the behavioral excess or deficit, and (3) reveal how the person's behavior functions to produce reinforcement. Although the antecedents, behaviors, and consequences in functional analyses are usually overt, they can be covert too.

We saw in Chapter 1 that *operant behavior* follows a standard A-B-C sequence in which antecedents lead to behaviors, which produce consequences. Obviously, functional analyses apply straightforwardly in programs to change operant behaviors. In the case of *respondent behavior*, the CS is the antecedent, and CRs in everyday life function to produce consequences (see Figure 1.2). Suppose, for instance, a child who is afraid of dogs comes across a dog (a CS), which arouses the CRs of fear and running away. What's the consequence of escaping? The child's feeling of fear decreases.

Functional analyses of respondent behavior include the consequences produced by respondent behaviors (Bernstein, Borkovec, & Coles, 1986; Emmelkamp, Bouman, & Scholing, 1992). Interventions to reduce fears and anxieties need to address the consequences individuals get by escaping or avoiding the situations that arouse these emotions. When people escape or avoid the antecedents that elicit fear or anxiety, they retain their inability to cope effectively with the situations and often increase the chances that these antecedents will arouse the same emotions in the future.

Recording Data for a Functional Analysis

In conducting a functional analysis, we maintain records of our assessments of the target behavior on a series of forms. Often there is a separate form for each of the following: (1) interview data, (2) observational data for the target behavior, (3) a summary of the observational data, and (4) an overall analysis and plan for changing the behavior. Gerald Groden (1989; Groden, Stevenson, & Groden, 1996) and Robert O'Neill and his coworkers (1990) have written excellent guides for conducting functional analyses and developing forms to record and organize the data. I used these guides as main sources in preparing the material for this section and constructing the two forms we will examine.

When the program will address a *behavioral excess*, observations of the target behavior in a functional analysis must be made until the behavior has occurred often enough to reveal patterns in the relationships between the behavior and its antecedents and consequences. Useful patterns in people's everyday behavior generally emerge after about 2 to 5 days of observation, with *about a dozen or more instances* of the behavior recorded. When a functional analysis is conducted under highly structured conditions, the observation period can be shorter (Kahng & Iwata, 1999; Watson & Sterling, 1998). Figure 2.6 presents a form for an **A-B-C Log**—a chronological record of the target behavior, along with the antecedents and consequences of each instance of the behavior. This form has been filled out with data on 4-year-old Ray's tantrum behaviors. When we conduct a functional analysis, we use an A-B-C Log to record data regarding the target behavior. For each instance of the behavior, we would record its *day*, *date*, *time*, and *place*. The place would be specified as precisely as necessary. For example, if the behavior tends to occur in certain rooms in the house, such as the bedroom or kitchen, we would use special codes for those places.

The A-B-C Log also includes three other sets of codes that should be recorded for each instance of the behavior. One of these sets of codes is used to indicate the *type of data* being recorded. Another set of codes describes the *types of consequences* the behavior produced. The final set of codes specifies the conditions that preceded the behavior, classified into the following seven *antecedent types*:

- *Activity:* what the person was doing immediately prior to the behavior. The activities should be specific—giving the name of a game the person was playing, for example.
- *Social:* which people were in the environment, and what specifically did they do or say immediately before the behavior occurred.
- *Covert:* what the person was thinking or imagining just before the behavior. Sometimes this can be determined by asking the person or noticing what he or she said prior to the behavior.
- *Emotion:* the type of emotion the person seemed to experience just prior to the behavior.
- *Physical events:* any nonsocial stimuli that occurred or that the person noticed, such as a loud noise or an object that came in view, immediately before the behavior.
- *Other:* any immediate antecedents that do not belong to the above categories.
- *Distant:* any conditions or events that happened "several minutes to 24 hours or more before the behavior occurred and which you feel may be related to the occurrence of the behavior" (Groden, 1989, p. 165). An example might be an argument the person had earlier in the day. Distant antecedents' relationships to behavior are usually speculative, but sometimes they can be useful in functional analyses.

A-B-C LOG: _Tantrum_ Behavior

Person: _Ray_   Age: _4_   Observer(s): _Ms. Ashcroft, Mother, Father_

Day/Date/Time	Place[1]	Antecedents		Behaviors		Consequences		Thoughts/Comments
		Description	Type[2]	Description	Data[3]	Description	Type[4]	
Mon/ 9 26 94/ 11:50 AM	H	Drawing trees, Ashcroft told him favorite food on table for lunch, parents had big argument before leaving for work, Ray sulked	A, S, D, E	Screaming, crying, hitting	11 min D	Ashcroft made Ray another lunch	+	Ray had been upset all morning
Mon/ 9-26/ 7:00 PM	H	Watching TV, mother told Ray it was time to take bath, Ray seemed anxious at dinner	A, S, E	Screaming, crying, kicking	15 min D	Parents let him watch TV longer	+	
Tues/ 9-27/	H			No tantrum				No family problems
Wed/ 9-28/ 9:30 AM	H	Ray and Ashcroft reading picture book, she told him it was time to practice his printing (he dislikes)	A, S	Screaming, crying	4 min D	Ashcroft said maybe he would print later, continued reading	− +	No family problems. Ray seemed OK before.

[1] Place: C = classroom, H = home, __ = _____, __ = _____, __ = _____
[2] Type: A = activity, S = social, C = covert, E = emotion, P = physical events, O = other, D = distant
[3] Data: record with F = frequency, D = duration, M = magnitude, Q = quality, or L = latency
[4] Type: + = get or obtain desirable or wanted object or activity
         − = escape, avoid, or reduce something unpleasant
         U = unpleasant consequence

Figure 2.6 Use an A-B-C Log to keep a chronological record of the behavior(s) in a functional analysis. This log is for tantrum behavior, with the boy's babysitter and parents as the observers. Although the format used in this log would work well for many behaviors, it can be modified for others. Codes are provided for place, antecedents, behaviors, and consequences; other codes can be added as needed.

A-B-C logs may vary in their format and degree of detail, but they are essential in designing a careful behavior change program and should be detailed enough to identify the main links between the target behavior and its antecedents and consequences.

After having observed at least a dozen or so instances of the behavior during a period of a few days or more, we use the data collected to fill out a **summary record** form. This form organizes, collates, and summarizes the data, allowing us to see patterns among the factors examined and the behavior. Figure 2.7 presents a summary record of Ray's tantrum behavior during a 2-week period, during which time he had 12 tantrums. As you examine this summary record, you'll probably notice several patterns, the clearest of which is that after a tantrum the boy always got his way.

If the program will address a *behavioral deficit,* we'll need to look for instances when the behavior *could have* or *should have* occurred, but didn't. If the behavior was physically possible to perform and the antecedents that usually work for other people were present, we can assume the person could have or should have performed the behavior. To do a functional analysis, we simply use *nonoccurrences* of the behavior rather than occurrences in the A-B-C Log.

How to Use a Functional Analysis

The patterns in a functional analysis summary record should give us information about three important relationships. First, they should enable us to predict when the target behavior is likely to occur or not occur—that is, the days and times, the places, and the immediate and distant conditions associated with the likelihood that the behavior will or will not happen. Second, we should be able to see how different consequences relate to the behavior. And third, we should be able to examine the situations when the behavior *does* or *does not* occur and discover *why.* All of this information will be useful in designing a program to change the behavior. If the patterns of relationships are clear, we can proceed to design the program.

What if the relationships are not clear? If the summary record of a dozen instances of the behavior does not reveal sufficiently clear patterns, we can do two things (O'Neill et al., 1990):

1. Check the data collection process for flaws, such as poorly defined behaviors, and determine whether the observers carried out the observation and recording correctly. If we find problems with the process, we'll need to correct the problems and collect the data again.

2. If there were no problems in the data collection, observe another dozen or so instances of the behavior. Doing so probably will clarify the patterns.

If the summary record still contains no clear patterns, the next step would be to conduct *systematic environmental manipulations*—that is, to introduce or alter antecedents or consequences of the target behavior. For example, we could make certain requests of the person, place the individual in particular settings, give him or her access to certain objects or activities, or withhold social attention when the person performs the

Fuctional Analysis

SUMMARY RECORD: A-B-C Log of _Tantrum_____ Behavior

Person: ___Ray___   Period covering: __9-26 to 10-9-94__ Observer(s): _Ms. Ashcroft, Mother, Father_

Factors Examined	Behavior Frequency (Duration)		Factors Examined	Behavior Frequency (Duration)
Day			**Immediate antecedents (cont)**	
Monday	4 (12 min avg)		Social (describe):	
Tuesday	2 (6 min avg)		Asking him to do	8 (7.25 min avg)
Wednesday	1 (8 min)		something he dislikes	
Thursday	3 (7 min avg)		Asking him to do	4 (11 min avg)
Friday	0 —		something he likes	
Saturday	1 (3 min)		or is neutral	
Sunday	1 (10 min)		Covert (describe):	
			none clear	
Time	AM / PM		Emotions (describe):	
12:00 - 1:59	1 (6 min) PM		Upset	4 (12 min avg)
2:00 - 3:59	2 (9 min avg) PM		Physical events	
4:00 - 5:59	1 (9 min) PM		(describe):	
6:00 - 7:59	1 (4 min) AM / 3 (12 min avg) PM			
8:00 - 9:59	3 (6 min avg) AM		Other (describe):	
10:00 - 11:59	1 (11 min) AM			
Place				
Home	12 (8.5 min avg)		**Distant antecedents**	
Other places	never		(describe):	3 (11 min avg)
Immediate antecedents			Parent arguments	
Activities when behaviors occur (describe):			**Consequences**	
Playing	2 (10 min avg)		+ (describe):	
Watching TV	3 (11 min avg)		Got food he wanted 2 times	
Reading	1 (4 min)		Got to continue playing, reading,	
Awakening from nap	2 (4.5 min avg)		or watching TV 7 times	
Printing or other	4 (9 min avg)			
academic traing			− (describe):	
Activites when it doesn't occur			Avoided academic training 5 times	
(describe): *Seems to happen*			U (describe): *Scolded at each tantrum,*	
regardless of activites he's doing			*but that didn't help*	

Figure 2.7 A functional analysis summary record sheet for summarizing the A-B-C Log data to see patterns more clearly. This form can be modified to suit the needs of other programs.

behavior. We can choose which specific manipulations to try by looking at interview and observational data and then generating hypotheses about why the behavior does or does not occur. By manipulating selected events, we can test whether they change the behavior; if they do, we will know how these events influence the behavior.

Researchers have used systematic environmental manipulations in functional analyses to discover why children with autism repeatedly perform behaviors that cause severe injury to themselves, for example, biting their arms hard enough to draw blood. These studies have found that performing self-injurious behavior often functions to gain *escape* from certain activities, such as toothbrushing or learning a new skill (Carr, Taylor, & Robinson, 1991; Sasso et al., 1992; Steege et al., 1990). It may be that the children dislike these activities, or just find them unpleasant momentarily. For instance, a child may feel overwhelmed by the cognitive demands of a task. Studies have also used systematic environmental manipulations to find out how self-injurious behaviors can be stopped. A study by Mark Steege and his coworkers (1990) found that self-injury can be reduced by identifying and rewarding a noninjurious alternative behavior that allows the children to escape from these activities for brief periods of time.

Performing a careful functional analysis is a critical step in designing a program to change behavior. It is carried out before or during the *baseline phase* of behavior modification. Once we have identified the antecedents and consequences for doing or not doing the target behavior, we can select the most appropriate behavioral and cognitive methods to use in the *intervention phase* of a program to improve a person's behavior. Ideally, the program also should have a *follow-up phase* to determine the degree to which improvements in the target behavior are maintained after the intervention ends. The follow-up phase usually extends for several months, but sometimes it may cover only a few weeks, and sometimes it continues for years. (Go to ☑)

Tips on Specifying and Assessing Behavior

Chapters 2 through 11 end with a section giving a set of tips on how the techniques discussed in the text are usually applied by professionals when they design or conduct behavior change programs. The following list provides helpful tips on specifying and assessing behavior.

1. Define the target behavior very carefully, giving details of where and when it occurs more than it should or doesn't occur as much as it should. Students often think "I know what the behavior is" and define it unclearly. Specifying the target behavior is the foundation for any program. Make the foundation strong.

2. For most interventions, once a reasonable and specific behavioral goal has been selected, it is helpful to set some subgoals so the behavior can advance toward the goal gradually. Trying to achieve too much in too short a time will be discouraging and undermine motivation.

3. If the target behavior is covert, look for overt signs to assess too. If no signs of the covert behavior seem obvious, find out whether close friends or family members agree.

✓

CONCEPT CHECK 2.3

1. The time period and data collected before an intervention begins are called _____ .
2. Studies that examine changes in behavior within individual subjects across time are classified as _____ designs.
3. A period of time in behavior modification research when the intervention is withdrawn is called a _____ phase.
4. Research approaches in which many subjects are separated into two or more groups and compared are called _____ designs.
5. A chronological record of antecedents, behavior, and consequences is called a(n) _____ .
6. An example of a distant antecedent we could identify from a functional analysis is _____ . ⇔

Answers: 1. baseline, 2. intrasubject, 3. reversal, 4. between-subjects, 5. A-B-C Log, 6. an accident that happened hours before the behavior

4. If the intervention will address a behavioral excess, find an alternative behavior to strengthen in its place. If the program will address a behavioral deficit, such as not exercising, it helps for the person to decide how to make time for the behavior in his or her schedule.

5. Use at least one direct assessment method if at all possible.

6. Some operant behaviors, such as smoking or studying, can depend on the person's emotional state—being bored or under stress, for example. Keep track of emotional behaviors if they apply.

7. Before using a data sheet or an A-B-C Log, compose a draft of it and try it out to find "bugs" to correct.

8. If the person will be using self-monitoring to keep track of his or her own behavioral excess, which is performed absentmindedly or habitually, use special procedures to assure the accuracy of the collected data. People are usually unaware when they perform such responses; biting fingernails and swearing are two examples. One way to help people pay attention to these responses is to use a technique called *negative practice*, in which clients deliberately perform the behavior over and over while paying close attention to every sensation it produces, such as the sounds they make or the exact position of their fingers. They can also use *prompts* to remind them to pay attention to the behavior and record each instance.

9. Make sure that all *data are recorded immediately* or very close in time to when the behavior occurs. The accuracy of the data will decline with each second or minute of delay. All record keeping instruments—data sheets, pencil or pen, or even a watch or device to

count frequency (such as a golf counter)—must be accessible and easy to use when the behavior occurs.

10. If the target behavior occurs in social situations, the person collecting the data may need to be ready to deal with questions about the record keeping. Telling people the truth is fine. But if telling them would be embarrassing or problematic, it is possible to devise ways to record data secretly.

SUMMARY

Target behaviors to be changed in behavior modification programs must be defined in terms of specific, objective, and measurable actions. Using pinpointing to define the behavior in this way makes it possible to specify a behavioral goal to be achieved by the end of the program and behavioral subgoals to be reached along the way. By achieving the behavioral goal, the person should accomplish the broad outcome goals that were selected for the program.

Three aspects of target behaviors should be considered in designing a program to change behavior. First, some target behaviors are very complex, often requiring a sequence of response links to be performed as a chain of behavior. Because learning to perform complex behaviors can be very difficult, it may be necessary to conduct a task analysis to identify the component responses. Second, changing a target behavior sometimes produces response generalization in which similar changes occur in another behavior that was not specifically addressed in the intervention. It may be possible to use this phenomenon to make behavior modification programs more efficient. Third, an effective way to reduce a target behavior involves encouraging the person to replace it with an alternative response.

The target behaviors and behavioral goals used in training the developmentally disabled are geared to each individual's abilities. Many of these individuals are classified into one of four levels of mental retardation: mild, moderate, severe, and profound. Other people with markedly impaired learning abilities are classified as autistic. The training individuals with autism and mental retardation receive stresses the use of behavioral methods to help these people acquire basic self-help skills, language and social behaviors, and, sometimes, vocational skills.

Assessments of a target behavior use one or more type of data, including frequency, duration, and magnitude. Observations of the behavior can be conducted through self-monitoring or can involve any of several direct and indirect assessment methods. Different approaches for timing of behavioral assessments can also be used, including continuous recording, interval recording, and time sampling. If people know their behavior is being observed, the accuracy and validity of behavioral assessments can be reduced by reactivity.

To conduct functional analyses, we observe target behaviors, record data in A-B-C Logs and summary records, and examine these data to identify connections between the behavior and its antecedents and consequences.

KEY TERMS

target behaviors	alternative responses	continuous recording
pinpointing	frequency	interval recording
outcome goals	duration	time sampling
behavioral goal	magnitude	reactivity
behavioral subgoals	self-monitoring	baseline
chain	direct assessment methods	functional analysis
task analysis	indirect assessment methods	A-B-C Log
response generalization		summary record

REVIEW QUESTIONS

1. What is pinpointing, and how is it used in defining target behaviors?
2. What are outcome goals and behavioral goals, and how are they different?
3. Define what behavioral subgoals are and give two examples of them. Why are subgoals useful?
4. What is a meta-analysis?
5. Describe the task analysis of public speaking reported by Fawcett and Miller (1975).
6. Construct a task analysis of making a peanut butter and jelly sandwich, identifying any chains and links within them.
7. Give two examples of alternative responses (that were not described in the text) and the behavioral excesses they might be helpful in reducing.
8. Describe the four levels of mental retardation.
9. Name five self-help skills one would probably need to teach a 7-year-old girl who is autistic or moderately retarded and had received little special training.
10. Define the three main types of data (frequency, duration, and magnitude) one can use in assessing behavior.
11. Distinguish between direct and indirect assessment methods and give two examples of each.
12. Define and give an example of continuous recording.
13. Define and give an example of interval recording.
14. Define and give an example of time sampling.
15. Describe the four phases we would use in an intrasubject design to study how reinforcement can be used to reduce hitting behavior in 4-year-old Janet.
16. What is a functional analysis, and what does it tell you?
17. How are A-B-C Logs and summary records used in functional analyses?
18. Describe the types of antecedents one can assess with an A-B-C Log.

RELATED READINGS

Ciminero, A. R., Calhoun, K. S., & Adams, H. E. (Eds.). (1986). *Handbook of behavioral assessment* (2nd ed.). New York: Wiley.

Groden, G. (1989). A guide for conducting a comprehensive behavioral analysis of a target behavior. *Journal of Behavior Therapy and Experimental Psychiatry, 20,* 163–169.

Gross, A. M., & Drabman, R. S. (1982). Teaching self-recording, self-evaluation, and self-reward to nonclinic children and adolescents. In P. Karoly & F. H. Kanfer (Eds.), *Self-management and behavior change: From theory to practice.* New York: Pergamon.

Ollendick, T. H., & Hersen, M. (Eds.). (1986). *Child behavioral assessment: Principles and procedures.* New York: Pergamon.

O'Neill, R. E., Horner, R. H., Albin, R. W., Storey, K., & Sprague, J. R. (1990). *Functional analysis of problem behavior: A practical assessment guide.* Sycamore, IL: Sycamore.

Modeling by this parent provides important antecedents that help his child learn new skills.

C H A P T E R THREE

Identifying, Developing, and Managing Operant Antecedents

66 I feel like such a social klutz. How is it you get so many dates, Dina, and I haven't had one for weeks?" Jen asked. "I don't know," Dina replied, "I guess I just go places where there are guys, and I flirt. When I flirt, guys ask me out." Dina has just described in casual terms that her flirting is an antecedent to guys' behavior of asking for a date. Most men and women look for cues or signs that the person they find attractive is interested in them. OK, but what exactly is flirting— what are the cues people look for that set the occasion for them to show interest? When Jen asked Dina what she does to flirt, Dina said, "Well, I guess I just show an interest in the guy—what he says and what his interests are. Stuff like that."

Dina's right, but her answer is incomplete and a bit vague. A study by Charlene Muehlenhard and her colleagues (1986) with male college students identified 36 flirting cues men look for to indicate that a woman would be interested in dating them. These men's ratings of videotaped male–female interactions showed that some of the strongest cues they perceived as indicating a woman's interest included her

- Complimenting the man.

- Asking him questions about himself.

- Making it clear that she noticed him in the past—for example, recalling something he wore on another occasion.

- Mentioning an activity that would be possible for them to do together—pointing out, for instance, that a movie she's interested in seeing will be playing at a local theater.

- Looking at him almost constantly during a conversation.

- Touching him briefly.

- Stopping what she is doing if he talks to her.

Men and women each behave in ways that can set the occasion for the other person to respond with interest, and they learn to use their behavior as antecedents to increase their chances of getting the consequences they want, such as being asked out on dates. One objective in behavior therapy for individuals with poor dating skills is to teach them how and when to behave in ways that serve as cues for other people to respond with interest (Conger & Conger, 1986).

This chapter focuses on the role of antecedents in producing operant behavior. We will study how antecedent cues set the occasion for behavior to take place, how we acquire these cues, what kinds of events can serve as cues, and how we can manage antecedents to increase or decrease operant behavior.

SETTING THE OCCASION FOR BEHAVIOR

Antecedents tend to "push" or "pull" us toward doing, thinking, or feeling something. If you notice *hunger pangs* when you see a *restaurant* and know that it is *supper time*, these three antecedent cues set the occasion for you to go into the restaurant and have supper. In the past, going into restaurants when these antecedents were present led to pleasant outcomes, such as tasty food. We learn the cues that tell us when and where to perform or not perform certain responses by linking the cues with the behaviors and the consequences that follow.

What Stimuli Can Be Antecedents?

People's behavior happens in a *context* that includes objects or other people, and anything in the context that arouses behavior is a *stimulus*. Almost any stimulus—any event, person, object, or place—can serve as an antecedent for operant behavior. For instance, we saw in the story about Jen and Dina that the things people do, in this case, flirting, can set the occasion for other people to behave in certain ways. Here are some other examples of antecedents influencing behavior:

- A teacher asking a question sets the occasion for students to raise their hands.
- Seeing some friends leads you to wave and call to them.
- Tasting a friend's ice cream persuades you to order some of your own.
- Hearing someone yell "Fire" gets you to leave a building.
- Feeling someone you like caress your neck leads you to hug him or her.
- Being in a bar sets the occasion for ordering a drink.
- Thinking about an argument you had makes you act like a grouch.
- Saying to yourself "I hate this book" makes you stop reading.
- Feeling tired induces you to take a nap.
- Friends' asking you to go to the gym with them leads you to get some exercise.

As you can see in this list, antecedents can be overt or covert and can involve any of our senses. You also may be wondering if a stimulus that serves as an antecedent for one person can have a different effect for other people. The answer is yes—the effects of particular antecedents can differ from one person to the next (Wahler & Fox, 1981). For instance, some students never raise their hands when a teacher asks a question, and some students raise their hands only when they are sure they know the answer. We learn when and when not to respond.

Most antecedents are present shortly before the behavior and are called *immediate antecedents,* such as when you head toward an exit quickly after hearing someone in the building yell "Fire" (Groden, 1989; Wahler & Fox, 1981). Most immediate antecedents are less dramatic, but they can also be very useful to learn. For instance, traffic lights are antecedents to behavior. Making it through a signal without having to stop is reinforcing for most drivers (some may even feel "victorious" at times), and having to stop for a long time can be unpleasant, or punishing. To reduce drivers' zipping through a signal when it is yellow or has just turned red, traffic engineers would need to alter the antecedents or the consequences. Researchers did this at an intersection in Chicago after collecting baseline data showing that more than half of the drivers approaching yellow or red lights at that intersection went through without stopping (Jason, Neal, & Marinakis, 1985). By altering the timing sequence of the two signals so that the second signal's yellow light came on sooner and the red stayed on for a shorter period, the researchers made driving safer: over 90% of the drivers now stopped for the yellow or red lights, and the accident rate declined by more than 36% at that intersection. This example describes a clearly successful application of principles of behavior change.

In another example, Susan Ziegler (1987) trained beginning tennis players to use cues to help them hit balls projected from a machine. She first found that simply saying "Concentrate" and "Keep your eye on the ball" brought no improvement. But skills in hitting the balls—with both forehand and backhand strokes—improved substantially when they were taught to give themselves four verbal cues. The cues were to say "Ready" when the machine was about to project the next ball, "Ball" when the ball shot out of the machine, "Bounce" when the ball hit the surface of the court, and "Hit" when they saw the racquet meet the ball. Training can help people learn the cues they fail to learn on their own.

Immediate antecedents don't have to be discrete events, such as saying a word. They can be continuing or ongoing conditions too. For example, a study found that elderly patients in a mental institution communicated more frequently with each other and staff when the institution made two environmental changes: the staff rearranged furniture on the wards so that the patients sat around small tables rather than along walls, and they served meals and snacks buffet style so the patients would serve themselves rather than being given their food on individual trays (Melin & Götestam, 1981). Another study found that having children play organized games, such as rope jumping and foot races, on the playground while they waited for school to open in the morning reduced their aggressive acts by more than half (Murphy, Hutchison, & Bailey, 1983).

Sometimes antecedents precede the behavior by several minutes, hours, or much longer amounts of time and are called *distant antecedents* (Groden, 1989; Wahler & Fox, 1981). Distant antecedents often continue to affect behavior for a long time after the occurrence of the actual antecedent because they have strong emotional components. Thus, the behavior of a child who is a witness to or a victim of violence at home might be influenced hours or days later by such events. (Go to)

CASE STUDY 3.1

The "Betrayed" Husband

Israel Goldiamond (1965) described the case of a 29-year-old male graduate student. He began behavior therapy in an effort to save his marriage 2 years after his wife had committed the "ultimate betrayal" with his best friend. This event was especially distressing to him because he

> had suggested that the friend keep his wife company while he was in the library at night. Since that time, whenever he saw his wife, [he] screamed at her for hours on end or else was ashamed of himself for having done so and spent hours sulking and brooding. (p. 856)

The antecedents that set the occasion for his behavior were probably both immediate (seeing his wife) and distant (the betrayal). Part of the therapy program to change this behavior involved altering the cues. For instance, to decrease the activity of sulking, the husband was told to sulk as much as he wanted, but not in the rooms at home where he usually sulked, and not in the presence of his wife. When he finished sulking, he could leave his sulking place and join his wife. This method helped decrease his sulking duration to about half an hour per day for the first couple of weeks, after which it stopped entirely. Similarly, individuals who worry chronically can successfully restrict their worrying to certain times or places (Borkovec et al., 1983).

Identifying Antecedents

Not all stimuli that precede a behavior set the occasion for the person to respond. Some stimuli may just happen now and then to coincide in time and place with the actual antecedents. To get a reliable picture of the relationships between behavior and the stimuli that precede it, we will need to make systematic observations in a functional analysis of the behavior. Although it's useful to have hunches about which stimuli are antecedents for the target behavior, *hunches should serve only as hypotheses, not conclusions.* We should do a functional analysis, looking for patterns in relationships between the behavior and its preceding stimuli, to confirm or disconfirm our hypotheses.

In programs to reduce behavioral excesses, antecedents that are *overt* and *immediate* are usually fairly easy to identify in a functional analysis because they are present and observable just before the target behavior occurs. But sometimes overt, immediate antecedents are not easily noticed. For instance, we saw in Chapter 1 that children in a classroom become distracted from their studies when they are seated too close together. This antecedent is overt and immediate, but it might be overlooked. Antecedents that are *covert* or *distant* can be relatively difficult to identify. Covert antecedents are not directly observable and consist of thoughts, feelings, and physiological states. Often the person whose target behavior is to be changed isn't aware of these cues. Careful direct observations, along with well-chosen and well-administered indirect assessment methods, such as interviews, are needed to discover covert and distant antecedents.

What if we want to correct a *behavioral deficit*? How do we identify cues to responses that rarely or never happen? We saw in Chapter 2 that functional analyses of behavioral deficits look for antecedents and consequences for *nonoccurrences* of responses that could have or should have occurred. Knowing what cues usually precede people's *not* performing the behavior when they could or should do so can help us decide how to alter those antecedents to make the behavior occur more frequently. For instance, individuals who could and should exercise may fail to do so partly because they think "But it's so boring" each time they consider exercising. They might begin exercising if they could change their thinking and find exercises that are more fun.

HOW WE LEARN ANTECEDENTS

Wouldn't it be wonderful if children knew how to behave correctly and maturely in all situations? In school, for instance, if a substitute teacher were to take over their class, they would sit politely and attentively, waiting to carry out the teacher's instructions. But often that's not what happens. Instead, students recognize from past experience that things will be different now—the rules and consequences established by their regular teacher are no longer in effect. How do they know this?

Learning Discrimination

Learning to distinguish between different stimulus conditions and respond differently toward them is called **discrimination learning.** For example, we learned as toddlers to say "Mommy" when we saw our mothers, but not when we saw other women or our fathers. In early childhood, we learned to say "ess" when we saw the letter S, but not when we saw the number 8 or the letters J or Z. And we learned later to step on the brake pedal of a car we are driving when a traffic light is red, but not when it is green. The stimulus conditions in these examples are antecedents for our behavior.

We learn to discriminate through the process of **differential reinforcement** in which responding in a certain way (such as by saying "Mommy") to a particular stimulus (mother) leads to a rewarding consequence (in this case, lavish attention and praise). But responding in the same way to other stimuli (father, uncles) does not. This process is called *differential reinforcement* because the consequence of making that response is different for different stimuli. Thus, differential reinforcement involves antecedent stimuli of two types (Michael, 1982):

- A stimulus that sets the occasion for a particular response and signals that the response will be followed by reinforcement is called a **discriminative stimulus,** or S^D (pronounced "ess-DEE"). Thus an S^D becomes a cue for performing the behavior, which past experience suggests will lead to reward.
- A stimulus that is associated with *not* being reinforced for a given response, or with being punished for performing it, is called an **S-delta,** or S$^\Delta$ (Δ is the fourth letter in the Greek alphabet). Thus the S$^\Delta$ becomes a cue for *not* performing that particular behavior.

An example of an S^D from everyday life is a person's smile. We've learned that talking to a person who smiles at us leads to a pleasant interaction, whereas a frown tends to serve as an S$^\Delta$ because it is not associated with pleasant interaction. For children in school, their regular teacher is usually an S^D for their paying attention; a substitute teacher is all too often an S$^\Delta$ for paying attention!

A study by William Redd and J. S. Birnbrauer (1969) demonstrated how people who dispense reinforcement can become discriminative stimuli (S^{D}s) for the behavior of others. The individuals in this study were 12- to 15-year-old boys with mental retardation who received praise and sweets (candy, bites of ice cream, or sips of cola) every minute or so in a playroom with toys and other boys. Two adults who provided the praise and sweets as reinforcers served as the stimuli. One of these adults was a woman who dispensed the reinforcers to the boys only when they engaged in cooperative play, moving or manipulating a toy with another boy. The other adult, a man, provided the same reinforcers, but at certain time intervals that had no relation to what the boys were doing. Because the man's reinforcers were not contingent on any particular behavior, playing cooperatively was unlikely to receive reinforcement very often from him. In later tests, the children showed much more cooperative play when the woman entered the playroom than when the man entered, indicating that the woman had become an S^D for cooperative play and the man had not. Then when the adults switched the ways they gave reinforcement, the man eventually became the S^D for cooperative play and the woman lost her influence on the boys' play behavior.

Another study showed a similar effect when the consequence was punishment (Rolider, Cummings, & Van Houten, 1991). Two teachers were present during training sessions, but only one reprimanded the students for misbehaviors. Later tests showed that the students' misbehaviors decreased only if the reprimanding teacher (the S$^\Delta$) was present. These findings indicate that teachers and other individuals can also become antecedents for the withholding or suppression of inappropriate behaviors. The effect of antecedents on behavior depends on the consequences with which they have been associated in the past.

In our discussion of discrimination learning so far, you may have gotten the impression that we learn to respond only to the particular, exact S^D we experienced in our learning. This is not the case. As we learn to make a particular response to a specific S^D, we also learn to respond in the same way to other stimuli that are similar to it. This phenomenon is called **stimulus generalization.** For example, children who have learned to say "dee" whenever they see the letter *d* may also say "dee" when they see a *b* or even a *p*. Because these letters are similar to one another, we may be tempted to think that generalization simply reflects a failure to discriminate carefully (Rilling, 1977). But stimulus generalization seems to be more than that. Why? When children learn to raise their hands to ask questions in kindergarten, they continue to use this convention when they enter first grade; similarly, when they learn to say "please" to request something from their parents, they tend to do the same with other people. These behaviors probably aren't mistakes, but they show stimulus generalization.

In a related phenomenon called *stimulus equivalence,* two or more physically different stimuli come to serve the same purposes and to be used interchangeably (Sidman & Tailby, 1982; Tierney & Bracken, 1998). For instance, suppose no one told you the numbers *4* and *IV* mean the same thing, but you had the following two experiences in childhood. First, when your father taught you about numbers, he showed you four dots and wrote next to them, "There are *4*." Then, when your teacher taught you about Roman numerals, she drew four dots on the board and wrote next to them, "There are *IV*." If you remembered both experiences, wouldn't you have assumed that, or at least wondered if, *4* and *IV* are interchangeable? If someone at that time asked you to count out *4* fingers on one hand and *IV* fingers on the other hand, you'd have counted four on each hand. Stimulus generalization and stimulus equivalence involve learning processes that allow us to connect a variety of antecedent stimuli to a single response without actual training for each stimulus.

Stimulus Control

Stimulus control refers to the ability of an antecedent to influence the individual's performance of the behavior (Albin & Horner, 1988; Rilling, 1977). After people have learned to discriminate between different stimuli and have associated a response with an S^D as an antecedent, this cue comes to exert stimulus control over the behavior. When an antecedent exerts a high degree of stimulus control, the behavior tends to occur mainly or always in the presence of the cue, and when the cue is present, the response is highly likely to occur.

Our everyday lives contain many examples of cues that have a high degree of stimulus control. For instance, when we hear a telephone ringing, we're very likely to answer it, even if we have an answering machine. And our answering the phone—that is, picking up the receiver and saying "Hello"—only happens when the phone rings. We don't go around answering the phone when it hasn't rung! Another example is when someone greets us, saying, "Hi. How are you?" Even if we're not feeling all that well, we're likely to reply, "Fine, thanks. How are you?" Many behaviors for which antecedents have a high degree of stimulus control are habitual and automatic—we give them very little thought or no thought at all. All habitual, automatic behaviors happen in response to antecedents with high stimulus control.

The everyday examples of antecedents we've considered were generally simple, involving only one stimulus. But our everyday lives often have much more complex antecedents, consisting of several relevant stimuli. For example,

> if you are driving on a two-lane road and you come up behind a slow-moving vehicle, you only pass when the center line is broken on your side *and* there are no oncoming cars in the opposite lane. [The antecedent] consists of at least three elements: (1) the slow-moving vehicle ahead, (2) the broken center line, and (3) the clear opposite lane. If any one of those elements were absent, you would be unlikely to pass. The combination sets the *context*. (Baum, 1994, p. 89, italics added)

Oftentimes the antecedent is the overall context rather than a collection of stimuli (Baer, Wolf, & Risley, 1987; Bouton & Nelson, 1998; Michael, 1982; Wahler & Fox, 1981). When this is the case, stimulus control is described as *contextual control* (Haring & Kennedy, 1990).

Principles of stimulus control have been used effectively in treating people with insomnia (Morin, Culbert, & Schwartz, 1994). An intervention was conducted with men and women who were over 60 years of age and had experienced insomnia for at least the past 6 months (Puder et al., 1983). The treatment consisted of teaching these individuals to reassociate the bed and bedroom with going to sleep quickly by having them (1) go to bed only when sleepy, leave the bed if they are awake for 10 minutes, and return to bed only when drowsy again, and (2) go to another room to engage in activities that are incompatible with sleep, such as reading, watching TV, and worrying. This treatment was effective for most of the clients, and the data across all clients showed that the average latencies in getting to sleep declined from over an hour per night to about half an hour. (Go to ☑)

SHORTCUT STIMULUS CONTROL METHODS

Using differential reinforcement methods alone to teach someone when, where, and how to perform behaviors can be very time consuming because the person doesn't know what responses to make. We would present the cues (the S^{D}s) that should lead to the behavior, but the person would not respond correctly very often. Fortunately, we can shortcut this process by capitalizing on the learning and cognitive abilities people develop in early childhood. These abilities enable people to use antecedents with existing stimulus control to help them learn or perform new or infrequent responses. We would still need to present the appropriate S^{D}s, monitor the target person's responses, and make sure reinforcement follows the correct behavior, but the person would be more likely to respond correctly. We commonly use shortcut stimulus control methods in everyday life. Let's see what they are.

Prompting and Fading

A **prompt** is a stimulus that *reminds* us to perform a behavior we already know how to do or *helps us perform* a behavior we don't do often or well. Our everyday lives contain

---

CONCEPT CHECK 3.1

1. An example of a fragrance or smell as an antecedent that leads to a behavior is _____ . ⇔
2. Antecedents are relatively easy to identify in a functional analysis if they are _____ and _____ .
3. We learn to respond differently to different stimuli through _____ learning.
4. An example of differential reinforcement in learning a sport skill is _____ . ⇔
5. In your last answer, the S-delta (S^Δ) might be _____ . ⇔
6. A child who uses a key to open a padlock after having learned only how to open a door lock is showing stimulus _____ .
7. An example of an antecedent with a high degree of stimulus control in a high school classroom might be _____ . ⇔

Answers: 1. the smell of food gets you to go to the kitchen, 2. overt, immediate, 3. discrimination, 4. rewarding a baseball batter for swinging at a "strike" pitch, 5. a pitch that is "high and outside," 6. generalization, 7. the end-of-class bell

---

many prompts, such as the sound a car makes to remind us to use our seat belts and the description a coach gives of how to perform a sport or dance movement. Most prompts are learned S^Ds. Using prompts to remind or help people to perform a behavior is called *prompting*. In behavior modification interventions, each prompt is presented along with S^Ds that should themselves set the occasion for initiating the behavior, minus the prompt, in the future. The purpose of prompting is to enable stimulus control to "shift" from the prompt to the S^D. Prompts of several types are used in behavior modification.

Physical Guidance Prompts   Suppose you were trying the help 3-year-old Cecily print the first letter of her name. You'd probably grasp her hand and guide her printing with your own hand. Manually moving part of the person's body through the desired action or sequence is called *physical guidance*.

This prompting method is often used in teaching simple tasks to children who have not yet developed very much language. For instance, infants who are physically guided to shake a rattle and hear its sound soon learn to perform that behavior on their own to produce the reinforcing sound. Older children who are retarded, autistic, or otherwise learning impaired also benefit from manual prompts for basic tasks, such as using a toilet or rolling balls to one another (Kazdin & Erickson, 1975; Lovaas, 1977; Strain, Shores, & Kerr, 1976).

Physical guidance is also very useful with older children and adults who are trying to learn or improve complex skills, such as swimming, playing a violin, or dancing. A violin teacher might put the violin in the playing position and manually move the

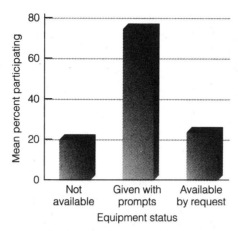

Figure 3.1 Mean percent of nursing home residents participating—that is, being engaged with recreational equipment, materials, or other people—while in a communal lounge. Data were taken on days when recreational material was either not available, given directly to individuals with prompts to encourage participation, or available only by request. *Source:* Data from McClannahan & Risley, 1975.

child's head so the chin clamps the instrument in place, position the hand to grasp the violin neck fingerboard correctly, position the hand to grasp the bow, and move the bowing arm back and forth. Elderly people in nursing homes are often unoccupied, even when recreational activities are available. Placing recreational equipment in their hands and helping them to use it can increase their involvement in these activities, as Figure 3.1 depicts (McClannahan & Risley, 1975).

Verbal Prompts   "Look at the doggie," parents might say to get their child to pay attention to what the animal is doing. Words that are spoken or written to induce a specific behavior are called *verbal prompts*. These prompts are useful with individuals who can understand the words and can be very helpful when learning new speaking skills and material. For instance, a director of a dramatic play might give the first few words of an actor's lines in rehearsal when the actor can't recall them. In such a case, the actor usually hasn't mastered the lines fully yet and simply needs a reminder.

Verbal prompts function as reminders and statements of the behavior to be performed and have been used effectively in many different ways, for instance:

- Researchers had a passenger in a car flash a sign that read, "Please buckle up— I care" to drivers of stopped cars who were not using their seat belts (Geller, Bruff, & Nimmer, 1985). Of the nearly 900 drivers who looked at the sign, 22% buckled up before driving on.
- Four brain-injured adults were able to modify their behavior to avoid accidents at home by using checklists that described potential hazards, such as a drinking glass

Figure 3.2   A pictorial prompt designed to accentuate the feature that distinguishes two stimuli children often find hard to discriminate. In this case, the distinctive feature is the diagonal leg of the *R*. Similar prompts can be made to help children discriminate between other letters, such as *F* and *E*, *c* and *e*, and *b* and *d*.

near the edge of a table, and steps to eliminate each hazard (O'Reilly, Green, & Braunling-McMorrow, 1990).

- Customers at an employee cafeteria were given the opportunity to play a game to make their diets healthier (Zifferblatt, Wilbur, & Pinsky, 1980). While they stood in the serving line, they got cards that had verbal prompts, such as "The idea is valid—have a salad." At the end of 6 weeks, the customers could use the cards they collected to win prizes. Even though winning prizes did not depend on the foods the customers bought, their diets improved during the intervention.

Verbal prompts don't have to be as direct as those we've considered so far. Sometimes they're less direct, as in the question, "What is the next thing you need to do?" Notice that the question doesn't say what the specific behavior should be, but it still serves to encourage the person to make the response.

Pictorial, Gestural, and Auditory Prompts   The knobs and buttons on the dashboards of new cars have drawings representing the function of each knob. These icons make it easier to learn how to operate the car. *Pictorial prompts* consist of pictures—for example, drawings, paintings, photographs, or video images. You can see other examples of pictorial prompts on coins of different denominations and books with different covers. Sometimes a pictorial prompt is just an element in the picture that is accentuated to make it more distinctive so that learning the discrimination is easier to learn, as Figure 3.2 illustrates (Gibson & Levin, 1975). Although pictorial prompts usually consist of a single picture to induce the person to perform a specific response, they can also show a sequence of pictures to prompt each link in a complex behavioral chain. Programs to teach the life-saving technique of cardiopulmonary resuscitation (CPR) usually provide pictorial prompts to help people learn the complex, step-by-step procedure.

Gestural prompts are physical motions that were previously learned SDs for specific behaviors. For example, a frown in certain contexts means "Stop that." An orchestra conductor signals to musicians to play louder by using gestures, such as turning his or her palms up and moving the hands in a high and upward direction. And teachers use pointing as a gesture to direct students' attention toward material on the chalkboard or in a diagram to enable students to learn the material and study it better on their own.

Auditory prompts are sounds other than words that were previously learned SDs for particular behaviors. An alarm beeping on your wristwatch during the first week or two of a semester to remind you to check your class schedule for the time and place of an upcoming class would be an example. An intervention demonstrated that auditory prompts can help incontinent children who are moderately to severely retarded learn toileting behaviors (Mahoney, Van Wagenen, & Meyerson, 1971). The procedure involved presenting an auditory signal through an electronic device repeatedly with each link the children practiced in the chain of toileting responses (walking to the toilet, lowering their pants, and so on). Once each child learned to perform the chain in response to the signal, that same sound was used in a urine alarm apparatus, like the one described in Chapter 1, that was placed in the child's pants. When the child released urine during regular activities, such as playing, the first drops triggered the signal, thereby prompting the child to perform the chain of toileting responses. This toilet training procedure was effective in eliminating "accidents" for four of the five children.

Fading   We saw earlier that prompts are useful because they already have a high degree of stimulus control to remind or help individuals to perform specific behaviors. If a prompt is presented along with one or more S^Ds that normally are antecedents for that behavior, stimulus control for the behavior will "shift" from the prompt to the S^Ds. When this shifting develops, we can reduce the person's reliance on the prompt through a process called **fading,** in which the prompt is gradually either removed or changed to become more and more like the normal antecedent for the behavior (Deitz & Malone, 1985; Demchak, 1990; Rilling, 1977).

Prompts can be faded in several different ways (Demchak, 1990). In one of the more commonly used fading approaches, *decreasing assistance*, the frequency or magnitude of the prompt's presentation is gradually reduced. To reduce its frequency, we would simply present it with the S^D less and less often until the person responds reliably to the S^D alone. For instance, a program that used physical guidance and other prompts to train women who were profoundly retarded to stamp return addresses on envelopes faded the prompts by gradually reducing the number of occasions on which the trainer helped the women perform parts of the task (Schepis, Reid, & Fitzgerald, 1987).

Reducing the prompt's magnitude can be accomplished in two ways. First, we could change the type of prompt from one that is very direct, such as physically guiding a child's printing the letter C on a sheet of paper, to one that is less direct, such as gesturing the shape of a C on the paper. Second, we can weaken the prompt's completeness or strength. If you were physically guiding a child's printing with your entire hand, you could reduce this prompt by (1) beginning to guide with only two of your fingers, (2) then using only one finger, and (3) eventually following, or "shadowing," the child's actions with your hand but not touching the child. If the prompt were pictorial, such as a drawing of the letter that the child was to trace, you could weaken the lines in the drawing, as Figure 3.3 illustrates. Teachers in a school for children with mental retardation used this fading approach to help 8-year-old Danny match digits he could already name, such as 5, with the number of objects each digit represented (Murrell, Hardy, & Martin, 1974). A digit and its corresponding number of circles were printed on a page, and Danny had to identify the digit and place circle cutouts on the printed

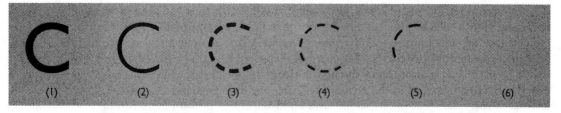

Figure 3.3 Illustration of fading a pictorial prompt. The child would start with the drawing that is darkest and most complete (level 1), tracing the letter with a marker pen. Once the child has mastered that level of prompt magnitude, he or she can progress to level 2, and so on to level 6 where no pictorial prompt is given.

circles. The lines of the circles were weakened over time until no circles were on the page, but Danny could still place on the page as many circles as were represented by the digit.

You may have noticed that progressing from one level to the next is fairly easy when decreasing assistance methods are used in fading prompts. This is done to promote *errorless learning*—fading is introduced gradually enough so that the person makes few or no errors while learning the task (Deitz & Malone, 1985; Rilling, 1977). Another commonly used fading technique, called *increasing assistance*, takes a very different approach (Demchak, 1990). For each instance of the target behavior, the trainer starts by giving a minimal prompt to see if the person will respond correctly. If the individual does not respond correctly, the trainer gradually introduces stronger prompts until the correct response occurs. For each subsequent instance of that behavior, the trainer starts again with a minimal prompt and uses stronger prompts only when necessary. Although the level of assistance increases when individuals do not respond correctly, they require less and less assistance as they learn the task. This is why the method of increasing assistance is considered a fading technique.

In the last method we will consider for fading prompts, *delayed prompting*, or *time delay*, a normal antecedent for the behavior and the prompt are presented together initially, but the prompt is delayed for increasing lengths of time as the person learns the task (Demchak, 1990; Touchette & Howard, 1984). If a delayed prompting procedure is designed appropriately, the person will begin to respond correctly during the delay period, before the prompt occurs, and will make few or no errors in learning the task. Technically, delayed prompting is not really a fading method because the prompt is not actually changed or removed (Deitz & Malone, 1985).

Designing an effective and efficient fading procedure for a particular person is more of an art than a science and requires some experience and skill. One of the most important concerns is the size of the "steps"—that is, the movement from one level to the next. If the steps are too large, the person will make many errors, and the usefulness of the prompts will be impaired. But if the steps are too small, the person may become too dependent on the prompts, and the learning process will become inefficient and tedious. Psychologist O. Ivar Lovaas (1977), who has worked extensively with children with autism, has recommended that the child's ability should determine the rate of fading:

> In some cases, very rapid, almost sudden, fading is appropriate and possible. In other cases, for certain children performing certain behaviors, fading is a slow process. The rule is to use the minimal number of prompts necessary to obtain the desired response. (p. 20)

The same recommendation probably applies to all fading methods with all individuals. Here are a few guidelines that can enhance the design of fading procedures:

- List the steps that are planned for the fading procedure and the criteria for advancing from one step to the next.
- The steps should be small enough to keep errors to a minimum, even when using increasing assistance methods.
- Monitor the person's performance carefully. When errors begin to occur, try going back to the previous step for a while and then advance again to the step at which errors occurred. If more errors occur at that step, consider revising the size of that step and perhaps others that were planned.

Therapists and teachers who help individuals acquire new skills typically intend for these people to function without prompts in their everyday lives. Fading not only reduces the reliance on prompts but also appears to enhance performance of target behaviors and generalization to new situations (Karlsson & Chase, 1996; Krantz & McClannahan, 1998).

Modeling and Instructions

Modeling and instruction are also shortcut methods by which we can use antecedents with a high degree of stimulus control to help a person learn and perform new or infrequent responses. We saw in Chapter 1 that *modeling* is a process by which people learn behaviors by watching what other individuals do. In modeling the antecedent is the modeled action, which *demonstrates* how to perform the behavior. For example, a woodshop teacher might show a student how to install a new sheet of sandpaper in an electric sander. **Instructions** are oral or written information that is designed to *describe* how to perform the target behavior. For instance, a VCR owner's manual describes how to set the device to record a program you won't be there to watch. Modeling and instructions occur very frequently in our everyday lives because they are easy to use and enable people to learn behavior with few or no errors. When these shortcut stimulus control methods are used in behavior change programs, they also indicate *when* to perform the behavior and *what consequences* are likely to follow it.

Applying Modeling and Instructions   Modeling and instructions often exert a high degree of stimulus control over behavior and can be thought of as "elaborate prompts."

They're prompts because they help the person perform a new or infrequent behavior; they're elaborate because they provide so much information: how to perform the behavior and often when to do it and what the payoff will probably be. Having people know the likely consequences is an important element in getting them to perform the behavior. In many cases, there are built in, "natural" rewards for behavior. For instance, we may want to learn to play a musical instrument because we enjoy the activity or see some utility in it. When strong rewards occur naturally in the person's environment, modeling or instructions can lead to improved performance without the need to provide additional rewards. But many behaviors people need to learn have inadequate or no natural rewards. For instance, researchers showed that second-graders' frequent classroom misbehavior didn't improve when the teacher simply wrote on the chalkboard the instructions, "We sit in our seats," "We raise our hands to talk," "We face the front of the room," and "We keep our desks clear" (O'Leary et al., 1969). But the students misbehaved only about half as often when the teacher specified and administered rewards for following the rules.

Instructions have been used effectively in changing a wide variety of behaviors. Charlotte Patterson and Walter Mischel (1975) used instructions to help preschoolers keep working on a task of copying X and O letters on a sheet of paper when they could be distracted by a Clown Box that contained a tape recorder that invited the children to play a game. Two of the instructions the children received to resist the invitations were these:

> When Mr. Clown Box says to look at him and play with him, you can just look at your work, not at him, and say, "No, I can't; I'm working." And when you say it, do it. That's Number One: he says "look" and you say, "No I can't; I'm working." The second thing you can do is . . . say to yourself, "I'm going to keep working so I can play with the fun toys and Mr. Clown Box later." (p. 371)

Not all children were given instructions on how to resist the invitations, but all were promised that they could play with the fun toys and Mr. Clown Box if they finished their work quickly while the researcher was out of the room; otherwise they could only play with broken toys. Those children who were given instructions on how to resist the invitations worked far longer on the task than the other children. Other researchers have shown that some cartoonists of well-known comic strips, such as *Blondie* and *Dennis the Menace*, increased their depiction of people in cars wearing seat belts after receiving letters from an advocacy group explaining the importance of modeling this behavior (Mathews & Dix, 1992).

Models and instructors who help to improve children's behavior do not need to be adults. Studies have found that children can provide very effective modeling and instructions to help other children learn and perform appropriate behaviors (Kohler & Strain, 1990; Lancioni, 1982; Strain, Shores, & Kerr, 1976). How practical it is to use children as models and tutors depends on the circumstances. For example, if students in a classroom will serve as models or tutors to teach specific skills to certain classmates, they will need to be trained to do this and monitored to see that they are applying these methods correctly (Kohler & Strain, 1990). And if the classroom has, say, 20 or 30 students and only one teacher, it can be very difficult or impossible for the instructor to monitor and provide feedback for several models or tutors. But modeling sometimes can be applied in less formal ways and still be reasonably effective. For instance, Marcia Broden and her coworkers (1972) were able to improve the conduct of two disruptive boys who sat next to each other in class by having the teacher reinforce with her attention and praise *one* boy's on-task behavior. The boy who received reinforcement improved more than the other—and when the second boy later received reinforcements for on-task behavior, his conduct showed further improvements.

Behavior modification interventions often combine modeling and instructions in a single program. As an example, three 10- to 13-year-old students who were moderately retarded were trained to prepare foods, such as scrambled eggs, by providing instructions to one student, the model, while the others watched (Griffen, Wolery, & Schuster, 1992). The teacher provided instructions to the model verbally and with a printed recipe with words and pictures. The teacher also reinforced the model for correctly performing the response links making up each food preparation chain and the other students for paying attention and for performing actions they had seen the model do. The model learned the instructed skill, and the observers learned most of the links they had seen. Similar approaches are also used in business and industry to teach workers new skills. Many other interventions have combined instructions and videotaped modeling. One program helped adults reduce their verbally abusive behavior (Frederiksen et al., 1976); another taught adults how to assert themselves in social situations, such as if someone cuts ahead in a grocery checkout line or if they receive a poorly prepared meal in a restaurant (Hersen, Eisler, & Miller, 1974). Professional videotapes are available to conduct modeling in behavior therapy, such as for people with sexual dysfunctions or social skills deficits (Dowrick & Jesdale, 1991).

Guidelines for Effective Modeling and Instructions   Several guidelines can be given to make modeling and instructions effective. First, because modeling and instructions are elaborate prompts, behavior change programs that use these methods often include *fading* procedures to eliminate clients' reliance on them. Second, the modeled behavior or instructions should be *matched to the abilities* of the individuals who must learn from them. If the methods are too hard, the person will make many errors; if they are too easy, the person may lose interest. Third, if few or no reinforcements occur naturally in the person's environment to strengthen the behavior, the modeling and instructions should *describe the consequences* for performing or not performing the behavior, and the consequences should be applied as specified. Fourth, whenever possible, the instructor should *describe reasons* for the behavior in terms of their natural consequences, as in "If you share your toys with her, she'll be nice to you" or "If you play with matches, you may get burned." Fifth, if the target behavior is complex, it should be *broken down into smaller tasks* that can be trained roughly in a sequence from easiest to most difficult.

In addition, we can use the following ways to enhance the effectiveness of modeling techniques:

- Provide reinforcing consequences for the model.
- Reinforce the observer for paying attention to what the model does.
- Use models who can perform the responses reasonably competently—but keep in mind that if the model appears too competent, the observer may think learning the behavior will be too difficult.
- Use models who are similar to the observer, perhaps in age and gender, and who have enough status to be admired by the observer. In fact, *self-modeling*—that is, showing the target persons videotapes of their own exemplary behavior—appears to improve people's behavior (Hartley, Bray, & Kehle, 1998).
- Use more than one model and make sure they all perform the target behavior in a consistent manner and show positive attitudes about the behavior.

Modeling is a frequently used technique in behavior therapy, and it is effective in reducing a wide variety of behavioral deficits, fears, and anxieties. (Go to ☑)

Using Cognitive Antecedents

Our cognitive activities of thinking and reasoning allow us to generate plans, ideas, expectations, beliefs, and rules that can serve as antecedents to our behavior. For instance, we generate self-efficacy beliefs about our abilities to learn or perform specific behaviors. Individuals whose sense of self-efficacy for a task is low are not likely to try to perform it. These cognitive antecedents usually take the form of covert statements we make to ourselves, and often we are not aware of them. To some extent the Patterson and Mischel (1975) study we discussed previously in which preschoolers tried to resist attractive invitations to play involved the children's using cognitive antecedents. But virtually all of the children who were instructed on how to decline the invitations did so aloud with no other people present and may well have been talking to Mr. Clown Box rather than to themselves.

Self-Instructions   "Watch the curb there—don't fall," 2-year-old Paul's mother shouted too late, and the toddler tripped over the curb. As she soothed her son's scraped knee, she said gently, "You need to watch for curbs, or you'll fall." At the next street they crossed he said to himself aloud, "Watch the curb—don't fall," and followed his advice. As you can see, covert or overt directions can regulate performance by specifying the act and its contingencies—that is, the likely reinforcers or punishers. This process is called **rule-governed behavior** (Skinner, 1969). Directions of this type can serve as antecedents if the person has received reinforcement in the past for following them. So, for example, a girl who has been praised for mixing chemicals correctly may think in the future, "If I pay close attention to the amounts I will need and use my math skills, my teacher will think I'm a good student."

CONCEPT CHECK 3.2

1. A father who manually moves his daughter's fingers to help her learn to tie her shoe-laces is using a _____ prompt.
2. An example of a verbal prompt you could use to remind yourself to take medicine before going to bed might be _____ . ⇔
3. Examples of pictorial prompts that are often used to designate men's and women's rest-rooms are _____ . ⇔
4. The process of gradually removing or changing a prompt to reduce someone's reliance on it is called _____ .
5. Beth's special education teacher had trained her with prompts to use a spoon to eat. To fade the prompts, he first pointed to the spoon—and when this didn't work, he asked her to use the spoon. Then he placed it in her hand. He was using the fading method called _____ .
6. Modeling and instructions often indicate how to perform a target behavior, when to do it, and what the _____ will be for doing it.
7. A model's characteristic that usually enhances the effectiveness of the modeling process is _____ . ⇔

Answers: 1. physical guidance, 2. put a sign saying "Take meds" with your toothbrush, 3. silhouettes of a man and a woman, 4. fading, 5. increasing assistance, 6. consequences, 7. same age or gender as the observer

A **self-instruction** is an antecedent statement people make to themselves that describes, directs, or guides the behavior they will perform. *Positive self-instructions* lead us to perform appropriate or desirable actions, as in the example with Paul. But we can also have *negative self-instructions* that lead us into undesirable behavior and prevent us from performing appropriate actions. Some negative self-instructions people commonly use are "They won't like me" or "I'm not good at this" or "I'm too tired to exercise" or "This reading is boring" or "I really shouldn't have dessert, but it looks so good."

When very young children, like Paul, use self-instructions, they usually say them aloud, and the statements are ones adults have said to them. As children get older, their self-instructions become more and more covert (Luria, 1961; Vygotsky, 1962). The speech young children use spontaneously to direct their behavior tends to be very simple, like verbal prompts, rather than elaborate, like full-scale instructions. For instance, Richard Roberts and Roland Tharp (1980) tape-recorded first-graders' speech as they worked on a task in school. The task required them to choose from a list of words to complete partial sentences they were given, then copy the words onto a sheet of paper. Although the children verbalized a lot, they rarely stated instructions that specifically referred to themselves or described the behavior they were to perform. More than three quarters of the things they said involved "sounding out" the words they were writing, as they had been taught to do in school. Other researchers compared what children of different ages think during stressful experiences, such as going to the dentist or giving a speech in school. They found that younger children tend to focus on their negative feelings—thinking, for instance, "I'm scared." Older children are much more likely to give themselves instructions that can help them cope—for example, thinking "I can take this" or "Be brave" (Brown et al., 1986).

How well do children learn and use self-instructions to improve their behavior? Researchers have examined this issue but found inconsistent results. Some studies were conducted to improve perceptual and motor skills in hyperactive, impulsive children, who today would be classified as having attention-deficit hyperactivity disorders (Davison & Neale, 1994; Meichenbaum, 1986; Meichenbaum & Goodman, 1971). These children have great difficulty keeping still, paying attention, and performing motor tasks that require fine coordination. In one of these studies, a trainer modeled how to copy drawings while using self-instructions in the following way:

> Okay, what is it I have to do? You want me to copy the picture with the different lines.
> I have to go slowly and carefully. Okay, draw the line down, down, good; and then to the right, that's it; now down some more and to the left. Good, I'm doing fine so far. Remember, go slowly. Now back up again. No, I was supposed to go down. That's okay. Just erase the line carefully. . . . Good. Even if I make an error I can go on slowly and carefully. I have to go down now. Finished. I did it! (Meichenbaum, 1986, p. 351)

After the children mastered using the self-instructions aloud, the overt statements were faded to become covert. For comparison, other hyperactive children spent time with a trainer but did not receive training in self-instructions. Compared with the children who received no training, those who were trained to use self-instructions showed markedly improved performance on a variety of perceptual and motor tasks, and this improvement continued when testing was repeated a month later. Another study found increased on-task behavior in hyperactive preschoolers who received self-instructions training (Bornstein & Quevillon, 1976).

But other studies with hyperactive children and with students having difficulty learning arithmetic skills have found that training in self-instructions produced little or inconsistent improvement in their academic skills and on-task behavior (Billings & Wasik, 1985; Bryant & Budd, 1982; Roberts, Nelson, & Olson, 1987). Although the reasons for these inconsistent findings are not fully clear, it seems likely that the children in some studies may not have used the self-instructions they were taught when their academic skills or on-task behaviors were tested. One study found support for this possibility with preschoolers whose on-task behaviors and independent work skills were deficient (Guevremont, Osnes, & Stokes, 1988). After being trained to use overt and covert self-instructions with a procedure like the one described for hyperactive children, the preschoolers' were given work sheets to complete in their classroom. At first the children didn't use the self-instructions they had been taught. When the teacher specifically prompted them to use the self-instructions, they did so, and the percentage of correct items on the work sheets improved substantially. Because self-instructions are overt or covert behaviors, newly learned instructions may need to be prompted so they can serve as antecedents for other behaviors. (Go to ▮)

Betty's Self-Instructions for Studying

A 19-year-old college student named Betty had a problem with studying (case described in Cohen et al., 1980). By talking on the phone, snacking, conversing with roommates, or listening to music, she often got sidetracked or distracted from studying. She decided to try to increase the percentage of time she actually studied during her regular study hours simply by using self-instructions. Before starting to study, she would read a card that stated:

> It's important to study to get good grades. I need to study to understand new material. I'm not going to talk to my roommates because it's important that I learn this material. . . . I will not talk on the phone. I will remain studying even though I feel the urge to eat or drink something. Because listening to music distracts me and its important that I learn this material I will not play the stereo. (pp. 447–448)

Every 15 minutes during studying she would read a similar statement.

Betty collected data during baseline and intervention phases using the time sampling method: every 5 minutes during her study hours she recorded whether or not she was studying. The data in her graph indicate that her studying increased from about 60% of the time during baseline to over 80% of the time during intervention.

Rules, Strategies, and Logical Thinking Many human behaviors require using higher order cognitive activities as antecedents; this is true, for example, when we must plan the most efficient way to solve an intellectual or academic problem. Suppose you are mixing a chemical solution and need only half as much of it as the directions would make. How would you know exactly what to do? To solve a problem like this one, you would need to understand concepts about measuring liquids and arithmetic rules. Robert Gagné (1985) has proposed that learning is a cumulative process in which acquiring complex intellectual skills, such as using arithmetic rules, requires mastery of relevant simpler skills, such as operant behaviors and discriminations. Thus, to learn the complex skills needed to mix the right amount of chemicals, you must have learned previously how to pour liquid from one container to another and discriminate among the numbers on a measuring beaker. All of these skills would be needed to plan how to mix the solution.

Young children typically lack most of the complex, logical skills and many of the simpler skills they would need to solve complex intellectual problems (Sarafino & Armstrong, 1986). For instance, preschoolers' abilities to count or use numbers are very limited, and they don't understand the concept of time very well. Because young children haven't acquired the necessary cognitive skills, they have a harder time solving logical problems than older children do. As an example, look at the two-by-four matrix in Figure 3.4. Suppose I were to present this challenge: determine which number from

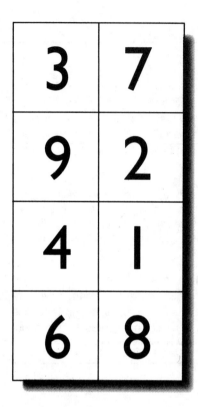

Figure 3.4   A matrix for studying children's strategies in solving problems. *Source:* Sarafino & Armstrong, 1986, Figure 8.4.

the matrix I am thinking of by asking me as few questions as possible, which I will answer only "yes" or "no." How would you solve this problem? The most efficient strategy would be to use three questions, with each paring the potentially correct cells in the matrix by half. Thus, you might ask, "Is the number in the bottom half?" And then, "Is it in the right two remaining cells?" This would leave two remaining cells, and you could simply guess, knowing that even if you guess wrong, you have found the correct number. Peter Eimas (1970) presented this problem to children and found that the older they were the more logical were their strategies. At about 8 years of age, they simply guessed haphazardly; at age 11, they tried systematic strategies but usually partitioned the matrix unevenly; at age 13, the children used very efficient strategies. The conclusion from this section is that if a behavior we want to change requires the individual to construct plans or strategies as cognitive antecedents, we must determine that the individual has the skills to construct them. (Go to 🕮)

Altering Antecedent Chains

Suppose you wanted to stop smoking cigarettes. Smoking a cigarette requires a chain of antecedent responses, such as reaching into a pocket, pulling out the pack, pulling out

CLOSE-UP 3.1

Can Young Children Think Logically?

 Try this task sometime with a preschooler, as one of my students did with her 5-year-old nephew. She mixed together seven same-sized writing instruments (you could use other items): two red felt-tipped pens and five red pencils. She had the boy state that the items were all "things to write with" and then separate the pens from the pencils. She next asked five questions: (1) "How many things to write with are there?" and he answered seven. (2) "How many pencils are there?" and he said five. (3) "How many pens are there?" and he said two. (4) "Are there more pencils than pens?" and he said yes. (5) "Are there more pencils than things to write with?" To her amazement, he answered "More pencils." Why did he answer the last question incorrectly? Is it because 5-year-olds can't think logically?

Theorist and researcher Jean Piaget (1929, 1952, 1970) conducted tasks like this one and found similar outcomes. From children's performance he came to believe children's thinking and reasoning abilities progress through a sequence of *stages*. He called the stage when children are about 2 to 7 years of age *preoperational* because he believed young children could not acquire the "operations," or logical mental actions, needed to think through the solution of a cognitive problem. According to Piaget's view, preoperational thinking is "intuitive"—it does not apply logic effectively and is determined largely by what they currently see or hear. Is young children's thinking really so intuitive?

Research has shown that Piaget's theory greatly underestimates the cognitive abilities of preschool-age children (Sarafino & Armstrong, 1986). Although it is true that young children have more difficulty than older ones in reasoning through logical problems, they are capable of acquiring and using logic for many tasks and situations. Children's thinking seemed so intuitive to researchers several decades ago mainly because the youngsters had not received training in the skills they needed to solve the problems Piaget presented to them. But we know today that preschoolers can learn many logical operations with modest amounts of relevant training and apply these skills to new problems they have not been trained on before (Dasen & Heron, 1981; Field, 1981; Gelman & Baillargeon, 1983).

a cigarette, putting it in the mouth, reaching for a lighter, and lighting the cigarette. In a *behavioral excess* it becomes harder and harder to stop yourself from performing the final, undesirable behavior with each advance through the antecedent chain. It is easier to stop yourself as you reach into your pocket than as you are about to light the cigarette.

One of the best ways to reduce the likelihood of performing an undesirable act that occurs at the end of an antecedent chain is to alter the chain of events in some way (Beneke & Vander Tuig, 1996). This approach, called **altering antecedent chains,** is especially effective if it is used *early* in the chain. Two basic methods can be used to alter chains. First, you can build *pauses* into the chain. For instance, in trying to reduce the number of snacks you eat, you can pause before going to get the snacks. What's more, you can use an early pause in the antecedent chain to assess the behavior you're about to do, marking the data in your records. Recording the behavior may help you to stop at that time (and you can cross out the data!). Pauses can also help while you're eating. At meals, for example, you can pause after cutting pieces of food, delay putting the food in your mouth, and put your utensils down. The second method for altering antecedent chains is to *reorder the links*. For instance, in smoking a cigarette you can reach for a lighter before reaching for the pack of cigarettes. Doing this can help break down the antecedent chain's stimulus control.

When the target response following a relevant antecedent chain is a *behavioral deficit*, the stimulus control of the chain needs to be increased. This can be accomplished in any of the ways we've already considered, such as by using prompts, modeling, or instructions. As an example, suppose a medical patient frequently failed to take the pills recommended by a physician. Putting a pill in one's own mouth is a step that occurs at the end of an antecedent chain. If we could get the chain started, the patient probably would take the pill. An effective way to accomplish this is to provide an auditory prompt, such as an alarm tone, to initiate the chain (Azrin & Powell, 1969). The alarm can turn off in a few seconds automatically or it can be built into the pill box and stay on until the box is opened. In either case, the prompt can be faded later.

We have examined a wide variety of shortcut stimulus control methods to improve people's operant behavior. You may have noticed that some of these methods seem to overlap, and to some degree this is true. For instance, if gestural prompts are fairly detailed, at what point do they become modeling? In a similar vein, at what point do verbal prompts become instructions? And couldn't self-instructions sometimes serve as part of a complex chain of behavior rather than as antecedents? There isn't any clear way to establish dividing lines between these phenomena. The purpose in separating these methods is to organize them in a way that will allow you to see the many different methods we can use, categorize most instances of methods we encounter, and describe efficiently most methods we apply.

MANAGING ANTECEDENTS TO INCREASE OR DECREASE BEHAVIOR

We have discussed many behavior modification techniques by which we can introduce or alter antecedent events to increase an operant target behavior when a deficit exists and to decrease a target behavior when an excess exists. To use these techniques effectively, we must first conduct a functional analysis to determine the antecedents for the current behavior pattern. When we design a behavior change program to modify our own or someone else's behavior, there's no substitute or shortcut for keeping an A-B-C Log and filling out a summary record. Sometimes we may be tempted to skip or abandon careful record keeping, thinking "I know what the behavior is and when and why it happens. Keeping records is just a waste of time." But students and professionals often find that there are important aspects of the antecedents, behavior, and consequences of a target behavior that they never realized before doing the functional analysis. Keeping records forces them to pay closer attention to what's going on. And don't forget that some factors that lead to a behavior are distant antecedents, which are very hard to identify without paying close attention.

The title of this section begins with the words "managing antecedents." To manage antecedents we must select the most appropriate stimulus control techniques and administer them carefully to change existing antecedents or to introduce new ones. A few additional methods we've not yet considered can be useful in changing existing antecedents. These methods are:

- *Reducing or avoiding antecedents.* Sometimes it's possible to reduce or avoid the antecedents that lead to behavioral excesses or deficits. For instance, if a person drinks too much alcohol, staying away from bars as much as possible would help a lot. Similarly, someone who must eat in restaurants often and consumes too much fatty food there can reduce the tempting nature of these situations by snacking on low-fat foods before going out to eat. If a college student fails to study because there are too many distractions in the dorm, it might be a good idea to study in the library.

- *Narrowing antecedent control.* It may be possible to limit an undesirable behavior to a smaller range of antecedents—a technique called **narrowing.** If someone watches too much TV, gradually reducing the times or places that TV watching may occur can help.

- *Using cognitive strategies.* Several cognitive strategies can help change existing antecedents, such as negative self-instructions. For instance, when we are tempted to perform an undesirable behavior, we can think about the *benefits of not doing it,* try to *distract* ourselves from the antecedents, or try to *reperceive the antecedents* we notice. When our perceptions of antecedents involve "hot" cognitions, such as "Oh, that chocolate looks so delicious," the unwanted behavior becomes very enticing and hard to resist (Mischel, 1981). We can reperceive the antecedents by substituting "cool" cognitions about them, such as "That candy is the same color as my belt and is about 1½ inches long, 1 inch wide, and 1 inch high." Reperceiving antecedents for a short while, sometimes just for several seconds, can be enough to get us past the temptation successfully. In people's efforts to quit smoking, combining cognitive and behavioral methods appears to be more effective than using methods of either approach alone (Shiffman, 1984).

- *Turning an S^D into an S^Δ.* One way to change existing antecedents (S^Ds) is to present them repeatedly while preventing them from being associated with reinforcements, thereby turning them into S^Δs. For instance, seeing or smelling alcoholic beverages can be a strong antecedent for drinking. Some research has found that presenting S^Ds that heavy drinkers of alcohol associate with drinking and simultaneously preventing reinforcement (consuming alcohol) of the behavior can help them quit drinking (Blakey & Baker, 1980).

Introducing new antecedents can be accomplished with the methods we've already seen, such as prompting and instructions. In most cases, these antecedents will be used

CONCEPT CHECK 3.3

1. One sentence in the self-instructions you might use when planning to run some errands is _____ . ⇔

2. Self-instructions, rules, and strategies are examples of _____ antecedents.

3. Research has found that Piaget's theory greatly _____ preschool children's abilities to learn and use logic.

4. An example of building in a pause to alter the antecedent chain for smoking is _____ . ⇔

5. The portion of an antecedent chain for a behavioral excess during which it becomes especially difficult to stop oneself from performing the behavior is _____ .

6. An example of narrowing antecedent control for snacking might be _____ . ⇔

Answers: 1. Buy some gas, 2. cognitive, 3. underestimates, 4. delaying pulling out a cigarette from the pack, 5. near the end, 6. eat snacks only in the kitchen

only temporarily to build stimulus control to normal antecedents; then they will be faded. In other cases, the new antecedents can become a permanent part of the normal ones, especially if the person cannot perform appropriately without them. When managing antecedents in an intervention, it is important to keep in mind that the desirable behavior the S^Ds elicit must be reinforced. (Go to ☑)

Tips on Managing Antecedents

Several tips in managing antecedents in behavior change programs are listed below. They are useful in conducting a functional analysis, interpreting the antecedents the analysis reveals, and finding ways to manage the antecedents in a program to change a behavior.

1. Look for immediate and distant antecedents carefully. Don't leave out information about particular stimuli in immediate antecedents simply because they don't seem to be important. Remember that preconceived "hunches" are useful, but they can be misleading.

2. Look for both overt and covert antecedents.

3. If possible, ask friends and relatives to help monitor the target person's behavior and identify antecedents. For instance, they can keep their own data for comparison with data that others collect.

4. If the antecedents for a behavioral deficit, such as not exercising, include thinking "I don't have the time," the target person should look in his or her usual schedule for when and where wasted time or "free" time occurs. This information can help to decrease those activities to make time for the target behavior.

5. When fading prompts, keep the steps small enough to minimize errors and monitor the behavior carefully.

6. Be creative in finding ways to manage antecedents, especially for reducing or avoiding ante-
    cedents, narrowing antecedent control, using cognitive strategies, and turning S^Ds into S^Δs.

SUMMARY

Almost any stimulus can serve as an antecedent for operant behavior. Immediate antecedents are present shortly before the behavior occurs, distant antecedents precede the
behavior by at least several minutes, and both types of stimuli can be overt or covert.

We learn to respond differently to different stimulus conditions through the process
of discrimination learning, which involves differential reinforcement in which responding to a discriminative stimulus (S^D) is regularly associated with reinforcement and
S-delta (S^Δ) stimuli are not. In this way, people who are regularly associated with
consequences of particular behaviors can become antecedents for those behaviors. Although individuals can learn to make fine discriminations and to make a certain response only when specific stimuli are present, the behavior often shows some degree of
stimulus generalization. Some antecedents exert a great deal of stimulus control, having
considerable influence on one's performance of a particular behavior. When the antecedent involves the overall context in which behavior occurs, the stimulus control is
called contextual control.

Many shortcut stimulus control methods can be used in modifying behavior. These
methods include a variety of prompts (physical guidance, verbal, pictorial, gestural, and
auditory) that are typically faded once the discrimination has been learned. Fading can
be done through decreasing assistance, increasing assistance, and delayed prompting.
Modeling and instructions are essentially elaborate gestural and verbal prompts that demonstrate or describe how to perform the behavior. One type of cognitive antecedent are
self-instructions, which can be either positive or negative, according to whether they lead
to desirable or undesirable behavior. Other cognitive antecedents include the rules and
logic people use to plan what they will do. Children's ability to learn and use cognitive
antecedents improves with age and is stronger than Piaget's theory suggests. Antecedent
chains can be altered by building in pauses between links and by reordering the links.

Behavior modification programs can manage antecedents by helping people reduce
or avoid them, narrowing antecedent control, using cognitive strategies, and turning
discriminative stimuli into S-deltas.

KEY TERMS

discrimination learning	stimulus control	self-instructions
differential reinforcement	prompt	altering antecedent chains
discriminative stimulus	fading	narrowing
S-delta	instructions	
stimulus generalization	rule-governed behavior	

REVIEW QUESTIONS

1. Describe the antecedents that might set the occasion for the following behaviors: calling the police, recycling trash, and cooking a gourmet dinner.

2. What is differential reinforcement, and how is it involved in children's learning to discriminate letters of the alphabet?

3. Define and give the abbreviations for the terms discriminative stimulus and S-delta.

4. Describe the study by Redd and Birnbrauer (1969) on how people can become discriminative stimuli.

5. Define stimulus generalization and give an example of it in the names children use for different flowers.

6. What is stimulus control? Give two examples of it from your current life.

7. A father complains to you that "Prompts don't work. I remind my kid all the time to clean up his room, and he never does." If you did a functional analysis of the boy's behavior, what reasons do you think you'd find for the failure of these prompts?

8. Describe how you might use physical prompts to teach a dog to respond correctly to the command, "Give me your paw."

9. Describe two gestural prompts a baseball coach might make.

10. Define "fading" and give an example of how you might fade (a) a verbal prompt to improve first-graders' classroom conduct and (b) a pictorial prompt to help a child discriminate between the numbers 3 and 8.

11. Define modeling and instructions and describe how you might use each method to teach an elementary school student how to use scissors to cut paper triangles.

12. Define positive and negative self-instructions and give an example of each from your own life.

13. What rules or other cognitive skills would be needed to play a card game, such as poker or gin rummy?

14. Describe an example of narrowing antecedent control from Case Study 3.1.

RELATED READINGS

Demchak, M. (1990). Response prompting and fading methods: A review. *American Journal on Mental Retardation*, 6, 603–615.

Gibson, E. J. (1969). *Principles of perceptual learning and development*. New York: Appleton-Century-Crofts.

Kohler, F. W., & Strain, P. S. (1990). Peer assisted interventions: Early promises, notable achievements, and future aspirations. *Clinical Psychology Review*, 10, 441–452.

Rilling, M. (1977). Stimulus control and inhibitory processes. In W. K. Honig & J. E. R. Staddon (Eds.), *Handbook of operant behavior*. Englewood Cliffs, NJ: Prentice-Hall.

Shiffman, S. (1984). Coping with temptations to smoke. *Journal of Consulting and Clinical Psychology, 52*, 261–267.

Posting stars provides this child with positive reinforcement for her behaviors. Stars are conditioned reinforcers.

Using Reinforcement to Increase Operant Behavior

S ome years ago, a newspaper I read printed a letter to "Dear Abby" that described how a woman got her teenaged stepson to keep his room neat. According to the letter, his room had been so messy that sometimes the teen had to "jump" from the door to his bed. The stepmother's program provided a nicely designed, moderately structured set of specified rules regarding the behavior needed to keep his room neat and consequences for doing so. She enforced the following rules:

- If his bed was made, he got breakfast.
- She would launder *only* the clothes he placed in a clothes basket in his closet.
- She would place anything left on the floor in a "mess box" located in the garage. If he wanted any of these items, *he* had to retrieve them.
- If his room was vacuumed on his "day for the car," he received the keys.

This letter was written in response to Abby's advice to a prior letter writer: she had advised the mother of very untidy teenagers to close the bedroom doors and "rake" their rooms weekly.

I don't know whether the stepmother had received training in behavioral methods, but, as you can see, much of the program involved creative common sense in making important consequences contingent on the boy's behavior. Three further points about this program should be mentioned. First, the boy initially "fought" the program, but eventually gave in. Second, once his room was consistently neat, he became proud of it and would take friends there. Third, it is instructive to contrast the stepmother's approach with the advice Dear Abby had given, which, if carried out, might have *reinforced messy behavior* if the teens happened to want their doors closed and their rooms "raked."

This chapter and the next focus on the role of consequences—reinforcement and punishment—in operant conditioning. In this chapter, we will concentrate on the process of *reinforcement*, the cornerstone and most reliable process in changing operant behavior. We will examine what reinforcement is, consider its many different types, and learn how to identify and administer reinforcers effectively in behavior change programs.

WHAT IS REINFORCEMENT?

To reinforce means to make stronger or more pronounced. In operant conditioning, **reinforcement** is a process whereby a consequence strengthens the behavior on which it is contingent. Increases in the strength of a behavior are reflected in its reduced latency or its increased frequency, duration, or magnitude. Of course, these measures may not improve much when reinforcement occurs for well-established behaviors— ones the person already performs very frequently or intensely, for instance. The term *reinforcer* refers to a stimulus that is introduced or changed when the behavior occurs; its introduction or change is the consequence in the process of reinforcement. Loosely speaking, reinforcers are things or events the person "wants" or finds "pleasant" or "satisfying." These are subjective qualities, but we will see later that it is sometimes possible to assess them objectively.

We previously used the terms *reward* and *reinforcer* as synonyms, which they are for the most part. But "reward" is an everyday word and has some excess meanings that can make it less precise. For instance, a prize or special payment for doing something unusual, like returning a wallet or doing a job especially well, is often called a reward. We don't usually think of rewards as subtle stimuli, such as casual praise or a warm smile, which are extremely frequent and very important reinforcers in our lives. What's more, the term *reward* tends to imply that most people find the stimulus pleasant or satisfying, but this isn't true of all reinforcers. For instance, masochists find pain very reinforcing, at least under some conditions, but most people do not. Thus, a reinforcer can be any stimulus that will strengthen an individual's behavior.

Keep this rule in mind: when reinforcement occurs, it *always* strengthens the behavior on which it is contingent. This means that if we provide a consequence for a behavior and find that the person subsequently does not perform the response at least as frequently, intensely, quickly, or persistently as in the past, reinforcement did *not* occur.

Positive and Negative Reinforcement

The process of reinforcement involves a pattern of events in which the behavior results in a consequence: a reinforcing stimulus being introduced or changed. This pattern of events can happen in two ways. One pattern these events can take is called **positive reinforcement,** in which the consequence involves introducing or *adding* a stimulus after the individual has performed the behavior. As we have seen, this consequence typically is something the person wants or finds pleasant or satisfying. Virtually all of the reinforcing consequences mentioned so far in this book have been examples of positive reinforcement. For one example of positive reinforcement, recall the Dear Abby story in which a boy got the keys to the car if he vacuumed his room. We've also seen examples of positive reinforcement given in the form of money, praise, and attention from parents or teachers for behaving appropriately.

But the pattern of events in reinforcement can happen in another way. For example, suppose you have a splitting headache, which is an *aversive stimulus*—that is, a painful, unpleasant, or injurious event. What could you do about it? One thing you could do is take a painkiller, such as aspirin. Performing this behavior changes the aversive stimulus: it reduces the pain. In this pattern of events, which is called **negative reinforcement,** the consequence of the behavior—in this case, taking aspirin—involves *reducing* or *removing* an aversive circumstance. To the extent that the aspirin reduces the headache, you are more likely to take aspirin when you have a headache in the future. The headache is the antecedent, and its reduction is the reinforcing consequence that strengthens the behavior of taking aspirin. (Go to 🔧)

Reward Value

The likelihood that a particular consequence will reinforce a response depends on the degree to which the person *values* it. The greater the value a consequence has, the more likely it will reinforce behavior. What aspects of a reward determine its value? Reinforcers can vary in their *quantity*, for example, the amount of candy a child receives for good behavior, and their *quality*, or character, for instance, different flavored candies.

To understand how these factors affect reward value, we need to consider positive and negative reinforcement separately. In positive reinforcement, the quantity and quality of a reinforcer determine its value. A large piece of chocolate candy generally has more reward value than a small piece, and chocolate candy may have more reward value than the same amount of licorice candy. Studies of positive reinforcement have found that reinforcers with greater value produce stronger responding than lesser reinforcers do, as reflected in the frequency or magnitude of the behavior (Crespi, 1942; Flaherty & Caprio, 1976; Green et al., 1991). In negative reinforcement, reward value seems to be determined mainly by the quantity factor—that is, the amount by which the aversive situation is reduced (Campbell & Kraeling, 1953). For instance, we are more likely to take aspirin to relieve a headache in the future if doing so in the past stopped most or all of the pain rather than just a little of it.

Our preferences for particular reinforcers differ from one person to the next and can change from one time to the next. For instance, getting tickets to a Whitney Houston concert as a reward for jogging might be very reinforcing for you, but a friend who jogs with you might prefer tickets to the Philadelphia Orchestra as a reward. And these preferences can change, given the "right" circumstances. If you are "in the mood" for classical music, Whitney Houston might be less appealing. What's more, to get a highly valued reward, such as going to a good concert, you may even be willing to endure unpleasant situations—traffic jams to get there, for example.

Unconditioned and Conditioned Reinforcers

Some consequences can serve as reinforcers because of innately determined processes. These consequences are called **unconditioned reinforcers,** or *primary reinforcers,* because little or no learning is needed for them to be reinforcing. Examples include satisfying basic physiological needs by eating food or scratching an itch. Unconditioned reinforcers are associated with internal stimuli, such as feelings of hunger, and the reward value they have depends on the individual's current physiological state—in this

Confusions About Negative Reinforcement

Many students and some professionals have difficulty understanding the concept of negative reinforcement (Kimble, 1993; McConnell, 1990). A common problem they have is *incorrectly equating* negative reinforcement and punishment. We saw in Chapter 1 that punishment *decreases* the behavior on which it is contingent, and we've just seen that negative reinforcement does the opposite.

To help clarify the distinction between punishment and negative reinforcement, let's look at an example of both processes happening in an everyday sequence of events. Suppose 9-year-old Sandra hits her younger sister Cheryl in an argument over what to watch on TV. Her father punishes Sandra's behavior by sending her to her room, where she has no TV to watch. But he also tells her she can come back to the TV room after half an hour *if* she writes Cheryl a note of apology. He has made Sandra's gaining release from her room contingent on her apology, thereby setting the stage for her to receive negative reinforcement for apologizing. But keep in mind that the *aversive event does not have to occur as a punisher*. Aversive events often happen without being contingent on our behavior. For example, your neighbors may be playing loud music when you are trying to sleep. If you call them and they comply with your request to turn it down, your calling them is negatively reinforced.

Why do people confuse negative reinforcement and punishment? One reason is that they both involve aversive situations, which people associate with punishment. But in punishment the unpleasant event occurs *after* the behavior on which it is contingent, whereas in negative reinforcement the aversive situation is present *before* the behavior that reduces it. An-

other reason for confusing these terms is that Skinner (1953) called negative reinforcement's aversive stimulus a "negative reinforcer," which makes it seem like the consequence occurred before the behavior. A third reason for confusion about negative reinforcement is that people often think the word "negative" refers to the unpleasantness of the aversive stimulus. It doesn't. In describing reinforcement, the words "positive" and "negative" refer to the arithmetic terms for *adding* (+) and *subtracting* (−): in negative reinforcement, a stimulus is *subtracted* from the situation if the appropriate behavior occurs; in positive reinforcement, a stimulus is *added* when the behavior occurs. Actually, both types of reinforcement result in a relatively pleasant state of affairs following the behavior on which they are contingent.

With all this confusion, you'd think someone would propose changing the terms to describe the patterns by which reinforcement happens. In 1975 a noted behavior modification researcher named Jack Michael proposed dropping the words "positive" and "negative" entirely and retaining the term *reinforcement* to refer to consequences of both types. He argued that it isn't very meaningful to distinguish between patterns of reinforcement in which stimuli are subtracted versus added because the end result is pleasant in both patterns. What's more, a single reinforcer can provide both types of reinforcement. For instance, we can probably agree that eating food can reinforce preparing meals, but is the reinforcement positive or negative? Eating tasty food is a pleasant activity that occurs after preparing a meal, but it also reduces hunger. Perhaps dropping the distinction between positive and negative reinforcement would be a good idea, but these terms still persist in the literature.

case, whether the person is or is not hungry. The reward value for an unconditioned reinforcer increases when the person has been deprived of it for a sufficient period of time. Other examples of unconditioned reinforcers include water, oxygen, normal body temperature, and sleep.

Other stimuli become reinforcing through learning and are called **conditioned reinforcers,** or *secondary reinforcers*. For instance, an infant who is given a hundred-dollar bill would probably not be very impressed. In fact, if the bill were brand new, the baby might even find it aversive because of its stiffness and sharp, prickly edges. Making receipt of a hundred-dollar bill contingent on some behavior, say, head turning, would not strengthen the baby's head-turning behavior. The baby hasn't learned to value money. But chances are you have, and you might suffer whiplash if someone offered you $100 to turn your head! Some evidence indicates that nonreinforcing stimuli can become reinforcers through respondent conditioning (Ormrod, 1990). The procedure generally involves pairing the stimulus that is nonreinforcing with one that is already able to strengthen behavior. Money probably became a reinforcer for you by being associated with many other stimuli that were already reinforcing, such as food and clothing.

Why Are Reinforcers Reinforcing?

Reinforcing consequences have certain properties that enable them to strengthen behavior. One property some reinforcers have is the ability to *reduce drives*. Learning theorist Clark Hull (1943) proposed that biological needs produce unpleasant internal drives, such as hunger, that can be reduced directly by performing behavior that leads to a relevant unconditioned reinforcer, in this case, food. This reduction in drive and biological need strengthens the connection between the successful behavior and its antecedents. Conditioned reinforcers, such as money, work indirectly through their associations with unconditioned reinforcers, such as food.

Although reducing drives seems to be an important property that enables some consequences to reinforce behavior, not all reinforcers reduce drives. As you read these research examples with animal subjects, ask yourself if the reinforcer could have reduced any *biologically based drive* directly or indirectly.

- *Visual exploration as a reinforcer*. Robert Butler (1954) placed a series of monkeys individually in a cage that was enclosed in a box that prevented the monkeys from seeing out. There was a small door in the box, however, and Butler trained the monkeys to open it. Each time they did so, they could see an empty laboratory room for a short time. The monkeys learned this behavior with no other reinforcers given. In later tests, opening the door allowed the monkeys to see the laboratory either empty or containing different stimulus conditions, such as an array of food, a moving toy train, or another monkey in a cage. Door opening occurred frequently under each of the stimulus conditions but was highest when they could see another monkey or the train.

- *Saccharin as a reinforcer*. Saccharin is a sweetener that has no calories or nutritional value. Researchers examined saccharin as a reinforcer with rats that had been fed in the past on an unsweetened grain mash with water always available in their home cages (Sheffield, Roby, & Campbell, 1954). The subjects, which were hungry but not thirsty, were trained three times a day for 2 weeks to run from one end to the other in a runway. Some got plain water for running, and others got a water-saccharin solution. Comparisons of the subjects' runway performance for the last few days of testing revealed that those trained with the water-saccharin reinforcer ran six times faster than those trained with just the plain water.

- *Sex without ejaculation as a reinforcer.* Ejaculation is the release of semen by males at orgasm, which appears to reduce the sex drive. Researchers trained sexually inexperienced male rats twice a day for 2 weeks to run a runway and cross a 4-inch-high hurdle to enter a large, circular chamber that contained a female rat in heat (Sheffield, Wulff, & Backer, 1951). In each training session, the male was allowed to copulate with the female, which typically occurs as a series of a dozen or more mountings and dismountings before ejaculation occurs. To prevent drive reduction, the researchers removed the female after several mountings before the male could mount her again and eventually ejaculate. During the last few days of testing, the males were running more than twice as fast down the runway as they had during the first few days. What's more, a comparable group of males that were trained in the runway with a *male* rat in the chamber increased their running speed across sessions too, but to a much lesser degree.

- *Brain stimulation as a reinforcer.* James Olds and Peter Milner (1954) implanted very thin electrodes deep in rats' brains to deliver tiny pulses of electrical current to specific locations. The researchers then trained the subjects to press a lever and receive an electrical pulse to the brain with each press. Not only did the subjects learn this operant task, but they would then perform the response at extremely high rates if the pulses were to a particular region (the septal area). For instance, one rat made 1,920 responses in a 1-hour period.

Although the reinforcing effects of at least some of these reinforcers may seem intuitively reasonable, the problem is that reinforcement occurred without reducing a biologically based drive directly or indirectly. This means that other properties of consequences must also enable them to strengthen behavior.

Another property of consequences is that they provide *sensory stimulation*, which may explain why they are reinforcing. If you are at home alone, you might feel you have nothing to do and become bored. At other times, the events around you become too stimulating, and you feel overwhelmed. Both feelings are unpleasant. Some evidence suggests that the reward value of sensory stimulation is greatest between these extremes, when there is enough going on to keep your interest and when the stimulation has some variety and meaning to it (Baldwin & Baldwin, 1981; Fiske & Maddi, 1961; Schultz, 1965). A third property of some consequences is that they involve performing *high-probability behaviors*, which may make them reinforcing (Premack, 1959, 1965). High-probability behaviors are responses the person performs frequently or for long periods of time when free to choose what he or she will do. Some common high-probability behaviors are eating, watching TV, having sex, dancing, and playing games. For the most part, these behaviors are ones the person enjoys doing. Finally, reinforcers of all types have specific *physiological effects*—for example, the release of a

CONCEPT CHECK 4.1

1. Reinforcement always _____ the behavior on which it is contingent.
2. In positive reinforcement the consequence is _____ after the behavior occurs.
3. If you stubbed your toe, a behavior you could perform that would produce negative reinforcement might be _____. ⇔
4. The terms "positive" and "negative" to describe reinforcement refer to _____ and _____ in arithmetic.
5. A reinforcer with high reward value for a typical child might be _____. ⇔
6. Another term for primary reinforcer is _____.
7. One property reinforcers often have that may enable them to strengthen behavior is that they involve _____. ⇔

Answers: 1. strengthens, 2. added, 3. to rub the toe, 4. adding, subtracting, 5. candy, 6. unconditioned reinforcer, 7. drive reduction, stimulation, or high-probability behavior

chemical called dopamine in the brain (Blum et al., 1996; White & Milner, 1992). (Go to ✔)

TYPES OF POSITIVE REINFORCERS

Choosing the reinforcers to change operant behavior is a pivotal consideration in any program to change behavior because they can have a very powerful impact on what people do. To make choices carefully, we need to know what reinforcers we have at our disposal. This section describes several different but somewhat overlapping categories of positive reinforcers. Most potential reinforcers belong to one or more of these categories. Knowing the types of reinforcers and examples of each type makes choosing reinforcers easier and more successful.

Tangible and Consumable Rewards

When asked to give examples of reinforcers, many things people first think of are items that are *tangible*, material objects we can perceive such as toys, clothing, or musical recordings, or *consumable*, things we can eat or drink such as candy, fruit, or soft drinks. Tangible and consumable rewards have a strong influence on our everyday actions and include both unconditioned and conditioned reinforcers. When you go to a store to buy a new pair of jeans, the jeans are a tangible reinforcer for your shopping behavior. When children in school obey their teacher's instructions to line up in a quiet and orderly fashion before they may go to the lunchroom, food is the reinforcer for their behavior.

Although food can be a useful reinforcer, it isn't used very often in behavior modification interventions for at least three reasons. First of all, food is most effective as a reinforcer when the individuals receiving it are hungry, and depriving people of food against their will can raise ethical and legal concerns. Of course, we could reserve using food until just before mealtime, but it would still have limited value to reward many instances of the target behavior because hunger will weaken as the individuals consume their rewards. Second, consumable reinforcers are often difficult and messy to carry around and dispense in everyday settings, such as at work, in classrooms, or in stores. This problem is compounded by the great differences in food preferences from one person to the next and for the same person from one time to the next. Thus, to use food effectively as a reinforcer, we would need to have a sufficient variety of foods with us at all times when the target behavior could occur. Third, people who receive and consume food as a reward for each instance of a target behavior are likely to be distracted from ongoing behaviors we're trying to train. For example, suppose we were trying to improve children's concentration while studying. Giving them food rewards every several minutes would disrupt their efforts.

Still, using food reinforcers is sometimes reasonable and practical. For instance, a parent or teacher could use food rewards for children's meeting specifically identified behavioral goals. An example of this approach would be a teacher providing snacks at specified times if students keep their disruptive behavior below a certain level. Another example comes from the Dear Abby story: the woman gave her stepson breakfast if he made his bed. And food rewards often are used when few or no other reinforcers are effective. For instance, some children with moderate retardation may respond only to edible reinforcers in the early phases of an intervention (Lancioni, 1982). In addition, a study found that using highly preferred foods as reinforcers was helpful in getting children to eat a wider range of foods after they had become malnourished because they refused to eat almost all other foods (Riordan et al., 1984).

Activities

"You may watch TV after you finish your homework," your parents may have promised. They were using an activity as a reinforcer for your doing homework. Watching TV is probably one of many activities you enjoy and do frequently when you have a free choice. We saw earlier that these kinds of activities are called high-probability behaviors. David Premack (1959, 1965) proposed that consequences are reinforcing because they involve performing high-probability behaviors, and these activities will only work as reinforcers for less frequent behaviors. This rule is known as the **Premack principle.**

Studies have shown that the Premack principle has some validity—having the opportunity to engage in high-probability behaviors can increase people's performance of infrequent behaviors. Here are some example research results:

- Adults with mental retardation increased the number of repetitions they performed of physical exercises, such as knee bends and toe touches, when researchers made the opportunity to participate in games contingent on increased exercising (Allen & Iwata, 1980).
- Toothbrushing at a summer camp increased when the campers' opportunity to go swimming was contingent on brushing their teeth (Lattal, 1969).
- Children's classroom conduct improved when their teacher made the opportunity to play with toys, games, and crafts contingent on increasing desirable behaviors and decreasing undesirable ones (Wasik, 1970).
- Female college students who were trying to lose weight by changing their eating habits were trained to think of undesirable aspects of being overweight and desirable aspects of losing weight. Some of these subjects were instructed to engage in a high-probability noneating activity, such as sitting in a frequently used chair, only if they practiced these thoughts. These subjects reported practicing the positive and negative thoughts more often and lost more weight than subjects who were not instructed to use activity rewards to increase these thoughts (Horan & Johnson, 1971).

An important implication of the Premack principle is that we can identify existing and potential reinforcers by looking for high-probability behaviors in people's naturally occurring activities, as we do in functional analyses. This approach is usually effective and easy to use, but deciding on how to assess and compare different behaviors can be tricky (Allison, 1989). For instance, suppose you wanted to determine if reading novels and drinking soft drinks are high-probability behaviors for a given person. Would you measure each activity's frequency or duration? Suppose you chose duration. Now, when assessing drinking, would you include the time between sips, such as while the person swallows or can still taste the drink? And how would you determine whether one activity involves a higher probability behavior than another if you decided that frequency is the best measure for one behavior and duration is the best measure for the other? Decisions like these generally do not present serious problems in applying the Premack principle, but they make using this approach a little harder than you might have suspected.

Although using high-probability behaviors, such as playing a game, usually works to reinforce performing low-probability behaviors, we're not entirely sure why. William Timberlake and James Allison (1974) have proposed an explanation called the *response deprivation hypothesis*. According to this view, using a high-probability behavior (for instance, playing a game) as a reward makes that activity contingent on performing an infrequent behavior (doing chores), thereby restricting or depriving the person of his or her usual opportunities to perform the high-probability behavior. So, if we used activities to reinforce a person's doing chores, the person would increase doing chores to overcome the restricted opportunities to do the restricted behavior, playing a game. A number of studies have found evidence supporting this explanation (Konarski et al., 1981).

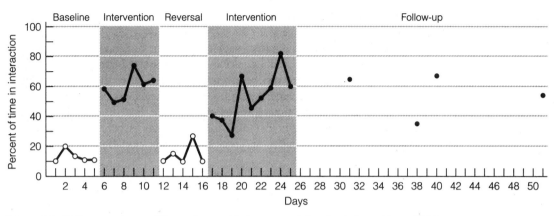

Figure 4.1 Daily percentages of time a 4-year-old who was socially retarded spent in social inter-action with other children during 2-hour morning sessions. In the intervention phases she received social reinforcement from her teachers for playing with her nursery schoolmates. The follow-up data indicate that her increased social interaction was durable. *Source:* Adapted from Harris, Wolf, & Baer, 1964, Figure 2.

Social Reinforcers

Do you know what "moshing" is? It's a dance craze that began in the early 1990s. To the outsider, it looks like a riot or street fight. Paul Tough (1993) describes it this way:

> torsos slam into one another, chests collide, heads recoil, noses bleed; clothing is ripped off, trampled underfoot, forgotten; bodies fall and disappear, sucked into the sweaty undertow. Occasionally a warrior is tossed above the crush and passed along from hand to hand. It's unspeakably hot, often painful, certainly claustrophobic. (p. 53)

What reinforces such behavior? The rewards are probably social, for the most part. We learn to value social reinforcers through conditioning.

Social reinforcers are consequences of behavior that involve interpersonal acts, such as smiling, nodding, praising, and giving attention or affectionate touches. These acts can be given directly to the person or indirectly, such as in a letter of appreciation or commendation at work. Social reinforcers usually are very subtle in our everyday lives, but they have very powerful effects on people's actions and often strengthen undesirable behaviors without our realizing it. As an example, a parent or teacher who pays atten-tion to children's misbehavior by trying to correct or "punish" it—saying, "Stop that," for instance—without attending to their desirable acts often increases their conduct problems (Harris, Wolf, & Baer, 1964; Madsen et al., 1970; Wahler et al., 1965). In one study, researchers found that preschool teachers were unknowingly reinforcing children's excessive crying, whining, and solitary play activities (Harris, Wolf, & Baer, 1964). The teachers were instructed to ignore such behaviors but to give social rein-forcers for alternative responses, such as playing with other children. Figure 4.1 presents the substantial effect the teachers' attention had on a 4-year-old girl's social interactions with other children.

Using social reinforcers to improve people's behavior has four main advantages over other rewards. First, social reinforcers can be administered easily and quickly in almost any setting. Second, they can be given immediately after the target behavior, thereby enhancing their effectiveness. Third, social reinforcers, such as praise or a pat on the back, generally disrupt ongoing behavior very little. Fourth, rewards like these occur "naturally" in people's everyday lives for most kinds of behavior. As a result, social consequences may continue to reinforce a target behavior after the intervention ends. (Go to)

CASE STUDY 4.1

Using Social Reinforcers to Overcome a Man's "Pain Behavior"

People in pain behave in characteristic ways, such as by moaning, grimacing, moving in a guarded or protective manner, or stooping while walking. These actions are called *pain behaviors*. Regardless of why these behaviors start, they often have reinforcing consequences, such as receiving attention and care from family and friends and getting certain benefits, called "secondary gains," like not having to go to work or do chores around the house. If these reinforcing conditions persist too long, the person who was in pain may continue to perceive or anticipate pain and show pain behaviors when little or no physical basis for pain exists. The person gets caught in a vicious circle of others' solicitous behavior leading to more pain behavior, which elicits more solicitousness, and so on. But don't misunderstand this phenomenon: the person and his or her family and friends are probably not aware this is happening.

This phenomenon may have led to the condition of a 42-year-old man who was admitted to a medical center in a wheelchair after having experienced years of medical treatment, including surgery, for back pain that had no medically detectable cause (case described in Kallman, Hersen, & O'Toole, 1975). He had retired from work 5 years earlier, and his wife was supporting the family. At admission, he was unable to walk or straighten his body, which was bent at the waist. The behavior modification treatment he received was very simple: a female assistant paid three 10-minute daily visits to his room, each time chatting with him and then asking him to stand and walk as far as possible. She assessed these behaviors and provided social reinforcers, saying, for instance, "You're standing straighter now" and "I'm very proud of you." During the first few days, the social reinforcers had little noticeable effect, but soon his standing and walking began to improve. After 18 days, he was walking normally and was discharged from the center. A month later, he was readmitted to the center, showing severe pain behaviors again. Because his family had socially reinforced these behaviors, they received training to ignore his pain complaints and praise his motor activities. Follow-up assessments in the 12 weeks after he was discharged from the center again revealed no further problems.

Feedback

Feedback refers to information that assesses or corrects people's performance. We get feedback continuously about our motor actions: as you reach to grasp an object, your senses give you information about how the movements are progressing. When we receive "positive" feedback, the information indicates that our behavior was correct or is being performed well. Feedback is implicit in many types of reinforcers we receive. If we receive praise or a gift for something we did, this reinforcement also tells us we performed well. Feedback essentially has the same advantages as using social reinforcers: feedback occurs naturally in people's lives, doesn't interrupt ongoing behavior, and can be administered easily, quickly, and immediately in almost any setting.

Although feedback alone sometimes is sufficient to strengthen or maintain a behavior, combining feedback with other rewards, such as praise, usually works better. The greater reinforcing effect of feedback plus praise was demonstrated in an intervention to decrease home heating-oil consumption (Seaver & Patterson, 1976). Heating-oil customers were divided into three groups. A feedback group received a form with information about their rate of oil use during the current delivery period, their rate for a comparable period in the preceding year, and what the difference in these rates means in dollars the household saved or lost. A feedback/praise group got the same type of feedback, but if their rate of oil use had declined, the information form had a decal that read "We are saving oil" in red letters and a note commending their efforts. The third group got no special information at all. Assessments at the next oil delivery revealed that the feedback/praise group used 10% less oil than either of the other groups, which did not differ.

A special feedback technique called *biofeedback* helps people gain voluntary control over body processes by giving them continuous and very specific information about the current functioning of a physiological process, such as heart rate or muscle tension. This technique has been used effectively in helping individuals reduce chronic headaches and asthma attacks (Sarafino, 1998). We will examine biofeedback in greater detail in Chapter 13.

Tokens

Tokens are symbolic rewards that represent or resemble money because they can buy, or be traded in for, goods or privileges. The tokens themselves can be tickets, small chips or buttons, check marks or stars on a chart, or points recorded in a log. The goods or privileges are called *backup reinforcers* and are generally some form of tangible, consumable, activity, or social reward. So, for example, someone who has earned enough tokens can buy a candy bar or the opportunity to watch TV as a backup reinforcer. Receiving stars or stickers for good performance, without being able to trade them in for backup reinforcers, would just be feedback or social reinforcement.

To use token reinforcers, we must determine the specific behavioral criteria to earn the tokens, what the backup reinforcers will be, and how many tokens will be needed to buy each backup reinforcer. For example, a simple token system was used as part of a program to reduce the frequent tantrums of an 8-year-old elementary school student named Diane (Carlson et al., 1968). Her teacher gave

> Diane a star (on the board) for each half-day of non-tantrum behavior. When four stars *in a row* were received there would be a little class party, with Diane passing out the treats. The latter provision was designed with the thought of increasing Diane's acceptance by her peers. (p. 118)

Although she had several tantrums in the first couple of weeks of the program, she had only three more in the remaining 2½ months before summer recess. Having the tokens buy a backup reinforcer that Diane and her classmates could share proved to be a useful approach. Another study found that earning tokens to provide backup reinforcers for all students in their class is more effective than children earning tokens to buy rewards for themselves alone (Kazdin & Geesey, 1977).

Token reinforcement systems can be much more complicated than the one used with Diane. They can involve more than one behavior, offer different numbers of tokens for different behaviors or levels of performance, and include a wide variety of backup reinforcers from which to choose. Using tokens as reinforcers has many of the advantages we've seen for social and feedback reinforcement. In addition, tokens have the advantages of (1) bridging the delay between performing the target behavior and getting tangible, consumable, or activity reinforcers for it and (2) offering the possibility of a variety of backup reinforcers, thereby maintaining the reward value of the tokens at a consistently high level. Tokens have no reinforcing value of their own—they become reinforcers because of the backup reinforcers they can buy. Simply explaining the token system is sufficient for most people to establish the link to the backup reinforcers. But individuals who are either very young or have severe learning impairments may need a little training to establish the value of the tokens.

One thing to keep in mind in designing a token reinforcement system is that the criteria for earning tokens should be neither too easy nor too difficult, and the number of tokens needed to buy backup reinforcers should be reasonable. Individuals should get attractive backup reinforcers when they perform at acceptable levels. In Chapter 12, we will discuss in detail how token reinforcement systems can be used with many individuals—for example, in institutional settings.

Covert Reinforcers

Covert reinforcers are consequences individuals experience for their behavior through imagination (Cautela, 1993a). These reinforcers are used in the following way: after you perform the target behavior, you might imagine a pleasant scene or engaging in a pleasant activity. For instance, the scene might involve your feeling proud and self-satisfied at having behaved correctly and saying to yourself, "Way to go! I knew you could do it" (Krop & Burgess, 1993). Or the scene might involve imagining how nicely proportioned your body will be because of the exercise routine you've begun. Covert reinforcers are different from other rewards because they are not actually or directly experienced when they occur. As a result, it is unlikely that they would have as much reward value as real life reinforcers or remain effective for very long if they are used without other reinforcers. But they have the advantage of always being available and easy to use. Like all other rewards, covert reinforcers work best if they occur soon after the target behavior.

IDENTIFYING AND STRENGTHENING REINFORCERS

"Different strokes for different folks" is the rule for selecting and applying reinforcers to change operant behavior. Because people differ in their reinforcer preferences, we must choose reinforcers with high reward values from the point of view of the individual whose problem behavior we're trying to help change. We must also determine through a functional analysis what consequences already exist in the person's life that strengthen or maintain the problem behavior (Groden, 1989; Iwata et al., 1982; O'Neill et al., 1990). For behaviors that are maintained by more than one existing reinforcer, we can assess the relative reward value of each through functional analysis methods (Lalli & Kates, 1998; Piazza et al., 1998). Thus, we need to know what reinforcers to apply in our program and what existing reinforcers we must overcome or eliminate to change the behavior.

Sometimes the actual consequences that reinforce behavior are surprising and would not be discovered if we simply asked the person or someone else. For example, one study had a woman named Peg who was profoundly retarded learn the behavior of placing a marble in a box when prompted to do so (Favell, McGimsey, & Jones, 1978). The only consequence used in teaching the response was placing her arms in splints for 30 seconds after each correct response. When this reinforcer was discontinued, Peg's performance deteriorated sharply; when it was reintroduced, her performance improved quickly and dramatically. These results suggest that placing self-injurious children in arm splints to restrain them when they start to harm themselves might sometimes serve as a reinforcer for self-injurious behavior.

Identifying Potential Reinforcers

Generating hunches about what consequences will have high reward value can be a useful first step in identifying potential reinforcers for a particular individual. We develop these hunches through our everyday observations, noticing, for instance, that many of the things people seem to like are related to broad demographic factors, such as their gender and age. For instance, Americans' reinforcer preferences change with age: Although kindergarten children tend to prefer tangible reinforcers, such as candy or trinkets, over social reinforcers, such as praise, this preference is reversed by third grade (Witryol, 1971). And survey data on spending patterns suggest that teens value entertainment, clothing, and music recordings as reinforcers (Minton, 1999). But hunches are not sufficient to decide what reinforcers to use in changing a person's behavior. To the extent that the everyday connections we observe between demographic factors and reward value are valid, they reflect overall trends and not necessarily what a *particular person* will value. How can we assess what consequences will serve as strong reinforcers for a given individual?

Direct Assessment Methods   One way to determine what consequences will reinforce a person's behavior is through *direct assessment methods:* observing and recording the individual's reactions toward the stimuli when they occur or are available. Direct assessment methods can be carried out in two ways. First, we can use *naturalistic observations,* observing the person in his or her natural environments and recording the frequency and duration of each behavior displayed. This is essentially the approach Premack (1959, 1965) proposed using to identify high-probability behaviors to serve as activity reinforcers. The activities that are likely to be good reinforcers are those that the person performs most frequently or for the longest amounts of time. Second, we can conduct *structured tests,* presenting a previously selected set of stimuli and assessing which ones the person prefers. The stimuli can be presented in two ways: (1) one at a time, with data collected on how soon the person approaches or reaches for them, or (2) two or more at a time, with data collected on which ones the person chooses (Green et al., 1988, 1991; Neef et al., 1992; Pace et al., 1985; Wong et al., 1987). The 1988 study by Carolyn Green and her coworkers demonstrated that reinforcers identified through structured tests are more effective in changing children's behavior than ones identified by asking staff who work with the children. Structured tests are especially useful when trying to identify reinforcers for individuals who have severe learning or motor handicaps.

Indirect Assessment Methods   A simple but indirect way to identify potential reinforcers is to ask individuals what items or experiences they like or find pleasurable. This can be done by asking probing questions in an interview or by having the person fill out a questionnaire, such as the one presented in Figure 4.2. This questionnaire provides some flexibility to the assessment process by allowing the person to add potential reinforcers that were not listed and to clarify the information he or she gives. A much more detailed and extensive questionnaire, called the Reinforcement Survey Schedule, is also available (Cautela & Kastenbaum, 1967).

Using indirect assessment methods to identify reinforcers has some limitations. First, like all self-report measurements, they may be less accurate than direct methods might be. Second, young children, people with mental retardation, and others whose verbal abilities are very limited may be unable to answer the questions. And third, people who are extremely depressed may feel that nothing gives them pleasure. When the latter two limitations arise, people who know the individual may be able to answer some of the questions, but it would be better to use direct assessment methods.

Enhancing Reinforcer Effectiveness

It is sometimes useful to strengthen the effectiveness of potential reinforcers, as in the case of token reinforcers that have no value in their own right. Individuals who cannot understand an explanation of a token reinforcement system will need to have the

PREFERRED ITEMS AND EXPERIENCES QUESTIONNAIRE (PIEQ)
FOR ADOLESCENTS AND ADULTS

Name _____ Age _____ Sex _____ Date _____

This questionnaire is designed to find out how much you like or get pleasure from various *items and experiences* in your life. The questionnaire contains lists of items and experiences many people enjoy, and each list has spaces in which you may add other things you like that the list left out. You may write on the questionnaire to clarify any information you give. For each item or experience, **rate** how much you like *to receive, have, or do it*. Use the folowing scale:

0	1	2	3	4
Not at all	A little	A fair amount	A lot	Very much

Items/Experiences	Ratings	Items/Experiences	Ratings
1. Tangible items:		5. Friends'/relatives' actions toward you:	
New clothes	_____	Praising your	
Sports equipment	_____	appearance	_____
Games	_____	competence	_____
Tools	_____	personality	_____
Beauty supplies	_____	Giving affection	_____
Music recordings	_____	Socializing with you	_____
Video recordings	_____	Inviting you for	
Other: _____	_____	a date	_____
Other: _____	_____	dinner	_____
Other: _____	_____	a party	_____
2. Foods:		Other: _____	_____
Ice cream	_____	Other: _____	_____
Candy	_____		
Fruit	_____	6. Leisure activities (passive):	
Pastry	_____	Watching TV	_____
Cookies	_____	Watching movies	_____
Popcorn	_____	Attending performances of	
Potato chips	_____	sports	_____
Other: _____	_____	music	_____
Other: _____	_____	drama	_____
Other: _____	_____	dance	_____
3. Beverages:		Listening to music	_____
Milk	_____	Lying in the sun	_____
Soft drinks	_____	Taking a leisurely bath	_____
Juices	_____	Other: _____	_____
Coffee	_____	Other: _____	_____
Tea	_____	Other: _____	_____
Other: _____	_____	7. Leisure activities (active):	
Other: _____	_____	Hobbies/crafts	_____
4. Outcomes for work, chores, or skills		Gardening	_____
at work, school, or home:		Hiking/camping	_____
Money	_____	Playing athletics	_____
Praise/feedback	_____	Exercising	_____
Input in decisions	_____	Playing games	_____
Flexible duties	_____	Reading	_____
Special privileges	_____	Socializing	_____
Other: _____	_____	Other: _____	_____
Other: _____	_____	Other: _____	_____
		Other: _____	_____

Figure 4.2 The Preferred Items and Experiences Questionnaire (PIEQ) for adolescents and adults to identify potential reinforcers. *Source:* Sarafino, 1995.

tokens associated repeatedly with the backup reinforcers. We can do this by giving these people tokens either for desirable behaviors they already perform readily or for no particular behavior at all, and then exchanging the tokens immediately for backup reinforcers.

Another way to enhance reinforcer effectiveness involves presenting a small or brief sample of the consequence *before* the behavior occurs to increase the likelihood that the person will make the response and get the reinforcer. This method is called **reinforcer sampling** (Ayllon & Azrin, 1968a). For instance, to encourage a child with mental retardation to repeat a word you say, you might show the child a small bit of candy he or she will receive after saying the word. Stores selling food sometimes use a similar method, allowing customers to sample items they can buy in larger quantities.

Modeling is another technique by which we can increase the effectiveness of reinforcers. Individuals who see others receiving and enjoying pleasant consequences for their behavior tend to increase the value they place on these consequences and copy the behavior they saw the other people do. Alan Kazdin (1973) demonstrated this effect with children with mild retardation in an elementary school. He had the teacher praise some children in the classroom when they were in their seats and paying attention to their work. Reinforcing attentive behavior in these children increased the attentive behavior of the children who were praised *and* of classmates who were sitting near them. (Go to ☑)

HOW TO ADMINISTER REINFORCEMENT

Once we have decided which reinforcers to use in changing someone's behavior, we need to consider exactly how and when to provide them. In this section we will look at many different procedures for administering reinforcement, beginning with the process of shaping behavior.

Shaping a Behavior

Shaping is a procedure by which an individual's behavior gradually improves because the criteria or standards for successive instances of reinforcement become more and more rigorous. For the individual to keep getting reinforced, his or her behavior must advance through a series of successively better approximations to the behavioral goal. For example, suppose 3-year-old Erin is learning to print the first letter of her name, with her father giving social reinforcers. Even though her first attempts are likely to be very distant or primitive approximations to a well-formed *E*, those initial attempts would receive praise. But then her father's standards would begin to increase, and Erin would be required to make successively better approximations to receive praise. Although shaping is usually used to train a behavior the person doesn't presently perform, it can also be applied to improve an existing skill—making a very good tennis backhand stroke excellent, for example.

CONCEPT CHECK 4.2

1. A favorite consumable reward of people you know is _____ . ⇔
2. Parents saying to a teenager, "You can go out tonight if you finish your chores," is an example of using a(n) _____ as a reinforcer.
3. An advantage of using feedback or social reinforcers is _____ . ⇔
4. Providing continuous information about the functioning of a person's physiological processes is called _____ .
5. A backup reinforcer for tokens might be _____ . ⇔
6. Identifying reinforcers by presenting different stimuli to the person and seeing which he or she prefers is called _____ .

Answers: 1. chocolate, 2. activity, 3. they are administered immediately/easily and quickly, 4. biofeedback, 5. watching TV, 6. structured tests

Types of Shaping   Shaping can be applied to improve qualitative and quantitative features of the behavior. In *qualitative shaping* (or "topographic" shaping), the successively higher standards for performance pertain to the degree to which the responses look, sound, or feel like the well-formed behavior. Erin's printing better and better *E*s is an example of qualitative shaping. *Quantitative shaping* refers to setting criteria for reinforcement to increase or decrease the quantity of the behavior, generally by changing its frequency, duration, or magnitude. An example of quantitative shaping can be seen in a study that used biofeedback methods to increase a 20-year-old man's heart rate by 17 beats per minute above baseline levels (Scott et al., 1973). The man could hear the audio portion of television programs at all times during the intervention, but the video portion remained on only if he kept his heart rate at certain levels. The initial criterion was 5 beats above baseline to keep the video portion on, but the criteria were raised once each level had been achieved. An older man's heart rate was decreased by 16 beats per minute in a similar fashion. These changes were temporary, of course. Another study used shaping to induce a girl with mental retardation, who rarely spoke at an audible level, to talk louder and louder (Jackson & Wallace, 1974).

Shaping "Steps"   Shaping advances the behavior through a series of levels, and movement from one level to the next is a *step*. Because the behavior that undergoes shaping is new to the person, it generally starts as a very primitive approximation to the desired action. It often is so primitive that its relationship to the desired behavior may be hard to see. Erin's first attempt to print an *E* might be a squiggle that has little resemblance to the letter. But as a first approximation, it's probably worth reinforcing.

How big should the steps be? There's no hard and fast answer to this question; step sizes depend on the difficulty of the task and the person's abilities. But a very general rule can be given: shaping steps should be large enough to produce some challenge and fairly quick progress but small enough to allow the person to succeed. If a step is too large, the person will fail. Here are three guidelines we can follow:

- Do not try to advance to the next step until the person has mastered the current one. If we do, the step is likely to be too big.
- If the person's behavior begins to deteriorate because we tried to advance too quickly, and various methods such as prompting do not help, reinforce an earlier approximation and build from there again.
- Try not to make the steps too small either. If we do, the task may become boring, the training will be inefficient and unnecessarily expensive, and the person may become "stuck" at a level of behavior that has produced inordinate reinforcement.

Perhaps the best advice in shaping behavior is to be flexible enough to speed up or slow down the shaping process as needed. Being able to shape behavior effectively is a skill that requires knowledge of the person's abilities and experience in training different people to perform various tasks. Individuals with very severe learning difficulties, such as children who are profoundly retarded, may even need to be trained to retrieve, use, or consume the reinforcer. Computer programs are now available that simulate important features of the shaping process and help train many skills needed to administer reinforcement effectively (Acker, Goldwater, & Agnew, 1990).

Shortcuts to Shaping   As you read the material on shaping, you may have recognized that there are ways to shortcut the process of shaping. Four of the approaches we discussed in Chapter 3 to shortcut stimulus control can be used to speed shaping too. One way to shortcut shaping is to use *physical guidance,* manually moving the person's body through the desired movements. Another method involves using *pictures* of the behavior or its product, such as the printed letter. The third approach is *modeling* the behavior. And the fourth way to shortcut shaping is to use *instructions* to describe how to perform the responses. Only this last approach requires that the learner have good language skills.

Timing and Schedules of Reinforcement

When we are helping someone change an existing behavior or learn a new one, we can maximize the effect of reinforcement by delivering it *immediately after each and every correct response* (Chung, 1965; Michael, 1986). This is an important rule. The longer we delay giving the reinforcer, the less effective it will be in strengthening the behavior—even if the delay is just a matter of several seconds. Suppose the reinforcers cannot be given immediately—for instance, when prizes are used for improved performance throughout a whole school day. We should find ways to *bridge the delay* in time between the behavior and the reinforcer. The best way to bridge the delay is to use additional reinforcers, such as tokens or praise, that can be delivered immediately and then describe instances of the target behavior when we give the prizes.

Thinning the Schedule of Reinforcement During an intervention to change or teach behaviors, we monitor the person's responses and try to time or "schedule" reinforcement for each and every correct response—a pattern called a **continuous reinforcement** (CRF) schedule. This approach is ideal and produces the fastest progress in modifying behavior. But we cannot monitor people's behavior and provide continuous reinforcement forever. Fortunately, it isn't necessary to do this. We can actually help individuals maintain the target behavior and strengthen their self-regulation by phasing out our use of reinforcement after the behavioral goal has been achieved and the target behavior is well established.

How can we phase out the reinforcers we use? We can gradually change the **schedule of reinforcement**—that is, the rule that determines which instances of a response, if any, will be reinforced. Most of our behaviors do not receive reinforcers from others each time they occur; sometimes they are reinforced, and sometimes they are not. If you clean your room, sometimes people notice and praise you, and sometimes they don't. At the end of behavior change programs, we try to copy everyday life by employing a procedure called **thinning** in which we gradually *reduce the rate* at which the behavior receives reinforcement. For example, we might start by reinforcing, say, 80% of the person's correct responses for a few days, and then slowly reducing the rate to 60%, 40%, 20%, and 10%. These gradual reductions make the schedule of reinforcement progressively "thinner." Reinforcing only some instances of a behavior is called **intermittent reinforcement,** or *partial reinforcement*. There are several types of reinforcement schedules, and we will discuss them in detail in Chapter 10.

Research by Frank Kirby and Frank Shields (1972) provides an example of thinning a schedule of reinforcement in an intervention to improve the arithmetic skills of a 13-year-old boy named Tom. Each day the researchers gave Tom a set of 20 math problems to do in 20 minutes. They reinforced Tom's correct arithmetic answers with simple statements of praise, such as "Good work" or "Great, you got 14 right today." Every couple of days they doubled the number of problems Tom needed to complete to receive praise, eventually requiring 16 correct problems. By the end of this program, the speed at which he correctly computed math problems tripled compared with his baseline performance. What's more, Tom's on-task behavior increased during the intervention, even though that aspect of his conduct was not specifically reinforced.

One of the main benefits of thinning the reinforcement schedule at the end of an intervention is that the *target behavior usually becomes even stronger*—that is, it occurs at a higher rate than it did under continuous reinforcement and persists longer when reinforcement is discontinued entirely. This is one of several ways to help maintain appropriate behavior after an intervention ends. Probably the simplest change we can make in a schedule of reinforcement is to stop rewarding a behavior entirely. *Extinction* is the condition in which a behavior no longer receives reinforcement, making the person less likely to perform it in the future. In Chapters 5 and 10, we will discuss in detail the effects of extinction on behavior and ways to maintain improved behaviors.

Delaying Reinforcement Another way to phase out a person's reliance on reinforcers and maintain the target behavior after the intervention ends is to increase the delay between the occurrence of the response and its reinforcer. As in thinning schedules of reinforcement, delaying reinforcement is begun after the behavior is well established and proceeds in gradual steps. This approach was used in an intervention to increase elementary schoolers' following rules of good classroom conduct, such as working quietly on assignments and following their teachers' instructions (Greenwood et al., 1974). The students received continuous feedback regarding their conduct during reading and mathematics sessions, and activity reinforcers were given immediately after each session if their behavior met certain criteria. When the students' good conduct was well established, the activity reinforcers were delayed more and more so that the students behaved well for longer periods of time before engaging in the reinforcing activities. Follow-up assessments taken a few weeks after the intervention ended showed that the children's good conduct remained at high levels.

Using Reinforcers to Develop Behavior Chains

When teaching a complex series of responses that forms a behavior chain, we often need to identify its links by doing a task analysis, as we saw in Chapter 2. Suppose we want to help a young boy who is retarded learn to dress himself, and we are teaching him to put on his sock while seated. This chain consists of four links, each containing an antecedent cue (an S^D) and a response. The responses are: (1) *grasp* the sock with one hand, making sure the heel points down; (2) *spread* the hole with the fingers of both hands; (3) *position* the foot up at the hole; and (4) *insert* the foot into the sock. Seeing each response completed serves as the cue for the next link, as depicted in the following diagram:

$$S^{D1} \rightarrow R_{(1)} \rightarrow S^{D2} \rightarrow R_{(2)} \rightarrow S^{D3} \rightarrow R_{(3)} \rightarrow S^{D4} \rightarrow R_{(4)} \rightarrow \text{Reinforcer}$$

see sock / grasp / see grasp / spread / see spread / position / see position / insert

Although the criterion for reinforcement will eventually require that the entire chain be performed, we can teach the links of the chain using one of three main methods.

- **Forward chaining** involves teaching one link at a time in sequence, beginning with the first. In our example, the child would first learn to grasp the sock correctly ($R_{(1)}$ in the diagram), and the reinforcer would be given just for that response. After the first link is mastered, the child would need to add the second link (spread the hole with the fingers) to the first to get the reinforcer. Then the next link is added, and so on, until the complete chain, with all links included, is required for the reinforcer.
- **Backward chaining** consists of teaching one link at a time in the reverse sequence, beginning with the last one. Referring again to the diagram, the child would first learn to insert the foot correctly, $R_{(4)}$, and the reinforcer would be given for that response. Then the child would need to add the next-to-last link (position the foot at the hole) to the last link to get the reinforcer, and so on, until the chain is complete.

■ **Total-task presentation** involves teaching all of the links together as a full sequence. From the start of training, the child would be required to make the entire series of links from beginning to end to receive the reinforcer.

In each of these training methods, the teacher may use prompts of all kinds, as they are needed to perform each link. Is one of these methods best? Studies with people with mental retardation have compared these methods and found that the total-task presentation method teaches behavior chains at least as quickly as backward or forward chaining methods (Kayser, Billingsley, & Neel, 1986; Spooner, 1984; Yu et al., 1980). But two reservations about this conclusion should be mentioned. First, some evidence suggests that individuals who are severely retarded show more disruptive behavior, such as aggression, when trained with total-task methods than with methods that break the task down (Weld & Evans, 1990). Second, for chains in which the last link is particularly difficult, using backward chaining methods may be the best approach (Ash & Holding, 1990).

Regardless of which method we use to teach a behavior chain, we can enhance training effectiveness by following a few guidelines. First, be sure that all the links the task analysis identifies are simple enough for the person to learn without too much difficulty. Second, design the approach to ensure that to receive reinforcement the person must perform all the links he or she has learned, and always in the correct order. Third, apply and then fade shortcut stimulus control methods—prompts, modeling, and instructions—to help the person learn the links. Last, use shaping and give reinforcement liberally when beginning to teach each link.

Using Group and Individual Contingencies

Most of the interventions we have seen so far in this book have involved *individual contingencies*—that is, the reinforcers received were contingent on the learner's own behavior and did not depend on the performance of other individuals. But it is possible to arrange contingencies in ways that involve the performance of groups of people. We will discuss some of these approaches in this section.

Reducing Extraneous Counterproductive Reinforcers   Picture this scenario. Almost every day for the past month Ms. Wu, the teacher of a sixth-grade class, has shown her displeasure when one student, Jeff, has come to class late, disrupting ongoing activities. When he arrives, the other students giggle, which reinforces Jeff's behavior of arriving late. Ms. Wu will want to stop that reinforcement to help eliminate Jeff's lateness.

Two approaches can stop people from reinforcing someone's inappropriate behavior. One way is to *reinforce them for not reinforcing* the person. This approach was used in the program we discussed earlier to reduce the classroom tantrums of a girl named Diane (Carlson et al., 1968). In addition to giving Diane tokens for nontantrum behavior, the teacher attempted to reduce the social reinforcers she might receive from other students for disruptive behavior. If Diane had a tantrum, she was taken to the back of the room so her classmates couldn't watch her, and the classmates were given candy treats if they didn't turn around. The second approach involves having the *other people share in the rewards* the individual earns for improved behavior. In the intervention for Diane's tantrums, the whole class would have a party if she did not have a tantrum for four half-days in a row. Similar approaches have been used effectively to reduce conduct problems in larger numbers of classroom students by providing token reinforcers to classmates for not socially reinforcing the problem behaviors (Broussard & Northup, 1997; Walker & Buckley, 1972). The backup reinforcers in these programs included snacks, watching cartoons, and taking field trips.

Lotteries   A **lottery** is a procedure in which all eligible individuals are entered in a drawing to determine one or more prizewinners on the basis of chance. In behavior change programs, eligibility to enter lotteries is based on people's behavior. Entering individuals into a lottery is often a simple process, such as giving one entry to each person whose behavior meets a certain criterion. But other methods to enter people can be more complicated—for example, by allowing more than one entry per person on the basis of the number of points (tokens) he or she earned and whether or not the behavior improved since the last lottery (Sarafino, 1977).

Lotteries can be used in many different settings, including schools, psychiatric hospitals, and workplaces. For instance, a lottery intervention by Michael Johnson and Stephen Fawcett (1994) was introduced to improve the courteousness of human service staff when they interacted with clients. The staff first received training in specific ways to be courteous—addressing clients by name and stating reasons for requesting information, for example. In the lottery, assessments of the staff members' courteousness determined how many entries they had in a weekly drawing for a $10 cash prize. As Figure 4.3 shows, the training alone increased courteous behavior substantially, and the lottery increased it a good deal more and made it more consistent. Other lottery interventions in workplaces have reduced employee absenteeism and unnecessary use of automobiles (Foxx & Schaeffer, 1981; Pedalino & Gamboa, 1974; Wallin & Johnson, 1976).

Group Contingencies   In a **group contingency,** the performance of *all members of the group* determines the consequences that befall its members. An everyday example is when restaurant workers share in pooled tips from customers. An intervention that used a group contingency for reinforcement was conducted with boys whose prior behavior indicated they were at risk for becoming habitual delinquents (Alexander, Corbett, & Smigel, 1976). The boys were living at a treatment center and were supposed to go to a high school during the day, but they skipped nearly half of their classes. To increase class attendance, lunch money was used as a reinforcer. The boys had been accustomed to receiving lunch money from the center with no strings attached. But a few weeks before the intervention began, the center started packing sack lunches for the boys instead. Then the boys were told that they could get lunch money instead of sack lunches if they attended all their classes. At first, this reinforcer was on an individual contingency: if a boy attended all his classes for the day, he received the money for the next day. Later, the lunch money was offered on a group contingency: the boys

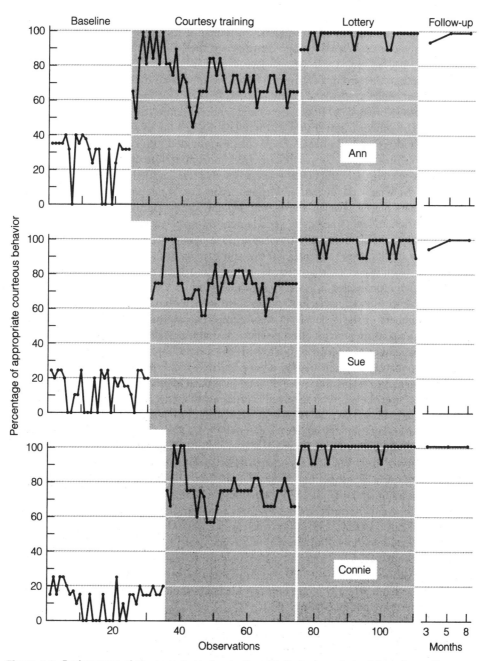

Figure 4.3 Performance of courteous behaviors by three staff members during interactions with clients, as reflected in the percentage of the 30 behaviors they received training to use in the courtesy training intervention phase. The data for the baseline, courtesy training, and lottery phases were collected over a 5-month period. *Source:* Johnson & Fawcett, 1994, Figure 1.

would receive the money only if *all* the boys attended *all* their classes for the preceding day. Under the individual contingency, attendance increased to an average of about 80% of the classes. With the group contingency, the boys' average attendance increased to nearly 100%.

Another way group contingencies can be used is to divide the individuals into teams that compete with one another for reinforcers. This approach has been used with employees (Kortick & O'Brien, 1996) and schoolchildren (Swain, Allard, & Holborn, 1982). The school intervention was implemented to improve first- and second-grade schoolchildren's toothbrushing. Each class was divided into teams to play the "Good Toothbrushing Game," in which four children from each team were chosen randomly each day to have their oral hygiene assessed with a standardized procedure. All members of the class team with the best oral hygiene score got "scratch n' sniff" stickers and had their names posted. The children's oral hygiene scores improved markedly during the intervention and remained quite good at a follow-up assessment 9 months later.

Group contingencies have three main advantages over individual contingencies in behavior modification programs. For one thing, programs with group contingencies are easier to administer. It is simpler to monitor and keep records on behavior and to dispense reinforcers for a group as a whole than to carry out these tasks for each individual in the group. Second, group contingencies have built-in incentives to prevent members of the group from reinforcing one another's inappropriate responses. Third, group contingencies often promote desirable side effects in the social behaviors of group members (Greenwood & Hops, 1981). For example, Frank Kohler and Charles Greenwood (1990) implemented a program in which elementary school classmates were assigned to teams that were divided into pairs of students to tutor each other in spelling. After the children received training in tutoring, they earned points for practicing these skills. The only reinforcer the teacher provided for tutoring was announcing at the end of each day which team, having earned the most points that day, was the winner. With this contingency, the children not only performed the tutoring skills they were trained to do but some students added helpful techniques they had not been trained to use, such as spelling the word more than once when correcting a teammate's errors. In a similar vein, a study of elementary schoolchildren found that group contingencies for candy rewards produced greater cooperation than individual contingencies did (Williamson et al., 1992). But one caution should be pointed out: group contingencies can sometimes have negative effects—for instance, by leading to negative peer-pressure tactics, such as threats or scolding (Greenwood & Hops, 1981; Romeo, 1998). Although it isn't entirely clear why these negative tactics occur, they are probably more likely when the program consequences include group *punishment* if behavioral criteria are not met. (Go to)

Who Will Administer Reinforcement?

In most of the interventions we have discussed so far, reinforcement was administered by teachers, therapists, or parents. But many behavior change programs have used peer-administered or self-administered reinforcement. How well do these approaches work?

Can Rewards Undermine Behavior?

 A study was done with preschool children in the early 1970s that produced surprising and provocative results suggesting that giving children rewards for a behavior they like to do may *reduce* their performance of that behavior in the future (Lepper, Greene, & Nisbett, 1973). Children who were already interested in drawing pictures with Magic Markers were asked to draw some pictures. Some of the children were shown a Good Player Award and told they would get that prize for drawing pictures. Other children got the same opportunity to draw pictures without being told about a prize. After doing the drawings, the children who expected the reward received it, and the others did not. Several days later, the researchers secretly observed the children while materials for drawing and other activities were freely available, with no prizes offered to anyone. At this time, the children who previously received the reward for drawing spent *less* time using the drawing materials than those who had not gotten the reward. Similar effects have been reported for older individuals, using a variety of tangible rewards (Sarafino, 1984). Does getting a reward for doing a preferred activity reduce people's interest in that activity?

The idea that rewards can reduce our interest in activities we enjoy contradicts common sense. After all, many people get paid for work they enjoy and continue to work hard despite receiving paychecks. Research since the 1970s has clarified the effects of rewards on preferred activities (Dickinson, 1989; Eisenberger & Cameron, 1996; Flora, 1990; Reitman, 1998). First of all, many studies have found no decrease in interest after people got rewards for performing enjoyable activities. Second, the conditions under which reduced interest sometimes occurs are very limited: the person's interest before being rewarded must be *very* high, the reward must be *tangible* or *consumable*, and the person must expect that people are *not normally given rewards* for the activity (Sarafino, 1984). Third, when reduced interest does occur, these

> *decrements are transient* if the individual continues to perform the task following the reward, and are not likely at all if individuals *meet or exceed specified performance standards*, or if rewards *increase the frequency* of the behavior and are delivered *repetitively*. (Dickinson, 1989, p. 12, italics added)

So, it appears that rewards can undermine people's interest in enjoyable activities, but the likelihood and durability of these effects are minimal.

Peer-Administered Reinforcement Studies have shown that children can monitor other children's behavior and provide reinforcement for correct responses. As an example, an intervention was introduced to improve arithmetic skills in underachieving fifth-grade students with classmates serving as tutors (Pigott, Fantuzzo, & Clement, 1986). The tutors' jobs included keeping score of the number of math problems each target student completed correctly, comparing that number with the current goal, and deciding whether the student had earned any backup reinforcers. During baseline, the students who were to receive the intervention had averaged only about half as many correct math problems as their classmates. But their performance improved dramatically, equaling that of their classmates by the end of the 3-week intervention and during the next 12 weeks of follow-up assessments. Other studies have shown that programs with same-age children serving as tutors and administering reinforcement can improve ninth-graders' reading skills and the social skills of children with mental retardation (Greer & Polirstok, 1982; Lancioni, 1982).

Using peers as tutors and administrators of reinforcement has some advantages. For one thing, the individuals requiring the intervention can receive more frequent and individualized help than is available with standard teaching procedures. Second, the peers who serve as tutors often gain from the experience themselves. For instance, the same target behaviors they are helping others improve, such as socialization with classmates, also tend to improve in themselves (Dougherty, Fowler, & Paine, 1985; Fowler et al., 1986). In addition, the general social relationships among the tutors and tutees also tend to improve as a result of the intervention experiences (Fantuzzo & Clement, 1981; McGee et al., 1992; Pigott, Fantuzzo, & Clement, 1986; Sanders & Glynn, 1977). A potential disadvantage of using peer-administered reinforcement with children is that they appear to be much more liberal than teachers in giving reinforcers. A study found that although child peers correctly gave reinforcers that were earned, they often provided reinforcers that were *not* earned too (Smith & Fowler, 1984). When children administer reinforcement, the professional who supervises them should monitor their decision making periodically and try to improve it when needed.

Self-Administered Reinforcement   Administering reinforcement to oneself is the cornerstone of self-management programs and is often used as a supplemental method in behavior therapy. This technique has been used in a variety of settings and to change many different behaviors, such as college students' studying and psychotherapy patients' feelings of anxiety (Gross & Drabman, 1982; Jones, Nelson, & Kazdin, 1977).

Several studies have examined the use of self-administered reinforcement in classroom settings. In an intervention to improve third-graders' story writing, the children wrote a story in class each day and assessed it for the number of sentences, verb variations, and modifying words (adjectives and adverbs) it contained (Ballard & Glynn, 1975). The children had been taught how to use verbs and modifying words, and these features were listed on a chart they could see while they scored their stories for the number of points they earned. Later, they could choose and exchange points for backup reinforcers, such as opportunities to have their stories displayed publicly or to play games or read. Self-reinforcement more than doubled the stories' number of sentences, verb variations, and modifying words over baseline levels. What's more, ratings of the stories by English instructors who knew nothing about the study revealed that the stories written when self-reinforcement procedures were in effect were of higher quality than those written during baseline.

One problem with using self-administered reinforcement is that sometimes people take unearned rewards (Gross & Drabman, 1982; McReynolds & Church, 1973; Santogrossi et al., 1973). It's difficult to know how deliberate these errors are. Although it may seem that the individuals must know they have not performed the behavior, oftentimes these reinforcement errors appear to result from people simply using very lenient standards in assessing their behavior. Three approaches can help reduce these errors. First, training by using modeling and instruction methods can teach the person to apply more rigorous or accurate standards in assessing personal behavior (Gross & Drabman, 1982; O'Brien, Riner, & Budd, 1983). Second, having the person make his or her target behavior and goals public appears to increase accuracy in self-reinforcement (Hayes et al., 1985). Third, using an accuracy checking procedure in a behavior change program increases the person's accuracy, especially if there are consequences for inaccuracies (Hundert & Batstone, 1978; McLaughlin, Burgess, & Sackville-West, 1982).

NEGATIVE REINFORCEMENT IN ESCAPE AND AVOIDANCE

If you were to ask cigarette smokers why they smoke, chances are many of them would implicate the role of negative reinforcement, saying, "It relieves my tension." We've seen that negative reinforcement strengthens behaviors we perform that reduce aversive circumstances in our lives. Tension is aversive, and the nicotine in cigarette smoke triggers the body to release chemicals that reduce feelings of tension, anxiety, and pain in a matter of seconds (Pomerleau & Pomerleau, 1989). Using other substances, such as alcohol, appears to have similar effects. The aversive stimuli we try to reduce can be *covert*, as in anxiety or depression, or *overt*, as when someone is physically hurting us. In these situations, we learn to perform behaviors that help us escape from the aversive stimuli.

Escape and Avoidance

In **escape conditioning,** we learn to make responses that reduce or eliminate aversive stimuli we are currently experiencing. If these responses succeed, they are strengthened through the process of negative reinforcement. Escape conditioning is clearly useful when the aversive stimuli we experience can harm us and when the behaviors we learn enable us to adapt well in our lives.

But escape conditioning can lead to maladaptive behaviors too. For example, children may learn that lying can help them escape from their teachers' or parents' threatening accusations or that being disruptive in school can help them escape from a class they don't like. A series of studies by Brian Iwata and his colleagues (1990) examined this process in children with developmental disabilities who frequently performed self-injurious behaviors, such as banging their heads or biting their arms. Part of this research essentially involved doing a functional analysis of the self-injurious behaviors by conducting systematic environmental manipulations—that is, introducing various antecedents and consequences to see whether they affected the behavior. Two findings from this research are relevant here. First, self-injurious behaviors were especially frequent when the children were asked to perform a behavior they were being trained to do, such as a self-help skill. Second, self-injurious behavior became more frequent when it resulted in the trainer stopping the training activity, removing the training materials, and turning away from the child. These findings indicate that training procedures can be unpleasant for children with developmental disabilities and that stopping the training when self-injury occurs negatively reinforces the escape behaviors.

How can we eliminate maladaptive escape behaviors? One way uses the process of extinction—that is, terminating the negative reinforcement. In another part of the research by Iwata and his coworkers, they no longer stopped the training when self-injurious behavior occurred; instead, they provided physical guidance in doing the task. This approach almost entirely eliminated the self-injurious behavior during training sessions. Another way to eliminate maladaptive escape behaviors is to use escape to negatively reinforce adaptive alternative responses. This was done with children who were very disruptive during dental treatment (Allen et al., 1992; Allen & Stokes, 1987). Their disruptive behavior decreased markedly when the dentist praised them and gave them "a little rest break" for being quiet and still but did not stop the treatment when disruptive behavior occurred.

What do people do if they can predict that an aversive event is likely to happen? They do something to try to avoid the unpleasant experience (Ayres, 1998). In **avoidance conditioning,** we learn to respond in ways that prevent us from experiencing aversive events. For instance, we learn to carry an umbrella when rain is likely and to give an excuse if asked to do something we find threatening, such as giving a speech. When I was a child, I learned to predict that I'd be in deep trouble if I didn't get home immediately when I heard my mother call, "Edward *Paul* Sarafino." The middle name signaled future trouble, which I learned to avoid by going home right away.

Learning to avoid aversive events appears to be a two-step process. According to O. H. Mowrer's *two-factor theory* (1947), the first step is to learn the signal as a conditioned stimulus in respondent conditioning. When my mother first used my middle name to call me, I didn't know what it meant, dallied a while, and encountered the "trouble"—the unconditioned stimulus—when I finally got home. The unconditioned response was feeling distress. Soon the signal (the CS) gained the ability to elicit distress, a covert aversive stimulus I could reduce by going right home. Thus, the second step involves operant conditioning: in my case, avoidance behavior (going home immediately) received negative reinforcement by reducing my feeling of distress.

A good deal of evidence supports the combined roles of respondent and operant conditioning in learning to avoid aversive events (Stasiewicz & Maisto, 1993). But two-factor theory does not fully explain avoidance behavior. For instance, people often learn to avoid events without having direct experience with these events, as children do when they stay away from a house they've heard is "haunted." In addition, research has shown that avoidance behavior that was learned by direct experience can be extremely persistent even though the aversive event has not occurred since the original experience (Solomon, Kamin, & Wynne, 1953; Herrnstein, 1969).

To explain such features of avoidance behavior, some researchers have proposed that cognitive factors are also involved. For instance, it may be that when people learn avoidance behaviors they also learn two *expectancies:* (1) "If *I make* the avoidance response, *I will not experience* the aversive event" and (2) "If *I do not make* the avoidance response, *I will experience* the aversive event" (Seligman & Johnston, 1973). By making the avoidance response consistently thereafter, individuals confirm the first expectancy and *fail to disconfirm* the second one. Although incorporating cognitive factors to explain avoidance behavior has some appeal, many researchers disagree that such factors are necessary or useful (McAllister & McAllister, 1995; Pear & Eldridge, 1984).

Factors Affecting Negative Reinforcement Effectiveness

Several factors can affect how effective negative reinforcement will be in our learning to escape or avoid aversive events. One factor is the *reward value* of the negative reinforcement, which appears to be determined by how much the escape or avoidance behavior reduces the aversive stimulus. The greater the degree to which the behavior removes the aversive event, the more effective the negative reinforcement is (Campbell & Kraeling, 1953). Thus, your behavior of taking aspirin when you have a headache is more strongly reinforced if it reduces your headache by 90% rather than by only 50%. Another factor is how strong the aversive stimulus is: negative reinforcement is more effective when the behavior reduces a very aversive stimulus than when it reduces a milder one (Piliavin et al., 1981). The last factor we'll consider is the delay of reinforcement: the more quickly the behavior results in removing the aversive stimulus, the more effective the negative reinforcement will be (Weiss, Cecil, & Frank, 1973).

Although negative reinforcement occurs very frequently in our everyday lives and influences much of our behavior, it isn't used very often in behavior modification programs. Professionals who design and administer interventions to change behavior typically try to minimize the use of aversive events, partly for humanitarian reasons and partly because of undesirable side effects in the person's behavior. When aversive events are used, the target person may become physically aggressive and make efforts to escape or avoid the program and the staff involved in it. In addition, the behaviors rewarded through negative reinforcement are often "superficial." For example, a child may apologize verbally for having been bad, thereby escaping or avoiding punishment, but the apology may be insincere. If it is, insincere behavior is reinforced. When negative reinforcement must be used, the person should receive clear instructions about the link between making the escape or avoidance response and reducing the aversive stimulus, and positive reinforcement should be provided for performing the target behavior. (Go to ☑)

Tips on Using Reinforcement

Professionals have applied these tips on using reinforcement in a wide variety of behavior change interventions. Most of these tips would be useful in designing almost any program to change operant behavior.

1. Be sure to select reinforcers with strong reward value and apply them consistently for performing operant target behaviors. If the target behavior is a respondent behavior, such as

✓

CONCEPT CHECK 4.3

1. A voice coach who reinforces gradual improvements in the "feeling" a student's voice projects is using _____ shaping.
2. A reinforcer that could bridge a delay between the target behavior and its main reinforcer is _____ . ⟺
3. Gradually reducing the rate at which a behavior is reinforced is called _____ .
4. An example of a behavior chain is _____ ; if we were teaching that chain using backward chaining, the first link we would train would be _____ . ⟺
5. An employer who gives special privileges to an entire department if they all come to work on time is using a _____ contingency for reinforcement.
6. Having classmates monitor and provide reinforcement for other students' behavior is called _____ .
7. According to two-factor theory, the first step in learning to avoid an aversive stimulus involves _____ conditioning.

Answers: 1. qualitative, 2. praise/tokens, 3. thinning, 4a. open a locked door, b. push the doorknob, 5. group, 6. peer-administered reinforcement, 7. respondent

an emotional response, we can apply reinforcers for performing the behavior modification activities to change that response.

2. Don't use reinforcers that could work against the behavioral or outcome goals. For instance, it's not a good idea to use sweets as a reward for meeting subgoals in a diet program to reduce caloric intake. This may seem obvious, but people who are first learning about behavior modification sometimes propose such rewards.

3. Make sure the person whose behavior is to be changed is aware that the reinforcers are contingent on and consequences for the target behavior.

4. Use a variety of reinforcers whenever possible (Bowman et al., 1997). One good idea is to allow the target person to select from a menu the reinforcer he or she wants when it has been earned.

5. Be sure to maintain a high degree of reward value during the intervention. If the program is using consumable reinforcers, be careful not to let the target person become satiated on them before a training session is over. To prevent this problem, either switch to other types of reinforcers periodically or give small portions of the food or drink for each instance of reward.

6. Use naturally occurring reinforcers, such as praise, whenever possible.

7. Make sure some kind of reinforcement can be presented immediately after the appropriate behavior that will not disrupt ongoing desirable responses very much.

8. Give reinforcement on a CRF schedule initially, and then thin the schedule after the behavior has become well established.

9. Watch for and try to eliminate counterproductive extraneous reinforcers.

10. Be wary of using reinforcers that are social activities, such as going to a concert with a friend. If the target behavior doesn't meet the criteria for earning the reward, what happens to the tickets if bought in advance? And what about the problems that now arise with the friend?

11. Check the behavior periodically to make sure the reinforcer is improving it.

SUMMARY

Consequences that provide reinforcement strengthen the behaviors on which they are contingent. This rule is true for positive and negative reinforcement. Unconditioned reinforcers satisfy basic physiological needs without having to be learned, but we learn to value conditioned reinforcers as they become associated with stimuli in our lives that are already reinforcing. Evidence suggests that reinforcers can strengthen behavior for any of three reasons: they reduce biologically based drives directly or indirectly, they provide sensory stimulation, and they involve performing high-probability behaviors.

The various types of positive reinforcers include tangible or consumable items, Premack principle activities, social reinforcers, feedback, tokens, and covert reinforcers. We can identify potential reinforcers to provide in an intervention by using direct assessment methods, such as naturalistic observations and structured tests, and indirect assessment methods, such as self-report instruments like the Preferred Items and Experiences Questionnaire. The effectiveness of reinforcers can be enhanced by the technique of reinforcer sampling in which a small or brief sample of the consequence is presented before the behavior.

Many different procedures are available for administering reinforcement. Shaping is a technique in which behavior improves because the standards for receiving reinforcement are increased gradually. Interventions generally apply a continuous reinforcement schedule initially. After the behavior is well established, the schedule of reinforcement undergoes a procedure called thinning; that is, the rate at which the behavior is reinforced is reduced within schedules of intermittent reinforcement. In the condition of extinction, reinforcement is terminated. When teaching chains, reinforcers can be administered within forward chaining, backward chaining, or total-task presentation procedures. Reinforcement also can be administered with individual and group contingencies and by using peer- and self-administered reinforcement methods. Negative reinforcement is involved in escape and avoidance conditioning.

KEY TERMS

reinforcement	conditioned reinforcers	shaping
positive reinforcement	Premack principle	continuous reinforcement
negative reinforcement	tokens	schedule of reinforcement
unconditioned reinforcers	reinforcer sampling	thinning

intermittent   backward chaining   group contingency
    reinforcement   total-task presentation   escape conditioning
forward chaining   lottery   avoidance conditioning

REVIEW QUESTIONS

1. Define positive and negative reinforcement, indicating how they are different. Give two examples of each.
2. What determines the reward value in positive and negative reinforcement?
3. What is the difference between unconditioned and conditioned reinforcers?
4. Describe two research examples suggesting that not all reinforcers directly or indirectly reduce biologically based drives.
5. What are tangible and consumable reinforcers? Give two examples of each.
6. Describe two examples of the Premack principle in your own life.
7. Give two examples each of teachers using social reinforcement and feedback in the classroom.
8. What are tokens and backup reinforcers?
9. Describe how direct and indirect assessment methods can be used to identify potential reinforcers.
10. Define and give an example of qualitative and quantitative shaping.
11. Describe a thinning procedure you might use to reduce the rate of reinforcement you give in an intervention.
12. Compare the procedures of forward chaining, backward chaining, and total-task presentation.
13. What are the advantages in using group contingencies for reinforcement?
14. What are the advantages and disadvantages in using peer- and self-administered reinforcement?
15. Describe the two-factor theory of avoidance conditioning, and give an example of how these processes may have happened in your own escape or avoidance behavior.
16. Describe three factors that determine the effectiveness of negative reinforcement.

RELATED READINGS

Bellamy, G. T., Horner, R. H., & Inman, D. P. (1979). *Vocational habilitation of severely retarded adults: A direct service technology.* Baltimore: University Park Press.

Dickinson, A. M. (1989). The detrimental effects of extrinsic reinforcement on "intrinsic motivation." *Behavior Analyst, 12,* 1–15.

Jones, R. T., Nelson, R. E., & Kazdin, A. E. (1977). The role of external variables in self-reinforcement. *Behavior Modification, 1,* 147–178.

Michael, J. (1975). Positive and negative reinforcement, a distinction that is no longer necessary; or a better way to talk about bad things. *Behaviorism, 3,* 33–44.

Premack, D. (1965). Reinforcement theory. In D. Levine (Ed.), *Nebraska Symposium on Motivation.* Lincoln: University of Nebraska Press.

The child seated alone at the top of the photograph was excluded from the group for a short time as punishment to decrease his misbehavior.

Methods to Decrease Operant Behavior

H elen was a psychiatric patient who had been hospitalized for several years
before Teodoro Ayllon and Jack Michael (1959) conducted a simple behavior modification intervention to reduce a problem behavior of hers.
That behavior was "psychotic talk," which refers to making statements based on delusional (false) beliefs. In Helen's case, she would talk mainly about an illegitimate child
she claimed to have and men who pursued her constantly. She had been making these
untrue statements for 3 years or more. What really made her psychotic talk a problem
was that it constituted almost all of her speech—91% of her baseline talking—and it

> had become so annoying during the last 4 months prior to treatment that other patients
> had on several occasions beaten her in an effort to keep her quiet. . . . Some of the nurses
> reported that, previously, when the patient started her psychotic talk, they listened to her
> to get to the "roots of her problem." A few nurses stated that they did not listen to what
> she was saying but simply nodded and remarked, "Yes, I understand." (p. 327)

Observations of Helen's behavior suggested that people's seeming to pay attention to
the psychotic talk was reinforcing it.

So the intervention simply consisted of *extinguishing* the psychotic talk by having
the nurses stop paying attention to those statements and *reinforcing* appropriate speech
by paying attention whenever Helen made sensible statements. With these new consequences, her psychotic talk declined rapidly, constituting only about 50% of her
speech after 2 days and 25% after another week. Interestingly, her psychotic talk then
began to increase again; probably other individuals at the hospital had begun to reinforce it: one time when Helen wasn't getting attention from a nurse, she said, "Well
you're not listening to me. I'll have to go and see . . . [a social worker] again, 'cause she
told me that if she would listen to my past she could help me."

In this chapter, we will focus on methods to decrease behavioral excesses. We will
examine what extinction and punishment are, their advantages and disadvantages,
and the factors that affect their effectiveness in decreasing undesirable behavior. We
will also discuss several other methods for changing unwanted operant behavior.

WHAT IS EXTINCTION?

When discussing operant behavior, the term **extinction** actually has two meanings. It is a *procedure* or *condition* in which reinforcement is terminated for a previously reinforced response and it is a *process* whereby the likelihood and vigor of performing the no-longer-reinforced response decrease. The verb form for extinction is *extinguish*. So we talk about a teacher or therapist extinguishing a child's disruptive behavior. When the behavior rarely or no longer occurs, we can say it has been extinguished. In reducing Helen's psychotic talk, the nurses used the procedure of extinction when they stopped paying attention to her delusional statements, thereby extinguishing that behavior.

Extinction can apply to behaviors that have received either positive or negative reinforcement. In either case, reinforcement is terminated and the behavior on which reinforcement was contingent declines. If the consequence of the behavior was *positive reinforcement*, such as receiving tangible or social reinforcers, the extinction procedure involves no longer providing those reinforcers. But if the consequence maintaining the behavior was *negative reinforcement*, the extinction procedure involves preventing the individual from escaping or avoiding the unpleasant situation. Because reducing the unpleasant situation provides negative reinforcement, that consequence must be stopped to use extinction to decrease the behavior. For example, children who do not want to be in school sometimes develop tantrums when they arrive there, leading their parents to take them home (Sarafino, 1986). Extinguishing their tantrums requires that these children not be allowed to escape or avoid school.

We know that behavior declines when reinforcement is terminated, but does extinction "erase" the original learning? No, it doesn't. After the response has been extinguished, the individual's memory retains at least part of what was learned in the original conditioning and in extinction (Bouton & Swartzentruber, 1991). Whether the person does or does not perform the behavior after extinction seems to depend on which memory is activated by antecedent stimuli. For instance, people who have quit smoking are much more likely to start smoking again if antecedents occur that are like those that were present during conditioning. These antecedents can be overt, such as seeing a pack of cigarettes, or covert, such as feeling tense. This means that behavior change programs need to prevent the return of an extinguished behavior by incorporating stimulus control techniques to modify the impact of antecedents. For example, programs to stop smoking need to make antecedents associated with extinction as strong as possible, and antecedents associated with smoking must be weakened or avoided when the program ends.

Extinction can occur as a haphazard condition in everyday life or as a careful and deliberate procedure in an intervention. In everyday life, for example, if children have parents who are quite indifferent toward or uninvolved in their parenting roles, many of the appropriate social behaviors children observe in school and elsewhere may not receive sufficient reinforcement to be maintained. At the same time, negative social behaviors, such as aggression, may produce quick rewards. These reinforcement patterns help to explain why children with indifferent, uninvolved parents tend to be aggressive, disobedient, and disagreeable (Sarafino & Armstrong, 1986). In contrast, extinction procedures in interventions are planned to accomplish certain behavioral goals. To start an extinction procedure for a target behavior, we must identify what the reinforcement is and be able to control its source. If we don't control the source of reinforcement very carefully, extraneous reinforcers may occur and reinstate the behavior.

Identifying and Controlling Reinforcement for Extinction

The first step in using extinction is to conduct a functional analysis to identify what the reinforcers have been for the behavior we want to eliminate. Although the reinforcers may seem obvious in some cases, often they are unclear or even surprising. Gary Sasso and his colleagues (1992) conducted a functional analysis to determine the reinforcers for aggressive behavior toward adults by a 7-year-old girl with autism named Molly. They discovered that her aggression was reinforced when the teacher allowed her to escape classroom activities she didn't like and to engage in activities she did like. They also found that social attention, such as saying "Please don't do that," did not affect Molly's aggression. This is surprising because attention is a common reinforcer for aggressive behavior. Her aggression was reduced with a program that centered around eliminating the negative reinforcement it had been getting.

Similarly, other researchers have found that escaping from academic and self-care training sessions can reinforce self-stimulation and self-injurious behavior and that preventing escape in these circumstances extinguishes the behavior (Iwata et al., 1990, 1994; Repp, Felce, & Barton, 1988). Self-injury and self-stimulation behaviors were very puzzling for many years because their reinforcers were unknown. Functional analyses allow therapists to identify the reinforcers and eliminate them when it is possible to control them. Sometimes the reinforcers for self-injury or self-stimulation are the sensations the behavior produces in the individual (Iwata et al., 1994; Lovaas, Newsom, & Hickman, 1987). When this is so, eliminating the reinforcement for self-stimulation behaviors may be possible—for example, by blindfolding the person (Rincover & Devany, 1982). But doing this is not always feasible.

Controlling the sources of reinforcement is essential in extinguishing a target behavior for two reasons. First, if other sources reinforce the behavior, extinction may not occur. This is often a problem in classrooms when classmates socially reinforce undesirable behavior in fellow students. One way to curb this situation is to reward classmates for not providing social reinforcement for problem behavior (Broussard & Northup, 1997). Second, if reinforcers appear again for a behavior that has already been extinguished, it will be reinstated. This is what happened in Helen's case when the social worker paid attention to her psychotic talk. A similar situation happened in an extinction procedure that was applied to eliminate a 21-month-old boy's tantrums at bedtime (Williams, 1959). The reinforcement for these outbursts was having one of his parents or an aunt stay with him for up to 2 hours each night until he went to sleep. To extinguish his tantrums, the adults put him to bed in a relaxed and pleasant fashion, left the room, closed the door, and did not reenter the room regardless of any screaming. Although his tantrum on the first night of extinction lasted for 45 minutes, the episodes declined rapidly in the following nights and were absent a week later. Several evenings later, the boy began to scream again, and his aunt returned to his room and stayed with him as in the past. This reinforcement reinstated the tantrums, which had to be extinguished again. Follow-up assessments during the next 2 years revealed no recurrence of this behavior.

Interventions using extinction to reduce an undesirable behavior often apply other techniques as supplements. A very useful supplement to extinction involves reinforcing a desirable *alternative response*—that is, a behavior that is incompatible with the target behavior. For example, extinction and reinforcement were combined in a program to reduce the pain behaviors of a young woman who suffered from migraine headaches (Aubuchon, Haber, & Adams, 1983). It appeared that such pain behaviors as complaining of pain were being reinforced by the enormous amounts of attention those behaviors received from her family, physician, and nurses. These individuals were instructed to ignore the pain behaviors (extinction) and reinforce alternative responses, such as exercising and doing household chores. The frequency of her pain behaviors dropped markedly in the first month from an average of almost 8 per day in baseline to less than 1 per day, and remained below an average of 1 per day at 6- and 12-month follow-up assessments. Similarly, an intervention succeeded in reducing children's destructive behavior by eliminating the negative reinforcement that had maintained it (extinction) and reinforcing alternative behaviors, such as playing quietly (Piazza et al., 1997).

An interesting combination of extinction and reinforcement was used in an intervention to reduce 3½-year-old Cain's aggressive behavior toward his classmates in preschool (Pinkston et al., 1973). These behaviors included choking, biting, pinching, hitting, and kicking. The teacher had been dealing with Cain's aggression by reprimanding him ("Cain, we don't do that here" or "Cain, you can't play here until you're ready to be a good boy"). But these statements seemed to be reinforcing the behavior. During the intervention, the teacher ignored Cain when he was aggressive and, instead, gave attention and activity reinforcers to his victim—for instance, by saying "I'm sorry that happened to you. Why don't you play with this nice truck?" In addition, the teacher began to give Cain social reinforcement for alternative responses such as interacting appropriately with other children. The intervention reduced his aggressive behavior in a couple of weeks or so from about 30 instances per day in baseline to about 5 per day, and his positive interactions with peers increased substantially too.

The Process and Characteristics of Extinction

Picture this scene. You're running late on your way to class one morning and have to skip breakfast. You expect from the many other times this has happened in the past that you'll be able to buy a snack from a conveniently located vending machine to take the edge off your hunger. You get to the machine, insert the correct change, and pull the lever for the snack you want, but nothing comes out. How will you react to not having your behavior reinforced? Chances are, you'll react initially by pulling the lever once again. When that produces the same result, you might pull the lever several times

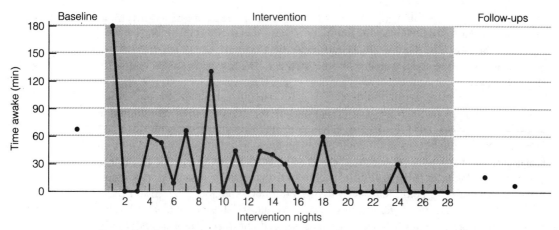

Figure 5.1 Number of minutes an infant was awake after having gone to sleep at night. Each data point for baseline and follow-up periods represents the average time awake across 14 nights for one infant (child 1). The intervention was conducted with seven 8- to 20-month-old infants who had been referred by nurses for treatment because of long-term sleep disturbances. The sole technique used in the intervention was extinction: after putting the child to bed, the parents did not return if the infant woke up unless the child was sick or might be injured. The infant whose awake time is presented in the graph was sick only on night 9 of the intervention. *Source:* Data abstracted from France & Hudson, 1990, Figure 2.

in rapid succession and very strongly. And when that doesn't work, you might kick the machine or pound on it.

This example illustrates two phenomena of the extinction process. First, when reinforcement fails to occur, the response often increases temporarily in its frequency and magnitude, for example, pulling the vending machine lever rapidly and strongly (Skinner, 1938). This phenomenon is called an **extinction burst.** Figure 5.1 gives an example of an extinction burst for the first night in an intervention to decrease the amount of time an infant was awake after having gone to sleep at night (France & Hudson, 1990). On that night, the infant was awake almost three times longer than the baseline average. People's responding in extinction does not always show a burst, but when it does, people who want to change the behavior but don't expect a burst may think that extinction does not work. Second, extinction often increases the target person's aggression and other emotional behaviors (Kelly & Hake, 1970; Kimble, 1961; Todd, Morris, & Fenza, 1989). If these phenomena occur when we try to extinguish an undesirable behavior, they can present problems in carrying out the extinction procedure, particularly if someone may be harmed physically or if the behavior is very annoying, such as the screaming of a child in a tantrum. Although aggression and extinction bursts occur in a substantial proportion of cases when extinction is used alone, these problems can be reduced markedly (Lerman, Iwata, & Wallace, 1999). Two ways to curb these problems are to combine extinction with other methods, such as reinforcement for alternative responses, and to instruct the person of the new contingencies in advance.

Extinction has two other characteristics that are quite typical of the process. For one thing, the behavior tends to decline gradually or irregularly rather than immediately and smoothly. You can see this in Figure 5.1: notice how the infant's awake time had a generally decreasing trend but fluctuated a lot during the first couple of weeks of the intervention. Although the awake times of the seven infants treated in that intervention didn't all show so much fluctuation, they all declined in a fairly gradual pattern, with some being extinguished in just a few days (France & Hudson, 1990). The other characteristic of the extinction process is that an extinguished behavior can reappear temporarily—a phenomenon called **spontaneous recovery.** This reappearance may happen partly because antecedents that were present when the behavior had received reinforcement in the past are present again (Bouton & Swartzentruber, 1991). When an extinguished response "recovers" without being reinforced, its strength—as reflected in its frequency, duration, or magnitude—is usually weaker than it was before extinction. Referring again to Figure 5.1, the infant's fairly brief durations of being awake during the follow-up assessments probably reflect spontaneous recovery. Some evidence indicates that spontaneous recovery is less likely to occur when extinction is carried out along with reinforcement of an alternative response (Lerman, Kelley et al., 1999).

What Factors Affect Extinction Effectiveness?

Several factors affect how quickly and completely extinction procedures will extinguish a behavior. We've already discussed some of these factors. That is, extinction is especially effective in stopping a target behavior when we have (1) carefully and fully identified the reinforcers that maintained the response in the past, (2) withheld all these reinforcers when the behavior occurs, and (3) supplemented these procedures by giving reinforcement for desirable alternative responses. When any of these conditions is lacking in an extinction program, the behavior will be more *resistant to extinction*, or harder to extinguish.

The reinforcement history of the target behavior can also affect its resistance to extinction in three ways. First, the more times the behavior was reinforced in the past, the longer it is likely to take to extinguish the response (Siegel & Foshee, 1953). Second, the greater the reward value of the reinforcers the behavior produced in the past, the harder extinguishing the response is likely to be (Lewis & Duncan, 1957). Third, behavior that was reinforced on an intermittent reinforcement schedule generally takes longer to extinguish than behavior reinforced on a continuous reinforcement schedule (Kimble, 1961; Lewis, 1960; Lewis & Duncan, 1956). For instance an intervention was conducted in which two male adults with mental retardation were instructed that they could earn token reinforcers if they conversed with other individuals (Kazdin & Polster, 1973). During a 5-week period, one man received tokens on a continuous schedule for conversing and the other man received tokens on an intermittent schedule. Later, when token reinforcement was withdrawn, conversing continued

CONCEPT CHECK 5.1

1. Terminating reinforcement for a previously reinforced response is called _____ .
2. Before introducing an extinction procedure, we should identify the reinforcers by conducting a(n) _____ .
3. Suppose a teacher terminated the social reinforcement that previously maintained a child's habit of blurting out questions in class. An alternative response the teacher might reinforce is _____ . ⇔
4. A temporary increase in a target behavior at the start of extinction is called _____ .
5. A relatively weak recurrence of a previously extinguished response is called _____ .
6. Behaviors previously reinforced intermittently rather than continuously tend to show greater _____ to extinction.

Answers: 1. extinction, 2. functional analysis, 3. hand raising, 4. extinction burst, 5. spontaneous recovery, 6. resistance

at a high rate during the next 5 weeks in the man who received intermittent reinforcement; in contrast, conversing declined rapidly in the man who received continuous reinforcement.

Another factor that can affect how quickly extinction procedures will eliminate a behavior is instruction in the new contingencies. Behavior often extinguishes much faster when target persons are told their responses will no longer be reinforced than when reinforcement simply ceases to appear (Weiner, 1970). The factors that affect the effectiveness of extinction lead to a couple of basic rules about using extinction procedures. Remember that the behavior we want to reduce may show an extinction burst and may fluctuate early in the process. If we have identified the reinforcers carefully and eliminated them, we shouldn't conclude from the burst or fluctuation that the extinction process isn't working. Behaviors sometimes get worse for a while before they get better. If we stop the extinction procedure and allow the behavior to be reinforced again, however, we'll reinforce the behavior's getting worse—that is, we'll fuel the burst. Also, keep in mind that most behaviors in everyday life receive reinforcement intermittently, making them harder to extinguish. As a result, we'll need to be patient when using extinction. (Go to ✔)

WHAT IS PUNISHMENT?

"Punishment doesn't work with Brian," the boy's parents told a neighbor who complained of the child's daily racket. "We've scolded him and spanked him for making so much noise. That stops him for the moment, but he starts making noise again in a while." Did Brian's parents punish his making noise when they scolded and spanked him? Probably not. Let's see why we should doubt it.

In operant conditioning, **punishment** is a process whereby a consequence *suppresses* the behavior on which it is contingent, decreasing its frequency, duration, or magnitude. The consequence that suppresses the behavior in this process is called a *punisher*. Punishers are aversive stimuli or conditions. Loosely speaking, the person finds these consequences "undesirable" or "unpleasant." Brian's behavior didn't seem to be affected by the consequences his parents applied. If a consequence must suppress behavior to be considered a punisher, it isn't likely that scolding or spanking punished Brian's making noise. The best way to determine whether a consequence is a punisher is to *apply it* and *assess carefully* whether the behavior declines. From casual reports like Brian's parents gave, we can't be sure whether a given behavior actually declined because parents typically don't assess their children's behavior carefully, and their impressions may be wrong.

You may be thinking, "But scolding and spanking *are* punishers. Everyone finds these things unpleasant!" Well, maybe Brian doesn't agree. If we're going to define punishers loosely as "consequences people find unpleasant," we must be sure to assess the unpleasantness from the *point of view of the person who will receive these consequences*. We've seen in earlier chapters that stimuli or conditions parents and teachers ordinarily think of as punishers, such as scolding, can actually *reinforce* the behavior they're intended to decrease. What's more, we know that some people dislike stimuli or conditions most other people like, and vice versa. For instance, some people seem to like physical pain—at least under some, usually sexual, situations—and are called *masochists*. It may be that pain becomes a conditioned reinforcer for these people through the process of respondent conditioning, for example, by participating in or viewing activities that associate pain with pleasure in a sexual context (Wincze, 1977).

There are two other reasons for not being certain whether scolding and spanking are punishers for Brian. First, the parents may have applied these consequences poorly, thereby severely weakening the punishing effects of these stimuli. We will see later that several factors affect how effective punishment is likely to be. Second, scolding and spanking may be punishers for Brian, but the reinforcement he gets from making noise may be so much stronger than the punishment being applied that his noise-making fails to change much after the scolding or spanking. The problems we have discussed in identifying punishers underscore, once again, the need for conducting a functional analysis in designing a behavior change program and collecting data carefully to assess the program's effects. Hunches are helpful, but not sufficient.

Types of Punishment

We saw in Chapter 4 that reinforcement can be delivered in two ways: When we give positive reinforcement, our *adding* a consequence strengthens the behavior on which such reinforcement is contingent. When we give negative reinforcement, our *subtracting* or taking away an aversive circumstance is the consequence, and it strengthens the behavior on which the reinforcement is contingent. The same "adding" versus

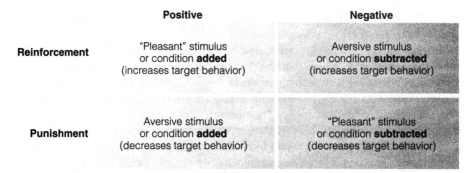

	Positive	Negative
Reinforcement	"Pleasant" stimulus or condition **added** (increases target behavior)	Aversive stimulus or condition **subtracted** (increases target behavior)
Punishment	Aversive stimulus or condition **added** (decreases target behavior)	"Pleasant" stimulus or condition **subtracted** (decreases target behavior)

Figure 5.2 Four types of behavioral consequences: positive reinforcement, negative reinforcement, positive punishment, and negative punishment. Notice that "positive" and "negative" refer to whether the stimulus or condition is *added* to or *subtracted* from the situation following a response.

"subtracting" distinction exists in punishment. As Figure 5.2 outlines, punishment can be delivered in two ways:

- In **positive punishment,** an aversive stimulus or condition is *added* as a consequence of the behavior. This is the kind of punishment Brian's parents tried to apply.
- In **negative punishment,** a stimulus or condition the person already has at the time the behavior occurs is *subtracted* as a consequence of performing the behavior. This stimulus or condition typically is something "pleasant" or valued—that is, receiving it for doing something would reinforce that behavior.

An example of negative punishment is having to pay money as a fine for a traffic violation. The money is something the person already has and was probably obtained as reinforcement for an earlier behavior, such as working.

People often confuse the processes of punishment and negative reinforcement. An example may help you distinguish between these types of consequences. Suppose 2-year-old Fran is curious about electrical outlets and keeps trying to pull plugs out of and stuff things into the little holes. This behavior justifiably frightens her parents, and they scold her each time. Scolding has helped—she stops immediately and has been playing with outlets less and less. In this case, scolding is positive punishment for Fran's behavior, but it is also an *escape* behavior for her parents because it stops her behavior, thereby reducing their fright. Scolding is negatively reinforced by reducing their fright.

All sorts of stimuli and conditions can serve as punishers to suppress behavior (Azrin & Holz, 1966; Matson & Taras, 1989; Van Houten, 1983). Most punishers can be classified into several categories that may overlap somewhat. The first few types of punishers we will consider involve positive punishment, and the last types involve negative punishment.

Physically Aversive Stimuli   I visited a stop-smoking clinic years ago and tried out a device that gave a mild electric shock to my finger. It was used to punish cigarette smoking to help people quit. The shock didn't hurt, but it produced a very unpleasant sensation, and I wanted it to stop. **Physically aversive stimuli** are events that cause physical pain, discomfort, or other unpleasant sensations. To be punishers, they must suppress behavior.

Physically aversive stimuli are very common consequences of behavior in our everyday lives. These consequences are often provided deliberately with the intention of correcting behavior—for instance, when parents and other adults hit children or animals for behaving in inappropriate or undesirable ways. But physically aversive stimuli can also be "naturally occurring events" that happen in our environment as consequences of our behavior (Azrin & Holz, 1966). Naturally occurring punishers that come to mind most easily involve careless behavior. Examples include bruising your head by walking into a post because you were looking at a physically attractive person, burning your hand by spilling hot coffee because you moved too quickly, and getting scratched by a pet because you played with it too roughly.

Using physically aversive stimuli as punishers in therapy is usually avoided for humanitarian reasons and because of their side effects on behavior, which we will consider later in this chapter. When the stimuli are strongly aversive, their use is controversial. One very controversial form of punishment is strong, painful electric shock (Goodman, 1994). The use of painful electric shock as a punisher in behavioral methods was pioneered in the 1960s in interventions with children with developmental disabilities, mainly to eliminate self-injurious and self-stimulatory behaviors (Corte, Wolf, & Locke, 1971; Lovaas, Schaeffer, & Simmons, 1965; Lovaas & Simmons, 1969). Although this method had some success, it is rarely used today and is reserved for those cases in which all other approaches have failed and the behavior must be suppressed quickly, as in cases of self-injury. Other approaches to stop self-injury and self-stimulation that often are successful include using *mild*, brief electric shock as punishment (Linscheid et al., 1990) and withdrawing negative reinforcement for these behaviors while giving positive reinforcement for alternative behaviors (Iwata et al., 1990, 1994; Repp, Felce, & Barton, 1988).

Milder forms of physically aversive stimuli are less controversial punishers. *Mild* electric shock as punishment was used effectively to eliminate a life-threatening behavior in a 9-month-old infant named Mark (Cunningham & Linscheid, 1976). The behavior is called *chronic ruminating* and consists of vomiting repeatedly after feeding. This behavior resulted in Mark's being hospitalized for malnutrition, dehydration, and severe weight loss. The shocks decreased his ruminating from 36 instances a day in baseline to 4 instances on the first day of the intervention, and only occasional instances after about a week. Figure 5.3 shows another infant who received this kind of therapy. Other relatively mild, physically aversive punishers include tasting a bitter or sour substance, such as unsweetened lemon juice; having water sprayed to the face; and smelling a pungent odor, such as ammonia (Altman, Haavik, & Cook, 1978; Dorsey et al., 1980; Sajwaj, Libet, & Agras, 1974; Singh, Watson, & Winton, 1986; Vargas & Adesso, 1976). (Go to ▓)

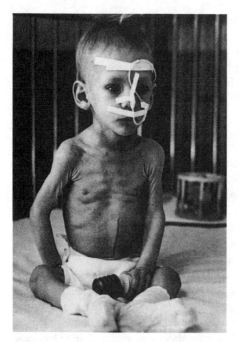 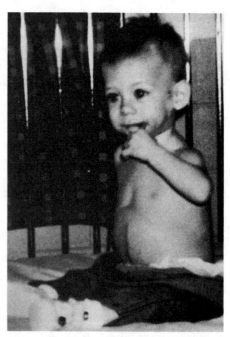

Figure 5.3   The photo of this infant boy on the left shows him when his chronic ruminating had reduced his body to skin and bones (the tape on his face was used for holding a tube to feed him through his nose). After punishment was used to suppress his ruminating, his weight increased by 26% in less than 2 weeks, and his face, body, arms, and legs had filled out, as shown on the right. *Source:* Photographic Media Center, University of Wisconsin-Madison archives.

CASE STUDY 5.1

Lemon Juice Therapy to Stop Public Masturbation

A 7-year-old boy with severe retardation had begun masturbating publicly when he was living in an institution and continued to display this behavior for the nearly 2 years since returning to live at home (case described in Cook et al., 1978). The behavior would occur at school and at home, causing his parents great embarrassment to the point that they were considering reinstitutionalization. Prior to the intervention, the boy's parents or teachers had tried to stop his public masturbating by shouting "No" and spanking his hand, but this didn't seem to be working. Because the parents were not concerned with his private masturbation in his bedroom or a bathroom, the intervention focused only on the target behavior's occurrence in all other places.

The lemon juice punishment was carried out in the following way. Whenever the boy "put either hand inside his pants and directed toward his penis," his parent or a teacher would squirt some unsweetened lemon juice

into his mouth with a plastic squirt bottle. . . . During the early stages of treatment the subject was under nearly constant observation, and the treatment procedure was always imple-

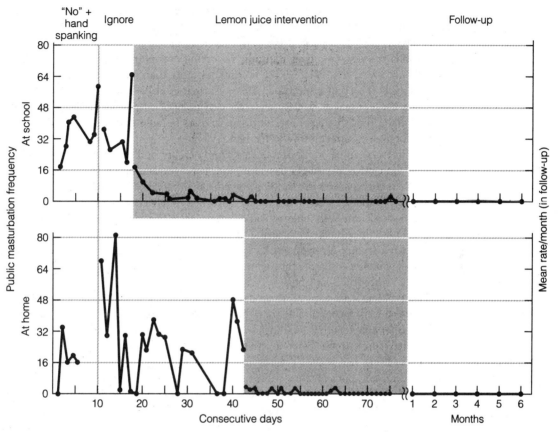

5CS.1 Public masturbation frequency at home and at school during four phases: "No" plus hand spanking, ignoring, lemon juice punishment intervention, and follow-up. Assessments were taken during six 5-minute observation periods in a day. For the first three phases, the data represent daily frequencies during the observation periods. For the follow-up phase, the data represent the mean frequency per day for each of 6 months. *Source:* Cook et al., 1978, Figure 1.

mented as soon as possible after the target behavior occurred. The subject's mother carried the lemon juice in her purse when she took her son to public places. (p. 132)

Data on the boy's target behavior were collected at school and at home during four phases of the treatment: a baseline in which the prior method ("No" plus hand spanking) was continued, a second baseline in which the target behavior was simply ignored, the intervention with lemon juice punishment, and a follow-up period. As Figure 5CS.1 shows, the boy's masturbatory behavior occurred at very high rates during both baseline periods, was almost completely eliminated quickly when the lemon juice intervention was used, and was totally absent in 6 months of follow-up assessments.

Reprimands   **Reprimands** are negative verbal statements or feedback—such as "No! That's bad"—sharply criticizing a behavior. Because these statements are added after the behavior, they provide positive punishment when they reduce operant behavior. Reprimands are very common, naturally occurring events in people's everyday lives. Studies have found that teachers use reprimands more than praise with their students, particularly after second grade (Bear, 1998; Thomas et al., 1978; White, 1975). Classmates also use reprimands, sometimes to the detriment of other students' learning: some students claim that they avoid speaking up in class because they've been ridiculed in the past for giving correct answers (Herbert, 1997).

Reprimands can be administered easily and quickly, and sometimes they are more effective than other punishers that are more time-consuming to use (Doleys et al., 1976). Their effectiveness in changing behavior is enhanced when the person receiving them is nearby and the statements are accompanied by a fixed stare and firm grasp, such as of the person's arm or shoulders (Van Houten, 1983; Van Houten et al., 1982). Their effects can also be enhanced by pairing them with other punishers, such as mild physically aversive stimuli (Dorsey et al., 1980). Reprimands that suppress responses are *conditioned punishers*—that is, they gained their ability to suppress behavior by having been paired with other punishers.

One problem with using reprimands by themselves to change behavior is that their effects appear to be more variable than those of other consequences. For instance, we've seen in earlier chapters that scoldings by parents and teachers often serve as reinforcers for children's undesirable behavior, *increasing* the behavior instead of decreasing it. Sometimes using reprimands creates an illusion of being effective: the misbehavior stops immediately, but only for a short time, and the frequency of the behavior actually increases later. If their effects are assessed periodically, reprimands can still be very useful as a part of programs to change behavior.

Aversive Activities   An 11-year-old boy named Mark who lived at a residential institution during the week used swear words about 11 times per dinner period (Fischer & Nehs, 1978). He went home on weekends. His "cottage parents" at the institution had been unsuccessful in trying to convince him to stop swearing, so they conducted an intervention requiring him to spend 10 minutes washing windows for each instance of swearing during dinner. His swearing declined sharply within a few days and remained infrequent during follow-up assessments taken in the 15 days after the intervention ended.

This example illustrates that aversive activities can serve as positive punishers. When we discussed the Premack principle and reinforcement in Chapter 4, we saw that engaging in high-probability behaviors can reinforce performing infrequent responses. Using aversive activities as punishers is essentially the other side of this coin—that is, being required to engage in a *low*-probability behavior as a consequence of performing a target response that occurs too frequently, such as Mark's swearing, can reduce the person's performance of the frequent response. As we saw in Mark's case, the low-probability behavior does not have to be related to the target behavior. Researchers found, for instance, that requiring grade-school children to perform arbitrarily chosen motor activities, such as repeatedly standing up and sitting on the floor, can serve as punishers to reduce their aggressive behavior (Luce, Delquadri, & Hall, 1980).

Of course, the aversive activities selected as punishers in interventions can be related to the behavioral excesses we're trying to reduce. A punishment approach called **overcorrection** requires the person to engage in aversive activities that correct or are the opposite of the undesirable target behavior when that misbehavior occurs (Foxx & Azrin, 1972). This approach includes two methods, restitution and positive practice, which can be used together or separately (Axelrod, Brantner, & Meddock, 1978; Ollendick & Matson, 1978). **Restitution** refers to correcting the effects of the misbehavior and restoring the environment, usually to a condition better than it was before the misbehavior. For example, a person who wrote graffiti on a wall might be required to paint the entire wall. In **positive practice,** when the misbehavior occurs, the person must repeatedly perform an appropriate or useful alternative or opposite response to that of the misbehavior. For instance, a girl who pushes her little brother down to get the toy he was playing with might have to practice over and over asking him nicely for the toy and offering to give him another toy in exchange.

An intervention to reduce stealing by institutionalized adults with mental retardation used restitution as punishment for the target behaviors (Azrin & Wesolowski, 1974). These 34 individuals stole from one another very frequently, and one of the main items they would steal was food at mealtimes and at snack times. No baseline assessment was made because it would require an ethically indefensible condition: the staff would not be able to intervene when they were aware of victims losing their property. Instead, the first few days of the intervention used a "simple correction" procedure in which staff only required that the thief return the food (or the part remaining, if some was already consumed). Because thefts often occurred as a "sudden grasping-biting movement," this procedure often didn't restore the original condition, and thefts continued at a high rate. The intervention used an overcorrection–restitution method that included the simple correction procedure *and* the requirement that the thief go to the food display area with a staff member, get an identical item, and give it to the victim. Nearly 20 thefts occurred each day when simple correction was the only consequence, but the thefts declined rapidly with the restitution method and were completely eliminated in a few days, as Figure 5.4 shows.

Positive practice was used in an intervention to reduce sprawling by adults with mental retardation—that is, sitting or lying about on the floors instead of sitting in available chairs at the institution where they were residents (Azrin & Wesolowski, 1975). This behavior was not just unsightly; it also created a hazard that had caused injuries. Other behavioral methods had been tried without success to change this behavior. Positive practice was conducted in the following way: residents who sat on the floor were told they could not do that and were required to get up, go to a nearby chair, sit there for about a minute, and then go and sit for a minute on each of several other chairs. They were left sitting on the last chair. Verbal prompts were given for each step in the sequence, and physical guidance prompts were used initially and then faded. This method eliminated floor sprawling in about 10 days, and a follow-up assessment found that the residents continued to use the chairs 6 months later.

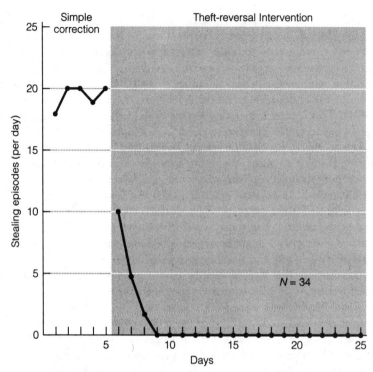

Figure 5.4 Frequency of stealing episodes each day by 34 adults with mental retardation during two phases: simple correction and an overcorrection theft-reversal intervention. *Source:* Azrin & Wesolowski, 1974, Figure 1.

Research has shown that overcorrection methods can be effective in reducing a variety of problem behaviors in hospital, classroom, and home settings (Axelrod, Brantner, & Meddock, 1978; Ollendick & Matson, 1978). Some research results indicate that overcorrection may be effective in classrooms even when the punishment (positive practice) is delayed until a lesson or the class is over (Azrin & Powers, 1975; Barton & Osborne, 1978). An advantage of overcorrection methods is that they have built-in alternative responses, thereby providing opportunities to learn appropriate behaviors instead of just suppressing misbehavior (Carey & Bucher, 1981). But these methods have some disadvantages as well. For example, they are complicated and very time-consuming to administer (Kelly & Drabman, 1977; MacKenzie-Keating & McDonald, 1990). In addition, problems may arise with any punisher that involves an aversive activity if the person who is being punished refuses to engage in the activity. Suppose the adults who were stealing food refused to make the required restitution. What then? Using physical prompts can help move the person into a given activity, but if such measures don't work, making other consequences contingent on engaging in the activity may have the desired effect. If not, however, we may have to abandon using the aversive activity as a punisher.

Time-Out   Most of us have heard parents command, "Go to your room!"—which they intended as punishment. If being in your room is not very stimulating and does not provide many opportunities for reinforcement, being sent there from someplace more reinforcing constitutes negative punishment. The method of punishing misbehavior by converting or moving the person's environment from one that is relatively reinforcing to one that is less reinforcing is called **time-out** (Brantner & Doherty, 1983; Van Houten, 1983).

How long should the time-out last? Jennie Brantner and Michael Doherty (1983) reviewed the results of many studies and found that effective time-out periods usually can be fairly short, lasting a matter of minutes rather than hours or days. Periods of between 1 and 15 minutes work well. One study compared the punishing effects of three time-out period lengths: 1, 15, and 30 minutes (White, Nielsen, & Johnson, 1972). The time-out procedures were applied with institutionalized individuals with mental retardation to reduce their deviant behaviors, such as aggression and tantrums. The results indicated that the 15- and 30-minute time-out periods reduced deviant behavior the most, but these two lengths were equally effective. In general, time-out periods should be as short as possible while still reducing the target behavior substantially. Sometimes just a minute or two is enough.

Brantner and Doherty (1983) have described three types or levels of time-out. In the most restrictive level, called *isolation time-out,* the target person is removed from the relatively reinforcing environment and placed in a separate, substantially less reinforcing environment. Being sent to your room would be an example of isolation time-out if it is a less reinforcing environment. Some schools or institutions have set up special "time-out rooms" where individuals are sent or taken when they misbehave (Barton et al., 1970). But using isolation time-out can have some disadvantages and is inadvisable in some cases. For instance, individuals who might harm themselves if left unattended may require a staff member to monitor their behavior in isolation. Isolating children with developmental disabilities may provide them with opportunities to perform self-stimulation or self-injurious behaviors that are undesirable and dangerous.

Exclusion time-out involves removing the target individual from opportunities for reinforcement without isolating him or her. A common way of using exclusion time-out is to move the person to a separate part of the same environment and not allow him or her to participate in ongoing reinforcing activities. Researchers used this method in a day-care center to reduce the children's disruptive behavior, such as being aggressive or damaging toys or other objects (Porterfield, Herbert-Jackson, & Risley, 1976). When an instance of disruptive behavior occurred, the caregivers described to the child both the misbehavior and an alternative behavior. "No, don't take toys from other children," the caregiver might say, "Ask me for the toy you want." Then the time-out would be started: the target child had to sit on the floor with no toys at the periphery of the other children's activities and watch how they interacted. After the child watched quietly for a minute or so, he or she was allowed to rejoin the other children. Although misbehavior occurred during the intervention with time-out punishment, the rate was only about 37% of the rate resulting when the children were simply told the behavior was wrong and given another activity to do.

Similar exclusion time-out procedures have been applied in interventions that effectively reduced oppositional behavior in preschoolers and disruptive behavior in adults with mental retardation (Bostow & Bailey, 1969; Roberts, Hatzenbuehler, & Bean, 1981). Exclusion time-out can also be applied by having the target person stay in the same environment while the materials or stimulation the person uses for reinforcement are taken away for a short period. For example, toys might be removed and the radio or TV might be turned off for a few minutes. This exclusion time-out approach was applied effectively to reduce spitting and self-injurious behaviors of a child with autism (Solnick, Rincover, & Peterson, 1977).

In *nonexclusion time-out*, the person who misbehaves is not removed from the ongoing activities at all but receives a signal indicating a period in which he or she cannot earn reinforcers that would have been available if the misbehavior hadn't occurred. An intervention using a nonexclusion time-out procedure was conducted with five boys with mental retardation in a special education class to reduce disruptive behaviors, such as aggression and yelling (Foxx & Shapiro, 1978). During the usual classroom activities, the boys could earn social and consumable reinforcers every few minutes for working quietly. Each child who was eligible for these reinforcers wore a colored ribbon around his neck to signify this status. When a boy misbehaved, the teacher removed the ribbon from his neck for 3 minutes. Thus, when the teacher gave the next reinforcers, he could not receive any. This procedure reduced disruptive behavior in all of the boys, and the two boys who had been most disruptive during baseline were misbehaving only about 5% as often by the end of the intervention.

In addition to being a punishment technique, time-out can also be extended to become extinction or negative reinforcement procedures. For example, suppose we sent Len to his room for hitting his sister, and he began to have a tantrum. Maintaining the time-out conditions until the tantrum ends would serve as extinction of that behavior. Or, if we required Len to apologize to his sister to gain release from time-out, apologizing would be negatively reinforced.

Time-out punishment appears to be effective in reducing unwanted behavior and may be a very good alternative to punishers of other types, especially those that apply physically aversive stimuli (Brantner & Doherty, 1983). Exclusion and nonexclusion time-out methods seem to be as effective as isolation time-out procedures in most situations, while having fewer disadvantages. Time-out punishment is likely to be most effective in suppressing behavior if the amount of reinforcement in the original environment is much greater than that in the time-out environment (Solnick, Rincover, & Peterson, 1977; Van Houten, 1983).

Response Cost   Response cost refers to a negative punishment procedure in which misbehavior results in the person losing something valued—that is, an item or privilege that was probably a reinforcer for an earlier behavior (Van Houten, 1983). Although the stimulus is usually something the person already has, it can also be a reinforcer he or she has earned but not yet received. Everyday examples of response cost include having to pay money as a fine for a traffic violation or as a penalty for writing a check that bounces or failing to pay a bill on time. The lost stimulus can also be an item the person owns, such as a favorite article of clothing or videotape or a privilege he or she ordinarily has, such as watching TV. Of course, losing something of value in a response cost procedure occurs only when the unwanted target behavior is performed.

Interventions usually apply response cost with fines in the form of money or tokens. In one example, Peter Miller (1972) applied response cost in behavior therapy to treat a man's alcohol abuse. The client and his wife agreed to two conditions: he should limit his drinking to no more than three drinks per day, and he must consume all drinks in her presence, whether they were at home or out. They also agreed to the following response cost procedure. If he drank outside the agreed upon conditions—as determined by her smelling liquor on his breath or seeing him drink or appear drunk—he had to pay her $20 that she would spend very frivolously. What's more, his wife's behavior was included in the program too: if she criticized her husband for his drinking, she had to pay him $20. They each reported that having to pay the fine would be very unpleasant. His drinking decreased from a baseline average of about seven and a half drinks a day to three or fewer in less than 2 weeks and remained at that level throughout follow-up assessments over the next 6 months. Although this simple approach effectively reduced this man's drinking, it would not be sufficient by itself to control drinking in most alcohol abusers.

Response cost has been applied very effectively in classrooms. One intervention used response cost to reduce off-task, distracted behaviors in children with conduct and learning problems (Sullivan & O'Leary, 1990). In this program, teachers would scan their classes periodically, checking to see whether individual children were working on class activities or performing *off*-task behaviors. In some classes, response cost was used in a way that punished performing off-task behavior during the scan with the loss of a token, which was worth 1 minute of recess. In other classes, reinforcement was used instead of punishment; thus performing *on*-task behavior was reinforced with a token that was worth 1 minute of recess. Both conditions improved the children's working on class activities, and using response cost was at least as effective as using reinforcement. Other classroom interventions have used response cost methods in token programs that effectively reduced off-task behavior in children who are hyperactive, stealing in second-graders, disruptive behavior in fourth- to sixth-graders, and spelling errors in adolescents (Barrish, Saunders, & Wolf, 1969; Harris & Sherman, 1973; Rapport, Murphy, & Bailey, 1982; Swizer, Deal, & Bailey, 1977; Truchlicka, McLaughlin, & Swain, 1998). The interventions for stealing and disruptive behaviors administered the consequences on the basis of group contingencies.

Response cost punishment is fairly easy to apply, especially when it is part of a token reinforcement program. One thing to keep in mind about the response cost approach is that taking away something of value contingent on misbehavior is not the same as withholding reinforcement until appropriate behavior occurs. Many students confuse the two circumstances. The former applies when the person *has performed* an unwanted response in a program to modify a behavioral excess, and the latter applies when the person *has not yet performed* the wanted response in a program to modify a behavioral deficit. (Go to ▮)

CASE STUDY 5.2

Response Cost to Stop "Lady Mary's" Blurting Out

A 29-year-old woman with mental retardation who worked in a sheltered workshop had a habit of blurting out statements that were either false or nonsensical in the context (case described in Kazdin, 1971). For instance, she would suddenly say "You can't take that away from me," when no one had tried to take anything, or "My name is Lady Mary," which it wasn't.

A response cost intervention was designed to reduce the frequency of "Lady Mary's" blurting out. To implement this intervention, a response cost procedure was added to a token reinforcement system that had already been in effect for 6 months to increase her job production rate, which was only 20% of the minimum industrial rate. She was informed that her blurting out now would cost her tokens. During the first week, no tokens were taken for the target behavior to see if the threat would be sufficient to reduce the behavior. It wasn't—her blurting out continued at the baseline rate of about 40 instances a week. Once the response cost was actually in force, her blurting out plummeted to about 3 per week. What's more, it remained at that level during the 4-week follow-up period when the response cost consequences were no longer applied.

The Process and Characteristics of Punishment

We've seen that there are many varieties of punishers and that punishment can suppress behavior effectively. But using punishment is very controversial, especially when the punisher is a physically aversive stimulus. The issues in these controversies focus on the advantages and disadvantages of using punishment in all applications of behavioral methods—in behavior therapy interventions, everyday parenting, education, business and industry, and so on (Brown, 1982; Singh, Lloyd, & Kendall, 1990; Walters & Grusec, 1977). Let's see what these issues are.

Advantages of Punishment   One of the main advantages of using punishment techniques lies in the *rapid results* that can be achieved in suppressing the undesired behavior (Dinsmoor, 1998). This advantage is especially important if the behavior is dangerous, as in the cases discussed earlier of self-injurious behavior and infant ruminative vomiting. Physically aversive stimuli have been applied to stop these behaviors, and *mild* stimuli are frequently sufficient to suppress them very quickly, sometimes with just a few applications (Cunningham & Linscheid, 1976; Linscheid et al., 1990). These effects are especially impressive because the target behaviors in these interventions had occurred for months or years before aversive stimuli were applied, and other methods had been tried to stop the behaviors without success.

Rapid results are also important when the target behavior is very embarrassing, as in the case considered earlier of a boy who masturbated in public. Using lemon juice as a punisher dramatically reduced this boy's public masturbation in just a few days and eliminated it almost completely in a couple of weeks (Cook et al., 1978). Interventions using time-out and overcorrection punishment methods have quickly and substantially decreased aggressive and self-stimulation behaviors (Marholin & Townsend, 1978; Wilson et al., 1979). Although speed in reducing these two behaviors may not be such a critical concern, it is certainly desirable.

Another advantage in using punishment are the *positive side effects* sometimes produced in nontarget behaviors. In the mild shock intervention Thomas Linscheid and his colleagues (1990) applied to decrease the long-standing self-injurious behaviors of individuals with mental retardation and autism, only certain types of self-injurious behaviors were targeted for punishment. Yet specific assessments indicated that several of the nontarget behaviors improved too. Anecdotal information suggested that social behaviors and independent feeding also improved in some individuals. Other studies using other kinds of punishment have found positive side effects on such nontarget behaviors as individuals' greater attentiveness when aggressive behavior was suppressed and increased play behavior when self-stimulation was suppressed (Van Houten, 1983).

The last advantage in using punishment we'll consider is that it often leads to a *complete suppression* of the unwanted response (Dinsmoor, 1998; Van Houten, 1983). For most of the studies of punishment effects we have examined, the data presented in the text or in graphs (see Figures 5.3 and 5.4) depict long-lasting, complete or near-complete suppression of the target behaviors. This durability is important for two reasons. First, when the target behavior is dangerous, the most appropriate behavioral goal is to stop it entirely. Although other behavioral methods frequently can reduce dangerous responses substantially, they may not eliminate them. Second, behaviors that have been strongly suppressed are less likely to recover and become problems again in the future.

Disadvantages of Punishment   Researchers have described several negative side effects punishment may sometimes produce. We will examine these disadvantages of punishment within three broad categories: emotional and escape/avoidance reactions, aggressive behaviors, and future use of punishment.

Emotional and Escape/Avoidance Reactions   People don't like to be punished—they don't like to receive unwanted or unpleasant consequences for their behavior. As a result, being punished sometimes produces negative emotional reactions, causing the person to cry or have tantrums, for instance. These reactions are not limited to punishment techniques that involve physically aversive stimuli, such as painful events, but may also occur with other methods, such as overcorrection (Axelrod, Brantner, & Meddock, 1978; Carey & Bucher, 1981). We might be concerned about causing negative emotions for many reasons, but one relates to the likely success of our intervention: negative emotions interfere with therapy and learning processes.

A related side effect of punishment is that the unpleasantness of the aversive stimuli may cause the target person to try to escape from the situation, even when the punisher is fairly mild (Azrin & Holz, 1966; Dinsmoor, 1998). What's more, associations the person is likely to make between the aversive stimuli and the therapy or training situation may lead him or her to try to avoid the situation or the people dispensing the punishment (Morris & Redd, 1975).

Aggressive Behavior   Sometimes individuals become physically aggressive toward the people who dispense punishment or toward other individuals in the environment (Azrin & Holz, 1966; Dinsmoor, 1998; Hutchinson, 1977; Mayhew & Harris, 1978; Oliver, West, & Sloane, 1974). In therapy sessions, this may take the form of hitting, kicking, or throwing objects at the therapist—behavior that disrupts the session, at least temporarily. To the extent that the target person's aggression leads to escape from the therapy or training session, that behavior will be negatively reinforced by virtue of the reduced discomfort from getting out of the session.

Future Use of Punishment   I remember seeing a cartoon years ago depicting a boy across his father's lap, being spanked. The caption read, "This will teach you to hit your sister." Although the father was using punishment to reduce the boy's physical aggression, he was also modeling the undesired type of behavior for his son to learn. Children often imitate the punishing acts they see, and the punishment can be physical or nonphysical, as in response cost (Gelfand et al., 1974; Walters & Grusec, 1977).

A dramatic example of the likely role of modeling in children's using physical punishment comes from a study of disadvantaged toddlers in four day-care centers that focused on helping battered children and nonabused children from "families under stress" (Main & George, 1985). The researchers observed the children for incidents in which a child showed distress by crying or behaving fearfully and assessed the reactions of the other children toward the distressed child. How did the abused and nonabused children react? Nonabused children tended to respond in a concerned or sad manner. In contrast, the abused boys and girls showed little or no concern—instead, they often reacted with physical attacks or anger. The following example describes one such episode:

> Martin [an abused boy of 32 months] tried to take the hand of the crying other child, and when she resisted, he slapped her on the arm with his open hand. He then turned away . . . and began vocalizing very strongly, "Cut it out! CUT IT OUT!", each time saying it a little faster and louder. He patted her, but . . . his patting became beating, and he continued beating her despite her screams. (p. 410)

Although these observations can't pinpoint why the abused children reacted this way, the similarity to their parents' abusiveness is both disturbing and provocative, suggesting a role of modeling. We know also that abusive parents often were abused or neglected as children (Kempe, 1976).

✓

CONCEPT CHECK 5.2

1. Punishment is a process whereby a consequence _____ the behavior on which it is contingent.
2. An example of positive punishment from your life is _____ . ⇔
3. An example of negative punishment from your life is _____ . ⇔
4. Washing a child's mouth out with soap for swearing is an example of using a(n) _____ stimulus as a punisher.
5. Overcorrection consists of two methods: _____ and _____ .
6. The length of time-out periods usually doesn't need to exceed _____ to be effective.
7. Having a student sit facing a rear corner of his or her classroom is an example of _____ time-out punishment.
8. An advantage of using punishment is _____ . ⇔
9. A disadvantage of using punishment is _____ . ⇔

Answers: 1. suppresses, 2. a scolding, 3. interest paid for not paying a credit card bill on time, 4. physically aversive, 5. restitution, positive practice, 6. 15 minutes, 7. exclusion, 8. behavior declines rapidly, 9. aggression.

But the recipient of punishment is not the only person in the aversive situation who can learn to use punishment more in the future—the person dispensing it can too. For example, parents or teachers who use punishment are likely to find that it stops the current misbehavior immediately and tends to reduce future instances of the response rapidly. When this happens, their punitive acts are reinforced, and they become more likely to use aversive consequences in the future.

The negative side effects of using punishment in changing behavior are serious concerns when they occur, but they don't appear to happen very often (Linscheid & Meinhold, 1990; Matson & Taras, 1989; Van Houten, 1983). For instance, children are not likely to become abusive individuals from having received punishment occasionally, even if some of it was fairly intense and physically aversive. The more excessive the punishment is in its frequency, duration, and intensity, the more likely long-lasting negative side effects will develop. Still, whenever we consider using punishment in interventions to change behavior, we should move cautiously and examine the likely advantages and disadvantages carefully. And if we use punishment and don't begin to see improvements in the target behavior quickly—usually in a matter of hours or days—we should reassess the situation and, perhaps, discontinue the aversive consequences. (Go to ✓)

When to Consider Using Punishment

Wouldn't it be nice if punishment occurred little or not at all in life? Punishment, like all forms of reinforcement, is a common and natural part of people's lives. When we do things carelessly or that are wrong, unpleasant consequences tend to happen. To end the need for punishment, we would have to control everyone's antecedents carefully and monitor their behavior constantly to make sure it is sufficiently reinforced. This is not a scenario that's likely to develop, nor is it one most people want. Instead, we encounter individuals whose prior behavior and reinforcement history is unknown. If we try to influence antecedents and consequences deliberately at all, we generally intervene haphazardly. But as psychologist Paul Brown (1982) has pointed out, sometimes just "catching people doing well" and then "accentuating the positive" with reinforcement isn't enough. Sometimes we need to consider using punishment.

When is using punishment a good idea? We will look at some issues that can help us judge whether to use punishment and what types of punishers to apply. The first issue to consider is whether *other behavior modification methods have been tried*. The other behavioral methods worth trying should have been identified with a careful functional analysis. These methods might include modifying antecedents, providing reinforcement for alternative responses, and using extinction procedures to eliminate the reinforcers that maintain the undesirable behavior. If all nonpunitive methods identified in the functional analysis failed to decrease the target behavior, we may want to consider using punishment (Axelrod, 1990; Guess, Turnbull, & Helmstetter, 1990). Unfortunately, functional analyses are not always conducted to help select the behavioral methods to use in interventions (Lennox et al., 1988).

The second issue we need to examine in deciding whether to use punishment relates to *characteristics of the target person's behavior*. An important characteristic of the behavior is its likelihood of causing injury to the person or others. The greater the likelihood of injury, the more acceptable using punishment becomes (Smith, 1990). Self-injurious behavior, severe aggression, and ruminative vomiting are three kinds of behavior for which punishment typically can be justified. In addition, behaviors that are highly embarrassing or bizarre, such as self-stimulation, have the effect of isolating the individual socially. For that reason, punishment may be an acceptable approach if other behavioral methods have not been successful. Many professionals have substantial reservations about using punishment even when injury is likely if the behavior is allowed to continue (Donnellan & LaVigna, 1990; Luiselli, 1990). But if other methods have failed to decrease behaviors that are dangerous or severely impair intellectual and social development, professionals who are trying to change the behaviors may find it necessary to consider using punishment.

The third issue in deciding on using punishment entails our ability to *control extraneous, counterproductive reinforcers* of the undesirable behavior. As researcher Ron Van Houten (1983) has pointed out, some behaviors may have intrinsic, or "built-in," reinforcers, as in cases of self-stimulation and public masturbation. Other behaviors, such as stealing or speeding, may result in naturally occurring reinforcement. And some behaviors may receive reinforcement from individuals over whom we have little control. When we cannot control extraneous reinforcement, nonpunitive methods may not be sufficient to decrease the behavior very much, and punishment may be necessary.

Our last issue relating to making decisions on using punishment has to do with the *types of punishers* available. Punishers that produce strong pain or tissue damage evoke humanitarian concerns and are often precluded or restricted by professional guidelines

---

CLOSE-UP 5.1

The "Gentle Teaching" Approach

 Controversies over the use of aversive stimuli with people with developmental disabilities have led to the design of a training approach called *Gentle Teaching* (McGee et al., 1987; McGee & Gonzalez, 1990). This approach assumes that teachers or therapists, called "caregivers," and the person with a disability must develop a social "bonding" as a prerequisite to training. To encourage this bonding, caregivers try to show the target person that other people are safe and that participating in training leads to rewards, not punishment.

Gentle Teaching uses no aversive consequences, and the only consequences the caregiver applies are social reinforcers such as praise, hugs, and smiles. Inappropriate behaviors are seen as examples of a failure to bond. When they occur, the caregiver withholds social reinforcers in an effort to extinguish them and tries to redirect the behaviors toward a desirable activity by giving the person new task materials. If self-injurious behavior begins, the caregiver tries to prevent harm by blocking the response, perhaps by deflecting the person's arm in the act of hitting, and then conveys calming messages such as "Everything's fine. No one will hurt you."

Research on the effectiveness of the Gentle Teaching approach with individuals with developmental disabilities has yielded mixed results. One study found that Gentle Teaching increases certain appropriate behaviors—participating correctly in training activities, for instance—and decreases inappropriate behaviors such as making errors and performing disruptive acts (McGee & Gonzalez, 1990). But studies using this approach to decrease self-injury and self-stimulation have found that Gentle Teaching either fails to decrease the behaviors or is less effective in decreasing them than are behavioral methods that include a wider range of reinforcers and some mild punishers (Barrera & Teodoro, 1990; Jones, Singh, & Kendall, 1990; Jordan, Singh, & Repp, 1989). One effective mild punisher is *visual screening*, in which the teacher covers the person's eyes briefly with a hand or piece of cloth when misbehavior occurs. Although Gentle Teaching offers some creative methods that can be tried in interventions before resorting to punishment, the evidence does not yet support relying on its methods alone in training individuals with developmental disabilities.

---

or law (Hamilton & Matson, 1992; Singh, Lloyd, & Kendall, 1990). In addition, the general public may have a voice in the choice of punishers that can be applied, particularly in schools. One study had adults rate different types of punishers for use in school and at home (Blampied & Kahan, 1992). Response cost and reprimands were rated as the most acceptable types, followed by time-out, overcorrection, and physical punishment. Although this order of acceptability held for both school and home, overcorrection and physical punishment were rated as more acceptable at home than at school. What's more, these acceptability ratings may be related to the punishers' likelihood of leading to negative side effects. For instance, studies have found relatively few negative side effects when using response cost rather than physical punishment methods (Kazdin, 1972). Of course, an important consideration in choosing a punisher is that it must be effective in decreasing the target behavior. But regardless of the type of punisher selected, its degree of severity or restrictiveness should be as mild as possible while still allowing the intervention to succeed in reducing the undesirable behavior. (Go to 🔲)

How to Use Punishment Well

If we decide to use punishment to change behavior, we should maximize its effectiveness. The more carefully we apply punishment, the less often it will be needed because the behavior will decline faster. The most basic rule in applying consequences is to be *systematic*. To apply punishment well, we'll need to use behavioral criteria consistently to determine when to apply a punisher, instead of waiting until we've "had enough" of the misbehavior (Hall et al., 1971). It is also important to eliminate or reduce as much as possible extraneous reinforcers that maintain the target behaviors. We'll turn now to examining several aspects in the application of punishment that can influence how effective it will be.

Reinforcing Alternative Responses   It's rarely a good idea to design an intervention that uses punishment by itself without providing reinforcement for alternative responses. There are three reasons to reinforce alternative responses when using punishment. First, punishment only teaches what *not* to do. It doesn't teach new, more appropriate behavior to take the place of the undesirable actions (Brown, 1982). Second, combining reinforcement of alternative responses with punishment for undesirable behaviors is more effective in decreasing target behaviors than punishment is alone (Van Houten, 1983). This approach can make relatively mild punishers more useful. For instance, a study used positive practice of alternative responses to decrease self-stimulation behaviors in adults with mental retardation (Carey & Bucher, 1986). When the activity in positive practice was reinforced, the positive practice method became more effective in suppressing undesirable behavior than when it was not reinforced. Third, the occasional negative side effects of punishment are less likely to appear if alternative responses are reinforced (Van Houten, 1983).

Using Instructions   Punishment appears to work best in suppressing unwanted behavior when the person receives specific instructions describing both the target behavior and the consequences. An intervention that used instructions was introduced to decrease negative social behaviors among unpopular boys in the first to third grades in school (Bierman, Miller, & Stabb, 1987). The program decreased these behaviors by describing the undesirable acts and applying response cost when they occurred. What's more, some of the boys also received instructions on and reinforcement for performing positive social behaviors as alternative responses. Only the boys who received instructions on positive and negative behaviors along with consequences for each type of behavior became more popular among their classmates.

Punisher Magnitude   In general and within limits, the more intense a punisher is, the more effective it is likely to be in suppressing the target behavior (Dinsmoor, 1998; Van Houten, 1983). But this relationship doesn't mean that it's a good idea to use highly aversive consequences as punishers. Intense punishers tend to produce more negative side effects than milder ones, and mild punishment is often quite effective when used in combination with reinforcement for alternative responses. To restate the rule presented earlier about applying punishment: we should use the mildest level we can to achieve the behavioral goals of the program (Brantner & Doherty, 1983).

The Timing of Punishment   Punishment is most effective in suppressing undesirable behaviors when it is delivered *immediately after every instance* of the behavior (Dinsmoor, 1998; Van Houten, 1983). Its effects are weakened when it is delayed or when it occurs only occasionally, particularly at the beginning of an intervention. After the behavior has declined substantially, the punishment can usually be thinned to an intermittent schedule and eventually eliminated. For instance, studies have found that delivering time-out punishment intermittently after the behavior has been decreased to a low frequency does not lead to an increase in the behavior (Calhoun & Lima, 1977; Clark et al., 1973). If the behavior involves a chain of responses, it's probably best to punish it as early in the sequence of responses as possible.

Varying the Punishers   We saw in Chapter 4 that reinforcement tends to be more effective when a variety of reinforcers are available to be given for appropriate behavior. A similar phenomenon exists for punishment—that is, varying the punishers applied for misbehavior appears to suppress the behavior more effectively than using the same punisher all the time. This phenomenon was demonstrated with three developmentally disabled 5- and 6-year-olds in an intervention to decrease specific deviant behaviors, such as aggression and self-stimulation (Charlop et al., 1988). During some training sessions, the children received one of four punishment methods: reprimands, overcorrection, time-out, and a loud noise. During other training sessions, the trainer alternated using three of the four punishers when misbehaviors occurred. Each of the punishers suppressed the deviant behaviors when presented singly in the sessions, but the children engaged in deviant behaviors even less often during sessions when the trainer varied the punishers. It may be that people adapt to the same punisher over time and that varying the punishers prevents this adaptation.

Self-Administering Punishment   An option in using punishment is to have people administer punishers to themselves, especially in self-management approaches. Will people do it? Yes, but probably not as reliably as they should. We saw in Chapter 4 that individuals often become lenient in giving reinforcers to themselves. The same problem seems to arise if punishment is self-administered. For instance, Jack James (1981) had a young man try to reduce his stuttering by using self-punishment. When the client stuttered, he was to take a very brief time-out period (about 2 seconds) from speaking. Although the intervention reduced his stuttering from baseline levels, he applied the time-out in less than half of the instances of stuttering, as reflected in periodic assessments. His accuracy in administering time-out was improved substantially later on by adding a response cost procedure: each time he failed to apply the time-out when he should, he lost a small amount of money.

We can increase the accuracy of applying self-administered punishment by monitoring its occurrence. A program to help a man reduce his smoking used this method with response cost punishment: when the man exceeded agreed-upon smoking limits, he had to write a $25 check to a charity he disliked and send it to the researcher, who would then forward it to the charity (Belles & Bradlyn, 1987). The man's wife kept collateral records of his smoking for verification. Another factor that influences the likelihood that self-punishment will be administered accurately is the magnitude of the punishers selected for use. Accuracy in applying self-punishment probably decreases as punisher magnitude increases. As we have seen, sometimes very mild punishers can help suppress behavior. One way to reduce the severity of a punisher is to make it *covert*. For instance, have the person imagine an aversive consequence, such as getting caught or being fined, for performing the undesirable behavior (Cautela, 1993a). Of course, we cannot verify that covert punishers have been applied, but we can assess whether the behavior changed.

OTHER STRATEGIES TO DECREASE UNDESIRED BEHAVIORS

Other strategies that do not withhold reinforcers or apply punishment can be included in programs to decrease undesired operant behaviors. The first of these strategies we will examine is called differential reinforcement.

Differential Reinforcement to Decrease a Behavior

It is possible to use reinforcement to decrease an undesirable behavior, and we will look at three ways to do this. We've discussed this method before without giving it a specific name: **differential reinforcement of incompatible behavior** (DRI, pronounced by spelling "d-r-i") is the systematic provision of reinforcers for performing an alternative response. An effective approach in using DRI involves doing a functional analysis to identify the reinforcing functions of the target behavior and making sure the alternative response receives the same reinforcers as the undesirable behavior. This approach was used in an intervention to decrease deviant behaviors, such as aggression and self-injury, in children with developmental disabilities (Carr & Durand, 1985). After it had been determined that the function of these behaviors was to communicate the need for help or feedback from their teachers, the intervention had the teachers provide attention for communicating the needs verbally, such as by saying, "I don't understand" or "Am I doing good work?" DRI methods can also be used by parents at home to decrease their children's disruptive behaviors and sibling conflicts (Friman & Altman, 1990; Leitenberg et al., 1977).

The second way to use reinforcers to decrease a target behavior is to give them if the behavior occurs less and less frequently. In this approach, called **differential reinforcement of low rates of responding** (DRL), reinforcement is only given when instances of the undesirable behavior fall below certain rates. For example, a teacher might reinforce students for being out of their seats in class fewer than three times in an hour. Although technically DRL methods could reinforce the first instance of the behavior after a minimum period of time in which it did not occur at all, DRL procedures are rarely used in this way in applied settings (Rolider & Van Houten, 1990). Interventions using DRL methods have successfully decreased a wide variety of inappropriate behaviors, such as sleeping and talking out in class and eating too quickly (Deitz, Repp, & Deitz, 1976; Lennox, Miltenberger, & Donnelly, 1987).

The third way to use reinforcers to decrease operant behaviors is a variation on the DRL approach called **differential reinforcement of other behavior** (DRO). In the DRO procedure, reinforcement is given when the target response, such as whining, *does not occur at all* during a certain time period—perhaps for the whole day. In a sense, reinforcement is given for doing anything except the target response, which is why the name of the method mentions "other behavior." DRO methods can successfully reduce a variety of unwanted behaviors, including sibling conflict at home, classroom misconduct, and thumb-sucking (Leitenberg et al., 1977; Repp, Deitz, & Deitz, 1976), but they seem to be less effective than other methods for decreasing operant behavior (Didden, Duker, & Korzilius, 1997; Whitaker, 1996).

Habit Reversal

A strategy called **habit reversal** includes several methods to decrease operant behavior, particularly repetitive motor "nervous" habits, such as muscle tics and stuttering (Azrin & Nunn, 1973; de Kinkelder & Boelens, 1998). One of its chief methods is called *competing response practice*, in which the target person engages for a few minutes in a response that is the opposite of the target behavior. For example, to reduce thumb-sucking or nail-biting, clients might be instructed to place their hands by their sides and clench their fists for 3 minutes when they find that the target behavior has begun or is about to happen. This method is like that of positive practice, which we saw earlier, but it is designed to "minimize any aversiveness of the required practice" (Azrin & Nunn, 1973, p. 623). The other methods in habit reversal include training the person to be more aware of the target behavior's occurrence and having family members reinforce improvements in the behavior at home. Several studies have found that habit reversal procedures often can eliminate highly frequent habits almost entirely (Azrin & Nunn, 1973; Azrin, Nunn, & Frantz, 1980; Azrin & Peterson, 1990; Finney et al., 1983; Miltenberger, Fuqua, & Woods, 1998).

Self-Monitoring and Self-Instructions

Sometimes simply using *self-monitoring* and *self-instructions* may help to decrease operant behaviors. For example, Clarke Harris and William McReynolds (1977) had college students self-monitor their nail-biting by marking each instance of it on a card. Other students also self-monitored their nail-biting, but some were instructed to say to themselves "Don't bite" periodically during the day and others were instructed to say

CONCEPT CHECK 5.3

1. An example of the type of punishment people generally find least acceptable to use in school or at home is _____. ⟺

2. The approach for training children with developmental disabilities by having teachers "bond" with the child and use only social reinforcers is called _____.

3. The most effective timing pattern for punishment is to deliver it _____ of the behavior.

4. Rewarding someone for smoking fewer than five cigarettes a day is an example of the strategy called differential reinforcement of _____.

5. The strategy for decreasing operant behavior that includes having the target person practice a competing response is called _____.

Answers: 1. spanking, 2. Gentle Teaching, 3. immediately after each and every instance, 4. low rates of responding, 5. habit reversal

"Don't bite" each time they found themselves doing so. The students' nail-biting behavior was assessed by measuring their fingernail lengths. Individuals in all of these conditions showed greater gains in nail length than other students who did not receive an intervention. The individuals who were told to say "Don't bite" contingent on nail-biting had the greatest gains, which suggests that the statement may have served as a punisher. Other studies have found that self-monitoring by itself improved students' academic performance (Wood et al., 1998) and helped a woman reduce her frequent upsetting thoughts about the possibility of developing cancer (Frederiksen, 1975). (Go to ✔)

Tips on Using Extinction and Punishment

Several tips on using extinction and punishment methods are listed here. These tips can be applied to decrease operant behavior in any behavior modification program to correct a behavioral excess.

1. Make sure the target person is aware of the changes in consequences and exactly what the target behavior is.

2. If at all possible, identify an alternative response to prompt and reinforce when methods are used to decrease the target behavior.

3. Think carefully about the reinforcers that maintain the behavioral excess and what can be done to eliminate them. Once the behavior starts to decline, watch for new sources of reinforcement that may cause the behavior to recover.

4. If extinction will be used, remember that extinction bursts sometimes occur at the beginning of the process.
5. If a punisher will be used, select the weakest level that is likely to be effective.
6. Make sure a punisher to be used in the intervention can be applied immediately after every instance of the target behavior to be decreased.
7. When using response cost punishment, make sure there is always a supply of things to lose. If the supply of things to lose is exhausted, the intervention will not have a punishing consequence to use.
8. Don't present punishment at about the same time as reinforcement. If this happens, one or both consequences may weaken. This could happen, for example, if we were to comfort the target person soon after a punisher is presented because he or she looks sad.
9. It's a good idea to precede instances of punishment with a warning cue, such as saying "No!" By doing this, we may strengthen the ability of the cue to suppress unwanted behavior.

SUMMARY

In the procedure or condition of extinction, the reinforcers that maintained an operant behavior are withdrawn and the behavior eventually declines. To conduct extinction effectively, a functional analysis should be done to determine what reinforcers to terminate. At the beginning of extinction, the behavior may increase temporarily in an extinction burst, and sometimes behaviors that have been extinguished show spontaneous recovery. The target behavior's reinforcement history can affect its resistance to extinction.

Punishment suppresses the behavior on which it is contingent. In positive punishment, an aversive stimulus or condition is added after the behavior; in negative punishment, a valued stimulus or condition is taken away after the behavior. Some types of punishment involve physically aversive stimuli or reprimands. Other punishers consist of aversive activities—as in the procedure of overcorrection, which includes the methods of restitution and positive practice. Still other punishers involve imposing a time-out from opportunities for reinforcement or applying response cost.

Punishment methods have several advantages and disadvantages that influence decisions on whether to use them and which types of punishers to select. To be very effective, punishment should be applied systematically, an alternative response should be identified and reinforced, and the person should be instructed about the target behavior and the new consequences. The magnitude, timing, and variety of aversive stimuli affect the suppressive effects of punishment. Self-punishment can work, but people may not administer punishers to themselves very reliably.

Strategies other than extinction and punishment that are also able to decrease operant behavior include differential reinforcement of incompatible behavior, differential reinforcement of low rates of responding, and differential reinforcement of other behavior. Habit reversal, self-monitoring, and self-instructions are other strategies that can reduce undesirable behavior.

KEY TERMS

extinction
extinction burst
spontaneous recovery
punishment
positive punishment
negative punishment
physically aversive stimuli
reprimands

overcorrection
restitution
positive practice
time-out
response cost
differential reinforcement
   of incompatible
   behavior

differential reinforcement
   of low rates of
   responding
differential reinforcement
   of other behavior
habit reversal

REVIEW QUESTIONS

1. What is extinction? Describe how it is conducted when the behavior has been maintained with positive and negative reinforcement.
2. Why is it important to conduct a functional analysis before using extinction?
3. Describe an undesirable behavior of someone you know and its likely reinforcers. Outline how you could, or why you couldn't, extinguish that behavior.
4. Define and give an example of an extinction burst and of spontaneous recovery.
5. What is punishment, and how do positive and negative punishment differ?
6. What are physically aversive stimuli? Give four examples.
7. How could you determine if a stimulus, such as a reprimand, is a punisher for a specific person?
8. Define overcorrection, and give an example of how a parent might use this method to decrease a child's misbehavior.
9. Describe the procedure and findings of the research by Azrin and Wesolowski (1974) on using restitution as punishment.
10. Distinguish among the three types of time-out punishment.
11. Define and give an example of response cost punishment from your own life.
12. What are the advantages and disadvantages of using punishment?
13. Describe five aspects of the way punishment is applied that influence its effects and what the effects of each aspect are.
14. Define and distinguish among DRI, DRL, and DRO procedures for reducing undesirable behavior.
15. Describe the strategy of habit reversal.

RELATED READINGS

Axelrod S., & Apsche, J. (Eds.). (1983). *The effects of punishment on human behavior*. New York: Academic Press.

McGee, J. J., Menolascino, F. J., Hobbs, D. C., & Menousek, P. E. (1987). *Gentle Teaching: A nonaversive approach for helping persons with mental retardation*. New York: Human Sciences Press.

Repp, A. C., & Singh, N. N. (Eds.). (1990). *Perspectives on the use of nonaversive and aversive interventions for persons with developmental disabilities*. Sycamore, IL: Sycamore.

Walters, G. C., & Grusec, J. E. (1977). *Punishment*. San Francisco: W. H. Freeman.

Airlines provide information and behavioral methods, such as systematic desensitization, to reduce people's fear of flying.

CHAPTER SIX

Behavioral Methods for Changing Respondent Behavior

C hild clinical psychologist Michael Rutter (1975) described the case of a 6-year-old boy named Martin who appeared to be a generally happy child with no psychological problems other than an extremely severe fear of dogs. He was so terrified of dogs that he couldn't go shopping or walking with his parents or on family outings, and he would run out to the road, heedless of traffic, to avoid encounters with dogs. If a dog came near,

> he screamed, cried, and ran away. The fear of dogs first started when Martin was a year old when he was repeatedly frightened by two very large and noisy hounds in the adjoining garden. The dogs never attacked Martin, but they would put their paws on top of the fence and snarl and bark at him. Martin would either stand still, screaming and terrified, or would rush into the house in tears. (p. 220)

Martin's parents protested, but the neighbors did not change the situation, which continued for a couple of years. The fear he developed was very intense and still persisted 3 years after the situation with the dogs at home had ended. Martin's case is an example of a learned fear. It had become so maladaptive that it interfered with the boy's general functioning and required treatment. He received successful treatment with behavior therapy procedures like those we will discuss in this chapter.

Martin learned his fear of dogs through respondent conditioning. In Chapter 1, we saw how John Watson and Rosalie Rayner (1920) demonstrated that an infant boy named "Little Albert" could learn to fear a gentle white rat. These researchers paired the rat, the *conditioned stimulus* (CS), with a loud noise, the *unconditioned stimulus* (US), that was already able to elicit in Albert an *unconditioned response* (UR) of fear. Martin's fear of dogs had become a *conditioned response* (CR) in real life in much the same way as Albert's fear was conditioned in a laboratory.

This chapter examines the process and characteristics of respondent conditioning and describes behavioral methods based on respondent conditioning that are useful in changing respondent behaviors. We'll start by examining the process and characteristics of respondent conditioning in everyday life.

RESPONDENT CONDITIONING IN REAL LIFE

Real life provides many opportunities for individuals to learn respondent behaviors, such as fears. For example, picture this scene that I observed some years ago on a beautiful day at a European beach. Two parents were trying to accustom an infant to seawater, which was most inviting to them. The father walked out to waist-deep water while holding the baby, who was perhaps 18 months old, in a prone position with his hands. He lowered the child, face down, into the water, producing at least the threat of difficult breathing. Although there was no actual danger, the baby was terrified and screamed and flailed about constantly during several of these dunkings, each lasting long enough for the child's skin to become flushed from the exhausting ordeal. After quite some time with no improvement in the infant's response, the father decided either he or the child had had enough and left the water. I don't know whether this infant developed a fear of water, but the situation was surely one that could produce an association between fear and water, as Figure 6.1 illustrates.

What We Learn in the Respondent Conditioning Process

Examples like those we've seen show us how we can develop respondent behaviors, but they don't tell us what exactly we learn in this process. Current research and theory indicate that what we learn in respondent conditioning consists of two components. First, we learn an *association* between the CS and the US, based largely or solely on their occurring "contiguously," or close in time. The CS does not need to *cause* the US to happen for an association to form—the two stimuli must simply be paired in some way. Each time the stimuli occur together, the CS gains in its ability to elicit the CR. Some researchers believe the association is based solely on the stimuli occurring together (Papini & Bitterman, 1990), but Robert Rescorla (1988; Rescorla & Wagner, 1972) has proposed another view. He has suggested that the association between the CS and US also involves a *contingency*, an "if–then" relationship. Thus, when we learn a respondent behavior, we learn that if the CS occurs then the US probably will occur. This is why the CS functions as an antecedent signal, enabling us to decide if the US is likely to occur. If a person repeatedly experiences a CS—a dog in Martin's case—and the CS always occurs with a US, such as barking or snarling, the CS would be a very reliable predictor of the US. As an antecedent signal, the dog would have a high degree of *stimulus control*—that is, it would elicit a fear response virtually always. If the dog only barked and snarled occasionally, it would have less stimulus control and would be less likely to elicit fear. In general, CSs that are paired consistently with a US are more likely to become strong antecedents for the CR than CSs that are paired only sometimes with the US.

The second component of what we learn in respondent conditioning is a CS *evaluation*, such as the degree to which we like or dislike the stimulus (Baeyens, Hermans, & Eelen, 1993; Davey, 1994; Martin & Levey, 1994). When Martin had his experiences with the dogs, he surely evaluated them quite negatively. But not all

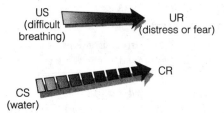

Figure 6.1 Diagram of the likely elements in the respondent conditioning of fear in the example of a baby placed face down in seawater.

respondent conditioning leads to negative evaluations. It's possible to like a CS more if it is associated with a very attractive US. For instance, a little girl might start to like the sound of a car pulling into the driveway if she learns that soon after she hears it her father would come in the door and play with her, as he regularly has done. (Go to 🔖)

Factors and Phenomena in Respondent Conditioning

Several factors and phenomena influence the development of respondent conditioning and the strength of the resulting respondent behavior. We have already discussed one of these factors, the *consistency* with which the CS and US are paired: CSs that are paired consistently with a US are more likely to elicit the CR than CSs that are paired only sometimes with the US. Another factor is obvious: the greater the *number of times the CS and US are paired*, the greater the ability of the CS to elicit the CR and the stronger the CR is likely to be (Kimble, 1961). In the development of Martin's fear, it's likely that the continued pairing of the dogs (the CSs) with their threatening behavior (the US) of snarling and barking made it more likely that the dogs would elicit the boy's fearful CR and that the response would be intense. Let's look at some other important factors and phenomena in respondent conditioning.

CS–US Timing and Intensity   In respondent conditioning, as in telling a joke, timing is a critical factor. The CS and US typically must occur *close enough in time* to allow the individual to connect the two. This makes sense. Imagine someone shouting to a toddler "Watch out!" (the CS) just before a ball hits her in the head (the US). It wouldn't take very many such events to teach her to take defensive action, such as ducking, to the CS alone. But she'd have a hard time learning the relationship if the ball hit her, say, 30 minutes after the warning. In general, respondent conditioning develops most quickly and strongly when the CS precedes the US by a fairly short amount of time, usually between a quarter-second and several seconds (Fitzgerald & Martin, 1971; Kehoe & Macrae, 1998; Kimble, 1961).

The *intensities* of the CS and US are also important in conditioning. Shouting "Watch out!" is a more intense CS than saying it in a moderate voice, and being hit hard is a more intense US than being tapped softly. Respondent conditioning develops more quickly and stronger when either or both of these stimuli are fairly strong rather than weak (Kimble, 1961; Lutz, 1994).

CLOSE-UP 6.1

What's What in Respondent Conditioning

 When students learn about respondent conditioning, they sometimes have difficulty distinguishing among its components, especially the CS and US. You can figure out what's what in an example of respondent conditioning by following three steps (Lutz, 1994):

1. Search the example for an overt or covert response made by the person or animal. Since the UR and CR are virtually identical, this response is the UR and CR.

2. Look for the antecedent stimulus that probably had the ability to elicit the response *before* the situation in the example occurred. This is the US. It often is a stimulus you'd expect to elicit the response "naturally"—that is, automatically or

without learning—but it can also be a learned antecedent with sufficient stimulus control to function as a US.

3. Now search the example for another stimulus (or more than one) that (a) occurred *before the response*, (b) probably did *not* have the ability to elicit the response before the situation occurred, but (c) seems to have *gained the ability* to do so in the example. This is the CS, and the response it now elicits is the CR. The CS usually occurs just before the US in respondent conditioning.

Go back to the case of Martin at the beginning of this chapter and use these steps to identify the US, UR, CS, and CR.

Relevance of the CS to the US   Have you ever gotten sick to your stomach after eating something? If so, you probably learned to associate the food as a CS for the US, becoming sick. Chances are, you learned this connection quickly, even though you may not have felt sick for hours after you'd eaten the food. And the one experience might have been enough to make you dislike the food you "blamed." Your newly acquired dislike of the food is the CR. This kind of learning is called **taste aversion.** Animals also learn quickly to associate foods they consumed with becoming sick and to avoid those foods in the future (Garcia, Ervin, & Koelling, 1966; Garcia, Hankins, & Rusiniak, 1974; Garcia & Koelling, 1966; Wilcoxin, Dragoin, & Kral, 1971). What's more, it's easier to learn to associate the taste of food (CS) with becoming sick (US) than with receiving an electric shock (US). These findings indicate that some CS–US combinations are more easily related than others.

Why would this be? Some CS–US combinations consist of stimuli that are more "relevant" to each other, either because of prior learning or as a result of some innate tendency to associate them (Davey, 1992; Hollis, 1997; Hugdahl & Öhman, 1977; Seligman, 1971). A study demonstrated the importance of CS–US relevance by presenting college students with an aversive loud noise and vibration just once and telling them this aversive event might occur shortly after some of the pictures that were about to be projected on a screen (Honeybourne, Matchett, & Davey, 1993). When each picture was shown, the students estimated the likelihood that the aversive event would happen, but the aversive event never actually occurred. Their estimates that the aversive event would happen were much higher when the pictures they saw were of fear-relevant objects, such as a snake or handgun, than when the pictures were of fear-irrelevant objects, such as a flower.

Overshadowing, Blocking, and Latent Inhibition   In real life respondent conditioning, the US occurs in a context with many stimuli, any of which could become a CS (Bouton & Nelson, 1998). The example described earlier of a father placing his infant face down in seawater had a threatening US for the baby that involved difficult breathing and unsteady physical support. Many stimulus elements of the context could have become CSs. Consider just the water—the baby could see, feel, hear (splashes), smell, and even taste it. Which of these elements will become a CS?

People tend to perceive one or more stimulus elements in a context as relatively prominent or noticeable, particularly when a stimulus is very intense or involves a sensory system the person relies on heavily. For instance, most people rely more on vision than smell. In contexts with many stimuli, two phenomena can occur. First, the most prominent stimulus will probably become the strongest CS, having the greatest control in eliciting the CR. This phenomenon is called **overshadowing** because one stimulus outweighs the others in importance (Kamin, 1969; Pavlov, 1927). In the example of the infant in seawater, the CS of *seeing* the water may overshadow the other stimuli, such as smelling it. Second, once a strong CS has been established, it tends to "block" other stimuli from becoming signals (CSs) for that US in the future. So, if the parents who tried to accustom their infant to seawater then tried the same method in a pool, the sight of the water might prevent other features of the situation from becoming CSs. **Blocking** refers to the phenomenon in which an existing CS prevents other stimuli from becoming effective signals of the US (Arcediano, Matute, & Miller, 1997; Halas & Eberhardt, 1987; Kamin, 1969). It may be that blocking occurs because the individual pays attention to the established CS and not the other stimuli or because the other stimuli are redundant—they simply offer no added predictive value to the existing CS.

A third phenomenon in respondent conditioning involves prior experience with potential CSs. In **latent inhibition,** prior experience with a potential CS in neutral circumstances—that is, without a US—makes later respondent conditioning involving that CS more difficult. For instance, if Martin had had prior experience with neutral or friendly dogs before encountering his neighbor's dogs, his fear would have been more difficult to condition. A study of the origins of fears found that adults who were afraid of dogs reported having had relatively little contact with dogs before their fear developed (Doogan & Thomas, 1992). These results and those of other studies suggest that early nonfearful exposure to potentially fearful events, such as dental treatment, can help prevent the development of fears later when aversive encounters happen (Lubow, 1998).

One other point should be made. The influence of overshadowing, blocking, and latent inhibition on a given conditioning situation can be complex, with more than one of these phenomena playing a role simultaneously (Blaisdell et al., 1998).

Discrimination and Generalization   When we discussed operant antecedents in Chapter 3, we saw that people learn to *discriminate* between different antecedent stimuli and respond differently toward them, even though the stimuli may be similar in some

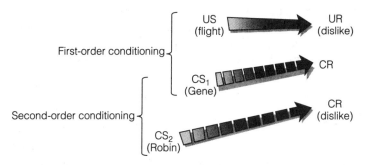

Figure 6.2 A comparison of first-order and second-order conditioning. Carla's disliking Gene (CS$_1$) developed in first-order conditioning, with their fight as the US. But her disliking Robin (CS$_2$) developed in second-order conditioning, building on her strong dislike of Gene—a strong CS that could function like a US.

respects. The same process happens in respondent conditioning: individuals learn to discriminate between a particular CS and other potential antecedents (Kimble, 1961). We can see this in Martin's case because he was afraid of dogs but not other animals, such as cats, which also have four legs, furry coats, and tails. He could discriminate between these animals and react fearfully only to dogs.

We also saw in Chapter 3 that people's reactions to antecedents show *stimulus generalization*, whereby we tend to respond to antecedents other than the exact ones we experienced in conditioning. Stimulus generalization occurs with respondent behaviors too. For instance, Martin was afraid of *all* dogs, not just the ones he encountered at home. The greater the similarity between a new antecedent stimulus and the actual CS the individual experienced in conditioning, the stronger the CR is likely to be (Kimble, 1961). Martin probably showed much more fear with dogs that looked like the ones at home than with dogs much different in size and color.

Second-Order Conditioning   Imagine this scenario. Carla and her boyfriend Gene have a nasty fight and split up, ending the relationship they began 2 years ago when they entered college. The fight (a US) made them dislike (the UR and CR) each other very much. Then Carla sees Gene walking and talking happily with Robin several times on campus. Gene and Carla neither liked nor disliked Robin before they split up. How does Carla feel about Robin now? Most students answer that Carla probably dislikes Robin. Why? Because Robin is now paired with Gene, whom Carla dislikes.

But Gene is not a US, he's a CS. Robin was paired with a CS that functioned like a US. When conditioning occurs with a true US, it is called *first-order conditioning*. This is the kind of respondent conditioning we've stressed so far in this book. But respondent conditioning can develop by building from a strong CS too, as Figure 6.2 illustrates. In **second-order conditioning** a new CS gains the ability to elicit the CR by being paired with a CS that can function as a US to elicit that respondent behavior (Rizley & Rescorla, 1972). Carla's disliking Robin would be a result of second-order conditioning.

Students sometimes confuse second-order conditioning and blocking. Both phenomena involve pairing an established CS and a potential CS, and the difference between the two is subtle—but critical. In blocking, an established CS is paired with a potential CS *in the presence of the US*, and the potential CS *does not* develop the ability to elicit the CR. In second-order conditioning, a strongly established CS and a potential CS are paired *without the original US*, and the potential CS *does* develop the ability to elicit the CR.

Processes Underlying Conditioned Emotional Responses

Experience and biology play important roles in respondent conditioning. Because most of the research on these roles has studied the acquisition of emotions, our discussion of how experience and biology are involved in conditioning will center on our acquiring fears. These respondent behaviors are examples of **conditioned emotional responses** (CERs, pronounced by spelling "c-e-r"). Some researchers distinguish between two categories of fear, defining **phobia** as an intense and irrational fear of something specific and **anxiety** as a fear that has a vague or unspecified source. Thus, Martin's fear of all dogs would be a phobia, and the fear that something awful might happen in social situations would be an anxiety. But these terms are often used interchangeably; in addition, the characteristic of vagueness or specificity is hard to assess, and distinctions among these terms don't seem to be useful in practice (Davison & Neale, 1994; Sarafino, 1986). I will use the term *fear* interchangeably with *phobia* and *anxiety*, selecting the two latter terms mainly when the specificity or vagueness is obvious.

The Role of Experience in CERs   Studies have shown that people can acquire CERs through direct or indirect respondent conditioning (Emmelkamp, Bouman, & Schooling, 1992; Milgrom et al., 1995; Rachman, 1991). Respondent conditioning is *direct* when the person actually experiences the CS and US; it is *indirect* when the person acquires a CER through modeling or cognitive processes.

Analysis of interviews and surveys of people with fears suggest that in perhaps two thirds or more cases fears were acquired mainly through direct respondent conditioning (Doogan & Thomas, 1992; Kleinknecht, 1994; Merckelbach et al., 1992; Merckelbach, Muris, & Schouten, 1996; Ost, 1987; Ost & Hugdahl, 1981; Wolpe, 1981). For instance, people reported having had negative experiences with the feared object—say, spiders—before the fear developed. But substantial proportions of these individuals also implicated modeling and verbal information they received as contributors to the development of their fears. Although these people's reports may have been inaccurate, being based on recollections of past events, some of which happened many years earlier, the proportions of individuals reporting direct and indirect sources of their fears have been similar across studies. Still, not all evidence supports the role of conditioning in the acquisition of fears (see Poulton et al., 1998), and the factors that affect the way direct and indirect respondent conditioning lead to CERs are unclear. Most of the existing evidence of indirect respondent conditioning has come from anecdotal reports, and many people who have had extremely frightening experiences, such as in war, do not appear to develop long-lasting, severe fears (Rachman, 1991).

Biological Processes in CERs   Little research existed before the 1980s on the role of biological processes in people's development of CERs (Emmelkamp, Bouman, & Scholing, 1992). But evidence from studies of fears across diverse cultures and within families suggests such processes are involved (Davey et al., 1998; Graham & Gaffan, 1997). We will look at two biological processes that appear to affect the conditioning of emotions.

The first of these processes involves *genetics*. Studies have compared the development of fears and anxieties in identical and same-sex fraternal twins. *Identical*, or "monozygotic," twins share exactly the same genetic inheritance because they result from the splitting of a single fertilized egg. *Fraternal*, or "dizygotic," twins arise from two separate eggs, each of which was fertilized by a separate sperm. If genetic factors are involved in the development of fears, researchers should find greater similarities in the fears of pairs of individuals who are identical twins than fraternal twins. These studies have generally found greater similarity in fears among identical than fraternal twins (Emmelkamp, Bouman, & Scholing, 1992). Such findings indicate that inborn, physiological factors may make some people more likely than others to develop fear reactions from their experiences. But we don't yet know what these physiological factors are or how they work.

The other biological processes pertain to *brain organization and function* in forming, storing, and using memories of conditioned emotions. For one thing, when we have emotional experiences, our brains release chemicals called "stress hormones" that enhance the memory of those events (Cahill et al., 1994). In addition, current evidence suggests that when we learn something, such as a respondent or operant behavior, the brain stores information about this learning in at least two different memory systems with separate, but connected, physiological structures (Petri & Mishkin, 1994; Schacter, 1992; Squire, 1987). These systems are (1) *implicit, or "nondeclarative," memory*, which refers to stored information about learned associations or procedures that is unavailable to our awareness, and (2) *explicit, or "declarative," memory*, which refers to stored information we are aware of and can report, indicating we know or have experienced something. Joseph LeDoux (1994) has described evidence that respondent conditioning of CERs usually produces memories of both types. He pointed out that we may store information from this conditioning

> within declarative memory, but it is kept there as a cold declarative fact. For example, if a person is injured in an automobile accident in which the horn gets stuck in the on position, he or she may later have a reaction when hearing the blare of car horns. The person may remember the details of the accident, such as where and when it occurred, who else was involved and how awful it was. . . . The person may also become tense, anxious and depressed, as the emotional memory is reactivated. (p. 57)

The reaction to horns results from the information in implicit, nondeclarative memory, but information about details of the accident is stored separately in explicit, declarative memory. According to LeDoux, this distinction may explain why some people's fears and anxieties do not respond to treatment or return after being treated successfully. It may be that partially successful treatments addressed one type of memory but not the other. (Go to ☑)

✔

CONCEPT CHECK 6.1

1. The association we learn in respondent conditioning is based largely on the CS and US occurring _____ .
2. In Martin's learning to fear dogs, the US, UR, CS, and CR were _____ , _____ , _____ , and _____ , respectively. ⟺
3. Respondent conditioning develops most strongly and quickly when the CS precedes the US by _____ seconds.
4. An example of one CS overshadowing another at the time of a car accident (the US) might be _____ . ⟺
5. Parents might use latent inhibition to reduce the likelihood that their child will learn to fear water by _____ . ⟺
6. A person who is fearful of all flying insects after being stung by a bee is showing stimulus _____ .
7. People who can describe the situation when they acquired a fear are using _____ memory.

Answers: 1. contiguously/close together in time, 2. snarling and barking, fear, dogs, fear, 3. one quarter to several, 4. the sound of a horn being a stronger CS than the rainy weather conditions at the accident, 5. giving the child pleasant early experiences with water, 6. generalization, 7. explicit or declarative.

Other Respondent Behaviors

Respondent conditioning is involved in many other behaviors people develop in real life. We will examine the role of conditioning in two of these behaviors: substance abuse and reactions to cancer chemotherapy.

Substance Use and Respondent Conditioning   Both respondent and operant conditioning appear to lead to people's continued and increasing use of mood altering substances, such as alcohol and narcotic drugs (heroin, etc.). Operant conditioning influences substance use in two ways. First, taking substances usually produces pleasant mood states that provide positive reinforcement for the behavior. Second, *not* taking the substance after having done so heavily for a long while produces unpleasant "withdrawal" symptoms—such as anxiety, headache, and tremors—that can be removed by taking the substance again. Removing these symptoms provides negative reinforcement for using the substance.

Respondent conditioning is involved in substance use in at least two ways. First, it develops CSs, such as the sight of heroin or a bottle of liquor, that produce internal CRs like the unconditioned reactions of actually taking the substance (Cunningham, 1998; Niaura et al., 1988; Rohsenow et al., 1994). For instance, alcoholics who are shown their favorite liquor respond with strong cravings to drink and increased salivation and physiological arousal. Individuals who quit using a substance and then encounter antecedents like these have a difficult time resisting the temptation to start using it again.

Second, respondent conditioning leads to increased substance use through the phenomenon of *tolerance*, in which the body adapts to the substance and requires more and more of it to achieve the same effect. As a result, heroin addicts typically take doses of the drug that would ordinarily kill individuals who had never or rarely used it. The body seems to acquire tolerance by trying to "protect" itself with physiological reactions that counteract the effects of the substance (Hinson, Poulos, & Cappell, 1982). But addicts sometimes die from their normal dose (normal, that is, in terms of amount and purity). Why would this be? Shephard Siegel and his colleagues (1982) reasoned that these deaths happen when the tolerance effect fails temporarily because the usual CSs that have come to elicit the protective reaction as a CR are not there—if, perhaps, the addict took heroin in a new environment. To test this hypothesis, the researchers injected rats with heroin every other day in a particular room until the animals reached a high level of tolerance. On alternate days, the rats were injected with a sugar-water solution in a distinctly different room. Then the animals received a larger-than-usual dose of heroin; half were in the room where they had received heroin in the past and half were in the room where they had gotten the sugar-water. If the "heroin room" had become a CS that would elicit a protective CR, fewer rats would die from the heroin overdose given in this room than in the other room. The results confirmed this expectation: 32% of the "heroin room" rats died, compared with 64% of the other rats.

People voluntarily use many illegal or unhealthful substances, including tobacco, alcohol, and drugs. Stopping these behaviors is often very difficult to do, but evidence indicates that some behavior modification techniques can help (Sobell, Toneatto, & Sobell, 1990; Tucker, Vuchinich, & Downey, 1992). One method, for example, that is used in treating alcohol abuse involves respondent conditioning and is called **emetic therapy** because it has the person take an *emetic*—that is, a drug that produces nausea as an unconditioned response (UR) when alcohol is consumed. In a typical half-hour session in a hospital, the person first receives an injection of the drug and then repeatedly drinks an alcoholic beverage, each time quickly becoming nauseated and vomiting (Miller & Hester, 1980). After several of these sessions, the person usually receives occasional "booster" sessions after being discharged from the hospital. Many studies have found that emetic therapy can be effective in treating alcohol abuse (Elkins, 1991). But one critic of this approach has noted that emetic therapy "has not been shown to be more effective than alternative, less costly methods" in behavior modification for treating alcohol abuse (Wilson, 1991, p. 415). Keep in mind also that quitting using a substance is more easily achieved than staying quit for good. Many people return to using tobacco, alcohol, or drugs weeks or months after quitting.

Chemotherapy Reactions and Respondent Conditioning Many cancer patients receive chemotherapy treatment in which powerful drugs are administered orally or by injection to circulate through the body and kill cells that divide rapidly, as cancer cells typically do (Laszlo, 1987; Williams, 1990). One of the difficult side effects of chemotherapy is the severe nausea (often with vomiting) many patients experience, which often produces two respondently conditioned reactions. One reaction is called *anticipatory*

Cancer patients who develop learned aversions to foods they like can become very demoralized by these experiences, feeling that they have suffered enough. Simply telling the patient why these aversions often develop doesn't seem to stop them from occurring. Can behavioral methods be used to prevent cancer patients from learning to dislike foods they normally eat?

A promising approach to prevent a patient's normal foods from becoming disliked uses the phenomenon of *overshadowing*. The procedure is simple: the patient just consumes a strongly flavored, unfamiliar food shortly before the chemotherapy session. Because it has been introduced as a very prominent item in the person's recent diet, the unfamiliar food will probably become the strongest CS if a taste aversion develops. In effect, this procedure makes this food a *scapegoat*, so that it "takes the blame" for the nausea. Studies using scapegoat candies and drinks with unusual, strong flavors, such as plum or coconut, have markedly reduced learned food aversions in adults and children who experienced nausea-producing events (Bernstein, 1991; Okifuji & Friedman, 1992).

nausea, in which the drug is the US and nausea is the UR and CR (Kvale et al., 1991; Taylor et al., 1992). By association, other related events, such as seeing the hospital or thinking about the procedure, become CSs and can then elicit nausea in the absence of the drug. The other reaction is called a *learned food aversion,* which is the same as taste aversion learning, discussed earlier: a food becomes distasteful because the person associates it as a CS with the US of becoming sick. Taste aversions can develop for foods eaten hours before the chemotherapy treatment and are more likely for foods with strong odors or tastes, such as chocolate and coffee, than for milder foods (Bernstein, 1991). Strong odors or tastes are relatively intense CSs, making conditioning more likely. (Go to ⚡)

PREPARING TO CHANGE A RESPONDENT BEHAVIOR

Designing an intervention to change a respondent behavior requires similar procedures and data gathering activities to those we've seen for changing operant behaviors. We need to assess the behavior and do a functional analysis of it before deciding exactly which methods to use and how to implement them.

Assessing Respondent Behaviors

For the most part, we can assess respondent behaviors by using the strategies and types of data we discussed in Chapter 2. Because most respondent behaviors addressed in interventions are CERs, we will focus our discussion of assessment methods on ways to measure fear. We can use *direct assessment methods* by observing the person's overt fearful behaviors, such as Martin's reluctance to approach a dog (the CS) or distress when one was present. And we can use *indirect assessment methods* by using self-reports, others' reports, or physiological measures of the person's reactions to the CS. Direct and indirect methods can be applied to collect various types of data that can reflect the presence or strength of the CER.

Frequency and *duration* data can be collected when it's important to know how often the fear CR occurs or how long it lasts when the CS is present. But the type of data most commonly used in interventions addressing CERs is *magnitude*—the degree or intensity of the CR. Two of the most frequently used measures of the magnitude of fear employ indirect assessment methods. *Physiological measures* assess internal events, such as heart rate, that are known to vary with outward signs and self-reports of fear. The greater the increase in heart rate when the CS appears, the stronger the fear is assumed to be. *Rating scales* assess the person's subjective feelings of fear. The higher the rating, the stronger the fear is assumed to be. In one common rating scale to measure fear, the **subjective units of discomfort scale** (SUDS, which is pronounced as a acronym), the person assesses fear experiences on a scale, usually ranging from 0 to 100 (Heimberg, 1990; Wolpe, 1973). The rating of 100 is usually defined something like, "the worst fear you have ever experienced or can imagine experiencing," and each unit in the scale is called a "SUD." Thus, a CR the person rates at 70 SUDs is subjectively much stronger than one rated at 20 SUDs. Because these are *subjective* ratings, we cannot assume that the same rating given by different people indicates that all raters experienced the same degree of discomfort. But we can assume that a person who gave the same rating to two CSs, such as taking an exam and giving a speech, experienced the same magnitude of fear in these two situations.

Functional Analyses of Respondent Behavior

Conducting a functional analysis is just as important in changing a respondent behavior as it is in changing an operant behavior. The A-B-C Log and summary record form can help us identify and describe in detail the antecedents, behaviors, and consequences to address in a program to change a respondent behavior (Emmelkamp, Bouman, & Scholing, 1992).

Antecedents   The antecedents for a respondent behavior represent either the actual CSs conditioned through the individual's overt or covert experiences or stimuli to which the CR has generalized. One approach for identifying problem CERs is to have individuals fill out questionnaires. For example, the Fear Inventory has people rate how much they are disturbed by various situations, such as seeing lightning and being criticized (Wolpe, 1973). Some instruments focus on assessing fears in children (Morris & Kratochwill, 1983).

But people's self-reports regarding how the antecedents came to elicit the CR will not necessarily be useful in changing the behavior. It is much more critical to know the specific recent antecedents for the behavior. A functional analysis of a CER, such as fear or anxiety, should try to answer these three questions about its antecedents (Emmelkamp, Bouman, & Scholing, 1992):

- Under what circumstances would the target person's CER tend to occur? These circumstances can include overt events or stimuli, such as certain places or people, or covert ones. We should identify a large number—say, two dozen or so— CSs for the target respondent behavior that could elicit at least a weak CER.
- What factors about the circumstances under which the CER occurs or the individual's general life, such as being unemployed or disabled, seem to affect how likely or strongly the CER will be performed?
- What thoughts tend to precede the CER? Interviews can help to identify these thoughts in two ways. First, we can ask clear questions, such as "What was going through your mind?" or "What did you think might happen?" Second, we can have the person close his or her eyes, imagine instances in which the CER occurred, and speculate out loud about what the antecedent thoughts were.

Material later in this chapter and the next one will describe several methods for changing respondent behaviors. Answers to the three questions about the antecedents help in deciding which methods to include in interventions and how to use them.

Behavior   The functional analysis should enable us to determine three characteristics about the respondent behavior we want to change (Emmelkamp, Bouman, & Scholing, 1992). First, we should try to identify what the person's bodily sensations and activities are at the time of the CER. For example, does the person tremble, become fidgety, bite his or her nails, blush, or hyperventilate when the fear or anxiety occurs? Second, we should determine what avoidance behaviors the CER evokes. For instance, does the person procrastinate in doing important behaviors, such as studying, or try to get out of them entirely? Does the person use mood-altering substances, such as alcohol, to reduce the fear or anxiety? Third, we may be able to identify related problem behaviors in the person's life. For example, a person who uses alcohol excessively to reduce his or her anxiety is likely to have social or employment difficulties as well.

Consequences   We saw in Chapter 1 that respondent and operant conditioning occur together in real life. In the case of CERs, the avoidance behaviors they evoke have consequences that can reinforce those behaviors. A functional analysis should allow us to identify the short-term and long-term consequences of avoidance behavior (Emmelkamp, Bouman, & Scholing, 1992). People often report that the avoidance behavior reduces the feelings of tension they experience in the CER, thereby providing negative reinforcement as a short-term consequence of the avoidance behavior. The long-term consequences of avoidance behavior usually are undesirable and affect the person's general functioning. For instance, a student who fears exams and then avoids studying may fail to learn important material, do poorly on tests, and flunk a course or miss graduating from school or college. Other CERs have little or no impact on the person's life and may not need to be addressed. Bostonians who are afraid of alligators are probably not affected very much by these fears.

BEHAVIORAL METHODS TO REDUCE RESPONDENT BEHAVIORS

Interventions to change respondent behaviors generally address behavioral excesses, such as when individuals react fearfully or angrily too frequently, too strongly, or for too long. These programs are designed to reduce the respondent target behavior and help the person function more adaptively. We will examine several behavioral methods that help achieve these behavioral and outcome goals.

Extinction and Counterconditioning

Our discussions of operant and respondent conditioning have revealed many parallels in these two learning processes. For instance, stimulus generalization and discrimination take place in both types of learning. Moreover, these types of learning have several other phenomena in common that can be applied to reduce unwanted respondent behaviors.

Extinction of Respondent Behavior   What do you suppose would have happened to Martin's fear of dogs if new neighbors had moved in next door with a very gentle, friendly dog? At first the child would have been very frightened, but eventually he would have learned that the new dog did not snarl and bark at him, and his fear would have begun to diminish. This example illustrates how extinction can happen with respondent behaviors in real life. In respondent conditioning, as in operant conditioning, the term **extinction** has two meanings: (1) a *procedure* or *condition* in which a CS is presented repeatedly *without the US* it had been paired with during conditioning and (2) a *process* in which the likelihood and vigor of the CR decrease when the US no longer occurs with the CS. Extinction probably plays a very substantial role in reducing respondent behaviors in everyday life. This is surely part of the reason early fears tend to decline as children get older (Sarafino, 1986).

The process of extinguishing a respondent behavior tends to proceed gradually rather than rapidly, just as it does for operant behavior. For instance, an intervention using extinction procedures to reduce people's strong CERs to social situations found that SUDS ratings for feared social CSs declined by about 3.2% per treatment session (Turner et al., 1992). By the end of the 16 sessions in the intervention, the clients' SUDS ratings had declined by about 50%. Sometimes extinction methods are carried out by exposing the person to very intense CSs for prolonged periods of time—a technique called *flooding*. For instance, someone who is receiving flooding therapy for an intense fear of insects might be taken to the insectary at a zoo and sit there surrounded by insects in glass enclosures for half an hour. This is a specialized variation of extinction that requires professional supervision, particularly during the early sessions of treatment (Stanley, 1992). We will examine flooding in detail in Chapter 13.

Another parallel to operant conditioning phenomena is the failure of extinction procedures to erase the memory of the original respondent learning (Bouton &

Swartzentruber, 1991). Our memories retain at least part of what we learned in the original conditioning and in extinction. As a result, *spontaneous recovery*—the reappearance of an extinguished response—can take place after a respondent behavior has been extinguished. And if the CS and US are presented together again after extinction has been carried out for a prolonged period, the strength of the CR often returns very rapidly (Bouton & Nelson, 1998; Bouton & Swartzentruber, 1991). So, if Martin's fear of dogs were successfully eliminated with extinction procedures, and he later had a very negative encounter with a dog, his strong fear might return.

Respondent extinction seems to be a promising approach for treating substance abuse. You'll recall that when people use mood-altering substances they develop CSs, such as the sight of liquor or the place where they usually drink, that produce internal CRs like the unconditioned reactions of actually taking the substance. Richard Blakey and Roger Baker (1980) applied extinction procedures with six male problem drinkers by having them repeatedly experience important CSs for their drinking, such as holding a can of beer, while not allowing them to drink. These sessions were carried out a few times per week for several weeks or months. Self-reports from most of these men suggested that their cravings for alcohol and drinking had decreased. More recent programs have had some success in treating substance abuse by applying respondent extinction alone or combining it with other behavioral or cognitive methods (Drummond & Glautier, 1994; Monti et al., 1994; Sitharthan et al., 1997). These programs have provided stronger evidence for the usefulness of respondent extinction by assessing drinking in more objective ways, such as by having the subjects take breath tests and having family members confirm drinking data.

Counterconditioning   Another similarity in behavioral methods for changing respondent and operant behavior can be seen in the use of alternative responses. We've discussed how operant behavioral excesses can be reduced more effectively if an alternative response is reinforced. A similar effect happens with respondent behaviors when we apply a technique called **counterconditioning,** in which the individual is trained to substitute a competing or incompatible behavior for the CR when the CS is present. Joseph Wolpe (1958, 1973) gave this technique the name "counterconditioning," based on the belief that it *reverses* a person's previous learning of fear. He proposed that "If a response [that inhibits] anxiety can be made to occur in the presence of anxiety-provoking stimuli, it will weaken the bond between these stimuli and the anxiety" (1973, p. 17). Of course, because counterconditioning is conducted by presenting the CS without the US, extinction is part of the process.

We saw an example of counterconditioning in Chapter 1 in which Mary Cover Jones (1924) reduced a fear of rabbits a boy named Peter had developed. When this fear was first evaluated, he would cry if he spotted a rabbit far away and in a cage. The intervention took place over the next several weeks, with Peter receiving counterconditioning therapy once or twice a day. The procedure simply involved bringing the rabbit a little closer each time while he ate some favorite foods in the presence of an assistant he liked. Eating and being calm were the alternative responses. By the end of the intervention, Peter would ask for the rabbit and play with it.

CONCEPT CHECK 6.2

1. Taking drugs to escape or avoid withdrawal symptoms provides _____ reinforcement for using the substance.
2. In the respondent conditioning technique of emetic therapy, what might be the US, UR, CS, and CR? ⇔
3. A cancer patient who becomes nauseated at the thought of the next chemotherapy treatment is experiencing _____ .
4. A food that might be a good candidate for a scapegoat to prevent learned food aversions to foods in an adult cancer patient's normal diet would be _____ . ⇔
5. A common rating scale for the assessment of fears is called _____ .
6. To extinguish the fear of bees a child developed after being stung twice, we would need to present a _____ without _____ . ⇔
7. An alternative response to replace fear or anger might be _____ . ⇔

Answers: 1. negative, 2. emetic drug, nausea, seeing a bottle of liquor or a drink, nausea, 3. anticipatory nausea, 4. strong grape-flavored Kool-Aid, 5. SUDS/subjective units of discomfort scale, 6. bee, the sting, 7. calm or laughter.

In another example of this method, counterconditioning was applied to reduce a social fear of a 20-year-old female college student: she was afraid she would humiliate herself at a banquet she planned to attend, knowing that her ex-boyfriend would also be there—with a date (Ventis, 1973). Their relationship had lasted 2 years when he ended it. To reduce her fear, she was asked to imagine various scenes at the banquet, each ending in a mildly absurd event. For instance, she was asked to imagine herself there waiting and watching for new arrivals until the ex-boyfriend "entered, dressed in leotards." When she heard that last detail, she smiled and looked surprised, but then imagined the scene with a smile on her face. Her jolly reaction was the alternative response. Later, after the student actually attended the banquet, she reported having experienced only mild apprehension while she was there. A similar approach was applied successfully to countercondition a woman's anger toward her husband and child (Smith, 1973). (Go to ✔)

Systematic Desensitization

The verb *to sensitize* means "to make someone highly responsive or susceptible to certain stimuli," and the prefix *de* means "remove or do the opposite of." So, a process of desensitization would remove a person's learned responsiveness, such as a CER, to a CS. Joseph Wolpe (1958, 1973) used his concept of counterconditioning as the basis in developing a technique to desensitize people's fears, which he described as proceeding in the following way:

A physiological state inhibitory of anxiety is induced in the patient by means of muscle relaxation, and he is then exposed to a weak anxiety-arousing stimulus for a few seconds. If the exposure is repeated several times, the stimulus progressively loses its ability to evoke anxiety. Then successively "stronger" stimuli are introduced and similarly treated. (1973, p. 95)

This technique, called **systematic desensitization,** is designed to reduce a CER by presenting CSs that are successively more fear-arousing while the individual remains in a physiologically calm state, which is induced by having the person perform relaxation exercises. It is called "systematic" because it is carried out as a gradual, step-by-step procedure. This procedure contains four important features:

- The person must remain very relaxed during the procedure.
- Each CS is presented briefly.
- The first CS presented is very mild, and succeeding ones are progressively stronger antecedents for the CER.
- Each CS is desensitized before advancing to a stronger one.

Let's look at how these features are designed and carried out.

Relaxation Exercises   Relaxation is an alternative response for fear because people rarely, if ever, feel afraid and relaxed at the same time. To become very deeply relaxed, people need to receive training in specific techniques, such as *muscle relaxation exercises*, and to practice them extensively. When doing these exercises, the people sit or lie down comfortably and then tense and relax each of the body's major muscle groups, one group at a time. They might start by tensing and relaxing the muscles in the hands and arms, then in the neck and shoulders, then in the abdomen, and so on. Doing these exercises produces a deeply relaxed feeling along with a calm physiological state, as reflected in reduced heart rate and blood pressure (Lichstein, 1988). After practicing these exercises very frequently, people are usually able to induce relaxation more and more easily and quickly. Because several techniques are available to produce relaxation and they are also used frequently by themselves—that is, without desensitization—we will examine them in more detail later (in Chapter 7).

Constructing a Stimulus Hierarchy   The functional analysis should have identified a large number of CSs related to the respondent target behavior that could elicit at least a weak CR. These stimuli can be of three types:

- *In vivo*, or real life, events, objects, or people. For instance, for people who are very fearful of wasps, a CS might be an actual wasp flying nearby or in a capped jar.
- *Imaginal*, or covert, representations of events, objects, or people, such as imagining a wasp is nearby.
- *Symbolic*, or overt, representations of events, objects, or people, such as seeing a picture of a wasp. Virtual reality technology can make symbolic stimuli more like in vivo presentations (North, North, & Coble, 1997).

One of the most important steps in using systematic desensitization is to pare these stimuli down to construct a **stimulus hierarchy**—a graded sequence of CSs that are rank-ordered in terms of the magnitude of the target behavior they are likely to elicit. Stimulus hierarchies commonly consist of between 10 and 15 rank-ordered stimuli.

Let's see how we would construct a stimulus hierarchy for a fear of fire a girl named Sue developed. Suppose we had identified 20 *in vivo* CSs in our functional analysis of her fear. We would use five tasks to pare down these stimuli:

1. Write each CS on an index card, giving enough information to picture or create the stimulus in detail.

2. Have Sue give each CS a SUDS rating on a scale of 0 to 100.

3. Set up "anchor points"—a weak CS and the most intense CS—making sure that all the intense CSs represent reasonable situations that might be encountered in real life and are not very dangerous. In Sue's stimuli, seeing a matchbook several feet away is the weak anchor, rated at 5 SUDs, and poking burning logs with fireplace tools is the intense anchor, rated at 90 SUDs.

4. The next step would be to rank order the remaining index cards on the basis of the SUDS ratings. Among these CSs, Sue might have included: seeing a burning candle across the room, placing a pot on a stove with the gas burner-flame lit, and walking to within 10 feet of a large fire in a fireplace.

5. Cull out 5 to 10 stimuli, trying to equalize the step "sizes"—that is, the number of SUDs—between the stimuli we retain for the hierarchy.

To make the progression through the hierarchy *gradual*, the distances separating stimuli should be fairly consistent and not more than 10 SUDs (Wolpe, 1973). If the ratings of the original set of stimuli contain a large gap, the person should identify an intervening CS. Table 6.1 presents two example stimulus hierarchies, one with all *in vivo* CSs and one with a combination of symbolic, imaginal, and *in vivo* CSs.

Performing Desensitization Once we've constructed the stimulus hierarchy, the procedure for desensitization is fairly straightforward. It starts by having the individual sit or lie down comfortably and perform the relaxation exercises. If the stimuli are imaginal, the person will be asked to picture each one as a scene and signal by raising a finger when the image is clearly formed (Wolpe, 1973). But if the stimuli are *in vivo* or symbolic, the person will need to experience each one—by approaching it, perhaps, or looking at it. The procedure for desensitization usually lasts between 15 and 30 minutes of a therapy session, and only some of the stimuli are used in a single session.

Let's see how we would proceed to desensitize Sue's fear of fire. When she is completely relaxed, we'd start by presenting the weakest stimulus from the hierarchy: we would have her look at a matchbook several feet away for several seconds and then say, "Stop." She would look away or close her eyes and state in SUDs how much discomfort the activity elicited. Her rating, say, "5," would end the first "trial" with that CS. We would immediately say "Go back to relaxing," and allow her to do so for 20 to 30 seconds. Then we'd start the second trial with the same stimulus, repeating

Table 6.1   Examples of Stimulus Hierarchies with Hypothetical SUDS Ratings for a Fear of Heights and a Fear of Dating

Heights: Stimulus hierarchy using all *in vivo* CSs:

1. Standing at a closed upper-floor window and looking out. (SUDS = 5)
2. Standing on a stepladder, 3 feet from the floor, to change a light bulb. (SUDS = 15)
3. Standing on a balcony near the railing, several stories above the ground. (SUDS = 25)
4. Walking on flat ground above a mountain cliff, 20 feet from the edge. (SUDS = 35)
5. Walking on flat ground above a mountain cliff, 5 feet from the edge. (SUDS = 45)
6. Hiking on a steep trail. When cliffs are very near, there are guard rails. (SUDS = 55)
7. Being a passenger in a car traveling at the speed limit on a narrow and winding mountain road. When cliffs occur, there are guard rails. (SUDS = 65)
8. Being on an extension ladder outside a house, cleaning a second-story window. (SUDS = 75)
9. Climbing up a 50-foot high water tower, using a ladder with handrails. (SUDS = 85)
10. Standing on a moderately sloped roof of a house. (SUDS = 95)

Dating: Stimulus hierarchy using symbolic, imaginal, and *in vivo* CSs:

1. Looking at a photograph of an attractive prospective person to date. (SUDS = 3)
2. Imagining meeting the person in the photograph (item 1) at a party. (SUDS = 10)
3. Looking at a photograph of a couple on a date. (SUDS = 17)
4. Imagining being at a movie with several acquaintances and sitting next to one of them who could be a prospective date. (SUDS = 25)
5. Imagining exchanging phone numbers with an attractive person who could be a prospective date. (SUDS = 35)
6. Imagining calling the item 5 person to chat. (SUDS = 40)
7. Imagining accidentally meeting the item 5 person at a shopping mall and going for coffee together. (SUDS = 48)
8. Imagining calling the item 5 person for a date. (SUDS = 55)
9. Imagining being on a date with item 5 person. (SUDS = 65)
10. Imagining a friend talking about helping to arrange a date with an actual mutual acquaintance who is an attractive person. (SUDS = 74)
11. Actually dialing the first several digits of the phone number of the attractive item 10 person, without completing the call. (SUDS = 80)
12. Dialing a number that always has a taped message, such as the phone at a movie theatre, then talking as if the call had gone through to the attractive item 10 person and asking for a date. (SUDS = 85)
13. Imagining an "awkward silence" when conversing on a date with the item 10 person. (SUDS = 92)
14. Actually calling the item 10 person for a date. (SUDS = 98)

the same procedure. We would continue with additional trials until she reported "0" *on two successive trials.* Once this "success criterion" is reached, we may advance to the next stimulus in the hierarchy. We would not advance to the next stimulus at any point in the desensitization process until this criterion has been met.

We would perform this same procedure for each CS, advancing through the hierarchy in sequence. Here are some guidelines to follow in desensitization (Sarafino, 1986; Wolpe, 1973):

- Reducing a moderately strong fear is likely to take at least several sessions, and stronger fears may require many more.

- Try to have each session end on a positive note, either successfully desensitizing a stimulus or making very good progress on it. If a success criterion is reached but there isn't enough time to complete the next stimulus, save it for the next session.

- The first stimulus used in each succeeding session should be the last one fully desensitized in the previous session, and the success criterion should be repeated.

Finally, it is important to be flexible and willing to revise the procedure to meet the individual's needs. Something may have happened in the person's life since the last session that may influence his or her reactions to the stimuli. (Go to)

CASE STUDY 6.1

Desensitizing a Boy's Fear of Loud Noises

A bright 4-year-old boy developed an extreme fear in which loud sounds, such as a siren or airplane noise, would send him running in unpredictable directions, sometimes toward the source of the noise and sometimes away from it (case described in Tasto, 1969). His parents were concerned for three reasons. First, his fear was restricting his social activities. Second, it could cause him to be injured if he ran into the street when a noise occurred. Third, new CSs, such as rain, were beginning to develop because of their association to noises such as thunder.

A stimulus hierarchy was constructed in which the strongest CS was a gun firing, and the weakest was a piece of paper being crunched. Intermediate CSs included a balloon breaking, thunder, and a board falling on the floor. The therapist taught the boy to perform relaxation exercises and then tried to desensitize the fear by having the boy *imagine* each stimulus. But the boy did not report any fear to these stimuli during the sessions, and his real life fears were not improving. So the therapist switched to *in vivo* stimuli, such as actually dropping a board to the floor and popping balloons.

The parents helped by having the boy practice relaxation exercises at home and presenting some of the stimuli. After the desensitization had progressed, the father got the boy to burst balloons by allowing him to keep coins that were inside them if he broke them. At first the balloons were only slightly inflated, but later the inflation—and noise—was increased. His father also took him target practicing: initially, the boy stayed a long distance from his father, got calm, and signaled his father to shoot. He then moved closer and closer until he could be near the gun when it was fired. Follow-up reports from the parents 1 and 4 months after therapy indicated no recurrence of the boy's fear.

Effectiveness of Systematic Desensitization   Systematic desensitization is a well-documented, highly effective method for helping people overcome fears and other CERs (Borden, 1992; TFPDPP, 1993; Wilson, 1982). Not only does this method usually succeed in reducing fears by the end of treatment, but these improvements are durable. Follow-up assessments taken for 2 years after treatment have found few recurrences in the fears (Paul, 1967; Rosen, Glasgow, & Barrera, 1977). What's more, many individuals who succeed in overcoming specific fears in treatment with systematic desensitization report improvements in other areas of emotional functioning in their lives as well (Paul, 1967). Desensitization has also been used successfully in treating other anxiety-related problems—for example, people's being unable to urinate in public restrooms and checking compulsively for potentially harmful circumstances, such as whether doors are locked (McCracken & Larkin, 1991; Overholser, 1991).

In the case study of the boy who was afraid of loud noises, using imaginal CSs didn't work. Are imaginal CSs useful? Although desensitization with imaginal stimuli can reduce people's fears, several studies have shown that direct exposure to the feared object or situation results in greater fear reduction (Barlow et al., 1969; Crowe et al., 1972; Menzies & Clarke, 1993; Sherman, 1972; Wilson, 1982). In the research by David Barlow and his colleagues, female college students who were afraid of snakes were pretested for their fear with a "harmless boa constrictor" that was kept in a glass box with a wire mesh cover. Then they were desensitized for their fear and posttested with the snake. The pretests and posttests included assessments of two types: (1) a *behavioral test* that contained 17 acts ranging from watching the snake in the cage 15 feet away to picking up the snake, and (2) a *physiological test* that measured Galvanic skin responses while the snake was in the box at various distances away. Desensitization was carried out with the CSs in the stimulus hierarchy presented by either an imaginal or an *in vivo* procedure. Posttests conducted with the snake revealed that the individuals desensitized with the *in vivo* stimuli were able to perform more of the items in the behavioral test and showed much less physiological arousal to the snake than those desensitized with the imaginal stimuli, as depicted in Figure 6.3.

Some controversy exists over the importance of two features of the systematic desensitization procedure. One of these features is relaxation. Findings from some studies suggest that relaxation during sessions enhances the desensitization process, but other findings are contradictory (Kazdin & Wilcoxon, 1976). The second feature is the need to use relatively weak CSs in the stimulus hierarchy. A study compared the use of a full stimulus hierarchy with the use of only the strongest stimuli in the hierarchy in desensitizing college students' mathematics anxieties (Richardson & Suinn, 1973). The two approaches were equally successful in reducing the students' fears. If using a small number of stimuli in a hierarchy produces an overly large "step" between CSs that entails too much discomfort for the target person, an intermediate CS can be added (Sturges & Sturges, 1998). Although there is some doubt about the importance of these features to the success of desensitization, the evidence against their use is not yet clear enough to warrant dropping them. Because relaxation exercises and full stimulus hierarchies don't seem to harm clients and may help the treatment process, it's probably best to include these features in systematic desensitization.

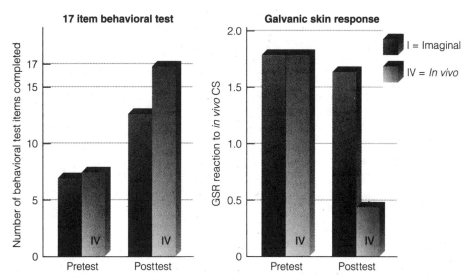

Figure 6.3 Number of items completed in a 17-item behavioral test and Galvanic skin response (GSR) with a real CS, a snake. The data are for snake-phobic adults before (pretest) and after (posttest) systematic desensitization to snakes conducted with imaginal (I) or *in vivo* (IV) CSs. High GSR scores indicate greater fear reactions. *Source:* Data from Barlow et al., 1969, Tables 1 and 2.

Vicarious Desensitization Through Modeling

A girl named Keisha was able to overcome her fear of cats by watching her parents play with one and later, with their encouragement, joining in and gradually contacting the cat. Notice that in this example the parents *modeled* fearless behavior for their child to watch. Modeling can be applied to desensitize fears in a *vicarious* manner. Keisha's parents reduced her fear with a method called **participant modeling** in which the fearful person watches someone else cope well in real life, increasingly threatening situations; then the person is encouraged to join in and is guided toward more and more contact with the feared object (Bandura, 1975; Bandura, Jeffery, & Gajdos, 1975). Guiding toward contact usually involves verbal and physical guidance prompts.

Studies of participant modeling have found it to be very successful in reducing fears and more effective than simply watching a filmed model cope with the feared situation (Borden, 1992; Wilson, 1982). Teaching individuals *how* to behave in fearful situations and *actually performing that behavior* in the modeling sessions seem to be critical components to overcoming fears. One study found that children who were asked to practice the coping behaviors they had seen in a video of children undergoing dental treatment were less disruptive in a subsequent dental visit than were other children who merely watched the video (Klingman et al., 1984). Other research findings indicate that the fear reduction produced through modeling can be fairly specific. For instance, a girl who was extremely afraid of dogs and cats was treated first for her

✓

CONCEPT CHECK 6.3

1. Systematic desensitization is based on Wolpe's concept of _____ .
2. The alternative response to fear in systematic desensitization is _____ .
3. An example of a weak *in vivo* CS for a fear of flying might be _____ . ⇔
4. An example of a strong imaginal CS for a fear of flying might be _____ . ⇔
5. Rank-ordering CSs in a stimulus hierarchy is based on the fearful person's _____ ratings.
6. The success criterion for desensitizing a CS is _____ .
7. Having a fearful person gradually contact a fearful object or situation while watching someone else cope well with it is called _____ .

Answers: 1. counterconditioning, 2. relaxation, 3. calling an airline ticket agent for information, 4. picturing being on a bumpy flight, 5. SUDS, 6. "0" on two successive trials, 7. participant modeling

fear of dogs, which participant modeling decreased (Matson, 1983). But her fear of cats continued until it was specifically addressed.

USING RESPONDENT-BASED TECHNIQUES: SOME CAUTIONS

All of the techniques we have examined to change respondent behavior have involved ways to *reduce* the occurrence or magnitude of CERs, and these techniques were based on respondent conditioning processes and phenomena. But other techniques have been used with varying degrees of success to *increase* people's CERs—that is, to *sensitize* individuals to certain CSs by pairing these stimuli with *aversive* USs. These approaches are called *sensitization techniques*, or *aversion therapy*. In an application of aversion therapy discussed earlier in this chapter, alcoholics take an emetic drug, which causes them to become nauseated and vomit when they consume alcohol. The nausea is the US, and alcohol-related stimuli, such as its taste or a bottle of liquor, become CSs for the CR of feeling nauseated. This approach is designed to impart negative sensitization to stimuli alcoholics ordinarily associate with drinking.

Some behavioral methods are potentially hazardous to an individual if applied by someone without extensive professional training. Aversion therapy and flooding techniques mentioned earlier are examples of methods that are potentially hazardous. Other methods, although perhaps not especially hazardous, require very special skills or circumstances that are accessible only to students who receive advanced graduate training. Taking this course will not give you sufficient training to use these techniques. All of these *advanced, specialized techniques* are examined in Part V in Chapters 12 to 14 of this book. (Go to ✓)

Tips on Using Respondent-Based Techniques

The tips on using respondent-based techniques listed here focus on using systematic desensitization to reduce problem CERs. Professionals generally apply these tips when they design programs to change overt or covert respondent behaviors.

1. Make sure all individuals directly involved in the program understand what the exact procedures will be, what their purposes are, and that clinical research has shown that the techniques work very well in reducing problem CERs for the great majority of people.

2. The stimulus hierarchy must be personalized to the needs of the target person; it should be based on a functional analysis of the behavior and the SUDS ratings of all CSs it includes.

3. All CSs should be presented in ways that maximize how clearly and fully the target person will experience them.

4. The stimulus hierarchy can contain imaginal CSs, especially for stimuli that cannot be presented in more concrete ways. Although desensitization with imaginal stimuli can reduce CERs, *in vivo* stimuli are more effective.

5. A target person who is experiencing *in vivo* CSs with very high SUDS ratings should have another person present as a precaution.

6. Number the index cards that describe the CSs in their rank order and keep them handy to consult during desensitization sessions.

7. Don't start the first desensitization session until the target person has practiced the relaxation exercises at least 5 times (preferably about 10 times). A person who has mastered the technique should experience deep relaxation within several minutes. (See Chapter 7 for additional information about relaxation exercises.)

8. Don't rush through the procedure. Make sure each CS is fully desensitized before moving on to the next. Some sessions may not get beyond one or two stimuli.

9. Don't make sessions too long. The desensitization procedure in a session should take, say, 20 minutes and should not exceed half an hour.

10. Desensitization sessions should take place at least once or twice a week, and they can be done as often as two or three times in any one day. Try to schedule between three and six sessions a week, if possible.

11. If the target person experiences too much discomfort with a newly introduced CS or a lot of difficulty relaxing during its presentation, withdraw the stimulus, practice relaxation for a couple of minutes, and try the CS again for a shorter time. If there are still difficulties, go back to the previous CS, achieve the success criterion again, and advance again to the problem CS. If the difficulties persist, stop the procedure and identify one or two intervening CSs to insert before the problem CS.

SUMMARY

Children and adults learn many respondent behaviors, such as fears, from experiences in everyday life. This learning includes an association between the CS and the US, as well as an evaluation (like/dislike) of the CS. Respondent conditioning develops most quickly and strongly when the CS and US are paired consistently, frequently, and close enough in time to permit them to be associated. An exception to this rule is taste aversion learning, which develops very quickly even though the CS and US occur far apart in time.

Three important phenomena in respondent conditioning are (1) overshadowing, in which one CS outweighs others in being able to elicit the CR; (2) blocking, whereby an existing CS prevents other stimuli from becoming conditioned to a CR; and (3) latent inhibition, in which past neutral experience with a CS makes it more difficult to associate it with a US in the future. People learn to discriminate between a particular CS and other stimuli that could serve as antecedents, and they also show stimulus generalization, responding to CSs that are not exactly the same as the one to which they were conditioned. People also learn respondent behavior through second-order conditioning in which an established CS functions like a US in conditioning a new CS to a CR.

Many of the respondent behaviors people learn are conditioned emotional responses, such as anger and fears of two types: anxieties and phobias. Although we acquire conditioned emotional responses through direct and indirect experiences, biological processes are also important. Genetic factors appear to influence the development of fears, and people appear to store the memories of conditioned emotions in separate structures of the brain. Respondent conditioning is important in many other behaviors too. For instance, it is involved in people's becoming dependent on mood-altering substances, such as alcohol and drugs; the respondent method called emetic therapy is used in treating alcohol abuse. It is also involved in the development of anticipatory nausea and food aversions in cancer patients who receive nausea-producing chemotherapy.

Respondent behaviors can be measured with direct and indirect assessment methods, using frequency, duration, and magnitude data. The magnitude of respondent behaviors can be assessed with physiological measures and rating scales, especially the subjective units of discomfort scale. Techniques that can reduce respondent behaviors include extinction, counterconditioning, systematic desensitization, and participant modeling. Systematic desensitization is a highly effective method for reducing fears and other emotional behaviors. It involves having the person become and remain relaxed while experiencing *in vivo*, imaginal, or symbolic CSs from a stimulus hierarchy. *In vivo* stimuli are usually more effective in reducing fears than imaginal or symbolic stimuli.

KEY TERMS

taste aversion	phobia	systematic desensitization
overshadowing	anxiety	stimulus hierarchy
blocking	emetic therapy	participant modeling
latent inhibition	subjective units of	
second-order conditioning	discomfort scale	
conditioned emotional responses	extinction	
	counterconditioning	

REVIEW QUESTIONS

1. Describe the associations and evaluations that occur in the respondent conditioning process.
2. How are CS–US intensity, pairing consistency, and timing important in respondent conditioning?
3. Why are taste aversions learned so quickly even though the CS and US occur far apart in time?
4. Define overshadowing, blocking, and latent inhibition and give an example of each phenomenon that happened or might have happened in your own life.
5. Define second-order conditioning and describe an example from your own life, pointing out the first- and second-order parts of the process.
6. What are conditioned emotional responses? How are experience and biological processes involved in their development?
7. Describe the research by Siegel and his colleagues (1982) on tolerance effects and drug overdoses.
8. Why is overshadowing helpful in preventing learned food aversions in cancer patients who receive chemotherapy?
9. Define extinction in respondent conditioning and give an example of how it might be used to reduce a person's anger.
10. How are counterconditioning and systematic desensitization related?
11. Describe the steps in constructing a stimulus hierarchy.
12. Describe the procedure for conducting systematic desensitization.
13. What are imaginal and *in vivo* CSs, and how were they used in the case study on desensitizing a boy's fear of loud noises?
14. Describe the research by Barlow and his colleagues (1969) on desensitizing snake phobias. What do the results mean in designing stimulus hierarchies?

RELATED READINGS

Borden, J. W. (1992). Behavioral treatment of simple phobia. In S. M. Turner, K. S. Calhoun, & H. E. Adams (Eds.), *Handbook of clinical behavior therapy* (2nd ed.). New York: Wiley.

Emmelkamp, P. M. G., Bouman, T. K., & Scholing, A. (1992). *Anxiety disorders: A practitioner's guide*. Chichester, UK: Wiley.

Morris, R. J., & Kratochwill, T. R. (1983). *Treating children's fears and phobias: A behavioral approach*. New York: Pergamon.

Rachman, S. (1991). Neo-conditioning and the classical theory of fear acquisition. *Clinical Psychological Review, 11*, 155–173.

Sarafino, E. P. (1986). *The fears of childhood: A guide to recognizing and reducing fearful states in children*. New York: Human Sciences Press.

Wolpe, J. (1973). *The practice of behavior therapy*. New York: Pergamon.

This young woman is using one of many types of meditation as a relaxation technique.

Covert Behavioral Methods for Changing Respondent Behavior

A 31-year-old divorced man named Dennis developed a severe anxiety condition called *panic disorder*, which is characterized by occasional, sudden, and irrational attacks with intense physiological symptoms and feelings of impending doom (Oltmanns, Neale, & Davison, 1991). The attack that led to his seeking therapy occurred while he and his fiancée, Elaine, were Christmas shopping at a mall. Being in large crowds had been a problem for him for years, and he soon had an attack with classic symptoms of panic disorder. He suddenly felt an overwhelming sense of apprehension but didn't understand why he should be so terrified. At the same time, he became physically ill, with symptoms that included trembling hands, blurred vision, general body weakness, huge pressure on his chest, and great difficulty breathing.

Without saying anything to Elaine, he turned and ran from the store, seeking safety in their car. There, the symptoms continued for about 10 minutes. Dennis had left Elaine so suddenly that she was unaware he had gone, and she looked for him in stores for over an hour before finding him in the car. When he explained to her what happened, she persuaded him to seek professional help.

Dennis's interviews with a therapist revealed that his first full-blown attack occurred 7 years earlier when he and his wife were with some of her professional colleagues at a dinner theater. He didn't know what was happening and was terrified in his seat when others noticed, tried to help, and eventually took him to a lounge where he could lie down. Dennis did not seek medical treatment, deciding that the attack resulted from something he had eaten. But this and subsequent attacks, such as one while he was driving alone, had the effect of making him even more anxious than he had been. For instance, Dennis became less and less socially active and very frightened of driving in rush hour and on bridges for fear of having another attack in those circumstances. Being in social situations and driving had become CSs for intense feelings of anxiety, the CR.

This chapter, like the last one, concentrates on changing respondent behaviors that have become problems for individuals. But the techniques we will examine to produce these changes focus relatively heavily on covert behaviors, such as people's thoughts and imagery processes, rather than overt conditioning or modeling processes. A major component of the successful treatment Dennis received was the training he got in relaxation—the first category of *covert behavioral methods* we will discuss.

RELAXATION TECHNIQUES

"Try to relax when hassles or pressures happen in your life," physicians often advise their patients who have high blood pressure. Does this advice help? Probably not, and it may actually make individuals' blood pressure worse if they try to relax without knowing how. Researchers demonstrated this possible effect with two groups of individuals who watched a videotape of physiologically arousing events (Suls, Sanders, & Labrecque, 1986). None of the individuals had been trained to relax, but some were asked simply to try to relax and keep their blood pressures low while they watched the TV, and others were asked to respond as they normally would. Those who were asked to relax showed greater blood pressure increases during the videotape than those who were given no such instructions. These findings suggest that people who have not been trained to relax may try too hard. Individuals who have received training in relaxation techniques are able to become psychologically and physiologically relaxed and to react less strongly when they experience arousing stimuli (Lichstein, 1988; Poppen, 1998).

The term **relaxation** refers to a state of reduced psychological and physiological tension or arousal. Techniques to produce relaxation gained wide acceptance in psychological therapy through their inclusion in successful systematic desensitization treatments of emotional respondent behaviors, especially anxieties and phobias. In the 1970s, relaxation techniques became recognized as therapeutic tools that were effective in their own right in helping to treat a variety of psychological and medical problems, such as people's fears, asthma, high blood pressure, migraine and tension headache, and cancer chemotherapy reactions (Carlson & Hoyle, 1993; Lichstein, 1988; Poppen, 1998).

People can use any of several techniques to achieve relaxation. Regardless of the particular methods the person uses, a few points should be kept in mind (Lichstein, 1988; Moore, 1987; Taylor, 1978). First, the procedure should be carried out with the person seated or reclining in a *quiet and comfortable setting*. It's usually best not to do relaxation exercises on a bed—the person should not be comfortable enough to fall asleep. Loosen any tight-fitting clothing. Second, sessions last between *10 and 30 minutes*, but the first 10 sessions or so are likely to take more time than later sessions because people get better at inducing relaxation with practice. Third, it's typically a good idea for the person to *set aside regular times* to practice the relaxation exercises once or twice a day as "homework" in a place that is *free of interruptions and distractions*.

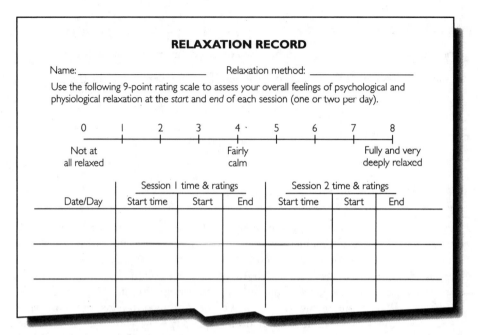

Figure 7.1   A data sheet for keeping relaxation records of progress made in practicing relaxation techniques. For each session, the person records the start time and the start and end ratings of relaxation.

The place can be at home, in a library, or anywhere else these conditions can be assured. To assure that these conditions will exist, the person may need to plan ahead or negotiate with other people, such as roommates. Fourth, you may not want to use relaxation techniques within an hour or so of going to bed. Some people report that doing relaxation exercises leaves them relaxed but *alert*, making it hard to go to sleep. Those individuals may not want to use relaxation exercises within an hour or so of bedtime. Finally, the person should collect data rating the magnitude of his or her relaxation during sessions, using a data sheet like the one in Figure 7.1. We'll turn now to descriptions of three of the most commonly used types of relaxation techniques: progressive muscle relaxation, autogenic training, and meditation.

Progressive Muscle Relaxation

The approach described briefly in Chapter 6 involved alternately tensing and relaxing separate muscle groups while resting comfortably. This technique, developed in the 1920s and 1930s by Edmund Jacobson (1938), is called **progressive muscle relaxation,** or just *progressive relaxation*. Because the original technique was extremely detailed, sometimes taking dozens of hours for training, a shorter, easier-to-learn version of this technique was eventually developed by Douglas Bernstein and Thomas Borkovec (1973). This shorter version, or some variation of it, is what is meant by progressive muscle relaxation today (Lichstein, 1988). Studies with follow-up assessments have shown that the positive psychological and physiological effects of using progressive muscle relaxation continue and may even get stronger in the weeks and months after individuals receive training in the procedure (Carlson & Hoyle, 1993). Children at just 3 or 4 years of age can learn muscle relaxation techniques and apply them to reduce their anxieties during stressful events, such as receiving dental treatment (Siegel & Peterson, 1980).

Before we examine an actual *protocol,* or script, for performing progressive muscle relaxation, we will consider two aspects of the procedure that currently are controversial. First, it is not certain whether it is necessary or desirable to *tense* the muscles as part of the process. For instance, a recent study found evidence that alternating tensing and relaxing muscle groups may not be as effective in inducing deep physiological relaxation as procedures that omit the tensing phase (Lucic et al., 1991). But other researchers have reported contradictory results, and it appears that having individuals tense their muscles is helpful *while they are being trained* in the technique (Lehrer, 1982). Tensing probably promotes their learning the skill of relaxing by teaching them to discriminate between relaxation and muscular tension. After people have mastered the skill, tensing the muscles can be eliminated (Moore, 1987).

The second controversial aspect of the progressive muscle relaxation procedure pertains to the value of using tape-recorded protocols during relaxation sessions. Many therapists either provide protocol tapes or advise clients to make tapes of the scripts that are used in relaxation exercises. Although these tapes are generally used for clients to practice relaxation as homework assignments, they have also been tried as a substitute for in-person training with a therapist. Studies have found that using taped protocols without supervised training can teach individuals to induce relaxation, but in-person training is more effective (Beiman, Israel, & Johnson, 1978; Lehrer, 1982). It may be that supervised training allows the therapist to notice difficulties and give the person corrective feedback. Other studies have shown that the beneficial effects of relaxation are greater when in-person training is conducted individually rather than in groups and that providing taped protocols for clients to use in practicing relaxation on their own appears to be very helpful (Carlson & Hoyle, 1993). Although clients tend to overstate their amount of homework practice with tapes, most appear to practice relaxation about as often as the therapist advises (Taylor et al., 1983).

Close-Up 7.1 contains a protocol that can be used to carry out progressive muscle relaxation training based on information from several sources (Bernstein & Borkovec, 1973; Lichstein, 1988; NJNPI, 1972; Taylor, 1978). You'll notice that the tensing and relaxing progresses through a series of different muscle groups. Breathing exercises are included, as well. If you want to use the protocol, make a tape recording of it, but do not say the numbering and time measurements (note that 7 s and 30 s mean 7 and 30 seconds). Tensing phases should be about 7 (between 5 and 10) seconds long, and relaxation phases should be about 30 (between 20 and 45) seconds. When you tape the

CLOSE-UP 7.1

A Protocol for Progressive Muscle Relaxation

 Please sit or lie back, get comfortable, and keep your eyes closed throughout these exercises. When I ask you to tense a certain set of muscles of your body, tense only those muscles, quickly make them *as tight as you can*, and keep them tight, noticing how tense they are. After several seconds, I will say "Now relax." And when I do, *release* those muscles immediately, letting them go completely limp. Keep them limp and relaxed for quite a while, *feeling* the relaxation *spread* through those muscles. Focus your attention on your sensations and think over and over to yourself something like, "I feel so peaceful, so wonderfully calm and beautifully relaxed. My whole body feels so warm and well. I'm so very relaxed, deeply relaxed." Keep relaxing until I say, "OK, stop," which will either signal the next exercise or the end of the session. We'll start with the muscles in your right hand.

1. Make a tight fist with your *right hand*. Squeeze it very tightly. Keep it tight and notice how it feels. . . . (7 s) Now relax. Release all that tension and let it flow out of those muscles so your hand is limp. Feel how limp your hand feels. . . . (30 s) OK, stop.

2. Clench your *left hand* to make a tight fist. Squeeze it tightly, very tightly. Hold that tension and notice how it feels. . . . (7 s) Now relax. Release the tension and let your hand go limp. Focus on how relaxed your hand feels. . . . (30 s) OK, stop.

3. Bend your *right arm* to make your biceps very hard. Tighten those muscles and make them hard, like steel. Keep them tight and feel the tension. . . .

(7 s) Now relax. Let your arm fall to your side and allow the tension to flow out. When your muscles seem relaxed, see if you can relax them even more. . . . (30 s) OK, stop.

4. Bend your *left arm* and make your biceps very hard. Keep them very, very hard and feel the tightness. . . . (7 s) Now relax. Let your arm fall to your side. Feel the tension flowing out and the wonderful tingling sensation in your limp arm. . . . (30 s) OK, stop, and let's move to the muscles in your head.

5. Pull your *eyebrows* together very tightly, wrinkling your forehead and squinting your eyes. Hold that tension and study it. . . . (7 s) Now relax. Let your forehead relax and feel so comfortable. . . . (30 s) OK, stop.

6. Now scrunch up the lower part of your *face*, raising your cheeks, elongating your lips, wrinkling your nose, and squinting your eyes. Make all those muscles tight. . . . (7 s) Now relax, just totally relax. Feel the tension flow out of your lower face and down your neck. . . . (30 s) OK, stop.

7. Stretch the *back of your neck* by bending your head forward so your chin is very close to your chest. As you stretch those muscles, tighten the ones in the front of your neck at the same time. Concentrate on the two sets of muscles tugging against each other. . . . (7 s) Now relax. Just let go and feel the wonderful relaxation in your neck and how it flows downward to your shoulders. . . . (30 s) OK, stop.

(continued)

protocol, simply leave blank tape for the amount of time you will use for each tensing or relaxing period. You may tape it in your own voice or have someone else do it. If possible, have someone who understands the purpose of the procedure supervise the first several sessions to provide feedback. We will discuss later how to shorten the procedure and leave out the tensing part of the process. (Go to 🔍)

8. Stretch the *front of your neck* by bending your head backward as far as you can. As you stretch those muscles, tighten the ones in the back of your neck. Notice how tight both sets of muscles are. . . . (7 s) Now relax. Let your neck muscles go limp, so limp that you think a breeze could move your head back and forth. Notice how the tingling and warmth of the relaxation is spreading downward in your body. . . . (30 s) OK, stop, and let's try a breathing exercise.

9. Take a deep *breath* and hold it, feeling the pressure in your chest. . . . (7 s) Now relax and exhale slowly. When all the air is out, take another deep breath, hold it, and notice the pressure again. . . . (7 s) Now relax, exhale slowly, and say in your mind "relax and let go." When all the air is out, rest a moment and take one more deep breath— a very, very deep breath. Hold it, hold it. . . . (7 s) Now relax and exhale slowly, very slowly. And think about how the air flowing out is like letting out all your tensions, your anxieties, and your frustrations. Notice how peaceful and calm you feel. Just relax and breathe normally. . . . (30 s) OK, stop, and let's move our exercises to your shoulders.

10. Hunch your *shoulders* forward, squeezing them toward each other so that you can feel the muscles of your upper back stretch tightly. Notice how tight the muscles are between your shoulder blades, across the top of your shoulders, and in your chest. Hold that tightness. . . . (7 s) Now relax, and feel the relaxation spread from your neck, shoulders, and chest to your whole upper body, especially your back. . . . (30 s) OK, stop.

11. Move your *shoulders* upward toward your head, pushing them as far up as you can. Feel the tension in your neck and shoulder muscles. . . .

(7 s) Now relax. Release the tension in those muscles, and let your shoulders sink back down. Think about how deeply and completely relaxed you're becoming. . . . (30 s) OK, stop.

12. Tighten your *stomach* muscles while pulling your shoulders back and arching your back backwards. Suck in your stomach as far as you can and feel the tension as you keep your stomach muscles tight as a drum. . . . (7 s) Now relax. Feel completely relaxed. . . . (30 s) OK, stop.

13. Lift both your *legs* a few inches and curl your toes so that the muscles of your arches and calves are very tight. Hold that tightness. . . . (7 s) Now relax. Let your legs fall as their muscles go limp. Feel the tension flowing out and calmness spreading up toward your stomach. . . . (30 s) OK, stop.

14. Lift both your *legs* again, but this time tighten the muscles in your thighs and lower abdomen. Make the muscles as tight as a drum. Feel how tense they are. . . . (7 s) Now relax. Let your legs fall as the muscles in your legs and abdomen go limp. Feel the tingling and warm sensations of relaxation flow down your legs and up your trunk. . . . (30 s) OK, stop, and let's do another breathing exercise.

15. In this exercise, you'll take a series of *five deep breaths*, inhaling and exhaling very slowly. You'll notice that when your lungs reach their peak of fullness, they seem to relax almost on their own. Each time the peak is reached, tell yourself to "relax and let go" as you start to exhale. Go ahead and take those five deep breaths. Each time you exhale very slowly, think about how peaceful, calm, and wonderfully well you feel. . . . (100 s) OK, stop. Breathe normally again and enjoy your refreshing feeling of well-being and calm throughout your body as this relaxation session ends.

Autogenic Training

Another approach for helping people relax has them imagine being in a pleasant and peaceful scene and experiencing specific bodily sensations, such as their arms feeling warm or heavy. This relaxation technique is called **autogenic training** and was developed in Germany by Johannes Schultz (1957; Schultz & Luthe, 1969). The name "autogenic" reflects Schultz's view that the technique's psychological and physiological effects are self-produced: *auto* means "self" and *genic* means "produced by."

In the standard autogenic training procedure, the person listens to instructions from a therapist or on tape and tries to imagine the events described. The procedure starts by asking the person to (1) adopt a passive and relaxed attitude, (2) allow changes in his or her bodily processes to evolve naturally, and (3) choose a pleasant, peaceful scene, such as lying on the beach or sitting in a meadow on a beautiful warm day. Then the training proceeds through a series of six phases, each with a theme regarding the type of sensation to imagine in the body. Of these themes, the two that are most commonly used in therapy involve feeling *heaviness* and *warmth* in parts of the body (Lichstein, 1988). The instructions specify the parts of the body to focus on and what to feel—for instance:

> My left arm is heavy. . . . I'm at peace. . . . My left arm is heavy. . . . My left arm is heavy. . . .
> I'm at peace. . . . My left arm is heavy. . . . My left arm is heavy. . . . My left arm is heavy.

Each instruction like this one is read very slowly. The person repeats the instruction to himself or herself while focusing attention on that part of the body and then receives a rest period. This sequence of reading/repeating/resting with the same instruction is repeated three times for a total of about 5 minutes. This same procedure then moves to six other parts of the body for 5 minutes each, still with the same theme. Covering the theme for all seven parts of the body takes about 35 minutes.

The next theme is warmth, and the instructions would include phrases like, "My abdomen is warm." Each of the six themes is covered in the same way we've seen, and whole phase takes about 35 minutes. Because the complete, standard procedure for autogenic training is so time consuming to carry out, researchers have developed shorter versions in which the repetition, the timing of each instruction sequence, or the number of themes is reduced (Lichstein, 1988). These versions take less than half an hour to carry out. Although some evidence indicates that the shorter versions do induce relaxation, more research is needed to determine whether the relaxation they produce is as deep as that achieved with the standard procedure of progressive muscle relaxation. Autogenic training doesn't require the tensing and relaxing of muscles, however, and it therefore has a clear advantage over progressive muscle relaxation for many people, particularly those who suffer from medical conditions like severe arthritis or low back pain, which make movement painful or difficult.

Meditation

The third approach for helping people learn to relax uses various forms of **meditation**— the process of contemplating or focusing one's attention on an object, event, or idea. The practice of meditation derives from Eastern philosophy and religion, especially Buddhism, and is intended to help people recognize but become detached from their physical states, thoughts, and feelings (de Silva, 1984, 1990; Hart, 1987; Solé-Leris, 1986; Thera, 1979). Although an important function of meditation is to produce relaxation, or "tranquility," it has a broader purpose: to develop a *clear and mindful awareness,* or "insight," unencumbered by cognitive or emotional distortions, regarding the essence of each experience.

An example of how mindful awareness may help individuals detach experiences from cognitive and emotional distortions comes from research on people with chronic pain. Jon Kabat-Zinn (1982; Kabat-Zinn, Lipworth, & Burney, 1985) trained chronic pain patients to use meditation techniques to focus on painful sensations as they happened, rather than trying to block them out, and to separate the physical sensations from the cognitive and emotional reactions that accompany pain. The patients were trained to pay close attention to their sensations, including pain, without reacting toward them in any way. By doing this, they could become aware of the pain itself, unembellished by their thoughts or feelings about it. This training reduced the patients' reported physical and psychological discomfort. As Kabat-Zinn described the rationale in using meditation treatment for pain, the sensory signals "may be undiminished, but the emotional and cognitive components of the pain experience, the hurt, the suffering, are reduced" (1982, p. 35).

We can achieve the relaxation component of meditation by doing exercises to focus attention on a *meditation stimulus*, which may be one or more of the following:

- A *static visual object*—something pleasing and simple, such as a flower, a bowl, or a symmetrical design. If you attempt to meditate with this type of stimulus, do not try to describe or evaluate the object; just try to see it as a whole and let its image rest in your awareness. Sometimes the objects seem to change or move, even though they are unchanging. Don't focus on these changes but simply accept them passively.

- A *mantra*, or spoken sound—such as *om*, *shirim*, or *wen*—that you say softly over and over to yourself. The mantra can be a word, but the word should be neutral.

- Your own *breathing*. For instance, breathe slowly and deeply through your nose in a natural, effortless manner and pay close attention to the air going into your nose as you inhale, and out of your nose as you exhale.

You may want to close your eyes if you're not using a visual object as your meditation stimulus. During meditation, your mind may sometimes wander to other thoughts. This is to be expected. When it happens, you should simply and gently coax your attention back to the meditation stimulus, without getting intellectually or emotionally involved in the intrusive thoughts. Don't get annoyed with the thoughts or try to keep them out; if they happen, they happen. The stimulus will return.

Individuals who are being trained to use meditation as a relaxation technique are instructed to practice it once or twice a day in a quiet environment, sitting upright in a relaxed and comfortable position. Each meditation session takes about 20 minutes. Some psychologists and psychiatrists advocate meditation exercises to reduce reactions to stress. For example, Herbert Benson has developed a widely known meditation procedure that incorporates breathing and mantra meditation stimuli. Benson instructs individuals who want to reduce stress to

relax all your muscles. . . . Become aware of your breathing. As you breathe out, say the word *one* silently to yourself. . . . Maintain a passive attitude and permit relaxation to occur at its own pace. Expect other thoughts. When these distracting thoughts occur, ignore them by thinking, "Oh well," and continue repeating, "One." (1984, p. 332)

According to Benson (1974, 1984, 1991), using meditation in this way increases people's ability in stressful situations to make a "relaxation response," which includes reduced physiological arousal, as an alternative to the CER they usually make. It is not clear to what extent this reduced physiological arousal develops in people from Western cultures who are trained to meditate (Holmes, 1984; Lichstein, 1988). Research has shown, however, that Buddhist monks in Southeast Asia can dramatically alter their body metabolism and brain electrical activity through meditation (Benson et al., 1990).

Regardless of whether we choose progressive muscle relaxation, autogenic training, or meditation as the standard technique for relaxation training, the procedure can be shortened to sessions of 10 or 20 minutes in length after the technique has been mastered. This can be accomplished in progressive muscle relaxation by combining a few of the exercises, such as doing both hands or arms together, and eliminating the tensing phases of all muscle exercises that are retained. Shortening autogenic training can be accomplished by using only the heaviness and warmth themes and combining parts of the body to which they are applied. Meditation sessions can be shortened simply by stopping sooner. There is one caution in shortening relaxation sessions: they should not become so brief that the target person is not achieving deep relaxation. If a tape-recorded protocol is being used for a relaxation technique, a new tape should be made for the shortened version, leaving out all instructions that no longer apply.

Rapid Relaxation Induction

The relaxation techniques we've seen help individuals to be less easily aroused by CSs that elicit CERs in their lives, allowing them to be calmer and more clear-headed in the general style with which they approach potentially arousing antecedent events. But many individuals who have problems with emotional behaviors also need to have an *alternative, quick way* to induce some level of relaxation when troublesome CSs arise— for instance, if they are about to give a speech in class. The alternative method is meant to supplement, not take the place of, deep relaxation.

The best way to develop an alternative procedure for rapid relaxation induction is by altering and shortening considerably the standard technique that has been mastered (Lichstein, 1988). There are four points to keep in mind in creating a rapid induction procedure. First, a rapid induction method is not a substitute for the standard procedure. The target person should continue practicing the standard relaxation technique in 10- to 20-minute sessions at least a few times a week. Second, we should try to make sure the person has mastered the standard relaxation technique on which the rapid method will be based. We can do this by reviewing the person's relaxation records and observing the person using the technique. Third, rapid induction methods generally do not induce relaxation as deeply as the standard techniques. And fourth, rapid induction methods work best if the target person can anticipate the need to use them by being aware of the antecedents that lead to the CER.

Useful Components for Rapid Relaxation Induction When we design a rapid relaxation method, we can enhance its effectiveness by trying to incorporate three useful components: verbal cues for relaxation, breathing exercises, and cognitive images. The standard relaxation techniques include having the target person make certain statements or sounds, which can serve as *verbal cues* for rapid relaxation. For instance, if the person says "relax," "feel calm," or a mantra such as "Om" in the standard procedure, he or she should use the same words or sounds softly or covertly as part of the rapid method.

Some standard relaxation techniques include *breathing exercises* that involve slowly inhaling and exhaling deep breaths. If we know before selecting the standard technique that we will want to use a rapid induction method, we should make sure the standard technique includes breathing exercises in which the person takes *deep* breaths and pays close attention to them. Sometimes deep breathing exercises can be added to the standard technique, thereby providing the opportunity to use breathing exercises in the rapid induction method. The deepness of the breathing is usually lessened to *moderately deep* breathing for a rapid induction method because the deep breathing might be noticeable to others, who may interrupt the process or make it embarrassing to use (Lichstein, 1988).

The third useful component involves using clear and detailed *cognitive images* of pleasant or relaxing scenes, which are called **calm scenes** (NJNPI, 1972). One of the standard relaxation techniques, autogenic training, already includes a pleasant scene for the individual to picture while doing imaginal exercises for six different themes, such as feelings of heaviness and warmth in parts of the body. But calm scenes can be used in the two other relaxation approaches as well. In meditation, a calm scene could be used as a meditation stimulus in place of a static visual object. In progressive muscle relaxation, a calm scene could be added to the breathing exercises as a focal object to imagine while relaxing. When using calm scenes with any of these standard approaches, it is helpful to include short, specific instructions, such as:

> With your eyes closed, picture yourself in your calm scene—the scene that makes you feel comfortable, peaceful, and relaxed. Experience the scene in all its details and with all your senses. Try to see aspects of the scene, hear them, smell them, and feel them on your body. As you picture this scene, you'll feel deeper and deeper relaxation.

Using calm scenes in relaxation exercises requires that the person select *one scene* to employ whenever a scene is applied. Two of the most common themes or types of calm scenes that people use are lying on a beach and walking or sitting in a forest. Although the scene can have almost any theme, it:

- Should be one the target person *has actually experienced* in the past, felt *very relaxed* in, and believes would *always help* him or her feel relaxed and calm.

- Should be one the target person *can imagine easily and clearly, with as many senses as possible*. For instance, in a scene of lying on the beach, one would try to see the water, sand, and clear blue sky; smell the water and hear it splashing; feel the warmth of the sun on the body; and see and hear gulls or other sea birds.

- Should *not* be one that portrays or includes (1) the use of mood-altering substances, such as alcohol or drugs, and (2) someone with whom the target person has or wants to have a strong emotional attachment. Although people we love usually make us feel calm and relaxed, such as when cuddling, if the relationship should change and become distressing, the scene will no longer be useful.

If we know we'll want to use verbal cues, breathing exercises, or calm scenes in a rapid induction method, we should incorporate those components in the standard relaxation technique the person masters originally. These components will be retained as the person learns to use the quicker method.

Creating a Rapid Induction Method: An Example   As an example of how we can create a rapid relaxation method, we'll use progressive muscle relaxation as the standard technique. Before moving toward creating a rapid relaxation method, the person should have practiced the full procedure for at least 10 sessions, mastered it, shortened it to a 10- to 20-minute version, and practiced the shortened version for several sessions. The target person should continue to practice that shortened version indefinitely.

We can create a rapid method of progressive muscle relaxation by introducing two intermediate steps, each of which involves making a new tape of a version that is further altered or shortened. Based on the protocol of Close-Up 7.1, these two tapes would contain the following exercises and alterations:

1. *Intermediate Tape 1:* exercises numbered 1, 2, 6, 9, 10, 12, 14, and 15 from the protocol (without tensing), including calm scenes. Use this tape in place of the tape with the shortened version for at least five sessions.
2. *Intermediate Tape 2:* exercises numbered 9, 10, 12, and 15 from the protocol, as used in Intermediate Tape 1, except for two changes: (a) deep breathing should be diminished to *moderately* deep breathing and (b) relaxation periods should be only *half as long* in each exercise. Use this tape in place of Intermediate Tape 1 for several sessions.

As an example, the final procedure to induce rapid relaxation might have three steps: (1) take a moderately deep breath, (2) say a verbal cue softly or covertly while exhaling—for instance, "Relax. Feel nice and calm," and (3) think of the calm scene. This induction procedure would not be taped and is short enough to elicit a relaxation CR in a matter of seconds. (Go to ☑)

COVERT CONDITIONING

The success of using imaginal procedures in relaxation and systematic desensitization techniques led psychologist Joseph Cautela (1966, 1993a) to develop an array of imagery-based conditioning methods called **covert conditioning.** Cautela refers to the methods as *covert* because the person is asked to imagine all components of the conditioning process—the antecedents, target behavior, and consequences. He considers the

CONCEPT CHECK 7.1

1. A medical condition for which relaxation techniques appear to be a useful component of treatment is _____ . ⇔
2. Alternately tensing and relaxing separate muscle groups while resting comfortably is called _____ .
3. The relaxation technique in which the individual imagines a pleasant scene and sensations in different parts of the body is called _____ .
4. The process of contemplating or focusing one's attention on an object, event, or idea is called _____ .
5. A static visual object you could use as a meditation stimulus in your own residence is _____ . ⇔
6. An example from the progressive muscle relaxation protocol of muscle groups you could combine to shorten the procedure is _____ . ⇔
7. An example of a verbal cue you could incorporate from autogenic training into a rapid induction method is _____ . ⇔
8. A calm scene you might use in designing your own relaxation exercises is _____ . ⇔

Answers: 1. asthma/migraine headache, 2. progressive muscle relaxation, 3. autogenic training, 4. meditation, 5. a painting, 6. tensing and relaxing both biceps together, 7. "I'm at peace," 8. walking in Tuolumne Meadows in Yosemite National Park

methods to be forms of conditioning because he views them as private or internal respondent or operant behaviors.

One covert conditioning method, called **covert sensitization,** pairs in the target person's imagination an existing antecedent, or CS, with aversive events that serve either as a US (in respondent conditioning) or as a punisher (in operant conditioning). Cautela applied covert sensitization to help a 29-year-old nurse overcome her alcohol abuse problem by having her imagine various scenes. In one scene, she was asked to imagine that she had ordered and got her favorite drink. Then,

> as you reach for the drink you start to feel sick to your stomach. As you hold the glass in your hand you feel yourself about to vomit. As you are just about to put the glass to your lips you vomit. It comes out your mouth all over the table and the floor. It is a real mess. (1966, p. 37)

In some scenes, she was told that she refused to take a drink, and she felt calm right away. In interviews with her after several sessions of covert sensitization and 8 months later, she reported having stopped drinking (the study did not include a way to validate her reports).

A similar covert sensitization approach was used in another study with men who were hospitalized for alcohol abuse (Ashem & Donner, 1968). Follow-up assessments 6 months later with confirmation by relatives revealed that 6 of the 15 men who received the treatment remained abstinent; but of an additional 8 men who did not get this treatment, none was abstinent. Other interventions incorporating covert sensitization have successfully reduced people's nail-biting (Daniels, 1974; Paquin, 1977) and sexually deviant behaviors, such as exhibitionism and excessive masturbation (Hayes, Brownell, & Barlow, 1978; Krop & Burgess, 1993).

Another covert conditioning method is like *desensitization,* but Cautela refers to it as a **covert positive reinforcement** procedure. Here the person imagines performing a target behavior that is followed by a pleasant event. Dennis Upper (1993) applied this method in a program to help a young woman named Joan overcome her severe anxieties about sexual contact. The therapist and the client constructed a stimulus hierarchy of sexual situations and started the procedure with the least anxiety-provoking stimulus. For each stimulus,

> the client is asked to imagine herself performing the behavior, experiencing mild anxiety, and using relaxation or some other procedure for decreasing the anxiety, and then is asked to switch in imagination to a pleasant (that is, reinforcing) scene. (p. 239)

The reinforcing scene involved skiing, which Joan enjoyed doing very much.

Joseph Cautela (1993c) described another intervention using covert positive reinforcement to treat 6-year-old Alice's unusual phobia of buttons. Her fear was so great that she would not wear clothes with buttons or stay in the same room with people who wore buttons. Cautela treated the fear with a program that included teaching Alice relaxation exercises and presenting stories for her to imagine. In one story that portrayed a family outing at the beach, she and her sister Amy were digging in the sand and found a treasure chest that contained

> coins, necklaces, rings and bracelets! Also there are some beautiful buttons [Alice winces]. The buttons are so beautiful they look like jewelry. . . . And then your sister says, "Oh, I want to hold and look at the buttons." Your father gives her some beautiful buttons while you look at your gold-and-diamond ring. You're all so happy. (p. 129)

The therapy advanced through increasingly fear-provoking stories and even included some *in vivo* stimuli. Alice's fear eventually disappeared after about a dozen sessions, and she had no more problems with buttons thereafter.

As you think about covert conditioning procedures, you'll realize that virtually all learning processes and conditioning phenomena can take place covertly. For instance, the imaginal scene used in treating Alice's fear of buttons included *covert modeling:* sister Amy asked for and held some buttons that her father had handed her. Scenes can also be designed to include covert instances of extinction, punishment, and negative reinforcement (Cautela, 1993a). Covert conditioning methods are probably not as effective as *in vivo* procedures in changing respondent behaviors —for instance, we saw in Chapter 6 that desensitization is more effective with *in vivo* stimuli than with imaginal ones. But covert methods may be especially useful when certain stimuli are too threatening or inconvenient to present in real life (Ascher, 1993). To enhance the success of covert procedures, Cautela (1993a) recommends having the target person rate the clarity of the image and the pleasantness or aversiveness of the events on 5-point scales, for example, ranging from "not at all clear" to "very clear." A scene would only be applied if both ratings are high.

COGNITIVE-BEHAVIORAL COPING TECHNIQUES

Have you ever expected to be very frightened or anxious by an experience, such as giving a speech, only to find that you weren't? People often expect to be more fearful in fear-arousing situations than they turn out to be (Rachman, 1994). Cognitive processes and people's respondent behaviors are intimately linked, and each can affect the other. For instance, a man who was very frightened of developing cancer examined his body frequently,

> especially his skin. During these periods of elevated anxiety the natural and permanent patches of his skin appeared to him to have become significantly enlarged. When the anxiety subsided, however, he was able to estimate the size of these skin patches correctly. He experienced similar fluctuations in his estimations of the size of various bumps and lumps. (Rachman & Cuk, 1992, p. 584)

In such cases, the CER seems to produce *perceptual distortions*, thereby making the situation seem worse than it actually is.

An experiment to investigate the possibility of perceptual distortions during fearful experiences was conducted with individuals who either were or were not very fearful of snakes or spiders (Rachman & Cuk, 1992). The individuals watched one of two harmless animals—a spider or a garter snake—in a glass enclosure and estimated its movement. Those who were fearful estimated that the creature showed far more movement toward them and efforts to leave the enclosure than the nonfearful individuals did. All the individuals then saw a video in which a therapist used participant modeling to reduce a person's fear of a snake or a spider. When again asked to watch a spider or snake in the enclosure and estimate its movement, the fearful and nonfearful individuals' estimates were far lower than before. These findings indicate that cognitive processes can exaggerate people's experience of a CS, almost certainly making these experiences more difficult.

But cognitive processes can also help people *reduce* the impact of a CS through the use of coping techniques. *Coping* refers to people's use of cognitive and behavioral processes in attempting to manage their experiences of emotionally arousing or stressful events in life. Psychologists have identified many coping techniques people commonly use (Cohen & Lazarus, 1979; Moos & Schaefer, 1986). These techniques often combine behavioral and cognitive methods, and are called *cognitive-behavioral coping techniques*. Some individuals seem to use these techniques more effectively than others do in managing their respondent behavior. Training individuals to use coping techniques can help them deal better with the antecedents to CERs, perhaps by making their perceptions more positive or by preventing fearful distortions from happening. Let's look at some cognitive-behavioral coping techniques that have been applied widely in interventions to change respondent behaviors.

Self-Statements

Suppose you were about to experience a painful medical procedure. Could you talk yourself into coping with this aversive situation? Many people in this kind of situation say things like "Be brave—you can take it" or "It will hurt, but having this done will make you walk better." These sentences are examples of **self-statements**—things we say to ourselves, which can be either *positive* or *negative*. Both of these sentences are examples of positive self-statements, with the former being a *coping statement*, and the latter being a *reinterpretative statement* (Fernandez, 1986). Interventions to train individuals to use positive self-statements instead of negative ones appear to be very successful in reducing anxiety in a variety of situations, such as taking tests and speaking in public (Dush, Hirt, & Schroeder, 1983). Let's look at coping and reinterpretative statements more closely.

Coping Statements   **Coping statements** are things people say to themselves that emphasize their ability to tolerate unpleasant situations. When feeling anxious about a paper you're writing, you might say to yourself, "Relax—you're in control" or "It's hard, but you'll get through it." Coping self-statements like these help us tolerate the anxiety and carry on. Unfortunately, many individuals do the opposite, saying to themselves self-defeating things like, "I'm not good at this" or "I'm gonna fail." People who make very frequent negative self-statements are likely to experience a lot of anxiety in stressful situations. (Go to 🔎)

Reinterpretative Statements   **Reinterpretative statements** are declarations people make to themselves that redefine a situation by negating unpleasant aspects of the situation or giving a reason to view it differently. For instance, a girl who had a phobia of elevators was instructed to say "The elevator doors cannot hurt me, they bounce back open" (Sturges & Sturges, 1998). Sometimes positive self-statements simply try to put a good face on a bad situation, such as by noting that things could be worse, making comparisons with individuals who are less well off, or seeing something good coming out of the problem. Thus, a woman with breast cancer remarked:

> What you do is put things into perspective. You find out that things like relationships are really the most important things you have—the people you know and your family—everything else is just way down the line. It's very strange that it takes something so serious to make you realize that. (Taylor, 1983, p. 1163)

Other reinterpretative statements can help individuals who "take things personally" see events as having nonpersonal reasons. For example, a person who thinks, "She just snubbed me," when an acquaintance passes by without saying anything could try to think, "What other reasons might explain her behavior?"

CLOSE-UP 7.2

Age Differences in Fears and Using Self-Statements

 The types of fears people have change with age. As children get older, the things they fear tend to become less *concrete* and more *abstract*, particularly after about 5 years of age (Sarafino, 1986). During the middle-childhood years, children become less afraid of tangible and immediate situations, such as noises and strange objects, and more afraid of such things as imaginary creatures (ghosts and witches), the dark, and signs of fear in others. In later childhood, these fears tend to decline, and anxieties relating to school and social relations become increasingly common. At the other end of the life span, the most prominent fears of people in old age are that they or loved ones will die or become ill or injured (Liddel, Locker, & Burman, 1991).

These changes in fears reflect the different experiences and levels of cognitive development of people at different ages. The factors of experience and cognitive level also relate to the use of self-statements when faced with stressful events. For example, a study had 8- to 18-year-old students describe what they say to themselves when they are about to get an injection at a dental visit (Brown et al., 1986). Of children at age 8 or 9, over 62% reported making *negative* self-statements, such as "I'm scared" or "I want to run away," and less than 43% said they used *positive* self-statements, such as "Be brave" or "I can take this." In contrast, adolescents' self-statements were much more positive. Of the 16- to 18-year-olds, only 44% reported making negative self-statements, and 86% reported using positive self-statements. These results show that children's cognitive coping skills improve with age and suggest that training young children to use positive self-statements would help them cope better with stressful events—a prediction that has been confirmed in research (Kanfer, Karoly, & Newman, 1975; Siegel & Peterson, 1980).

But reinterpretative statements must be declarations the person can *believe*. For instance, the man we discussed earlier named Dennis who suffered from panic attacks tried to cope with his unfounded anxieties about his ability to sell insurance by using the following pep talk he tape-recorded and played in his car:

> Go out there and charm 'em, Dennis. You're the best damn salesman this company's ever had! They're gonna be putty in your hands, big fella. Flash that smile. . . . They'll love you! (Oltmanns, Neale, & Davison, 1991, p. 19)

Listening to this declaration made his tension worse. Even though he really was a very successful agent, he didn't believe it. Saying these things probably just reminded him of what he feared. More believable reinterpretative statements were used in covert conditioning therapy with another man who also had severe anxieties about his work performance. He was asked to imagine being at a business meeting and thinking, "I hope I don't do anything wrong at the meeting," followed by the reinterpretative statement, "I haven't in the past, there is no reason to believe that I will in the future." He was also asked to imagine thinking, "I know that I'm going to perspire at the meeting and everyone will notice," followed by "People are too self-absorbed to notice a subtle change in your appearance" (Ascher, 1993, p. 18). This therapy helped him cope better at business meetings.

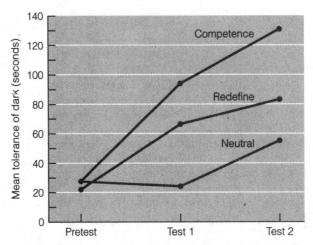

Figure 7.2   Mean duration (in seconds) children tolerated being in darkness at a pretest and at two tests after receiving training in using self-statements that either expressed competence in coping with darkness, redefined the darkness situation, or were neutral (i.e., unrelated to darkness). *Source:* Adapted from Kanfer, Karoly, & Newman, 1975, Figure 1.

Training to use positive self-statements can help young children cope with their fears too. Researchers trained 5- and 6-year-old kindergartners who were afraid of the dark to make various self-statements to help them cope in the dark (Kanfer, Karoly, & Newman, 1975). The children were pretested in a dark room by giving them a dimmer switch to use to turn on a light and increase its brightness and asking them to "Try to keep the room as dark as you can, for as long as you can." Then some of the children were taught to say, "I am a brave boy [girl]. I can take care of myself in the dark." These statements reflected a sense of competence and ability to control the situation. Other children were taught to say, "The dark is a fun place to be. There are many good things in the dark," which might simply redefine the situation. And a third group of children was just told to recite, "Mary had a little lamb. Its fleece was white as snow." When they were tested later in the dark room two more times, all three groups improved in their ability to remain in the dark and use low illumination. Figure 7.2 shows that this improvement was greatest by far among the children who were taught the competence self-statements and lowest among those who recited "Mary had a little lamb." These results highlight how important the *content* of self-statements can be in helping people cope.

Thought Stopping and Distraction

The last two cognitive-behavioral coping techniques we'll consider simply involve interrupting or diverting one's attention from antecedents that elicit overt or covert CERs.

Thought Stopping   "Stop!" the therapist shouted sharply as Phil described a depressing thought he often has about his ex-girlfriend. The therapist had asked Phil to describe the thought so they could use a simple procedure called **thought stopping** in which the word "stop" is said suddenly and emphatically soon after the person starts to describe or concentrate on an unwanted thought (Cautela & Wisocki, 1977; Wolpe, 1973). Individuals can also apply thought stopping as a self-management technique. If they do, the person either says "stop" aloud or very clearly in the mind as soon as the unwanted thought occurs.

Although thought stopping has been used widely as a component in successful interventions to reduce respondent behavior, research demonstrating its utility by itself has either involved very few clients or produced mixed results (Arrick, Voss, & Rimm, 1981; Hackman & McClean, 1975; Stern, Lipsedge, & Marks, 1973; Tryon, 1979). Thought stopping seems to be most useful in combination with other methods—replacing the unwanted thought with a positive self-statement immediately after saying "stop," for example. (Go to)

CASE STUDY 7.1

Thought Stopping and Self-Statements to Reduce Depressive Thoughts

After Carol's boyfriend of 3 years left her for another woman, she began to have recurrent thoughts about him and about herself that made her depressed (case described in Martin, 1982). Although she was attractive and had good social skills, she would think such things as, "I feel that I am a failure. I feel ugly and useless. I keep thinking about not being able to 'keep a man,' and not being able to have a husband." Then she would cry, sometimes for long periods of time, even at her job as a secretary.

Carol was referred by a friend for therapy, which consisted of training her to use thought stopping and positive self-statements when the troublesome thoughts arose. She carried these techniques out in two steps: First she'd use thought stopping by closing her eyes, covertly yelling "Stop!" to herself, and counting to 10 silently. Then she'd take out a few photographs she had selected, read statements she had written on the back of each one, and think about each picture while looking at it for several seconds. One picture, for example, showed Carol at the airport before leaving on a trip by herself. The message on the back said, "I'm my own boss. My life is ahead of me. I can do what I want to do."

Carol had been taught to evaluate "how bad" her days were in terms of the thoughts she experienced, using a 6-point rating scale in which 5 equaled a "very bad day" and 0 equaled a "very good day." Her average daily rating per week declined from slightly over 4 in baseline to under 1 after several weeks of therapy. A follow-up assessment 4 months later revealed no recurrence of problem thoughts about her ex-boyfriend.

Distraction **Distraction** is a technique in which individuals shift their attention from a CS that elicits a CER to overt or covert stimuli that are unrelated to the CER. Distraction can be used for just a moment, such as by focusing on a picture on a wall as you receive an injection, or for a longer time, perhaps by watching a TV show when

✓

CONCEPT CHECK 7.2

1. Imagery-based techniques that have individuals think about scenes of an existing CS being paired with an aversive US are called _____.

2. A person who always avoided using elevators because of a phobia of enclosed spaces might benefit from a *covert extinction* procedure in which he or she imagined _____. ⇔

3. A perceptual distortion a fearful dental patient might experience when getting an injection is _____. ⇔

4. "Relax—the traffic will let up eventually" is an example of a _____ statement.

5. When faced with a stressful experience, young children tend to make more _____ self-statements than _____ self-statements.

6. Saying "It could be worse" is an example of a _____ statement.

7. Thought stopping tends to be more useful when it is followed by a _____.

Answers: 1. covert sensitization, 2. riding the elevator safely and calmly, 3. the needle appearing larger than it is, 4. coping, 5. negative, positive, 6. reinterpretation, 7. positive self-statement

feeling anxious about giving a speech you've practiced many times. All sorts of stimuli and activities can distract us from unpleasant antecedents to respondent behavior. In the study we considered earlier of children coping with their fears of the dark, reciting "Mary had a little lamb" probably served as a distraction. As we saw, however, this activity was not nearly as effective as using self-statements. Distraction techniques tend to work best for momentary, mildly or moderately stressful experiences, rather than severe, recurrent, and long-lasting ones (Greene, Seime, & Smith, 1991; McCaul & Malott, 1984). (Go to ✓)

Tips on Using Covert Behavioral Methods

The tips listed here for using covert behavioral methods to change respondent behavior basically consolidate and recap recommendations already presented in this chapter.

1. As a general rule, procedures to change respondent behavior should use *in vivo* stimuli rather than imaginal ones whenever possible.

2. When considering which type of relaxation technique to use, consider whether any type would be uncomfortable to practice. For instance, it might be uncomfortable to use progressive muscle relaxation if suffering from muscular or joint pain and autogenic training with a warmth theme if suffering from some forms of internal disorders, such as ulcers.

3. Learning a relaxation technique takes a lot of practice. It is important to adhere very closely to a planned schedule of practice sessions. Try to establish a high priority for doing

relaxation exercises, thereby diminishing the temptation to skip sessions because "I don't have the time."

4. Use tapes for practicing relaxation whenever possible.

5. Relaxation exercises should be conducted in a quiet environment that is not brightly lit, if possible. Sometimes this ideal cannot be achieved. If the environment is less than ideal, do the exercises anyway. Earplugs may help.

6. The mind may sometimes wander during progressive muscle relaxation, autogenic training, or meditation sessions. Be aware that this happens and simply bring the focus back to the technique gently.

7. Don't try to introduce a rapid relaxation method before completing at least 10 sessions with the standard technique and mastering it.

8. Assess the degree to which relaxation develops during sessions. Decisions about how fast to progress in the training or whether to advance to a rapid method should be based on those data.

9. When selecting a calm scene, don't include anyone for whom an emotional attachment exists or is desired.

10. Make sure the clarity of scenes is assessed when using imaginal procedures, such as those used in covert conditioning.

11. When developing new positive self-statements, select statements that are reasonable and believable.

SUMMARY

Relaxation is a state of diminished psychological and physiological tension. Relaxation techniques should be practiced in quiet settings with no interruptions. Progressive muscle relaxation uses a protocol for tensing and relaxing separate muscle groups. In autogenic training, individuals imagine a pleasant scene and the experience of certain bodily sensations, such as heaviness in the limbs. Meditation involves focusing one's attention on a meditation stimulus, which may be a static visual object, a mantra, or one's own breathing. Although sessions using these techniques usually take close to half an hour during training, they can be shortened to 10 or 20 minutes after mastery has been achieved. Breathing exercises and calm scenes generally should be included in relaxation techniques if rapid relaxation induction methods will be used.

Covert conditioning methods involve having individuals imagine scenes that include respondent and operant conditioning procedures. These methods include covert sensitization, in which the person imagines an existing CS followed by an aversive event, and covert positive reinforcement, which is like desensitization. Other covert conditioning methods include covert modeling, extinction, punishment, and negative reinforcement.

Self-statements can help or hinder our ability to cope with difficult events—that is, they can be positive or negative. Coping statements emphasize our ability to tolerate troublesome events, and reinterpretative statements redefine the situation, making these events easier to face. Thought stopping and distraction are cognitive-behavioral coping techniques that involve interrupting or diverting attention from troublesome stimuli. Training in these coping techniques seems to help people reduce problem CERs.

KEY TERMS

relaxation
progressive muscle
    relaxation
autogenic training
meditation

calm scenes
covert conditioning
covert sensitization
covert positive
    reinforcement

self-statements
coping statements
reinterpretative statements
thought stopping
distraction

REVIEW QUESTIONS

1. Near the beginning of the discussion of relaxation techniques, several guidelines were described. Describe three of those guidelines.
2. Define progressive muscle relaxation, and discuss the pros and cons of including muscle tensing in the procedure.
3. Describe in a few sentences an overview of the procedure for conducting progressive muscle relaxation as outlined in the protocol of Close-Up 7.1.
4. What is autogenic training, and how is it similar to progressive muscle relaxation?
5. Describe the three types of meditation stimuli and how you might use each if you practiced meditation.
6. After a standard relaxation technique has been mastered, how might we go about shortening it?
7. What guidelines should we follow in selecting a calm scene?
8. Describe the three steps in the rapid relaxation induction method.
9. Define covert sensitization, and give an example.
10. Describe the research by Rachman and Cuk (1992) showing how perceptual distortions occur when fearful stimuli are present.
11. Define coping statements and reinterpretative statements, and give two examples of each.
12. How might you use distraction as a coping technique when a nurse draws a sample of blood from your arm?

RELATED READINGS

Benson, H. (1974). Your innate asset for combating stress. *Harvard Business Review, 52,* 49–60.
Carlson, C. R., & Hoyle, R. H. (1993). Efficacy of abbreviated progressive muscle relaxation training: A quantitative review of behavioral medicine research. *Journal of Consulting and Clinical Psychology, 61,* 1059–1067.

Cautela, J. R., & Kearney, A. J. (Eds.). (1993). *Covert conditioning handbook*. Pacific Grove, CA: Brooks/Cole.

Hart, W. (1987). *The art of living: Vipassana meditation*. New York: HarperCollins.

Kabat-Zinn, J. (1996). Mindfulness meditation: What it is, what it isn't, and its role in health care and medicine. In Y. Haruki, Y. Ishii, & M. Suzuki (Eds.), *Comparative and psychological study on meditation* (pp. 161–170). Eburon: Netherlands.

Lichstein, K. L. (1988). *Clinical relaxation strategies*. New York: Wiley.

A multidimensional program with several behavior modification techniques can effectively reduce classroom misconduct like that shown in this photo.

CHAPTER EIGHT

Putting Techniques Together to Design a Program

M r. W. had walked in his sleep four or five times a week since he was 15 years of age; when he was 24 years old, he entered therapy to stop this behavior (Meyer, 1975). His wife had tolerated his sleepwalking, complaining only if his fumbling around awakened her. But her view changed

> because during a recent act of sleepwalking he took down a shotgun, loaded it, and prepared to fire at imaginary burglars. Luckily, his wife's screaming woke him before he could fire. (p. 167)

She insisted that he get professional help immediately. In therapy, Mr. W. revealed that his sleepwalking was related to feelings of anxiety about taking tests and that he had become extremely anxious about taking an upcoming bar examination to be licensed as a lawyer. A decision was made to disable the shotgun for the time being by dismantling the firing pin.

The therapist decided to stop Mr. W.'s sleepwalking by applying two behavioral methods, each focusing on a different aspect of the problem. One method focused on sleepwalking as an operant behavior. This method was punishment: the sound of a loud whistle when he walked in his sleep. Because Mrs. W. was a light sleeper, they moved their furniture so he would have to crawl over her to get out of bed. She would blow the whistle if she awoke and he was sleepwalking. The other method focused on the underlying respondent behavior of anxiety, which seemed to be an antecedent to sleepwalking. Systematic desensitization was applied to reduce Mr. W.'s test anxiety. He learned to practice relaxation exercises, helped in constructing a stimulus hierarchy of imaginal CSs, and received 10 sessions of desensitization. This intervention combining two techniques was effective. Not only did it almost completely eliminate his sleepwalking, but he was able to study better and passed the bar examination easily. Follow-up assessments revealed only four sleepwalking episodes during the next year.

Designing a behavior modification intervention typically involves putting together several techniques to form a program to change a target behavior. To maximize the program's effectiveness, the techniques it includes should be directed at all three *dimensions* of the problem behavior: the target behavior itself, its antecedents, and its consequences. In this chapter, we will describe how to select from and combine the techniques we've discussed so far to design successful programs to change behavior.

COMBINING METHODS FOR A BEHAVIOR CHANGE PROGRAM

Behavior therapists recognize the need to combine appropriate techniques to maximize treatment effectiveness, and they tend to use several intervention techniques with each client (Swan & McDonald, 1978). If you think back to the techniques discussed in the preceding chapters, you'll notice that each one is useful in addressing a specific dimension of a problem behavior we may want to change. Interventions that combine techniques to address more than one dimension of a problem behavior are called **multidimensional programs** (Friedman, Campbell, & Evans, 1993). In designing an effective multidimensional program to change a behavior, we need to consider techniques to address the

- *Antecedents*—for example, by altering antecedent physical or social stimuli to reduce the likelihood of the problem behavior occurring.
- *Behavior*—perhaps by teaching the person a desirable, alternative response.
- *Consequences*—that is, by changing the existing consequences of the behavior through reinforcement, extinction, or punishment methods.

In addition to addressing the antecedents, behavior, and consequences, it is important to include procedures to maintain the newly acquired desirable behavior and prevent the unwanted behavior from returning (Friedman, Campbell, & Evans, 1993). Chapter 10 will examine techniques to maintain behavior changes over long periods of time. These techniques can be added to the program once the intervention is under way.

Identifying Possible Techniques to Use

Chapters 3 through 7 present all of the basic techniques to consider using in designing a multidimensional program to change behavior. The starting point in identifying techniques that might be appropriate for a program is the functional analysis. We would begin by asking two questions. First, does the target behavior involve operant behaviors, respondent behaviors, or both? Different techniques apply to different types of behavior. As we saw in the case of Mr. W.'s sleepwalking, an intervention can combine techniques that focus on each type of behavior when both types need to be addressed.

The chapters in Part II of this book describe methods to change operant behavior, and Part III covers methods to change respondent behavior.

The second question is: Is the program being designed to change a behavioral excess or a behavioral deficit? Once again, the answer will suggest different techniques to apply. For instance, reinforcement methods are extremely important to correct an operant behavioral deficit or to increase an alternative response; extinction and punishment procedures might be very useful in decreasing a behavioral excess. Bear in mind that keeping records, performing relaxation exercises, and other activities a person does in self-management procedures are all behavioral deficits. It's often a good idea to reinforce these activities.

Once we've answered these questions, we can proceed with the task of designing the program as a problem-solving activity. The most efficient strategy to arrive at the best solution to a problem begins by *generating many alternative solutions* (D'Zurilla & Nezu, 1982; Nezu, Nezu, & Perri, 1989). Generating a large number of alternatives increases the likelihood that the most appropriate or most effective techniques will be considered for inclusion in the program. A good way to generate alternative solutions is to use the method of **brainstorming,** which has three rules:

- *Aim for quantity.* The more alternative solutions we produce, the more likely we'll have good ones from which to select.
- *Defer judgment.* When brainstorming, don't stop to evaluate any of the ideas generated, saying things like "I'll never make that technique work" or "I don't like the idea of . . ." We can evaluate the ideas later.
- *Start with strategies, then tactics.* Initial ideas can be general strategies, which can be refined later to specific tactics. A strategy might be to "use reinforcement," and some tactics might include using "tokens" and "activities as backup reinforcers."

Figure 8.1 presents a checklist of methods we've discussed in the preceding chapters. You can find those discussions by using the index at the end of the book, and most of the terms are defined in the glossary. These materials can help in the brainstorming process and in selecting the techniques to use. The next step in designing a multidimensional program is to pick the most promising alternatives from the ones generated. Before we consider how to select techniques from these alternatives, let's look at some example programs.

Examples of Multidimensional Programs

To illustrate how various techniques to change behavior can be combined, we will look at a variety of multidimensional programs with very different goals and settings. Some of these programs were designed to apply relatively broad resources with many clients, and other programs were designed for specific individuals.

Broad, Community-Based Programs   Community-based programs to change behavior are designed with the view that serious behavior problems, such as alcohol abuse,

CHECKLIST OF BEHAVIOR CHANGE METHODS

This checklist can be used to generate and select ideas in designing programs to change behavior. Use the index at the end of this book to find descriptions of the techniques listed. The techniques are separated on the basis of whether their most common uses are to manage the antecedents, the behavior, or the consequences. Some techniques may be directed toward managing more than one dimension of the behavior change process. If you use the checklist to design a program, you may want to make a photocopy of it and write *yes* or *no* in the spaces preceding the methods to indicate if you think they may be useful.

Managing the Antecedents

_____ Discrimination learning
_____ Prompting/fading
_____ Modeling
_____ Instructions
_____ Self-instructions/rules
_____ Altering antecedent chains
_____ Reducing/avoiding antecedents
_____ Narrowing antecedent control
_____ Cognitive strategies
_____ Systematic desensitization
_____ Participant modeling
_____ Self-statements
_____ Thought stopping
_____ Distraction

Managing the Behavior

_____ Subgoals
_____ Shaping
_____ Shortcuts to shaping
_____ Chaining
_____ Alternative responses
_____ Counterconditioning
_____ Relaxation techniques
_____ Covert conditioning

Managing the Consequences

_____ Positive reinforcement
_____ Tangible/consumable
_____ Activities
_____ Social reinforcers
_____ Feedback
_____ Tokens
_____ Covert reinforcers
_____ Negative reinforcement
_____ Extinction (operant/respondent)
_____ Reducing counterproductive reinforcers
_____ Lotteries/group contingencies
_____ Punishment
_____ Physically aversive stimuli
_____ Reprimands
_____ Aversive activities
_____ Time-out
_____ Response cost
_____ Differential reinforcement
   (DRI, DRL, DRO)
_____ Habit reversal
_____ Self-monitoring/self-instruction

Figure 8.1 Checklist of behavior change methods.

result from factors that operate in and are affected by the community in which the individual lives. This view suggests that the best way to treat substance abuse is to rearrange these factors in the community rather than trying to correct the problem in a hospital. Using this view, Nathan Azrin and his colleagues have designed the *community-reinforcement approach* to treat alcoholism (Azrin, 1976; Azrin et al., 1982;

Hunt & Azrin, 1973; Sisson & Azrin, 1989). The program has evolved over the years, but these main features have endured:

- Daily doses of the emetic drug *disulfiram*. An emetic produces nausea; disulfiram has this effect if the target person drinks. Taking the drug is monitored and verbally reinforced by the person's spouse or other intimate individual.
- Marital counseling, job counseling, and a program aimed at getting work.
- Reinforcers for taking the disulfiram and attending counseling sessions.
- Assistance in developing hobbies and recreational activities in which alcohol is not available.
- Training in refusing drinks that are offered to the problem drinker.
- Training in relaxation exercises and ways of handling social problems that have led to drinking in the past.

If you examine this list carefully and look back at the checklist in Figure 8.1, you'll see that the program includes techniques directed at the antecedents, behavior, and consequences of drinking. Several interventions using the community-reinforcement approach have been used with high rates of success in maintaining sobriety (Smith, Meyers, & Delaney, 1998; Tucker, Vuchinich, & Downey, 1992). Data from one of these interventions showing its success relative to other approaches are presented in Figure 8.2.

Classroom Programs   Multidimensional programs have been used extensively in classrooms to enhance students' academic learning and to improve their social behavior and general conduct. One program was designed to improve the social skills of nine 8- and 9-year-old deaf children with language disabilities (Rasing & Duker, 1992). The program focused on increasing several specific behaviors, such as waiting to speak without interrupting someone; calling a hearing person's name once or twice in a moderate voice to get his or her attention; and providing help, praise, or comfort to someone. It also focused on reducing certain other behaviors—aggression, screaming, and teasing other people, for example. A variety of behavioral methods were included in the program, which the children's teachers were trained to implement. These methods included providing (1) prompts for appropriate social behaviors, (2) verbal and modeled instruction regarding the specific behaviors to perform, (3) negative feedback and corrective instruction for inappropriate behaviors, and (4) immediate reinforcement for appropriate behaviors by giving praise and tokens, which the children could redeem for tangible and activity reinforcers. All of the children showed substantial increases in the appropriate social behaviors and decreases in the inappropriate behaviors.

Interventions Implemented on an Individual Basis   A wide variety of operant and respondent target behaviors have been addressed very successfully with multidimensional programs. For example, a program to increase the operant behavior of dental

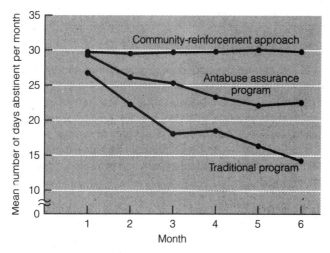

Figure 8.2 Mean number of days per month on which alcoholic clients who had received treatment with an emetic drug (disulfiram) did not drink during a 6-month follow-up period. Each of 41 clients received one of three treatments: the *community-based reinforcement approach* (a multidimensional program that included the use of disulfiram), the *antabuse assurance program* (which focused only on having the client take disulfiram in the presence of a significant other at scheduled times and places), and the *traditional program* (which simply provided the client with disulfiram and instructions on how, when, and why it should be administered). *Source:* Azrin et al., 1982, Figure 2.

flossing was conducted in the homes of four 7- to 11-year-old boys and girls (Dahlquist & Gil, 1986). In addition to providing each child with training in correct flossing procedures, the program included the following techniques. First, the intervention used prompts of two types: cards stating "Remember to Floss" were hung in the child's room and a poster describing the steps in flossing was hung in the bathroom. Second, self-monitoring was used: each child had to record instances of flossing on a calendar in the bathroom and save used floss in a bag. Third, parents were trained to evaluate their child's flossing and give praise or corrective feedback. Fourth, the child received tangible reinforcers three times a week if his or her self-monitoring and flossing quality met certain criteria. These criteria were low initially but were increased periodically during the intervention.

Functional analyses of problem CERs often determine that both respondent and operant behaviors need to be addressed. For example, a 9-year-old boy's fears relating to school resulted in his avoiding the classroom, either by refusing to go to school or hiding once there (Lazarus, Davison, & Polefka, 1965). The intervention included the use of distraction techniques to divert the boy's attention on the way to school, *in vivo* desensitization for the school situation itself, and a variety of reinforcers for going to school and interacting with classmates. Interventions have also helped children cope with fears concerning medical treatment. (Go to ▓)

A Multidimensional Program to Reduce a Fear of Upcoming Surgery

At 7 years of age, Robert had developed an intense fear of undergoing a surgical procedure that was scheduled to remove nonmalignant tumors from his legs and arms (case described in Friedman, Campbell, & Evans, 1993). The tumors, a recurrent condition that resulted from a rare disease called osteochondroma, were impairing his walking and the use of his left hand. Robert had undergone surgery to remove earlier tumors with no complications, but he vividly remembered the pain he had experienced during his recovery. Recalling one particularly salient experience provoked a great deal of anxiety: He was told that he would

> have "steel sutures" removed. He became highly agitated, making removal of the sutures more difficult and painful. Medical records reflect his level of pain, noting that "plain Tylenol is not holding him." The parents were very distressed about the amount of pain and finally requested a change in medications. This experience appeared to form the core of his current anxieties. (p. 243)

A multidimensional program was implemented to treat Robert's fear before he underwent the new round of surgery. The program included several components. First, the boy was trained to practice progressive muscle relaxation at home and to use the technique when he was afraid. Second, imaginal systematic desensitization was used to reduce his fear of the surgical environment. Third, he was taught to use self-statements, such as using "Ninja powers" to "fight off scary thoughts" when he was afraid. Fourth, his parents were instructed to prompt his use of these fear reduction techniques. Fifth, his parents were instructed to praise his brave behaviors and to reduce their attention to his fearful acts. Finally, he was promised a "Ninja-pizza" dinner and a trophy if he completed the surgery. This intervention markedly reduced his fearful behavior in presurgical medical visits, at the surgery itself, and during the following year when other medical procedures were done.

Self-Management Programs   Self-management procedures are often applied as a part of behavior therapy interventions with a therapist (Swan & McDonald, 1978). For instance, the therapist might have the client practice relaxation techniques at home, keep self-monitoring records, or provide self-reinforcement for improvements in an operant behavior. In contrast, individuals who initiate, design, and conduct self-management projects to change their behavior—for instance, as part of a college course—usually devise and implement almost all of the techniques themselves. These projects typically are multidimensional programs that include 6 to 12 different techniques (Hamilton, 1980).

A fine example of a self-management program was designed and conducted by a student of mine named Diane, the mother of a 2-year-old boy, who wanted to improve her parenting behaviors. She and her husband had decided before Andrew was born that they intended to "take a nonviolent, rational, and positive approach" toward parenting. However, Diane found that she was using more and more yelling and spanking to discipline the child. Her functional analysis of the problem revealed three antecedents to her behavior. First, she had a very hectic lifestyle so that "being a mother, wife, student, and employee leaves me very little time to relax." Second, Diane's behavior of yelling at her son and spanking him usually occurred when she was in a hurry, especially when she was getting Andrew ready to go out. Third, her rush to get the child ready initiated a chain of events: Andrew would struggle against getting dressed or groomed; his mother would yell at him; he'd scream; she'd spank his hand; he'd cry; she'd try to ignore his crying; and he'd become infuriated and cry more. These encounters left Diane "feeling horrible."

Diane's program contained many different behavioral methods, some of which are listed here:

1. Substituting the alternative responses of using calm explanations or brief time-out punishments in place of yelling and spanking when Andrew misbehaved.
2. Using self-instructions to prompt using these alternative responses.
3. Praising Andrew for behaviors that helped in the process of getting ready to go out.
4. Using thought stopping to replace negative self-statements, such as "Oh no, we're going to be late," with positive ones, such as "In the long run it isn't worth it."
5. Meditating each morning before Andrew woke up.
6. Providing a system of reinforcers, with separate rewards for (a) increasing her calm parenting behaviors while decreasing her yelling and spanking, (b) praising Andrew's help, and (c) practicing meditation.

By the end of the month-long intervention, Diane was using calm parenting 100% of the time in these interactions with Andrew, compared with only 25% of the time in baseline. She no longer yelled and spanked her little boy, and he rarely misbehaved when getting ready to go out.

FEATURES OF A GOOD PROGRAM

A "good program" to change behavior is not simply an intervention that succeeds. If someone makes a New Year's resolution to quit smoking and just stops "cold turkey," we cannot say the person used a good program. We should be able to judge whether or not a program is good before it is even conducted. We would make this judgment on the basis of the processes used in designing it and the techniques that it included. Smokers rarely succeed in quitting the first time they try, and most attempts end in returning to smoking (Sarafino, 1998). As Mark Twain noted: "To cease smoking is the easiest thing I ever did; I ought to know because I've done it a thousand times." Smokers who quit and stay quit use better designed programs than those who don't succeed.

What Makes a Behavior Change Program Good?

First and foremost, a good behavior change program has been designed on the basis of data collected in a carefully done *functional analysis*. As such, the program should be *multidimensional*, containing techniques to address the behavior itself, its antecedents, and its consequences. If the program is designed to change more than one behavior, such as a person's diet and exercise patterns, each one probably should be addressed with separate methods, such as different reinforcers. Several other features will also increase the quality of the program (Kanfer & Grimm, 1980; McLaughlin, Burgess, & Sackville-West, 1982; Morris & Ellis, 1997; Passman, 1977; Prue et al., 1980). A good program to change a person's behavior should:

1. Identify and clearly specify the target behavior(s), alternative responses, behavioral goals, and subgoals.
2. Describe the rules or criteria that will determine what consequences will apply to the behaviors to be changed.
3. If possible, involve the target person as an active participant in designing and implementing the program to change his or her behavior.
4. Provide training and reinforcers for any staff or helpers (teachers, friends, or relatives, and so on) the program may employ or enlist.
5. Assess the person's behavior carefully and arrange for some way to check that the data are accurate. When possible, enlist the help of more than one staff member or of a friend or relative to provide data to confirm self-monitoring data the person collects.
6. Use the data collected to provide feedback to the person regarding improvements in his or her behavior and progress toward goals.
7. Provide feedback to staff or helpers regarding their performance.
8. Allow for the possibility of making adjustments to the program if conditions change.
9. Introduce techniques to increase the ability of the behavior change to continue after the intervention ends and to generalize to appropriate new environments.
10. Try to maximize the person's commitment to the program and motivation for carrying out the tasks and for achieving the behavioral goals.

Deciding Which Techniques to Use

The first consideration in deciding which techniques to use in changing a behavior is which ones are likely to be highly effective. Whenever possible, of course, choose the most effective methods for the type of problem to be addressed. For instance, when trying to increase an operant behavior, it is essential to include a strong system of reinforcers. When trying to reduce a fear with systematic desensitization, *in vivo* stimuli should be used in preference to imaginal ones if possible.

Another consideration in choosing techniques is practicality, especially in the time or effort they require and their financial cost. Some techniques are very economical of

CONCEPT CHECK 8.1

1. Interventions that contain techniques to address the antecedents, behavior, and consequences are called _____ programs.
2. A technique that could be useful for reducing a behavioral excess but not for changing a behavioral deficit might be _____ . ⇔
3. To generate alternative solutions in designing an intervention, it is helpful to use the method of _____ .
4. A component of the community-reinforcement approach for treating alcohol abuse that is directed at managing behavioral consequences is _____ . ⇔
5. The first consideration in deciding to use a technique for a behavior change program is this: Is it likely to be _____ ?
6. Techniques that are moderately or highly _____ should be considered for a behavior change program only as a last resort.

Answers: 1. multidimensional, 2. punishment/extinction, 3. brainstorming, 4. reinforcing taking disulfiram, 5. highly effective, 6. aversive

time and money. Shortcut methods for shaping or stimulus control are examples of very effective, economical techniques. Other methods are complicated or burdensome to implement, sometimes requiring tremendous amounts of time to carry out properly; overcorrection punishment procedures are an example (Kelly & Drabman, 1977). Time-consuming methods are often rejected if they will be implemented by paid staff or therapists, thereby adding to the cost of the intervention, or by friends or relatives, who may be unwilling or unable to give very much of their time. High expenses for materials, such as tangible reinforcers, may also influence our choice of specific methods in designing a given program.

Decisions to use punishment or other aversive procedures should be made very carefully in designing programs to change behavior. In most cases, aversive methods are rejected because the behavior can be changed effectively with other methods. Using moderately or highly aversive procedures should be considered only as a last resort and only when the (1) behavior is very maladaptive, (2) intervention is carried out under professional supervision, (3) the program has gotten appropriate ethical approval, and (4) the procedure contains safeguards to protect the client. Punishment procedures that are only mildly unpleasant, such as covert punishment or some forms of time-out, are usually more acceptable, but a program that includes them should be approved by a professional or other supervisor. Keep in mind that one of the drawbacks in using aversive procedures is that they can reduce the person's motivation to participate in the program (Wilson et al., 1975; Wilson & Tracey, 1976). (Go to ✔)

SCALE OF MOTIVATION TO CHANGE BEHAVIOR

Use these seven questions to evaluate a client's motivation to change his or her behavior. On the basis of information from direct and indirect assesment methods, *rate* each item in the space preceding it, using a 5-point scale on which 0 = "Not much or often," 2 = "Fairly much or often," and 4 = "Very much or often."

_____ How *often* has the client clearly stated he or she wants to change?

_____ How *much* strength in a desire to change do the client's verbal and gestural expressions suggest he or she may have?

_____ How *often* has the client canceled, delayed, or been late for therapy appointments?

_____ With how *much* care and regularity has the client kept requested records of his or her behavior and its antecedents and consequences?

_____ With how *much* care and regularity has the client completed therapy homework assignments, such as doing relaxation exercises or developing a list of feared stimuli?

_____ How *much* openness and cooperation has the client shown in answering questions in therapy sessions?

_____ How *much* attentiveness has the client shown during therapy sessions?

_____ **Total Score** (The sum of the ratings reflects the client's overal motivation to change. Low ratings of individual items may suggest the need for specific efforts to address relevant factors.)

Figure 8.3 The Scale of Motivation to Change Behavior is designed to assess client motivation in individual therapy, but similar items could be rated in other types of interventions. *Source:* Based on Cautela & Upper, 1975.

MOTIVATIONAL FACTORS TO CONSIDER

People who are highly motivated to change their behavior are more likely to participate in and succeed in interventions for making the change (Cautela & Upper, 1975; Granlund et al., 1998; Hamilton, 1980; Kanfer & Grimm, 1980; Perri & Richards, 1977). Assessing motivation to change is important in individual therapy, especially if the client will be using self-management techniques, such as doing homework assignments that involve self-monitoring, covert conditioning, or relaxation exercises. A therapist can assess the client's motivation by using the Scale of Motivation to Change Behavior presented in Figure 8.3.

People's Readiness to Change

An important factor in people's motivation to change a behavior is their level of *self-efficacy*—that is, their belief that they have the ability to succeed at a specific task they

---

CLOSE-UP 8.1

The Stages of Change Model

The **stages of change model** is a theory that describes five potential *stages* through which people's motivation and intention to modify their behavior can progress (DiClemente et al., 1991; Prochaska & DiClemente, 1984; Prochaska, DiClemente, & Norcross, 1992). These stages are arranged from lowest to highest readiness to change:

1. *Precontemplation*. People in this stage are not seriously considering changing the behavior in question—smoking, for instance—at least during the next several months or so. These people may never have thought about changing or may have decided against it.

2. *Contemplation*. During this stage, people are aware a problem exists and are seriously considering trying to change within the next several months. But they are not yet ready to make a commitment to take action.

3. *Preparation*. At this stage, individuals plan to pursue a behavioral goal, such as stopping smoking, within the next month and have tried to reach that goal in the past year without being fully successful.

4. *Action*. This stage spans a period of time, usually 6 months, from the start of a successful effort to change a behavior.

5. *Maintenance*. People in this stage work to maintain the successful behavior changes they achieved.

According to the stages of change model, people who are currently in one stage show different behavioral and cognitive characteristics from people in other stages. For instance, people in the precontemplation stage regarding a behavior, such as smoking, are likely to have less self-efficacy and see more disadvantages than advantages for changing that behavior. People's own efforts or those of others to change the behavior are not very likely to succeed in that stage.

---

want to do. In the case of changing a behavior, people need to believe they can carry out the necessary activities to achieve their behavioral goals. Self-efficacy is a critical element in people's "readiness" to begin and participate in self-management activities. The role of people's readiness to change their behavior is the main focus of a motivational theory called the stages of change model. (Go to 🔎)

Ways to Enhance Motivation to Change

What can be done to strengthen a person's motivation to participate in and complete an intervention to change a problem behavior? The intervention can contain provisions to help the person have *realistic expectations* about the behavior change process, a *sense of commitment* to the program's goals, and *social support and supervision*.

Realistic Expectations   At the start of an intervention to change behavior, the target person needs to develop realistic expectations about the procedures that will be used, the effort they will require, and how quickly and smoothly the progress toward the behavioral goal is likely to be (Kanfer & Grimm, 1980). One expectation that can enhance motivation is that the burdensome requirements of the program generally are temporary and brief. For example, collecting detailed data for a functional analysis is over in several days, and the amount of time one needs to spend practicing relaxation exercises decreases after a week or two. In addition, the person should be informed that improvements in behavior are usually slower to emerge early in the intervention than later on and that setbacks or lapses in progress are commonly experienced. A **lapse** is an instance of backsliding —sort of a "mistake"—in the person's performance. For instance, a person who has stopped smoking might have a cigarette one day. People should expect to have occasional lapses, especially when they are trying to change habitual or lifestyle behaviors.

People's motivation to change a behavior can also be enhanced by knowing the program has provisions or techniques they can use to reduce the usual temptations they experience as antecedents to the unwanted behavior. For instance, individuals who are trying to limit their intake of fattening foods might eat low-calorie foods either before going to a party or restaurant or early in the meal, thereby decreasing the temptation to have dessert. Other methods we've discussed for dealing with antecedents can also help. Because people who want to change their behavior often have doubts about their self-efficacy to deal with tempting antecedents, they need to know what techniques they can use and how to use them when temptations arise.

Another way to enhance people's motivation to participate in an intervention to change their behavior is to include in the program a provision called a **rule-release,** in which the person is *released* from restrictive *rules* of the program under certain *specific and limited conditions*. Rule-releases are especially useful when the program restricts behaviors the person enjoys, such as eating fattening foods, or requires behaviors the person doesn't enjoy, such as studying. The rule-release should identify *in advance* the specific conditions under which the restrictive rules won't apply. For example, rule-releases that could be used in programs to decrease calorie intake, reduce excessive drinking, and increase studying are:

- "I can have dessert on Friday and Saturday nights if I go out to dinner or to a party. I can overeat on Thanksgiving Day."
- "I can drink four beers at a party, and I can go to a maximum of two parties in any week. Beer is the only alcoholic beverage I can have."
- "I don't have to study on Thursday nights or on Saturdays."

The purpose of rule-releases is to eliminate individuals' making negative self-statements, such as "I can never eat what I like" or "I never have time to enjoy myself." Statements like these demoralize people and decrease their motivation to adhere to the program. Rule-releases are not appropriate for all behaviors one might want to change, but they can be useful in some cases.

When designing rule-releases, keep two guidelines in mind. First, the release from the program's rules must be *guaranteed*. Reinforcers are contingent on the target person's behavior, but rule-releases are not. So, in the increased studying example of rule-releases listed, no matter how much the student studied during the week, Thursday nights and Saturdays were free. The consequences a program provides to increase study-ing would apply to all other times. Second, rule-releases *should not include lapses*. That is, they should not be described as allowing an unwanted behavior whenever the antecedents for backsliding are very strong. For example, someone who is trying to stick to an exercise routine should not have a rule-release that says, "I don't have to exercise if I have too much work to do." Rule-releases should describe conditions that are predetermined, specific, and limited.

A Sense of Commitment to Change   Having a sense of commitment to the goals of a behavior change program increases the person's motivation to adhere to it. One way to increase people's commitment to stick to the program is to have them simply state to others the goals they want to achieve and the actions they intend to take to reach those goals. Research has found that asking people to state verbally or in writing what they will do increases the likelihood that they will do it (Griffen & Watson, 1978; Kulik & Carlino, 1987; Ward & Stare, 1990). Writing out one's intentions makes the commitment more formal and concrete, as illustrated in this *commitment statement:*

> I plan to exercise more, and will eventually walk 2 miles five times a week and do 20 minutes of aerobics three times a week. I am committed to changing my behavior to reach the goal I've chosen and will work hard to carry out the program.

Making a public commitment that describes the behavioral goals and consequences may be especially important when the person will self-administer reinforcement (Hayes et al., 1985). It may be that having others know the contingency makes the person more careful in judging whether reinforcers have been earned.

Another simple approach individuals can use to increase their commitment to a behavior change program is to have them write out a list of *pros and cons*—the advantages of changing and the disadvantages of not changing. Long- and short-term advantages and disadvantages should be included. The list of pros and cons can be posted on a wall to serve as a prompt or on a card and kept handy to consult when temptations arise.

People's commitment to completing a behavior change intervention can also be enhanced by having them *invest a great deal* of effort or money in the program. For instance, doing a functional analysis represents an investment of time, and sometimes the person needs to buy equipment to carry out a program. When tempted to lapse, the person can reflect on how much he or she has already invested. Probably a better approach for many people is to deposit items of value—such as clothing, jewelry, or money—with a friend or relative (Wysocki et al., 1979). The person must then earn these items back by performing activities required in the program. Whatever the person does not earn back can be given away. For instance, leftover money could go to a charity the person respects to some degree but ordinarily would not support.

Social Support and Supervision   Interventions appear to be more effective in changing behavior if the person receives social support and supervision for performing activities in the program (Passman, 1977). For instance, a study of married cigarette smokers found that those who quit and did not smoke again during the next 6 months reported greater helpfulness on the part of their spouses in the effort to quit than did smokers who either never quit or quit but returned to smoking later (Mermelstein, Lichtenstein, & McIntyre, 1983). Other studies have shown that individuals who use a manual to carry out a self-management program without supervision of any kind are unlikely to follow the program or succeed in changing their behavior (Marshall, Presse, & Andrews, 1976; Zeiss, 1978). Having someone with training in behavior management programs to consult with, even for a few minutes a week by telephone, appears to improve people's motivation and success in carrying out the program.

ASSEMBLING MATERIALS FOR THE PROGRAM

Before starting an intervention, we need to prepare and assemble all of the materials we plan to use in carrying out the program. These materials may include data sheets, any supplies or equipment for performing the behavior, and reinforcers. In addition, it's often useful to formalize the elements of the program into a *behavioral contract*, which is sometimes called a "contingency contract."

Developing a Behavioral Contract

A **behavioral contract** is a formal, written and signed agreement that states explicitly what the target behavior is, the conditions under which it should or should not be performed, and the outcomes for performing that behavior. In other words, a behavioral contract describes the behavior and its antecedents and consequences (DeRisi & Butz, 1975; Homme, 1971; O'Banion & Whaley, 1981; Stuart, 1971).

The agreement generally is made between and signed by at least two parties: the *person* whose behavior is to change and a *mediator*, an individual who can and will monitor the behavior and dispense the consequences. The mediator can be the target person's therapist, teacher, coworker, friend, or relative. In some cases, more than one mediator is involved, and in self-management programs, the two parties may be the same person. The contract should indicate the roles of all parties, and each one should sign. From this description, we can state that a good behavioral contract should contain or clearly describe the following elements:

1. Target behaviors and antecedents, specifying the behaviors, the occasions when they should be performed, and behavioral improvements that may be required. The reasons for the intervention and the behavioral goals can be indicated. Rule-releases should be clearly specified.

2. Monitoring process, including who will observe the behavior, the type of data to be collected, and how these data will be recorded and made available to determine the consequences.

3. Consequences, which ideally should include immediate and delayed reinforcers for meeting the terms of the contract, as well as penalties for not doing so. Penalties usually take the form of time-out or response cost punishment. The contract should specify who will dispense the consequences, and when.

BEHAVIORAL CONTRACT

Between Dick and his roommate Bob
Date: _____

1. *Target behaviors and antecedents:* Dick's anxieties in taking tests in college have impaired his performance. As part of an intervention he helped design to reduce his test anxiety to manageable levels, he must practice progressive muscle relaxation for 30 minutes each morning for 2 weeks, after which the sessions will be shortened to 10 minutes each.

2. *Monitoring process:* Bob will serve as the mediator, observing and keeping records of Dick's frequency of doing relaxation exercises.

3. *Consequences:* If Dick does his exercises for the day, he will earn a token and be allowed to watch TV that night. When he has earned five tokens, he can rent a videotape of his choosing to watch with Bob. If Dick does not do the exercises on any day, he must pay Bob one dollar that night.

4. *Bonus reward:* If Dick does the relaxation exercises at least six mornings in a given week, Bob will do some of Dick's housekeeping chores for one half hour.

5. *Schedule for reviewing progress:* Every Sunday with Bob.

6. *Signatures:* By signing below, I agree to follow the terms of this contract.

Dick _____

Bob _____

Figure 8.4 Sample of a fairly simple behavioral contract to encourage a young man to perform progressive muscle relaxation exercises.

4. Bonus rewards for high-level, consistent compliance with the terms of the contract. A study found that supplementing a standard token reinforcement program with bonus rewards produced further improvements in performance (Swain & McLaughlin, 1998).

5. A schedule for reviewing the target person's progress, the rate at which reinforcement has been given, and any problems that may need to be addressed.

6. Signatures of all parties involved.

The terms of the agreement should be negotiated by the parties, not simply imposed on the person by someone who has power. The terms can also be adjusted if any of the parties discovers problems or flaws when trying to carry out the agreement. A new contract can be negotiated when the current one expires. Figures 8.4 and 8.5 give samples of behavioral contracts and illustrate that they can vary in complexity.

BEHAVIORAL CONTRACT

Between Jo and Her Teacher and Mother

Date: _____

1. *Target behaviors and antecedents:* Jo has refused to go to school for the past 3 weeks, and when she was going she often failed to do her homework, claiming she "forgot" to take home the books she needed. The five target behaviors she must do are: (a) not fussing at home when getting ready to go to school, (b) arriving at school each day on time, (c) attending all classes as scheduled, (d) taking home all of her books, and (e) submitting acceptable homework on time.

2. *Monitoring process:* Jo's mother will observe and keep records of her getting ready for school and bringing home her books. Her teacher will observe the three in-school behaviors and write his initials at the end of each day on a card next to any of the three listed behaviors she performed acceptably.

3. *Consequences:* At the end of each school day that Jo earns two or more initalings on her card, she may feed the class hamster or choose a book for the teacher to read to the class on the next school day. She will take the card home. Jo's mother will review with her each day's card and records regarding Jo's fussing and bringing home books. When Jo has accumulated ten acceptably performed behaviors, she may choose one of the following rewards: (a) have a friend over to play, (b) eat a candy bar, (c) have first choice of what to watch on TV for an hour that night, (d) help her mother make cookies, (e) take some homemade cookies as a treat for her class. If Jo's records show fewer than three acceptably performed behaviors on any school day, she cannot have her usual snack before bedtime. Rule-release: If Jo is clearly ill (e.g., has a fever), these rules are suspended until she is well.

4. *Bonus rewards:* If Jo's records show all five behaviors performed acceptably on each of three school days in one calendar week, she may choose a videotape for her mother to rent and watch it that night.

5. *Schedule for reviewing progress:* Every day with her teacher at school and mother at home. Her teacher and mother will talk on the phone every Friday.

6. *Signatures:* By signing below, I agree to follow the terms of this contract.

Jo _____

Mother _____

Teacher _____

Figure 8.5 Sample of a moderately complex behavioral contract for an 8-year-old girl with school-related behavior problems.

You can see in Figure 8.5 that agreements can involve more than one behavior, more than one mediator, and several reinforcers. In addition, agreements can designate separate reinforcers for different behaviors. For example, Richard Stuart (1971) helped develop a contract for a delinquent 16-year-old girl named Candy and her parents. It stated that (1) Candy could go out one weekend evening until 11:30 p.m. and not have to account for her whereabouts if she maintained "a weekly average of 'B' in the academic ratings of all her classes" and that (2) she could go out in the afternoons on weekend days and holidays if she "completed all household chores *before* leaving" and agreed to call her parents once while she was out.

Negotiating the Terms of a Behavioral Contract   Behavioral contracts generally provide for outcomes that are wanted by all parties. In Candy's case, she wanted some freedom to socialize with friends, and her parents wanted her delinquent behavior to decrease and her performance of schoolwork and household chores to improve. In the contract presented in Figure 8.4, Dick and Bob were good friends, and Bob wanted to help.

Because the conditions of the agreement affect all parties, each should have a say in the contract's provisions (Kanfer & Grimm, 1980; O'Banion & Whaley, 1981). Being a mediator is an imposition: it takes time and effort, and often there is no pay. Thus, a mediator's motivation to follow the agreement will depend on provisions the contract contains. Sometimes it's useful to include provisions for reinforcing the mediator's activities. Because the motivation of the target person is also critical to the success of the behavior change program, he or she should have a say in which reinforcers the program will use and the criteria for earning them. Standards that are simply imposed by others lead to smaller changes in behavior than standards the person has helped to develop (Dickerson & Creedon, 1981; Lovitt & Curtiss, 1969). The parties to a contract usually negotiate among themselves to reach an agreement they think is fair and reasonable for them to follow. Having a therapist supervise the negotiations can help in developing a contract that contains few or no flaws in it and will achieve what each party wants.

An intervention to improve the homework performance of four 9- to 11-year-old students employed negotiated behavioral contracts between each child and one of his or her parents (Miller & Kelley, 1994). Two types of negotiation occurred throughout the intervention. First, for each homework assignment, the parent and child negotiated the division of the task into "challenging, yet attainable" goals for the child to complete. Each party would suggest a goal and then negotiate a compromise, which was recorded. For instance, they might agree that the child should complete five math problems in the next 10 minutes. Second, each week the parent and child negotiated the rewards for the child's bringing home the needed homework materials and achieving the goals agreed upon for each assignment. For these negotiations, the parent was to

identify several rewards from which the child could choose and to change the rewards occasionally to prevent the child from becoming bored with reward choices. Rewards were different for each child and included special snacks, small amounts of money (e.g., 25 cents), stickers, and late bedtime as daily rewards, and renting a videotape, having a friend spend the night, or a trip to a shopping mall as weekly rewards. (p. 78)

The parents received instructions on listening carefully to the child's views, offering a variety of solutions, avoiding criticism, and being willing to compromise. All four of the children showed substantial improvements in their homework performance during the intervention.

Benefits of Using Behavioral Contracts   Using behavioral contracts to formalize the procedures to change behavior has several advantages. First, a contract ensures that the parties know what their roles are and what the conditions of the program are, thereby minimizing disagreements and errors in implementing the roles and conditions. Second, having all parties sign the contract enhances their commitment to fulfilling their roles. Third, putting the conditions in writing makes it easier for the parties to see how much progress is being made in changing the target behavior and how close the program is to meeting its goals. Fourth, negotiating a contract increases the likelihood that the program will contain elements that will lead to success. Fifth, negotiating a contract and structuring difficult interpersonal relationships may help to improve the way the parties interact. Finally, using a contract enables each party to estimate more clearly the costs in time and money for participating in the program.

Preparing Other Program Materials

To carry out a program to change behavior, we must prepare and assemble all materials *in advance* of their use (Homme, 1971). At least a week's supply of all data sheets and other needed forms should always be available. Reinforcers that are planned for use must be available as soon as they are scheduled to be given. We mustn't run out and have to delay a reinforcer or substitute another. In addition, various materials may be necessary for the person to perform the target behaviors or other program activities. For instance, if the target behavior involves a child's homework assignments from school, all books and stationery items must be ready to use at each study session. If the behavior involves household chores, the cleaning materials and equipment must be available when needed. If the target person will be doing relaxation exercises, any taped protocols to be used should be ready when needed. We must plan for and anticipate all items we'll need for all aspects, phases, and procedures of the intervention. (Go to ✔)

Tips on Designing a Program

Selecting the techniques to use for an intervention and putting them together are the most critical tasks in designing a program to change behavior. We must do these tasks very carefully. Research has identified several factors that can help in this process (Charlop et al., 1988; Gross & Drabman, 1982; Hamilton, 1980; Heffernan & Richards, 1981; Perri & Richards, 1977). These factors are included in these tips on designing a program.

CONCEPT CHECK 8.2

1. The motivational theory that focuses on people's readiness to change their behavior is called the _____ model.
2. Cigarette smokers who realize they should quit for health reasons and are thinking about ways to do it, but have not yet decided when they might start, are probably in the _____ stage of readiness to change. ⇔
3. An instance of backsliding for a program's target behavior is called a(n) _____.
4. An example of a rule-release you might use in a program to reduce TV watching is: _____. ⇔
5. A formal written agreement describing the target behavior and the antecedents and consequences that will apply in an intervention is called a(n) _____.
6. An example of materials that should be assembled before starting an intervention is _____. ⇔

Answers: 1. stages of change, 2. contemplation, 3. lapse, 4. "I can watch any amount of TV on Saturdays," 5. behavioral contract, 6. data sheets/reinforcers

1. Use techniques to address the target behavior itself as well as its antecedents and consequences.
2. If more than one target behavior is involved in the program, use separate reinforcers and behavioral criteria for each to make sure each improves.
3. Use several techniques from Figure 8.1 for each behavior, but using more than 10 usually doesn't add much to a program's effectiveness.
4. In assessing the behavior, try to have some way to confirm the accuracy of the data that are collected. Although the best way to do this is to have a second observer make independent assessments at the same time, this ideal is not always possible. A useful but less precise approach is to have someone who has many opportunities to observe the behavior make assessments of it at convenient times, thereby permitting comparisons of the two sets of data.
5. Make sure each instance of the desired behavior will receive some form of reinforcer immediately, even if it's just a covert or token reinforcer, and that at least one relatively more powerful reinforcer will be given each day that the behavior meets the criterion that was set. The criterion can become more rigorous during the intervention if there is reason to believe that doing so would help achieve the behavioral goals.
6. It may be useful to vary the specific reinforcers or punishers used if it seems likely that they will become "boring" or in some other way less powerful.
7. It's usually a good idea to provide reinforcers for performing self-management activities, such as keeping records carefully or doing relaxation exercises.

8. Estimate the likely costs of the program in time and money and make adjustments to the design if the costs will be more than is feasible.

9. Make lists of the responsibilities and activities of each party involved in carrying out the program, and set a schedule for reviewing progress and discussing problems that may arise.

SUMMARY

Interventions can direct techniques at the three dimensions of a problem behavior: the behavior itself, its antecedents, and its consequences. Multidimensional programs address more than one dimension of the problem behavior. When designing a multidimensional program, it's usually a good idea to generate many alternative solutions by using the brainstorming method. Multidimensional programs have been applied to improve a wide variety of behaviors, including classroom conduct problems, children's self-help skills, parenting skills, children's fears, and excessive alcohol use. "Good" behavior change programs usually are multidimensional and contain features to ensure that the program is carried out carefully, provide ways to collect and use accurate data effectively, and motivate all involved parties.

Highly motivated individuals are more likely to participate in interventions to change their behavior and are more likely to succeed. People's motivation and readiness to participate in a behavior change program are likely to be fairly high if they have high levels of self-efficacy. According to the stages of change model, individuals' readiness to change can progress through five stages: precontemplation, contemplation, preparation, action, and maintenance. One way to enhance people's motivation to change their behavior is to make sure they have realistic expectations about the procedures that will be used, the effort required, and the progress that is likely to be seen. For instance, they should be aware that lapses are likely to occur. Additional ways to enhance motivation include providing rule-releases in the program design, using techniques to increase the person's sense of commitment, and making sure the person has sufficient social support and supervision for completing the intervention.

A behavioral contract is a negotiated agreement that describes the conditions of the intervention. It describes the target behaviors and antecedents, the monitoring process, the consequences, the bonus reward(s), and a schedule for reviewing progress in the intervention. It also contains the signatures of all parties. All materials, including any behavioral contracts, to be used in the program should be prepared and assembled before the intervention begins.

KEY TERMS

multidimensional programs	stages of change model	rule-release
brainstorming	lapse	behavioral contract

REVIEW QUESTIONS

1. What are multidimensional programs?
2. Describe the three rules to use when applying the brainstorming method.
3. Outline the community-reinforcement approach to treating alcoholism, and illustrate the multidimensional components of this program.
4. Describe the multidimensional components of the program Friedman, Campbell, and Evans (1993) used to reduce the fear of surgery of a boy named Robert.
5. List several characteristics of a "good" program to change behavior.
6. What factors go into deciding which techniques to use in a program to change behavior?
7. Describe the stages of change model, using examples related to increasing a person's exercising.
8. Define "lapse" and give two examples.
9. Define "rule-release" and give two examples.
10. What two guidelines should be kept in mind when designing a rule-release?
11. What is a behavioral contract, and what six elements should it have?
12. Describe four benefits of using behavioral contracts.

RELATED READINGS

DeRisi, W. J., & Butz, G. (1975). *Writing behavioral contracts: A case simulation practice manual.* Champaign, IL: Research Press.

Hamilton, S. B. (1980). Instructionally-based training in self-control: Behavior-specific and generalized outcomes resulting from student-implemented self-modification projects. *Teaching of Psychology, 7,* 140–145.

Heffernan, T., & Richards, C. S. (1981). Self-control of study behavior: Identification and evaluation of natural methods. *Journal of Counseling Psychology, 28,* 361–364.

Kanfer, F. H., & Grimm, L. G. (1980). Managing clinical change: A process model of therapy. *Behavior Modification, 4,* 419–444.

Stuart, R. B. (1971). Behavioral contracting within the families of delinquents. *Journal of Behavior Therapy and Experimental Psychiatry, 2,* 1–11.

Organizing and using data in tables or graphs can be done manually or with the aid of computers.

CHAPTER NINE

Organizing and Using Data

Try to picture the work schedule of a creative person, such as a famous novelist. Do you picture this person sitting down to write when he or she feels inspired with a great idea? If no rush of inspiration exists on a particular day, does the novelist simply do something else? You might believe, as many others do, that people can't be creative "on call" or at will because creativity happens spontaneously. If you believe this, you may also feel we can't set behavioral goals for creativity— it happens when it happens.

Maybe these beliefs hold true for some authors, but many famous novelists work on a regular schedule, keep track of how much they produce, and set behavioral goals and subgoals for their work (Wallace & Pear, 1977). For example, when American novelist Ernest Hemingway was interviewed, he revealed how he kept

> track of his daily progress—"so as not to kid myself"—on a large chart. . . . The numbers on the chart showing the daily output of words differ from 450, 575, 462, 1250, back to 512, the higher figures on days Hemingway puts in extra work so he won't feel guilty spending the following day fishing on the Gulf Stream. (Plimpton, 1963, p. 219)

Looking at these data, you can see that Hemingway paced himself at about 500 words a day, plus or minus, say, 50 or so.

Other great authors have used similar self-monitoring methods to set numerical writing goals and stick to them. The British novelist Anthony Trollope described in his autobiography that he

> allotted myself so many pages a week. The average number has been about 40. It has been placed as low as 20, and has risen to 112. And as a page is an ambiguous term, my page has been made to contain 250 words. . . . I have had every word counted as I went. (Trollope, 1946, p. 117)

He clearly kept close track of his progress. Trollope worked at a fairly steady pace and at perhaps twice Hemingway's rate in pages. He felt that falling below his writing goals for a week or more was "a blister to my eye" and "a sorrow to my heart." He noted in his autobiography that others had chided him for keeping data to motivate his writing, saying it was "beneath the notice of a man of genius." But he knew he would not be nearly as productive otherwise.

Data serve many useful functions. They make a permanent record of what currently exists and what has occurred in the past. By comparing current and past data, we can clarify our understanding of the whole situation and tell precisely how much change has taken place over time. We have seen in earlier chapters that using data in these ways enables us to assess a target behavior and tell whether an intervention has changed it. The present chapter examines how to use and organize data to enhance their usefulness in evaluating and improving programs to change behavior.

WAYS TO USE AND ORGANIZE DATA

We can't really know a target behavior very clearly or fully until we've assessed it by collecting data. The data we collect provides more detailed and accurate information about the behavior than we've ever had before. This information is most useful when we know what to look for and how to organize it.

What the Data Tell Us

Data tell us the current status and history of **variables**—or characteristics of people, objects, or events that can *vary* or change. Behavior is a variable, and its antecedents and consequences are variables too. The data we collect on these variables can clarify different issues or concerns at different points in planning and conducting a program to change a target behavior.

When we do a functional analysis, the data tell us what antecedents and consequences are associated with the behavior. By seeing these connections, we can choose the most appropriate techniques to use in a program to change the behavior. Baseline data give us a representative picture of the extent or severity of the problem behavior before the intervention begins. Sometimes these data will tell us that the behavior is not as serious a problem as we had believed. Without these data, we might have implemented a program for a behavior that didn't really need to be changed. But the main role of baseline data is to give a reference point for comparison during the intervention phase. Data collected during the intervention tell us how well the behavior change program is working.

Organizing Data

To find out what the data can tell us about a behavior and whether it is changing, we'll need to organize the data so they present a clear picture. Obviously, we'll need to organize the data chronologically to see whether the behavior has changed over time. Other approaches to organizing data are also used, but the need to use them may be less obvious. Choosing approaches to organize data entails a consideration of characteristics of the data and an awareness of what we are trying to find out about the behavior. We'll begin looking at ways to organize data by considering how arithmetic calculations can help.

Using Arithmetic Calculations   Suppose the data we collected fluctuated quite a lot from one observation or time block to the next. For instance, suppose the data pertained to cursing behavior, and they were as follows for 14 successive days: 38, 9, 3, 22, 7, 40, 21, 31, 5, 9, 23, 4, 39, and 8. How much did the person curse overall? Did the target behavior decrease over time? It's hard to tell, isn't it? The picture these data present is not at all clear because they vary so much.

When the collected data vary a great deal, we can clarify the picture they present by calculating the average, or **mean,** value for a set of data. To calculate the mean, add up the scores and divide the total by the number of scores you added up. In the cursing data, the overall total is 259, which, when divided by 14, gives a mean of 18.5 instances of cursing per day. In the first and second weeks, the means are 20 and 17, respectively. Cursing occurred frequently and decreased somewhat from the first to the second week. Calculating the mean organizes the data by smoothing out the record to estimate the general level of the behavior. Probably the most common approach for calculating means involves grouping the data by weeks, as we just did. This is because many behaviors fluctuate by the day of the week. A person might curse very frequently on, say, Mondays and Thursdays, and rarely on Sundays.

Suppose a different problem exists in our data: we want to compare a person's behavior for two time periods or circumstances, but the *opportunities* to perform the behavior were different for the two sets of data. For instance, suppose an intervention was implemented to reduce a clerk's impatient behavior toward indecisive customers. To check the progress of the program, we decide to compare the frequencies of impatient behaviors in the baseline week and the first week of intervention. These data were 12 and 4, respectively. This drop might suggest that the clerk's behavior had improved, but the number of indecisive customers who came into the store when the clerk was on duty also dropped sharply from 30 to 10 in those weeks.

How can we clarify whether the clerk's behavior improved? We can solve this problem by comparing percentages, as we discussed in Chapter 2. *Percentages* organize data by combining instances of when the behavior did and did not occur when it ordinarily would or should have, thereby taking into account opportunities for the behavior to occur. By calculating a percentage, we can find out *how much* the behavior occurred *in proportion to the opportunities* for it to occur. To calculate a percentage, divide the data representing the behavior's instances of occurrence by the opportunities to

Table 9.1 Frequency of cigarette smoking each day for 2 weeks of baseline

Day of Week	Weeks	
	One	Two
Monday	19	15
Tuesday	16	17
Wednesday	16	18
Thursday	17	16
Friday	17	17
Saturday	24	25
Sunday	21	20

occur in the corresponding time period or circumstances and multiply by 100. In our example, we would separate the sets of data—that is, baseline and intervention. For each set, divide the number of behaviors by the corresponding number of indecisive customers the clerk served and then multiply by 100. Doing this with the data already discussed reveals that the percentage of indecisive customers with whom the clerk was impatient stayed at 40% in baseline and also in the first week of intervention. Thus, the target behavior had not improved.

Whenever we design a behavior change program and think the opportunities to perform the behavior might fluctuate across the time periods or circumstances we will want to compare, we must collect data on the opportunities to perform the behavior. Without these data, we won't be able to calculate percentages. Interventions of many types can use percentages to evaluate behavioral improvements. For instance, programs to increase the amount of studying students do often find that the opportunities to study—that is, the amount of time available after excluding necessary commitments, such as to attend class or work—vary widely for different days and different weeks. To calculate percentages for a set of data, we would collect data on the amount of time available and the duration of studying for each day. We would then divide duration by time available to yield a percentage.

Calculating means and percentages can also be useful in comparing data that cover unequal lengths of time, such as if you want to compare the target behavior during 2 weeks of baseline and 4 weeks of intervention.

Using Tables A **table** is a systematic arrangement of data in rows and columns for easy reference. It organizes the data visually, giving a whole picture, so we can see patterns and make comparisons in the data plainly and quickly. The data in tables are usually numerical, and the rows and columns can be divided on the basis of any variable we want to examine, such as different periods of time or different types of antecedents, behaviors, or consequences. Table 9.1 presents an example of tabular data that a student named Tom compiled for the baseline phase of a self-management project to reduce cigarette smoking gradually.

Notice four features about this table. First, not only do we get a sense of how much Tom smoked, but we can see that he smoked more on weekends than during the week. This is an example of how tables can help us see patterns and make comparisons. Second, an array of data like this one is called a "Table" and given a number that reflects the order in which it was first mentioned in the text material. Third, the text material refers to Tom's tabular material by number ("Table 9.1 presents . . ."). Fourth, the table has a descriptive title. A table should always have a title and be referred to by its number in the text material.

A quotation in the beginning of this chapter revealed Ernest Hemingway's self-monitoring technique: the famous author recorded in a "chart" the number of words he had written each day. The term *chart* has a very broad meaning—it can mean a table, a graph, a diagram, a map, or just a sheet of paper that has a grid printed on it for use in recording data. As a result, the term *chart* is rarely used in scientific papers.

GRAPHING OUR DATA

A **graph** is a drawing that depicts variations within a set of data, typically showing how one variable changed with changes in another variable. Throughout this book, graphs have illustrated the effectiveness of different interventions in changing behavior. Data collection and precise records are essential parts of the scientific method and assessments of programs to change behavior. A graph that is constructed in a careful and direct way provides the clearest picture of any changes that occurred in the target behavior over chronological time or when particular techniques were applied.

Types of Graphs

Graphs can take several forms, and we will discuss three: line graphs, bar graphs, and cumulative graphs. Each of these graphs is constructed with a *horizontal axis*, or "abscissa," and a *vertical axis*, or "ordinate." In graphs of data from behavior change programs, the vertical axis typically represents some measure of behavior, such as frequency or duration, and the horizontal axis represents another variable, such as chronological time or the type of procedure applied.

Line graphs use straight lines to connect successive data points that represent the intersects of plotted values for the variables scaled along the horizontal and vertical axes. Line graphs are the most common type of graph used in assessing programs to change behavior, and the horizontal axis almost always scales chronological time, spanning baseline and intervention phases of a program. That axis is usually divided into and labeled to indicate periods in which intervention techniques were used or not used. Figure 9.1 gives an illustration of a line graph based on data from Tom's self-management project to reduce his cigarette smoking. Each data point in the graph reflects the number of cigarettes he smoked on a given day. Tom didn't quit entirely by the end of the semester, but you can see that his smoking declined markedly: the mean

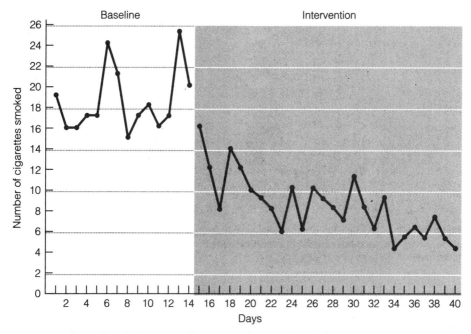

Figure 9.1 Illustration of a line graph. The data are from a self-management project conducted by Tom, a student who wanted to quit smoking.

number of cigarettes he smoked per day was 18.43 in baseline and 5.14 in the last week shown in the graph. Tom planned to continue the program after the semester ended. In some programs, the horizontal axis of a line graph covers several phases, such as when two or more intervention techniques are used in sequence.

Bar graphs use vertically arranged rectangles to represent data points scaled along the vertical axis. The rectangles, or "bars," are usually spaced along and extend up from the horizontal axis to the appropriate point represented on the vertical axis. The bar graph illustrated in Figure 9.2 shows that each bar reflects the behavior of individuals categorized by the groups or circumstances in which they were assessed. Sometimes the rectangles in bar graphs are arranged horizontally instead of vertically. If so, the axes are switched so that the measure of behavior runs along the horizontal axis and the categories are spaced along the vertical axis.

Cumulative graphs, or *cumulative records,* are line graphs in which the measure of behavior accumulates across units scaled along the horizontal axis. Figure 9.3 gives an example of a cumulative graph, using Tom's data on cigarette smoking again. Notice how the number of cigarettes smoked on any day is added to the preceding total. For instance, we know from Figure 9.1 that on the first two days of baseline Tom smoked 19 and 16 cigarettes, respectively. Thus, on the cumulative graph, the data point for the second day reflects the total, 35. Because the data accumulate, the graph is

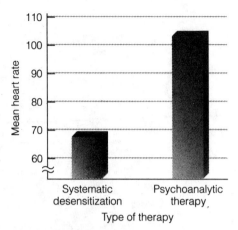

Figure 9.2   Illustration of a bar graph showing the magnitude of fear response (mean heart rate in beats per minute, hypothetical data) of individuals after receiving two types of therapy for their fear. In the graph, high heart rate reflects high fear.

smoother, and the line can never turn downward. If the number of responses declines, the graph just goes up by a smaller amount. If no responses occur on a particular day, the line would not go up at all—it would parallel the horizontal axis. The *steeper the slope* of the line, the *higher the response rate*. In Figure 9.3, the slope of the line is steeper for the baseline data than for the intervention data. This means that the number of cigarettes smoked per day was greater in baseline than intervention. If Tom had quit smoking entirely, the line would have stopped going up. (Go to 🏃)

Making a Graph

Graphs can be prepared by hand or with computer graphics programs (see, for example, Carr & Burkholder, 1998). When preparing a graph by hand, it's a good idea to use graph paper and a ruler to make all lines neat and straight. Start by making a sketch of what the graph will look like, including all labels it will have and a caption, which describes what the graph contains. In a report or book, each graph is numbered and referred to as a "figure." The figure number, which also appears in the caption, reflects the order in which the graph was mentioned in the text. The text material should refer at least once to the graph by number (for instance, "Figure 1 presents . . ."). Label each axis clearly with measurement units and a name that communicates the nature of what the axis represents. A well-planned and well-prepared figure

- Is easy to read and understand.
- Contains only essential information and leaves out visually distracting detail.
- Creates a clear and fair picture of what the data indicate.
- Uses distinct geometric forms, such as circles or squares, for data points. Don't use color to distinguish different sets of data.

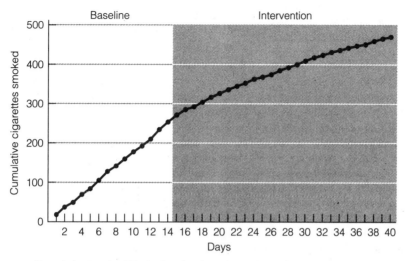

Figure 9.3 Cumulative graph of Tom's data for cigarette smoking. Compare this graph with the one in Figure 9.1, which plots the same data.

Use the figures contained in this book as models. The remainder of this section describes the preparation of a line graph because it is the most common type of graph used in behavior change programs.

The *vertical axis* will represent a measure of the behavior. Make this axis about 4 to 6 inches long. To create a scale for the vertical axis, find the largest and smallest values of the data collected. If the smallest value is much higher than zero, we may break the axis with double slash marks (as was done in Figure 9.2) and start the scale at a value that is lower than the smallest value of the data collected. Divide the remainder of the axis into equal segments to reflect units of the scale, which should include the largest and smallest values collected. The *horizontal axis* typically will represent chronological time, usually in units of days or weeks. Each baseline and intervention phase is plotted separately and chronologically along this axis. If we're using days, and the data fluctuate widely from one day to the next across most of the graph to the point that it's difficult to see whether the behavior is increasing or decreasing, we can consider combining data from successive days and plotting the means. As we saw earlier, organizing data in this way will smooth out the graph and create a clearer picture of the change that has occurred.

Using Graphs

Graphs can be used in two ways. First, we can use graphs to assess the effectiveness of an intervention. This assessment is done simply by detailed visual inspection—a procedure called **graphic analysis.** We would examine the graph to see whether the behavior changed substantially when intervention techniques were implemented. If the changes shown in the graph are very pronounced, we would conclude that the intervention

CLOSE-UP 9.1

Which Type of Graph Should We Use?

In considering when to use line, bar, and cumulative graphs, we can start by describing the general rule of thumb for selecting between line and bar graphs. Line graphs should usually be selected when the variable arranged along the horizontal axis is *continuous*—that is, values along the scale on that axis represent a numerical progression of number, amount, or degree. Chronological time is a continuous variable, and graphs of data from behavior change programs typically scale this variable along the horizontal axis in graphs to show how the target behavior changed across time in the baseline and intervention phases. As a result, the line graph is the most commonly used type of graph to represent data from programs to change behavior. Other continuous variables that can be scaled along the horizontal axis of a line graph are age, income, and the amount of a particular medication or therapy a person received.

Bar graphs should be used when the variable represented along the horizontal axis involves *discrete*, or separate, categories, rather than a progression of numerical values. As we saw in Figure 9.2, the *type* of therapy individuals receive is an example of a discrete variable; systematic desensitization and psychoanalytic therapy are separate approaches to therapy and are not related to each other as part of a progression. Other discrete variables for which bar graphs are appropriate are gender, college major, religion, and political party affiliation.

Cumulative graphs are used occasionally in programs to change behavior. They are most useful when the *rate* of responding or the *total* number of responses must be monitored constantly as critical aspects of the behavior. For instance, a therapist might need to monitor constantly the self-injurious behaviors of a child with autism to see how many of these responses the child has made and to see whether the response rate is reduced when different behavioral methods are introduced. Changes in response rates and totals show up more clearly and quickly with cumulative graphs than with other graphs.

has affected the behavior. If the changes are not very clear, we would conclude that the program has not been effective. Although there is no widely accepted, specific criterion for deciding whether the changes are or are not pronounced enough, these evaluations require the use of rigorous standards. Only very clear and marked changes should be accepted as reflecting a successful intervention.

The second way graphs can be used is to provide feedback as reinforcement and as a motivator to improve the target behavior. For instance, teachers can post a graph of the children's conduct or academic performance so the teacher and children can see how much progress has been made. Seeing concrete evidence of improvement can be reinforcing for all individuals who want the behavior to change. This approach can be very reinforcing and motivating in self-management programs too. If you were to try to change your own behavior, consider starting a graph when you begin the intervention and add data points to it each day. Display the graph where you can see it, especially if it can serve as a reminder to monitor, record, and regulate your behavior. Depending on what your target behavior is, you might want to post the graph on the refrigerator or food cabinet, above your desk, on the door to your room or closet, in your medicine chest, or above your alarm clock. If the behavior is not highly personal, display the graph where others can see it and tell them about your project. Doing this seems to help improve the target behavior (McKenzie & Rushall, 1974). Friends and family members usually want to help. (Go to ✔)

IS THE PROGRAM WORKING?

As soon as we begin the intervention phase of a program to change a behavior we'll be wondering if the program is working. In most cases, we can wait until about a week or so of the intervention before we try to find out. The process of finding out whether the program is working is based mainly on inspecting the data to see how much progress has been made, but other approaches can help in making this judgment too.

Ways to Assess a Program's Progress

Three approaches can be used to assess how well a program is working. First, we can interview individuals who must deal with the behavioral problem on a day-to-day basis (Baer, Wolf, & Risley, 1968). These people may include the target person him- or herself, as well as his or her teachers, parents, or coworkers. Have they noticed any change at all? Are they pleased with the changes they've seen? Second, we can consult experts and research literature on the particular behavioral problem we're trying to change. From these sources, we can try to determine how much change we should expect in the time since the intervention began.

The third and most critical approach is to conduct a *graphic analysis* of the data. We saw earlier that a graphic analysis is done by visually inspecting a graph of the data to judge whether it depicts pronounced changes in the behavior that can be attributed to the intervention. This judgment involves assessing two *trends*, or general patterns of change in the behavior over time, shown in the data. One trend reflects whether the behavior *improved from baseline to intervention*, and the second trend reflects whether the behavior has continued *to improve across time during the intervention*.

To see how to assess these trends in a graphic analysis, we will use the data graphed in Figure 9.4. These data are from a self-management program that a student named Jennelle conducted to reduce her nail-biting. At the end of 8 days of intervention, she did a graphic analysis to assess whether her program was working. This assessment is fairly clear just by looking at the graph: her nail-biting frequency had dropped after baseline, but it hadn't declined very much after the first day of the intervention. We'll see later how Jennelle used this assessment.

A graphic analysis to determine whether a program is working can be made even clearer by carrying out three procedures. First, we would calculate the means for the baseline and intervention data we want to compare. In Jennelle's data, the mean frequencies of nail-biting were 9.62 for baseline and 4.25 for the first 8 days of the intervention. Second, we would mark each of those means on the graph with a data point placed halfway across the corresponding time period, using a geometric form that is different from any other forms we've used in the graph. Figure 9.4 uses small open circles, one at day 11 (halfway across the 21 days of baseline) and one between days 25 and 26 (halfway across the first 8 days of intervention). Third, for each time period we're comparing, we would draw a **trend line**—that is, a straight line that best "fits" or represents all of the data points in a time period. Each trend line should pass through or very near the data point for the corresponding mean; we would draw it very lightly in pencil initially, in case we want to change it. If the trend line is positioned correctly, it will look like it carves the data points in half, with about the same number of points above and below the line. We would then use a ruler to darken the line, making it distinctly different from any other lines in the graph, such as by using short dashes.

If Jennelle's nail-biting had been declining across time during the intervention, the trend line for those data would slope sharply downward. As you can see, the line slopes only slightly. Analysis of the two trends in the graph suggests that the program had helped but might benefit from some adjustments to improve its effectiveness. The graph notes that Jennelle revised her intervention after the eighth day, and her nail-biting declined more sharply thereafter.

Problems in Graphic Analyses

Trends in the data we collect when conducting programs to change behavior may not always be as clear as Jennelle's, thereby making a graphic analysis more difficult to

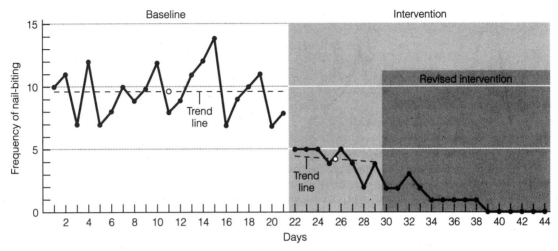

Figure 9.4 Illustration of data used to assess if a program to reduce nail-biting was working. The data are from a self-management project conducted by a student named Jennelle. The two open-circle data points represent the means for the two time periods being compared: baseline and the first 8 days of intervention. The trend lines for these periods are represented by short dashes.

interpret. Difficulties in evaluating trends can arise from data problems of three types: *excessive variability*, a *decreasing baseline trend* (for a behavioral excess), and an *increasing baseline trend* (for a behavioral deficit). Each type of problem is illustrated graphically with three graphs in Figure 9.5, using hypothetical data for 1 week of baseline and 1 week of intervention. Let's look at these problems by examining the graphs. As we do this, you'll see that the problems illustrated in the graphs are compounded when data are collected for an insufficient amount of time.

Figure 9.5a presents data for a program to reduce the frequency of a person's anger episodes. The excessive variability in the baseline data makes it difficult to interpret whether any real change has occurred thus far in the intervention phase, even though the trend lines suggest that the number of anger episodes per day has declined. This difficulty exists because the baseline data are very unstable, containing sharp fluctuations. Is the declining trend in anger frequency depicted in the intervention data just an extension of the baseline fluctuations, or has the behavior really decreased? Was the high variability an unusual circumstance? If so, collecting baseline data for at least another week might help to stabilize the data. As we saw earlier, it may also be possible to stabilize the data by averaging them across days. But this approach usually requires more than seven data points so that enough averages can be plotted to show a trend.

In Figure 9.5b, the data represent a person's frequency of gossiping. Notice that the baseline data for this behavioral excess show a clear decreasing trend that existed before the intervention was introduced to reduce the gossiping behavior. Is the decrease in gossiping after baseline due to the intervention, or is it just a continuation of the existing trend? If the declining trend during the intervention phase had been much

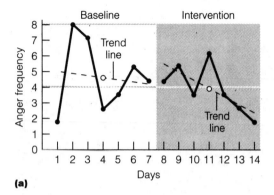

(a)

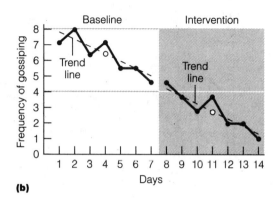

(b)

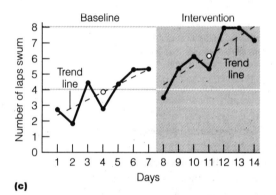

(c)

Figure 9.5 Graphs illustrating three types of problem data: (a) excessive variability, (b) decreasing baseline trend for a behavioral excess, and (c) increasing baseline trend for a behavioral deficit. The means (open circles) and trend lines (dashes) for each set of data (hypothetical) are plotted. These graphs assume that the evaluations of whether the programs were working were undertaken 1 week after the start of the intervention.

sharper than the trend in baseline, we could assume that the difference resulted from the intervention. But the two trends in this graph are very similar. As a result, we can't determine whether the program is working or whether the decreasing trends in both phases are due to some other factor, such as a temporary change in the person's general social experiences. Again, collecting baseline data for another week might clarify the situation, perhaps by showing a reversal in the baseline trend.

Figure 9.5c presents data for a program to increase the number of laps a person swims in a pool each day. The problem in these data is similar to the one we just saw for the gossiping data. For the swimming behavior, the baseline data for this behavioral deficit depict a clear increasing trend before the intervention was introduced to increase swimming. Once again, the trends in both phases are not very different, so we can't tell whether the program is working or whether some other factor is responsible for the increases in swimming in both phases.

In general, whenever baseline data show excessive variability or an increasing or decreasing trend in relation to the behavioral goal, we should consider delaying the start of the intervention and collecting additional baseline data.

TROUBLESHOOTING AND IMPROVING A PROGRAM

Each program to change behavior is unique and designed to meet the needs of a specific individual whose problem behaviors, prior learning experiences, and current life situations are typically different from those other people. As a result, conducting an intervention is an experiment or test of the program design, which may contain flaws that impair its effectiveness. In addition, new circumstances can arise that affect the target behavior. This is why, starting after about a week of the intervention, we assess whether a program is working. The graph of Jennelle's data (Figure 9.4) showed that she revised her program after seeing that her nail-biting had not decreased during the first 8 days of her intervention. Her revision was fairly simple: she deposited with her friend a large amount of money, which she would earn and use to shop for items she wanted if she achieved her behavioral goal. Once she made that revision, her nail-biting declined more sharply. Problems in the initial designs of programs are common. When a program isn't working, we must find out why and improve it. (Go to)

CASE STUDY **9.1**

Revising Monica's Dietary Program

A student named Monica designed and conducted a self-management program to reduce her daily consumption of junk food snacks, such as cookies and ice cream, in favor of healthy snacks, such as fruits and vegetables. Although Monica's initial design was very good and included techniques that were directed at the snacking behavior itself and its antecedents and consequences, she found that the program wasn't working as well as she wanted. Her behavioral excess and deficit had improved moderately from baseline to intervention but showed no improvements in more than a week of her intervention.

Monica decided to revise her intervention in three ways. One change she made was to use the technique of narrowing antecedent control by deciding:

> "If I'm going to eat junk food, it had to be at a table made for eating." Dining room tables or tables in cafeterias would be examples. I allowed myself to eat healthy snacks anywhere at all. This strategy helped eliminate eating unhealthy goodies while driving, studying in the student center, watching TV, or just hanging out being bored.

She also introduced using the strategy of "cool" cognitions to reperceive junk foods as neutral items when they tempted her. Last, she increased the amount of the monetary reward she would earn if she ate no junk food on a given day. By the end of Monica's month-long intervention, her daily junk food intake had declined to less than one third of her baseline intake. Also, her daily consumption of healthy snacks had increased substantially, becoming about three times that of junk food snacks.

Discovering Why a Program Isn't Working

There are several reasons programs to change behavior may not be as effective as they could be. For one thing, sometimes programs are designed without doing a careful functional analysis of the target behavior and its antecedents and consequences. In the absence of data from a functional analysis, the program design is likely to be based on misperceptions or misunderstandings of the factors that control the target behavior. This leads to choosing incorrect intervention techniques and rules for their use.

But even when a good functional analysis has been done, design problems can reduce a program's effectiveness. For instance, the techniques the intervention includes may not be the best ones available or as powerful as they might be. Using less-than-optimal techniques is a fairly common problem that can usually be corrected easily. For example, both Jennelle and Monica initially used reinforcement systems that were not as powerful as needed. Making the reinforcers more powerful enhanced the success of their programs. It's hard to know in advance how many reinforcers to use, what types they should be, and how much reward value each should have to maximize the success of a behavior change program. Skill in choosing and designing optimally effective techniques improves with experience.

Finally, the individuals who administer program techniques may not implement them as carefully or rigorously as they should. This may happen partly because many of the techniques that are used in changing behavior are commonly used in everyday life, but usually in a haphazard manner and for behaviors that have not been carefully defined. Parents and teachers apply reinforcers and punishers to influence children's behavior, but these adults typically do not apply consequences consistently and immediately for every correct instance of a behavior they want to change. Sometimes individuals fail to apply consequences consistently or immediately because the behavior is not well defined. It is also true, however, that people tend to fall back into their habitual ways of doing things, and that carrying out procedures haphazardly is easier than implementing them carefully and rigorously. It takes a lot of time, effort, motivation, and training to carry out a behavior change program effectively.

How to Improve a Program

To improve a program that is not as effective as it could be, we will need to ascertain how the intervention has been conducted, determine what problems have impaired its success, and decide what to do about these problems. These activities begin with the process of *troubleshooting*—that is, investigating to find problems—for all aspects of the existing program (DeRisi & Butz, 1975; Holmes, 1977).

Troubleshooting the Program   In troubleshooting the program, we should answer the diagnostic questions discussed in the following sections concerning the program's design and execution. Answers are written down *only for those questions that pertain to the way the program was actually designed or conducted.* The questions are categorized under headings that reflect the dimensions to which the techniques apply or the procedures the program has involved.

Methods of Managing the Antecedents   Examine the effectiveness of methods for management of the antecedents of the target behavior by answering these questions about methods the program has been using:

- Were the prompts, modeling, or instructions used in the intervention (a) noticed by the target person and (b) effective?
- Were there difficulties in trying to alter chains, reduce or avoid antecedents, or narrow antecedent control?
- Were the CSs in the stimulus hierarchy for desensitization (a) applied effectively and (b) appropriately spaced?

Methods of Managing the Behavior   Examine the effectiveness of methods directed toward managing the behavior by answering these questions about the methods the program has been using:

- Was the target behavior clearly defined for the target person?
- Were the shaping steps appropriate to the skills and abilities of the target person?
- Did the target person lack any prerequisite skills for learning the new behavior?
- Was the target person able to use the relaxation techniques effectively?
- When using covert conditioning, was the target person able to form clear images of the scenes?
- Were the alternative responses used in the program appropriate and effective?

Methods of Managing the Consequences   Examine the effectiveness of methods to manage the consequences of the target behavior by answering these questions about methods the program has been using:

- Did the reinforcers lose some of their appeal or become undermined by external factors, such as other people providing stronger, counterproductive reinforcers?
- Were some reinforcers provided immediately after appropriate behaviors, and were these rewards given frequently and in small amounts?
- Were any punishers functioning as reinforcers—that is, did they seem to maintain a behavioral excess instead of decreasing it?
- Were there difficulties implementing extinction procedures for positive or negative reinforcement in an effort to decrease undesirable behavior?
- Did lottery or group contingency procedures for administering reinforcers lead to any difficulties?

Procedural Aspects of the Program   Examine various procedural aspects of the program by answering these questions:

- Were assessment methods performed correctly, and were data calculated or charted without errors?
- Was it possible to verify the accuracy of the data?
- Was the data collection process overly difficult, complex, or time consuming?
- Were the program's techniques or procedures, such as reinforcement, implemented correctly and as planned?
- Were all mediators or program administrators using the techniques in the same way?
- Was the behavioral contract mutually negotiated, and were its terms clear and fair?
- Did some unexpected outside factor interfere with or disrupt the program?
- Were there reasons to suspect that motivational problems or a lack of training hampered the performance of the individuals who administered the techniques?

Correcting the Program   To decide how to correct the problems discovered by troubleshooting the program, we would use the written answers to the questions to stimulate rethinking of decisions we made in designing the intervention. It is generally useful to consult the functional analysis materials, relevant sections of this text, and the Checklist of Behavior Change Methods (see Figure 8.1). Consulting the checklist would help us determine whether our program left out any useful techniques. If there were problems with the program's system of reinforcers, it may be useful to consult the Preferred Items and Experiences Questionnaire (see Figure 4.2) to decide how to improve the design.

Once we have decided how to revise the program's design, we would make sure to have any materials needed to incorporate the new methods into the intervention. We can then begin the revised program and reevaluate the program's progress after several days by conducting another graphic analysis. Chances are, one revision is all we'll need to do if the initial design did not work as well as expected. Revising a program shouldn't be construed as indicating a "failure" in the design. It is a positive and reasonable step toward fine-tuning the program's effectiveness. (Go to ☑)

Tips on Using Data and Improving Programs

When performing and evaluating an intervention, we need to keep in mind the following helpful tips on using data and improving programs:

1. Transfer data from data sheets to a table on a regular basis, daily if possible, and check that no errors were made in this process.
2. Look for problems in the data, such as excessive variability and increasing or decreasing baseline trends.

CONCEPT CHECK 9.2

1. A general pattern of change in a behavior over time is called a(n) _____ .
2. A trend line is a straight graph line that best _____ the data points within a time period.
3. An example of a set of data showing excessive variability for 5 days might be _____ , _____ , _____ , _____ , _____ . ⇔
4. An example of a set of data showing a decreasing baseline trend for 5 days might be _____ , _____ , _____ , _____ , _____ . ⇔
5. One revision Monica made to her dietary program was to introduce _____ . ⇔
6. Answering diagnostic questions to find problems in the way a program was actually conducted is part of the process of _____ .

Answers: 1. trend, 2. fits/represents, 3. 9, 2, 0, 7, 3, 4, 9, 8, 6, 5, 5. narrowing antecedent control/"cool" cognitions/stronger reinforcer, 6. troubleshooting

3. Make sure all tables and graphs are neat and accurate. Don't draw any lines freehand—use a ruler.
4. Keep track of any unusual circumstances, such as sickness, that may have affected the target person's performance. If necessary, add footnotes to the graph to explain peculiar data.
5. When constructing a graph, sketch it out freehand on scratch paper first to see what it will look like. Redraw it until it is clear, uncluttered, and appropriately proportioned.
6. When composing the final version of a graph, label trend lines (if any), baseline and intervention phases, and points at which revisions were introduced to the intervention.
7. After the intervention has been in force for about a week, do a full graphic analysis with trend lines. Troubleshoot and make revisions, if needed.
8. When troubleshooting a program, write down all answers to relevant diagnostic questions and ideas about improving the program.
9. Add data points to the graph periodically, and evaluate the progress being made each week.

SUMMARY

Data in a behavior change program provide a record of variables related to the target behavior and clarify whether and how much the behavior has changed. Several methods for organizing data can clarify the picture data present. A mean combines data into an average and is an especially useful way of organizing data when they vary a great deal from one collection period to the next. A percentage is a useful way of organizing data when the opportunities to perform the behavior differ for two or more sets of data. Transferring data to a table organizes the data visually, allowing you to see patterns.

Data can also be presented in line graphs, bar graphs, and cumulative graphs. Line graphs are the most commonly used way of presenting data from programs to change behavior because the horizontal axis typically scales units of chronological time, such as days or weeks, which are continuous variables. The most common way of determining whether a behavior change program is working is to inspect graphs of the data using a process called graphic analysis. We can improve the clarity of the data in a graphic analysis by computing means for the baseline and intervention data we want to compare and then drawing trend lines to represent the general pattern of change in the behavior over time.

When a graphic analysis indicates that an intervention to change behavior is not as effective as it should be, we will need to revise the program. This process begins with troubleshooting the program by answering diagnostic questions about the way it was designed and carried out. This information is then used in deciding what revisions to make.

KEY TERMS

variables	graph	cumulative graphs
mean	line graphs	graphic analysis
table	bar graphs	trend line

REVIEW QUESTIONS

1. Define the term variables and give three examples.
2. Two arithmetic ways to organize data involve calculating the mean and the percentage. Define both terms and indicate when these calculations are useful.
3. What is a data table, and how is it useful?
4. Describe the axes used when presenting graphical data for a behavior change program.
5. What are line graphs, bar graphs, and cumulative graphs? How are they similar and different from one another?
6. Describe how to decide when line graphs are more appropriate to use than bar graphs.
7. Describe how to construct a line graph.
8. Describe in detail how to do a graphic analysis using trend lines.
9. Draw graphs of the three problems in the data that can make interpreting a graphic analysis very difficult.
10. Write a hypothetical account of the troubleshooting process Monica (in the case study) might have used in revising her dietary program.

RELATED READINGS

American Psychological Association (1994). *Publication manual* (4th ed.). Washington, DC: Author.

DeRisi, W. J., & Butz, G. (1975). *Writing behavioral contracts: A case simulation practice manual.* Champaign, IL: Research Press.

Many people make healthful lifestyle changes such as getting more physical exercise. The likeli-hood of maintaining those changes can be improved with behavior modification techniques.

Maintaining Behavior Changes

I magine that you are one of the therapists in this intervention to train eight 4-to 13-year-old children with autism to perform basic classroom behaviors, such as looking at the teacher and imitating the teacher's actions when requested (Koegel & Rincover, 1974). Children must be able to do these things so they can learn in a classroom. But these children have very poor basic classroom skills. For instance, four of them are mute, and the others can only echo words they hear others say. All of them have extremely low IQ scores.

In an effort to teach the children several basic classroom skills, the therapists worked on a one-to-one basis with the children, using a training procedure in which

> responses were shaped by first rewarding the child for establishing eye contact with the teacher until the child would consistently (90% correct trials for three consecutive days) look at the teacher for a period of at least 5 seconds when the teacher commanded, "Look at me." Then, nonverbal imitation was gradually established by prompting and reinforcing copying behaviors until the subject could consistently imitate. . . . Imitation was then used as a prompt to teach other nonverbal responses to instructions. For example, the teacher would say, "Touch your nose" and prompt the correct response by saying "Do this" and modelling the correct response. The prompts were then faded. (p. 47)

After 2 to 4 weeks of this training, all of the children were able to perform the skills correctly at least 80% of the time. Then came the crucial test to see if the children would use these skills when the situation was more like a classroom setting—that is, if they were tested with all eight children present in the same room, instead of alone. The average correct responding when alone—nearly 89%—dropped to about 28% when they were tested with other children present.

If you had spent weeks in one-to-one training of basic classroom behaviors, only to have the skills fall apart when the children were tested together, you'd probably be very discouraged. Why didn't these behaviors generalize to the group situation? What can we do to increase the likelihood that the behaviors we train will be maintained in and generalize to other appropriate situations? These are the issues we will examine in this chapter.

WILL BEHAVIOR CHANGES LAST?

A student named Kevin conducted a self-management project to increase his exercising and decrease eating high-fat foods as a permanent lifestyle change. A few months later, he stopped by to tell me that he had stuck to the program and felt great about having done so. Another student, Jane, chose to do a self-management project to lose about 11 pounds so she would fit into a size 8 bridesmaid's gown for her sister's wedding in May. Jane's was a short-term goal, and she succeeded in losing the weight, but she gained it right back in a few months. Short-term goals can be of value, but behavior change programs are usually undertaken with long-lasting goals in mind. We have seen that programs consisting of behavioral and cognitive methods can succeed in changing behavior. But will the change last?

Relapses in Behavior

Even when the goal of an intervention is to produce a permanent improvement in the person's behavior and he or she agrees with the goal, the behavior sometimes regresses after the intervention ends. You undoubtedly know individuals who seemed to have succeeded in stopping smoking or reducing their intake of fattening foods but then went back to their old habits. Falling back to one's former, full-blown pattern of an undesired behavior is called a **relapse.** We saw in Chapter 8 that a *lapse* is an instance of backsliding—a relatively isolated or temporary regression to the former behavior. People often can bounce back from a lapse fairly easily if they know that backsliding commonly happens and should be expected. Relapses are likely to occur when the person is not very committed to changing the target behavior, especially when it involves changing his or her lifestyle or long-standing habits. Let's look at a few different examples of relapses occurring after the behaviors had improved.

The first example of a relapse comes from an intervention to improve the feeding skills of a 6-year-old girl with profound retardation (O'Brien, Bugle, & Azrin, 1972). Before the intervention began, she was eating without utensils, using her hands to grasp some food, crush it, and put it in her mouth. As you might imagine, her feeding was both unsightly and messy. The intervention used two main techniques to teach her to eat with a spoon: (1) physical guidance prompts, in which the teacher held and moved the girl's hand through the feeding movements, and (2) interruption-extinction, in which the teacher stopped an incorrect response, such as trying to eat with the hands, and prevented reinforcement by cleaning the food from the girl's hands so she couldn't eat it. When physical guidance was used, the guidance was withheld for the next response following a correctly performed guided response to assess her skill in independent feeding with a spoon. Figure 10.1 shows that the girl's performance in using a spoon to eat improved greatly when the interruption-extinction method was added to the physical guidance but dropped sharply when the intervention techniques were withdrawn in the reversal phase. Even though the girl had learned how to eat with a spoon, she did not continue to eat properly when the intervention ended.

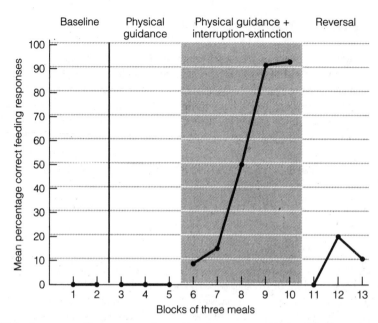

Figure 10.1   Percentage of correctly performed feeding responses by a child with profound retardation during four phases of the training program. The mean percentages were calculated across three meals. All data plotted are for feeding responses the child performed independently. During phases in which physical guidance was used, the guidance was withheld for some responses to assess independent feeding. *Source:* Based on data abstracted from O'Brien, Bugle, & Azrin, 1972, Figure 1.

O. Ivar Lovaas and his coworkers (1973) conducted a program in which 20 children with developmental disabilities received intensive individual training to reduce undesirable behaviors, such as engaging in self-stimulation, and to increase desirable behaviors, for example, using speech, playing with other children, and performing self-care activities. The program applied behavioral methods over many months and succeeded in improving the target behaviors in all of the children, with some showing very large gains. Then, 1 to 4 years after their discharge from the program, follow-up assessments were made on each child. These assessments revealed that the environment *after* the intervention is crucial to maintaining the children's behavioral improvements. Some of the children went to live at home upon leaving the program, and their parents received training in behavioral methods. These children's behaviors continued to improve. Those who could not be placed at home went to institutions, where they received basic custodial care with no behavioral methods, and their behavior relapsed.

The third example of relapse comes from interventions to prevent or reduce juvenile delinquency in problem adolescents by using behavioral methods to increase their performance of socially and academically desirable behaviors and decrease their performance of activities that lead to social, academic, and legal problems. In some of these interventions, youths with problem behaviors have attended separate classes in a public school, and their teachers and parents administered token reinforcement systems (Heaton & Safer, 1982; Safer, Heaton, & Parker, 1981). Other interventions have housed the youths in community-based group homes while they attended public schools. Behavioral methods with token reinforcers were administered mainly by trained supervisors at the group home, with feedback from teachers regarding school performance (Fixsen et al., 1978; Phillips, Phillips, Fixsen, & Wolf, 1973; Wolf, Braukmann, & Ramp, 1987). Although each of these programs has produced impressive improvements in the youths' target behaviors during the many months in which the intervention was in effect and for about a year after it ended, the behavioral improvements for many of the participants were lost after a couple of years. Relapse seems very likely if problem adolescents are returned to their original life circumstances without continued treatment or support to encourage them to maintain the improved behaviors.

Why Relapses Occur

Have you ever had an experience like this one? I bought a new refrigerator with a special bin on the door for a gallon milk container. Months later I found myself still occasionally looking for the milk container on a shelf in the body of the refrigerator or starting to return it there, as I had done for years with the old appliance. Automatic or habitual behaviors die hard. Why? We continue to perform the obsolete behaviors even though we know the correct actions because we have learned the old behaviors so thoroughly. In addition, the antecedent cues and chain of responses, such as opening the door and thinking "Get milk," are much the same as they had been. If we then were to perform the old behavior and often receive reinforcing consequences, we may revert to the old habit entirely. This account describes some of the factors that can lead to relapses.

The strength of the old behavioral tendency and the circumstance of encountering antecedents for that behavior are important factors in determining whether a relapse will happen after a behavioral excess has been reduced (Bouton, 2000). People who have succeeded in stopping smoking or drinking for a few weeks or longer may return to the habit again if they do not or cannot control the antecedents for that behavior. For instance, individuals frequently report having gone back to smoking because they experienced high levels of frustration or stress or strong social temptations to smoke, all of which are common antecedents for smoking (Shiffman, 1986).

And relapses happen for many other reasons, such as the strength or persistence of responses the program tried to enhance. These behaviors include alternative responses used in the intervention and new behaviors that were trained to address behavioral deficits, as in the program we discussed that trained a girl with severe retardation to use a spoon to feed herself. The stronger or more persistent these desirable behaviors are, the less likely relapses become. Other factors that can lead to relapses involve cognitive processes, for example, a diminution in the target person's sense of self-efficacy for being able to maintain the behavior change. The remainder of this chapter concentrates on describing methods that programs can include to maintain behavior changes and overcome the many factors that can lead to relapses. (Go to)

CLOSE-UP 10.1

Relapse and the Abstinence Violation Effect

 One way by which cognitive processes may lead to a relapse has been described by G. Alan Marlatt and his colleagues (Marlatt & Gordon, 1980; Marlatt & Parks, 1982). As we consider the course of events these processes follow in producing a relapse, we will use an example of a man named Victor, who had stopped drinking alcohol. According to Marlatt, the course of events leading to a relapse starts with the experience of a high-risk antecedent situation:

1. *High-risk situation.* Victor encounters two tempting antecedents for drinking: he was feeling upset by events at his job, and he was invited to go to a bar.
2. *Poor coping with the risk.* He decides to accept the invitation, promising himself he will only drink nonalcoholic beverages.
3. *Negative self-statements and thoughts.* At the bar, Victor begins to feel a strong craving for a drink. He begins to doubt his self-efficacy, thinking "It's no use—the booze is gonna win." And he thinks about how good a drink would taste and make him feel.
4. *Lapse.* He orders a drink and starts to consume it, rationalizing that "With the day I've had, who could blame me." (He'll find out who: himself!)

5. *Perceived violation of abstinence rule.* Because Victor believed the slogan "You are always only one drink away from a drunk," he had been committed to the rule of *total abstinence*: he would never drink again, ever. Now he starts to realize he has violated that rule. He feels guilty, blames himself for the transgression, and concludes that ordering the drink was a sign of personal failure: "I don't have enough willpower to control my drinking. I'm really just an alcoholic after all." This series of thoughts and feelings is called the **abstinence violation effect** and can precipitate a full relapse. Strictly speaking, the abstinence violation effect applies only when the person is committed to a rule of total abstinence, but violating less severe rules can have similar effects.
6. *Increased likelihood of relapse.* Once Victor felt weak-willed and powerless to resist that first drink, his ability to resist subsequent drinks was greatly reduced that night. The abstinence violation effect carried over into the next day, and he drank several drinks again. A relapse had begun.

Programs to change behavior often need to include techniques to prevent these kinds of cognitive events from undermining the gains the person has made, leading to a relapse.

THINNING AND DELAYING REINFORCEMENT

To prevent a relapse, we need to apply methods that will enable the improved behavior to persist after the intervention ends. We saw in Chapter 4 that one way to maintain a behavior change involves *thinning* (sometimes called "fading" or "leaning") the schedule of reinforcement used in the program. Once a target behavior is learned and well established under a *continuous reinforcement* (CRF) schedule, we can thin the schedule by gradually reducing the rate at which the behavior is reinforced. Thinning the reinforcement schedule makes the consequences for the behavior more like the conditions people experience in everyday life. For instance, when you place a phone call, sometimes you reach the party and sometimes you don't. When you do a good job in your chores at home or at work, sometimes you are praised and sometimes you're not. Behavior changes produced in an intervention are likely to receive *intermittent* or *partial reinforcement* in the target person's daily life.

The reason for decreasing reinforcement *gradually* rather than suddenly is to guard against deterioration of the behavior. If reinforcement is reduced too quickly, the person may not be sufficiently motivated to continue responding appropriately. Thus, the behavior may decline rapidly, necessitating the introduction of a CRF schedule again to reestablish the behavior. How gradual should the thinning be? As with the gradual processes of shaping a behavior and fading prompts, there are no fixed rules. Sometimes the reinforcement schedule can be thinned very quickly, and other times the process takes weeks (Sulzer & Mayer, 1972). It seems reasonable to assume that thinning can progress rapidly for individuals who can understand the need to reduce the rate of reinforcement and who have some control—perhaps through negotiations for a behavioral contract—over how quickly these reductions take place.

Probably the most common approach for thinning a schedule of reinforcement is to reduce the percentage or ratio of correct responses that receive rewards. In a CRF schedule, 100% of correct responses receive reinforcement. Beth Sulzer and G. Roy Mayer conducted a program to teach a child to name various items in a set of objects. They thinned the reinforcement schedule, starting

> by *skipping* reinforcement for about one correct response out of four. As time went by, more and more trials went unreinforced until eventually the child had to label the whole set before the . . . reinforcer was delivered. (1972, p. 109)

This thinning process began by reducing reinforcement to about three of every four correct responses, or 75%, by skipping one reward. When the schedule was thinned to 50%, the child had to name two objects correctly to get a reinforcer. Gradually, the child had to name more and more objects correctly for each instance of reinforcement.

Other strategies can be used in thinning reinforcement schedules. For example, one intervention trained children to identify and request nutritious snacks, such as fruit, to receive reinforcers of various types on a CRF schedule (Baer, Blount, et al., 1987). In the process of thinning, the children continued to get reinforcement on a CRF schedule on days when rewards were made available, but the percentage of days when rewards were available was reduced from 100% of the days to 67%, and then 33%. A reinforcement schedule can also be thinned by decreasing the frequency of assessment. For instance, an intervention was conducted to discourage a boy from stealing the belongings of other students in his classroom (Rosen & Rosen, 1983). Initially, token reinforcers and punishers were administered by assessing his stealing every 15 minutes, but this schedule was thinned by increasing the interval between assessments to once every 2 hours.

Decreasing the rate of reinforcement is a very flexible process that can progress at different speeds and follow different strategies. To determine whether the thinning procedure we are using is advancing too quickly, we monitor the person's performance carefully and frequently. If the behavior seems to be regressing, we may be reducing the reinforcement rate too quickly, hence may need to slow the pace. Choosing a strategy for thinning reinforcement should be based on and be coordinated with the intermittent reinforcement schedule we plan to use in the program.

Types of Intermittent Reinforcement Schedules

Thinning a reinforcement schedule means that only some instances of the behavior will be reinforced. The rule specifying the circumstances under which some instances of the behavior will be reinforced is called an **intermittent reinforcement schedule,** or *partial reinforcement schedule*. For example, a rule in my everyday life specifies that I will be paid every other Friday during the academic year for my work as a college instructor. Although the rules governing intermittent reinforcement schedules in our everyday lives may be stated and clear, most often they are not. The matrix in Figure 10.2 outlines the four basic intermittent reinforcement schedules; the two in the top row are *ratio schedules*, and the two in the bottom row are *interval schedules*. Let's examine these types of reinforcement schedules.

Ratio Schedules   In **ratio schedules,** the rule for administering each instance of reinforcement is based on the *number of correct responses* made since the last reinforcer was given. This rule can describe one of two patterns: the number of responses required for reinforcement can be *fixed*, or constant, for every instance of reinforcement, or it can be *variable*, changing from one instance to the next.

In a **fixed-ratio** (FR) schedule of reinforcement, the criterion for receiving each instance of reinforcement is performance of a constant number of correct responses by the individual. Typically, the reinforcer is given immediately after the individual makes the last response in the fixed criterion. An everyday example of a fixed-ratio schedule is the practice of factories to pay employees on a piecework basis—garment workers might have to sew five pullover shirts to earn one dollar. Although these workers are not paid immediately, they probably keep track of their earnings. In this example, the ratio of the number of responses (shirts sewn) for each dollar is 5:1, which is abbreviated as FR 5. Note that an FR 1 schedule is a CRF schedule, but it isn't intermittent. People's rate of responding for fixed-ratio intermittent reinforcement is usually very high because the more rapidly they respond the more rewards they'll get.

The process of thinning reinforcement to a fixed-ratio schedule was used in an intervention to improve a boy's arithmetic skills by providing praise, such as "Good work," for correctly solved math problems (Kirby & Shields, 1972). The number of correct math problems required for each statement of praise was doubled every couple of days, until an FR 16 schedule was reached. In fixed-ratio schedules, the rule governing when reinforcement is given is often stated explicitly or is easy for the person to detect after many instances of reward. Of course, people with insufficient intellectual abilities may not notice the pattern or understand it when told; still, the schedule seems to affect their behavior.

In a **variable-ratio** (VR) schedule, the rule governing when reinforcement will be given requires an unspecified and changing number of correct responses for each instance of the reward. As with fixed-ratio schedules, the reinforcer is typically given

Response or Time Pattern

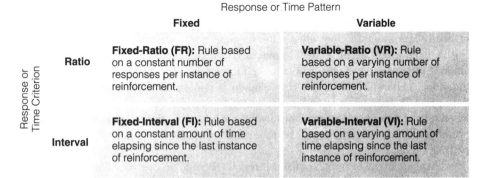

Figure 10.2 Four basic types of intermittent reinforcement schedules: fixed-ratio, variable-ratio, fixed-interval, and variable-interval. Each reinforcement schedule is defined by a rule based on two factors: (1) the *response* or *time criterion* (the number of responses or elapsed time) since the last instance of reinforcement, and (2) the *response* or *time pattern* (fixed or variable) required for the criterion.

immediately after the individual makes the last response in the varying criterion. Thus, for a series of six instances of reinforcement, the person might be required to perform the following number of responses: 4, 12, 23, 8, 11, and 2, respectively. This is an example of a VR 10 schedule because the *average* number of responses required for reinforcement is 10. Notice that the required number of responses varies from one instance of reinforcement to the next. Variable-ratio schedules keep the person guessing about whether or when a payoff will happen because instances of reinforcement are unpredictable. But responding rapidly increases the frequency of reward. As a result, people usually respond at high rates for variable-ratio reinforcement.

Gambling pays off on variable-ratio schedules. When playing a slot machine for a few hours, for instance, the number of times you would need to perform the chain of dropping a coin into the slot and pulling the lever would vary from one jackpot to the next—the machine is programmed to ensure this. Telemarketing work provides another example of behavior being reinforced on a variable-ratio schedule: telephoning people to sell products or services earns a commission for each sale, but the number of calls the person will need to make before selling something varies from one sale to the next.

Interval Schedules   In **interval schedules,** the rule for administering each instance of reinforcement is based on the *elapsed time* since the last reinforcer. A reinforcer is given for the *first correct response* following some period of time since the last reinforcement occurred. In other words, reinforcement is not available for a period of time after each reward is given. When reinforcement becomes available, however, the first correct response is reinforced. As with ratio schedules, the specific rule for an interval schedule can describe one of two patterns: the amount of time when reinforcement is not available can be *fixed*, or constant, for every instance of reinforcement, or it can be *variable*, changing from one instance to the next. Refer to Figure 10.2 to compare interval and ratio schedules. Thinning reinforcement to an interval schedule is generally done by gradually extending the time when reinforcement is not available.

A **fixed-interval** (FI) schedule makes reinforcement unavailable for a constant amount of time after each instance of reinforcement. The first correct response the individual makes after that time has elapsed is reinforced immediately. Because the time period is fixed, people and animals usually can learn to predict fairly accurately when reinforcement will be available again. It appears that they learn to respond slowly or not at all early in the interval and to increase the rate of responding toward the end of the interval.

There are many examples of fixed-interval schedules in everyday life. For instance, checking my mail is rewarded on a fixed-interval schedule because it is delivered at the same time every weekday (getting mail I want is a reward). Going to campus every other Friday is rewarded by getting my salary. These are examples of FR 24-hours (or 1-day) and FR 2-weeks schedules. Notice that with interval schedules the abbreviation must specify the time units, such as seconds, minutes, or hours. Another everyday example of a fixed-interval schedule entails watching TV. If you are watching a show you enjoy and are not interested in the commercials, reinforcement for looking at the TV is not available during the time commercials are aired. Because commercial interruptions tend to have a standard duration, you can leave the room or engage in some other activity for about that amount of time and start looking at the TV again toward the end of the interval.

In a **variable-interval** (VI) schedule, the rule governing when the reinforcer will not be available involves an unspecified and changing amount of elapsed time after each instance of the reward. As with fixed-interval schedules, the reinforcer is typically given immediately after the individual makes a single correct response after reinforcement is again available. Thus for a series of, say, six instances of reinforcement, the reward might be unavailable for the following amounts of time: 4, 12, 23, 8, 11, and 2 minutes, respectively. This would be an example of a VI 10-minutes schedule because the *average* time that reinforcement was unavailable is 10 minutes. Variable-interval schedules, like variable-ratio schedules, make instances of reinforcement unpredictable and keep the person guessing about whether or when a payoff will happen. But in variable-interval schedules, responding at a continuously rapid rate will not speed up the reinforcement. As a result, people tend to respond at a steady, moderate rate when this type of schedule is in effect.

Montrose Wolf and his colleagues (1970) used a variable-interval reinforcement schedule in an intervention to increase grade schoolers' sitting in their seats in class. The teacher set a kitchen timer for varying amounts of time on a VI 20-minutes schedule and provided token reinforcement for students who were in their seats when the timer sounded. An everyday example of a variable-interval schedule can be seen in grilling steaks on a barbecue. The amount of time needed to cook steak to the desired doneness can vary a lot, depending on how hot the coals are, how cold the meat was before it went on the grill, and how thick the steak is. Another everyday example of a behavior being reinforced on a variable-interval schedule is looking to see when a red traffic light turns green. If you arrive at a traffic light after it has already turned red, you don't know when it will change. And looking at it a lot won't make it turn green faster! When it turns green, looking at it is reinforced by being able to proceed.

Although most examples of intermittent reinforcement schedules from everyday life probably fit into the four basic types, not all do. For instance, the so-called *duration schedules* require that the person engage in the target behavior for certain amounts of time before being reinforced. Being paid an hourly wage is an example because work behavior is required during each hour. Sometimes interval schedules have an extra requirement that the person must respond within a certain amount of time after reinforcement becomes available or lose the chance. This added requirement is called a *limited hold* because reinforcer availability is "held" for a limited time. Consider a train that has a regular, fixed-interval schedule. The "limited hold" aspect of the rule is that the train will wait at the station for only a limited amount of time.

Other everyday reinforcement schedules involve combinations of the types we've discussed. For example, taking full advantage of a department store's weekly sales requires that you arrive there when they open, and arriving much earlier probably won't matter. So far, this is just a fixed-interval schedule. Once you're in the store, a variable-ratio schedule will apply: the number of rummaging behaviors you'll need to perform in finding items you want at bargain prices will vary from one item to the next.

Effects of Intermittent Reinforcement Schedules

So far, I have described the effects of intermittent reinforcement on behavior rather broadly. We will look next at the effects of the four basic intermittent reinforcement schedules in more detail, examining them first while the schedules are in force during an intervention, and then after reinforcement has been discontinued—that is, after the intervention ends.

Effects of Schedules During an Intervention   Our discussion of the effects of various schedules of reinforcement on behavior during interventions will assume that the target responses have progressed to the point of being well established and the reinforcement schedules have been thinned. In general, all intermittent reinforcement schedules produce higher rates of responding than CRF schedules do while they are in force.

Ratio Schedules   Ratio schedules produce very high rates of responding, with response rates being somewhat higher under variable-ratio than fixed-ratio reinforcement schedules, as Figure 10.3 illustrates. The two cumulative graphs present hypothetical data contrasting the usual kinds of effects of fixed- and variable-ratio schedules, as we might find in an intervention to increase a child's performance in reading words from a list. Notice three features of these graphs. First, the two reinforcement schedules are equated for the average number of responses, 20, required for reinforcement. By equating the two schedule types in this way, we can compare their effects without being concerned that one schedule provided more reinforcement than the other. Second, although the slope is steep in both cases, the variable-ratio graph is somewhat steeper than the fixed-ratio graph. In cumulative graphs, the steeper the slope, the higher the response rate. Third, individuals receiving reinforcement on fixed-ratio schedules tend to pause briefly

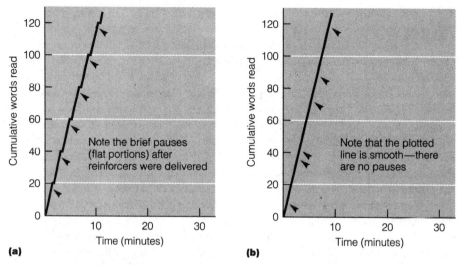

Figure 10.3 Illustration of hypothetical *cumulative graphs* of the number of words a child might read correctly in interventions using (a) a fixed-ratio (FR 20) reinforcement schedule or (b) a variable-ratio (VR 20) reinforcement schedule. The arrowheads pointing at the plotted lines indicate instances of reinforcement.

in their responding, usually just after obtaining the reward. These **postreinforcement pauses** tend to be longer when many responses are required for each reward than when few responses are required. Although it's tempting to conclude that these pauses result because the individual is using the reinforcer, such as eating a food reward, there are two reasons to think other factors must be involved. First, the pauses don't happen with variable-ratio schedules. Second, pauses also occur with reinforcers of other types, such as praise and money. It's as if the individual sees completing each set of responses for a reward as a "goal" and "takes a break" after achieving each one.

Research using ratio schedules has shown that increasing the number of responses required for each instance of reinforcement increases people's response rates, within limits (Schroeder, 1972; Stephens et al., 1975). But at some point, the number of responses may become too large, and the behavior may begin to deteriorate. This is called **ratio strain** because the ratio of responses to reinforcement has become so large that the behavior isn't reinforced enough to be maintained (Miller, 1980). Although we can't predict the point at which ratio strain will happen, it appears to depend on several factors, such as the reward value, how gradually the thinning procedures advanced, and how much effort the response requires. Still, individuals will often perform at very high rates for fairly modest reinforcers. For instance, researchers used variable-ratio token reinforcement to increase exercising on a stationary bicycle on the part of obese and nonobese 11-year-old boys (De Luca & Holborn, 1992). The backup reinforcers included a kite, a model car, a flashlight, and comic books. The schedule of reinforcement was thinned for each boy to at least a VR 100 schedule, in which one point was earned for every 100 pedal revolutions on the bicycle, with no deterioration

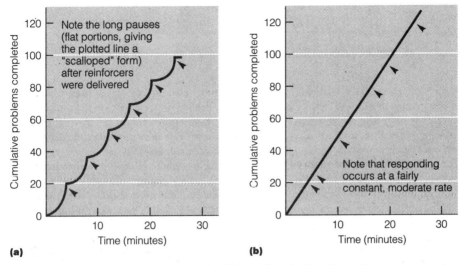

Figure 10.4 Illustration of *cumulative graphs* of the number of arithmetic problems a teenager might complete in interventions using (a) a fixed-interval (FI 4 minutes) reinforcement schedule or (b) a variable-interval (VI 4 minutes) reinforcement schedule. The arrowheads pointing at the plotted lines indicate instances of reinforcement.

in the behavior. What's more, when the 30-minute exercise sessions were over, the boys often asked if they could continue exercising to "get more points."

Interval Schedules   As Figure 10.4 illustrates, interval schedules produce moderately high response rates that are stronger and more constant with variable-interval than with fixed-interval schedules. Like the graphs for ratio schedules, these two cumulative graphs present hypothetical data contrasting the usual effects found with fixed- and variable-interval schedules. In this case, the intervention involves increasing the number of arithmetic problems a teenager completed in half-hour sessions. Notice that the two reinforcement schedules are equated for the average interval length, 4 minutes, when reinforcement is not available. Once again, equating the two schedule types in this way enables us to compare effects without being concerned that one schedule provided more reinforcement than the other.

An important phenomenon tends to occur with fixed-interval schedules. As the cumulative record in Figure 10.4a shows, fixed-interval schedules produce a prolonged pause in responding after each instance of reinforcement, causing the graph to resemble a series of *scallops*, or arcs. These pauses occur because the individual learns that the response will not lead to reinforcement soon after a reward was received. After a while, responding begins to accelerate because the end of the interval is approaching and reinforcement will be available again. These pauses have the obvious effect of slowing down the rate of responding, thereby making variable-intervals preferable to fixed-intervals. Although variable-interval schedules don't produce response rates that are as high as those produced with ratio schedules, they have a practical advantage for use in

CLOSE-UP 10.2

Cognitive Factors and Intermittent Reinforcement Effects

 The effects and phenomena relating to intermittent reinforcement and behavior were shown originally with animals, especially pigeons and rats, as subjects in research. Later, they were applied toward changing human behavior. But we now know that the effects of intermittent schedules of reinforcement are not always the same for animals and humans (Baron & Galizio, 1983; Lowe, 1979). One of the clearest differences is that humans who are being reinforced under a fixed-interval schedule sometimes don't show the prolonged pauses in responding after reinforcement that are usually found with this schedule. Why should this be?

The answer almost certainly involves the greater cognitive abilities of humans. People often try to figure out the rules governing their experiences and verbalize these rules in regulating their behaviors (Baron & Galizio, 1983; Michael, 1987). But the rules figured out are not necessarily correct. When people decide on the wrong rule, their response patterns are likely to follow the rule they believe exists rather than the actual rule. Three lines of evidence support the view that cognitive factors can affect people's performance under intermittent reinforcement. First, the cumulative graphs of children under fixed-interval reinforcement schedules show less and less scalloping as the subjects get older and their cognitive and verbal skills develop (Bentall, Lowe, & Beasty, 1985; Lowe, Beasty, & Bentall, 1983). Second, when adults are prevented from using verbal instructions to regulate a target behavior—for example, by having them subtract numbers in their heads—cumulative graphs of their behavior under fixed-interval reinforcement show very pronounced scalloping (Laties & Weiss, 1963). Third, simply giving adults rate-related instructions, such as to "go fast" or "go slow," can greatly affect their response rates in operant tasks with various reinforcement schedules (Catania, Matthews, & Shimoff, 1982; Hayes et al., 1986).

certain settings, especially in classrooms: administering the schedule doesn't require us to keep track continuously of all instances of the target behavior. Keeping track of more than one person's behavior simultaneously and continuously is difficult and time consuming. (Go to)

Effects of Schedules After the Intervention Ends   After an intervention ends and the reinforcement given in the behavior change program is discontinued, the everyday life of the person may provide little or no reinforcement for the target behavior. If this happens, ratio strain or extinction may cause a relapse in the behavior. We saw in Chapter 4 that giving reinforcement on an intermittent schedule rather than a CRF schedule makes the behavior more persistent, more *resistant to extinction*. This effect has been found with animals and humans (Kazdin & Polster, 1973; Kimble, 1961; Lewis, 1960; Lewis & Duncan, 1956). In general, behaviors that have been reinforced on variable schedules rather than on their fixed counterparts appear to be especially resistant to extinction (Shaw, 1987). To maintain a behavioral change and prevent a relapse, interventions should reinforce the target behavior on an intermittent schedule of reinforcement.

A reanalysis by John Nevin (1988) of data from several studies conducted with animals has raised some controversy regarding the impact of intermittent reinforcement schedules on extinction. According to this reanalysis, resistance to extinction may be *greater* after CRF than after intermittent reinforcement schedules when the behavior involves a "free operant" response—that is, a behavior one can engage in freely, with few or no constraints on the opportunity to act. Probably most behaviors people perform would qualify as free operant responses. On the basis of this reanalysis, some researchers (for example, Epstein, 1992) have recommended that interventions to change most problem operant behaviors in humans should use CRF rather than intermittent reinforcement schedules. But following this recommendation at this time seems premature. A large body of research supports using intermittent reinforcement to promote the persistence of free operant behavior, and Nevin's compelling reanalysis was conducted on only a small number of studies, all of which were conducted with rats or pigeons. To justify changing the current practice of using intermittent schedules to prevent relapses, we would need to have much more evidence, particularly in studies with humans.

Delaying Reinforcement

Reinforcement in everyday life is often delayed. For instance, when you do a fine job on an essay exam or a paper, you may not get your "A" grade for several days or longer. Although immediate reinforcement is important in learning to perform new behaviors, once the behavior is well established, the delay before reinforcement occurs can be increased without impairing performance. In fact, some evidence indicates that gradually delaying reinforcement after the behavior is well established can enhance its persistence after an intervention ends (Dunlap & Plienis, 1988; Fowler & Baer, 1981). To use delayed reinforcement in an intervention, we should wait until the behavior is well established, increase delays gradually, and monitor the person's performance carefully to make sure improvements in the behavior are not lost. (Go to ☑)

PROMOTING NATURAL REINFORCEMENT

One of the best ways to prevent relapses is to make sure the target behavior receives reinforcement in the target person's everyday environment. **Natural reinforcers** are rewards people receive in their usual life situations. In contrast to the programmed reinforcers in interventions, natural reinforcers happen spontaneously as a normal part of our daily lives. Enjoying a TV show is a natural reinforcer for turning on the set, selecting the channel the show is on, and sitting there to watch. Other examples of natural reinforcers include obtaining needed information by reading some material, receiving praise for good work in school or on a job, getting continuous feedback from your senses that your movements in performing a motor action are correct, and having someone laugh at a joke you tell. Interventions generally teach behaviors and skills that are expected to produce natural reinforcers in the person's everyday life.

Behaviors a person acquires in an intervention surely were not sufficiently reinforced in his or her everyday life in the past. If the behaviors had been reinforced, the

✓

CONCEPT CHECK 10.1

1. Regressing into one's former full-blown pattern of unwanted behavior is called a(n) _____ .

2. In the series of cognitive events leading a person to return to smoking after quitting, a high-risk situation might be _____ . ⇔

3. Thinning is recommended after the behavior has been well established under a(n) _____ schedule.

4. An everyday example of a variable-ratio schedule that doesn't involve gambling or selling products might be _____ . ⇔

5. The abbreviation for a reinforcement schedule in which the reward is unavailable for 2 minutes after each reinforcer is given would be _____ .

6. The reinforcement schedule that produces the highest response rate is the _____ schedule.

7. Temporary halts in responding after receiving rewards are called _____ .

8. People don't always show prolonged pauses after reinforcement under fixed-interval schedules, as animals do; this difference is probably because people's _____ abilities are different from those of animals.

Answers: 1. relapse, 2. someone offering a cigarette, 3. CRF, 4. asking new acquaintances on dates, 5. FI 2 minutes, 6. variable-ratio, 7. postreinforcement pauses, 8. cognitive/verbal

person would have been performing them already, and the intervention wouldn't have been needed. Studies have examined the occurrence of natural reinforcement in people's everyday lives and found that desirable behaviors often don't produce the kinds of consequences that would support or maintain them. For instance, observations in elementary and high schools have found that teachers tend to use more reprimands than praise with their students (Bear, 1998; Thomas et al., 1978; White, 1975). If a person whose behavior has been improved in an intervention is returned to an environment that does not reinforce the improved behavior, the gains will be lost.

The importance of natural reinforcers in preventing relapses can be seen in people who have quit smoking. Researchers have found that individuals who continue to abstain from smoking after quitting tend to receive more reinforcement and less punishment from their spouses for their efforts to abstain than individuals who relapse (Mermelstein, Lichtenstein, & McIntyre, 1983). Because natural reinforcement of the improved behavior is so important in maintaining it, behavior change programs should include procedures that promote its occurrence and effects. Let's see how this can be done.

Applying Natural Reinforcers

Ending an intervention involves a transition to naturally occurring reinforcers. A behavior change program can help the target person make this transition by applying natural reinforcers in the intervention. For instance, social reinforcers, such as praise, are among the most common types of reinforcers in daily life. Deliberately programming and applying social reinforcers in an intervention is likely to ease the person's transition to his or her natural environment. This is one reason behavior change programs often plan and include social reinforcers as consequences of target behaviors. For example, programs to improve the social behaviors of children have had more mature classmates model, initiate, and praise appropriate social behavior, such as smiling and inviting another child to play (Cooke & Apolloni, 1976; Strain, Shores, & Timm, 1977). To the extent that these positive social behaviors become part of the mutual interactions of the children in class, the behaviors will be maintained by natural reinforcement (Fowler, 1988).

Assessing and Increasing Natural Reinforcement

A critical step in promoting the occurrence of natural reinforcement for the improved behavior is to assess the target person's everyday environment for two characteristics. First, the natural environment should provide opportunities to perform the changed behavior so that it can be reinforced (Horner, Williams, & Knobbe, 1985). This would be especially important for maintaining alternative responses and newly trained responses to correct behavioral deficits. Second, the environment must provide sufficient natural reinforcement to maintain the target behavior. These characteristics can be assessed in several ways, one of which is by doing a functional analysis of the behavior during or soon after the process of ending the intervention (Durand & Carr, 1991; Favell & Reid, 1988; Kohler & Greenwood, 1986). If these assessments indicate that the target person's current environment is not likely to maintain the behavior, efforts should be made to modify the environment. One of the best ways to increase the opportunities for the person to perform the changed behavior is to instruct other people, such as parents and teachers, to make sure these opportunities occur. For instance, teachers of children whose social behaviors have been improved can schedule classroom activities and provide materials that encourage rather than constrain the desired behaviors.

There are basically two approaches for increasing the occurrence of natural reinforcement in the everyday life of someone whose behavior has been changed in an intervention. First, we can train the target person to seek out or *recruit* natural reinforcement. Because individuals often fail to get the feedback and praise they need to maintain appropriate behavior, it may be useful to train them in ways to elicit the reinforcement they need. This approach was used in an intervention to improve the work skills of three individuals with mental retardation in a sheltered workshop (Hildebrand et al., 1990). Training these workers to recognize when they reached a productivity goal and then ask their supervisors to give them feedback increased the production rates of two of the individuals. Similarly, children with developmental disabilities have been trained to recruit teacher attention and feedback for their classroom work (Craft, Alber, & Heward, 1998).

The second approach for increasing natural reinforcement after an intervention involves training other people in the target person's everyday life to watch for the behavior and reinforce it. Although these other people are usually family members or teachers, anyone with whom the person has contact regularly can assist in monitoring and reinforcing the behavior. Here are three examples. First, programs to improve classroom conduct have included procedures to train teachers to incorporate token reinforcement in their classrooms on a regular basis (Walker & Buckley, 1972; Walker, Hops, & Johnson, 1975). Second, an intervention to improve speaking and self-care skills in children with autism trained their parents in behavioral techniques (Lovaas et al., 1973). Third, after a man's pain behaviors had been reduced and then relapsed when he returned home, his family was trained to ignore his pain complaints and praise his motor activities (Kallman, Hersen, & O'Toole, 1975). In each of these interventions, training people in the target person's natural environment to apply behavioral methods helped the improved behavior persist.

PROMOTING GENERALIZATION OF THE BEHAVIOR

To assure that a person's improved behavior will persist after an intervention, behavior change programs should include steps to help the response generalize to the antecedents that are likely to be encountered in everyday life. We saw in Chapter 3 that when individuals learn to perform behaviors in association with specific antecedents they also tend to make those responses to stimuli they encounter that are similar to the antecedents they have learned. This phenomenon is called *stimulus generalization*. Although there are many other forms of generalization (see Allen et al., 1991), we will focus on eliciting the behavior in a variety of appropriate situations that were not explicitly trained in the intervention.

How well do improved behaviors generalize to everyday appropriate situations? Some behavior change programs have assessed the occurrence of target behaviors in nontrained situations without having included specific steps to promote generalization. Sometimes the behavior did generalize; for example, it occurred in nontrained settings or with different antecedent cues (Baer, Peterson, & Sherman, 1967; McNeil et al., 1991; Stokes & Baer, 1976). In other programs, the behavior did not generalize (Guevremont, Osnes, & Stokes, 1988; Hersen, Eisler, & Miller, 1974). Interventions can use several techniques to promote generalization (Landrum & Lloyd, 1992; Stokes & Baer, 1977; Stokes & Osnes, 1988, 1989). Let's see what these techniques are.

Training with Everyday Antecedents

Interventions often occur in settings and with antecedent stimuli that are very different from those that will be present in the target person's everyday life when he or she will need to perform the target behavior. For instance, the settings in therapists' offices and psychiatric hospitals are quite different from those clients will encounter in their natural environments. The greater the differences between intervention and natural settings, the less likely it is that the behavior will generalize. As a result, programs to change behavior need to ensure that training occurs under conditions that are as similar as possible to those in the person's usual environment (Bouton, 2000; Favell & Reid, 1988; Landrum & Lloyd, 1992; Stokes & Osnes, 1989).

There are three ways of making the intervention and natural conditions similar, thereby promoting generalization of the target behavior. One approach involves fading any prompts that are being used in training a behavior that will not be available in the person's everyday environment. The second way involves conducting some or all of the intervention training in the person's natural environment. As an example, a program to improve the strained communication patterns of parents and their adolescent children initially provided training in therapists' offices (Serna at al., 1991). Although the parents and adolescents learned the skills and could demonstrate them when assessed in the office settings, they didn't use these skills effectively at home until training was moved to the home situation. Other studies with different behaviors and different individuals have also found that carrying out training in settings like those in which the behavior is intended to occur promotes generalization to those situations (Corte, Wolfe, & Locke, 1971; Stark et al., 1986).

In the third approach for making the intervention and natural conditions similar to promote generalization of the target behavior, aspects of the everyday environment are brought into the therapy setting. An intervention used this approach to get children with autism to generalize to the classroom situation basic classroom behaviors they were taught individually in a different room (Koegel & Rincover, 1974). These behaviors included looking at the teacher and imitating the teacher's actions upon request. To promote generalization, the training conditions were changed to be more like a classroom by gradually adding other children to the intervention sessions. This procedure was very effective in getting these children to generalize the target behaviors to the classroom. (Go to)

Getting Alice to Speak Up in Class

Alice was a very withdrawn 15-year-old girl with mild retardation who almost never spoke at a level others could hear (case described in Jackson & Wallace, 1974). A program was undertaken to increase the loudness of Alice's speech by using tokens to reinforce her when she read words at acceptable loudness levels while sitting inside an enclosed booth in a laboratory. Although the intervention succeeded in the therapy setting, Alice still spoke too softly in the classroom when tested each day of the intervention. To promote generalization of audible speech, the therapists made the therapy setting more and more like the classroom by introducing the following changes during the next 15 training sessions:

1. Two classmates were brought into the laboratory to study silently several feet away from the booth and out of Alice's view while she read words.
2. The side of Alice's booth was opened part way, thereby reducing her privacy.

3. The side of the booth was removed, exposing Alice to the two classmates who studied silently.

4. The teacher and five students conducted a study period in the laboratory while Alice read words in the booth, still with the side removed.

These steps to promote generalization succeeded. Soon Alice was speaking at normal loudness levels in the classroom.

Widening Stimulus Control

Another reason for the failure of people's improved behaviors to generalize to everyday life is that during the intervention the behaviors may have become associated with too small a range of antecedent stimuli. For example, suppose a child receives training in naming objects, and only one teacher and that set of materials are used. The stimulus control exerted by that teacher and that set of materials may become overly strong because these discriminative stimuli (S^Ds) have been associated with reinforcement frequently and consistently, but other stimuli have not. As a result, the child may respond correctly only when these S^Ds are present and not when other teachers or materials are used. Programs can avoid this kind of problem and promote generalization of the behavior by taking steps to widen stimulus control.

The basic approach used in widening stimulus control involves including a range of antecedent stimuli in the intervention. The program can use more than one teacher, for example, and a variety of materials, activities, or settings. The effects of using this approach were tested in a study of ways to increase the positive comments students made to one another at a residential home for delinquent and disturbed teenagers (Emshoff, Redd, & Davidson, 1976). All of the students in the study received token and social reinforcers for making positive comments to a peer during seven 30-minute sessions. Half of the students experienced these sessions with varying antecedent stimuli (trainers, locations, time during the day) and activities (at dinner, for instance, or while playing cards, word games, or Ping-Pong). For the remaining students, the sessions always occurred with the same trainer, location, time of day, and activity (Ping-Pong).

To test whether generalization was greater when training was carried out with varied antecedents, positive comments were assessed during other home activities, such as watching TV. Not only did the students who received training with varied antecedents show far more generalization of the behavior to other home activities, but during follow-up assessments in the 3 weeks after the intervention ended, their positive comments continued to occur at higher rates than those with constant antecedents. Other studies with different behaviors and individuals have also found high levels of generalization when the interventions used varied antecedent stimuli (Poche, Brouwer, & Swearingen, 1981; Stokes, Baer, & Jackson, 1974).

This approach of using a range of antecedent stimuli to widen stimulus control has been refined and formalized into a procedure called *general case training* (Albin & Horner, 1988; Horner, Eberhard, & Sheenan, 1986). General case training begins with a specification of the exact situations in which the behavior should occur after the program has ended, as well as the extent to which antecedent stimuli and the person's behavior can be allowed to vary. The next step is to identify a series of teaching examples that sample the full range of stimulus and response variations within each situation in which the behavior should be performed. For instance, if the general case involved using ballpoint pens of different types, we might use pens that expose the writing tip by taking off a cap, or pushing a button, or twisting the shaft. Last, training is given with the teaching examples. Studies that have tested the general case training approach have found not only that it is effective in promoting the generalization of target behaviors but that it is more effective in promoting generalization than several other commonly used approaches (Ducharme & Feldman, 1992; Horner, Eberhard, & Sheenan, 1986; Neef et al., 1990).

Enhancing Self-Regulation Skills

According to Frederick Kanfer and Laurence Grimm (1980), therapy using behavior change techniques proceeds through a series of phases, the last of which focuses on the generalization and maintenance of treatment gains as

> the culmination of the therapy process, since the overall goal is to help the client become his or her own therapist by extending treatment gains beyond the time limits of therapy and to problems that may occur after termination. (p. 436)

Some research suggests that enhancing individuals' abilities to direct and modulate their own target behavior—their *self-regulation skills*—tends to promote generalization of that behavior to everyday life.

In one study, adolescents who were emotionally disturbed were trained to increase their on-task behavior in the classroom and decrease their socially undesirable behavior, such as fighting and cursing (Ninness et al., 1991). The behavior change program included modeling, reinforcement, and self-management techniques. After 5 weeks of training, the students' classroom conduct had improved substantially, and this conduct generalized to between-class periods when they were asked to apply newly acquired self-management skills, such as self-monitoring. In another study, adults and adolescents received participant modeling treatment to reduce their fear of snakes (Bandura, Jeffery, & Gajdos, 1975). Some of them spent an additional hour on their own handling the snake. Subsequent follow-up assessments revealed that, compared to individuals who received participant modeling alone, those who spent time with the snake on their own reported greater reductions in a number of other, nontreated fears. These results suggest that interventions that provide individuals with opportunities to self-regulate their behavior promote generalization.

One additional point should be made about promoting the generalization and persistence of improved behavior: the techniques we've examined can be used in combination. One example of a program that used a combination of these techniques was aimed at improving institutionalized adolescents' social skills, such as waiting to ask for materials and not interrupting others (Foxx, Faw, & Weber, 1991). This program faded the prompts that were used in training, widened stimulus control by training for a variety of social antecedents the teenagers were likely to encounter, thinned the monetary reinforcement given for attendance and performance at training sessions, and used some self-management techniques, such as self-monitoring.

POSTTREATMENT PROGRAMS

Many people think of emotional and behavioral problems in the same framework they use in thinking about infectious illnesses: When you're sick, you become cured—free of the infection—by killing the microorganisms that caused the illness. Emotional and behavioral problems don't really conform to this view, however, partly because these problems usually result mainly from our learning, and we retain memories of what we have learned. Even after an unwanted operant or respondent behavior has been extinguished and replaced, we retain the memory of the behavior (Bouton & Swartzentruber, 1991; LeDoux, 1994). This means there's always some risk of relapsing into the unwanted behavior. If we recognize this and prepare for the possible return of the behavior, it may be possible to head off a relapse.

There are two main approaches for heading off relapses, and each involves some form of posttreatment program. One of these approaches involves having the person participate in a **booster program**—that is, a set of additional intervention phases or sessions to shore up or refresh the original program's effects. These phases or sessions usually are similar to the original ones, and the person may need to participate in them periodically, perhaps every few months. Stan Paine and his colleagues (1982) used a booster program to refresh the training socially withdrawn schoolchildren received in an intervention that reinforced social behaviors with tokens. Because the children's improved social behavior tended to decline after the original training, the intervention was reintroduced three times as separate phases, with reversal phases in between. Across successive intervention phases, the children lost less and less of the improved behavior during the reversal phases and continued to show social behaviors that were within the normal range after the booster program ended. Other booster programs have also been successful, helping individuals maintain their improvements in assertiveness, problem drinking, and classroom conduct (Baggs & Spence, 1990; Connors, Tarbox, & Faillace, 1992; Maletzky, 1974).

The second approach, called the **relapse prevention method,** is based on G. Alan Marlatt's view that relapses develop through a series of cognitive events that often follow the occurrence of a lapse. We saw earlier that these events lead to an abstinence violation effect, in which feelings of guilt and reduced self-efficacy after a lapse can precipitate a relapse (Marlatt & Gordon, 1980; Marlatt & Parks, 1982). The relapse prevention approach is basically a self-management program that is supervised by a therapist. The program consists of having the person take the following steps:

1. *Learn to identify high-risk situations* by generating a list and descriptions of antecedent conditions in which lapses are most likely to occur.
2. *Acquire competent and specific coping skills* through training in specific behaviors and thought patterns that will enable the person to deal with high-risk situations and avoid lapses.

CONCEPT CHECK 10.2

1. A natural reinforcer people might receive after starting an exercise program and becoming more physically fit is _____ . ⇔
2. One way to promote generalization of the training given to institutionalized alcoholics to enhance their ability to refuse drinks at a party might be to _____ . ⇔
3. The formal procedure for widening stimulus control is called _____ .
4. If we provided treatment phases or sessions after an intervention ended, we'd be using a(n) _____ to head off a relapse.
5. The first step in the relapse prevention approach is to have the person _____ .

Answers: 1. compliments, 2. simulate a party atmosphere during training, 3. general case training, 4. booster program, 5. learn to identify high-risk situations

3. *Practice effective coping skills in high-risk situations* under a therapist's supervision. For example, problem drinkers might go with their therapists to a bar and practice ways to avoid drinking.

The relapse prevention method was developed to address the high relapse rates that often follow treatment for substance abuse. Research has shown that it is successful in reducing relapse after substance abuse treatment, especially for alcohol use (Irvin et al., 1999). It has been applied to other behavior problems too. (Go to)

Tips on Maintaining Behavior Changes

We have discussed several ways interventions can help individuals maintain behavior changes after the intervention is over. Here are some tips to consider when designing a program:

1. Try to focus interventions on target behaviors that will be useful in the person's natural environment, thereby leading to reinforcement after the program is over.
2. Train the target behavior(s) with a variety of antecedent stimuli that are likely to be encountered in the natural environment. If possible, start the training with simple tasks, such as with antecedents that are easy to discriminate, and then progress to harder ones.
3. Monitor the behavior very carefully when fading prompts, thinning reinforcement, or introducing other procedural changes.
4. Thin the reinforcement gradually, preferably with the goal of establishing a variable schedule.
5. Assess the likelihood of natural reinforcement for the target behavior(s) before the intervention ends.
6. Make sure the target person will have opportunities to perform the target behavior in everyday life after the intervention ends.

SUMMARY

Although some behavior changes produced in interventions are permanent, other changes are not. Relapses in behavior are not unusual. They can occur for several reasons. First, the former behavior was probably learned very thoroughly. Second, the target person is likely to encounter the old antecedent cues and chains again. Third, sometimes the behavioral improvements the intervention produced are not learned strongly enough. And fourth, cognitive factors can lead to a relapse: encountering a high-risk situation may lead to a lapse; this can trigger a series of thoughts and feelings called the abstinence violation effect, which can precipitate a relapse.

Thinning the reinforcement to an intermittent reinforcement schedule tends to make the behavior more persistent, or more resistant to extinction, after an intervention ends. In ratio schedules, the occurrence of reinforcement is based on the number of correct responses made. For each instance of reinforcement, a fixed-ratio (FR) schedule requires a constant number of responses, but a variable-ratio (VR) schedule requires an unspecified and changing number of responses. Responding under fixed-ratio schedules generally shows postreinforcement pauses. Ratio schedules of reinforcement produce very high rates of response while the schedules are in force, especially if the ratio is variable. In interval schedules, rewards are given following the first correct response after an interval of time has elapsed. For each instance of reinforcement, a fixed-interval (FI) schedule sets a constant length of time when the reward is not available, whereas a variable-interval (VI) schedule makes rewards unavailable for an unspecified and changing period of time. Interval schedules produce moderate response rates, with cumulative graphs of responses showing a scalloping pattern. Cognitive factors appear to affect whether scalloping is seen in the graphs in studies of humans. If the number of responses required for each instance of intermittent reinforcement becomes too large, ratio strain may occur, causing the behavior to deteriorate.

Natural reinforcers occur as a normal part of everyday life and can play an important role in maintaining changes in behavior. Before an intervention ends, the target person's natural environment should be assessed to determine what the likelihood is of natural reinforcers occurring and whether they will need to be enhanced. To help prevent relapses, programs can promote generalization of the behavior by conducting training with everyday antecedents and with a variety of stimuli and situations. Booster programs and relapse prevention methods are posttreatment approaches for maintaining behavior changes.

KEY TERMS

relapse	fixed-ratio	postreinforcement pauses
abstinence violation effect	variable-ratio	ratio strain
intermittent reinforcement schedule	interval schedules	natural reinforcers
ratio schedules	fixed-interval	booster program
	variable-interval	relapse prevention method

REVIEW QUESTIONS

1. How are relapses different from lapses? Why do relapses occur?
2. Define the term intermittent reinforcement schedules, and describe how ratio and interval schedules differ.
3. What is an FR schedule? Give an example from your everyday life that doesn't involve piecework.
4. What is a VR schedule, and how is it different from an FR schedule?
5. Explain what an FI schedule is, and give two examples from everyday life that are not in the text.
6. Explain what a VI schedule is, and give two examples from everyday life that are not in the text.
7. What are duration schedules, and how are they different from interval schedules?
8. Describe the effects of ratio schedules of reinforcement on behavior.
9. Describe the effects of interval schedules of reinforcement on behavior.
10. What is ratio strain?
11. How are natural reinforcers important in maintaining a behavior change?
12. Describe how interventions can promote generalization of the target behavior.
13. Describe the research by Emshoff, Redd, and Davidson (1976) on generalization. What do the results mean?
14. Describe the two main approaches for heading off relapses after an intervention ends.

RELATED READINGS

Horner, R. H., Dunlap, G., & Koegel, R. L. (Eds.). (1988). *Generalization and maintenance: Lifestyle changes in applied settings*. Baltimore: Paul H. Brookes.

Landrum, T. J., & Lloyd, J. W. (1992). Generalization in social behavior research with children and youth who have emotional or behavioral disorders. *Behavior Modification, 16,* 593–616.

Marlatt, G. A., & Parks, G. A. (1982). Self-management of addictive behaviors. In P. Karoly & F. H. Kanfer (Eds.), *Self-management and behavior change: From theory to practice*. New York: Pergamon.

Stokes, T. F., & Osnes, P. G. (1989). An operant pursuit of generalization. *Behavior Therapy, 20,* 337–355.

The accuracy of research data can be enhanced by videotaping behavior through a one-way mirror and having two or more observers make direct assessments from the taped recordings.

Research Methods in Behavior Modification

Each semester, students in Mrs. Quinn's fifth-grade classes try to improve their public speaking skills by giving short speeches. In one semester, a boy named Cassius was doing poorly in the first week of these activities, performing at a much lower level than any other classmate. Because Mrs. Quinn wanted very much to have all her students do well, she met with the boy individually to provide training in several speaking skills. The teacher identified certain behavioral deficits in the way her student introduced and ended his speeches—for instance, he didn't smile or look at the audience—and trained him in doing these things. And she addressed another deficit by giving Cassius a few specific rules for organizing speeches, such as "Present an overview first" and "Cover the topics in the stated order." Mrs. Quinn's techniques included verbal prompts, modeling, and token and praise reinforcers. After just three individual sessions in the first week, the grades Cassius received on his classroom speeches were higher than the class average.

Did the student's improved grades result from the intervention techniques Mrs. Quinn used? Although it's very tempting to think they did, other factors might have been responsible. For instance, maybe he started the semester with good speaking skills, but illness or difficulties at home impaired his performance in the first week and ended soon after. Or maybe his speeches improved because his parents helped him compose them. Or maybe he hadn't done any preparation for his speeches in the first week, but he became motivated to prepare them in the second week because of the individual attention he was getting. And maybe the boy's performance didn't really improve at all, but the teacher perceived better skills because she believed her methods would work. Since the improved grades could have resulted from any of these reasons and many others, we cannot be certain that the intervention techniques produced the changes.

In evaluating the success of a program to change behavior, we can have two purposes in mind. First, we'll want to know *whether* the behavior has changed. We saw in Chapter 9 that we can do a graphic analysis to make such a determination. Second, we may want to know *why* the behavior changed. Research in behavior modification is designed to demonstrate unambiguously that changes in the behavior resulted from the intervention's techniques, rather than from some other factors. This chapter focuses on this second purpose and describes various research methods used in demonstrating that the techniques in the intervention, rather than other factors, were responsible for any changes we observe in the behavior.

ACCURACY OF THE DATA

To evaluate clearly whether behavior changes have occurred and, if so, why, we must have data that accurately reflect the status of the behavior. Several types of problems can reduce the accuracy of the data collected in a behavior modification program.

Sources of Data Inaccuracies

Suppose Vera is trying to control her weight, and the bathroom scale she uses to weigh herself gives widely different readings, even when her true weight hasn't changed. For instance, when she got on and off the scale three times in row without doing anything to change her true weight, the scale read 148, 153, and 145. Because the scale doesn't give the same reading each time the same poundage is weighed, Vera's weight data are *unreliable*. The source of these inaccuracies lies in the measuring instrument—the scale. If the data vary unpredictably, there isn't any good way to decide which reading is correct. Sometimes people in everyday life simply decide that the correct reading is the one that pleases them. Beth Sulzer and G. Roy Mayer (1972) described how a dieting woman they knew would get on and off her unreliable scale repeatedly until the reading pleased her. Then she would walk away smiling and thinking, "The diet is working." Deluding oneself doesn't make the data any more accurate. Of course, measurement accuracy is never perfect, but variations from the true reading should be very slight or rare. Whenever possible, unreliable instruments should be replaced or corrected.

Assessments of behavior can be unreliable too. Indirect assessment methods can lead to inaccuracies in assessing behavioral changes for at least three reasons. First, some indirect assessments measure the outcomes of behavior, not the target behavior itself. For example, part of an intervention to reduce cash-register shortages resulting from theft or careless change-counting by cashiers in a store consisted of assessing discrepancies between sales receipts and cash in the register (Marholin & Gray, 1976). While the intervention was in force, these discrepancies decreased. But this doesn't necessarily mean thefts or change-counting errors were reduced. As the researchers noted, it may be that the victim became the customer instead of the employer; i.e., the employees resorted to short-changing the customer rather than taking money directly from the cash register. Another possibility is that the cashiers may have increasingly been underringing sales. (pp. 28–29)

Given the procedures used in this intervention, the underlying target behavior may not be reflected in the data collected. Second, when indirect assessment methods involve rating scales or questionnaires, the data are likely to be unreliable if the questions or labels they use can be interpreted in different ways. Third, data from self-report instruments depend on people's memories, which can be faulty. Reports about a specific event can vary from one assessment to another because what people remember about it can change.

Direct assessment methods of behavior can produce unreliable data for several reasons. For one thing, as we saw in Chapter 2, people's behavior can be affected by *reactivity*—that is, actions may change when individuals know they are being observed (Baum, Forehand, & Zegiob, 1979; Monette, Sullivan, & DeJong, 1990). These effects often are temporary; they may occur during just a few initial observations and tend to disappear as the person becomes accustomed to being observed. When reactivity occurs, the assessments will either over- or underestimate the behavior during those observations, making the data less reliable across time periods. As an example, reactivity may reduce a behavioral excess—for example, cursing—during baseline but disappear by the time the intervention starts. If there is reason to think reactivity has been occurring, it is usually a good idea to collect baseline data until the data stabilize.

Three other problems can lead to unreliable data in direct assessments (Hawkins & Dotson, 1975; Sulzer & Mayer, 1972). First, the *definition of the target behavior* may be unclear. When the operative definition is stated vaguely or incompletely, it is hard for an observer to be sure whether or to what extent the behavior occurred. Second, the *observer* may not have received enough training and practice or be sufficiently motivated to watch for the behavior carefully and to detect and record the behavior accurately. Third, *detectability* may be impaired because the behavior is very subtle or because distractions or other factors may interfere with the observation process. Although we can reduce many of these problems by clarifying the definitions of behaviors, providing sufficient training, or removing distractions, we may not eliminate them entirely. As a result, it is often important to assess the reliability of the data.

Assessing Data Reliability

Assessing the accuracy of data collected with direct assessment methods should begin while observers are being trained and continue throughout baseline and intervention phases of behavior change programs. The general approach for assessing the accuracy of such data involves examining the records collected by two or more observers to ascertain their degree of consistency, which is called **interobserver reliability** (or *interrater reliability* or *interobserver agreement*). Observer consistency or reliability is not exactly the same as accuracy, but data are more likely to be reliable if they are accurate. To use this approach, we must have the observers collect data simultaneously for the same behaviors. We must also make sure the observers record their data independently, without being able to tell what is being recorded by the other observer(s) at any given time. Although there are several ways to evaluate the consistency of the data different observers have collected, two methods are especially common (Foster & Cone, 1986).

In the *session totals method* of assessing interobserver reliability, all the data collected by each of two observers in an observation session or period are added, the smaller total is divided by the larger, and a percentage of agreement or consistency is obtained by multiplying by 100. For example, suppose Todd and Kim observed and recorded a worker's frequency of complimenting customers for an entire day at work. Todd recorded 40 acts of complimenting, and Kim recorded 36. We would divide 36 by 40 (which equals .90), and multiply by 100, which yields 90% agreement. What does this percentage mean?

Interobserver reliability evaluated with the session totals method should be interpreted with caution. Although the percentage gives us a sense of the extent of overall agreement for the amount of complimenting Todd and Kim observed the worker perform, it does not necessarily mean that they both saw the same 36 compliments, with Todd seeing 4 additional ones that Kim missed. It is possible that Todd was mistaken about the 4 extra ones. And it is possible that the worker actually made 50 compliments, and only 30 of them were seen by both Todd and Kim. Still, a percentage as high as 90% gives us reason to believe that the total number of acts recorded is a reliable estimate of the actual behavior, even though the observers may have disagreed on some individual instances.

The Todd and Kim example used frequency data. But the session totals method can also be used with other types of data, such as duration or magnitude. For instance, Tim Wysocki and his colleagues (1979) used this method to compare the total points awarded by observers to 12 individuals for the intensity and duration of their exercising. As an example, someone who ran a mile in about 9 minutes got 4.0 points, and someone who swam 200 yards in 4 minutes got 1.5 points. To calculate the percentage of agreement, the smaller number of points given by two observers for an individual's exercising was divided by the larger and multiplied by 100. Across all individuals, agreements ranged from about 83% to 100%. In this study, interobserver reliability evaluations with two observers were done for about one fourth of the observations. Assessing data reliability on only some of the possible observations is a fairly common practice, but the number of observations should be substantial and distributed evenly over the time the study is conducted to get a representative sample of the behavior.

The second commonly used approach for assessing interobserver reliability is the *interval-recording method*. We saw in Chapter 2 that, in interval recording, only one instance of the target behavior is recorded for each particular, specified time interval in an extended observation period, even if many more instances occurred. Let's suppose Todd and Kim collected their data on the worker's complimenting by using the strategy of interval recording. They watched the worker for 30 minutes and were to record if an instance of complimenting a customer occurred during each 15-second interval. Their records might agree that complimenting occurred for some intervals and disagree with respect to other intervals. To calculate the interobserver reliability with the interval recording method, we would divide the number of intervals for which Todd and Kim agreed that a compliment occurred by the total number of intervals in which their records agreed and disagreed. Suppose that for eight of the intervals both observers said that the worker complimented customers in each interval, but for two intervals there was disagreement (Todd's records said complimenting occurred in one of the intervals and Kim's said complimenting occurred in another interval). We would calculate the percentage of agreement by dividing 8 (agree intervals) by 10 (agree + disagree intervals) and multiplying by 100, yielding 80% agreement.

At this point you may be wondering why all the intervals in which Todd and Kim recorded no complimenting are not included in the analysis. After all, they both seemed to agree that the behavior did *not* occur in those intervals. Many researchers do not include data for nonoccurrences of the behavior because these data are more likely to be faulty or inaccurate than data for occurrences (Foster & Cone, 1986; Hawkins & Dotson, 1975). For instance, both records might show no complimenting even though it actually occurred if both observers missed seeing it because of a distraction in the environment. By including inaccurate records in assessing interobserver reliability, we would be biasing the evaluation. As a result, the interval-recording method generally excludes nonoccurrence data. One exception to this rule is when the target is a behavioral excess, such as an emotional reaction, and we need to determine if the observers agree that the behavior no longer occurs when the antecedent cues are present (Foster & Cone, 1986). In this case, we would use nonoccurrences in place of occurrences in the calculations.

Five additional points can be stated about assessing data accuracy. First, some evidence indicates that letting observers know their records will be checked against those of other observers appears to increase their accuracy (Foster & Cone, 1986). Second, methods to test interobserver reliability can be used in training observers before they begin to collect data for the research itself. In one study, observers received training until they showed 90% agreement during three consecutive observation periods (Zohn & Bornstein, 1980). Third, the general rule of thumb is that 80% agreement is the minimum acceptable level of reliability (Sulzer & Mayer, 1972). Fourth, data collected with indirect assessment methods can be compared for interobserver reliability in a similar manner. Fifth, interobserver reliability can be used to assess data accuracy in self-management programs, too, by having one or more observers collect data on the person's behavior to compare against the person's self-monitoring records.

Collecting reliable data is essential in evaluating changes in behavior. Without reliable data, research projects start out with weak foundations and produce ambiguous results that can have more than one plausible interpretation. When research is well designed and conducted, one interpretation of why the changes occurred is clearly more convincing than any other. Research designs can take many different forms, but the most commonly used designs in evaluating behavior changes can be classified into two categories: *intrasubject research*, which focuses on behavioral changes in individual subjects across time, and *group-based research*, which examines changes or differences in behavior across many individuals. Sometimes research is conducted simply to determine *whether and to what extent an intervention has changed behavior*, and sometimes it is conducted *to isolate the cause of the change*. The purpose of the research is a major consideration in deciding which type of research design to use. (Go to ✓)

INTRASUBJECT RESEARCH

Research using **intrasubject designs,** or *single-subject designs,* examine changes in the behavior of individual subjects across time, while interventions are either in effect or absent (Hilliard, 1993; Monette, Sullivan, & DeJong, 1990). Sometimes intrasubject research is conducted with more than one subject, but the data collected for the target behaviors are usually evaluated for each subject separately, using graphic analysis methods. Researchers have developed methods to combine data from many intrasubject studies to evaluate the overall effectiveness of specific behavior modification techniques (Scruggs & Mastropieri, 1998). In our examination of intrasubject designs, we will see that researchers name and describe some types of these designs by using the first two letters of the alphabet to signify different phases of the research. The letter A indicates a baseline or reversal phase in which the intervention was absent, and the letter B symbolizes a phase in which a specific form of intervention was in effect. Other letters, such as C or D, sometimes are used to indicate phases in which intervention techniques different from those in B were in effect.

AB Designs

The **AB design** is the simplest type of intrasubject research, consisting of one baseline phase and one intervention phase. Earlier we saw an example of an AB design in which Mrs. Quinn used several techniques to improve the public speaking skills of a student named Cassius. As we noted in that discussion, we cannot determine whether the teacher's intervention was responsible for the boy's improved grades. This is because having just one baseline and one intervention phase doesn't allow us to rule out other factors in the person's life that may actually be responsible for the behavior changes observed. As a result, the AB design may be useful when the purpose of research is simply to determine the extent to which the behavior changed, but it is less than ideal when we want to isolate the cause of the change.

Drew Erhardt and Bruce Baker (1990) used an AB design to evaluate behavioral changes in two 5-year-old hyperactive children after their parents began a training program in behavior modification techniques. The parents learned how to identify and define target behaviors, collect data, determine relevant antecedents and consequences, and apply various types of reinforcement for appropriate behavior. Although the target behaviors observed for each child were somewhat different, noncompliance to adult requests was targeted as a problem behavior for both children. Noncompliance declined modestly and continued to fluctuate for each of the children across the several weeks of the intervention. Even though this study does not allow us to isolate the causes of the behavior changes, its outcome is important because it provides preliminary evidence that parent training in behavioral methods may be useful in treatment programs for hyperactive children.

Reversal, ABA or ABAB Designs

Reversal designs involve a series of phases in which an intervention is alternately present and absent. Reversal designs of two types are commonly used. The **ABA design** consists of three phases: baseline, intervention, and reversal. In the reversal phase, the intervention is withdrawn to reinstate the baseline conditions. The reversal phase allows us to see if the behavioral changes that occurred during intervention revert toward baseline levels when the intervention is withdrawn. The **ABAB design** contains four phases: baseline, intervention, reversal, and intervention. By reinstating the intervention, we can see whether the behavior responds again to the program's techniques. Reversal designs have a distinct advantage over AB designs—they can demonstrate increases and decreases in the behavior that correspond to the presence and absence of the intervention. Because these corresponding increases and decreases would be unlikely to result from factors other than the conditions in the research, they provide strong evidence that the intervention *caused* the behavior to change. As a result, reversal designs not only show changes in the behavior but indicate why the changes occurred.

To illustrate intrasubject research using an ABAB design, I will describe an intervention to reduce the excessive, loud, and abusive statements of a 58-year-old institu-

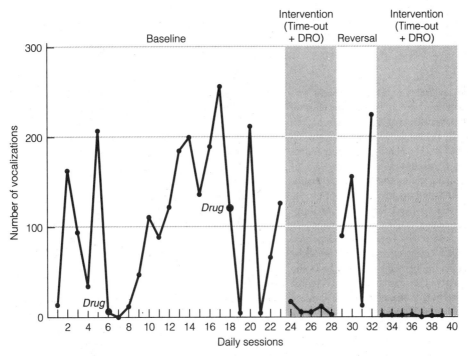

Figure 11.1 Number of loud verbal outbursts (vocalizations) a woman with mental retardation named Ruth made in each 1-hour observation session in baseline and intervention phases in an ABAB design. The intervention consisted of time-out punishment for outbursts and differential reinforcement of other behavior (DRO). On two occasions during the baseline phase (labeled "Drug"), Ruth was given a tranquilizer because her tirades had been so extreme. *Source:* Bostow & Bailey, 1969, Figure 1.

tionalized woman with mental retardation named Ruth (Bostow & Bailey, 1969). Her tirades tended to focus on demands for various items, such as articles of clothing or favorite objects that she frequently dropped but couldn't retrieve from her wheelchair. Ruth's verbal tirades were particularly severe at mealtimes: she would scream violently when she wanted her meal tray delivered, her tray removed when she was finished, and so on. To reduce the frequency of her verbal outbursts, the intervention applied two techniques: (1) time-out punishment, which involved wheeling her to a corner of the room when outbursts occurred and leaving her there for 2 minutes, and (2) differential reinforcement of other behavior (DRO), in which she would receive reinforcers for *not* having an outburst for certain periods of time. The researchers monitored Ruth's outbursts by using a tape recorder that had a device to activate it only when a sufficiently loud noise occurred. As Figure 11.1 shows, the frequency of her loud vocalizations dropped sharply during both times the intervention was in force and returned to baseline levels during the reversal phase. These data clearly indicate that the combined consequences of time-out and DRO caused her outbursts to decrease. (Go to 🖈)

CLOSE-UP 11.1

Problems in Using Reversal Designs

 Using reversal designs can present two problems for researchers. First, the effect of the intervention may not be fully or substantially reversible. That is, when the intervention is withdrawn, the behavior sometimes does not or cannot revert back toward baseline levels. Under such conditions, our ability to interpret the results unambiguously is impaired because we cannot be certain why the behavior changed during the first intervention phase. For example, the target behavior may fail to regress because it has been changed permanently by the original intervention phase, as might occur if the target person learned a skill that he or she finds useful in a variety of settings. For instance, tennis players who learn effective strategies for performing excellent forehand and backhand strokes are not likely to stop using these strategies just because their trainers stop reinforcing that behavior.

If we think that the target behavior we plan to change could not be expected to regress when the intervention is withdrawn, we should not use a reversal design. But it is not always possible to predict that an intervention will produce a quick and permanent change in a behavior. For example, an intervention consisting only of punishment with mild electric shock was used to reduce a 14-year-old boy's frequent and chronic cough (Creer, Chai, & Hoffman, 1977).

The cough had become so severe that his classmates ridiculed the boy, and he was expelled from school at his teachers' request. Various other therapies had been applied without success, and the boy and his parents agreed to try the shock. The researchers planned to use an ABAB design. During the 1-hour baseline period, the boy coughed 22 times. In the initial intervention phase, the boy coughed once, which

> was followed immediately by a mild (5mA) electric shock of 1 second duration to the forearm. . . . Because the boy did not cough again for the remainder of the hour or the next 2 hours, a reversal procedure could not be instituted. (p. 108)

The boy returned to school the next day and experienced no recurrence of the chronic cough in follow-up assessments over a 2½-year period.

The second problem researchers can face in using reversal designs is that it may be undesirable or unethical to withdraw an intervention that appears to have produced a beneficial effect. Suppose, for example, an intervention successfully reduced severe self-injurious behaviors in a child with autism. It would not be desirable or ethically appropriate for the researcher to withdraw the treatment to meet the needs of a research design. Fortunately, other intrasubject research designs do not involve reversal phases and can be used in such situations.

Multiple-Baseline Designs

Research using **multiple-baseline designs** basically conduct more than one AB design, with all baselines starting simultaneously and proceeding together for a while. Each baseline period continues for a different length of time before the intervention begins. As a result, multiple-baseline designs have three important characteristics. First, there are no reversal phases. This feature makes multiple-baseline designs useful when the behavior change is permanent or when withdrawing the intervention is undesirable. Second, introduction of the intervention is staggered across the separate AB designs.

Third, a baseline phase in at least one AB design can overlap an intervention phase in at least one other design. You can see this overlap in the following multiple-baseline design with three AB designs, where each letter represents a period of time—say, one day—in either the baseline phase (A) or the intervention phase (B):

AB Design #1: **A, B, B, B**

AB Design #2: **A, A, B, B**

AB Design #3: **A, A, A, B**

This overlap enables us to compare the target behavior in baseline with the behavior in the intervention simultaneously within and across designs. We can assess the effect of the intervention on the target behavior by making comparisons with baseline data after the introduction of each intervention phase. By making these comparisons, we can see how the intervention selectively affects the target behavior in each AB design. Multiple-baseline designs can be carried out across different *behaviors*, individual *subjects*, or *situations*.

Multiple-Baseline, Across-Behaviors The **multiple-baseline, across-behaviors** research design uses separate AB designs for each of two or more different *behaviors* for a single individual in a particular setting. In using this research design, we would monitor simultaneously two or more different behaviors—for instance, a factory worker's daily frequency of arriving to work on time, number of items made, and amount of time spent in idle conversation—starting in baseline. Once the baseline data have stabilized for each behavior, we would apply the intervention techniques, such as token reinforcement, to *one* of them. Soon we should see in our graph that this behavior has changed. When the change is clear, we would apply the intervention to the next behavior, and so on. Assuming that the *only* behavior that changes at any given time is the one newly exposed to the intervention, we can infer with strong certainty that applying the techniques caused the change.

A multiple-baseline, across-behaviors design was used to examine the effects of an intervention to help children with asthma learn to use a device that sprays medication into their airways when an asthma episode has begun (Renne & Creer, 1976). Four 7- to 12-year-olds were having trouble learning to use the device and, after baseline, received training with reinforcement for three behaviors. The training for each child started with eye fixation behavior (looking constantly at the device), then facial posturing (inserting the device in the mouth at the right angle and with the lips and nostrils correctly formed), and then diaphragmatic breathing (using the stomach muscles correctly to breathe in the medication). Figure 11.2 depicts the sequencing of training for each behavior and the outcome of the intervention, as reflected in the mean number of inappropriate behaviors the children made. Notice three aspects in the graph. First, like all multiple-baseline designs, the baseline phases started together but lasted for different amounts of time (the baseline lengths increased from the first-, to the second-, to the third-trained behavior). Second, the children's inappropriate behaviors in facial posturing and diaphragmatic breathing did not diminish until each

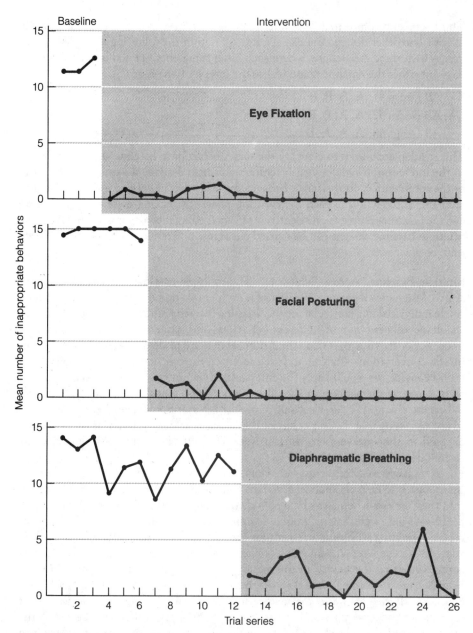

Figure 11.2   Mean number of inappropriate behaviors four children made in learning to perform the behaviors of eye fixation, facial posturing, and diaphragmatic breathing when using a device to control asthma episodes. The maximum number of inappropriate behaviors per trial was 15 for each behavior. In this study, the data for the four subjects were combined rather than presented for each child. *Source:* Renne & Creer, 1976, Figure 1.

behavior was subjected to the intervention. Third, each behavior responded quickly once the intervention started.

The target behaviors of research using multiple-baseline, across-behaviors designs can vary in the degree to which they are related or unrelated. You can see different degrees of relatedness in the pairs of behaviors in the following examples: studies have examined the effects of interventions on articulation errors in producing *th* and *z* sounds (Bailey et al., 1971), classroom behaviors of being out of one's seat and making inappropriate statements or sounds (Calhoun & Lima, 1977), and sleeping problems of a child not going to sleep on time and entering her sister's bed (Ronen, 1991). Some of these studies examined several behaviors, not just the two listed, and each specific behavior was observed in a baseline phase and an intervention phase.

Multiple-Baseline, Across-Subjects   The **multiple-baseline, across-subjects** research design uses separate AB designs for each of two or more *individuals* for a particular behavior in a particular setting. In this design, each individual receives a baseline phase and an intervention phase for the same target behavior. Once the baseline data have stabilized for each target individual, the intervention is applied to *one* of these people. When graphed data indicate the behavior has changed for this person, we would apply the intervention to the next person, and so on. Assuming that the *only* individual whose behavior changes at any given time is the person newly exposed to the intervention, we can infer with strong certainty that applying the intervention techniques caused the change.

A study used a multiple-baseline, across-subjects design to examine the effects of an intervention to prevent HIV (the AIDS human immunodificiency virus) infection among hospital nurses (DeVries, Burnette, & Redmon, 1991). The target behavior was wearing rubber gloves in hospital activities where there is a high probability of contact with a patient's body fluids. If the patient is infected with HIV, wearing gloves reduces nurses' risk of becoming infected. The intervention, consisting of biweekly performance feedback and encouragement to wear gloves in these activities, was introduced with one nurse first, then another nurse, and so on. Figure 11.3 illustrates the design and results of this study. Notice that the target behavior improved in each nurse only after the intervention was introduced, which indicates that the feedback caused the behavior to change. Other studies have used this type of multiple-baseline design to demonstrate the beneficial effects of interventions to improve school students' skills in math and spelling (Swain & McLaughlin, 1998; Truchlicka, McLaughlin, & Swain, 1998) and in recruiting teacher attention and feedback (Craft, Alber, & Heward, 1998).

Multiple-Baseline, Across-Situations   The **multiple-baseline, across-situations** research design uses separate AB designs for each of two or more different *situations* for a single individual and a specific behavior. In this design, the individual receives a baseline phase and an intervention phase in each of two or more situations—for example, in different places or with different people present. As with the other multiple-baseline designs, the baselines in all situations begin at much the same time. Once the baseline

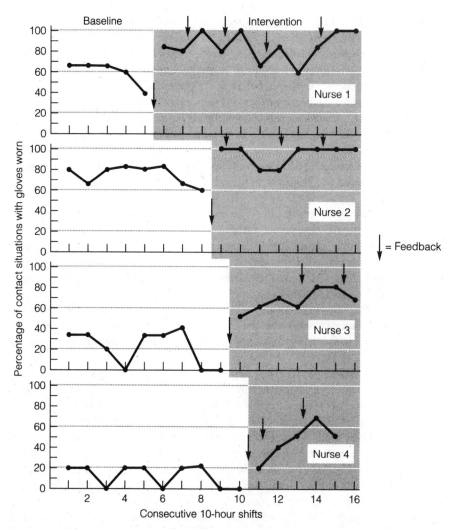

Figure 11.3   Percentage of occasions in which four nurses wore rubber gloves during 16 consecutive 10-hour shifts when contact with a patient's body fluids was likely. The intervention in this multiple-baseline, across-subjects design involved feedback about the nurses' recent use of gloves and encouragement to wear them more often. Arrows indicate points at which feedback was given by a nurse specializing in the control of the spread of infection in hospitals. *Source:* DeVries, Burnette, & Redmon, 1991, Figure 1.

data have stabilized in each situation, the intervention is applied in *one* of them. When the change is clear on a graph, the intervention is applied in the next situation, and so on. Assuming that the behavior *only* changes at any given time in the situation with the newly presented intervention, we can conclude that applying the techniques caused the change.

Jack James (1981) conducted a study using a multiple-baseline, across-situations design to test the effects of an intervention of brief (2-second) time-out punishment procedures on a young man's stuttering. In both the baseline and intervention phases, the client talked while a tape recorder was running in five situations: in the laboratory talking alone, in the laboratory conversing with a researcher, at home talking with an adult, on the telephone talking with an adult, and in various business settings talking with clerks or agents. The results demonstrated that his stuttering decreased in each situation, but only when the time-out consequences were applied there. Similarly, a study used a multiple-baseline, across-situations design to demonstrate the effectiveness of self-monitoring methods in improving students' on-task behavior in three different settings: language arts, reading, and computer classes (Wood et al., 1998).

I hinted earlier at a potential problem in using multiple-baseline designs: a target behavior may begin to change during a baseline phase, before the intervention has been introduced. This occurred in a multiple-baseline, across-behaviors design to test the effects of an intervention to reduce a 29-year-old male patient's three delusional beliefs (Lowe & Chadwick, 1990):

- He was to be married to a woman called Amanda, with whom he had not been in contact for many years, and who supposedly was reading his mind and controlling many of the things that happened to him.
- He had been Jesus Christ in a prior life.
- He had been Leonardo da Vinci in a prior life. (p. 466)

The beliefs were treated in the listed sequence. Although the man's beliefs that he had been Jesus and Leonardo in past lives did not change while the Amanda belief declined, the Leonardo belief began to decline in baseline, paralleling the decline in the Jesus belief that was currently receiving the intervention. When this happens, we can't be certain why the untreated behavior has begun to decline. Perhaps the decline in the Leonardo belief resulted from response generalization because the Jesus and Leonardo beliefs were so similar. But the effects of the intervention would have been clearer if the Leonardo belief had not begun to change in baseline.

Similar problems can arise in other multiple-baseline designs. In the multiple-baseline, across-subjects design, changes in the target behavior for the person receiving the intervention may lead to changes in the behavior of other individuals who are still in baseline. And in the multiple-baseline, across-situations design, changes in the target person's behavior in the situation where the intervention was introduced may lead to changes when the person is in other situations still lacking the intervention. Even though some potential exists for these problems to arise, they do not seem to be very common.

Changing-Criterion Designs

Another useful approach for demonstrating that intervention techniques caused changes in a behavior is called the **changing-criterion design.** As the name implies, the criterion for successful performance changes over time, usually becoming more rigorous. For instance, when we start the intervention, we may require a fairly lax level of performance for receiving reinforcement. After the behavior has stabilized at that level, we may raise the criterion to a higher level, and when the behavior stabilizes again, we may raise the criterion again, and so on. If the behavior increases or decreases in accordance with each change in the criterion, we can conclude that the reinforcement is responsible for the behavioral changes.

Rayleen De Luca and Stephen Holborn (1992) used a changing-criterion design to study the effects of a token reinforcement system on exercising among 11-year-old obese and nonobese boys. Once each boy's pedaling rate on a stationary bicycle had stabilized in baseline, the researchers began to reinforce pedaling on a variable-ratio schedule in each 30-minute exercise session. The number of pedaling revolutions required for each instance of reinforcement at the start of the intervention for each boy was set roughly 15% above his average rate in baseline. So, if the boy had pedaled in baseline at the rate of 70 revolutions per minute, the intervention began by requiring an average rate of 80 revolutions per minute. Each subsequent increased criterion for reinforcement was set at 15% above the average pedaling rate he achieved in the preceding phase. Whenever a boy earned "a point" token while pedaling, a bell would ring and a light would go on, announcing the success. The tokens could be exchanged later for backup rewards.

Figure 11.4 shows the data for two of the six boys in the exercise bicycle study. Notice how their pedaling increased in accordance with each increase in the criterion for reinforcement. This pattern occurred for all six boys. Although the reversal (BL) phase was not necessary in the design, the corresponding decrease in performance makes the effects of the reinforcement clearer. Other researchers have used changing-criterion designs to study the effects of consequences introduced for meeting or not meeting specific criteria for smoking fewer and fewer cigarettes (Axelrod et al., 1974; Belles & Bradlyn, 1987).

Alternating-Treatment Designs

Alternating-treatment designs (also called *simultaneous-treatment* or *multi-element designs*) examine the effects of two or more treatments, each of which is conducted within the same intervention phase with the same person. Although both treatments are applied in the same phase, they are separated in time and alternated. Thus, each treatment might be applied on different days or at different times during the day throughout the intervention phase. By examining graphs of the data, we can determine if one treatment is consistently more effective than another in changing the person's target behavior.

An example of an alternating-treatment design was reported by Frank Kohler and Charles Greenwood (1990), who examined the tutoring behaviors of schoolchildren, each of whom received training in two tutoring procedures to help classmates in spelling. The *standard tutoring procedure* involved having the tutor give the student feedback

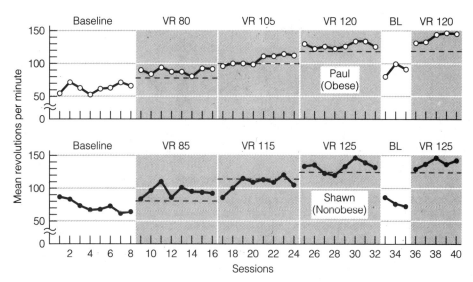

Figure 11.4 Mean (average) number of revolutions per minute pedaled on a stationary bicycle by two boys, Paul, who was obese, and Shawn, who was not obese. (Data for four other boys, not included here, showed similar patterns.) A changing-criterion design was used, with each increased criterion (dashed horizontal lines) being set at 15% above the average pedaling rate the boy achieved in the previous phase. After the initial baseline phase, token reinforcement was given on increasingly rigorous variable-ratio (VR) schedules. The BL phase is a reversal baseline phase. *Source:* DeLuca & Holborn, 1992, Figure 1.

and token reinforcers for correct spellings and provide corrective feedback when a word was misspelled. The *modified tutoring procedure* had the tutor use praise and token reinforcers for correct spelling and give corrective feedback as soon as a student gave an incorrect letter in a word. During the intervention phase, the tutors were told which procedure to apply in each tutoring session. The 10-minute tutoring sessions in all phases were observed for instances of a type of tutoring behavior called "help," which involved spelling a word *more than once* during corrective feedback for an error. The training the tutors received had them spell the word only once. Figure 11.5 presents the number of help behaviors per tutoring session by Karen, one of the tutors. Notice that she rarely performed help behaviors in baseline and during the intervention phase when told to use the standard tutoring procedure. But her help behaviors occurred very frequently when she was told to use the modified tutoring procedure during intervention. In the "choice" phase, the tutors were allowed to use the procedure of their choice, and she continued to use help behaviors.

Alternating-treatment designs have two principal advantages. First, as in some other designs, no reversal phases are needed. Second, two or more treatments can be compared to see if one is more effective than another. But a problem can arise in

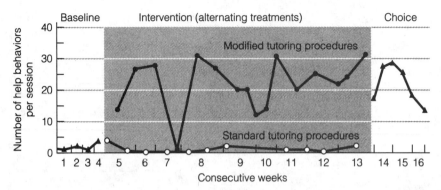

Figure 11.5 Number of "help" behaviors per 10-minute tutoring session by a tutor named Karen, as examined in an alternating-treatment design. Help behaviors were assessed in baseline, during training in two different tutoring procedures in the intervention phase, and later when Karen could use the tutoring procedure of her choice. (Data for two other tutors, not included here, showed similar patterns.) *Source:* Kohler & Greenwood, 1990, Figure 2.

alternating-treatment designs that cannot happen with other designs: the effects of the treatments may "interact." For example, if a subject receives two treatments, the effect of one of the treatments may be influenced if the person contrasts it with the second treatment (Barlow & Hayes, 1979; Hains & Baer, 1989). If only one of these treatments had been implemented during the intervention, its effects on behavior might have been different. (Go to ☑)

GROUP-BASED RESEARCH

Most research on learning and psychology is *group-based*, with observations taken on large numbers of individuals instead of just one or a few. In group-based research, the data for the target individuals are combined rather than examined separately. Combining data is usually accomplished by computing the average, or *mean*, across all individuals. These means are then compared. To evaluate whether two or more means differ, researchers compute complex statistics to evaluate the "significance" of the difference. A *significant difference* indicates that given the pattern of data in each of the groups the difference in the mean scores is sufficiently great that it probably didn't happen by chance or accident.

Keep two things in mind about these statistical procedures. First, the term *significant* describes a mathematical concept and doesn't mean "important." It is possible to find a statistically significant difference in the data for two or more groups even if the problem being studied is trivial. Second, the *average* response across a group of individuals may be very different from the behavior of any specific individual in the group.

CONCEPT CHECK 11.2

1. Studies that examine changes in the behavior of individuals across time are examples of _____ designs.
2. Isolating the causes of changes in behavior is especially difficult in intrasubject research when a(n) _____ design is used.
3. A preschool child's behavior that might not regress when a reversal phase is in effect is _____ . ⇔
4. Research that begins an intervention to improve three different job skills in a single individual at work would be using a(n) _____ design.
5. A potential problem with multiple-baseline designs is that the behavior may begin to change during _____ .
6. In a changing-criterion design seeking to determine the effects of rewards on lifting weights in an exercise program, we might change the criterion by requiring more _____ . ⇔

Answers: 1. intrasubject, 2. AB, 3. learning to play with other children, 4. multiple-baseline, across-behaviors, 5. baseline, before the intervention, 6. weight/repetitions

Still, research with many subjects is very useful in showing effects that may apply to a wide range of individuals and can be conducted as within-subjects designs and between-subjects designs.

Within-Subjects Designs

We saw in Chapter 1 that *within-subjects designs* test many individuals in more than one condition of the study. The data collected for all individuals in each condition are combined, and the means are compared for the significance of the difference. In research conducted to examine the effects of methods for changing behavior, these designs are generally structured like intrasubject designs, with all individuals being observed in each phase of the design. As with intrasubject designs, the intervention's success in behavior modification research is usually evaluated by doing a graphic analysis. Let's see how this approach works.

Dennis Upper (1973) performed a study using a within-subjects design with 30 patients in a psychiatric hospital. A token system had already been established in a ward of the hospital to reinforce self-care and sociable behaviors, but the patients had been violating ward rules that were not part of the reinforcement program. The rule violations included spitting on the walls or floor, sleeping in unauthorized areas, engaging in indecent exposure, and stealing. To decrease rule violations, consequences for obeying the rules were added to the existing token system: the patients earned 15

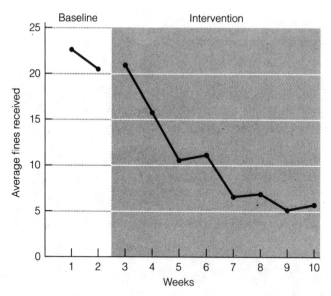

Figure 11.6 Average number of tokens taken per week in fines from 30 psychiatric patients during baseline and intervention phases for infractions of ward rules. *Source:* Data from Upper, 1973, Table 2.

tokens each day for not violating any of the specified rules, but those who violated rules were fined from 3 to 15 of those possible tokens per infraction, depending on its severity. Patients who lost more than 15 of those tokens, had to pay tokens they had earned under the original token system. This study was structured like an AB design, with a baseline phase and an intervention phase, but the data were combined across all 30 individuals by calculating the *average* number of tokens per patient that they lost as *fines* for their violations. Figure 11.6 shows that the average fines for each week declined markedly across the 8 intervention weeks.

Within-subjects designs can follow the structure used in any of the intrasubject designs we have considered. For instance, a study used a within-subjects design that was structured like an ABAB design to examine the effects of a peer tutoring program to improve low-performing students' arithmetic skills (Pigott, Fantuzzo, & Clement, 1986). The peer tutoring intervention greatly increased the students' average number of correctly calculated arithmetic problems compared with their averages for baseline and reversal phases. Also, Elizabeth Barton and her colleagues (1970) used a multiple-baseline, across behaviors design to examine the effects of a time-out intervention on undesirable mealtime behaviors of 16 individuals with mental retardation. Each target behavior (stealing food, eating with fingers, and so on) improved across the group when the intervention was applied to it.

Between-Subjects Designs

Between-subjects designs involve collecting data on the behavior of many target individuals who are separated into two or more groups. The data for all individuals in each group are then combined, and the means are compared to see whether there is a significant difference. Separating the individuals into groups can be accomplished in more than one way, and the method chosen can determine whether the research is viewed as an *experiment* or as a *quasi-experiment*.

Experiments An **experiment** is a controlled study in which the researcher manipulates—that is, determines or controls the level of—a variable to examine its effect on another variable. The manipulated variable is called the *independent variable*; the other variable is called the *dependent variable* because its value is expected to *depend* on the manipulated level of the independent variable. In behavior modification research, the independent variable is typically an intervention or behavior change technique, and the dependent variable is the target behavior.

Our description of experiments will focus on the simplest and very commonly used form that consists of two groups: one group receives the intervention and is called the *experimental group*, the other group does not receive the intervention and is called the *control group*. By administering the intervention to one group but not the other, the researcher is manipulating the independent variable. To separate individuals into these two groups in an experiment, the researcher assigns the individuals *randomly* to the groups. The term *random* means that the assignment of each individual is determined by chance alone. One way to assign individuals randomly is to put their names on cards, shuffle the deck of cards thoroughly, and draw cards from the deck without looking. The first name drawn would be assigned to one group, the second name to the other group, and so on. This process distributes characteristics of the individuals in an unbiased manner and tends to produce groups that, overall, are very similar with respect to their abilities and other characteristics that might affect their performance in the research. As a result, these characteristics usually will have about the same impact on the behavior of individuals in each group, thereby allowing us to conclude that the independent variable is responsible for—that is, the *cause* of—any differences we find in the dependent variable. In experiments, researchers manipulate the independent variable while controlling other variables that are not being studied, such as characteristics of the individuals; therefore, *cause–effect* relationships between variables can be discovered.

Thomas Burling and his colleagues (1991) conducted an experiment with a between-subjects design to assess the effects of an intervention to induce pregnant women to stop smoking for their own health and that of their babies. The 139 women in the study, patients at a medical clinic, were randomly assigned to two groups. Seventy women were assigned to the experimental group and received standard prenatal care plus antismoking materials and a letter stating that "abnormalities in the chemistry of your blood . . . pose a risk to both you and your unborn child. This abnormality will disappear if you stop smoking." The 69 women in the control group received only the standard prenatal care. Although most of the women in both groups did not quit smoking, the number of women who quit was significantly greater in the experimental group than in the control group.

Another experiment using a between-subjects design was performed by Nathan Azrin and Alan Peterson (1990) to test the effects of an intervention to reduce motor and vocal tics in patients with a neurological disease called Tourette's syndrome. The intervention applied the method of habit reversal, which consists of several techniques, such as competing response practice and relaxation training. The patients, recruited through newspaper articles and an association for people with Tourette's syndrome, were randomly assigned to the experimental group and a *waiting-list control* group, with five individuals in each group. Waiting-list control groups are frequently used in clinical research; the intervention is not denied to them, but it is postponed until after it is clearly successful in the experimental group. Statistical analyses were carried out on data collected in the 3 months when the habit reversal treatment was in effect for the experimental group, but not the control group. These analyses revealed that patients in the experimental group had significantly fewer tics per month than patients in the control group.

Quasi-Experiments   Sometimes researchers who perform studies with between-subjects designs are unable to randomly assign people to groups. Random assignment may not be feasible for many reasons. For instance, the researcher may want to see how changes in the living environments at a nursing home would affect the residents' behavior. To randomly assign individuals to the changed environments would require relocating the people to different living quarters—a procedure that is unlikely to be strategically and ethically acceptable. Or a researcher may be examining the role of an existing variable and may use that variable to categorize people into one of two or more groups: male and female adults, for example, or delinquent and nondelinquent teenagers. Studies of this type are called **quasi-experiments**—they "look" like experiments because they have separate groups of individuals, but they are not. The variable that forms the groups—such as gender or living quarters—is not manipulated, and the people who participate in the study cannot be randomly assigned to the groups (Goodwin, 1995; Monette, Sullivan, & DeJong, 1990). As a result, we cannot arrive at cause–effect conclusions from the data, even if the behavioral differences between the groups are huge.

Quasi-experiments are very common in psychological research. For instance, many studies have been done to determine if meditation techniques enable individuals to achieve states of profound rest. In the typical between-subjects design, individuals are selected and assigned to two groups: experienced meditators and nonmeditators. Physiological arousal is then assessed while the meditators practice meditation and the nonmeditators simply try to rest. Reviews of these studies have revealed no consistent differences in blood pressure, heart rate, or respiration rate between the meditating and the resting individuals (Holmes, 1984; Lichstein, 1988). But the quasi-experimental nature of these studies leaves open the possibility that the failure to find consistent differences in arousal may be due to other differences between individuals who do and do not meditate.

EVALUATING THE RESULTING CHANGES IN BEHAVIOR

Until now, we have focused on ways to evaluate the success of interventions in terms of whether and why the target behavior changed. Researchers have used these approaches to test an enormous variety of interventions, some using behavior modification techniques and some using other methods. Not all methods have been effective, and occasionally they may even have made the behavioral or emotional problems worse (Bangert-Drowns, 1988; Shaffer et al., 1990). But knowing whether and why an intervention has changed behavior is not enough. In addition to discovering prominent graphical or statistical differences in behavior when the intervention was present and absent, we need to evaluate the value of intervention techniques in terms of several practical considerations.

Dimensions of Evaluation

Professionals commonly evaluate three dimensions of practical considerations that relate to the behavioral changes produced by intervention techniques. These dimensions entail the *generalization and durability* of the behavioral changes in the target person's natural environment, the *amount and importance of the changes* to the person's everyday life and functioning, and the *costs and benefits* of the intervention.

Generalization and Durability of the Changes   For a behavior change intervention to be viewed as effective and useful, the improved behavior must generalize to the target person's natural environment, and it must be durable. Thus, someone who has mastered a relaxation technique and learned to use a rapid relaxation induction method must be able to apply these skills as the need arises in everyday anxiety-provoking situations. Similarly, someone who has learned how to avoid antecedents that lead to an unwanted behavior, such as smoking or drinking, must use these skills in his or her usual environment. We considered the importance of generalization and durability in Chapter 10 and described methods programs can use to enhance these outcomes.

When ending an intervention, it is often a good idea to phase it out gradually by thinning reinforcement schedules, for example, or withdrawing some techniques earlier than others. Gradually withdrawing behavior change techniques offers two potential benefits. First, it tends to promote generalization and durability of the improved behavior. Second, we can monitor the target behavior during this process to assess the degree to which each component of the program is critical for maintaining the behavior after the intervention has ended (Rusch & Kazdin, 1981). To evaluate the durability of a behavioral change, the program must conduct follow-up assessments periodically after the intervention ends. Follow-up data will reveal changes in the target behavior. If the behavior is deteriorating, a posttreatment program may be needed to maintain the gains produced in the intervention.

Amount and Importance of the Changes   The *amount of change* an intervention produces in the target person's problem behavior and the *importance of the changes* to the person's everyday life and functioning are critical dimensions in evaluating a program's effectiveness. We can assess these dimensions by considering two outcomes of the behavior change: its clinical significance and its social validity.

The concept of **clinical significance** refers to the degree to which the change in behavior is *meaningful* to the target person's life and functioning, where a meaningful change is one that is *large* and brings the behavior into the *normal range* (Jacobson, Follette, & Revenstorf, 1984; Jacobson et al., 1999; Kendall et al., 1999; Speer, 1992). As an example, let's consider a hypothetical case of an 8-year-old boy who stutters, on average, about 10% of the syllables he speaks. Suppose that an intervention reduces his stuttering to 6% of his spoken syllables. This would be a large change, but the behavior would not yet be in the normal range. Now suppose that the intervention were continued or strengthened and reduced his stuttering to 3% of his spoken syllables. This level would represent a clinically significant change because it is both large and the behavior is within the normal range (Gagnon & Ladouceur, 1992). Determining the normal range can be accomplished in two ways. First, research may have previously identified a *norm* for the behavior—that is, its usual level among a large population of individuals of the same age and gender (Trull, Neitzel, & Main, 1988). Second, the researcher may identify and test a control group to assess their average level of the behavior (Dush, Hirt, & Schroeder, 1983).

The second outcome of behavior change that indicates the amount or importance of the change is its **social validity**—that is, the utility and adaptiveness of the change for the target person's everyday functioning (Foster & Mash, 1999). According to Montrose Wolf (1978), a behavior change program can be evaluated for its social validity by collecting data to answer three questions:

- Are the behavioral goals of the program desired by society and appropriate for the target person's life?

- Are the target person and significant individuals in his or her life, such as relatives, teachers, or coworkers, satisfied with the amount and utility of the behavioral changes the program has produced?

- Are the treatment techniques and procedures acceptable to the target person, significant individuals in his or her life, and the community at large?

Answers to these questions can be obtained in several ways (Foster & Mash, 1999). For instance, we can ask for assessments or opinions from relevant individuals—the person and people in his or her life who have frequent contact with the person and might be affected by the behavioral changes the program produces (Schwartz & Baer, 1991). We can also have independent judges make evaluations of the person's behavior after the intervention and other aspects of the program (Fawcett & Miller, 1975). And we can examine measures of the outcome that show a clear social impact of the changes, such as improved communication and friendships after reductions in stuttering. For a program to modify delinquent behavior, we might assess social impact in terms of the person's future use of drugs or arrests for criminal activity (Bank et al., 1991). By evaluating the clinical significance and social validity of behavioral changes, we can get a sense of the degree to which the intervention has made a real difference in the lives of the target person, and other individuals who are affected by the outcomes of the program. (Go to)

CASE STUDY 11.1

Assessing Social Validity in Reducing a Boy's Tics

Hugh had developed multiple tics at the age of 3 and was 11 years old when he entered a behavioral treatment program to correct this problem (case described in Finney et al., 1983). In the recent months prior to beginning the program, there had been an increase in the frequency and intensity of four tics: head-shaking, head-jerking, mouth-grimacing, and eye-blinking. The intervention, which was based on the habit reversal technique, produced dramatic reductions in each of these tics within several weeks, and follow-up assessments indicated that these decreases were maintained over the next year.

People commonly seek treatment for tics because of the unusual appearance and social embarrassment these motor behaviors produce. To evaluate the program within a social validity framework, the researchers made videotapes of Hugh during baseline and intervention phases of the treatment. These tapes were rated by two groups of judges: 12 teachers from a junior high school and 36 graduate students in pediatric fields, such as nursing and special education. These judges did not know Hugh but were chosen because of their regular contact with children of Hugh's age. When the panel rated his tics, using a 7-point scale (1 = not distracting; 7 = very distracting), the average ratings were as follows: about 6.5 for the baseline tapes and 1.6 for the intervention tapes. This assessment of social validity suggests that Hugh's tics became far less embarrassing as a result of this treatment.

Costs and Benefits in Producing the Changes   Lastly, we can evaluate the value of an intervention by assessing its **cost–benefit ratio,** or the extent to which the costs of providing the treatment are outweighed by the money saved in the long run (Jospe, Shueman, & Troy, 1991; Kaplan, 1989). In medical settings, for example, studies have shown that providing behavioral interventions to reduce anxiety enables surgery patients to recover more quickly and use less medication than patients who do not receive these interventions (Sarafino, 1998). The financial savings in medical costs far exceed the costs of administering these interventions.

Composing a Report

After an intervention has been completed, the professionals who supervised the project usually write a report to describe the target behavior(s), intervention techniques, and

✓

CONCEPT CHECK 11.3

1. Studies that test many individuals in more than one condition use _____ designs.
2. An independent variable that might be used in a between-subjects design in behavior modification is _____ . ⇔
3. An example you have seen in everyday life of a person being randomly chosen might be _____ . ⇔
4. A group of individuals in an experiment for whom treatment is postponed is called a _____ group.
5. A norm for infant or child motor development might describe the age at which most children _____ . ⇔
6. Determining whether an intervention's treatment procedures are acceptable to the person can be part of an evaluation of a program's _____ .

---

outcomes of the program. Often, these reports are published in professional journals; in other cases, they are kept on file in counseling offices or institutions. The outcomes of a behavior modification program are presented graphically, showing data from baseline and intervention phases, and in words. When possible, the outcomes should provide data on follow-up assessments too. (Go to ✓)

Tips on Doing Behavior Modification Research

Some of the research methods used in behavior modification are unique to this field, but other methods are used widely in psychology and other disciplines. Let's look at some tips on doing research in behavior modification.

1. It's important to use more than one observer to collect data on a target behavior; the observers should work simultaneously and independently. Try to have simultaneous recording for as much of the data as possible—at least 25% is desirable.
2. Let observers know other observers will be collecting data simultaneously as a check on the accuracy of the data.
3. It's important to have a practice period for collecting data before the actual records for research will be collected. Not only does this provide training for the observer, but the person under observation has an opportunity to adapt to being watched, thereby reducing subsequent reactivity.
4. Before moving from one phase to another, wait for the behavior to stabilize, or reach a fairly constant level, if possible.

5. When planning to do a research project, consider whether the target behavior is likely to regress if a reversal phase is introduced. If there is reason to suspect there will be no regression, use a research design other than ABA or ABAB.

SUMMARY

Collecting accurate data is critical in evaluating the success of programs to change behavior, but inaccuracies can develop for many reasons. One way to assess the accuracy of collected data is to have a second observer collect data simultaneously with and independently from the primary observer and compare the two sets of records. The degree to which the records agree is called interobserver reliability.

Research using intrasubject designs examines behavioral changes over time in one individual at a time, while interventions are either in force or absent. Intrasubject designs include the AB, ABA, and ABAB types. AB designs, which consist of a baseline phase and an intervention phase, do not indicate unequivocally whether the intervention caused changes in the behavior. Reversal designs yield stronger evidence than AB designs for cause–effect links between interventions and changes in behavior, but only for target behaviors that regress upon introduction of a reversal phase.

Multiple-baseline designs start baselines simultaneously but begin the interventions in sequence, thereby showing patterns of behavior change that correspond to the introduction of the intervention. Such approaches can be applied as three different designs: multiple-baselines, across-behaviors; multiple-baselines, across-subjects; and multiple-baselines, across-situations. In changing-criterion designs, the criterion for success changes, generally by becoming increasingly rigorous. We can conclude that the intervention is responsible for behavioral changes if the behavior increases or decreases in accordance with criterion changes. Alternating-treatment designs allow the comparison of two or more treatments presented in the same intervention phase.

Group-based research collects data on many individuals and then combines and compares the data by computing means, or averages. Within-subjects designs test each individual in more than one condition of the study, and between-subjects designs separate the individuals into groups. Between-subjects designs are called experiments when an independent variable is manipulated, individuals are randomly assigned to experimental and control groups, and changes in the dependent variable are assessed. Quasi-experiments use or select for an existing variable, which becomes the basis for categorizing the individuals into groups. Because true experiments manipulate the independent variable and equate the groups through random assignment, they can yield cause–effect conclusions about the link between variations in the independent and dependent variables.

Behavior modification programs can be evaluated not only for whether and why they produced behavioral changes but also for three practical dimensions. First, the improved behavior should generalize to the person's everyday environment, and it should be durable. Second, the amount and importance of the change in behavior should be substantial, which can be evaluated by assessing the clinical significance of the change and the social validity of the program and its outcomes. Third, programs should strive to have a favorable cost–benefit ratio, demonstrating that in the long run the intervention saves more money than it costs.

KEY TERMS

interobserver reliability	multiple-baseline, across-behaviors	alternating-treatment designs
intrasubject designs		experiment
AB designs	multiple-baseline, across-subjects	quasi-experiments
reversal designs	multiple-baseline, across-situations	clinical significance
ABA designs		social validity
ABAB designs	changing-criterion designs	cost–benefit ratio
multiple-baseline designs		

REVIEW QUESTIONS

1. Describe four sources of inaccuracies in recording data on behavior.
2. Define the concept of interobserver reliability.
3. In calculating interobserver reliability, how are the session totals and interval-recording methods different?
4. What are intrasubject designs, and how are they different from group-based designs?
5. Define ABAB designs, and indicate why they can be superior to AB designs.
6. Describe the two problems with the use of reversal designs, and include the research by Creer, Chai, and Hoffman (1977) as an example.
7. Define multiple-baseline designs, and indicate how they can be carried out across individuals and situations.
8. Describe the research design and results of DeVries, Burnette, and Redmon (1991).
9. Define changing-criterion designs, and give an example of how this approach might be used in an intervention to improve a child's spelling skills.
10. How are experiments and quasi-experiments different?
11. Define clinical significance.
12. Describe the three questions by which one can assess the social validity of a behavior change program.

RELATED READINGS

Monette, D. R., Sullivan, T. J., & DeJong, C. R. (1990). *Applied social research: Tool for the human services* (2nd ed.). Fort Worth, TX: Holt, Rinehart & Winston.

Schwartz, I. S., & Baer, D. M. (1991). Social validity assessments: Is current practice state of the art? *Journal of Applied Behavior Analysis, 24,* 189–204.

Wolery, M., & Gast, D. L. (1990). Re-framing the debate: Finding middle ground and defining the role of social validity. In A. C. Repp & N. N. Singh (Eds.), *Perspectives on the use of nonaversive and aversive interventions for persons with developmental disabilities.* Sycamore, IL: Sycamore.

Wolf, M. M. (1978). Social validity: The case for subjective measurement *or* how applied behavior analysis is finding its heart. *Journal of Applied Behavior Analysis, 11,* 203–214.

Token economy programs at worksites can use convenient parking spaces as backup reinforcers.

Token Economies

L ocated in Mexico about 175 miles south of the Arizona border is a private community called Comunidad los Horcones (Rohter, 1989). Its approximately 40 adult and child residents have constructed a set of social rules and consequences to build and maintain a society based on cooperation and equality rather than competition and discrimination. The community is self-supporting and sustains itself by farming and by providing educational programs for children from a nearby city. The entire community shares the money these activities bring in and engages in discussion and democratic vote to make decisions about how to spend their income.

One of the community's founders, Juan Robinson, had studied psychology and read B. F. Skinner's (1948) *Walden Two*. This novel by the famous behaviorist describes a utopian society that used operant conditioning principles to create an environment that promoted positive social conduct and relationships. To achieve these goals for los Horcones, Juan and his fellow residents have used democratic procedures to develop a detailed code of behavior that applies to all residents and all major facets of life in their community. The code for children, for instance, has 24 categories of outcome goals that include about 150 specific, defined behaviors. By behaving in accordance with the code—for example, by performing the work needed for the community to function—individual residents earn token reinforcers. As you might guess, the token reinforcement system applied at los Horcones is very complex.

In the present chapter and the next two, we shift our attention from methods that can be used fairly easily in many different everyday situations to techniques that are more advanced and specialized in their application. You will see that these techniques are relatively *specialized* with respect to appropriate settings for their use and *more advanced* with regard to the skills needed to carry them out effectively. Training in an undergraduate course on principles of behavior change is not sufficient to develop the needed skills to design programs using these methods. Individuals who use or directly supervise the use of these methods typically have graduate degrees. This chapter introduces you to complex systems of token reinforcement called *token economies*.

THE TOKEN ECONOMY APPROACH

In discussing programs that have applied token reinforcement, we've seen that using tokens as reinforcers has several advantages over using rewards of some other types. For instance, the tokens can be given immediately after a desirable behavior to bridge the delay between performing the behavior and getting the tangible, consumable, or activity reinforcer that has been earned. Token reinforcers can also be applied more easily than other rewards with groups of individuals, and because tokens can be exchanged for a variety of attractive backup reinforcers, their reward value is likely to remain high. Advantages like these have made token reinforcers very popular in behavior change programs.

This chapter focuses on the token economy approach in providing consequences for people's behavior. What is a token economy, and what makes it different from the token reinforcement approaches we've seen so far? A **token economy** is a method of using a complex system of consequences that is typically applied with groups of individuals for a wide range of target behaviors (Ayllon & Azrin, 1968b). Token economies differ from other token systems in three ways. Compared with other token systems, token economies generally:

- Try to change the behaviors of groups of people, rather than just one person.
- Attempt to change relatively wide ranges of target behaviors.
- Use relatively complex systems of consequences for those behaviors.

Although these characteristics help to define "token economies," there are no definite criteria that determine if a program qualifies as a token economy. The number of target individuals included in the intervention, the range of behaviors to be changed, and the complexity of the system of consequences can vary.

Usual Settings for Token Economies

One of the earliest recorded instances of using a token economy approach occurred in a 19th-century prison (Pitts, 1976). Alexander Meconochie, a captain in the British Royal Navy, was placed in charge of

> one of the worst British penal colonies, Norfolk Island, located about 1000 miles off the coast of Australia. The inmates were two-time losers, having committed major crimes in both England and Australia. (p. 146)

To control the inmates' behavior, he implemented a point system by which they could earn their way out of the penal colony by performing appropriate tasks and social behaviors. The number of points the inmates needed depended on the seriousness of the crimes they had committed. Meconochie had a motivational rationale for using this approach: "When a man keeps the key of his own prison, he is soon persuaded to fit it into the lock." Even though his approach seemed to be successful in controlling the behavior of the Norfolk Island prisoners, Meconochie's superiors criticized it and recalled him to England.

Because token economies are usually implemented to change the behaviors of groups of individuals, they are applied mainly in organizational or institutional settings. Token economies have been used in a great variety of settings, including classrooms for normal students of all ages, classrooms and institutions for people with mental retardation, hospitals for psychiatric patients and drug abusers, group homes for teenagers who have committed antisocial acts and are at risk of becoming delinquents, and work settings to enhance job performance (Kazdin, 1985). Los Horcones, described at the beginning of this chapter, is one of several similar communities, such as those located in Kansas, Michigan, Virginia, and Canada, that have been established with token economies to structure their social behaviors (Rohter, 1989).

What's Needed to Start a Token Economy

Starting a token economy requires that several tasks be completed in advance. One of the main steps to take is to decide on the target behaviors that the behavior modification program will try to change. Decisions about which behaviors to include will depend on the types of problem behavior the group appears to have, the specific needs of individual group members, and the needs of the organization or institution where the program will be implemented. If the individuals in the group are very similar to one another in their problem behaviors and personal characteristics, the target behaviors and rules about them can apply broadly to all members of the group. Having similar target individuals in the group is a fairly common circumstance, as might be expected from the examples of settings just mentioned. For instance, each child who is mentally retarded is likely to have many behavioral deficits and excesses that are like those displayed by other children with mental retardation, and many of these problems are likely to be different from those found among children in regular classrooms.

Once the target behaviors have been identified, they must be defined carefully and in detail so that the members of the group and the staff who administer the program will know exactly what the behaviors are and can determine reliably whether they occurred. At that point, four tasks should be initiated. First, functional analyses should be conducted to determine the antecedents and consequences that seem to be involved in each of the behaviors. Second, because token economies usually require several staff members to administer the program, these individuals must be recruited. Third, the staff must receive extensive training in identifying the target behaviors, using methods to reduce the antecedents and consequences that have promoted inappropriate behaviors in the past, recording data, and administering the token system. Fourth, the staff must collect baseline data. Let's see what the next steps would be to set up a token economy and implement it.

SETTING UP AND IMPLEMENTING A TOKEN ECONOMY

After the functional analyses have been conducted, all the materials, equipment, and facilities that will be needed to implement the token economy can be set up while the baseline data are being collected. The materials and equipment might include a supply of tokens, data sheets to record each person's behaviors and tokens earned, behavioral contracts, backup reinforcers, timing devices, and so on. Any special facilities that will be needed must be set up in advance. For instance, token economies in large institutions often have a special room, set up like a store, where tokens can be exchanged for tangible or consumable backup reinforcers. In smaller token economies, the store may be kept in a cabinet or large box. To set up all of these prerequisites, it is necessary to plan various features of the program, starting with what the "tokens" will be.

The Tokens: Choosing Them and Monitoring Their Use

Tokens can take many different forms. For instance, they can be poker chips, stars or stamps attached to a chart, check marks in a table, data entries in logs that are like bank books, or specially printed paper money. Tokens can be color-coded to reflect some important dimension, such as their value or the type of behavior for which they were earned. Because tokens function like money, they serve as points or credits toward the exchange cost for backup reinforcers. Sometimes tokens are specifically designed to operate timers or automatic dispensers. For example, Leonard Jason (1985) used coin-like tokens in a program that had TV watching as an activity backup reinforcer for several behaviors, such as doing chores or homework. A timer was connected to the TV set, and each token activated the timer for 30 minutes.

Ideally, tokens should have certain practical characteristics: they should be durable, convenient to store and handle, easy to carry around and dispense, and difficult to steal or counterfeit. Stealing tokens can be a major problem in some settings and must be prevented. It is also a good idea to provide some way for each person to store the tokens he or she earns, such as in a purse or wallet. (Go to ▓)

CASE STUDY **12.1**

Not-So-Funny Money

Because token economies are usually carried out with groups of people, presenting a single person as a case study might be misleading. So the "case" in this case study box is a type of token that was nicely designed by Daniel Logan (1970) to serve in a token economy at a psychiatric hospital. The tokens were printed on paper to serve as "paper money" receipts that could not be easily counterfeited, or redeemed, if stolen, partly because each one had to be filled out by a staff member, as shown in Figure 12CS.1. Each money receipt

> was color-coded according to broad classes of behavior. Money bearing the labels "Self-Care," "Ward Work," and "Social Contact" was printed in different colors to facilitate easy recognition and quick sorting. The money was also stamped according to the denomination (1 cent, 5 cents, and 10 cents). (p. 183)

The space labeled *Task* on the receipt was filled in by staff to indicate the specific behavior that was reinforced, such as "emptying the trash" or "playing checkers."

Figure 12CS.1   Sample of the "paper money" receipts used in a token economy. *Source:* Based on information in Logan, 1970.

The receipts also had other advantages. Because of the information staff wrote on them, the receipts were worth saving as records of behavior. That is, when target persons exchange the tokens for the backup reinforcers, the receipts can be sorted and stored according to their denominations and resorted by color to see quickly which classes of behavior are being reinforced. And sorting by the specific behavior or by the issuing staff member can indicate the kinds of behaviors each staff member has been rewarding.

Backup Reinforcers and Punishers

Making decisions about which backup reinforcers and punishers to include in a token economy program can be accomplished by using the information we discussed in Chapters 4 and 5. To identify potentially strong backup reinforcers, we can use two approaches: *direct assessment methods,* such as observing the target person's preferences in naturalistic or structured tests, and *indirect assessment methods,* such as by asking the person probing questions in an interview or having the person fill out a questionnaire, like the Preferred Items and Experiences Questionnaire (see Figure 4.2). The larger the variety of reinforcers available for exchange in the token system, the greater the chance that the tokens will maintain their effectiveness and provide strong reinforcement for all individuals under the token economy. A related issue to keep in mind is that reinforcement is more effective in a token economy when target individuals can select their reinforcers from an array of items rather than having items assigned to them (Karraker, 1977).

A type of punishment that often dovetails easily into token economies is response cost, in which the target person pays fines, in tokens, for instances of misbehavior. Although problems can arise if a person runs out of points or credits to lose, the reinforcement system can be designed to provide enough credits for appropriate behavior so that the person will almost always have enough to cover any amount of misbehavior he or she performs. Some research findings suggest that earning and losing tokens—that is, reward and punishment methods—may be equally effective in changing behavior (Sullivan & O'Leary, 1990).

Managing the Consequences

Once we have decided what reinforcers and punishers to include in the program, we will need to keep a large supply of backup reinforcers available and devise a system for managing the distribution of the consequences. To manage the consequences effectively, we should follow a few important guidelines and decide certain critical questions in advance.

Guidelines for Administering Tokens   Five general guidelines can be followed in managing all token economy programs. First, specify clearly to everyone involved the behavioral criteria for earning tokens and the exchange rates for backup reinforcers. Post the criteria and rates prominently, if possible. Second, be sure to award tokens as soon as possible after the desired behavior occurs. Third, use natural reinforcers, such as praise, in conjunction with dispensing tokens. Fourth, keep careful and accurate records of the target behaviors performed and the reinforcers dispensed. Fifth, provide bonus rewards for high-level performance, if possible.

Who Will Administer Consequences?   Who will deliver and keep track of the tokens each target person earned or lost and the backup reinforcers or punishers received? The individual(s) bearing these responsibilities will need to monitor the target behaviors and record data carefully and deliver tokens promptly. Staff members of the organization or institution—for example, attendants, teachers, or supervisors—usually have these responsibilities. When more than one staff member is involved simultaneously in administering consequences, each member should have a separate role in the process and know what that role is (Ayllon & Azrin, 1968b). Otherwise they may duplicate each other's actions or fail to act, thinking that the other staff member will do it. If the token economy includes self-management procedures, there must be methods to check the accuracy of the data and the judgments the target person makes when administering the consequences to him- or herself (Hundert & Batstone, 1978; McLaughlin, Burgess, & Sackville-West, 1982).

How Many Tokens Will a Behavior Earn?   The goal in deciding how many tokens a behavior will earn is to maximize each target person's performance of the target behaviors. Several factors should be taken into account when deciding the number of tokens a behavior will earn. First, the laws of supply and demand are relevant (Ayllon & Azrin, 1968b). Behaviors or chores that are less attractive than others—perhaps because they are relatively time consuming, strenuous, fearful, or tedious to do—may require more tokens to enhance the reward value of the reinforcer. And there is a fairness issue too. People tend to feel that they deserve more pay for performing less attractive behaviors. So, for example, in a token economy in which college students earned tokens for doing chores in their residence, the number of tokens each student received for completing a task was directly related to the amount of time the chore took per week to do (Johnson et al., 1991).

Three other factors are also considered when deciding on the number of tokens to give for a behavior. First, target individuals with lesser abilities to learn or perform the needed behaviors may be given more tokens per behavior to equalize the potential for getting backup reinforcers. Second, it is sometimes useful to reinforce the behavior with more tokens in the first few days of a person's participation in a token economy rather than later on in the program. Third, after the behaviors have become well established, the schedule of reinforcement can be thinned to an intermittent schedule (Stainback et al., 1973).

What Will the Exchange Rates Be?   Decisions about the number of tokens needed to buy each backup reinforcer depend on four factors. First, these decisions are tied to the number of tokens target individuals can earn for each behavior. If the number of tokens earned per behavior is small, the cost of the backup reinforcers should be low, and vice versa. Second, some reinforcers cost the program money to buy. The number of tokens needed to get a particular reinforcer should be related to the monetary cost of that item. Third, the laws of supply and demand may apply again. Some reinforcers are in greater demand than others; those with high demand and low supply can cost more than those with low demand and high supply. This factor may apply especially well to activity reinforcers, such as going into town. Suppose several individuals like to go to town and often choose that as a backup reinforcer, but there are only five seats in the car regularly used for the trip. The high demand and low supply for this reinforcer may provide a rationale for making its cost higher than that of an activity with an unlimited supply. Fourth, some backup reinforcers may have more therapeutic relevance than others, and charging a relatively small number of tokens for these reinforcers can encourage individuals to choose them. For example, going on a shopping trip might cost only a few tokens because participants may learn valuable skills from that experience.

How Often Will Backup Reinforcers Be Available?   Another decision to be made in implementing a token economy concerns the availability of the backup reinforcers— that is, how often and when tokens can be redeemed for backup reinforcers. A factor here is the intellectual ability of the target individuals in the token economy. Very young children and low-functioning individuals, such as the mentally retarded, will probably need to have the backup reinforcers available at least twice a day, at least when they first enter the program. For other children, the token exchanges for backup reinforcers

> should probably take place once or twice each day during the first three or four days of a token economy. In this way the children are made aware of the real value of the tokens shortly after receiving them. (Stainback et al., 1973)

After the first few days, reinforcer availability should be reduced gradually toward the goal of allowing the children to redeem their tokens infrequently, perhaps only once a week. In general, regardless of the age of the target individuals in a token economy, the greater their cognitive abilities, the more quickly the availability of backup reinforcers can be reduced. The frequency with which tokens can be redeemed should be based on the characteristics of the individuals who receive them and on the rate that maintains the target behavior best.

Will the Program Use Group or Individual Contingencies? Like most other reinforcement programs, token economies can use group or individual contingencies for administering reinforcers. When a token economy uses a group contingency, tokens are given on the basis of the group's performance as a whole. With an individual contingency, tokens are given to each person based on his or her own performance. As we discussed in Chapter 4, group contingencies have the advantages of being relatively easy to administer and having built-in incentives to prevent group members from reinforcing one another's inappropriate behaviors. But negative peer pressure tactics, such as threats, seem to be more likely to happen with group than with individual contingencies, especially if the consequences include group punishment if behavioral criteria are not met. Keep in mind that a program can be a hybrid, in which some behaviors are rewarded with group contingencies and others with individual contingencies.

Phasing Out the Program

Although token economies are sometimes used just to maintain appropriate conduct or high performance while people are in organizational and institutional settings, they can also be applied in programs with broader, long-term goals. For instance, the goals of token economies in psychiatric hospitals may involve helping individuals function better in natural environments, outside the institution. The methods we discussed in Chapter 10 for maintaining improved behavior after an intervention ends can help achieve these long-term goals. One of these approaches involved using natural reinforcers, such as praise and feedback, along with tokens. Later in the program, the natural reinforcers can gradually replace the tokens.

Other approaches for maintaining improved behavior after an intervention ends include thinning and delaying reinforcement. These methods can be implemented by:

- Decreasing the number of tokens each target behavior earns.
- Decreasing the number of target behaviors that earn tokens.
- Increasing the number of tokens required to buy backup reinforcers.
- Increasing the delays between receiving tokens and having opportunities to redeem them for backup reinforcers.

These approaches can be used separately or in combination, but it is not yet clear which method or combination of techniques will enhance maintenance of behaviors best. (Go to ✔)

AN EXAMPLE OF TOKEN ECONOMY: ACHIEVEMENT PLACE

Now that we have seen the general features of token economies and how they are set up and implemented, we will examine in some detail a fine example of a token economy program to see how one functions. This token economy, called Achievement Place, was developed in Kansas in the 1960s and 1970s by Elery Phillips (1968) and several

CONCEPT CHECK 12.1

1, A behavior change program designed to change a wide range of behaviors in groups of individuals by using a complex system of reinforcers is called a _____ .

2. An example of the materials or equipment to be obtained and set up before starting a token economy is _____ . ⇔

3. An example of tokens that could be used in a token reinforcement program is _____ . ⇔

4. A type of punishment that can fit into a token economy especially easily is _____ .

5. To equalize the potential for getting backup reinforcers among target individuals who differ in their abilities to perform the target behaviors, those with lesser abilities can be given _____ per behavior.

6. People who are likely to need opportunities to exchange tokens for backup reinforcers very frequently are likely to be individuals with lesser _____ abilities.

Answers: 1. token economy, 2. backup reinforcers, 3. poker chips, 4. response cost, 5. more tokens, 6. cognitive/intellectual.

colleagues, particularly Montrose Wolf and Dean Fixsen (Phillips et al., 1971; Phillips, Phillips, Wolf, & Fixsen, 1973).

The Purpose and Structure of Achievement Place

Achievement Place was designed as a residential token economy program for juvenile boys who were classified as "predelinquent." The term *predelinquent* reflects the belief that a juvenile's home life and record of minor offenses, such as petty thefts and fighting, indicates he or she is likely to become a habitual lawbreaker if no corrective action is taken. The purpose of Achievement Place was to rehabilitate the boys who were placed by the courts in the program to prevent them from becoming delinquents. The approach this program developed became a model for over 200 other programs to prevent delinquency in the United States, including *Boys Town* (Fixsen et al., 1978; Wolf, Braukmann, & Ramp, 1987). Although most of these programs have been for boys, many have been for girls. The average age at entry into and exit from these programs has been 14.1 and 15.0, respectively, for boys, and 14.8 and 15.4 for girls (Kirigin et al., 1982).

Achievement Place was set up in a large house and received predelinquent boys from the local community. The house served as the residence for several boys at a time and a pair of *teaching parents*, who supervised the program. The boys continued to go to their own schools, and their teachers completed brief "report cards" daily. Each day the boys could earn or lose points based on their performing specific social, academic, and

Table 12.1   Some target behaviors in the achievement place program and the number of points each one earned or lost

Behaviors That Earned Points	Points
1. Watching news on TV or reading the newspaper	300 per day
2. Cleaning and maintaining neatness in one's room	500 per day
3. Keeping one's person neat and clean	500 per day
4. Reading books	5–10 per page
5. Aiding house-parents in various household tasks	10–1000 per task
6. Doing dishes	500–1000 per meal
7. Being well dressed for an evening meal	100–500 per meal
8. Performing homework	500 per day
9. Obtaining desirable grades on school report cards	500–1000 per grade
10. Turning out lights when not in use	25 per light
Behaviors That Lost Points	**Points**
1. Failing grades on the report card	500–1000 per grade
2. Speaking aggressively	20–50 per response
3. Forgetting to wash hands before meals	100–300 per meal
4. Arguing	300 per response
5. Disobeying	100–1000 per response
6. Being late	10 per minute
7. Displaying poor manners	50–100 per response
8. Engaging in poor posture	50–100 per response
9. Using poor grammar	20–50 per response
10. Stealing, lying, or cheating	10,000 per response

Source: Phillips, 1968, Table 2.

everyday living behaviors both at the house and in school. Whenever points were earned or lost, the behavior and number of points were recorded on an index card each boy carried with him. Table 12.1 describes some of the target behaviors in the program and the number of points the behaviors earned or lost. The backup reinforcers, or "privileges," as they were called, were mainly activities, such as being allowed to go downtown, and consumable items, such as snacks, that would be naturally available in most teenagers' everyday lives.

An important feature of this program was a gradual transition toward self-regulation. The boys made this transition by advancing through three levels or phases of the program. When a boy entered the program, he started on a *daily point system* in which the points he earned were tallied up at the end of each day and could be exchanged for privileges he would receive on the following day. This arrangement allowed him to learn how the system worked and the value of earning tokens. As soon as the boy could function with less structure, he advanced to the second level, the *weekly point system*, in which his points were tallied for a full week and exchanged for

Table 12.2   Privileges (backup reinforcers) that could be earned at achievement place and the number of points needed to purchase them on the daily and weekly point systems

Privileges	Price in Points	
	Weekly System	Daily System
Basics (hobbies and games)	3000	400
Snacks	1000	150
TV	1000	150
Allowance (per $1.00)	2000	300
Permission to leave Achievement Place (home, downtown, sports events)	3000	*
Bonds (savings for gifts, special clothing, etc.)	1000	150
Special privileges	Variable	*

*Not available

Source: Phillips et al., 1971, Table 1.

reinforcers he would receive for the following week. In the last level in the program, called the *merit system*, the point system was phased out and the privileges became freely available as long as improved social, academic, and everyday living behaviors were maintained with social reinforcement alone. Boys were placed on the merit system only if their behavior was consistently good, and they appeared to be almost ready to leave Achievement Place to return home.

The token economy for the daily and weekly point systems was designed so that boys who performed all of the target behaviors and lost few points in fines could expect to earn essentially all of the privileges available. Table 12.2 lists the privileges the boys could earn at Achievement Place and the number of points needed to purchase each one on the daily and weekly point systems. The privileges called "basics" were exchanged as a package that included the use of a telephone, a radio, the recreation room, and tools. The number of points needed to purchase each privilege stayed fairly constant but could change occasionally if the reward value varied. For example, watching TV cost more tokens during the winter than in other seasons. Various "special privileges" could be available. One special privilege the boys could buy at an auction each week was the opportunity to serve as *manager*—the person with authority to assign chores and award tokens to the other boys under his supervision. The manager's behavior earned or lost points for him, depending on how well the other boys performed their household chores and everyday living behaviors, such as brushing their teeth and getting up on time in the morning.

A Day in One's Life at Achievement Place

Because the boys lived in a house with two "teaching parents," and the social structure and activities were like those of a family, the Achievement Place approach came to be known at the *teaching-family model*. The daily routine was designed to be like the routines of most families. As Elery Phillips (1968) has described, the boys got up at a standard time in the morning, showered and dressed, and cleaned their rooms. Then,

> after breakfast, some of the boys had kitchen clean-up duties before leaving for school. After school the boys returned home and prepared their homework, after which they could watch TV, play games, or engage in other recreational activities if these privileges had been earned via the token economy. Some boys were assigned kitchen clean-up duties after the evening meal. (p. 214)

A "family conference" was held each evening to enable the boys and teaching parents to discuss the day's events, the manager's performance, and problems with the token economy program (Phillips, Phillips, Wolf, & Fixsen, 1973). These conferences gave the boys chances to contribute to and learn from the way the program was administered. During the rest of the evening, the boys could engage in individual and group recreational activities before going to bed at a standard time.

How Effective Is the Achievement Place Approach?

Studies have shown that the Achievement Place approach is very effective in improving a wide variety of behaviors while predelinquent juveniles are in the program and for a year or so after it ends. For instance, a 2-year follow-up study found that, compared with boys who were placed either in a large institution for delinquents or on probation, Achievement Place boys had substantially fewer police and court contacts, greater school attendance, and higher grades (Fixsen et al., 1978).

Another study compared the effects of two types of group homes: 13 homes that followed the teaching-family model and 9 homes that used other approaches to prevent delinquency (Kirigin et al., 1982). The court and police records of each boy or girl were examined for instances of alleged criminal offenses during the intervention period and for the year before and the year after the group home intervention. The *rate* of offenses was then determined by taking the average number of offenses per month. The researchers then compared the rates of offenses for the three periods—before, during, and after intervention. For the juveniles in the homes using the teaching-family model, the rate of offenses dropped by about half during the intervention and did not increase in the subsequent year. For those in the homes using other approaches, the rate of offenses *increased* sharply during the intervention and dropped in the subsequent year to the same rate as that of the teaching-family homes. This means that the teaching-family homes were much more effective in controlling delinquent behaviors while the juveniles were in group homes, but the two types of programs did not differ in being able to prevent delinquency in the subsequent year.

Despite the success of the teaching-family model for improving the behavior of predelinquent juveniles while they are in the program and for the year after, it is now clear that these improvements are often lost after a couple of years (Wolf, Braukmann, & Ramp, 1987). In addition, the rate of criminal offenses after completing a teaching-family intervention is, on average, still well above national norms for juveniles of matching ages.

The failure of short-term interventions to prevent delinquency fully and durably should not be very surprising. Juveniles who complete a teaching-family program typically are returned to the same environment that reinforced antisocial behavior in the past. Little encouragement exists in that environment for the kinds of behaviors that were reinforced at the group home. Even among teenagers who are receiving group therapy sessions with peers, members of the group often promote deviant behavior in each other (Dishion, McCord, & Poulin, 1999). The solution to the problem of maintaining the gains interventions produce in predelinquent juveniles may be to provide longer term contact with environments that support positive social behavior, perhaps by training parents and foster parents in behavior modification skills to help them supervise these teens during adolescence (Wolf, Braukmann, & Ramp, 1987). This possibility has received support in research (Chamberlain & Reid, 1998; Dishion & Andrews, 1995).

OTHER SETTINGS FOR TOKEN ECONOMIES

Three of the many other settings in which token economies have been used successfully are in school classrooms, places of employment, and institutions for individuals with psychiatric and developmental disabilities. We will look briefly at some representative interventions and the target behaviors they addressed.

Token Economies in Classrooms

The use of rewards to influence classroom behavior has a long history. Your parents and grandparents probably remember teachers who gave "stars" to students for academic achievement and extra recess time to children who had "been good." These reinforcers are still used today. They basically give social reinforcement or feedback because they are generally not exchanged for backup reinforcers. Using tokens as rewards in schools has a shorter history. It began in the 1960s and has continued in many regular and special education classrooms since then, usually in programs conducted to improve students' general conduct and academic performance. Some of these programs qualify as token economies because they addressed several target behaviors and used fairly complex reinforcement systems.

One early example of a token economy applied in a school setting was carried out in a special education classroom with mildly and moderately retarded 8- to 14-year-olds (Birnbrauer et al., 1972). Although token and social reinforcement were given mainly for correct performance on academic assignments, such as vocabulary and arithmetic tasks, the students could also earn tokens for being cooperative or doing some extra activity. Reprimands and time-out were used as punishment for disruptive behaviors. The tokens were marks the teacher put in squares that divided up sheets of paper in a student's "mark book" folder. At the end of the daily token economy class, the students could exchange fully marked sheets for backup reinforcers (balloons, trinkets, pencils, and so on). Sheets that had any squares unmarked could be carried over to the next day. In some cases, a child would save up sheets to buy a special, relatively expensive item that was included as a backup reinforcer specifically for him or her. After the students had spent more than 3 months in the token economy, the token reinforcement was suspended for more than 3 weeks. Only a third of the children continued to perform well during that time, but the higher performance levels returned when the token economy was reinstated.

Another token economy program was applied for a full academic year in an entire elementary school, spanning from kindergarten through sixth grade (Boegli & Wasik, 1978). The target behaviors differed somewhat for the younger and older children, but in all cases they called for students to be at assigned areas on time, have needed supplies and books for the day's activities, talk or move about quietly so as not to disturb others, help other individuals, and successfully complete assigned work. All teachers and all other staff of the school, including librarians and aides, were trained in the token economy method and could distribute tokens for appropriate behaviors. Although token exchanges could occur at various times during any day, the child's teacher supervised all exchanges, and children could save their tokens across days if they wished. Sometimes auctions were held in which the children could bid on various items—such as musical recordings, magazines, comic books, toys, and jewelry—donated by parents and merchants. Data analyses revealed decreases in student disruptions and suspensions, and the students' scores on reading and mathematics achievement tests showed greater improvements during the year of the program than during the preceding year.

Token Economies in Worksites

The owner of a company that manufactures egg cartons in Massachusetts introduced a token economy to improve several behaviors, with a focus on decreasing absenteeism and discipline problems (Nelton, 1988). The point system worked in this way: each employee would earn 25 points for excellent attendance for an entire year, 20 points for having no formal disciplinary action for a year, and 15 points for having no injuries requiring an absence in a year. They could also earn points for submitting suggestions that improved safety or reduced costs and lose points for being absent from work. When workers accumulated 100 points, they became members of the company's "100 Club" and were awarded a jacket with the name of the club and company logo printed on it. Although the backup reinforcer is limited and may appear a bit corny, individuals who received it seemed quite proud.

A more complex worksite token economy was introduced at two open-pit mines to improve worker safety in the hazardous jobs associated with mining (Fox, Hopkins, & Anger, 1987). Each year hundreds of mining workers are killed and many thousands are injured in the United States. The two mines that received the intervention had very poor safety records, with the numbers of days workers lost due to work-related injuries being several times higher than the national mining average. The tokens were trading stamps that were awarded monthly with paychecks and could be redeemed at stores for hundreds of different items, such as a spice rack, bowling ball, gas-fired barbecue grill, and microwave oven. Workers received the tokens mainly for not having had any injuries requiring a physician's care in the prior month, but they could also earn tokens for safety suggestions. The token economy divided the workers into four groups on the basis of how hazardous their jobs were. Although injuries had occurred in all job groups, most injuries were in jobs associated with the use and maintenance of heavy machinery. The more hazardous the job, the more tokens workers received for avoiding injury. What's more, a group contingency was added so that all workers under the same supervisor got tokens if none of those workers was injured during a month. As Figure 12.1 depicts, the rates of work-related injuries dropped after the token economies were introduced and remained relatively low at both mines during the many years the interventions remained in effect.

Token Economies in Institutional Settings

The structure and usefulness of the token economy approach for changing behavior was first described by Teodoro Ayllon and Nathan Azrin (1968b), based on the program they applied in a psychiatric hospital. In this groundbreaking program, patients could earn tokens for a variety of activities and chores, such as helping to serve meals or clean the kitchen, gathering clothes to be laundered, and performing personal hygiene tasks. The tokens were specially made metal coins that could only be obtained inside the ward. The patients could exchange the tokens for reinforcers of two types: (1) candies, magazines, or other items at a "store" on the ward and (2) opportunities to watch movies or TV programs, choose the people to dine with, and attend extra religious services. (We'll see later that some of these reinforcers cannot be used in hospitals today because of legal or ethical concerns.) After this program provided a model structure for a token economy and demonstrated that this approach could be implemented successfully in psychiatric settings, token economies were applied in other psychiatric hospitals and in institutions of many other types (Glynn, 1990; Welch & Gist, 1974).

A long-term and extensive research project compared the effectiveness of a token economy program with two other commonly used approaches in treating middle-aged psychiatric patients who had been in mental institutions most of their adult lives (Paul & Lentz, 1977). The researchers randomly assigned a large number of patients to the three treatment approaches and evaluated many outcome measures over several years. The token economy was very carefully designed and applied and included many different backup reinforcers for a wide range of socially relevant behaviors. The patients who were treated with the token economy program showed greater improvements in their behaviors in the institution, used less medication to control their psychological functioning, were released sooner, and adjusted better to living outside the institution than the patients who were treated with the other approaches. But despite the clear effectiveness of the token economy approach in treating psychiatric patients, it has not yet been widely adopted in mental hospitals. (Go to ⬛)

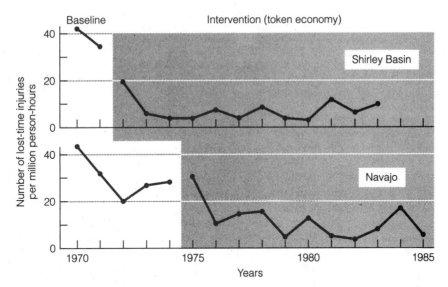

Figure 12.1 Baseline and intervention rates of serious work-related injuries, as reflected in the yearly number of injuries, per million person-hours worked, that resulted in the loss of 1 or more days from work. The token economies were studied with a variation of a multiple-baseline, across-subjects design, comparing employees at two open-pit mines: the Shirley Basin uranium mine in Wyoming and the Navajo coal mine in Arizona. *Source:* Fox, Hopkins, & Anger, 1987, Figure 2.

BENEFITS AND PROBLEMS OF TOKEN ECONOMIES

The token economy has been clearly established as an effective treatment approach for changing problem behaviors (TFPDPP, 1993). Target individuals tend to perform a program's target behaviors at high rates when the token economy is in effect. But these gains are often temporary if the program is discontinued, as when individuals are re-leased from an institution that uses a token economy. Although the loss of these gains is an important problem, a useful question to ask is whether improved behaviors are maintained better after interventions with token economies than with other ap-proaches. As we have seen in programs with predelinquent adolescents and psychiatric patients, token economies are at least as effective and are sometimes more effective than other approaches in maintaining improved behaviors.

Not all behavioral improvements are likely to be lost when a token economy ends. For instance, children who acquire new academic skills in classroom token economies are likely to retain these skills, especially if the skills are reinforced in other classes or outside the academic environment. Skills in reading or arithmetic are useful in many situations children encounter. In contrast, improvements in people's general conduct or lifestyle behaviors may be harder to maintain after a token economy has ended because the natural environment may not reinforce the new behaviors.

CLOSE-UP 12.1

Why Are Token Economies Not Used Widely with Psychiatric Patients?

 Token reinforcement approaches have been successful and widely adopted for changing problem behavior in many different settings. Given the success of token economies in treating psychiatric patients, why are they not used widely in mental hospitals in the United States? Researcher Shirley Glynn (1990) has described five reasons:

- *Staff resistance.* Sometimes staff who work in mental hospitals resist using token economies because of the intensive supervision and monitoring these approaches require and for philosophical reasons—some, for example, may view reinforcers as "bribes."
- *Economic factors.* The immediate costs of backup reinforcers and extra staff needed to carry out a token economy may preclude the use of this approach, despite the likelihood of a favorable cost–benefit ratio in the long run.
- *Reduced length of hospitalization.* Token economies often take several months or longer to achieve success with psychiatric patients. Because of cost-containment policies at most institutions, however, patients remain in hospitals only for short stays and return periodically when they relapse.

- *Emphasis toward community-based treatment.* Coinciding with having patients stay in hospitals for brief periods has been an emphasis on outpatient treatment. Although there are some advantages to outpatient treatment, token economies for psychiatric patients are harder to supervise and appear to be less effective in correcting problem behaviors when administered on an outpatient basis.
- *Legal/ethical concerns.* Legal rulings in the United States and ethical concerns have had the effect of restricting the types of backup reinforcers that can be used with psychiatric patients. In some states, for instance, institutions are required to give free access to personal property, cheerful furnishings, television, and so on. And ethical concerns have been expressed about using some backup reinforcers, such as cigarettes: Is it acceptable to use a highly effective reinforcer if it is known to have negative health effects? Although these constraints do not prevent token economies from being used, they make it more difficult to apply powerful reinforcers to change behavior in institutions.

One solution to this problem may be simply to continue the token economy. But the feasibility of continuing a program, especially if it is expensive to run, will surely depend on the cost–benefit ratio and the speed with which the savings can be realized. For example, the token economies we discussed earlier that were applied to increase workers' safety in mining jobs continued for many years. By maintaining safety behaviors, industries with hazardous jobs can save money in the costs of insurance and absenteeism. These savings can offset the costs of running an effective program to change behavior.

Sometimes people criticize token economies as being "demeaning" to the target individuals, especially if the individuals are adults who should be able to control their behavior on their own. If this criticism is correct, assessments of the program's social validity by the target individuals and others should indicate dissatisfaction with the

CONCEPT CHECK 12.2

1. In the Achievement Place program, the last level toward self-regulation is called the _____ system.
2. A likely task of an Achievement Place manager might be to have other boys _____ . ⇔
3. The rate of criminal offenses of juveniles after receiving a teaching-family intervention in a group home is _____ than the national norm for teens.
4. In the token economy applied at the two mines, workers received token reinforcers mainly for _____ .
5. An example of a backup reinforcer one may *not* be allowed to use with patients in some U.S. institutions is _____ . ⇔
6. An improved behavior that might be relatively difficult to maintain after a token economy ends is _____ . ⇔

Answers: 1. merit, 2. clean bathrooms, 3. higher, 4. not having injuries, 5. watching TV, 6. obeying rules

methods used. But this does not seem to be a problem. For instance, predelinquent adolescents in programs to improve their behavior evaluated the interventions with 7-point rating scales, where a 7 reflected high satisfaction. Teenagers who received interventions in group homes gave ratings that averaged 6.5 out of 7 points for the homes using the teaching-family model and only 5.0 points for the homes using other approaches (Kirigin et al., 1982). Perhaps individuals in token economy programs realize that the system is not very different from their earning pay for working or grades for studying. Perhaps they also realize that any "demeaning" aspects to the program, if such exist, are easily offset by the sense of self-esteem and pride to be gained from improving personal problem behaviors. (Go to ☑)

SUMMARY

A token economy is a complex system of consequences that is usually applied to change a wide range of behaviors in groups of people. Token economies have been used mainly in organizational and institutional settings, such as classrooms for normal students, institutions for people with mental retardation and psychiatric patients, group homes for predelinquent teenagers, and worksites. They have also been applied to structure and encourage positive social conduct in private communities.

Starting a token economy requires that many detailed decisions be made; in addition, staff must be trained, and baseline data collected. Setting up a token economy is a very complex process. It involves choosing the tokens, the backup reinforcers, and the punishers to be used. It also entails assigning one or more persons to administer conse-quences and deciding the number of tokens a behavior will earn, the exchange avail-ability and rates for reinforcers, and whether individual or group contingencies will be used. Phasing out a token economy can promote the maintenance of the improved behavior by using natural reinforcers and by thinning and delaying reinforcement.

Achievement Place was designed as a residential token economy in which "teach-ing parents" supervised the behavior of predelinquent juveniles. This approach is called the teaching-family model. It features a gradual transition toward self-regulation by requiring the teenagers to progress through three levels: the daily point system, the weekly point system, and the merit system. Although the teaching-family model ap-pears to be more effective in reducing antisocial behavior than other group home approaches while the juveniles are in the program, the gains are often lost within 2 years after the teenagers are returned to their home environments.

Token economies have been applied successfully to improve a wide variety of behaviors, including classroom conduct and academic achievement, job performance and safety, and social behaviors of many types. Because improved behaviors often are not maintained after people leave the program, it may be necessary to continue the program in some form to prevent relapses.

KEY TERMS

token economy   Achievement Place

REVIEW QUESTIONS

1. What is a token economy, and how is it different from other token reinforcement systems?
2. Describe the steps that need to be completed before a token economy can start to function.
3. What kinds of tokens are there?
4. State the four general guidelines for administering tokens.
5. What issues do we need to consider when deciding who will administer conse-quences in a token economy?
6. Describe the factors to consider when deciding how many tokens to give for tar-get behaviors.
7. Describe the factors to consider when deciding on the exchange rate for backup reinforcers.
8. How can token economies be phased out while enhancing the likelihood that desirable behaviors will be maintained after the participants have left the program?

9. Describe the levels of transition Achievement Place provides toward self-regulation.

10. Describe the study by Kirigin et al. (1982) comparing the outcomes of group homes using the teaching-family model with homes using other approaches.

11. Describe the study by Fox, Hopkins, and Anger (1987) on applying token economies to improve worker safety in mining.

12. Describe the research by Paul and Lentz (1977) comparing a token economy with other approaches in treating psychiatric patients. What did they find?

13. Discuss why token economies are not used widely with psychiatric patients.

RELATED READINGS

Ayllon, T., & Azrin, N. H. (1968b). *The token economy: A motivational system for therapy and rehabilitation*. Englewood Cliffs, NJ: Prentice-Hall.

Glynn, S. M. (1990). Token economy approaches for psychiatric patients: Progress and pitfalls over 25 years. *Behavior Modification, 14*, 383–407.

Phillips, E. L. (1968). Achievement Place: Token reinforcement procedures in a home-style rehabilitation setting for "pre-delinquent" boys. *Journal of Applied Behavior Analysis, 1,* 213–223.

Stainback, W. C., Payne, J. S., Stainback, S. B., & Payne, R. A. (1973). *Establishing a token economy in the classroom*. Columbus, OH: Charles E. Merrill.

Wolf, M. M., Braukmann, C. J., & Ramp, K. A. (1987). Serious delinquent behavior as part of a significantly handicapping condition: Cures and supportive environments. *Journal of Applied Behavior Analysis, 20*, 347–359.

People can gain voluntary control of bodily processes through biofeedback training. In this photo, the woman is receiving electromyographic biofeedback with sounds delivered through earphones to reflect the level of muscle tension in her forehead.

Advanced Behavioral Methods
for Therapy

When getting on an escalator, does it ever occur to you that the moving handrail might move too fast and pull you forward, making you trip and fall? This idea formed part of a female college student's phobia when she entered therapy (Nesbitt, 1973). Her fear of riding on escalators had developed several years earlier at a shopping mall: she had ridden on one of the familiar people-movers to an upper floor with relatives with no difficulty, but when the family began to board the escalator later to descend, she said she was afraid because of the apparent height. The relatives may have thought she was "being silly," so they forced her onto the escalator. Ever since that experience, she avoided escalators and always took the stairs or elevator instead. If she was with other people who suggested taking an escalator, she bluntly refused.

On one subsequent occasion, she approached an escalator unexpectedly while shopping and became so overcome by anxiety that she nearly vomited. Because of the problems she experienced with escalators, she had tried, before entering therapy, to reduce her fear

> by attempting, in the company of friends, to get on an escalator. On those occasions when she could bring herself to stand at the foot of the escalator, she would not step on for fear that by holding on to the handrail she would be pulled downward and so miss her step. (p. 405)

The therapist helped her overcome her fear in one very intense session in which she had to ride on a department store escalator repeatedly with him. Getting her to board the escalator the first time was very difficult and required a great deal of coaxing and "a little physical force." Once on board, she held onto the therapist's shirt tightly, said she felt she'd vomit, and seemed on the verge of crying. The next escalator ride was somewhat easier. After nearly half an hour of riding escalators continuously, she could ride on her own comfortably. Months later, she reported rarely experiencing anxiety when on escalators.

As you read about this fear reduction method, you probably noticed how different it was from other methods discussed earlier in which individuals encounter fearful stimuli gradually. You may have also thought that it was a good idea to have a therapist there in case the client "freaked out." Experienced therapists usually can gauge how anxious a client is and help prevent the person from feeling overwhelmed.

This chapter examines behavioral methods that require professional supervision. Although supervision is necessary throughout all applications of most of these methods, some techniques may need professional supervision mainly in early sessions or just to provide training for clients who will use the techniques in self-management programs. The first behavioral method we will examine is biofeedback, which clients can usually apply in self-management programs after training by a professional.

BIOFEEDBACK

Imagine that you have asthma, a respiratory condition whose symptoms include recurrent episodes of impaired breathing that results when tissue inflammation causes the airways to narrow, develop spasms, and produce mucus (McClintic, 1985; Sarafino, 1997). Now, suppose you had some way to tell that an episode is just starting, and you had learned a skill that enabled you to keep the airways open. If you could receive feedback about the status of your respiratory processes, you might be able to learn to control them and avoid future asthma episodes or reduce their severity. Receiving information about the status of our bodily functions is the basis of biofeedback.

What Is Biofeedback?

Biofeedback is a technique in which an electrical/mechanical device monitors the status or changes of a person's physiological processes, such as heart rate or muscle tension, and immediately reports that information back to the individual. This information allows the person to *gain voluntary control over these bodily processes* through operant conditioning. If, for instance, we were to use biofeedback to lower your blood pressure or heart rate, and the device reports that the pressure or rate has just decreased a bit, this information would reinforce whatever you had done to accomplish this decrease (Weems, 1998).

Measuring blood pressure provides a clear and familiar example of how biofeedback devices work. You've surely seen a physician or nurse apply the basic device, called a sphygmomanometer, to measure a patient's blood pressure. A cuff on the person's arm is filled with air until it is tight enough to stop the blood from flowing through the main artery in the arm (AMA, 1989). The cuff is then slowly deflated so that the medical worker can hear through a stethoscope the first beat forcing its way along the main artery as the blood flow overcomes the pressure in the cuff. The cuff pressure at that first beat can be seen on a gauge and indicates the person's maximum (called "systolic") blood pressure at that time, which occurs when the heart contracts to pump the blood. The medical worker continues the procedure by deflating the cuff until the beating sound has disappeared. The pressure shown on the gauge at this time reflects the resting ("diastolic") pressure in the artery while the heart chambers fill with blood between contractions. Blood pressure biofeedback sessions can be conducted in several different ways (Olson & Kroon, 1987). In one approach, many sphygmomanometer readings may be taken, with the person receiving each pressure reading. Some devices can inflate and deflate the cuff and take readings automatically (Goldstein, Jamner, & Shapiro, 1992).

The feedback individuals receive in biofeedback can take many different forms. For instance, the level of physiological functioning can be reflected by high or low numbers on a gauge, pitches of tones produced by an audio speaker, degrees of loudness of a tone from a speaker, or degrees of brightness of a light. Status and functioning can be measured for many different physiological processes, enabling the use of biofeedback on each process (Olson, 1987; Peek, 1987). For some body functions, such as heart rate or temperature, measurements can be taken continuously, without having to cycle through a procedure. Specific names are given for biofeedback techniques for different physiological processes, such as *blood pressure* (BP). Some of the other commonly used types of biofeedback are:

- *Heart rate* (HR), or heartbeats per minute.
- *Galvanic skin response* (GSR, also called *electrodermal activity*, EDA), which measures sweat gland activity by testing how readily the skin conducts minute levels of electricity. Sweaty skin conducts more readily than dry skin.
- *Electroencephalograph* (EEG), which assesses electrical activity in the brain.
- *Electromyograph* (EMG), which measures muscle tension by assessing the electrical activity of muscles when they contract.
- *Skin temperature*, which measures the flow of blood, which is warm, in part of the body, such as a foot or hand, by assessing the skin temperature in that region of the body.

Note that all these measures are indirect. They are taken on the outside of the body or just below the skin to reflect changes deeper in the body, such as brain activity. Sometimes the measure only allows us to *infer* internal changes, as when we assume that skin temperature changes suggest that blood flow changes have occurred.

Learning to regulate one's own bodily processes with biofeedback requires training. The training clients get incorporates a shaping procedure in which tiny physiological changes in the desired direction are reinforced initially; as the training progresses, larger and larger changes are required for reinforcement. Clients are usually encouraged to practice biofeedback techniques at home when they receive training. Home practice appears to enhance the success of biofeedback in certain applications, such as in treating headache (Gauthier, Côté, & French, 1994), but it may not help people learn the methods better or faster during training (Blanchard et al., 1991).

CLOSE-UP 13.1

"Mind Control" with EEG Biofeedback?

 In the early 1970s, the findings of research on EEG biofeedback seemed to suggest that training to increase a specific type of brain electrical activity, called *alpha brain waves*, enabled individuals to achieve an "alpha experience" of deep relaxation and well-being (Olson & Schwartz, 1987; Stern & Ray, 1980). Alpha waves are a normal component of wakeful brain activity that tend to increase during certain conditions, such as daydreaming or meditating. The news media quickly publicized the findings about biofeedback, and many people rushed to get some training or to buy equipment with instructions so they could achieve that experience, and with it, some level of "mind control."

The idea of being able to control one's own mind to decrease feelings of anxiety and increase feelings of relaxation through EEG biofeedback is quite intriguing, but research results have not supported this possibility (Olson & Schwartz, 1987; White & Tursky, 1982). For instance, studies have shown that people who receive training to increase alpha activity are likely to report that they have had the "alpha experience" only if they were told it would happen (Plotkin, 1976). EEG training to increase alpha wave activity does not seem to help people reduce to their anxiety or to experience feelings of relaxation and well-being.

Biofeedback Applications

As we will soon see, biofeedback techniques have been applied successfully to produce many medical and psychological benefits for people—for example, helping individuals with asthma to control episodes (Sarafino, 1997). Because of such successes, biofeedback therapists and commercial companies have advertised "miracle" cures for all sorts of problems, sometimes even when little or no good evidence has been found that these techniques are effective. For instance, one company advertised tape recordings by stating "Let your cancer disappear with image rehearsal and biofeedback," "Image rehearsal and biofeedback to let your joints be normal and comfortable if you have arthritis," and "Feel wonderful without the urge to drink alcohol excessively with image rehearsal and biofeedback" (Stern & Ray, 1980, p. v). We will look at several effective biofeedback applications. (Go to 📖)

Biofeedback and Epilepsy *Epilepsy* is a neurological condition marked by recurrent, sudden seizures that result from electrical disturbances in the brain (EFA, 1990). In the most severe form of epileptic seizure, called a *grand mal attack*, the person loses consciousness and has muscle spasms. EEG biofeedback has been used successfully with many patients in helping them learn to control their brain electrical activity and reduce their seizures (Goldstein, 1990; Sterman, 1986). The general approach in using EEG biofeedback with epileptics involves training the patient to increase or decrease certain kinds of brain wave activities in specific areas of the brain. If the person can gain some measure of control over these brain waves in the areas of the brain where the disturbances occur, seizures should diminish. Although not all patients benefit from this approach, many do. One problem in using biofeedback to reduce seizures is that there is no good way to predict which patients will benefit from this approach and which will not. This is an important problem because the procedure is costly, requiring many hours of individually supervised training with expensive equipment.

Biofeedback and Hypertension   *Hypertension* is the medical condition of having high blood pressure consistently over several weeks or more. Medical treatment for hypertension usually includes having the person use prescription drugs and make lifestyle changes, such as exercising and making dietary changes designed to lower weight. BP biofeedback is a useful supplement to medical treatment. It appears to help people control their blood pressure, thereby enabling them to use less medication (McCaffrey & Blanchard, 1985; Olson & Kroom, 1987). The drugs used in treating hypertension can cause side effects, such as increased blood sugar levels or feelings of weakness or confusion, that may be very difficult for some patients to tolerate. Using behavioral methods may be especially useful for these people in helping to reduce their blood pressures while minimizing the use of drugs.

Biofeedback and Anxiety   In earlier chapters, we have discussed how anxiety and other conditioned emotional responses can be reduced through procedures that relax the muscles, particularly by using progressive muscle relaxation techniques. Because EMG biofeedback can help people learn to relax specific muscle groups, studies have investigated the utility of this form of biofeedback in treating anxiety. Most of these studies have focused on applying biofeedback to reduce tension in the *frontalis*, the large rectangular-shaped sheets of muscle that span the forehead. These studies focused on tension in this muscle because some evidence suggested a link between frontalis relaxation and general body relaxation (Surwit & Keefe, 1978). Robert Gatchel (1982) has reviewed the research using EMG biofeedback and concluded that although the procedure is effective in reducing anxiety it is not more effective than other, more easily administered relaxation methods, such as progressive muscle relaxation.

Biofeedback and Chronic Headache   Two biofeedback approaches have been used for treating patients who suffer from severe, recurrent headaches (Andrasik, Blake, & McCarran, 1986). One approach is used with *muscle-contraction* (or "tension") *headaches*, which seem to result from persistent contraction of the head and neck muscles. Patients with muscle-contraction headaches receive EMG biofeedback training to control the tension in specific muscle groups, such as those in the forehead. The other approach is used with *migraine headaches*, which appear to result from the dilation of blood vessels surrounding the brain. Patients with migraine headaches receive temperature biofeedback training (usually monitoring the hand) to help them control the constriction and dilation of arteries. Research has shown that biofeedback methods and relaxation methods are about equally effective in reducing chronic headache, and using both methods together can be more effective than using either one alone, at least for some patients (Andrasik, Blake, & McCarran, 1986; Holroyd & Penzien, 1985). What's

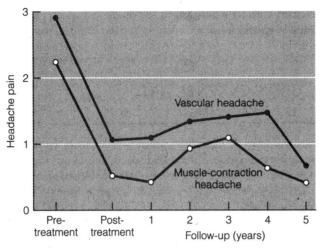

Figure 13.1 Mean ratings of headache pain (0 = no headache; 5 = intense, incapacitating head-ache) for muscle-contraction and vascular (migraine, often with muscle-contraction) headache pa-tients who completed treatment with either progressive muscle relaxation or both relaxation and biofeedback. The graph plots patients' ratings at pretreatment, posttreatment, and follow-up years 1 through 5. *Source:* Data from Blanchard et al., 1987, Table 1.

more, the results of several follow-up studies have shown that treating chronic head-ache with relaxation techniques or with relaxation and biofeedback methods together provides durable relief for at least 2 years (Blanchard, 1987). The data from one study with five yearly follow-up assessments are presented in Figure 13.1 (Blanchard et al., 1987). Children acquire skills in EMG and skin temperature biofeedback as easily as adults, and they appear to get at least as much headache relief from biofeedback proce-dures as adults do (Sarafino & Goehring, 2000).

Biofeedback and Neuromuscular Disorders *Neuromuscular disorders* are medical conditions that affect the muscles and the nerves that carry information directing the muscles to move. Some neuromuscular disorders involve paralysis, which may have resulted from a spinal cord injury or a stroke that damages the brain, and other disorders cause the muscles to become rigid or to have spasms. Such conditions have been treated successfully with EMG biofeedback (Brudny, 1982; Fogel, 1987; Krebs, 1987). This procedure involves monitoring muscles in the affected body parts, such as the legs, with sensitive electronic equipment to detect tiny changes in muscular function. In the case of patients with paralysis of part of the body, the paralysis cannot be total, as happens when the spinal cord is completely severed. Incomplete paralysis can occur if nerves are damaged but not severed. For patients whose muscles are incompletely paralyzed—that is, the nerves are damaged, but the spinal cord is not completely severed—EMG biofeedback is conducted by showing the patient that the muscle has tensed a bit and encouraging him or her to tense it more and more, thereby gradually increasing its strength. For patients with rigid muscles, the feedback focuses on relaxing the muscles. Patients with muscle spasms focus on trying to get the EMG pattern to match that of normal muscle action.

METHODS USING INTENSE AND PROLONGED EXPOSURE

Several methods have been developed to reduce people's fears. Some methods, such as systematic desensitization, proceed very gradually in exposing the person to fearful situations to minimize the degree of fear experienced. Other techniques take a very different approach: they deliberately expose the target person to high levels of fear while preventing the possibility of escape or avoidance behaviors. The purpose of this approach is to extinguish the escape or avoidance behaviors the person has relied on in the past when the fear was aroused. Because these methods are designed to arouse high anxiety, they are called **anxiety-induction therapies.** There are two basic types of anxiety-induction therapies: flooding and implosive therapy.

Flooding

At the beginning of this chapter, we considered the case of a woman who was afraid of escalators. Her therapist helped her overcome her fear by accompanying her as she rode on a department store escalator repeatedly for about half an hour. This treatment is an example of a technique called **flooding** (or *response prevention*), in which the person is exposed to a highly feared situation for prolonged periods of time under the direction of a therapist. In flooding, the therapist tries to prevent the person from using avoidance or escape responses to reduce anxiety; relaxation exercises usually are not included. Because negative reinforcement is prevented, flooding is categorized as an extinction procedure. Therapists typically explain to their clients the rationale for having to experience the highly feared situation intensely for prolonged periods without avoiding or escaping. By receiving this explanation, clients know what to expect and can decide whether they are willing to receive this treatment approach and to try hard to tolerate emotionally difficult periods in the treatment. When the source of a fear is fairly specific, such as escalators, it is often possible to complete flooding treatment in one session. When the source is broad, complex, or vague, however, as it is with most social anxieties, many sessions may be needed to present a wide range of possible CSs.

Flooding Procedures   In the example we saw of the woman who was afraid of escalators, getting her to board the escalator initially was very difficult. Once she was on board the first time, the woman appeared very frightened. It is not unusual for clients to be highly emotional initially in flooding procedures, but these reactions decrease with exposure. Still, some clients are not able to tolerate extremely intense initial exposures, and a therapist may need to present the feared situation somewhat gradually, advancing through a short stimulus hierarchy that contains several fear-arousing situations (Borden, 1992). Requiring an exposure that is too threatening may lead the client to drop out of treatment and retain the fear. Obviously, the therapist should make certain that exposure to the feared situation (the CS) will *not* be accompanied by an unpleasant US. For instance, a client who is fearful of dogs should not be exposed to a dog that might bite.

Fearful situations in flooding can be presented *in vivo*—that is, in real life, as in the therapy for the fear of escalators—or in other ways, using virtual reality technology or scenes in the person's imagination, for example. Sometimes *in vivo* presentations can be more complicated to set up than the escalator example. In one case, a woman had developed an obsessive-compulsive disorder, in which she was extremely preoccupied (or "obsessed") with anxiety-provoking ideas or events and compulsively performed maladaptive rituals to reduce her anxiety. This woman had developed an idea she found very distressing: objects *associated* with death were "contaminated" with death (Meyer, Robertson, & Tatlow, 1975). After her father died, she took a suitcase of his belongings to her apartment. Because she believed his personal things were contaminated, she carefully washed the suitcase, placed it in the back of a closet, and took a bath. These actions made her feel better, and she never touched the suitcase again. Other items she thought were contaminated were pictures of dead people, newspaper articles about death, and her fiancé, whose ex-wife had died recently. The successful *in vivo* flooding treatment included a visit to a hospital mortuary where she had to touch a dead body in the presence of her therapist.

Research comparing *in vivo* and imaginal flooding procedures has found that both methods can successfully reduce many different anxieties and phobias, and neither approach is clearly more effective than the other (Borden, 1992; James, 1986; Mathews et al., 1976). Thus, imaginal procedures can be used effectively when it is difficult or impossible to present feared situations in their real-life form. For example, it may be difficult to use real-life stimuli when a person is afraid of flying in airplanes, especially if the fear is greatest when turbulence or strange noises occur. Also, it would be impossible to present *in vivo* stimuli to reduce the fears individuals develop from experiencing extremely traumatic events, such as in war, natural disasters, or a rape. In such cases, flooding may provide more effective treatment than systematic desensitization because the latter approach is less effective with imaginal than *in vivo* procedures. (Go to)

CASE STUDY 13.1

Imaginal Flooding for War Trauma

Joseph was a 6½-year-old Lebanese boy who was referred for therapy by his teacher because he had developed frequent temper outbursts, memory problems, and inattention behaviors in class after experiencing a bomb blast (case described in Saigh, 1986). Interviews and clinical assessments revealed that he showed similar behavior problems at home, had trauma-related nightmares, and was very depressed. Imaginal flooding was applied to reduce his emotional condition.

The therapy Joseph received combined a flooding procedure with relaxation, using progressive muscle relaxation exercises and a calm scene of being on a beach. (As noted earlier, using relaxation with flooding is unusual.) Each session began with relaxation exercises and then focused mainly on flooding one of several trauma-related scenes, two of which were: "hearing a loud explosion and seeing injured people and debris" and "being led away from the site against background calls for help and automobile horns." Joseph had assessed each of the trauma-related scenes on a subjective units of discomfort scale (SUDS) as being extremely uncomfortable to imagine. No mild or moderately strong CSs were used. During the flooding procedure, he was asked to imagine a traumatic scene in great detail for over 20 minutes and give it a SUDS rating every minute. The remainder of the session was spent briefly imagining the other traumatic scenes and doing more relaxation exercises. The SUDS ratings Joseph gave were reduced dramatically in about three sessions for each traumatic scene. Follow-up assessments made during the 6 months after treatment showed only mild discomfort for any of the scenes.

Effectiveness of Flooding   Research has shown that flooding is a highly effective technique for reducing a wide variety of anxiety and phobic conditions (TFPDPP, 1993; Trull, Nietzel, & Main, 1988). Flooding is about as effective as systematic desensitization, but imaginal flooding appears to be more effective than imaginal desensitization (Marshall et al., 1977; Wilson, 1982).

A recent study examined the success of a combination of *in vivo* and imaginal flooding in treating social phobias, which are marked by extreme levels of anxiety in social situations (Turner, Beidel, & Jacob, 1994). People with social phobias may worry excessively that they will say something stupid in social situations or that other people will notice their nervousness. These individuals often experience strong physiological symptoms, such as trembling, heart palpitations, and sweating, in social situations that others do not find particularly distressing. This study compared the effects of three treatment conditions: (1) flooding therapy, (2) drug therapy in which clients took a commonly prescribed drug (atenolol) for helping them cope with social situations, and (3) a *placebo* condition in which clients took inert tablets they thought were atenolol. All three conditions were administered for 3 months, and the effects were assessed in several ways—for example, by having the clients fill out tests measuring their anxiety and asking them to speak for 10 minutes to an audience of three individuals. The results showed that flooding was generally more effective than the drug and placebo conditions in reducing the clients' anxiety problems and maintaining their gains in the 6 months after the treatment ended. For example, Figure 13.2 depicts that the mean length of the speeches the clients gave increased much more for clients who received flooding therapy than for those in the two other treatment conditions.

Studies have also examined two important questions about using flooding techniques. First, is it necessary for a therapist to accompany clients when they are exposed to the fearful situations? The outcome of research on this question indicates that the success of flooding is not enhanced by having therapists present for most of their clients'

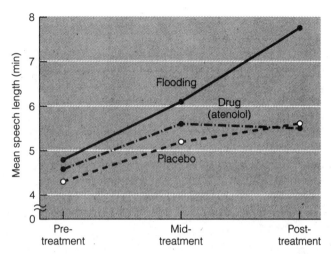

Figure 13.2 Mean speech length in minutes at pretreatment, midtreatment, and posttreatment assessments for social phobic clients under three treatment conditions: flooding therapy, drug (atenolol) therapy, and placebo drug therapy (clients took inert tablets that were described as atenolol). At each assessment, the clients were asked to give a 10-minute speech. As a social comparison, normal (nonphobic) individuals who were assessed in the same manner spoke for an average of 8.1 minutes. *Source:* Data from Turner, Beidel, & Jacob, 1994, Table 3.

exposures to highly fearful situations (Al-Kubaisy et al., 1992). It may be important for therapists to be present during the most fearful encounters, but their main roles in flooding therapy involve assessing the problem, designing the treatment, instructing the client on how to perform flooding, and monitoring the client's progress. Second, how safe is flooding? When anxiety-induction therapies were originally described, many therapists were concerned about the possibility of serious side effects, perhaps making their clients' conditions worse, rather than better. But a survey of therapists who had used anxiety-induction therapies with clients in the intervening years revealed that the procedures are quite safe, with negative outcomes being reported in only 9 out of nearly 3,500 cases (Shipley & Boudewyns, 1980).

Implosive Therapy

Implosive therapy is a variation of imaginal flooding in which the person is asked to imagine scenes that include unrealistic, exaggerated, or physically damaging events that are unlikely to happen in real life (Morganstern, 1973; Stampfl & Levis, 1967). When Thomas Stampfl developed this technique, he wanted it to address unrealistic beliefs that often seem to underlie or maintain people's anxieties. Here are some scenes that have been used in implosive therapy:

- A client with an extreme fear of heights imagined being in a roof garden atop a 40-story building, leaning against a wall that collapses, and falling down to the street (Crowe et al., 1972).

✓

CONCEPT CHECK 13.1

1. Biofeedback involves giving individuals information about the _____ of their physiological systems.
2. Receiving information about the status or changes in muscle tension is called _____ biofeedback.
3. EEG training to increase _____ wave brain activity does not seem to help people reduce their anxiety.
4. A medical condition for which biofeedback training can be helpful is _____ . ⇔
5. An example of a fear for which *in vivo* flooding would be difficult or impossible to conduct is the fear of _____ . ⇔
6. Having clients who are afraid of elevators imagine they are in one that is plunging down 20 stories is an example of _____ therapy.

Answers: 1. status or changes, 2. electromyograph (EMG), 3. alpha, 4. neuromuscular disorders/headache/epilepsy/hypertension, 5. being mugged or shot, 6. implosive.

- A person with a phobia of spiders imagined a spider having crawled on "your face and that it starts biting your cheek and chewing your eyes" (Marshall et al., 1977).
- A client with a phobia of snakes imagined being bitten and slithered on by a large, slimy snake (Mealiea & Nawas, 1971).

Although several studies have shown that implosive therapy can reduce people's anxiety and phobic conditions, flooding techniques without including unrealistic aversive events are at least as effective as implosive therapy (Marshall et al., 1977; Morganstern, 1973; Wilson, 1982). Having clients imagine exaggerated or physically damaging events does not appear to reduce their fears any better than techniques without such events. (Go to ✓)

SPECIALIZED MODELING APPLICATIONS

We have seen in previous chapters that modeling is a straightforward and very useful method for changing operant and respondent behaviors. In efforts to change operant behaviors, modeling serves as a shortcut stimulus control technique in demonstrating how to perform the responses. In changing respondent behaviors, modeling shows adaptive behaviors that can be applied in a fearful situation and enables the fear to become desensitized vicariously. We will examine a few ways modeling has been applied in specialized settings and circumstances.

Training Professional Skills

Modeling is often applied in training specific skills professionals need to use in their work (Dowrick & Jesdale, 1991). Videotapes are commonly employed to present the modeled professional skills. For instance, videotapes have been developed to show health care workers in hospitals how to handle psychiatric emergencies they tend to encounter, including patients who threaten to kill themselves. Other tapes have been developed for training graduate students to serve as teaching assistants and training counselors in skills needed to mediate divorces. Research investigating the effectiveness of videotaped modeling in training professional skills has shown that this approach is often more effective than live *role-playing*—that is, having two or more individuals enact interpersonal scenes.

Sometimes the videotapes used in professional training are designed around a story or issue of high interest to the viewer, but there is a danger in doing this. Some research findings indicate that "modeling videotapes purposely designed to maintain high viewer interest may cause so much attention to be focused on the issue presented that the modeled behaviors themselves may be overlooked" (Dowrick & Jesdale, 1991, p. 69). In a videotape on how to handle psychiatric emergencies, for example, the story of why a person wants to commit suicide may be so absorbing that the viewer doesn't notice the modeled skills for preventing suicide.

Assertion Training

Being *assertive* involves speaking up and reacting openly when among other people, expressing both positive and negative opinions and feelings. **Assertion training** refers to programs of behavioral methods that train individuals to be assertive in appropriate and adaptive ways. Assertiveness need not be accompanied by inconsiderate or aggressive acts. One view of the ways appropriate and adaptive assertion differs from aggression is that assertion involves

> expressing thoughts, feelings, and beliefs in direct, honest, and appropriate ways which respect the rights of other people. In contrast, aggression involves self-expression which is characterized by violating others' rights and demeaning others in an attempt to achieve one's own objectives. (Lange & Jakubowski, 1976, pp. 38–39)

Although assertion training can be applied to tone down people's excessive assertive behaviors, it is generally used with individuals who are unassertive. People may fail to assert themselves for many reasons. For instance, they may not know what to say, may fear something awful will happen if they speak up, or may not believe being assertive is proper in many situations.

Types and Assessment of Assertion   Individuals who are relatively assertive are not likely to be assertive in all situations. One factor that can influence whether people will be assertive is the type of assertion a given situation calls for (Christoff & Kelly, 1985; Lange & Jakubowski, 1976). Here are four common types of assertive behavior:

- *Refusing others' requests*—being able to say no when others ask you to do them a favor or service, especially when it is an unreasonable request. For instance, if a friend asks you to run an errand that would make you late for an appointment, you might say, "I'm sorry, I can't do that right now because I'll be late for my exam. I could do it later, if that would help."

- *Standing up for one's rights*—being able to object when you think your rights are being abridged or someone is cheating you. Say you've been waiting for service in a store and another customer comes in and gets the clerk's attention. You might say, "I suppose you didn't notice, but I was here first."

- *Voicing one's opinions or feelings*—being able to express positive or negative ideas or judgments. For instance, you might express your liking or admiration for someone, such as by saying, "That answer you gave in class was really insightful." Or, you might express a political or moral viewpoint to a group with the knowledge that others in the group disagree strongly.

- *Expressing one's desires or requests*—being able to voice your needs or goals to others. For example, you might ask someone for help or suggest doing some activity you would enjoy.

Some people have an easy time showing some types of assertion, such as voicing their opinions, but have difficulty showing other types of assertion, such as saying no. Other people have problems showing all types of assertion. For some people, being assertive is only difficult in certain situations or with certain people.

Therapists usually assess a client's assertiveness on the basis of interviews and one or both of two other measures. One measure involves observing the client either in real assertion situations or in simulated situations, using a *role-playing* method. The second measure has the client fill out a questionnaire that measures assertion. On some questionnaires, clients rate the degree to which each of many different assertive behaviors describes the way they react in everyday life. For instance, clients might rate statements such as "I speak up easily when I am in a group" on a 5-point scale, where 0 = never and 4 = always. Two instruments that use this approach are the Assertion Inventory (Gambrill & Richey, 1975) and the College Self-Expression Scale (Galassi et al., 1974). Other questionnaires have clients predict from several listed responses how they would react to very specific situations. For example, the Conflict Resolution Inventory (McFall & Lillesand, 1970, 1971) presents 35 hypothetical situations in which the respondent receives a request, such as:

> A slight acquaintance of yours asks to borrow $5 until next week. You have the money, but you would have to postpone buying something you wanted until the loan was repaid.

The respondent chooses from five statements ranging from "I would *refuse* and would not feel uncomfortable about doing so" to "I would *not refuse* because it seems to be a reasonable request."

Assertion Training Techniques Modeling plays a critical role in assertion training programs (Hersen et al., 1979; McFall & Twentyman, 1973). Although modeling procedures are usually carried out *overtly* in individual therapy or in group therapy sessions, they can be very effective when applied *covertly* too. In *overt* modeling, the therapist, another client, or some other person models assertive behavior live or on videotape for scenarios in which assertion would be appropriate or adaptive. After each scenario, the client is asked to imitate the observed behavior and receives feedback on his or her performance. The client's acting out the behavior is called **behavior rehearsal.** This procedure is carried out for a variety of everyday scenarios, and the client may also be asked to demonstrate how he or she would react in situations that were not specifically modeled.

In *covert* modeling, the therapist describes the full scenario and has the client visualize the appropriate assertive behavior in his or her imagination (Cautela, 1993a). The individual performing the behavior in the scene can be the client or some other person. The therapist instructs the client on the assertive behavior to visualize and what features it should have. For instance, if the client is the assertive person in the scene, the therapist might state (Hersen et al., 1979, p. 372):

- You must be looking directly at the person to whom you are speaking.
- You should respond promptly to the other person.
- Talk long enough so that the person fully understands what you are saying.
- Be sure that your tone of voice reflects how you feel about the situation.

The client is asked to relax and imagine the complete scene. When the client signals, such as by raising a finger, that the imagery is clear, the therapist describes a positive consequence for the client to imagine as an outcome of the assertive interaction.

A few other points can be made about assertion training. First, the therapy typically includes *homework assignments* to have clients engage in overt and covert assertive behaviors. Often these assignments are arranged in a hierarchy, beginning with easy assertive situations and advancing gradually to more difficult ones. For instance, in a restaurant, a very unassertive client might start by simply asking a waiter for a menu, then asking the waiter to repeat a description of some food, and then asking the waiter to bring something, such as a fork, that the waiter should have brought to the table already. Second, assertion training tries to be realistic in preparing clients for events in which being assertive doesn't work—if a client asks for a favor and receives a refusal, for instance. Modeling and role playing are used in teaching clients how to deal with such situations. Last, although many clients appear to relapse into unassertiveness after successful assertion training, research has found that clients who receive monthly booster sessions are much more likely to maintain their gains and improve further as compared with clients who receive no booster sessions (Baggs & Spence, 1990).

Reducing Anxiety in Medical Patients

Videotaped modeling is a very effective method for reducing patients' anxieties before, during, and after receiving frightening medical treatments, such as surgery or invasive dental work (Parrish & Babbitt, 1991). Reducing patients' anxieties is important for humane reasons, but it can also have two other desirable effects: (1) it tends to increase the likelihood that patients will cooperate with and not disrupt the medical procedures, and (2) it tends to decrease the amount of time patients spend in the hospital to recover and the amount of medication they take while there (Sarafino, 1998).

Preparing Patients for Nonsurgical Procedures   Many medical procedures that don't involve surgery are very difficult to undergo, sometimes because they produce pain or discomfort. One such procedure is an *endoscopy*, which is used in diagnosing ulcers and other disorders of the digestive tract. The most aversive aspect of an endoscopic examination is that a long, flexible, fiber-optic tube, almost half an inch in diameter, must be passed through the patient's mouth and down to the stomach or intestine. This tube remains in the digestive tract to transmit images of the lining for about 15 to 30 minutes. The person is awake throughout the procedure but has received tranquilizing medication and has had the throat swabbed with a local anesthetic.

Videotaped modeling has been applied in research to show patients who were awaiting endoscopic examinations what the procedure consists of and how to reduce their anxiety (Shipley et al., 1978). The tape was 18 minutes long and showed an adult

> patient actually receiving an endoscopy. The patient in the tape showed an "average" amount of distress during the examination, gagging several times and requiring a moderate amount of "calming talk" by the nurse. (p. 502)

Some patients saw the tape three times before having the procedure themselves, other patients saw it only once, and other patients saw a different videotape that was not related to having any medical procedure. After each endoscopy, the physicians and nurses rated the degree of anxiety the patient showed during the procedure, without knowing which videotape condition the patient had experienced. The findings indicated that seeing the videotape of the endoscopy just once reduced the patients' signs of anxiety substantially, and seeing it three times reduced their anxiety even more.

Preparing Patients for Surgical Procedures   The application of videotaped and filmed modeling to reduce anxieties prior to undergoing surgery has focused mainly on pediatric patients (Parrish & Babbitt, 1991). Barbara Melamed and Lawrence Siegel (1975) conducted an experiment with 4- to 12-year-old hospital patients who were scheduled for elective surgery, a tonsillectomy, for instance. The researchers assigned the children to two groups, matching the children for age, sex, race, and type of operation. One group saw a film that was relevant to having surgery, and the other group saw a film about a boy who goes on a nature trip in the country. The relevant film, entitled "Ethan Has an Operation," portrays the hospital experience of a 7-year-old boy,

> showing various events that most children encounter when hospitalized for elective surgery from the time of admission to time of discharge including the child's orientation to the hospital ward and medical personnel such as the surgeon and anesthesiologist; having a blood test and exposure to standard hospital equipment; separation from the mother; and scenes in the operating and recovery rooms. . . . Both the child's behavior and verbal remarks exemplify the behavior of a coping model so that while he exhibits some anxiety

and apprehension, he is able to overcome his initial fears and complete each event in a successful and nonanxious manner. (p. 514)

To assess the emotional adjustment of the children in the two groups the evening before surgery and at a follow-up visit about 3 weeks after the operation, the researchers used measures of three types: the children's hand sweating, questionnaire self-reports of fear, and ratings of their emotional behavior by trained observers.

The results with all three measures revealed that the children who saw the film about Ethan's operation experienced less anxiety before and after surgery than those who saw the irrelevant film. Several studies have found similar benefits in using video presentations to reduce children's medical fears (Parrish & Babbitt, 1991), but other studies have discovered that the effects of video preparation for surgery may depend on the age and prior medical experiences of the child (Sarafino, 1998). Still, video preparations for surgery are usually helpful and appear to be cost-effective: a study of children in the hospital for elective surgery found that those who received video preparation recovered more quickly than those who did not get the preparation (Pinto & Hollandsworth, 1989). The savings from being released from the hospital sooner amounted to several times the cost of providing the preparation.

AVERSION THERAPY

The powerful 1971 science fiction movie A Clockwork Orange portrayed an extremely violent young man who was convicted of a vicious crime and underwent a form of therapy to reduce his violent behavior. The procedure entailed propping his eyelids open with splints and forcing him to watch violent scenes projected on a screen while he became nauseated from the effects of an emetic drug. After many of these sessions, he could no longer bear the idea of aggression and became so meek that he could not defend himself when he was released to his original environment. This movie presents some interesting and compelling concerns about the use of aversive techniques in behavior therapy. It has been known for some time, however, that the effects these techniques produce on behavior are far weaker than those portrayed in the movie and that these methods are not very effective when applied with individuals against their will (Barlow, 1978). Nevertheless, aversive therapeutic techniques can be helpful under certain circumstances in programs to change behavior.

In **aversion therapy,** an unpleasant or painful stimulus is introduced while the client engages overtly or covertly in an undesirable behavior. The aversive stimulus is generally terminated as soon as the person stops the behavior. This procedure may be repeated over and over again within each of many therapy sessions. The purpose in using this therapy approach is to have the client begin to associate the behavior or its antecedents with the aversive stimulus, through respondent conditioning, so that performing that response becomes unpleasant. Thus, the procedure is a form of *counter-conditioning*, in which the attractiveness of inappropriate behavior or stimuli is reduced and replaced with unpleasantness.

Aversion therapy procedures can apply almost any aversive stimulus the client finds unpleasant or painful, including nausea-producing drugs, disgusting odors, feelings of humiliation, and painful (but not dangerous) electric shock. When electric shock is used, the level of shock is individually predetermined for each client by starting with a low level of shock and increasing it until he or she finds it very uncomfortable or somewhat painful (Barlow, 1978). An advantage in using shock is that it can be turned on and off exactly as needed. The technique of aversive therapy was developed mainly as a way of modifying behaviors that produce powerful reinforcers, as occur in smoking cigarettes and drinking alcohol.

Aversion Therapy in Stopping Smoking

Aversion therapy to help people stop smoking has applied aversive stimuli of three main types: electric shock, imagined negative scenes, and cigarette smoke itself. When electric shock is used, the therapist first determines the appropriate voltage to use and then pairs the shock with smoking plus stimuli associated with smoking. When imagined negative scenes are used, the client thinks about a sequence of negative events, such as getting ready to smoke but becoming nauseated and vomiting.

Cigarette smoke can be made into an unpleasant stimulus in several ways. One way, called *rapid smoking*, requires the person to take a puff, or "drag," of a cigarette every several seconds while concentrating on the unpleasant sensations the smoke produces (Tiffany, Martin, & Baker, 1986). In *satiation*, the smoker doubles or triples his or her usual smoking rate at home for some period of time. Using cigarette smoke as an unpleasant stimulus in aversion therapy for controlling smoking appears to be more effective than imagined scenes or electric shock (Kamarck & Lichtenstein, 1985; Lichtenstein & Mermelstein, 1984). Stopping smoking is hard to do. For some smokers, aversion therapy techniques may be useful as a first step in a treatment program for quitting.

Aversion Therapy in Stopping Drinking

Like quitting smoking, stopping excessive drinking is difficult. Using aversive stimuli may help. In aversion therapy to stop drinking, unpleasant stimuli of two main types have been used: electric shock and nausea-producing drugs. Electric shock has not been a very successful aversive stimulus, however, in stopping problem drinking (Miller & Hester, 1980).

A much more effective aversion therapy strategy has been to have the person take an *emetic drug,* such as emetine, that induces nausea when alcohol is consumed. In a typical half-hour session, the person first receives an injection of emetine and then repeatedly drinks an alcoholic beverage, each time quickly becoming nauseated and vomiting (Miller & Hester, 1980). The person undergoes several of these sessions, typically as an inpatient in a hospital, and then receives booster sessions periodically after discharge. A study of hundreds of problem drinkers who received emetine therapy revealed that 63% of the men and women remained abstinent during the 12 months after

CONCEPT CHECK 13.2

1. The therapy method of having two or more people enact interpersonal scenes is called _____ .
2. As an example of being unassertive, someone might want to _____ but does not speak up. ⇔
3. A client's practicing a behavior that someone modeled is called _____ .
4. An example of a nonsurgical medical procedure (other than endoscopy) for which patients might benefit by having their anxieties reduced through the method of video-taped modeling might be _____ . ⇔
5. Using videotaped modeling to reduce children's anxieties about prospective surgery is known to be cost-effective because the children _____ .
6. The approach of applying an unpleasant or painful stimulus while the client engages in an undesirable behavior is called _____ .

Answers: 1. role playing, 2. compliment a friend/suggest changing the TV channel others are watching, 3. behavior rehearsal, 4. childbirth/dental work, 5. recover and leave the hospital sooner, 6. aversion therapy

treatment, and half of these individuals remained abstinent for the next 2 years (Wiens & Menustik, 1983). Other studies using emetine in aversion therapy have also demonstrated high rates of success (Elkins, 1991; Miller & Hester, 1980). Although the effectiveness of emetine therapy is far from ideal, it is high for this type of problem behavior.

Despite the success aversion therapy has had in modifying various behaviors, it is not widely used for at least three reasons (Wilson, 1991). First, there are important ethical concerns in using aversive stimuli in treatment, particularly when research has not yet demonstrated that aversion therapy is clearly superior to other approaches for changing the target behaviors, in this case, drinking. Second, aversion therapy can be more expensive to carry out than other approaches for changing behavior, especially if the treatment must be done in a hospital or under continual supervision of a therapist. Third, some evidence indicates that clients who receive aversion therapy are more likely to drop out of treatment or fail to administer the aversive stimulus, perhaps by not taking the emetine (Wilson, Leaf, & Nathan, 1975; Wilson & Tracey, 1976). (Go to ✔)

SUMMARY

This chapter describes specialized behavioral methods that typically require professional supervision. In the technique of biofeedback, an electrical/mechanical device monitors the status or changes of a person's physiological processes. The device immediately reports that information to the person, enabling him or her to gain voluntary control over those internal processes through operant conditioning. Training in biofeedback can be given for a wide variety of physiological systems, using such measures as blood pressure, heart rate, muscle tension, and skin temperature. This technique has been used with some success in treating epilepsy, hypertension, anxiety, chronic headache, and neuromuscular disorders.

Anxiety-induction therapies are designed to arouse high levels of fear while preventing the client from escaping or avoiding the fearful situations presented. Flooding is a technique in which the target person experiences intense, prolonged exposure to feared situations under the direction of a therapist. The exposure can be *in vivo* or imagined, both of which are highly effective in reducing strong fears and obsessive-compulsive behaviors. Implosive therapy is an imaginal procedure to reduce fears by means of having a client picture exaggerated events that are unlikely to happen in real life. The exaggerated scenes used in this anxiety-induction therapy method do not seem to make the technique more effective than imaginal flooding.

Modeling techniques have been applied in specialized ways and settings to train workers in professional skills, to help people be more assertive, and to help individuals cope well with frightening or uncomfortable medical procedures. In assertion training, clients are helped to become more appropriately and adaptively assertive in their everyday lives by learning to stand up for their rights, refuse unreasonable requests, and so on. This training often involves overt and covert modeling, behavior rehearsal, role playing, and homework assignments. Using videotaped modeling to reduce medical patients' fears of surgical and nonsurgical procedures increases the likelihood that they will cooperate with and not disrupt the procedures and decreases patients' recovery time and length of hospital stay, or both.

Aversion therapy is a specialized technique in which an unpleasant or painful stimulus is applied while the client engages overtly or covertly in an undesirable target behavior. This therapy method was developed as a way of reducing problem behaviors that produce powerful reinforcers. Aversion therapy has shown some success in helping people stop smoking cigarettes or drinking excessively.

KEY TERMS

biofeedback	flooding	behavior rehearsal
anxiety-induction therapies	implosive therapy	aversion therapy
	assertion training	

REVIEW QUESTIONS

1. What is biofeedback, and what can it enable the person to do?
2. Describe four different types of biofeedback.

3. Discuss the usefulness of biofeedback training of alpha brain waves.
4. Describe how a physical therapist might use biofeedback to help a patient gain strength in her legs after being unable to walk for a few months as a result of an injury that damaged (but did not sever) the spinal cord.
5. Define the basic approach used in anxiety-induction therapies.
6. Describe how a therapist might use imaginal flooding to help a man overcome his extreme fear of going outside at night, a phobia he developed after being mugged and assaulted one evening.
7. What is implosive therapy, and how useful is its feature of including exaggerated events in its scenes?
8. Define being assertive, and give one example each of three different types of assertive behavior.
9. What is assertion training, and what techniques does it include?
10. Describe the methods a therapist could use to assess a client's assertiveness.
11. Describe the research by Melamed and Siegel (1975) on reducing anxiety in children who are awaiting surgery.
12. What is aversion therapy, and what is its general objective?
13. Describe the types of unpleasant stimuli that have been used in aversive therapy to help people stop smoking.

RELATED READINGS

Bandura, A. (1969). *Principles of behavior modification*. New York: Holt, Rinehart & Winston.

Barlow, D. H. (1978). Aversive procedures. In W. S. Agras (Ed.), *Behavior modification: Principles and clinical applications* (2nd ed.). Boston: Little, Brown.

Dowrick, P. W. (Ed.). (1991). *Practical guide to using video in the behavioral sciences*. New York: Wiley.

Schwartz, M. S. (Ed.). (1995). *Biofeedback: A practitioner's guide* (2nd ed.). New York: Guilford.

A teenage boy who is feeling depressed. Therapists can use cognitive-behavioral methods to reduce clinical depression—that is, when a person's sadness is severe, frequent, and long-lasting.

Cognitive-Behavioral Therapies

J oseph Cautela (1993b) has described the case of a man who didn't seem to be trying very hard to overcome his intense fear of flying. The man was not picturing very well the scenes he was asked to imagine and hadn't been listening to the tapes the therapist had asked him to use at home. Cautela tried to find out why.

The therapist asked the man if he believed the therapy techniques would work, and the client said he was sure they would because a friend who recommended Cautela had overcome the same fear. So the therapist asked the client what would happen if he didn't have his fear, and the man replied that he would be promoted at work. At first Cautela thought the promotion would be an incentive for overcoming the fear, and said so, but the ensuing conversation indicated otherwise. The client responded to the idea that the promotion should be a motivator by saying,

> "Yeah, I guess so." I [Cautela] said, "What would the promotion mean to your job description?" He replied that he would have to fly more often. I said, "O.K., then we should get on with it." Then I asked what was wrong with flying a lot. He looked surprised and said, "Well, some of my co-workers who got promoted and flew a lot ended up getting heart attacks." I asked him if he was afraid of dying if he got promoted. He said, "Yes, I guess that's it." (p. 157)

Understanding the antecedent beliefs leading to the fear enabled them to continue with the therapy procedures and succeed in overcoming the problem at hand. Ultimately, he was able to fly without being afraid.

This example illustrates how cognitive processes can influence the problem behaviors people develop. The way we perceive and think about events in everyday life has a strong impact on how we behave and what we feel. Because of the role covert cognitive processes can play in initiating and maintaining people's overt behavior, the techniques used in therapy often include cognitive methods to modify people's thought processes. This chapter focuses on cognitive-behavioral therapy approaches for helping people change their overt and covert behavior.

WHAT ARE COGNITIVE-BEHAVIORAL THERAPIES?

The term **cognitive-behavioral therapy** refers to a broad class of therapy approaches to change overt and covert behaviors by applying both cognitive and behavioral methods (Dobson & Block, 1988). We examined the individual cognitive-behavioral techniques of self-statements, thought stopping, and distraction in Chapter 7. These techniques are often used in cognitive-behavioral therapy.

According to Donald Meichenbaum (1986), all cognitive-behavioral therapies share several characteristics. For instance, they provide a good deal of structure to the therapy process and enlist the clients as active participants in that process, by having them do homework assignments, for example. What's more, all cognitive-behavioral therapies apply to some degree procedures that can help clients to

- Understand the nature of the problems they have come into therapy to overcome.
- See their usual patterns of "automatic" thoughts, beliefs, and feelings as events that can be questioned and tested rather than as facts.
- Try out different overt and covert behaviors and then review their outcomes as "evidence" to disconfirm the incorrect expectations and beliefs they previously held.
- Learn new skills and strategies that promote self-regulation of their overt and covert social, cognitive, and emotional behaviors.

The various forms of cognitive-behavioral therapies differ in the extent to which they emphasize each of these characteristics. Sometimes these therapies are called *cognitive-behavior therapies* or simply *cognitive therapies*, and many psychologists use these names interchangeably (Davison & Neale, 1994; Dobson & Block, 1988; Kazdin, 1978). The terms for these forms of therapy have not yet been standardized. In fact, one form of cognitive-behavioral therapy is named "cognitive therapy," as we shall see.

Why Cognitive Processes Can Be Important

Several lines of evidence illustrate the role cognitive processes can play in people's problem behaviors and indicate why therapy approaches may find it helpful to address those processes (Williams et al., 1988). An example comes from the case of the man who was afraid of flying, which opened this chapter. Cautela's client was not participating fully in his therapy because he believed two things: first, that he would have to fly often if he overcame his fear, and second, flying a lot causes heart attacks. He had deduced the second belief incorrectly from his observation that other individuals who had flown a lot got heart attacks (Cautela, 1993b). This case provides clinical evidence that such beliefs have the potential to prevent clients from cooperating in therapy and may need to be addressed. Let's look at other lines of evidence showing a role of cognitive processes in problem behavior.

Thought Processes and Depression   Research has shown that cognition is involved in or related to the development of several clinical disorders, such as depression and anxiety (Stein & Young, 1992). Let's consider *depression*. We all feel "depressed" at times, although we may call the feeling something else, perhaps "sad" or "blue" or "unhappy." Occasional feelings of unhappiness are normal and differ from the disorder we are discussing here. Basically, depression is considered a clinical disorder when the person's feelings of sadness or loss of interest and pleasure become very severe, frequent, and long-lasting (Craighead, Evans, & Robins, 1992; Davison & Neale, 1994).

Overt behavioral symptoms of depression include large changes in eating and sleeping habits and a loss of energy and interest in usual activities. In addition to having a generally unhappy mood, clinically depressed people typically feel *hopeless* and *pessimistic* about the future and have *low self-esteem*, often blaming themselves for the stressful, negative events they experience (Rosenhan & Seligman, 1984). Feelings of hopelessness, pessimism, and low self-esteem involve cognitive processes, such as thinking and believing, that can also lead individuals to thoughts or attempts of suicide. Studies of depressed adults and children have found that feelings of hopelessness are more closely related to whether people consider or attempt suicide than are other characteristics of depression, such as the degree of sadness they feel (Beck, Kovacs, & Weissman, 1975; Kazdin et al., 1983).

Behavior therapy for depression often includes both cognitive and behavioral methods (Craighead, Evans, & Robins, 1992; Freeman, 1990). Depressed people typically have distorted beliefs, such as "Everything I do turns out wrong" or "They all think I'm incompetent, and they're probably right" or "I can't live without a mate." Cognitive methods are designed to alter these thought patterns, for example, by questioning the evidence the person uses to support these beliefs or by showing the person that "the worst thing that could happen" really wouldn't be so terrible (Freeman, 1990). People who are depressed also tend to be inactive and listless, often because they feel they lack necessary social skills. Behavioral methods can help clients acquire the needed skills by showing them how to perform the behavior and giving them feedback as they practice it. The overall treatment for depressed clients usually includes medication as well, particularly if the disorder is so severe that it seriously impairs the therapy process (Freeman, 1990).

Thought Processes and Fear   Cognitive processes can underlie links between expectations and fear. Let's consider two examples. First, people often become excessively fearful of unlikely events, such as being mugged, after mass media reports of a few high-profile cases (Kristof, 1996). Second, researcher Gerry Kent (1985) had dental patients fill out a brief anxiety scale while waiting for their dental appointments. They were then asked to rate the pain they expected to experience when receiving their dental treatment. After their appointments, the patients rated the pain they actually experienced, and rated it again by mail 3 months later. The ratings suggested that anxiety had played a role in the patients' expectations of pain and in their memories of it 3 months later. For the patients with high dental anxiety, the ratings for the pain they expected *and* the pain they remembered months later were four times as high as their ratings of the pain they experienced (the ratings they gave right after the appointments). In contrast, the low-anxiety patients' ratings of expected and remembered pain were less than twice as high as their ratings of the pain they experienced. The results of this study suggest that high-anxiety patients' memories of pain are determined far more by what they expect than by what they actually experience.

Thought Processes and Aggression   In the cognitive process called *attribution*, people try to identify causes or make judgments regarding their own or others' actions, motives, feelings, or intentions. The attributions individuals make can affect their behavior. Kenneth Dodge (1993) has described a large body of evidence showing a link between people's attributional patterns and their physical aggressiveness. For instance, studies have shown that highly aggressive boys appear to be *biased* toward making *hostile attributions*. That is, they are far more likely than are boys who are not very aggressive to interpret an accidental event, such as being bumped in a crowded mall, as having been intentional and motivated by hostility. What's more, the results of several studies indicate that having this bias leads individuals to develop aggressive behavior problems in childhood and commit violent crimes in the future. Individuals with this attributional bias are more likely to perceive a nonaggressive accident as hostile and to respond aggressively.

Memory Processes   One other line of evidence illustrating why it can be useful to consider and address people's cognitive processes in programs to change behavior relates to the organization and function of brain structures. As we saw in Chapter 6, the results of research on memory and physiology support the view that people's memory systems consist of two parts (Petri & Mishkin, 1994; Schacter, 1992; Squire, 1987). When we learn an operant or respondent behavior, we appear to store information about this learning in at least two different memory systems with separate, but linked, physiological structures. One of these systems, called *implicit* or *nondeclarative memory*, stores the basic associations for these learned behaviors. These associations link antecedents and behaviors—connecting, for example, a CS and a CR in a person's fear—but we are unaware of and cannot describe them. Nevertheless, associations stored in implicit, nondeclarative memory seem to trigger our habitual and emotional reactions to antecedents.

In contrast, *explicit* or *declarative memory* contains factual information and details that we are aware of and can describe. If we know what antecedents trigger our behaviors, it's presumably because this knowledge is stored as factual information in explicit, declarative memory. So, for example, this information enables us to know that we are afraid of something and describe how we acquired the fear. Presumably, then, we use our explicit or declarative memory systems in our cognitive processes when we think or have expectations about our fears. The distinction between these two memory systems may have important implications for therapy insofar as it offers an explanation of why some people's fears do not respond to therapy or relapse after successful treatment (LeDoux, 1994). That is, a therapy that failed to eliminate a fear may have addressed the fear representation in only one memory system, leaving the other largely intact.

Historical Roots of Cognitive-Behavioral Therapy

The idea that altering the way people think about events in their lives can change their behavior has a long history that has been documented in ancient Buddhist and Greek writings (de Silva, 1984; Mahoney, 1993). For instance, Buddhist writings describe the case of a woman named Kisa Gotami who suffered intense grief after her infant son had died. She would not allow anyone to take his body from her and carried him around as she roamed the streets asking people if they could suggest a remedy to bring him back to life. One man directed her to consult Siddhartha Gautama, the founder of Buddhism, whose followers often call "the Buddha," who suggested that she bring back to him some white mustard seeds from any house that had not experienced death. She went to a great many houses without success, and then

> began to realize what the Buddha had meant. She realized that death comes to all, that she was not the only one to have lost a child. When she returned to the monastery, the Buddha asked: "Have you got the mustard seed?" "No," she replied, "nor shall I try to find it anymore. In every village and every household, the dead are more than the living. My grief had made me blind. Now I understand." (de Silva, 1984, p. 673)

The approach used in this example enabled this woman to perceive her situation differently and, by doing so, change her behavior.

As we discussed in Chapter 1, the field of behavior therapy developed in the second half of the 20th century. In the first decade or so of its development, behavior therapy treatments focused almost exclusively on applying behavioral methods. By the early 1970s, however, behavior therapy had begun to incorporate a variety of cognitive methods as well (Dobson & Block, 1988; Kazdin, 1978; Mahoney, 1993). The introduction of cognitive methods in behavior therapy came about for at least two reasons. First, many behavior therapists had come to the conclusion that behavioral methods were too limited in their scope and impact. Hence, they were appropriate and effective only for certain kinds or aspects of clients' problems. Second, the focus of psychology as a whole had begun to move toward a cognitive orientation for understanding and explaining human behavior. By the end of the 1980s, the application of cognitive methods had become widespread in behavior therapy and well established in research (Linden & Pasatu, 1998).

Not all experts in behavior modification techniques believe the growth of the cognitive perspective has benefited the field. Some researchers have argued that theories incorporating cognitive factors are stated too vaguely to be of scientific value (Lee, 1992). Other researchers have argued that the role of cognitive processes is limited and has been overstated both in the development and maintenance of behavioral problems, such as phobias and anxieties, and in the treatment of these problems (Latimer & Sweet, 1984; Sweet & Loizeaux, 1991; Wolpe, 1993). Still, a good deal of evidence exists to indicate that some cognitive-behavioral therapies are useful in treating problems of certain kinds, such as clinical depression, some chronic pain disorders, and some forms of anxiety (TFPDPP, 1993). Indeed, the effectiveness of these methods can usually be assessed by measuring overt behaviors, and this is one reason many

CLOSE-UP 14.1

Intellectual Capacity and Cognitive Methods

 For theoretical and intuitive reasons, we might expect that the effectiveness of cognitive methods in changing behavior would depend on the client's intellectual capacity or development, even if we excluded individuals who are developmentally disabled (Braswell & Kendall, 1988; Garfield, 1986). Is this expectation correct?

Researchers have examined this question in two ways. First, researchers conducted a meta-analysis for the results of over 60 prior studies that examined the effectiveness of cognitive-behavioral therapy with children at different levels of cognitive development (Durlak, Fuhrman, & Lampman, 1991). The children's problems varied, but each child showed substantial behavioral or social maladjustment. To examine the role of cognitive development in the success of cognitive-behavioral therapy, the analysis assumed that the children's developmental levels were higher among older children than among younger children. The researchers separated the children into three age groups—about 6 years, 9 years, and 12 years of age—and then compared the groups at the end of therapy for relative degree of improvement. The analysis revealed that the children in each age group showed at least a moderate degree of improvement, but the oldest group improved far more than the two youngest groups, which did not differ. These results suggest that older, more cognitively advanced children are likely to benefit more from cognitive-behavioral therapy than are younger, less cognitively advanced children.

The second way researchers have examined the role of intellectual capacity in the success of cognitive-behavioral therapy entails seeing whether the degree of improvement clients gained from treatment is related to their intelligence. One study used this approach with 106 adult clients who were being treated for depression and anxiety disorders (Haaga et al., 1991). The researchers assessed each client's disorder and intelligence with appropriate and widely used standardized tests at the start of the therapy process. The intelligence of the clients was in the "high average" range. The clients then received an average of about 20 cognitive-behavioral therapy sessions. The final session included a reassessment of the client's disorder to permit the researchers to derive an improvement score by taking the original assessment of the disorder into account. No relationship was found between intelligence and improvement scores for clients with depression or with anxiety disorders.

An overview of these studies suggests that the intellectual skills people generally acquire in childhood play an important role in the likely success of cognitive-behavioral therapy for them, but having greater than normal intellectual skills in adulthood does not enhance the success of cognitive-behavioral treatment.

behavior therapists have accepted cognitive methods in their treatment approaches. (Go to)

COGNITIVE RESTRUCTURING APPROACHES

Some cognitive-behavioral therapies focus on *reducing an excess of covert behaviors*: maladaptive or "dysfunctional" thought patterns. These therapies try to reduce problem thoughts through the process of **cognitive restructuring** in which methods are applied to alter the way clients perceive and think about events in their lives, thereby enabling them to modify their problem behaviors and emotions. As an example, cognitive restructuring methods might be used to help depressed clients think about their life circumstances in more hopeful and less negative ways. Two widely applied types of cognitive-behavioral therapy that stress the use of cognitive restructuring approaches are *rational-emotive therapy* and *cognitive therapy* (Dobson & Block, 1988).

Rational-Emotive Therapy

Albert Ellis (1962, 1977, 1987, 1993) developed the cognitive restructuring approach called **rational-emotive therapy** (RET) in the 1950s from the premise that emotional difficulties often arise from faulty and irrational thinking. These thinking processes lead individuals to have unrealistic misperceptions, interpretations, and attributions about the experiences they have and the people they know. Ellis devised these terms to describe some commonly used irrational ways of thinking:

- *Awfulizing*—for example, "It's *awful* if I get less than an 'A' on a test."
- *Can't-stand-itis*—as in, "I *can't stand* getting turned down when I ask for a date."
- *Musterbating*—for instance, "People I like *must* like me, or I'm worthless."

Suppose a man we'll call Alex has the strong belief that "Candice absolutely, really, really *must* like me," but she doesn't care for him. He is likely to exaggerate the situation with unrealistic ideas, such as "She hates me," "It's *awful* and I can't stand it if she hates me," and "I'm worthless if she hates me." These thoughts exaggerate the person's negative view of the situation and are upsetting. The main purpose of RET is to change such thoughts and beliefs.

The Process of Rational-Emotive Therapy   A bright 8-year-old boy named Robert had become terrified of going to school because he was afraid of not doing well and of having others think he was incompetent. Part of the treatment he received used rational-emotive therapy, which involved discussions to alter his beliefs and the way he perceived events in school. In one session with his therapist, Robert described how terrible he felt when he answered incorrectly on a test. The therapist then had Robert imagine his teacher returning to him a test on which he had made a mistake and then report the thoughts he would have at that moment. Robert's face showed his distress, and he said the teacher thought he was "a dope" and didn't like him anymore. The following dialogue ensued (Oltmanns, Neale, & Davison, 1991, p. 281):

THERAPIST: Hmm, that's heavy stuff, little friend. Is that what you'd really think to yourself?

ROBERT: Well, I think so. I give myself a hard time when I make a mistake, and I'm sure other people think I'm a jerk.

THERAPIST: Do *you* think other people are jerks when they make mistakes?

ROBERT: Well, sometimes I do. I mean, if you're careful about what you do, won't you always be right?

Table 14.1 Illustration of Ellis's A-B-C-D-E paradigm for rational-emotive therapy

A	The *activating* experience, the event Sue describes as having precipitated her upset: Her boss said, "I've warned you time and again about your lateness and sloppy work. I don't want you to work here anymore. You're fired."
B	The *beliefs* and thoughts that go through the person's mind in response to A. These thoughts may be rational, as in "I guess I deserved being fired. I need to be more responsible and careful about my work." But Sue focused on irrational beliefs, thinking "I can't do anything right. I wish I had behaved better; that was a good job. I'm totally worthless and useless. I can't stand myself, and I can't bear facing people and telling them I was fired."
C	The emotional and behavioral *consequences* of feelings of disappointment and a determination to improve in her next job. Sue's consequences were inappropriate. She felt depressed, ashamed, and helpless and has not tried to find a new job in the several months since being fired.
D	*Disputing* irrational beliefs in therapy. It includes discriminating between valid ideas, such as "I wish I had behaved better," and irrational ones, such as "I'm totally worthless." Irrational beliefs are critically and logically examined in RET so that they can be disproven.
E	The therapy's *effect,* which consists of a restructured belief system and philosophy. With this effect, Sue should be able to cope with her world more sensibly in the future.

Source: Sarafino, 1998, Table 5.4.

> THERAPIST: I don't think so. I make lots of mistakes, but I don't think I'm a jerk for doing that. That's part of being a human being. Aren't you one of those? (Pokes Robert playfully in the ribs.)

The dialogue continued to point out that even if Robert's teacher was displeased that he made a mistake that wouldn't make him a "total jerk." After all, he usually performs well in school and behaves nicely with other children. The purpose of this kind of dialogue is to *dispute* irrational beliefs and disprove them (Beal, Kopec, & DiGiuseppe, 1996).

RET is often applied with clients who have severe problems with anxiety, anger, or depression. The procedures used in RET focus on several aspects or stages of the client's thought processes, using Ellis's (1977) A-B-C-D-E paradigm. Table 14.1 illustrates the basic outline of this paradigm by using the case of a woman we'll call Sue, a therapy client who is upset at having been fired from a job. Therapists who use RET vary in the style they use in disputing clients' beliefs. Some try to lead clients gently toward discovering alternative ways of thinking, as Robert's therapist did. Others, like Ellis himself, are much more direct and forceful, arguing with clients and teasing them about their beliefs, such as by describing their ideas as "nutty" and so on (see Ellis & Dryden, 1987, pp. 143–149). Many therapists use a variety of strategies to dispute irrational beliefs (Beal, Kopec, & DiGiuseppe, 1996). An important feature of RET is that it includes homework assignments, such as having the client read materials about irrational beliefs, engage in making positive self-statements, or do relaxation exercises.

How Effective Is Rational-Emotive Therapy? Dozens of studies have been conducted to assess the effectiveness of RET for treating a variety of behavioral and emotional disorders (Engels, Garnefski, & Diekstra, 1993; Gossette & O'Brien, 1993; Haaga & Davison, 1989, 1993; Lyons & Woods, 1991). An overview of this research suggests five conclusions. First, RET appears to be an effective therapy for several disorders, such as anxieties, producing clear improvements over baseline or in comparison to receiving no treatment. Second, RET is not superior to and is often less effective than other treatment approaches, such as systematic desensitization, for treating phobias and anxieties. Third, little evidence exists regarding the durability of improvements RET produces because few studies have done long-term follow-up assessments. Fourth, many studies of RET have been poorly designed or reported, making their results ambiguous. For instance, some studies did not report the number of clients who dropped out of treatment, and other studies did not indicate or define exactly the therapy techniques used. Fifth, research is lacking with regard to the specific aspects or components of RET that are effective. RET often applies a variety of cognitive and behavioral methods, and the style of disputing clients' beliefs can vary greatly. Are certain methods or styles more effective than others?

Cognitive Therapy

Cognitive therapy is a cognitive restructuring approach for treating behavioral and emotional disorders that was developed by Aaron Beck independently of but at about the same time as RET (1967, 1976, 1993; Beck et al., 1990; DeRubeis & Beck, 1988). Like RET, cognitive therapy is based on the view that emotional disorders develop because of faulty and negativistic thought patterns that must be altered in treatment.

A fundamental cognitive therapy concept called a **schema,** refers to a basic cognitive structure or unit of knowledge that serves to organize individuals' experiences and affect their perceptions, interpretations, and attributions of everyday events. Schemata (the plural form of schema) can be thought of as "core beliefs." We all have schemata to organize our knowledge of the world. But in people who develop emotional problems, many core beliefs tend to become negative **automatic thoughts**—erroneous and maladaptive thought patterns that occur habitually and frequently. Clients generally report that these thoughts seem to arise "automatically," like "reflexes." For instance, people with a schema of personal incompetence will tend to expect failure in many situations, particularly ones that resemble situations in which the schema was learned; they won't reflect on or reason about these thoughts. Cognitive therapy attempts to discover what the negative automatic thoughts are, point them out to the client, and change them.

According to Beck, individuals who develop emotional disorders engage in erroneous and maladaptive thought patterns excessively. Their automatic thoughts can contain any of several types of cognitive errors, including:

- *Dichotomous thinking* (thinking in absolute, all-or-none terms). For instance, people are either saints or sinners; objects are either perfect or defective.
- *Overgeneralization* (arriving at a sweeping conclusion or general rule on the basis of a single or small number of events and applying the conclusion in judging other people or events). For example, a mother who discovers her son has stolen

something might decide she is a terrible and useless mother or that her child is evil.

- *Arbitrary inference* (drawing a specific conclusion from insufficient, ambiguous, or contrary evidence). For instance, a worker might interpret his boss's bad mood as meaning the supervisor is unhappy with his performance when she is actually just preoccupied with a personal matter.
- *Magnification* (greatly exaggerating the meaning or impact of an event). For example, a student who receives a "B" on a test and defines the grade as a "catastrophe."

Beck believes people who become clinically depressed develop a *negative triad*—three clusters of schemata that involve erroneous, negative views of the *self*, the *world*, and the *future*.

The Process of Cognitive Therapy   Although cognitive therapy and RET both try to alter the client's incorrect thought patterns, the procedures they use differ in several ways. We will consider two of the clearest ways in which they differ. First, the treatment in cognitive therapy is more of a *collaborative effort* between therapist and client than it is in RET. That is, therapist and client in cognitive therapy actively share in the effort to discover and change automatic thoughts. The therapist tries to build a trusting relationship early in therapy and then guides the client toward discovering and examining the cognitive errors that underlie the person's thought patterns. Although some degree of collaboration occurs in RET, the focus on shared effort is more pronounced in cognitive therapy.

Second, cognitive therapy uses a *hypothesis testing* technique. Once the therapist and client discover an erroneous belief or thought, they treat it as a hypothesis rather than a fact and go about trying to test its validity. They question the belief in terms of (1) the evidence for and against it, (2) alternative explanations for or ways of looking at specific situations or feelings, and (3) the actual implications the belief carries if it were basically true. They also seek hard evidence regarding the belief by making observations in real-life situations. Suppose a male client is attracted to a female classmate in college but believes she dislikes him because she rarely looks at or talks to him. The therapist and client would devise an actual test of this belief—perhaps by having the client keep track of how often she looked at or talked to other male classmates. If she didn't look at or talk to most or all other males in class, they would have evidence that the client's belief is unwarranted.

To see how hypothesis testing might be used, we can look at an example of dialogue from a cognitive therapy session with a 33-year-old depressed client named Sharon who had low self-esteem. She believed she was "fat and ugly" and thought she had mannerisms that were "peculiar and annoying" to others. In the dialogue, the therapist asked:

THERAPIST: . . . what evidence do you have that all this is true? That you are ugly, awkward? Or that it is not true? What data do you have?

SHARON: Comparing myself to people that I consider to be extremely attractive and finding myself lacking.

THERAPIST: So if you look at that beautiful person, you're less?

SHARON: Yeah.

THERAPIST: Or if I look at that *perfect* person, I'm less. Is that what you're saying? . . .

SHARON: Yeah. I always pick out, of course, the most attractive person and probably a person who spends 3 hours a day on grooming and appearance, clothes shopping, and I only compare myself to them. I don't compare myself to the run-of-the-mill—I have begun to try to contradict all this stuff. . . .

THERAPIST: I would like to hear some of that.

SHARON: Well, I have done very well this whole week. I'm a lot less depressed. I have done a couple of really tough dysfunctional thought analyses, which I feel I have made very good progress on, and . . . I find myself contradicting the negative thoughts almost automatically, especially the ones I have written out. I have enjoyed what I have been doing this week. (Freeman, 1990, p. 83)

Cognitive therapy typically entails homework assignments: a client may be asked to list and analyze maladaptive or "dysfunctional" thoughts or to collect data to test a hypothesis (Freeman, 1990; Thase & Wright, 1991). These assignments may also include the solo application of various behavioral methods—having the client do relaxation exercises, for instance.

How Effective Is Cognitive Therapy?   Cognitive therapy was originally developed as a treatment for depression. Research has shown that cognitive therapy is clearly an effective and durable approach for treating this disorder (Craighead, Evans, & Robins, 1992; DeRubeis & Beck, 1988; Dobson, 1989; Hollon, Shelton, & Davis, 1993; Robins & Hayes, 1993; TFPDPP, 1993). For most clients, it is at least as effective in reducing depression and maintaining improved emotional functioning as other forms of psychological therapy and various drug therapies. Studies with follow-up assessments 1 and 2 years after cognitive therapy for depression have reported low rates of relapse. About one third of depressed clients do not improve substantially with cognitive therapy. Some evidence indicates that clients who are least likely to improve in cognitive therapy are those who have very severe initial levels of depression, serious family problems, or additional psychological disorders.

Since the 1970s, cognitive therapy has expanded its scope to treat a wide variety of emotional problems, including anxiety, panic, and eating disorders (Beck, 1993; Beck et al., 1990). Although relatively few studies have been done to evaluate the effectiveness of cognitive therapy in treating these disorders, existing research indicates that it is a very promising approach (Chambless & Gillis, 1993; Wilson & Fairburn, 1993). Still, as with RET, research is lacking with regard to the aspects or components of cognitive therapy that are effective. Cognitive therapy typically applies a variety of cognitive and behavioral methods. Which methods are responsible for the effectiveness of cognitive therapy? (Go to ☑)

CONCEPT CHECK 14.1

1. A characteristic of clinical depression in addition to feeling unhappy is _____ . ⇔
2. The cognitive process by which people try to identify causes of events in their lives is called _____ .
3. Information that explicit, declarative memory might include about a fear we have is _____ . ⇔
4. The effectiveness of cognitive-behavioral therapy with children appears to increase as children become _____ .
5. _____ processes in therapy alter the way clients perceive and think about events in their lives.
6. In RET, "It would be awful if I applied for a job and didn't get it" is an example of an irrational thought pattern called _____ .
7. In cognitive therapy, erroneous and maladaptive thought patterns that arise habitually are called _____ .
8. Having a client collect data in everyday situations to disconfirm a maladaptive belief is an example of the _____ technique.
9. Cognitive therapy is most clearly effective for treating the psychological disorder called _____ .

Answers: 1. feeling hopeless/pessimistic, 2. attribution, 3. when the fear started/how strong the fear is, 4. older or more cognitively advanced, 5. cognitive restructuring, 6. awfulizing, 7. automatic thoughts, 8. hypothesis testing, 9. depression.

COGNITIVE SKILLS TRAINING APPROACHES

We have just seen that cognitive-behavioral therapies in which cognitive restructuring methods are the main techniques applied focus on reducing an excess of maladaptive covert behaviors—thought patterns that maintain the client's emotional problems. Other cognitive-behavioral therapies take a different approach, trying to *correct a deficit of adaptive covert behaviors* by training clients in *cognitive skills* they don't yet possess or use. The purpose in trying to correct cognitive deficits in clients is to enable them to apply these new skills to reduce their overt and covert emotional difficulties. We will discuss two widely applied types of cognitive-behavioral therapy that focus on training clients in adaptive cognitive skills. These approaches are *stress inoculation training* and *problem-solving training* (Dobson & Block, 1988).

Stress Inoculation Training

People encounter many stressful circumstances in their lives, ranging from major serious events, such as the death of a close family member or being fired from a job, to everyday hassles, such as being late for an appointment or misplacing important items. We often can't control whether these circumstances occur, but we can learn cognitive skills to help us cope with or adjust to them. When we cannot cope well with stress, we tend to feel anxious, angry, or depressed. Frequently, people who enter therapy for anxiety, anger, or depressive disorders lack important cognitive skills to help them cope with stress. Donald Meichenbaum developed a therapy procedure called **stress inoculation training** that is designed to teach clients cognitive skills to help them cope with the stressful events they experience (Meichenbaum, 1977; Meichenbaum & Cameron, 1983; Meichenbaum & Deffenbacher, 1988).

The Process of Stress Inoculation Training   The term *inoculate* denotes the use of procedures that can enable individuals to defend themselves from disease. Stress inoculation training is designed to give clients the skills to defend themselves from stressful experiences. This form of therapy teaches coping skills and has clients practice them in training programs that proceed through three phases.

In the first phase, called *conceptualization*, clients learn about the nature of stress and how people react to it. This learning occurs in individual or group sessions through discussions of past stressful experiences. Clients consider such questions as:

- Under what specific circumstances do you experience stress?
- What have you done in the past to reduce your stress, and what do you believe could be done instead?
- What seems to make the problem worse or better?

They also try to identify antecedents for the problem behavior. In this dialogue, a therapist leads a highly anxious client to see the need for determining which situations do and do not make him anxious and encourages him to collect relevant data.

THERAPIST: Any notions about how we might be able to better figure this out?

CLIENT: I suppose I could keep track . . . you know, make some notes or something about when I get really uptight and when I just get upset.

THERAPIST: Keep track? How might you do that?

CLIENT: Well I could get a notebook, and, you know, write down what I was feeling.

THERAPIST: That sounds like a really good idea. You could get a notebook and write down what you were feeling and the situation you were in at the time. (Meichenbaum & Deffenbacher, 1988, p. 75)

You may have recognized that the therapist was getting the client to conduct part of a functional analysis of his anxiety.

In the second phase of stress inoculation training, *skills acquisition and rehearsal*, clients learn specific behavioral and cognitive coping skills, such as relaxation, systematic desensitization, self-statements, and coping statements. Some statements clients might learn to help them cope with stress are:

- "Easy does it. Getting upset won't help."
- "These are some anxiety cues I knew I could experience. They should remind me to use the coping skills I learned."
- "Stay cool and relax. If I need to, I can use my calm scene to help."

Other skills may depend on the individual's problems and personal circumstances. Thus, clients might learn communication skills or study skills or parenting techniques. Clients practice their newly learned skills under the therapist's supervision.

In the third phase, called *application and follow-through*, stress inoculation training helps clients make the transition to using the learned coping skills in the natural environment. To achieve this transition, clients respond to stress-provoking events that are introduced in the therapy setting in a graded sequence, as in a stimulus hierarchy. Various events are used in an effort to promote generalization of the skills to a variety of real-world situations. Clients also receive homework assignments that expose them to increasingly stressful situations in their everyday lives. Follow-up sessions are held periodically during the subsequent year or so as part of an effort to prevent relapse.

How Effective Is Stress Inoculation Training?   The methods used in stress inoculation training are well thought out and include a number of well-established techniques, such as relaxation, systematic desensitization, and modeling. Most studies of the effectiveness of stress inoculation training have been done with clients who had anxiety or stress problems (Meichenbaum & Deffenbacher, 1988). These studies have generally found that stress inoculation training reduces anxiety and stress and is at least as effective as less comprehensive programs, such as those that trained clients only in systematic desensitization or cognitive coping skills. Other studies have applied stress inoculation training successfully in helping abusive parents and police officers control their anger (Nomellini & Katz, 1983; Novaco, 1976, 1977). Although stress inoculation training is a very promising cognitive-behavioral therapy for emotional problems, more evidence is needed to demonstrate its value relative to other treatment approaches.

Problem-Solving Training

Another approach that trains clients in adaptive cognitive skills is designed to help them solve problems. In this context, a *problem* is a life circumstance that requires one or more effective, adaptive responses that the person can make after thinking about and planning what to do. Difficulties arise in daily life if the person does not know what to do or how to do it (D'Zurilla, 1988; D'Zurilla & Goldfried, 1971). Suppose, for instance, you had deadlines to meet for college exams and papers and didn't know how you were going to find the time to do it all. You'd be faced with a problem.

As a rule, individuals who do not know how to solve most of their everyday problems tend to become very anxious, frustrated, or depressed. **Problem-solving training** is a form of cognitive-behavioral therapy in which clients learn a strategy for identifying, discovering, or inventing effective or adaptive ways of addressing problems they face in their everyday lives. This form of therapy can be used to reduce clients' emotional disorders or simply to improve their adaptive social functioning (D'Zurilla, 1988; Nezu, Nezu, & Perri, 1989).

The Process of Problem-Solving Training   There are two widely used therapy approaches for providing problem-solving training, and each approach teaches clients a strategy for solving problems that is divided into a series of stages or steps (D'Zurilla, 1988; Spivack & Shure, 1974, 1982). We will examine the problem-solving training approach developed by Thomas D'Zurilla and Marvin Goldfried (1971; D'Zurilla, 1988). Their approach teaches clients a five-step strategy for solving problems.

In the first step in this problem-solving strategy, *problem orientation*, individuals develop a general mind-set to be alert to or watchful for problems that arise. To deal with problems effectively, we must first know they exist. Training clients in problem orientation begins by encouraging them to notice problems and helping them to realize that problems are both normal and inevitable. Clients are also taught ways to stop themselves from taking the easy way out and doing nothing or from acting impulsively. For instance, they might be taught to use self-statements, such as "OK. Slow down and think." Then they learn to proceed calmly and cautiously in addressing the problems they find.

Problem definition and formulation is the second step in the strategy for solving a problem. This step involves defining the problem in concrete, clear terms rather than in vague, abstract terms. You may have noticed that this process is essentially the same as defining a target behavior in a behavior change program. Clients tend to describe the problems they face in their lives in very general or vague terms, such as "I get upset by my roommate's attitude." By looking more carefully at the roommate's behavior, we might find out that the "attitude" is actually inferred from very specific, concrete behaviors, such as leaving the kitchen a mess and not doing her chores around the shared apartment. It's these behavioral deficits in the roommate that are upsetting.

The third step in solving a problem is the *generation of alternative solutions*. Once the behavior has been clearly defined, the client should make a list of possible solutions by using the process of *brainstorming*, which we considered in Chapter 8. The purpose in brainstorming is to identify as many alternative solutions as possible, even if some are not very good. For instance, in trying to deal with the problem of a roommate who is messy and doesn't do her chores, the client might come up with these alternatives:

- Yell at her louder and more often.
- Ignore the situation to see if she will eventually realize how useful it would be to clean her messes.
- Enlist the pressure of other roommates against her.
- Reinforce her for cleaning up and doing her chores, perhaps using praise or suggesting an activity she likes to do.
- Punish her by dumping the kitchen mess on her bed.

- Hang pictures of pigs around the apartment.
- Find another apartment.

As you can imagine, the list of alternative solutions can be quite long and contain some very creative ideas.

In the fourth step, called *decision making*, the client examines the list of alternatives and eliminates ones that are clearly not acceptable: "Find another apartment" might be unacceptable, for example, if it would require breaking a lease for the current apartment. Then the client would try to assess the short- and long-term consequences of each remaining alternative to the roommate and herself. Using these factors, she would be able to select the alternatives that seem most likely to provide the best solution. During the earlier sessions of therapy, she and the therapist would have made the decisions together; later, the client becomes able to make the decisions more and more on her own.

The last step in problem solving is called *solution implementation and verification*. Once the solution has been in effect for a while, the client tries to evaluate its success. If the problem seems to have been solved—say, if the roommate is no longer messy and does her chores—nothing more needs to be done. If the problem continues to exist, the client can choose other alternative solutions from the existing list or generate additional alternatives. Sometimes it is necessary to go back up to the step of problem definition and formulation to redefine the problem. (Go to)

CASE STUDY **14.1**

Problem-Solving Training for Neglectful Parents

Three mothers who were judged by welfare authorities as "child neglectful" were referred for treatment. The intervention applied problem-solving training and used a multiple-baseline, across-subjects design to assess treatment effects (Dawson et al., 1986). All three mothers were in their 20s, were receiving public assistance, and had no more than a 10th-grade education; one mother was currently married. The mothers had been brought to the attention of authorities for different reasons. One mother had left her 5-year-old asthmatic son with an unwilling caretaker for 3 days. Another mother had to give up her two children, aged 3 and 5, to foster care because of past child abandonment. The third mother, who had four young children, had failed to provide her epileptic son with needed medication and had left the children unattended in potentially dangerous conditions and with unsuitable caretakers, such as a sister who was multiply handicapped.

Part of the problem-solving training involved discussing a variety of vignettes in which a mother is faced with a problem in child care. The vignettes were written based on actual difficulties these parents had experienced in the past. For example:

> You and your mother have an argument on the phone. She tells you that you can just forget about bringing your children over tonight for her to babysit while you go out with your boyfriend (husband). It's 5:00 p.m. You don't have any money to hire a babysitter. The story ends with you and your boyfriend (husband) going out for the evening. (p. 213)

Each mother was asked to define the problem in each vignette, generate possible solutions, describe the pros and cons of each solution, and choose the best one—and her problem-solving performance was rated for quality.

Before the intervention began, about eight 60- to 90-minute baseline sessions were conducted with vignettes. The problem-solving performance ratings revealed poor problem-solving skills in baseline, but the ratings began to improve for each mother as soon as the intervention was introduced, reaching over four times the baseline levels for the last six intervention sessions. Other assessments indicated that the effects of problem-solving training generalized to the home situation and were long-lasting. Ratings by social workers of each mother's parenting performance at home revealed substantial improvements by the end of the intervention. What's more, follow-up evaluations 15 months later showed continued success of the training. Although two mothers had moved and were no longer available for testing on the vignettes, they had regained full custody of their children and had no further reports of neglect. One mother was available for testing and continued to demonstrate high levels of skill in problem solving.

How Effective Is Problem-Solving Training?   The rationale for applying problem-solving training to improve clients' functioning in everyday life situations and reduce their emotional difficulties has a good deal of intuitive appeal. Evidence indicates that depression and anxiety disorders are linked to the inability to solve everyday problems (D'Zurilla, 1988; Nezu, Nezu, & Perri, 1989). In addition, problem-solving strategies appear to be very easy for adults and children to learn and are often mastered in a single session, particularly by adults. For instance, the neglectful mothers in Case Study 14.1 showed improved skills in the very first session of the intervention (Dawson et al., 1986). And an adult client who was being treated for severe anxiety learned a problem-solving strategy in a single 1-hour session (Mayo & Norton, 1980). This client also provides a good example of the link between a lack of problem-solving skills and anxiety: being a mother and a student, problems in child care would arise in her life and make her very anxious about meeting her classes and tests

> because she was unable to identify effective strategies which would alter the problematic situations. For example, if her babysitter called saying she couldn't care for the baby the next day, [the client] would become very anxious and would have difficulty identifying solutions which would allow her to attend class. (p. 288)

Studies have shown that problem-solving training produces beneficial effects for clients with depression and anxiety disorders and for clients with difficulties in their general functioning, such as those doing poorly in school and those who are undecided about career goals (D'Zurilla, 1988). Research shows that the improvements from problem-solving training carry over into clients' natural environments and are durable, at least for adults. Some research with children, however, indicates that the effects of problem-solving training sometimes are variable, do not generalize well, and may not be long-lasting (Nelson & Carson, 1988; Yu et al., 1986). Few studies have compared problem-solving training with other forms of therapy. As a result, the relative effectiveness of this treatment modality is not clear.

COMBINED THERAPY APPROACHES

Therapists often find that clients who enter therapy have problems that have many different dimensions or aspects. As a result, a single technique or type of therapy may not be sufficient in designing a behavior change program for any given person; the most effective approach may draw on many different methods. For example, treatments for social phobia that combine cognitive restructuring and flooding (prolonged exposure) techniques are more effective than either approach alone (Taylor, 1996). We saw in discussing cognitive restructuring and cognitive skills training techniques that therapy programs usually use a variety of behavioral and cognitive methods. Programs that have combined therapy approaches can be seen in these examples:

- A program combining several techniques successfully treated two girls whose anxieties about being separated from their parents were reflected in their refusing to sleep in their own beds (Ollendick, Hagopian, & Huntzinger, 1991). The program consisted of behavioral methods, such as reinforcement and extinction, and "self-control training" with cognitive methods, such as training in relaxation exercises, problem-solving strategies, and using positive self-statements. As Figure 14.1 shows, self-control training by itself was not very effective, but the combined treatment was.

- An intervention that combined stress inoculation and problem-solving training was moderately successful in improving anger control among junior high school delinquents (Feindler, Marriott, & Iwata, 1984).

- A program provided treatment for highly aggressive, antisocial children and their parents by using one or both of two approaches: problem-solving training and parent management training, which consisted of teaching the parents how to use behavioral methods, such as reinforcement, shaping, and time-out (Kazdin, Siegel, & Bass, 1992). Although each form of training improved the children's behavior, combining the two approaches produced even greater improvements and placed a larger proportion of the children in the normal range for aggressive and antisocial behavior.

In an effort to promote the use of multidimensional approaches in therapy, Arnold Lazarus (1981) introduced the concept of **multimodal therapy,** in which the therapist identifies different dimensions or parts of the client's problems and chooses appropriate techniques for each one. A therapist using multimodal therapy would consider several specified dimensions of the client's problems, four of which are: *behavior*, such as excessive eating; *affect*, for instance, severe anxiety or depression; *cognitions*, such as irrational thoughts; and *interpersonal relationships*, for example, hostile behavior. The therapy would then be tailored to the client's specific problems.

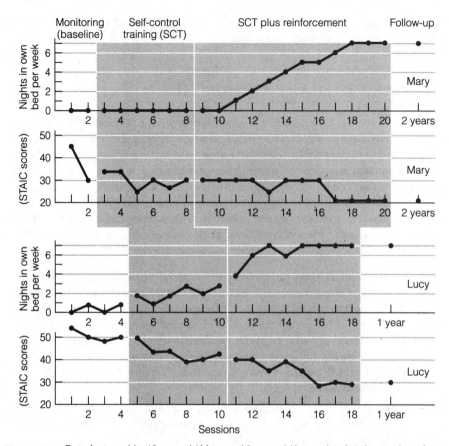

Figure 14.1 Data for two girls, 10-year-old Mary and 8-year-old Lucy, showing the number of nights per week each girl spent in her own bed, rather than with her parents, and the levels of anxiety (the STAIC scores, where high scores reflect high anxiety) each girl reported when thinking about being in her bed alone. Assessments in this multiple-baseline, across-subjects design were made in baseline (monitoring), self-control training (SCT), SCT plus reinforcement, and follow-up phases. *Source:* Ollendick, Hagopian, & Huntzinger, 1991, Figure 1.

Most of us are probably tempted to believe behavior change programs that combine techniques known to be individually effective will produce greater behavioral improvements than each technique applied by itself. Although there are many examples of interventions that support this belief, there are also examples that contradict it. For instance, a number of studies have found that the addition of cognitive methods to behavioral methods in treating emotional problems does not necessarily increase the effectiveness of the therapy (Sweet & Loizeaux, 1991). What's more, one study found that combining methods can worsen treatment: in treating eating disorders, therapists used two methods that had each reduced disordered eating patterns in prior interventions and found that combining the methods was less effective than using one method

CONCEPT CHECK 14.2

1. The first phase in stress inoculation training is called _____ .
2. If stress inoculation training were being used in helping clients control their anger, a coping statement they might be trained to apply in their lives is _____ . ⇔
3. A life circumstance that requires a response that, ideally, follows the application of cognitive skills (thinking and planning) is called a _____ .
4. The first step in the problem-solving methods outlined by D'Zurilla and Goldfried is called _____ .
5. In the case study about the neglectful mothers, an alternative solution they might propose for the vignette about not having a babysitter when they planned to go out might be to _____ . ⇔
6. The treatment approach of Arnold Lazarus in which the therapist identifies different dimensions of a client's problem and chooses methods to address each one is called _____ .

Answers: 1. conceptualization, 2. "Stay cool," 3. problem, 4. problem orientation, 5. take the children with them, 6. multimodal therapy

by itself (Agras et al., 1989). Whether combining particular therapy methods produces more effective treatment than each one singly for a specific disorder is an empirical issue that must be tested in research. (Go to ✔)

SUMMARY

Cognitive-behavioral therapy is a broad class of therapeutic approaches for the modification of overt and covert behaviors through the use of behavioral and cognitive methods. These forms of therapy are based on the view that cognitive processes play an important role in people's behavioral and emotional problems, such as excessive aggression, anxiety, and depression. The idea that modifying people's thoughts and beliefs can help change their behaviors and emotions has a long history. Research has shown that the success of cognitive methods improves with children's age, but having greater than normal intelligence in adulthood does not enhance the success of these methods.

Cognitive restructuring approaches are designed to reduce the client's excess of covert behaviors. One of these approaches, called rational-emotive therapy (RET), uses discussion to dispute irrational thought patterns—for example, patterns that have been termed awfulizing, can't-stand-itis, and musterbating. Cognitive therapy is based on the view that each schema a person develops to organize his or her experiences forms a "core belief." Schemata can give rise to negative automatic thoughts, which are erroneous and maladaptive patterns of thinking that seem to maintain emotional and behavioral problems. There are several types of negative automatic thoughts, including dichotomous thinking, overgeneralization, arbitrary inference, and magnification. Cognitive therapy uses a more collaborative process than RET to change thought patterns and has clients subject their automatic thoughts to hypothesis testing. Studies have found that both RET and cognitive therapy are promising approaches for treating anxiety disorders, and cognitive therapy is clearly effective in reducing depression.

Cognitive skills training approaches attempt to correct clients' deficits in adaptive covert behaviors. Stress inoculation training is designed to teach clients cognitive skills to help them cope with stress. The training has three phases: conceptualization, skills acquisition and rehearsal, and application and follow-through. Problem-solving training attempts to teach clients a strategy for solving everyday problems. One widely used problem-solving strategy involves five steps: problem orientation, problem definition and formulation, generation of alternative solutions, decision making, and solution implementation and verification. Both stress inoculation training and problem-solving training seem to be effective in helping people improve their behavioral and emotional functioning.

More research is needed to demonstrate the effectiveness of cognitive-behavioral therapies, particularly whether they are more effective than other therapy approaches. Many therapy programs combine different therapy approaches, often with improved effectiveness. Multimodal therapy is a cognitive-behavioral therapy approach in which the therapist evaluates the client's problems within specified dimensions and chooses a variety of behavioral and cognitive methods to ensure that each dimension will be addressed.

KEY TERMS

cognitive-behavioral therapy	cognitive therapy	stress inoculation training
cognitive restructuring	schema	problem-solving training
rational-emotive therapy	automatic thoughts	multimodal therapy

REVIEW QUESTIONS

1. What is cognitive-behavioral therapy, and what characteristics do all these approaches share to some degree?
2. Describe two reasons for assuming that cognitive processes can be important in overt and covert behavior.
3. Discuss the role of intellectual capacity and development in the success of cognitive methods.
4. What is cognitive restructuring?

5. Describe two examples each of the irrational thoughts Ellis calls awfulizing, can't-stand-itis, and musterbating.

6. What are schemas and automatic thoughts? Give an example of how a schema forms the basis of automatic thoughts.

7. Describe two examples each of overgeneralization and arbitrary inference.

8. What is hypothesis testing in cognitive therapy?

9. Discuss whether RET and cognitive therapy are effective therapies.

10. How are cognitive skills training approaches different from cognitive restructuring?

11. Describe the three phases of stress inoculation training and give an example of each.

12. Describe the five-step strategy in D'Zurilla and Goldfried's approach to problem-solving training.

13. Describe how problem-solving training was used to improve the parenting skills of the three neglectful mothers discussed in Case Study 14.1.

14. Discuss whether stress inoculation training and problem-solving training are effective therapies.

15. What is multimodal therapy?

RELATED READINGS

Beck, A. T., Freeman, A., & Associates (1990). *Cognitive therapy of personality disorders*. New York: Guilford.

Dobson, K. S. (1988). (Ed.). *Handbook of cognitive-behavioral therapies*. New York: Guilford.

Ellis, A., & Dryden, W. (1987). *The practice of rational-emotive therapy*. New York: Springer.

Meichenbaum, D., & Cameron, R. (1983). Stress inoculation training: Toward a general paradigm for training coping skills. In D. Meichenbaum & M. E. Jaremko (Eds.), *Stress reduction and prevention*. New York: Plenum.

Nezu, A. M., Nezu, C. M., & Perri, M. G. (1989). *Problem-solving therapy for depression: Theory, research, and clinical guidelines*. New York: Wiley.

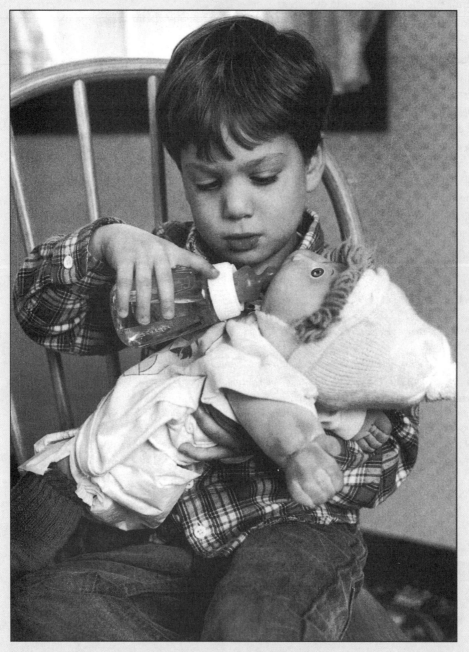

A boy engaging in a behavior that is considered feminine in many cultures of the world. Is reducing or stopping children's nontraditional sex-role behavior an acceptable behavior change goal?

C H A P T E R   F I F T E E N

Current Concerns and Future Challenges

Suppose this book were recorded on a computer compact disk, a CD-ROM, and you could glance through all of the behavior change examples it described. As you reviewed the examples, you might notice that lots of decisions needed to be made to carry out the interventions: What will the target behaviors be? What behavioral goals will the program try to achieve? Which techniques will the program use? For the most part, you'd see these decisions as pretty straightforward and noncontroversial. But this isn't always the case.

Let's consider the case of a patient with schizophrenia named Margaret (Oltmanns, Neale, & Davison, 1991). Schizophrenia is characterized by pervasively disordered thinking, perception, attention, and affect. Some of the many clinical symptoms commonly displayed by patients with schizophrenia are *hallucinations*, such as hearing nonexistent voices, and *delusions*, or beliefs that are contrary to reality. For example, Margaret claimed she heard "two saints" talking about her and that security personnel were monitoring her thoughts. Because of such cognitive and emotional disturbances, patients with schizophrenia typically have very poor social and occupational skills.

Suppose you were a therapist and wanted to improve Margaret's ability to function in society and, perhaps, make it possible for her to hold a job. Obviously, you'd have to stop some of her symptoms, especially the cognitive disturbances. Today there is a way of doing that: have the patient take antipsychotic drugs regularly on a long-term basis, as prescribed by a physician. But some of these drugs can have the serious and often irreversible long-term effect of causing a motor disorder called *tartive dyskinesia*, which is characterized by trembling and lip-smacking. Now we have a dilemma: Would it be acceptable to risk the development of this motor disorder by having Margaret take the antipsychotic drug on a long-term basis to permit some gains to be made in her social and occupational skills?

As we are about to see in this chapter, efforts to change behavior can present dilemmas of many different types to therapists and other professionals. After we have considered some of these dilemmas, we will examine ethical and legal issues in behavior modification therapy and research. Then we will consider some important challenges the discipline faces for the future.

DILEMMAS IN EFFORTS TO CHANGE BEHAVIOR

The dilemmas therapists and other professionals often face in their efforts to change behavior can be classified into two categories: those that pertain to the behavior change goals and those that pertain to the behavior change methods of the intervention.

Are the Behavior Change Goals Acceptable?

Most interventions involve target behaviors and behavioral goals that almost everyone would agree are appropriate and useful. Few people would disagree with the goals of improving children's academic performance, reducing excessively disruptive classroom conduct, decreasing severely aggressive behavior, reducing serious anxiety problems, eliminating self-injurious behavior among children with autism, and increasing behaviors that promote health and fitness. **Goal acceptability** refers to the degree to which the outcome or behavioral goals are fair, appropriate, and reasonable. What factors determine the acceptability of behavior change goals?

Deciding If Behavior Change Goals Are Acceptable   We are likely to think the goals of a behavior change program are acceptable if they meet two broad *goal acceptability criteria:* First, the goals should have a high degree of *social validity*—that is, they should be desired by society and appropriate for the target person's life (Wolf, 1978); second, the goals should involve a *clinically significant* improvement that we can realistically hope to achieve. We can evaluate whether the goals of a behavior change program meet these acceptability criteria by answering several relevant questions:

- Is achieving the goals a likely prospect?
- Will achieving the goals greatly improve the target person's general adaptive functioning, by, for example, enabling him or her to socialize more effectively?
- Will achieving the goals greatly decrease the likelihood of physical or psychological harm to oneself, such as from self-injurious behavior?
- Will achieving the goals greatly reduce the likelihood that the target person will physically or psychologically harm someone else, for instance, a spouse or a child?
- Will achieving the goals greatly decrease reasonable difficulties other people experience with the target person's behavior?
- Will achieving the goals bring the target behavior to a normal level for the target person's age and gender?

Although an affirmative answer to at least one of these questions suggests that the behavior change goals are likely to be acceptable, a "no" answer to the first question severely limits goal acceptability. Keep in mind that these are not the only criteria societies have invoked in deciding whether a program's behavior change goals were acceptable, and sometimes these other criteria have led to strong controversies. (Go to 🎯)

CLOSE-UP 15.1

Trying to Make Gays Straight

Society's criteria for the acceptability of behavior change goals are profoundly affected by current beliefs. This can be seen in the history of efforts to change the sexual orientation of gay males and females (lesbians), based on the belief that being a homosexual is a "wrong," learned "choice" that can be changed.

What Causes Homosexuality?   Two of the most widely believed views on the development of homosexuality propose that people become gay because of the experiences they have. One theory is based on respondent conditioning: homosexual preference is learned through conditioning. This view proposes that a person might acquire such conditioning if a same-sex person (the CS) were paired with the individual's sexual arousal (the US), perhaps through seduction or sexual exploration. The other theory is based on the Freudian psychodynamic view that parent–child relationships determine sexual orientation. For instance, males become gay because their fathers are detached and ineffectual, providing a poor role model, and their mothers are dominating and overprotective. Extensive research on the upbringing and experiences of homosexuals has failed to find much support for either of these theories (Bell, Weinberg, & Hammersmith, 1981; Garnets & Kimmel, 1991; O'Donohue & Plaud, 1994; Storms, 1983).

Rather, this research has revealed three critical findings. First, the parent–child relationships experienced by homosexuals and heterosexuals while growing up are not very different. Second, although siblings share the same parents, who might in fact consist of an ineffectual father and dominating mother, the siblings of a child who turns out to be gay will not necessarily be gay too. Third, gay men and women very often report being able to trace their homosexual feelings to their childhood years, long before they ever had sexual relations or even knew what sex was. What's more, recent but tentative evidence suggests a substantial influence of biological factors, such as genetics, in the development of homosexuality (Angier, 1995; Byne, 1994; LeVay & Hamer, 1994).

The Failure of "Conversion" Therapies   Many different *conversion therapies* have been designed and applied to change clients' sexual preferences from gay to heterosexual (Haldeman, 1994). Some of these therapies follow psychodynamic procedures; others use behavioral methods, mainly involving aversion therapy; and others use fundamentalist Christian programs of "reorientation counseling." In aversion therapy methods, electric shock or other aversive stimuli have been paired with sexually arousing photographs or thoughts (Barlow, 1978). Research on conversion therapies has shown that *none of these therapies is effective in changing sexual orientation,* even among individuals who want very much to change (Haldeman, 1994). Perhaps this should not be surprising. After all, would you expect conversion therapy to be effective in changing people's sexual preferences from *heterosexual* to *homosexual?*

In clinical practice, Gerald Davison is a prominent psychologist who pioneered the use of behavioral methods to try to change sexual orientation. In 1976, 3 years after the American Psychiatric Association had declared that homosexuality would no longer be considered an illness, he wrote an article questioning the effectiveness of conversion therapy and detailing ethical objections to applying those therapies. Other professional organizations—including the American Medical Association, American Psychological Association, and National Association of Social Workers—have arrived at similar conclusions and recommend against the use of conversion therapies. These forms of therapy clearly do not meet the goal acceptability criteria outlined earlier in this chapter.

Examples of Dilemmas in Behavior Change Goals   Occasionally, social and moral questions regarding the behavior change goals in therapy make the choice of goals controversial. We will look at three very different examples in which choosing the goals of therapy might present dilemmas for many people. We will begin each example by expressing the dilemma with a question.

The first dilemma is: Should therapy programs pursue the goal of making children's sex-role behaviors adhere strictly to traditional concepts of masculinity or femininity? George Rekers and O. Ivar Lovaas (1974) designed a program of behavioral methods to be applied by the parents of a 5-year-old boy named Kraig, whose behaviors were highly effeminate. Kraig liked to cross-dress, use cosmetics, walk and talk in a feminine manner, and take the role of the mother when playing house with a neighbor girl; he engaged in virtually no masculine, rough-and-tumble behaviors. Kraig's parents were concerned because he was becoming more and more socially isolated and ridiculed, and they were afraid his behavior would lead to sexually deviant behavior in adulthood.

The therapists trained his parents to provide social and token reinforcers for masculine behaviors and to ignore all feminine behaviors, which the parents had inadvertently reinforced in the past. The program succeeded in stopping his feminine behaviors and increasing his masculine behaviors, and these changes were maintained at a follow-up assessment 3 years later.

Other psychologists have criticized the goals of the program of Rekers and Lovaas, however, saying that by promoting overly strict adherence to social stereotypes one may in fact impair psychological health (Nordyke et al., 1977; Winkler, 1977). In this case, for instance, Kraig stopped playing with dolls entirely and no longer chose girls as playmates. Promoting highly traditional sex-role behavior to the exclusion of other gender behaviors is a value-laden course of action that many people today would argue benefits neither the client nor society.

The second dilemma is: Should a therapy program pursue the goal of helping obese individuals achieve normal weight levels by dieting? Considerable evidence indicates that being obese—that is, being more than 20% overweight for one's gender, height, and frame size—puts individuals at high risk of developing and dying from heart disease, hypertension, and diabetes (Sarafino, 1998). This evidence has provided the basis for the development of weight control programs in many nations to promote health. But researchers Kelly Brownell and Judith Rodin (1994) have described a controversy about the value of dieting that developed around 1990 when an antidieting movement formed. This movement claims that (1) diets almost always fail, (2) genetic factors make permanent weight reduction impossible for many people, and (3) obese people who do manage to lose weight and keep it off do not necessarily live longer.

Although the foregoing claims are extreme, they are not entirely wrong. For instance, most people who lose weight do not succeed in keeping it off for more than a year. But many succeed, and behavioral methods are more effective than other treatments in helping people lose weight and keep it off. Is it worth pursuing in therapy the goal of losing weight if many people fail? Would the goal be worth pursuing if people who kept the weight off didn't live very much longer than they otherwise would have?

The third dilemma is: Should a therapy program pursue the goal of decreasing children's extremely oppositional and aggressive behavior if doing so requires getting them to play alone much of the time? Robert Wahler and James Fox (1980) applied behavioral methods with four 5- to 8-year-old boys to reduce their problem behaviors, which included failing to comply with requests, teasing other people, temper tantrums, destroying property, fighting, and hitting their parents. After the baseline phase, each child experienced more than one type of intervention in separate phases lasting a few weeks each. In the *solitary play* intervention, being reinforced required that the child play alone, quietly, and without interacting with others in any way. In the *cooperative play* intervention, being reinforced required that the child play with family members in a cooperative manner, with no rule violations. During the phases in which the different interventions were applied, the children's social behaviors were observed at home in 30-minute sessions with no encouragement given for play behavior. The observational data were collected to assess whether the effects of the interventions carried over into the children's general social behavior.

The data revealed that the children's oppositional behavior decreased during solitary play phases, but not during cooperative play phases. In addition, all other social interactions decreased during solitary play phases too. The researchers concluded that treatment approaches emphasizing solitary behaviors may be more effective in reducing oppositional behavior than approaches stressing appropriate social interaction. They also pointed out that critics might feel that encouraging oppositional children simply to become less sociable would not be an acceptable way of correcting the behavior problem.

Dilemmas are often hard to resolve. When we arrive at a resolution, we do so on the basis of our value systems. For example, you may believe making a child less sociable is too high a "price to pay" for being able to decrease oppositional behavior as effectively as possible. If so, your value system differs from that of Wahler and Fox (1980), who argued that encouraging social interaction at high rates is "questionable in value to the developing child" (p. 38).

Are the Behavior Change Treatments Acceptable?

Another issue of importance in therapy is popular acceptability of the behavior change treatments. **Treatment acceptability** refers to the extent to which the client and the community consider the methods of a behavior change program to be *fair, appropriate,* and *reasonable* for the circumstances (Kazdin, French, & Sherick, 1981; Wolf, 1978). Treatment acceptability is part of the assessment of social validity in which the goals, procedures, and outcomes of interventions are evaluated. Evaluating treatment acceptability is important for two principal reasons: to protect clients' rights and to make the intervention agreeable to clients so they will participate fully in the treatment (Singh, Lloyd, & Kendall, 1990; Wacker et al., 1990).

Treatments Involving Aversive Stimuli   Probably the greatest concerns regarding treatment acceptability relate to methods that apply physically aversive stimuli, either as punishers or as USs in aversion therapy. As we have seen in earlier chapters, there are compelling reasons to avoid procedures that use physically aversive stimuli and reserve them for cases in which all other methods derived from careful functional analyses have failed to change the behavior. When aversive stimuli are used as punishers, the degree of their severity or restrictiveness should be as mild as possible while still allowing the intervention to succeed in reducing the unwanted behavior. Two useful procedures can be used to protect clients from harm and safeguard their rights (Green, 1990). First, the therapist should identify an appropriate professional committee that can review the plan to use aversive methods and seek their approval. Second, the therapist should describe the aversive methods to the client or guardian fully and seek their consent to use those methods.

Careful scrutiny regarding the use of aversive stimuli has been applied to programs for improving the behaviors and skills of children, particularly those who are developmentally disabled (Singh, Lloyd, & Kendall, 1990). In some cases, advocacy groups and professional organizations have issued policy statements to guide or restrict the use of punishment techniques of certain types. Unfortunately, the recommendations these organizations have developed are often contradictory. For instance, the Association for Persons with Severe Handicaps opposes all uses of painful stimuli with handicapped individuals, but the American Psychological Association Division on Mental Retardation and Developmental Disabilities takes the position that painful stimuli may be used under very restricted circumstances. An example of such circumstances is when the target behavior is harmful to the client or others and has not been reduced by other methods. When contradictory recommendations exist, which ones should therapists follow? In practice, therapists most probably follow the recommendations of the organization with the closest match to their own value systems or beliefs.

Dilemmas often arise when therapists recognize that alternative treatments have failed to decrease a potentially harmful behavior and physically aversive punishment may be the only alternative to doing nothing. In such instances, it is helpful to consider whether the ends justify the means. Israel Goldiamond (1974) has described a very thought-provoking case. A little girl in an institution was being made to wear a padded football helmet and had her hands tied to her crib to protect her from self-injurious head-banging behavior. In her efforts to take off the helmet, she would toss her head violently and pull her hair out whenever she got the chance. Her head was constantly bruised and bald. Eventually the child was placed in a different program in which punishment was introduced for her self-injurious behaviors. The punishment consisted of the therapist shouting "Don't!" and administering a sharp slap on the cheek. After fewer than a dozen instances of this punishment method, the self-injurious behavior stopped, the helmet was removed, her hair began to grow back, and her social behaviors began to improve. When the original institution and the girl's parents learned of the slapping, however, they removed her from the new program and returned her to the institution, where her behavior regressed and she was again restrained in her crib and required to wear a helmet. We can now ask ourselves two questions: Was using physical punishment acceptable in this case? Was it acceptable to return her to the original treatment conditions?

Sometimes schools and psychiatric institutions place restrictions on the use of aversive procedures that are not painful but are *intrusive,* or forced on individuals without their permission. For instance, some schools have taken the position that intrusive punishers may only be used with the most severe forms of behavior. There are three problems with this position. First, there is no standard criterion for knowing which methods will be viewed as intrusive. Second, the position may be interpreted so restrictively that no punishers of any kind would be permitted. Third, the effect of limiting the application of punishers only to extreme behaviors may be to diminish drastically the effectiveness of otherwise useful punishers. (Go to)

CASE STUDY 15.1

A Dilemma in Using Intrusive Punishment Only for Extreme Behaviors

Cory, an 11-year-old boy with mental retardation, was a student in a school that would permit the use of intrusive punishment only when he performed an extreme act of aggression or property destruction, which he did often (case described in Grace, Kahng, & Fisher, 1994). To test the effects of following the school's restriction, researchers applied a nonpainful punishment technique, which the school defined as "intrusive." The punishment consisted of crossing Cory's arms across his chest, guiding him to a seated position on the floor, and holding him there for 3 minutes.

During some phases of the intervention, the therapist applied this punishment technique only after Cory performed very severe aggressive or destructive acts, such as forcefully striking another person or throwing furniture. In other phases, the therapist used the technique after very severe acts *and* moderately severe acts, such as shoving someone or pushing objects off a table. Cory's aggressive and destructive behaviors in these different phases were compared. Punishing *both* the very severe and moderately severe acts resulted in an almost total elimination of Cory's aggressive and destructive behaviors. Punishing only the very severe acts was much less successful in decreasing his aggressive and destructive behaviors. These findings present a dilemma: should the school change its policy about the use of punishment?

Assessing Treatment Acceptability   The procedure used in assessing treatment acceptability involves having individuals fill out rating scales to evaluate the methods applied in interventions (Elliott, 1988). Several rating instruments have been developed for this purpose and are becoming more and more widely used. The instruments can be filled out by clients, relatives or friends of clients, teachers or coworkers of clients, hospital staff, or members of the general community (Schwartz & Baer, 1991). Because the assessments can serve various purposes, the intended purpose determines whose judgments would be sought. Thus, we would have clients rate the treatment methods if we wanted to know whether they would participate fully in their own therapy, and we would have teachers or hospital staff rate the treatment methods if we wanted to know how motivated they would be to learn the techniques and administer them carefully.

✓

CONCEPT CHECK 15.1

1. When behavior change goals involve clinically significant improvement and have a high degree of social validity, they meet the two main _____ criteria.
2. A finding that disconfirms the psychodynamic view of the causes of homosexuality is that the parent–child relationships homosexuals and heterosexuals have when growing up are _____ .
3. All types of _____ therapies to change clients' sexual preferences appear to be ineffective.
4. A claim that the antidieting movement makes to argue against dieting is that _____ . ⇔
5. The extent to which the client and the community consider the methods of a behavior change program to be fair, appropriate, and reasonable is called _____ .
6. One way therapists can take action to protect clients from harm and safeguard their rights is to _____ .
7. An example of a potentially intrusive punisher is _____ . ⇔

Answers: 1. acceptability, 2. not very different, 3. conversion, 4. diets almost always fail, 5. treatment acceptability, 6. obtain the client's consent, 7. time-out

The idea of assessing treatment acceptability may seem simple on the surface, but the factors affecting the ratings are actually very complex. The ratings people give depend on the exact wording used in describing the treatments, and the ratings tend to be higher if a rationale for the method is given and the rater has a good understanding of the treatment procedures (Elliott, 1988). Ratings of treatment acceptability also tend to be higher when the client's behavior problem is very severe, there are few undesirable side effects from the treatment, the methods involve reinforcement rather than punishment, and the cost in time and effort is low (Jones et al., 1998; O'Brien & Karsh, 1990; Wacker et al., 1990). Acceptability ratings also tend to be higher if the therapist has obtained the consent of the client or guardian and approval from an appropriate committee (see later) to use the techniques. (Go to ✓)

ETHICAL AND LEGAL ISSUES IN THERAPY AND RESEARCH

Many different ethical concerns and issues can emerge when psychology professionals conduct therapy, diagnostic assessments, and research, and improper actions regarding some ethical issues can make the professional subject to legal action. Professionals engaged in therapy, assessments, and research try to carry out these activities at a high level of competence, and they take measures to protect the rights and safety of the individuals involved. An important mechanism that is available to protect individuals is the *institutional review board* (IRB, or other review committee). In the United States, the Department of Health and Human Services introduced the requirement that all institutions receiving direct or indirect funding from the government establish an IRB for the evaluation of proposals for conducting research to assure that individuals will be protected from harm. These committees consist of at least five people who are not connected to the therapy or research in question and who can represent the views of significant and relevant elements of society, such as the general community, child welfare groups, and the fields of medicine and law. What's more, major professional organizations have developed guidelines as standards of general professional conduct and as rules to guide the process of conducting therapy and research. We will examine some guidelines that currently exist for professionals who study or apply principles of behavior change.

General Principles for Psychologists

The American Psychological Association (APA, 1992) has developed a detailed set of ethical principles and codes of conduct to guide the behavior of psychologists in nearly all facets of their work. For instance, there are specific standards for explaining to the client the results of diagnostic assessments and for maintaining confidentiality. These guidelines begin with this set of six general principles:

- *Competence*. Psychologists should carry out their work competently, recognizing the limits of their abilities and providing only those services they are sufficiently trained to do.
- *Integrity*. Psychologists should strive to be honest and fair toward others and in presenting descriptions of their qualifications and activities.
- *Professional and Scientific Responsibility*. Psychologists should consult with colleagues and other professionals to prevent unethical conduct and to serve the interests of their clients, students, or others who receive their services.
- *Respect for People's Rights and Dignity*. Psychologists should respect people's rights to privacy, confidentiality, and autonomy and be aware of cultural and individual differences, particularly those related to "age, gender, race, ethnicity, national origin, religion, sexual orientation, disability, language, and socioeconomic status."
- *Concern for Others' Welfare*. Psychologists should promote the welfare of their clients, students, or others who receive or are affected by their services by trying to prevent them from harm or exploitation.
- *Social Responsibility*. Psychologists should exercise professional responsibility to the larger community and society by trying to reduce human suffering, prevent the misuse of their work, and promote enactment of laws and social policies that benefit their clients and the public.

More specific guidelines have been established to guide the way in which professionals conduct therapy and research.

Ethical Safeguards in Therapy

Various groups and organizations have issued specific guidelines to protect clients from harm in therapy processes. We will examine the guidelines for therapy developed by the Association for the Advancement of Behavior Therapy (AABT) and the APA.

The AABT published in a 1977 issue of their journal *Behavior Therapy* an extensive set of questions that therapists and other individuals can consider in evaluating the ethical standards of an intervention. Table 15.1 paraphrases these questions and gives an introductory explanation by the committee that developed them. Keep in mind that the questions were designed to apply broadly to professionals who provide all types of human services, not just those who conduct behavior therapy. As you examine these questions, you may notice that some touch on topics we have considered at various points in this book. Other questions cover issues we've not mentioned before but are also important, such as the possibility of coercion to participate in therapy. If a therapist is planning or conducting an intervention, he or she should try to answer each question in the list. Answering "no" to any of these questions suggests that the program contains one or more features that may be ethically questionable. If ethical problems exist, revisions generally are in order.

In the 1970s, the APA commissioned a committee to develop detailed guidelines that would be specific to the practice of behavior modification in therapy and several other settings, such as schools and prisons (Stolz & Associates, 1978). Some of the issues this committee addressed were:

> How and by whom are problems to be defined and goals set? Does the psychologist serve established power structures in modifying an individual's behavior, or is the psychologist obligated primarily (or exclusively) to the interests of the person whose behavior is being changed? Can the psychologist ethically serve both the power structure and the target individual? (pp. 1–2)

Although the recommendations this committee made were designed specifically with the practice of behavior modification in mind, they actually apply to psychologists using intervention methods of all types. The following list presents these recommendations, separated into eight issues and updated from more recent APA guidelines.

1. *Identification of the client.* From the psychologist's point of view, the term *client* can have two meanings: (a) the person whose behavior is the target for change and (b) the psychologist's employer, such as the institution or community that pays the psychologist's salary or fee. In many therapy settings with adult clients, these two roles are filled by one person. When different individuals or entities fill these roles, the rights of the person whose behavior is to change must be protected from potential abuses that may be perpetrated, perhaps unwittingly, by the individual who controls the purse strings. (In this book, the term *client* has been reserved for the person whose behavior is to change, unless specifically clarified otherwise.)

2. *Definition of the problem and selection of the goals.* When considering changing a person's behavior, the psychologist must determine whether a problem exists, what it is, and what the behavioral goals should be. Various people may have

Table 15.1 Questions for evaluating interventions

The eight questions listed here were developed by a committee of the AABT for professionals to consider when evaluating therapeutic interventions in all types of human service. In this table, the term *client* refers to the individual whose behavior is to be changed, but a guardian may be substituted if the client cannot understand the issues to be considered; *therapist* refers to the professional in charge of providing the treatment. Ideal interventions generally allow clients maximum involvement in planning and carrying out the treatment while taking into account societal pressures on the clients, the therapists, and the therapists' employers. Although ideal interventions would receive "yes" answers for all eight questions, exceptions to this rule are possible while still maintaining high ethical standards. As you examine these questions, assume that the evaluation is being conducted after the intervention has already begun.

1. *Have the client and therapist considered the goals of treatment adequately?* An answer of yes is based on whether (a) the goals were made explicit to the client, preferably in writing, (b) the therapist had the client restate the goals orally or in writing, (c) the therapist and client agreed on the goals, (d) the immediate interests of or benefits for the client are consistent with his or her long-term interests, and (e) the interests of the client are compatible with those of other relevant individuals.

2. *Has the therapist examined the choice of treatment methods adequately?* A yes answer is based on whether (a) the published literature indicates that the methods in the intervention are the best ones for treating the client's problem, (b) the methods used are consistent with the accepted therapeutic practice, (c) the client was informed of alternative methods and their relative advantages and disadvantages, and (d) for treatment methods that are professionally, legally, or societally controversial, the therapist obtained approval through an ethical review by independent professionals.

3. *Is the client participating in treatment voluntarily?* Answering yes involves considering whether the client (a) is being coerced to participate, (b) was offered a choice of methods and therapists if the treatment was legally mandated, and (c) can withdraw from therapy without penalties beyond the loss of costs incurred for the treatment received.

4. *If some person or agency is legally empowered to arrange for treatment, have the interests of the client been considered adequately?* An answer of yes is based on whether (a) the client, although subordinated legally, was told of the treatment objectives and has had some input in the choices of treatment methods, (b) the empowered person or agency has discussed the goals and methods with the therapist and approved them, and (c) efforts were undertaken to make the interests of the client and those of the empowered person or agency compatible when their interests were in conflict.

5. *Does the intervention include procedures to assess treatment effectiveness?* A yes answer is based on whether (a) the intervention includes methods to assess the client's problem quantitatively and chart its progress and (b) the client has access to these assessments during treatment.

6. *Is the confidentiality of the therapeutic relationship adequately protected?* An answer of yes is based on whether (a) the client's records are accessible only to authorized individuals and (b) the client knows who has access to those records.

7. *Has the therapist referred the client to other professionals when necessary?* A yes answer is based on whether the client (a) was informed that he or she would receive a referral to another therapist if dissatisfied with the treatment and (b) received an appropriate referral if the treatment was unsuccessful.

8. *Is the therapist qualified to perform the treatment?* Answering yes depends on whether (a) the therapist has had appropriate training or experience in treating problems like those of the client, (b) the client was informed of any deficits in the therapist's qualifications, (c) an unqualified professional referred the client to or obtained careful supervision from a therapist who is qualified, and (d) the client was informed that a professional providing treatment was doing so under the supervision of a qualified therapist if such a circumstance existed.

Source: Based on AABT, 1977.

input into these decisions, and they may reach conflicting conclusions, as we saw in the dilemmas posed earlier. Although the recommendations do not specify how to resolve such disagreements, they suggest that having all parties describe their values openly would help. As an addendum to these recommendations, the 1992 APA guidelines suggest that IRBs or other ethical review committees might be contacted to help resolve disagreements.

3. *Selection of the intervention method.* Psychologists should choose the most effective methods that offer the least possible restriction, intrusiveness, and unpleasant side effects (or none). For instance, whenever possible, positive reinforcement approaches should be chosen in preference to punishment or other methods that use aversive stimuli. If neither reinforcement nor mild punishment changes the behavior, it may be necessary to apply stronger forms of punishment.

4. *Accountability.* Psychologists have the responsibility to produce satisfactory therapy outcomes and to document the intervention's success. Being accountable requires that reliable data on the behavior be collected and available for the client to examine.

5. *Evaluation of the quality of the psychologist and the intervention.* Performing any type of psychological therapy requires that the professional who is supervising the intervention have appropriate training and certification in clinical or counseling psychology. But procedures specifically for assessing skills in applying behavior modification techniques are lacking. Although a professional organization called the Association for Behavior Analysis has developed some guidelines to assess these skills, there are currently no generally accepted or used standards or processes for accrediting behavior modification skills.

6. *Record keeping and confidentiality.* All interventions should include procedures for keeping accurate and up-to-date records. Although clients and their guardians must have access to those records, psychologists should exercise great discretion in disclosing information about clients to anyone else. The 1992 APA guidelines also recommend that psychologists discuss the issue of confidentiality with clients and indicate its limits.

7. *Protection of the client's rights.* Three mechanisms should be used to protect the rights of clients. First, whenever possible, an IRB or other ethical review committee should oversee and evaluate the ethics of an intervention. Second, the social validity of the treatment methods should be assessed during and at the end of therapy. Third, psychologists who provide therapy are expected to obtain from clients or guardians **informed consent**—that is, approval to carry out the planned procedures based on knowing what they will be and the positive and negative effects the procedures may have. The 1992 APA guidelines clarify the process of informed consent by indicating that the individuals giving consent should (a) have the cognitive capacities to do so, (b) have received relevant information concerning the techniques to be used, and (c) be permitted to decline freely and without undue influence. When clients are legally incapable of giving informed

consent, therapists should still try to explain the procedures to them in simple terms, request their consent, and consider their preferences as well as possible. When the client is a child, the parent or guardian must give informed consent.

8. *Assessment of the place of research in therapeutic settings.* Conducting therapy and doing research are complementary processes that often occur simultaneously. But the goals and methods of research should not take precedence over the progress of therapy or the rights of clients. So, for example, a research design used during therapy should not include a reversal phase if withdrawing treatment would restrict the client's progress.

Ethical Safeguards in Research

The APA has also developed guidelines to safeguard individuals' rights and protect from harm those who serve as participants in research (APA, 1982, 1992). These guidelines parallel and are similar to those used in therapy. The ethical safeguards in research include these eight principles:

1. All individuals, regardless of their ages or other characteristics, have rights that supersede those of the researcher.

2. The researcher should (a) inform the participant of all features of the research that may affect his or her willingness to participate and (b) answer the individual's questions in terms that are appropriate to his or her abilities to comprehend.

3. *Informed consent* should be obtained from the participant, if possible. If the individual is a child, informed consent should be obtained, preferably in writing, from his or her parents or individuals who can reasonably act *in loco parentis* (teachers or directors of institutions, for example). Individuals giving consent should be informed of all features of the research that may affect their willingness to consent.

4. The researcher should respect the individual's freedom to choose *not* to participate in the research or to discontinue participation at any time without undue coercion to reconsider such decisions.

5. The researcher should not use any procedure that may harm the participant physically or psychologically. When harm seems possible, the researcher must consult an IRB for guidance and approval. This often means that the research will need to be postponed and redesigned or abandoned.

6. Concealing important information from participants or deceiving them should be avoided whenever possible. If such procedures are contemplated, the researcher must consult an IRB, demonstrate that alternative procedures are not feasible, and show that the research outcome will have considerable scientific or applied value. If the use of concealment or deception is allowed, the researcher must *debrief* the participants to correct misconceptions, preferably as soon as their participation has been completed. Debriefing entails describing the purpose of the research and explaining the need for deception (which may then be self-evident).

7. The researcher should keep confidential all information obtained about participants unless the participants had agreed in advance to the open use of the
   information.
8. When research procedures result in unforeseen undesirable circumstances for the
   participant, the researcher should take immediate action to correct the circumstances, including any long-term effects they may have on the individual.

FUTURE CHALLENGES FOR BEHAVIOR MODIFICATION

We've covered a lot of ground in our examination of principles of behavior change,
and we've seen that these principles have great potential for benefiting individuals and
societies. You now have a clear picture of what these principles are and how to apply
them successfully. We've seen that the techniques of behavior modification are highly
effective and produce obvious improvements in behavior fairly quickly, sometimes in
just a few sessions. We've also seen that these techniques can be applied in a wide
variety of settings to change almost any problem behavior. These techniques are generally at least as effective as other approaches in changing behavior. It should be clear
that behavior modification methods possess many very significant strengths, but there
are some limitations too (Goldfried & Castonguay, 1993). In the remainder of this
chapter, we will look at a few challenges the discipline faces for the future.

Improving the Effectiveness of Behavior Modification

Despite the clear success of behavioral and cognitive methods in changing behavior,
some important challenges remain for the future. One way to improve the success of
behavior modification techniques is to enhance the care with which interventions are
designed and implemented. For instance, many professionals who design behavior
change programs use "intuitive" processes in choosing treatment methods rather than
doing thorough functional analyses (Lennox et al., 1988). In addition, staff members
who administer interventions may become lax in applying the techniques if they are not
carefully and periodically trained and monitored in their efforts (Harchik et al., 1992).

Not only are behavior modification techniques useful in correcting behavioral
problems that already exist, but they have also shown some promise in the *prevention* of
human suffering and problem behaviors. For example, interventions have been conducted with some degree of success in preventing teenagers from developing unhealthful addictive behaviors, such as smoking cigarettes or using drugs (Botvin et al., 1990;
Flay et al., 1989; Murray et al., 1989). Some behavioral and cognitive methods were
designed specifically to prevent future behavior problems by training individuals in
skills to help them function better in everyday life. Self-management methods, in
general, as well as the approaches of stress inoculation training and problem-solving
training also qualify as preventive methods. Although some tentative evidence suggests

that behavior modification programs may be useful in efforts to prevent medical and psychological problems, much more research is needed to demonstrate these effects convincingly.

We have seen that *relapse* is an important problem in the success of programs to change behavior. In many cases, behavior modification interventions are successful in changing problem behaviors while the programs are in effect, but the behaviors sometimes regress after the programs have ended. Although some progress has been made in developing methods to reduce the likelihood of relapse, the problem of relapse remains a critical challenge for the future.

Another challenge for the future of behavior modification will be to justify its application in relation to its financial costs (Baer, Wolf, & Risley, 1987; Yates, 1994). Research needs to be conducted to demonstrate a favorable *cost–benefit ratio*—that is, the extent to which providing the intervention saves more money in the long run than it costs (Jospe, Shueman, & Troy, 1991; Kaplan, 1989). These "bottom line" issues often are used in deciding whether to apply certain procedures or whether insurance will pay for an intervention. Many behavior modification interventions have the potential to produce far more financial benefits than costs. For instance, we considered research findings earlier in this book that hospital patients who receive help in coping with medical procedures recover more quickly and use less medication than those who don't receive such help. However, most therapeutic techniques that we know are effective have not yet been subjected to cost–benefit analyses (Yates, 1994). A promising approach involves using the mass media: an intervention that provided training in behavior modification techniques, such as progressive muscle relaxation, on television and radio greatly reduced the headaches and medication usage of people with chronic headaches (de Bruijn-Kofman et al., 1997). This approach is likely to be cost-effective, reaching large numbers of people at low cost.

Integrating Therapy Approaches

Because of the central role of research and data in behavior modification, many professionals who use behavioral and cognitive methods have been willing to consider using new techniques that research has shown are effective in changing behavior. In the first decade or so of the discipline, behavior modification research and therapy tended to apply a single technique, such as reinforcement, by itself. Then the discipline began to combine different behavioral methods, and soon behavioral and cognitive methods were used in the same interventions (Linden & Pasatu, 1998; Wilson, Hayes, & Gifford, 1997).

By the 1970s, therapists had become increasingly eclectic in their orientations (Swan & MacDonald, 1978). These changes marked the beginning of a movement to integrate therapy approaches from widely different theoretical bases, such as medicine and psychoanalysis (Wilson, 1990). A chief argument that has led to an integration of therapy approaches is that research has found support for the effectiveness of many different methods of therapy (Beitman, Goldfried, & Norcross, 1989; Smith & Glass, 1977). A common form of integration with behavior therapy is the use of medication, for example, in treating anxiety disorders, depression, and hyperactivity (Emmelkamp, Bouman, & Scholing, 1992; Roth et al., 1982; Satterfield, Satterfield, & Cantwell, 1981; Simons et al., 1986). Although psychologists cannot prescribe medication, they often provide therapy in conjunction with professionals who can—that is, medical doctors (physicians or psychiatrists). But combining methods is not necessarily a good idea. In the case of treating depression, for instance, research indicates that cognitive-behavioral therapy is at least as effective as medication, and it costs less too (Antonuccio, Danton, & DeNelsky, 1996; Antonuccio, Thomas, & Danton, 1997). The value of integrating therapy approaches is a very controversial issue at this time, and the speed and direction it will take are currently unclear.

Enhancing the "Image" of Behavior Modification

The early years of behavior modification got off to a rocky start in terms of public and professional acceptance of its approach. The field received very sharp criticism for two of its defining characteristics. First, its philosophical foundations seemed to reject the role of cognitive and biological processes in behavior. Second, the techniques it used seemed simplistic, cold, and impersonal. For instance, a great deal of the early research and application involved the use of punishment, sometimes using intense, physically aversive stimuli with children with developmental disabilities. We have seen in this book that the field of behavior modification has evolved, discarding and replacing unacceptable and untenable features with perspectives and methods that are more consistent with the mainstream of psychological thought.

The negative impact of the early characteristics of behavior modification on its image continued at least until the 1980s (O'Leary, 1984). The extent of people's biases against the use of behavioral methods was shown in a fascinating study (Woolfolk, Woolfolk, & Wilson, 1977). Undergraduate and graduate students at a large state university watched a videotape in which a teacher of children in a special education class used reinforcement techniques, including social and token reinforcers. Before watching the tape, half of the participants (university students) were told they would see a teacher using *behavior modification* techniques with her students and half of the participants were told they would see a teacher using *humanistic psychology* teaching methods. The participants were then asked to rate the teacher and her methods. As you may suspect, those who were told the techniques were humanistic rated the teacher much more favorably than those who were told the techniques were behavioral. In addition, the "humanistic" teacher's methods were rated as being more likely to promote academic and emotional growth than the "behavioral" teacher's methods.

Since the early 1980s, professionals who use behavior modification techniques have been working to correct the negative image of the field. One way they have tried to achieve this goal has been to challenge incorrect statements and misconceptions about behavior modification that have appeared in the news media (O'Leary, 1984). Another approach for enhancing the image of behavior modification has been to publicize how widely accepted and used the techniques are within the field of psychology. Along with the evolution of the field of behavior modification since the 1970s, the

CONCEPT CHECK 15.2

1. Committees mandated by the U.S. Department of Health and Human Services to review the ethics of research are called _____ .

2. The APA recommends that psychologists recognize the limits of their abilities and provide only those services in which they are well trained. This recommendation is part of the general principle called _____ .

3. A question the AABT recommends professionals ask in evaluating the ethics of an intervention is _____ . ⇔

4. A client's approval for therapy to proceed after learning what the procedures will be is called _____ .

5. Whenever possible, researchers should avoid using _____ . ⇔

6. A common form of integration with behavior therapy is the use of _____ in treating anxiety and depression.

Answers: 1. institutional review boards, 2. competence, 3. Is the client's participation voluntary?, 4. informed consent, 5. deception, 6. medication

image of the field has probably been improving—but the pace of this improvement continues to be slow (Axelrod, 1996).

As the final chapter comes to a close, I want to say that I hope you have enjoyed reading this book. You may find it useful to refer to in the future when and if you are working as a professional or when you want to design a program to change your own behavior. (Go to ✔)

SUMMARY

Although most behavior change interventions involve outcome and behavioral goals that are generally acknowledged to be desirable, sometimes questions arise about the acceptability of certain goals for behavior change programs. An intervention's goals are likely to be viewed favorably if they meet two goal acceptability criteria: the goals should have a high degree of social validity, and they should propose achieving a clinically significant improvement. As an application of these criteria, we saw that although psychologists have used conversion therapies in attempts to change the sexual orientation of homosexuals these efforts have not been successful and the behavioral goals do not meet the acceptability criteria. Value systems play a large role in people's acceptance of the goals of an intervention.

Treatment acceptability refers to assessments of the fairness, appropriateness, and reasonableness of the behavior change methods. Using physically aversive stimuli in interventions presents problems for treatment acceptability and should be avoided whenever possible. If aversive stimuli are used, their severity and restrictiveness should be as mild as possible while still allowing the program to succeed in changing the target behavior. The acceptability of treatment methods can be assessed by having individuals fill out rating scales.

Because many ethical concerns can arise in conducting psychological therapy and research, institutional review boards or other review committees can be used to examine the plans and protect the rights of clients and research participants. The American Psychological Association and the Association for Advancement of Behavior Therapy have developed principles to guide the behavior of psychologists in research and therapy activities. These guidelines discuss broad issues, such as competence and integrity, and outline codes of conduct in very specific activities, such as selecting intervention methods and maintaining confidentiality. Clients' rights in therapy can be protected with three mechanisms: (1) using institutional review boards, (2) assessing the social validity of the treatment, and (3) obtaining informed consent from the client or guardian. Ethical safeguards are also applied to protect the rights of participants in research.

Several challenges remain for the future of behavior modification. They include improving the effectiveness of behavioral and cognitive methods, integrating effective approaches from other disciplines into behavior therapy, and enhancing the image of behavior modification.

KEY TERMS

goal acceptability   treatment acceptability   informed consent

REVIEW QUESTIONS

1. What two acceptability criteria apply toward deciding if behavior change goals are acceptable?
2. Describe the questions one should ask in deciding if behavior change goals are acceptable.
3. Describe the evidence against the view that homosexuality is caused by children's experiences with their parents.
4. Pick one of the three dilemmas in behavior change goals discussed in the chapter and present two arguments each for and against the goals.
5. Define treatment acceptability.
6. Describe the case study of Cory, and discuss the meaning of the outcome of the intervention for policies on using punishment.
7. What is an institutional review board (IRB)?
8. Describe four of the APA's general principles of ethics for psychologists.

9. Describe how you might use the AABT questions in Table 15.1 to judge the ethics of therapy.
10. Discuss the three mechanisms for protecting the rights of clients in therapy.
11. Describe the ethical guidelines for doing psychological research.
12. Describe the research by Woolfolk, Woolfolk, and Wilson (1977) on the public image of behavior modification.

RELATED READINGS

APA (American Psychological Association). (1982). *Ethical principles in the conduct of research with human participants*. Washington, DC: Author.

APA (American Psychological Association). (1992). Ethical principles of psychologists and code of conduct. *American Psychologist, 47*, 1597–1611.

Stolz, S. B. & Associates (1978). *Ethical issues in behavior modification*. San Francisco: Jossey-Bass.

Glossary

A-B-C Log A chronological record of each instance of the target behavior, along with the antecedents and consequences that accompanied it.

AB design Intrasubject research involving one baseline phase and one intervention phase.

ABA design A reversal design consisting of three phases: baseline, intervention, and reversal (baseline).

ABAB design A reversal design consisting of four phases: baseline, intervention, reversal (baseline), and intervention.

abstinence violation effect A cognitive process whereby a lapse leads the individual to feel guilt and reduced self-efficacy, which then precipitate a relapse.

Achievement Place A residential token economy program for predelinquent teenagers in which live-in teaching parents supervise the behavior and administration of reinforcers.

altering antecedent chains A method for managing operant antecedents by changing the sequence of events that leads to a behavior.

alternating-treatment design A type of intrasubject research design in which two or more treatments are conducted during the same intervention phase to compare their effectiveness. Also called *simultaneous-treatment* or *multi-element designs*.

alternative responses Behaviors that interfere or compete with other responses, making the other responses unlikely to occur. Also called *competing responses*.

antecedents Cues that precede and set the occasion for particular behaviors.

anxieties Fears with vague or unspecified sources.

anxiety-induction therapies Treatment approaches to reduce phobias and anxieties that expose the client to intense levels of the CS for prolonged periods of time under the supervision of a therapist.

assertion training Programs using modeling and other behavior modification techniques to train clients in being more appropriately or adaptively assertive in social situations.

autogenic training A technique designed to induce psychological and physical calm by having the person imagine being in a pleasant scene and experiencing certain calming body sensations.

automatic thoughts In cognitive therapy, habitual erroneous and maladaptive thought patterns that arise from inappropriate schemata and occur frequently in individuals with emotional problems.

aversion therapy A treatment approach to reduce an operant or respondent behavior by associating it with a highly unpleasant stimulus.

avoidance conditioning Learning a behavior that prevents the occurrence of an aversive circumstance.

backward chaining A method for teaching a chain of behavior by having the person master one link at a time, starting with the last link and adding each new one in the reverse sequence of the chain.

bar graphs Diagrams that use rectangles to represent data points to show how one variable changes with another.

baseline A period of time before an intervention is introduced *or* the data collected during a baseline period.

behavior Any measurable response a person makes; it can be overt or covert.

behavioral contract A formal agreement in a behavior change program describing the target behavior explicitly and stating where and when it should or should not be performed and what the consequences for doing so will be.

behavioral deficit An appropriate behavior that the person does not perform often enough, long enough, well enough, or strongly enough.

behavioral excess An inappropriate response that the person performs too often, too strongly, or for too long.

behavioral goal The desired level of the target behavior to be reached by the end of a behavior change program.

behavioral methods Behavior modification techniques that apply principles of operant conditioning, respondent conditioning, and modeling, especially toward altering overt behaviors.

behavioral subgoals   Specific intermediate levels of the target behavior to be achieved in the process of reaching a behavioral goal.

behaviorism   The school of thought that stresses the study of observable, measurable responses and proposes that behavior can be explained mainly by principles of learning, especially operant and respondent conditioning.

behavior modification   A discipline that focuses on using principles of learning and cognition to understand and change behavior.

behavior rehearsal   A technique used with modeling in which clients perform the modeled behavior and receive feedback on the performance.

biofeedback   A technique that enables individuals to regulate the functioning of their physiological systems by providing moment-to-moment information about the status of each system.

blocking   A respondent conditioning phenomenon in which having learned a CS as a signal for a particular US makes it difficult to learn a new CS for that US.

booster program   A program to maintain improved behaviors that is introduced after an intervention has ended and consists of periodic sessions of the intervention methods to refresh the effects of the original intervention.

brainstorming   A method of generating a large number of ideas that might be useful in solving a problem.

calm scenes   Cognitive images of pleasant events that are relaxing.

chain   A sequence of operant responses that leads to a consequence.

changing-criterion design   A type of intrasubject research design in which the effect of an intervention is examined by altering the standards for correct performance periodically and seeing if the behavior matches the new standards.

clinical significance   An evaluation of an intervention's success in terms of how meaningful the change in behavior is to the person's everyday life. A highly meaningful change is one that is large and brings the behavior into the normal range.

cognition   Covert events, particularly thinking and reasoning.

cognitive-behavioral therapy   Treatment approaches that use both cognitive and behavioral methods to change overt and covert behaviors.

cognitive methods   Behavior modification techniques that are used to change people's thought processes to modify associated overt and covert behaviors.

cognitive restructuring   A type of approach used by some cognitive-behavioral therapies that involves reducing behavioral excesses of thinking maladaptive thoughts by altering the way clients perceive or think about events in their lives.

cognitive therapy   A cognitive restructuring treatment approach that engages clients and therapists in a collaborative effort of hypothesis testing as a method of changing clients' maladaptive automatic thoughts.

computer-assisted instruction (CAI)   A form of programmed instruction in which a series of questions or problems is presented on a computer, which can provide immediate feedback for the individual's answers and give examples and explanations of concepts.

conditioned emotional responses (CERs)   Respondent behaviors that reflect emotions, such as fear and anger.

conditioned reinforcers   Consequences that developed their ability to strengthen behavior by way of conditioning, typically by being associated with established reinforcers. Also called *secondary reinforcers*.

conditioned response (CR)   A specific behavior that can be elicited by a conditioned stimulus as a result of prior learning.

conditioned stimulus (CS)   An event that has gained the ability to elicit a specific response through repeated pairing with a stimulus that already elicits that response.

continuous recording   A measurement strategy of keeping records of a target behavior by recording data on all instances of its occurrence in a specified time period.

continuous reinforcement (CRF)   A schedule of reinforcement in which a reinforcer is given after each and every instance of the correct response.

coping statements   Positive self-statements that emphasize our ability to handle difficult situations.

cost–benefit ratio An assessment of the extent to which the cost of treatment is exceeded by the amount of money it saves in the long run.

counterconditioning A respondent learning process in which the person substitutes a competing or incompatible response for the previously learned CR when the CS is present.

covert conditioning An array of imagery-based techniques in which individuals learn a behavior by imagining the components of operant or respondent conditioning events.

covert positive reinforcement A covert conditioning technique that is used to reduce people's fears by having them imagine performing the feared behavior (the CR) and having a pleasant event occur.

covert sensitization A covert conditioning technique in which a person learns to dislike an existing positive CS or suppress a previously liked behavior by associating an aversive stimulus with either of these events in imagined respondent or operant conditioning situations.

cumulative graphs Line graphs in which the measure of one variable accumulates across units scaled along the horizontal axis. Also called *cumulative records*.

differential reinforcement A discrimination learning process in which making a specific response to one stimulus is reinforced consistently, but making the same response to another stimulus is not reinforced.

differential reinforcement of incompatible behavior (DRI) Delivering reinforcers contingent on the individual performing an alternative response to an undesirable target behavior.

differential reinforcement of low rates of responding (DRL) Delivering reinforcers contingent on the individual performing an undesirable target behavior at a rate that is below a certain level.

differential reinforcement of other behavior (DRO) Delivering reinforcers contingent on the individual not performing an undesirable target behavior at all during a certain time period.

direct assessment methods Measuring behavior in a straightforward manner, usually by observing it directly.

discrimination learning Learning to distinguish between and respond differently toward different stimuli.

discriminative stimulus (S^D) A stimulus that has been associated as an antecedent for a specific reinforced response.

distraction A technique in which individuals shift their attention from stressful overt or covert events to other stimuli.

duration A measure of behavior that assesses the length of time an instance of it lasts.

emetic therapy A behavior modification approach for reducing alcohol abuse by having clients take a drug that makes them nauseated if they then drink alcohol.

escape conditioning Learning a behavior that reduces or eliminates an existing aversive circumstance.

experiment A type of group-based research in which individuals are randomly assigned to different conditions and the researcher manipulates the independent variable to determine its effect on a dependent variable.

extinction In operant conditioning, the process or procedure in which a previously reinforced behavior no longer receives reinforcement, making it less likely to occur in the future.

extinction In respondent conditioning, the process or procedure in which the CS occurs repeatedly without the US it was paired with, making the CR less likely to occur in the future.

extinction burst A temporary increase that sometimes occurs in the frequency or magnitude of a response soon after an extinction procedure is introduced.

fading Process of gradually removing or changing a prompt to decrease the person's reliance on it.

fixed-interval (FI) A type of interval reinforcement schedule in which the time period after each reinforcer is given when reinforcement is no longer available remains constant from one instance of reward to the next. The first correct response made after that period of time has elapsed is reinforced.

fixed-ratio (FR) A type of ratio reinforcement schedule in which the number of correct responses that must be made for each instance of reward remains constant.

flooding   An anxiety-induction therapy in which exposure is given to one or more CSs based on a real-life feared situation; exposure can be *in vivo* or imaginal. Also called *response prevention*.

forward chaining   A method for teaching a chain of behavior by having the person master one link at a time, starting with the first link and adding each new one in the sequence.

frequency   A measure of behavior that assesses how often it occurs.

functional analysis   A procedure to assess the connections between the target behavior and its antecedents and consequences.

goal acceptability   The extent to which the outcome or behavioral goals of a behavior change program are fair, appropriate, and reasonable.

graph   A diagram that generally shows how one variable changes as a function of another variable.

graphic analysis   A procedure used in examining graphs of data from behavior change programs to evaluate whether the program succeeded in changing the behavior substantially.

group contingency   A procedure for administering reinforcers in which the behavior of all members of a group determines the consequences they receive.

habit reversal   An array of methods designed to decrease operant behavior, especially ones that are habitual or automatic, such as motor tics. The methods include competing response practice and training to make the person aware of the behavior's occurrence.

health psychology   A field of psychology introduced to study psychosocial processes in the development, prevention, and treatment of illness.

implosive therapy   An anxiety-induction therapy in which clients imagine highly exaggerated, unrealistic, or physically damaging events related to their fears or anxieties.

indirect assessment methods   Measuring behavior by using abstract or roundabout approaches, rather than observing it directly.

informed consent   Approval by the participants or their guardians to the planned procedures in therapy or research after being told what the procedures will be and any negative effects they may have.

instructions   Oral or written description of how to perform a behavior.

intermittent reinforcement   A type of reinforcement schedule in which only some instances of a behavior are reinforced. Also called *partial reinforcement*.

interobserver reliability   An assessment of the degree to which the data from two or more observers agree regarding the occurrence of a target behavior. Also called *interrater reliability* or *interobserver agreement*.

interval recording   A measurement strategy in which observation periods are divided into fairly short intervals of equal length and a record is kept of whether the target behavior occurred in each interval.

interval schedules   Schedules of reinforcement in which delivery of each instance of reward is based on a rule that involves a period of time after each reinforcer is given when reinforcement is no longer available. The first correct response made after that period of time has elapsed is reinforced.

intrasubject designs   A type of research approach that examines changes in behavior for one individual at a time while an intervention is either in effect or absent. Also called *single-subject designs*.

lapse   An instance of backsliding—that is, performing an unwanted behavior—after having started or completed a program to improve that behavior.

latent inhibition   A respondent conditioning phenomenon in which prior experience with a specific stimulus in neutral circumstances retards the subsequent learning of that stimulus as a CS for a US.

learning   A relatively permanent change in behavioral tendency as a result of experience.

line graphs   Diagrams that use straight lines connecting data points to show changes of one variable in relation to another.

lottery   A procedure for administering reinforcers by entering all eligible individuals in a drawing to win one or more prizes.

magnitude   A measure of behavior that assesses its intensity, degree, or size.

mean   The arithmetic average for a set of data.

meditation   A technique designed to induce psychological and physical calm by having the person focus attention on a meditation stimulus, such as an object, event, or idea.

modeling   Learning a behavior by watching another individual perform it. Also called *observational learning, social learning,* and *vicarious learning.*

multidimensional programs   Behavior change programs that combine several methods to address the problem behavior and its antecedents and consequences.

multimodal therapy   A treatment approach that selects and employs various cognitive and behavioral methods to address several dimensions of a client's problems.

multiple-baseline designs   Intrasubject research designs in which two or more AB designs are conducted, with all baseline phases starting simultaneously but continuing for different lengths of time.

multiple-baseline across behaviors   A type of multiple-baseline design in which each AB design examines the effects of the intervention on a *different behavior* for a single individual in a particular situation.

multiple-baseline across situations   A type of multiple-baseline design in which each AB design examines the effects of the intervention on a particular behavior in a *different situation* for a single individual.

multiple-baseline across subjects   A type of multiple-baseline design in which each AB design examines the effects of the intervention on a particular behavior in a particular setting for a *different individual.*

narrowing   Limiting a target behavior to a relatively small range of antecedent conditions.

natural reinforcers   Unprogrammed rewards people receive as a natural part of their everyday lives.

negative punishment   A process in which subtracting or reducing a stimulus or condition suppresses the behavior on which it is contingent.

negative reinforcement   A process in which subtracting or reducing a stimulus as a consequence of a behavior strengthens that behavior.

operant conditioning   A form of learning in which behavior can be changed by its consequences.

organizational behavior management   An approach for improving employee behavior and functioning by applying behavior modification techniques in employment settings.

outcome goals   Broad or abstracted results to be achieved in a behavior change program.

overcorrection   A punishment procedure that has the person engage in activities that correct (see **restitution**) or are the opposite of the undesirable behavior (see **positive practice**) when the misbehavior occurs.

overshadowing   A respondent conditioning phenomenon in which one of multiple CSs outweighs the others in the ability to elicit the CR.

participant modeling   A fear reduction technique in which a fearful individual watches a therapist or other person engage in a feared activity and is encouraged and guided to join in the activity.

personalized system of instruction (PSI)   A method of teaching in which the course material is divided into a series of units, and students study and take tests at their own pace and receive immediate feedback on their performance.

phobias   Intense and irrational fears, usually of something specific.

pinpointing   Translating broad or vague descriptions of people's behavior into specific, objective, and measurable responses.

physically aversive stimuli   Punishers that cause physical discomfort, pain, or other unpleasant sensations.

positive practice   A component of the overcorrection method of punishment in which the misbehaving person must engage repeatedly in a response that is the opposite of the misbehavior.

positive punishment   A process in which adding or introducing an aversive event suppresses the behavior on which it is contingent.

positive reinforcement   A process in which adding or introducing a consequence for a behavior strengthens that behavior.

postreinforcement pauses   Brief pauses in responding that individuals often show after each instance of reward when they are reinforced on a fixed-ratio schedule.

Premack principle Activities that are high-probability behaviors for a particular individual can reinforce responses that occur less frequently.

problem-solving training A cognitive-behavioral treatment approach that trains clients in a strategy for identifying and dealing with life circumstances that require actions based on effective decision-making processes.

programmed instruction A self-teaching process in which individuals learn material by working at their own pace through a series of questions or problems and receive immediate feedback for their answers.

progressive muscle relaxation A technique designed to induce psychological and physical calm by having the person alternately tense and relax separate muscle groups. Also called *progressive relaxation*.

prompt An antecedent that reminds the person to perform a behavior or helps the person learn how to perform it.

punishment A process whereby a consequence of an operant response suppresses that behavior.

quasi-experiments Research designs that have different groups of participants and "look" like experiments but lack the requirement of manipulating an independent variable or randomly assigning individuals to conditions.

rational-emotive therapy (RET) A cognitive restructuring treatment approach in which the therapist challenges clients' irrational beliefs and trains them to substitute thoughts that are more adaptive and rational.

ratio schedules Schedules of reinforcement in which delivery of each instance of reward is determined by a rule that specifies the number of correct responses that must have been made since the last reinforcer was given.

ratio strain Deterioration of a behavior when the number of responses required in a ratio schedule of reinforcement becomes too large.

reactivity The tendency for people's behavior to change when they know they are being watched.

reinforcement A process whereby a consequence of an operant response strengthens that behavior.

reinforcer sampling A procedure that involves presenting a small or brief sample of a reinforcing consequence before a target behavior is performed to enhance the effectiveness of the reinforcer.

reinterpretative statements Positive self-statements that redefine a difficult situation by nullifying its unpleasant aspects or providing reasons for seeing it differently.

relapse Returning to one's former level of an undesirable behavior.

relapse prevention method A self-management program individuals learn as part of an intervention that is designed to help them maintain their improved behavior by learning how to identify and deal effectively with situations that tend to lead to relapses.

relaxation A psychological and physical state of calm.

reprimands Verbal statements expressing strong criticism of one's behavior.

respondent conditioning A learning process in which a stimulus gains the ability to elicit a particular response by its repeated pairing with an unconditioned stimulus that already elicits that response. Also called *classical conditioning*.

response cost A punishment procedure in which the misbehaving person loses an item or privilege he or she values.

response generalization A phenomenon in which modifying a target behavior leads to similar changes in another response that was not specifically addressed in the behavior change program.

restitution A component of the overcorrection method of punishment in which the misbehaving person must correct or restore the environmental situation, often to a condition that is better than it was previously.

reversal designs Intrasubject research formats with a series of phases that involve alternations in the presence and absence of the intervention.

rule-governed behavior An action that is controlled by an antecedent rule that describes the contingency between performance of the behavior and specific consequences.

rule-release   A provision in a behavior change program in which the person is exempt from its restrictive rules during certain predefined limited conditions.

schedule of reinforcement   A rule that determines which instances of a response will result in a reinforcer.

schema   In cognitive therapy, a cognitive structure that organizes one's knowledge and affects one's perceptions and interpretations of everyday experiences. The plural form is *schemata*.

S-delta (S$^\Delta$)   A stimulus that has been associated consistently with nonreinforcement of a specific response.

second-order conditioning   A respondent conditioning phenomenon in which a new CS gains the ability to produce a CR by becoming associated with an existing CS that already elicits that response.

self-control   The ability to exercise restraint over our own emotions, impulses, or desires. (Sometimes used interchangeably with **self-regulation.**)

self-efficacy   People's beliefs about their ability to succeed at performing a particular behavior they want to do.

self-instruction   An antecedent statement people make to themselves that guides, directs, or describes the behavior they will perform.

self-management   Applying behavioral or cognitive methods to change one's own behavior.

self-monitoring   Assessing one's own target behaviors.

self-regulation   The ability to direct and modulate one's own responses to behave appropriately. (See **self-control.**)

self-statements   Things people say to themselves either overtly (aloud) or covertly to influence their overt or covert behaviors.

shaping   A process or procedure in which a new behavior becomes increasingly well developed when the criteria for being reinforced for successive instances of the response become increasingly rigorous.

social validity   An evaluation by the client and individuals in his or her life of the social utility and adaptiveness of the change in behavior produced by an intervention.

spontaneous recovery   The reappearance of a previously extinguished behavior. If extinction continues, the response is weak and temporary.

stages of change model   A theory that incorporates people's motivations and intentions to describe five stages in their readiness to change their behavior.

stimulus control   The ability of an antecedent stimulus to affect one's performance of a specific behavior.

stimulus generalization   The tendency to perform a learned behavior in response to an antecedent stimulus or condition that is similar but not identical to the actual discriminative stimulus for that behavior.

stimulus hierarchy   A series of CSs that are rank-ordered in terms of the degree of fear each one arouses.

stress inoculation training   A cognitive-behavioral treatment approach that focuses on teaching specific skills clients can use in coping with stressful experiences in their everyday lives.

subjective units of discomfort scale (SUDS)   A rating scale by which a fearful person can assess the feelings of fear aroused by particular CSs.

summary record   A form that, when filled out using the A-B-C Log data, organizes and summarizes the data, allowing patterns to be seen in the relationships among the antecedents, behavior, and consequences.

systematic desensitization   A respondent conditioning technique for reducing fear by presenting increasingly strong CSs and replacing the CR with a calm response.

table   A chart that systematically arranges a set of data in rows and columns.

target behaviors   The responses to be changed in a behavior modification intervention.

task analysis   A process used in identifying the component responses and required sequences that make up a complex action.

taste aversion   A specific form of learning in which the taste of a previously liked food becomes disliked very easily through respondent conditioning, even though the CS and US are separated by a substantial period of time.

thinning   Gradually reducing the rate at which a behavior is reinforced.

thought stopping   A technique in which individuals interrupt their disturbing thoughts by saying "Stop" emphatically, either aloud or covertly.

time-out   A form of punishment in which the misbehaving person's reinforcing environment is converted or moved to one that is less reinforcing.

time sampling   A measurement strategy in which observation periods are divided into subperiods of equal length, and a record is kept of the occurrence of the target behavior during a short interval at the start of each subperiod.

token economy   A method that uses a complex system of consequences with tokens as reinforcers to modify a wide range of behaviors in groups of individuals.

tokens   Symbolic rewards that serve as conditioned reinforcers by virtue of their being traded for and associated with already established backup reinforcers.

total-task presentation   A method for teaching a chain of behavior by having the person learn all of the links together as a complete sequence.

treatment acceptability   The extent to which the treatment methods in a behavior change program are considered fair, appropriate, and reasonable by the client and the community.

trend line   A "best fitting" straight line applied in a graph to represent the overall or general changes in one variable across a set of data points plotted as a function of another variable.

unconditioned reinforcers   Consequences that require little or no learning for them to have the ability to strengthen behavior. Also called *primary reinforcers*.

unconditioned response (UR)   A specific behavior made automatically to a particular stimulus.

unconditioned stimulus (US)   A specific event that elicits a particular response automatically.

urine alarm apparatus   A device that applies operant and respondent conditioning principles to eliminate the release of urine during sleep or at other inappropriate times.

variables   Any characteristics of people, events, or objects that can change.

variable-interval (VI)   A type of interval reinforcement schedule in which the time period when reinforcement is no longer available changes and is unspecified from one instance of reward to the next. The first correct response made after each period of time has elapsed is reinforced.

variable-ratio (VR)   A type of ratio reinforcement schedule in which the number of correct responses that must be made for each instance of reward changes and is unspecified from one instance to the next.

References

AABT (Association for Advancement of Behavior Therapy). (1977). Ethical issues for human services. *Behavior Therapy, 8*, v–vi.

Acker, L. E., Goldwater, B. C., & Agnew, J. L. (1990). Sidney Slug: A computer simulation for teaching shaping without an animal laboratory. *Teaching of Psychology, 17*, 130–132.

Ackerman, M. D., & Carey, M. P. (1995). Psychology's role on the assessment of erectile dysfunction: Historical precedents, current knowledge, and methods. *Journal of Consulting and Clinical Psychology, 63*, 862–876.

Ackerman, M. D., D'Atillio, J. P., Antoni, M. H., Rhamy, R. K., Weinstein, D., & Politano, V. A. (1993). Patient-reported erectile dysfunction: A cross-validation study. *Archives of Sexual Behavior, 22*, 603–618.

Ackerman, M. D., D'Attilio, J. P., Antoni, M. H., Weinstein, D., Rhamy, R. K., & Politano, V. A. (1991). The predictive significance of patient-reported sexual functioning in RigiScan sleep evaluations. *Journal of Urology, 146*, 1559–1563.

Agras, W. S., Schneider, J. A., Arnow, B., Raeburn, S. D., & Telch, C. F. (1989). Cognitive-behavioral and response prevention treatments for bulimia nervosa. *Journal of Consulting and Clinical Psychology, 57*, 215–221.

Albin, R. W., & Horner, R. H. (1988). Generalization with precision. In R. H. Horner, G. Dunlap, & R. L. Koegel (Eds.), *Generalization and maintenance: Life-style changes in applied settings* (pp. 99–120). Baltimore: Paul H. Brookes.

Alexander, R. N., Corbett, T. F., & Smigel, J. (1976). The effects of individual and group consequences on school attendance and curfew violations with predelinquent adolescents. *Journal of Applied Behavior Analysis, 9*, 221–226.

Al-Kubaisy, T., Marks, I. M., Logsdail, S., Marks, M. P., Lovell, K., Sungur, M., & Araya, R. (1992). Role of exposure homework in phobia reduction: A controlled study. *Behavior Therapy, 23*, 599–621.

Allan, R. W. (1998). Operant-respondent interactions. In W. O'Donohue (Ed.), *Learning and behavior therapy* (pp. 146–168). Boston: Allyn & Bacon.

Allen, J. S., Tarnowski, K. J., Simonian, S. J., Elliott, D., & Drabman, R. S. (1991). The generalization map revisited: Assessment of generalized treatment effects in child and adolescent behavior therapy. *Behavior Therapy, 22*, 393–405.

Allen, K. D., Loiben, T., Allen, S. J., & Stanley, R. T. (1992). Dentist-implemented contingent escape for management of disruptive child behavior. *Journal of Applied Behavior Analysis, 25*, 629–636.

Allen, K. D., & Stokes, T. F. (1987). Use of escape and reward in the management of young children during dental treatment. *Journal of Applied Behavior Analysis, 20*, 381–390.

Allen, L. D., & Iwata, B. A. (1980). Reinforcing exercise maintenance: Using existing high-rate activities. *Behavior Modification, 4*, 337–354.

Allison, J. (1989). The nature of reinforcement. In S. B. Klein & R. R. Mowrer (Eds.), *Contemporary learning theories: Instrumental conditioning and the impact of biological constraints on learning* (pp. 13–39). Hillsdale, NJ: Erlbaum.

Altman, K., Haavik, S., & Cook, J. W. (1978). Punishment of self-injurious behavior in natural settings using contingent aromatic ammonia. *Behaviour Research and Therapy, 16*, 85–96.

AMA (American Medical Association). (1989). *The American Medical Association Encyclopedia of Medicine*. New York: Random House.

Anderson, K. O., & Masur, F. T. (1983). Psychological preparation for invasive medical and dental procedures. *Journal of Behavioral Medicine, 6*, 1–40.

Andrasik, F., Blake, D. D., & McCarran, M. S. (1986). A biobehavioral analysis of pediatric headache. In N. A. Krasnegor, J. D. Arasteh, & M. F. Cataldo (Eds.), *Child health behavior: A behavioral pediatrics perspective* (pp. 394–434). New York: Wiley.

Angier, N. (1995, October 31). Gene hunters pursue elusive and complex traits of mind. New York Times, pp. C1, 3.

Antonuccio, D. O., Danton, W. G., & DeNelsky, G. Y. (1996). Psychotherapy versus medication for depression: Challenging the conventional wisdom with data. *Professional Psychology Research and Practice, 26*, 574–585.

Antonuccio, D. O., Thomas, M., & Danton, W. G. (1997). A cost-effectiveness analysis of cognitive behavior therapy and fluoxetine (prozac) in the treatment of depression. *Behavior Therapy, 28*, 187–210.

APA (American Psychological Association). (1982). *Ethical principles in the conduct of research with human participants*. Washington, DC: Author.

APA (American Psychological Association). (1992). Ethical principles of psychologists and code of conduct. *American Psychologist, 47*, 1597–1611.

Arcediano, F., Matute, H., & Miller, R. R. (1997). Blocking of Pavlovian conditioning in humans. *Learning and Motivation, 28*, 188–199.

Arrick, M. C., Voss, J., & Rimm, D. C. (1981). The relative efficacy of thought-stopping and covert assertion. *Behaviour Research and Therapy, 19*, 17–24.

Asbell, B. (1984, February 26). Writers' workshop at age 5. *New York Times Magazine*, pp. 55–72.

Ascher, L. M. (1993). Treating recursive anxiety with covert conditioning. In J. R. Cautela & A. J. Kearney (Eds.), *Covert conditioning handbook* (pp. 13–21). Pacific Grove, CA: Brooks/Cole.

Ash, D. W., & Holding, D. H. (1990). Backward versus forward chaining in the acquisition of a keyboard skill. *Human Factors, 32*, 139–146.

Ashem, B., & Donner, L. (1968). Covert sensitization with alcoholics: A controlled replication. *Behaviour Research and Therapy, 6*, 7–12.

Aubuchon, P., Haber, J. D., & Adams, H. E. (1983). Can migraine headaches be modified by operant pain techniques? *Journal of Behavior Therapy and Experimental Psychiatry, 16*, 261–263.

Axelrod, S. (1990). Myths that (mis)guide our profession. In A. C. Repp & N. N. Singh (Eds.), *Perspectives on the use of nonaversive and aversive interventions for persons with developmental disabilities* (pp. 59–72). Sycamore, IL: Sycamore.

Axelrod, S. (1996). What's wrong with behavior analysis? *Journal of Behavioral Education, 6*, 247–256.

Axelrod, S., Brantner, J. P., & Meddock, T. D., (1978). Overcorrection: A review and critical analysis. *Journal of Special Education, 12*, 367–391.

Axelrod, S., Hall, R. V., Weis, L., & Rohrer, S. (1974). Use of self-imposed contingencies to reduce the frequency of smoking behavior. In M. J. Mahoney & C. E. Thoresen (Eds.), *Self-control: Power to the person* (pp. 77–85). Pacific Grove, CA: Brooks/Cole.

Ayllon, T., & Azrin, N. H. (1968a). Reinforcer sampling: A technique for increasing the behavior of mental patients. *Journal of Applied Behavior Analysis, 1*, 13–20.

Ayllon, T., & Azrin, N. H. (1968b). *The token economy: A motivational system for therapy and rehabilitation.* Englewood Cliffs, NJ: Prentice-Hall.

Ayllon, T., & Michael, J. (1959). The psychiatric nurse as a behavioral engineer. *Journal of the Experimental Analysis of Behavior, 2*, 323–334.

Ayres, J. J. B. (1998). Fear conditioning and avoidance. In W. O'Donohue (Ed.), *Learning and behavior therapy* (pp. 122–145). Boston: Allyn & Bacon.

Azrin, N. H. (1976). Improvements in the community-reinforcement approach to alcoholism. *Behaviour Research and Therapy, 14*, 339–348.

Azrin, N. H., & Foxx, R. M. (1971). A rapid method of toilet training the institutionalized retarded. *Journal of Applied Behavior Analysis, 4*, 89–99.

Azrin, N. H., & Holz, W. C. (1966). Punishment. In W. K. Honig (Ed.), *Operant behavior: Areas of research and application* (pp. 380–447). New York: Appleton.

Azrin, N. H., Hontos, P. T., & Besalel-Azrin, V. (1979). Elimination of enuresis without a conditioning apparatus: An extension by office instruction of the child and parents. *Behavior Therapy, 10*, 14–19.

Azrin, N. H., & Nunn, R. G. (1973). Habit-reversal: A method of eliminating nervous habits and tics. *Behaviour Research and Therapy, 11*, 619–628.

Azrin, N. H., Nunn, R. G., & Frantz, S. E. (1980). Habit reversal vs. negative practice treatment of nervous tics. *Behavior Therapy, 11*, 169–178.

Azrin, N. H., & Peterson, A. L. (1990). Treatment of Tourette Syndrome by habit reversal: A waiting-list control group comparison. *Behavior Therapy, 21*, 305–318.

Azrin, N. H., & Powell, J. (1969). Behavioral engineering: The use of response priming to improve prescribed self-medication. *Journal of Applied Behavior Analysis, 2*, 39–42.

Azrin, N. H., & Powers, M. A. (1975). Eliminating classroom disturbances of emotionally disturbed children by positive practice procedures. *Behavior Therapy, 6*, 525–534.

Azrin, N. H., Sisson, R. W., Meyers, R., & Godley, M. (1982). Alcoholism treatment by disulfiram and community reinforcement therapy. *Journal of Behavior Therapy and Experimental Psychiatry, 13*, 105–112.

Azrin, N. H., & Thienes, P. M. (1978). Rapid elimination of enuresis by intensive learning without a conditioning apparatus. *Behavior Therapy, 9*, 342–354.

Azrin, N. H., & Wesolowski, M. D. (1974). Theft reversal: An overcorrection procedure for eliminating stealing by retarded persons. *Journal of Applied Behavior Analysis, 7*, 577–581.

Azrin, N. H., & Wesolowski, M. D. (1975). The use of positive practice to eliminate persistent floor sprawling by profoundly retarded adults. *Behavior Therapy, 6*, 627–631.

Baer, D. M., Peterson, R. F., & Sherman, J. A. (1967). The development of imitation by reinforcing behavioral similarity to a model. *Journal of the Experimental Analysis of Behavior, 10*, 405–416.

Baer, D. M., Wolf, M. M., & Risley, T. R. (1968). Some current dimensions of applied behavior analysis. *Journal of Applied Behavior Analysis, 1*, 91–97.

Baer, D. M., Wolf, M. M., & Risley, T. R. (1987). Some still-current dimensions of applied behavior analysis. *Journal of Applied Behavior Analysis, 20*, 313–327.

Baer, R. A., Blount, R. L., Detrich, R., & Stokes, T. F. (1987). Using intermittent reinforcement to program maintenance of verbal/nonverbal correspondence. *Journal of Applied Behavior Analysis, 20*, 179–184.

Baeyens, F., Hermans, D., & Eelen, P. (1993). The role of CS-US contingency in human evaluative conditioning. *Behaviour Research and Therapy, 31*, 731–737.

Baggs, K., & Spence, S. H. (1990). Effectiveness of booster sessions in the maintenance and enhancement of treatment gains following assertion training. *Journal of Consulting and Clinical Psychology, 58*, 845–854.

Bailey, J. S., Timbers, G. D., Phillips, E. L., & Wolf, M. M. (1971). Modification of articulation errors of pre-delinquents by their peers. *Journal of Applied Behavior Analysis, 4,* 265–281.

Baldwin, J. D., & Baldwin, J. I. (1981). *Beyond sociobiology.* New York: Elsevier.

Ballard, K. D., & Glynn, T. (1975). Behavioral management in story writing with elementary school children. *Journal of Applied Behavior Analysis, 8,* 387–398.

Bandura, A. (1965). Vicarious processes: A case of no-trial learning. In L. Berkowitz (Ed.), *Advances in experimental social psychology* (Vol. 2, pp. 3–55). New York: Academic Press.

Bandura, A. (1969). *Principles of behavior modification.* New York: Holt, Rinehart & Winston.

Bandura, A. (1975). Effecting change through participant modeling. In J. D. Krumboltz & C. E. Thoresen (Eds.), *Counseling methods* (pp. 248–265). New York: Holt, Rinehart & Winston.

Bandura, A. (1977). Self-efficacy: Toward a unifying theory of behavioral change. *Psychological Review, 84,* 191–215.

Bandura, A. (1986). *Social foundations of thought and action: A social-cognitive theory.* Englewood Cliffs, NJ: Prentice-Hall.

Bandura, A., Jeffery, R. W., & Gajdos, E. (1975). Generalizing change through participant modeling with self-directed mastery. *Behaviour Research and Therapy, 13,* 141–152.

Bangert-Drowns, R. (1988). The effects of school-based substance abuse education—a meta-analysis. *Journal of Drug Education, 18,* 243–264.

Bank, L., Marlowe, J. H., Reid, J. B., Patterson, G. R., & Weinrott, M. R. (1991). A comparative evaluation of parent-training interventions for families of chronic delinquents. *Journal of Abnormal Child Psychology, 19,* 15–33.

Barlow, D. H. (1978). Aversive procedures. In W. S. Agras (Ed.), *Behavior modification: Principles and clinical applications* (2nd ed., 86–133). Boston: Little, Brown.

Barlow, D. H., & Hayes, S. C. (1979). Alternating treatments design: One strategy for comparing the effects of two treatments in a single subject. *Journal of Applied Behavior Analysis, 12,* 199–210.

Barlow, D. H., Leitenberg, H., Agras, W. S., & Wincze, J. P. (1969). The transfer gap in systematic desensitization: An analogue study. *Behaviour Research and Therapy, 7,* 191–196.

Baron, A., & Galizio, M. (1983). Instructional control of human operant behavior. *Psychological Record, 33,* 495–520.

Barrera, F. J., & Teodoro, G. M. (1990). Flash bonding or cold fusion? A case analysis of Gentle Teaching. In A. C. Repp & N. N. Singh (Eds.), *Perspectives on the use of nonaversive and aversive interventions for persons with developmental disabilities* (pp. 199–214). Sycamore, IL: Sycamore.

Barrera, M., & Glasgow, R. E. (1976). Design and evaluation of a personalized instruction course in behavioral self-control. *Teaching of Psychology, 3,* 81–84.

Barrish, H. H., Saunders, M., & Wolf, M. M. (1969). Good behavior game: Effects of individual contingencies for group consequences on disruptive behavior in a classroom. *Journal of Applied Behavior Analysis, 2,* 119–124.

Barton, E. J., & Osborne, J. G. (1978). The development of classroom sharing by a teacher using positive practice. *Behavior Modification, 2,* 231–250.

Barton, E. S., Guess, D., Garcia, E., & Baer, D. M. (1970). Improvement of retardates' mealtime behaviors by timeout procedures using multiple-baseline techniques. *Journal of Applied Behavior Analysis, 3,* 77–84.

Baum, C. G., Forehand, R., & Zegiob, L. E. (1979). A review of observer reactivity in adult-child interactions. *Journal of Behavioral Assessment, 1,* 167–178.

Baum, W. M. (1994). *Understanding behaviorism: Science, behavior, and culture.* New York: HarperCollins.

Beal, D., Kopec, A. M., & DiGiuseppe, R. (1996). Disputing clients' irrational beliefs. *Journal of Rational-Emotive Therapy, 14,* 215–229.

Bear, G. G. (1998). School discipline in the United States: Prevention, correction, and long term social development. *Educational and Child Psychology, 15,* 15–39.

Beck, A. T. (1967). *Depression: Clinical, experimental, and theoretical aspects.* New York: Harper & Row.

Beck, A. T. (1976). *Cognitive therapy and the emotional disorders.* New York: International Universities Press.

Beck, A. T. (1993). Cognitive therapy: Past, present, and future. *Journal of Consulting and Clinical Psychology, 61,* 194–198.

Beck, A. T., Freeman, A., & Associates (1990). *Cognitive therapy of personality disorders.* New York: Guilford.

Beck, A. T., Kovacs, M., & Weissman, A. (1975). Hopelessness and suicidal behavior: An overview. *Journal of the American Medical Association, 234,* 1146–1149.

Beck, A. T., Ward, C. H., Mendelson, M., Mock, J. E., & Erbaugh, J. K. (1961). An inventory for measuring depression. *Archives of General Psychiatry, 4,* 561–571.

Becker, W. C., Madsen, C. H., Arnold, C. R., & Thomas, D. R. (1972). The contingent use of teacher attention and praise in reducing classroom behavior problems. In K. D. O'Leary & S. G. O'Leary (Eds.), *Classroom management: The successful use of behavior modification* (pp. 91–114). New York: Pergamon.

Beiman, I., Israel, E., & Johnson, S. A. (1978). During training and posttraining effects of live and taped extended progressive relaxation, self-relaxation, and electromyogram biofeedback. *Journal of Consulting and Clinical Psychology, 46,* 314–321.

Beitman, B. D., Goldfried, M. R., & Norcross, J. C. (1989). The movement toward integrating the psychotherapies: An overview. *American Journal of Psychiatry, 146,* 138–147.

Bell, A. P., Weinberg, M. S., & Hammersmith, S. K. (1981). *Sexual preference: Its development in men and women*. Bloomington, IN: Indiana University Press.

Belles, D., & Bradlyn, A. S. (1987). The use of the changing criterion design in achieving controlled smoking in a heavy smoker: A controlled case study. *Journal of Behavior Therapy and Experimental Psychiatry, 18*, 77–82.

Beneke, W. M., & Vander Tuig, J. G. (1996). Improving eating habits: A stimulus-control approach to lifestyle change. In J. R. Cautela & W. Ishaq (Eds.), *Contemporary issues in behavior therapy: Improving the human condition* (pp. 105–121). New York: Plenum Press.

Benson, H. (1974). Your innate asset for combating stress. *Harvard Business Review, 52*, 49–60.

Benson, H. (1984). The relaxation response and stress. In J. D. Matarazzo, S. M. Weiss, J. A. Herd, N. E. Miller, & S. M. Weiss (Eds.), *Behavioral health: A handbook of health enhancement and disease prevention* (pp. 326–337). New York: Wiley.

Benson, H. (1991). Mind/body interactions including Tibetan studies. In The Dalai Lama, H. Benson, R. A. F. Thurman, H. E. Gardner, & D. Goleman (Eds.), *Mindscience: An East-West dialogue*. Boston: Wisdom.

Benson, H., Malhotra, M. S., Goldman, R. F., Jacobs, G. D., & Hopkins, P. J. (1990). Three case reports of the metabolic and electroencephalographic changes during advanced Buddhist meditation techniques. *Behavioral Medicine, 16*, 90–94.

Bentall, R. P., Lowe, C. G., & Beasty, A. (1985). The role of verbal behavior in human learning: II. Developmental differences. *Journal of Applied Behavior Analysis, 43*, 165–181.

Bernstein, D. A., & Borkovec, T. D. (1973). *Progressive relaxation training: A manual for the helping professions*. Champaign, IL: Research Press.

Bernstein, D. A., Borkovec, T. D., & Coles, M. G. H. (1986). Assessment of anxiety. In A. R. Ciminero, K. S. Calhoun, & Adams, K. E. (Eds,), *Handbook of behavioral assessment* (2nd ed., pp. 353–403). New York: Wiley.

Bernstein, I. L. (1991). Aversion conditioning in response to cancer and cancer treatment. *Clinical Psychology Review, 11*, 185–191.

Bierman, K. L., Miller, C. L., & Stabb, S. D. (1987). Improving the social behavior and peer acceptance of rejected boys: Effects of social skill training with instructions and prohibitions. *Journal of Consulting and Clinical Psychology, 55*, 194–200.

Billings, D. C., & Wasik, B. H. (1985). Self-instructional training with preschoolers: An attempt to replicate. *Journal of Applied Behavior Analysis, 18*, 61–67.

Birnbrauer, J. S., Wolf, M. M., Kidder, J. D., & Tague, C. E. (1972). Classroom behavior of retarded pupils with token

reinforcement. In K. D. O'Leary & S. G. O'Leary (Eds.), *Classroom management: The successful use of behavior modification* (pp. 293–311). New York: Pergamon.

Blaisdell, A. P., Bristol, A. S., Gunther, L. M., & Miller, R. R. (1998). Overshadowing and latent inhibition counteract each other: Support for the comparator hypothesis. *Journal of Experimental Psychology: Animal Behavior Processes, 24*, 335–351.

Blakey, R., & Baker, R. (1980). An exposure approach to alcohol abuse. *Behaviour Research and Therapy, 18*, 319–325.

Blampied, N. M., & Kahan, E. (1992). Acceptability of alternative punishments. *Behavior Modification, 16*, 400–413.

Blanchard, E. B. (1987). Long-term effects of behavioral treatment of chronic headache. *Behavior Therapy, 18*, 375–385.

Blanchard, E. B., Applebaum, K. A., Guarnieri, P., Morrill, B., & Dentinger, M. P. (1987). Five year prospective follow-up on the treatment of chronic headache with biofeedback and/or relaxation. *Headache, 27*, 580–583.

Blanchard, E. B., Nicholson, N. L., Radnitz, C. L., Steffek, B. D., Applebaum, K. A., & Dentinger, M. P. (1991). The role of home practice in thermal biofeedback. *Journal of Consulting and Clinical Psychology, 59*, 507–512.

Blum, K., Cull, J. C., Braverman, E. R., & Comings, D. E. (1996). Reward deficiency syndrome. *American Scientist, 84*, 132–145.

Boegli, R. G., & Wasik, B. H. (1978). Use of the token economy system to intervene on a school-wide level. *Psychology in the Schools, 15*, 72–78.

Borden, J. W. (1992). Behavioral treatment of simple phobia. In S. M. Turner, K. S. Calhoun, & H. E. Adams (Eds.), *Handbook of clinical behavior therapy* (2nd ed., pp. 3–12). New York: Wiley.

Borkovec, T. D., Wilkinson, L., Folensbee, R., & Lerman, C. (1983). Stimulus control applications to the treatment of worry. *Behaviour Research and Therapy, 21*, 247–251.

Bornstein, P. H., Hamilton, S. B., & Bornstein, M. T. (1986). Self-monitoring procedures. In A. R. Ciminero, K. S. Calhoun, & Adams, K. E. (Eds.), *Handbook of behavioral assessment* (2nd ed., 176–222). New York: Wiley.

Bornstein, P. H., & Quevillon, R. P. (1976). The effects of a self-instructional package on overactive preschool boys. *Journal of Applied Behavior Analysis, 9*, 179–188.

Bostow, D. E., & Bailey, J. B. (1969). Modification of severe disruptive and aggressive behavior using brief timeout and reinforcement procedures. *Journal of Applied Behavior Analysis, 2*, 31–37.

Botvin, G. J., Baker, E., Dusenbury, L., Tortu, S., & Botvin, E. M. (1990). Preventing adolescent drug use through a multimodal cognitive-behavioral approach: Results of a 3-year study. *Journal of Consulting and Clinical Psychology, 58*, 437–446.

Bouton, M. E. (2000). A learning theory perspective on lapse, relapse, and the maintenance of behavior change. *Health Psychology, 19*(Suppl.) 57–63.

Bouton, M. E., & Nelson, J. B. (1998). The role of context in classical conditioning: Some implications for cognitive behavior therapy. In W. O'Donohue (Ed.), *Learning and behavior therapy* (pp. 59–84). Boston: Allyn & Bacon.

Bouton, M. E., & Swartzentruber, D. (1991). Sources of relapse after extinction in Pavlovian and instrumental learning. *Clinical Psychology Review, 11*, 123–140.

Bowman, L. G., Piazza, C. C., Fisher, W. W., Hagopian, L. P., & Kogan, J. S. (1997). Assessment of preference for varied versus constant reinforcers. *Journal of Applied Behavior Analysis, 30*, 451–458.

Brantner, J. P., & Doherty, M. A. (1983). A review of timeout: A conceptual and methodological analysis. In S. Axelrod & J. Apsche (Eds.), *The effects of punishment on human behavior* (pp. 87–132). New York: Academic Press.

Braswell, L., & Kendall, P. C. (1988). Cognitive-behavioral methods with children. In K. S. Dobson (Ed.), *Handbook of cognitive behavioral therapies* (pp. 167–213). New York: Guilford.

Brigham, T. (1982). Self-management: A radical behavioral perspective. In P. Karoly & F. H. Kanfer (Eds.), *Self-management and behavior change: From theory to practice* (pp. 32–59). New York: Pergamon.

Broden, M., Bruce, C., Mitchell, M. A., Carter, V., & Hall, R. V. (1972). Effects of teacher attention on attending behavior of two boys at adjacent desks. In K. D. O'Leary & S. G. O'Leary (Eds.), *Classroom management: The successful use of behavior modification* (pp. 249–256). New York: Pergamon.

Broussard, C., & Northup, J. (1997). The use of functional analysis to develop peer interventions for disruptive classroom behavior. *School Psychology Quarterly, 12*, 65–76.

Brown, J. M., O'Keeffe, J., Sanders, S. H., & Baker, B. (1986). Developmental changes in children's cognition to stressful and painful situations. *Journal of Pediatric Psychology, 11*, 343–357.

Brown, P. L. (1982). *Managing behavior on the job.* New York: Wiley.

Brownell, K. D., & Rodin, J. (1994). The dieting maelstrom: Is it possible and advisable to lose weight? *American Psychologist, 49*, 781–791.

Brudny, J. (1982). Biofeedback in chronic neurological cases: Therapeutic electromyography. In L. White & B. Tursky (Eds.), *Clinical biofeedback: Efficacy and mechanisms* (pp. 249–275). New York: Guilford.

Bryant, L. E., & Budd, K. S. (1982). Self-instructional training to increase independent work performance in preschoolers. *Journal of Applied Behavior Analysis, 15*, 259–271.

Burgess, R. L., & Richardson, R. A. (1984). Coercive interpersonal contingencies as a determinant of child maltreatment: Implications for treatment and prevention. In R. F. Dangel & R. A. Polster (Eds.), *Parent training: Foundations of research and practice* (pp. 239–259). New York: Guilford.

Burling, T. A., Bigelow, G. E., Robinson, J. C., & Mead, A. M. (1991). Smoking during pregnancy: Reduction via objective assessment and directive advice. *Behavior Therapy, 22*, 31–40.

Butler, R. A. (1954). Incentive conditions which influence visual exploration. *Journal of Experimental Psychology, 48*, 19–23.

Byne, W. (1994). The biological evidence challenged. *Scientific American, 270*(5), 50–55.

Cahill, L., Prins, B., Weber, M., & McGaugh, J. L. (1994). β-adrenergic activation and memory for emotional events. *Nature, 371*, 702–704.

Calhoun, K. S., & Lima, P. P. (1977). Effects of varying schedules of timeout on high- and low-rate behaviors. *Journal of Behavior Therapy and Experimental Psychiatry, 8*, 189–194.

Campbell, B. A., & Kraeling, D. (1953). Response strength as a function of drive level and amount of drive reduction. *Journal of Experimental Psychology, 45*, 97–101.

Cantwell, D. P., & Baker, L. (1984). Research concerning families of children with autism. In E. Schopler & G. B. Mesibov (Eds.), *The effects of autism on the family* (pp. 41–63). New York: Plenum.

Carey, R. G., & Bucher, B. (1981). Identifying the educative and suppressive effects of positive practice and restitutional overcorrection. *Journal of Applied Behavioral Analysis, 14*, 71–80.

Carey, R. G., & Bucher, B. D. (1986). Positive practice overcorrection: Effects of reinforcing correct performance. *Behavior Modification, 10*, 73–92.

Carlson, C. R., & Hoyle, R. H. (1993). Efficacy of abbreviated progressive muscle relaxation training: A quantitative review of behavioral medicine research. *Journal of Consulting and Clinical Psychology, 61*, 1059–1067.

Carlson, C. S., Arnold, C. R., Becker, W. C., & Madsen, C. H. (1968). The elimination of tantrum behavior in a child in an elementary classroom. *Behaviour Research and Therapy, 6*, 117–119.

Carr, E. G. (1988). Functional equivalence as a mechanism of response generalization. In R. H. Horner, G. Dunlap, & R. L. Koegel (Eds.), *Generalization and maintenance: Lifestyle changes in applied settings* (pp. 221–241). Baltimore: Paul H. Brookes.

Carr, E. G., & Durand, V. M. (1985). Reducing behavior problems through functional communication training. *Journal of Applied Behavior Analysis, 18*, 111–126.

Carr, E. G., Taylor, J. C., & Robinson, S. (1991). The effects of severe behavior problems in children on the teaching behavior of adults. *Journal of Applied Behavior Analysis, 24*, 523–525.

Carr, J. E., & Burkholder, E. O. (1998). Creating single-subject design graphs with Microsoft Excel™. *Journal of Applied Behavior Analysis, 31*, 245–251.

Carson, T. P. (1986). Assessment of depression. In A. R. Ciminero, K. S. Calhoun, & K. E. Adams (Eds.), *Handbook of behavioral assessment* (2nd ed., pp. 404–445). New York: Wiley.

Carter, N., Holmström, A., Simpanen, M., & Melin, L. (1988). Theft reduction in a grocery store through product identification and graphing of losses for employees. *Journal of Applied Behavior Analysis, 21*, 385–389.

Catania, A. C., Matthews, B. A., & Shimoff, E. (1982). Instructed versus shaped human behavior: Interactions with nonverbal responding. *Journal of Applied Behavior Analysis, 38*, 233–248.

Caudill, B. D., & Lipscomb, T. R. (1980). Modeling influences on alcoholics' rates of alcohol consumption. *Journal of Applied Behavior Analysis, 13*, 355–365.

Cautela, J. R. (1966). Treatment of compulsive behavior by covert sensitization. *Psychological Record, 16*, 33–41.

Cautela, J. R. (1981). *Behavior analysis forms for clinical intervention* (Vol. 2). Champaign, IL: Research Press.

Cautela, J. R. (1993a). Covert conditioning: Assumptions and procedures. In J. R. Cautela & A. J. Kearney (Eds.), *Covert conditioning handbook* (pp. 3–9). Pacific Grove, CA: Brooks/Cole.

Cautela, J. R. (1993b). Insight in behavior therapy. *Journal of Behavior Therapy and Experimental Psychiatry, 24*, 155–159.

Cautela, J. R. (1993c). The use of covert conditioning in the treatment of a severe childhood phobia. In J. R. Cautela & A. J. Kearney (Eds.), *Covert conditioning handbook* (pp. 126–134). Pacific Grove, CA: Brooks/Cole.

Cautela, J. R., & Kastenbaum, R. (1967). A reinforcement survey schedule for use in therapy, training, and research. *Psychological Reports, 20*, 1115–1130.

Cautela, J. R., & Upper, D. (1975). The process of individual behavior therapy. In M. Hersen, R. M. Eisler, & P. M. Miller (Eds.), *Progress in behavior modification* (Vol. 1, pp. 276–305). New York: Academic Press.

Cautela, J. R., & Wisocki, P. A. (1977). The thought stopping procedure: Description, application, and learning theory interpretations. *Psychological Record, 2*, 255–264.

Chamberlain, P., & Reid, J. B. (1998). Comparison of two community alternatives to incarceration for chronic juvenile offenders. *Journal of Consulting and Clinical Psychology, 66*, 624–633.

Chambless, D. L., & Gillis, M. M. (1993). Cognitive therapy of anxiety disorders. *Journal of Consulting and Clinical Psychology, 61*, 248–260.

Charlop, M. H., Burgio, L. D., Iwata, B. A., & Ivancic, M. T. (1988). Stimulus variation as a means of enhancing punishment effects. *Journal of Applied Behavior Analysis, 21*, 89–95.

Christoff, K. A., & Kelly, J. A. (1985). A behavioral approach to social skills training. In L. L'Abate & M. A. Milan (Eds.), *Handbook of social skills training and research* (pp. 361–387). New York: Wiley.

Christophersen, E. R., Arnold, C. M., Hill, D. W., & Quilitch, H. R. (1972). The home point system: Token reinforcement procedures for application by parents of children with behavior problems. *Journal of Applied Behavior Analysis, 5*, 485–497.

Chung, S-H. (1965). Effects of delayed reinforcement in a concurrent situation. *Journal of the Experimental Analysis of Behavior, 8*, 439–444.

Ciminero, A. R. (1986). Behavioral assessment: An overview. In A. R. Ciminero, K. S. Calhoun, & H. E. Adams (Eds.), *Handbook of behavioral assessment* (2nd ed., pp. 3–11). New York: Wiley.

Clark, H. B., Greene, B. F., Macrae, J. W., McNees, M. P., Davis, J. L., & Risley, T. R. (1977). A parent advice package for family shopping trips: Development and evaluation. *Journal of Applied Behavior Analysis, 10*, 605–624.

Clark, H. B., Rowbury, T., Baer, A. M., & Baer, D. M. (1973). Timeout as a punishing stimulus in continuous and intermittent schedules. *Journal of Applied Behavior Analysis, 6*, 443–455.

Cohen, F., & Lazarus, R. S. (1979). Coping with the stresses of illness. In G. C. Stone, F. Cohen, & N. E. Adler (Eds.), *Health psychology—a handbook* (pp. 217–254). San Francisco: Jossey-Bass.

Cohen, R., De James, P., Nocera, B., & Ramberger, M. (1980). Application of a simple self-instruction procedure on adults' exercise and studying: Two case reports. *Psychological Reports, 46*, 443–451.

Cone, J. D. (1997). Issues in functional analysis in behavioral assessment. *Behaviour Research and Therapy, 35*, 259–275.

Conger, J. C., & Conger, A. J. (1986). Assessment of social skills. In A. R. Ciminero, K. S. Calhoun, & H. E. Adams (Eds.), *Handbook of behavioral assessment* (2nd ed., pp. 526–560). New York: Wiley.

Connors, G. J., Tarbox, A. R., & Faillace, L. A. (1992). Achieving and maintaining gains among problem drinkers: Process and outcome results. *Behavior Therapy, 23*, 449–474.

Cook, J. W., Altman, K., Shaw, J., & Blaylock, M. (1978). Use of contingent lemon juice to eliminate public masturbation. *Behaviour Research and Therapy, 16*, 131–134.

Cook, P. S., Petersen, R. C., & Moore, D. T. (1990). *Alcohol, tobacco, and other drugs may harm the unborn.* Rockville, MD: United States Department of Health and Human Services.

Cooke, T. P., & Apolloni, T. (1976). Developing positive social-emotional behaviors: A study of training and generalization effects. *Journal of Applied Behavior Analysis, 9,* 65–78.

Cooper, L. J., Wacker, D. P., Thursby, D., Plagmann, L. A., Harding, J., Millard, T., & Derby, M. (1992). Analysis of the effects of task preferences, task demands, and adult attention on child behavior in outpatient and classroom settings. *Journal of Applied Behavior Analysis, 25,* 823–840.

Correa, E. I., & Sutker, P. B. (1986). Assessment of alcohol and drug behaviors. In A. R. Ciminero, K. S. Calhoun, & K. E. Adams (Eds.), *Handbook of behavioral assessment* (2nd ed., pp. 446–495). New York: Wiley.

Corte, H. E., Wolfe, M. M., & Locke, B. J. (1971). A comparison of procedures for eliminating self-injurious behavior of retarded adolescents. *Journal of Applied Behavior Analysis, 4,* 201–213.

Craft, M. A., Alber, S. R., & Heward, W. L. (1998). Teaching elementary students with developmental disabilities to recruit teacher attention in a general education classroom: Effects on teacher praise and academic productivity. *Journal of Applied Behavior Analysis, 31,* 399–415.

Craighead, W. E., Evans, D. D., & Robins, C. J. (1992). Unipolar depression. In S. M. Turner, K. S. Calhoun, & H. E. Adams (Eds.), *Handbook of clinical behavior therapy* (2nd ed., pp. 99–116). New York: Wiley.

Creer, T. L., Chai, H., & Hoffman, A. (1977). A single application of an aversive stimulus to eliminate chronic cough. *Journal of Behavior Therapy and Experimental Psychiatry, 8,* 107–109.

Crespi, L. P. (1942). Quantitative variation of incentive and performance in the white rat. *American Journal of Psychology, 55,* 467–517.

Crowe, M. J., Marks, I. M., Agras, W. S., & Leitenberg, H. (1972). Time-limited desensitization, implosion and shaping for phobic patients: A crossover study. *Behaviour Research and Therapy, 10,* 319–328.

Cunningham, C. E., & Linscheid, T. R. (1976). Elimination of chronic infant ruminating by electric shock. *Behavior Therapy, 7,* 231–234.

Cunningham, C. L. (1998). Drug conditioning and drug-seeking behavior. In W. O'Donohue (Ed.), *Learning and behavior therapy* (pp. 518–544). Boston: Allyn & Bacon.

Dahlquist, L. M., & Gil, K. M. (1986). Using parents to maintain improved dental flossing skills in children. *Journal of Applied Behavior Analysis, 19,* 255–260.

Daniels, L. K. (1974). Rapid extinction of nail biting by covert sensitization: A case study. *Journal of Behavior Therapy and Experimental Psychiatry, 5,* 91–92.

Dasen, P. R., & Heron, A. (1981). Cross-cultural tests of Piaget's theory. In H. C. Triandis & A. Heron (Eds.), *Handbook of cross-cultural psychology: Developmental psychology* (Vol. 4, pp. 295–341). Boston: Allyn & Bacon.

Davey, G. C. L. (1992). An expectancy model of laboratory preparedness effects. *Journal of Experimental Psychology: General. 121,* 24–40.

Davey, G. C. L. (1994). Is evaluative conditioning a qualitatively distinct form of classical conditioning. *Behaviour Research and Therapy, 32,* 291–299.

Davey, G. C. L., McDonald, A. S., Hirisave, U., Prabhu, G. G., Iwawaki, S., Jim, C. I., Merckelbach, H., de Jong, P. J., Leung, P. W. L., & Reimann, B. C. (1998). A cross-cultural study of animal fears. *Behaviour Research and Therapy, 36,* 735–750.

Davison, G. C. (1976). Homosexuality: The ethical challenge. *Journal of Consulting and Clinical Psychology, 44,* 157–162.

Davison, G. C., & Neale, J. M. (1994). *Abnormal psychology* (6th ed.). New York: Wiley.

Dawson, B., de Armas, A., McGrath, M. L., & Kelly, J. A. (1986). Cognitive problem-solving training to improve the child-care judgment of child neglectful parents. *Journal of Family Violence, 3,* 209–221.

de Bruijn-Kofman, A. T., van de Wiel, H., Groenman, N. H., Sorbi, M. J., & Klip, E. (1997). Effects of a mass media behavioral treatment for chronic headache: A pilot study. *Headache, 37,* 415–420.

Deitz, S. M., & Malone, L. W. (1985). On terms: Stimulus control terminology. *Behavior Analyst, 8,* 259–264.

Deitz, S. M., Repp, A. C., & Deitz, D. E. D. (1976). Reducing inappropriate classroom behaviour of retarded students through three procedures of differential reinforcement. *Journal of Mental Deficiency Research, 20,* 155–170.

de Kinkelder, M., & Boelens, H. (1998). Habit-reversal treatment for children's stuttering: Assessment in three settings. *Journal of Behavior Therapy and Experimental Psychiatry, 29,* 261–265.

De Luca, R. V., & Holborn, S. W. (1992). Effects of a variable-ratio reinforcement schedule with changing criteria on exercise in obese and nonobese boys. *Journal of Applied Behavior Analysis, 25,* 671–679.

Demchak, M. (1990). Response prompting and fading methods: A review. *American Journal on Mental Retardation, 6,* 603–615.

DeRicco, D. A., & Niemann, J. E. (1980). In vivo effects of peer modeling on drinking rate. *Journal of Applied Behavior Analysis, 13,* 149–152.

DeRisi, W. J., & Butz, G. (1975). *Writing behavioral contracts: A case simulation practice manual.* Champaign, IL: Research Press.

DeRubeis, R. J., & Beck, A. T. (1988). Cognitive therapy. In K. S. Dobson (Ed.), *Handbook of cognitive-behavioral therapies* (pp. 273–306). New York: Guilford.

de Silva, P. (1984). Buddhism and behavior modification. *Behaviour Research and Therapy, 6,* 661–678.

de Silva, P. (1990). Buddhist psychology: A review of theory and practice. *Current Psychology: Research and Reviews*, 9, 236–254.

DeVries, J. E., Burnette, M. M., & Redmon, W. K. (1991). AIDS prevention: Improving nurses' compliance with glove wearing through performance feedback. *Journal of Applied Behavior Analysis*, 24, 705–711.

Dickerson, E. A., & Creedon, C. F. (1981). Self-selection of standards by children: The relative effectiveness of pupil-selected and teacher-selected standards of performance. *Journal of Applied Behavior Analysis*, 14, 425–433.

Dickinson, A. M. (1989). The detrimental effects of extrinsic reinforcement on "intrinsic motivation." *Behavior Analyst*, 12, 1–15.

DiClemente, C. C., Prochaska, J. O., Fairhurst, S. K., Velicer, W. F., Velasquez, M. M., & Rossi, J. S. (1991). The process of smoking cessation: An analysis of precontemplation, contemplation, and preparation stages of change. *Journal of Consulting and Clinical Psychology*, 59, 295–304.

DiClemente, C. C., Prochaska, J. O., & Gilbertini, M. (1985). Self-efficacy and the stages of change of smoking. *Cognitive Therapy and Research*, 9, 181–200.

Didden, R., Duker, P. C., & Korzilius, H. (1997). Meta-analytic study on treatment effectiveness for problem behaviors with individuals who have mental retardation. *American Journal of Mental Retardation*, 101, 387–399.

Dinsmoor, J. A. (1998). Punishment. In W. O'Donohue (Ed.), *Learning and behavior therapy* (pp. 188–204). Boston: Allyn & Bacon.

Dishion, T. J., & Andrews, D. W. (1995). Preventing escalation in problem behaviors with high-risk young adolescents: Immediate and 1-year outcomes. *Journal of Consulting and Clinical Psychology*, 63, 538–548.

Dishion, T. J., McCord, J., & Poulin, F. (1999). When interventions harm: Peer groups and problem behavior. *American Psychologist*, 54, 755–764.

Dobson, K. S. (1989). A meta-analysis of the efficacy of cognitive therapy for depression. *Journal of Consulting and Clinical Psychology*, 57, 414–419.

Dobson, K. S., & Block, L. (1988). Historical and philosophical bases of the cognitive-behavioral therapies. In K. S. Dobson (Ed.), *Handbook of cognitive-behavioral therapies* (pp. 3–38). New York: Guilford.

Dodge, K. A. (1993). Social-cognitive mechanisms in the development of conduct disorder and depression. *Annual Review of Psychology*, 44, 559–584.

Dodge, K. A., & Frame, C. L. (1982). Social cognitive biases and deficits in aggressive boys. *Child Development*, 53, 620–635.

Doleys, D. M. (1977). Behavioral treatments for nocturnal enuresis in children: A review of the recent literature. *Psychological Bulletin*, 84, 30–54.

Doleys, D. M., Wells, K. C., Hobbs, S. A., Roberts, M. W., & Cartelli, L. M. (1976). The effects of social punishment on noncompliance: A comparison with timeout and positive practice. *Journal of Applied Behavior Analysis*, 9, 471–482.

Donahue, J. A., Gillis, J. H., & King, K. (1980). Behavior modification in sport and physical education: A review. *Journal of Sport Psychology*, 2, 311–328.

Donnellan, A. M., & LaVigna, G. W. (1990). Myths about punishment. In A. C. Repp & N. N. Singh (Eds.), *Perspectives on the use of nonaversive and aversive interventions for persons with developmental disabilities* (pp. 33–58). Sycamore, IL: Sycamore.

Doogan, S., & Thomas, G. V. (1992). Origins of fear of dogs in adults and children: The role of conditioning processes and prior familiarity with dogs. *Behaviour Research and Therapy*, 30, 387–394.

Dorsey, M. F., Iwata, B. A., Ong, P., & McSween, T. E. (1980). Treatment of self-injurious behavior using a water mist: Initial response suppression and generalization. *Journal of Applied Behavior Analysis*, 13, 343–353.

Dougherty, B. S., Fowler, S. A., & Paine, S. C. (1985). The use of peer monitors to reduce negative interaction during recess. *Journal of Applied Behavior Analysis*, 18, 141–153.

Dowrick, P. W. (1991). Analyzing and documenting. In P. W. Dowrick (Ed.), *Practical guide to using video in the behavioral sciences* (pp. 30–48). New York: Wiley.

Dowrick, P. W., & Jesdale, D. C. (1991). Modeling. In P. W. Dowrick (Ed.), *Practical guide to using video in the behavioral sciences* (pp. 64–76). New York: Wiley.

Drummond, D. C., & Glautier, S. (1994). A controlled trial of cue-exposure treatment in alcohol dependence. *Journal of Consulting and Clinical Psychology*, 62, 809–818.

Ducharme, J. M., & Feldman, M. A. (1992). Comparison of staff training strategies to promote generalized teaching skills. *Journal of Applied Behavior Analysis*, 25, 165–179.

Dunlap, G., & Plienis, A. J. (1988). Generalization and maintenance of unsupervised responding via remote contingencies. In R. H. Horner, G. Dunlap, & R. L. Koegel (Eds.), *Generalization and maintenance: Life-style changes in applied settings* (pp. 121–142). Baltimore: Paul H. Brooks.

Durand, V. M., & Carr, E. G. (1991). Functional communication training to reduce challenging behavior: Maintenance and application in new settings. *Journal of Applied Behavior Analysis*, 24, 251–264.

Durlak, J. A., Fuhrman, T., & Lampman, C. (1991). Effectiveness of cognitive-behavior therapy for maladapting children: A meta-analysis. *Psychological Bulletin*, 110, 204–214.

Dush, D. M., Hirt, M. L., & Schroeder, H. (1983). Self-statement modification with adults: A meta-analysis. *Psychological Bulletin*, 94, 408–422.

D'Zurilla, T. J. (1988). Problem-solving therapies. In K. S. Dobson (Ed.), *Handbook of cognitive-behavioral therapies* (pp. 85–135). New York: Guilford.

D'Zurilla, T. J., & Goldfried, M. R. (1971). Problem solving and behavior modification. *Journal of Abnormal Psychology*, 78, 107–126.

D'Zurilla, T. J., & Nezu, A. (1982). Social problem solving in adults. In P. C. Kendall (Ed.), *Advances in cognitive-behavioral research and therapy* (Vol. 1, pp. 201–274). New York: Academic Press.

Edelbrock, C. (1984). Developmental considerations. In T. H. Ollendick & M. Hersen (Eds.), *Child behavioral assessment: Principles and procedures* (pp. 20–37). New York: Pergamon.

EFA (Epilepsy Foundation of America). (1990). *Epilepsy: You and your child.* Landover, MD: Author.

Eimas, P. D. (1970). Information processing in problem solving as a function of developmental level and stimulus saliency. *Developmental Psychology, 2*, 224–230.

Eisenberger, R., & Cameron, J. (1996). Detrimental effects of reward: Reality or myth? *American Psychologist, 51*, 1153–1166.

Elkins, R. L. (1991). An appraisal of chemical aversion (emetic therapy) approaches to alcoholism treatment. *Behaviour Research and Therapy, 29*, 387–413.

Elliott, S. N. (1988). Acceptability of behavioral treatments: Review of variables that influence treatment selection. *Professional Psychology: Research and Practice, 19*, 68–80.

Ellis, A. (1962). *Reason and emotion in psychotherapy.* New York: Lyle Stewart.

Ellis, A. (1977). The basic clinical theory of rational-emotive therapy. In A. Ellis & R. Grieger (Eds.), *Handbook of rational-emotive therapy* (pp. 3–34). New York: Springer.

Ellis, A. (1987). The impossibility of achieving consistently good mental health. *American Psychologist, 42*, 364–375.

Ellis, A. (1993). Reflections on rational-emotive therapy. *Journal of Consulting and Clinical Psychology, 61*, 199–201.

Ellis, A., & Dryden, W. (1987). *The practice of rational-emotive therapy.* New York: Springer.

Emmelkamp, P. M. G., Bouman, T. K., & Scholing, A. (1992). *Anxiety disorders: A practitioner's guide.* Chichester, UK: Wiley.

Emshoff, J. G., Redd, W. H., & Davidson, W. S. (1976). Generalization training and the transfer of prosocial behavior in delinquent adolescents. *Journal of Behavior Therapy and Experimental Psychiatry, 7*, 141–144.

Engel, G. L. (1977) The need for a new medical model: A challenge for biomedicine. *Science, 196*, 129–136.

Engel, G. L. (1980). The clinical application of the biopsychosocial model. *American Journal of Psychiatry, 137*, 535–544.

Engels, G. I., Garnefski, N., & Diekstra, R. F. W. (1993). Efficacy of rational-emotive therapy: A quantitative analysis. *Journal of Consulting and Clinical Psychology, 61*, 1083–1090.

Epstein, L. H. (1992). Role of behavior theory in behavioral medicine. *Journal of Consulting and Clinical Psychology, 60*, 493–498.

Erhardt, D., & Baker, B. L. (1990). The effects of behavioral parent training on families with young hyperactive children. *Journal of Behavior Therapy and Experimental Psychiatry, 21*, 121–132.

Evans, I. M., & Nelson, R. O. (1986). Assessment of children. In A. R. Ciminero, K. S. Calhoun, & H. E. Adams (Eds.), *Handbook of behavioral assessment* (2nd ed., pp. 601–630). New York: Wiley.

Fantuzzo, J. W., & Clement, P. W. (1981). Generalization of the effects of teacher- and self-administered token reinforcers to nontreated students. *Journal of Applied Behavior Analysis, 14*, 435–447.

Favell, J. E., McGimsey, J. F., & Jones, M. L. (1978). The use of physical restraint in the treatment of self-injury and as positive reinforcement. *Journal of Applied Behavior Analysis, 11*, 225–241.

Favell, J. E., & Reid, D. H. (1988). Generalizing and maintaining improvement in problem behavior. In R. H. Horner, G. Dunlap, & R. L. Koegel (Eds.), *Generalization and maintenance: Life-style changes in applied settings* (pp. 171–196). Baltimore: Paul H. Brooks.

Fawcett, S. B., & Miller, L. K. (1975). Training public-speaking behavior: An experimental analysis and social validation. *Journal of Applied Behavior Analysis, 8*, 125–135.

Feeney, E. J. (1972, November). Performance audit, feedback and positive reinforcement. *Training and Development Journal,* 8–13.

Feindler, E. L., Marriott, S. A., & Iwata, M. (1984). Group anger control training for junior high school delinquents. *Cognitive Therapy and Research, 8*, 299–311.

Feldman, M. A., Case, L., Garrick, M., MacIntyre-Grande, W., Carnwell, J., & Sparks, B. (1992). Teaching child-care skills to mothers with developmental disabilities. *Journal of Applied Behavior Analysis, 25*, 205–215.

Fernandez, E. (1986). A classification system of cognitive coping strategies for pain. *Pain, 26*, 141–151.

Field, D. (1981). Can preschool children really learn to conserve? *Child Development, 52*, 326–334.

Finney, J. W., Rapoff, M. A., Hall, C. L., & Christophersen, E. R. (1983). Replication and social validation of habit reversal for tics. *Behavior Therapy, 14*, 116–126.

Fischer, J., & Nehs, R. (1978). Use of a commonly available chore to reduce a boy's rate of swearing. *Journal of Behavior Therapy and Experimental Psychiatry, 9*, 81–83.

Fiske, D. W., & Maddi, S. R. (1961). A conceptual framework. In D. W. Fiske & S. R. Maddi (Eds.), *Functions of varied experience.* Homewood, IL: Dorsey.

Fitzgerald, R. D., & Martin, G. K. (1971). Heart-rate conditioning in rats as a function of interstimulus interval. *Psychological Reports, 29*, 1103–1110.

Fixsen, D. L., Phillips, E. L., Baron, R. L., Coughlin, D. D., Daly, D. L., & Daly, P. B. (1978, November). The Boy's Town revolution. *Human Nature,* 54–61.

Flaherty, C. F., & Caprio, M. (1976). Dissociation between instrumental and consummatory measures of incentive contrast. *American Journal of Psychology, 89*, 485–498.

Flay, B. R., Koepke, D., Thomson, S. J., Santi, S., Best, A., & Brown, K. S. (1989). Six-year follow-up of the first Waterloo school smoking prevention trial. *American Journal of Public Health, 79,* 1371–1376.

Flora, S. R. (1990). Undermining intrinsic interest from the standpoint of a behaviorist. *Psychological Record, 40,* 323–346.

Fogel, E. R. (1987). Biofeedback-assisted musculoskeletal therapy and neuromuscular re-education. In M. S. Schwartz (Ed.), *Biofeedback: A practitioner's guide* (pp. 377–409). New York: Guilford.

Foster, S. L., & Cone, J. D. (1986). Design and use of direct observation procedures. In A. R. Ciminero, K. S. Calhoun, & H. E. Adams (Eds.), *Handbook of behavioral assessment* (2nd ed., pp. 253–324). New York: Wiley.

Foster, S. L., & Mash, E. J. (1999). Assessing social validity in clinical treatment research: Issues and procedures. *Journal of Consulting and Clinical Psychology, 67,* 309–319.

Fowler, S. A. (1988). The effects of peer-mediated interventions on establishing, maintaining, and generalizing children's behavior changes. In R. H. Horner, G. Dunlap, & R. L. Koegel (Eds.), *Generalization and maintenance: Life-style changes in applied settings* (pp. 143–170). Baltimore: Paul H. Brookes.

Fowler, S. A., & Baer, D. M. (1981). "Do I have to be good all day?": The timing of delayed reinforcement as a factor in generalization. *Journal of Applied Behavior Analysis, 14,* 13–24.

Fowler, S. A., Dougherty, B. S., Kirby, K. C., & Kohler, F. W. (1986). Role reversals: An analysis of therapeutic effects achieved with disruptive boys during their appointments as peer monitors. *Journal of Applied Behavior Analysis, 19,* 437–444.

Fox, D. K., Hopkins, B. L., & Anger, W. K. (1987). The long-term effects of a token economy on safety performance in open-pit mining. *Journal of Applied Behavior Analysis, 20,* 215–224.

Foxx, R. M., & Azrin, N. H. (1972). Restitution: A method of eliminating aggressive-disruptive behaviors of retarded and brain damaged patients. *Behaviour Research and Therapy, 10,* 15–27.

Foxx, R. M., Faw, G. D., & Weber, G. (1991). Producing generalization of inpatient adolescents' social skills with significant adults in a natural environment. *Behavior Therapy, 22,* 85–99.

Foxx, R. M., & Schaeffer, M. H. (1981). A company-based lottery to reduce the personal driving of employees. *Journal of Applied Behavior Analysis, 14,* 273–285.

Foxx, R. M., & Shapiro, S. T. (1978). The timeout ribbon: A nonexclusionary timeout procedure. *Journal of Applied Behavior Analysis, 11,* 125–136.

France, K. G., & Hudson, S. M. (1990). Behavior management of infant sleep disturbance. *Journal of Applied Behavior Analysis, 23,* 91–98.

Frankel, F. (1993). A brief test of parental behavioral skills. *Journal of Behavior Therapy and Experimental Psychiatry, 24,* 227–231.

Franks, I, M., & Maile, L. J. (1991). The use of video in sport skill acquisition. In P. W. Dowrick (Ed.), *Practical guide to using video in the behavioral sciences* (pp. 231–243). New York: Wiley.

Frederiksen, L. W. (1975). Treatment of ruminative thinking by self-monitoring. *Journal of Behavior Therapy and Experimental Psychiatry, 6,* 258–259.

Frederiksen, L. W., Jenkins, J. O., Foy, D. W., & Eisler, R. M. (1976). Social skills training to modify abusive verbal outbursts in adults. *Journal of Applied Behavior Analysis, 9,* 117–125.

Frederiksen, L. W., & Lovett, S. B. (1980). Inside organizational behavior management: Perspectives on an emerging field. *Journal of Organizational Management, 2,* 193–203.

Freeman, A. (1990). Cognitive therapy. In A. S. Bellack & M. Hersen (Eds.), *Handbook of comparative treatments for adult disorders* (pp. 64–87). New York: Wiley.

Freud, S. (1933). *New introductory lectures in psychoanalysis* (W. J. H. Sprott, trans.). New York: Norton.

Freud, S. (1949). *An outline of psychoanalysis* (J. Strachey, trans.). New York: Norton.

Friedman, A. G., Campbell, T. A., & Evans, I. M. (1993). Multi-dimensional child behavior therapy in the treatment of medically-related anxiety: A practical illustration. *Journal of Behavior Therapy and Experimental Psychiatry, 24,* 241–247.

Friedrich-Cofer, L., & Huston, A. C. (1986). Television violence and aggression: The debate continues. *Psychological Bulletin, 100,* 364–371.

Friman, P. C., & Altman, K. (1990). Parent use of DRI on high rate disruptive behavior: direct and collateral benefits. *Research on Developmental Disabilities, 11,* 249–254.

Gagné, R. M. (1985). *The conditions of learning and theory of instruction* (4th ed.). New York: Holt, Rinehart & Winston.

Gagnon, M., & Ladouceur, R. (1992) Behavioral treatment of child stutterers: Replication and extension. *Behavior Therapy, 23,* 113–129.

Galassi, J. P., DeLo, J. S., Galassi, M. D., & Bastien, S. (1974). The College Self-Expression Scale: A measure of assertiveness. *Behavior Therapy, 5,* 165–171.

Gambrill, E. D., & Richey, C. A. (1975). An assertion inventory for use in assessment and research. *Behavior Therapy, 6,* 550–561.

Garcia, J., Ervin, F. R., & Koelling, R. A. (1966). Learning with prolonged delay of reinforcement. *Psychonomic Science, 5,* 121–122.

Garcia, J., Hankins, W. G., & Rusiniak, K. W. (1974). Behavioral regulation on the milieu interne in man and rat. *Science, 185,* 824–831.

Garcia, J., & Koelling, R. A. (1966). Relation of cue to consequence in avoidance learning. *Psychonomic Science, 4*, 123–124.

Garfield, S. L. (1986). Research on client variables in psychotherapy. In S. L. Garfield & A. E. Bergin (Eds.), *Handbook of psychotherapy and behavior change* (3rd ed., pp. 191–232). New York: Wiley.

Garnets, L., & Kimmel, D. (1991). Lesbian and gay male dimensions in the psychological study of human diversity. In J. D. Goodchilds (Ed.), *Psychological perspectives on human diversity in America* (pp. 143–189). Washington, DC: American Psychological Association.

Gatchel, R. J. (1982). EMG biofeedback in anxiety reduction. In L. White & B. Tursky (Eds.), *Clinical biofeedback: Efficacy and mechanisms* (pp. 372–396). New York: Guilford.

Gauthier, J., Coté, G., & French, D. (1994). The role of home practice in the thermal biofeedback treatment of migraine headache. *Journal of Consulting and Clinical Psychology, 62*, 180–184.

Gelfand, D. M., Hartmann, D. P., Lamb, A. K., Smith, C. L., Mahan, M. A., & Paul, S. C. (1974). The effects of adult models and described alternatives on children's choice of behavior management techniques. *Child Development, 45*, 585–593.

Geller, E. S., Bruff, C. D., & Nimmer, J. G. (1985). "Flash for Life": Community-based prompting for safety belt promotion. *Journal of Applied Behavior Analysis, 18*, 309–314.

Gelman, R., & Baillargeon, R. (1983). A review of some Piagetian concepts. In P. H. Mussen (Ed.), *Handbook of child psychology* (4th ed., Vol. 3, pp. 167–230). New York: Wiley.

Gibson, E. J., & Levin, H. (1975). *The psychology of reading*. Cambridge, MA: MIT Press.

Glynn, S. M. (1990). Token economy approaches for psychiatric patients: Progress and pitfalls over 25 years. *Behavior Modification, 14*, 383–407.

Goetz, E. M., & Baer, D. M. (1973). Social control of form diversity and the emergence of new forms in children's blockbuilding. *Journal of Applied Behavior Analysis, 6*, 209–217.

Goldiamond, I. (1965). Self-control procedures in personal behavior problems. *Psychological Reports, 17*, 851–868.

Goldiamond, I. (1974). Toward a constructional approach to social problems: Ethical and constitutional issues raised by applied behavior analysis. *Behaviorism, 2*, 1–84.

Goldfried, M. R., & Castonguay, L. G. (1993). Behavior therapy: Redefining strengths and limitations. *Behavior Therapy, 24*, 505–526.

Goldstein, I. B., Jamner, L. D., & Shapiro, D. (1992). Ambulatory blood pressure and heart rate in healthy male paramedics during a workday and a nonworkday. *Health Psychology, 11*, 48–54.

Goldstein, L. H. (1990). Behavioural and cognitive-behavioural treatments for epilepsy: A progress review. *British Journal of Clinical Psychology, 29*, 257–269.

Goodman, W. (1994, March 20). A few scary pictures can go a long way. *New York Times*, pp. 28, 34.

Goodwin, C. J. (1995). *Research in psychology: Methods and design*. New York: Wiley.

Goodwin, D. W. (1986). Heredity and alcoholism. *Annals of Behavioral Medicine, 8*(2–3), 3–6.

Gormally, J., Black, S., Daston, S., & Rardin, D. (1982). The assessment of binge eating severity among obese persons. *Addictive Behaviors, 7*, 47–55.

Gossette, R. L., & O'Brien, R. M. (1993). Efficacy of rational-emotive therapy (RET) with children: A critical reappraisal. *Journal of Behavior Therapy and Experimental Psychiatry, 24*, 15–25.

Grace, N. C., Kahng, S. W., & Fisher, W. W. (1994). Balancing social acceptability with treatment effectiveness of an intrusive procedure: A case report. *Journal of Applied Behavior Analysis, 27*, 171–172.

Graham, J., & Gaffan, E. A. (1997). Fear of water in children and adults: Etiology and familial effects. *Behaviour Research and Therapy, 35*, 91–108.

Granlund, B., Brulin, C., Johansson, H., & Sojka, P. (1998). Can motivational factors predict adherence to an exercise program for subjects with low back pain? *Scandinavian Journal of Behaviour Therapy, 27*, 81–96.

Green, C. W., Reid, D. H., Canipe, V. S., & Gardner, S. M. (1991). A comprehensive evaluation of reinforcer identification processes for persons with profound multiple handicaps. *Journal of Applied Behavior Analysis, 24*, 537–552.

Green, C. W., Reid, D. H., White, L. K., Halford, R. C., Brittain, D. P., & Gardner, S. M. (1988). Identifying reinforcers for persons with profound handicaps: Staff opinion versus systematic assessment of preferences. *Journal of Applied Behavior Analysis, 21*, 31–43.

Green, G. (1990). Least restrictive use of reductive procedures: Guidelines and competencies. In A. C. Repp & N. N. Singh (Eds.), *Perspectives on the use of nonaversive and aversive interventions for persons with developmental disabilities* (pp. 479–494). Sycamore, IL: Sycamore.

Greene, P. G., Seime, R. J., & Smith, M. E. (1991). Distraction and relaxation training in the treatment of anticipatory vomiting: A single subject intervention. *Journal of Behavior Therapy and Experimental Psychiatry, 22*, 285–290.

Greenspoon, J. (1955). The reinforcing effect of two spoken sounds on the frequency of two responses. *American Journal of Psychology, 68*, 409–416.

Greenwood, C. R., Carta, J. J., & Kamps, D. (1990). Teacher-mediated versus peer-mediated instruction: A review of educational advantages and disadvantages. In H. C. Foot,

M. J. Morgan, & R. H. Shute (Eds.), *Children helping children* (pp. 177–205). Chichester, UK: Wiley.

Greenwood, C. R., & Hops, H. (1981). Group-oriented contingencies and peer behavior change. In P. S. Strain (Ed.), *The utilization of classroom peers as behavior change agents* (pp. 189–259). New York: Plenum.

Greenwood, C. R., Hops, H., Delquadri, J., & Guild, J. (1974). Group contingencies for group consequences in classroom management: A further analysis. *Journal of Applied Behavior Analysis, 7,* 413–425.

Greer, R. D., & Polirstok, S. R. (1982). Collateral gains and short-term maintenance in reading and on-task responses by inner-city adolescents as a function of their use of social reinforcement while tutoring. *Journal of Applied Behavior Analysis, 15,* 123–139.

Griffen, A. K., Wolery, M., & Schuster, J. W. (1992). Triadic instruction of chained food preparation responses: Acquisition and observational learning. *Journal of Applied Behavior Analysis, 25,* 193–204.

Griffin, D. E., & Watson, D. L. (1978). A written, personal commitment from the student encourages better course work. *Teaching of Psychology, 5,* 155.

Groden, G. (1989). A guide for conducting a comprehensive behavioral analysis of a target behavior. *Journal of Behavior Therapy and Experimental Psychiatry, 20,* 163–169.

Groden, G., Stevenson, S., & Groden, J. (1996). *Understanding challenging behavior: A step-by-step behavior analysis guide.* Worthington, OH: IDS Publishing.

Gross, A. M. (1984). Behavioral interviewing. In T. H. Ollendick & M. Hersen (Eds.), *Child behavioral assessment: Principles and procedures* (pp. 61–79). New York: Pergamon.

Gross, A. M., & Drabman, R. S. (1982). Teaching self-recording, self-evaluation, and self-reward to nonclinic children and adolescents. In P. Karoly & F. H. Kanfer (Eds.), *Self-management and behavior change: From theory to practice* (pp. 285–314). New York: Pergamon.

Guess, D., Sailor, W., Rutherford, G., & Baer, D. M. (1968). An experimental analysis of linguistic development: The productive use of the plural morpheme. *Journal of Applied Behavior Analysis, 1,* 297–306.

Guess, D., Turnbull, H. R., & Helmstetter, E. (1990). Science, paradigms, and values: A response to Mulick. *American Journal on Mental Retardation, 95,* 157–163.

Guevremont, D. C., Osnes, P. G., & Stokes, T. F. (1988). The functional role of preschoolers' verbalizations in the generalization of self-instructional training. *Journal of Applied Behavior Analysis, 21,* 45–55.

Haaga, D. A. F., & Davison, G. C. (1989). Slow progress in rational-emotive therapy outcome research: Etiology and treatment. *Cognitive Therapy and Research, 13,* 493–508.

Haaga, D. A. F., & Davison, G. C. (1993). An appraisal of rational-emotive therapy. *Journal of Consulting and Clinical Psychology, 61,* 215–220.

Haaga, D. A. F., DeRubeis, R. J., Stewart, B. L., & Beck, A. T. (1991). Relationship of intelligence with cognitive therapy outcome. *Behaviour Research and Therapy, 29,* 277–281.

Hackman, A., & McClean, C. (1975). A comparison of flooding and thought stopping in the treatment of obsessional neurosis. *Behaviour Research and Therapy, 13,* 263–269.

Hains, A. H., & Baer, D. M. (1989). Interaction effects in multielement designs: Inevitable, desirable, and ignorable. *Journal of Applied Behavior Analysis, 22,* 57–69.

Halas, E. S., & Eberhardt, M. J. (1987). Blocking and appetitive reinforcement. *Bulletin of the Psychonomic Society, 25,* 121–123.

Haldeman, D. C. (1994). The practice and ethics of sexual orientation conversion therapy. *Journal of Consulting and Clinical Psychology, 62,* 221–227.

Hall, R. V., Axelrod, S., Foundopoulos, M., Shellman, J., Campbell, R. A., & Cranston, S. S. (1971). The effective use of punishment to modify behavior in the classroom. *Educational Technology, 11,* 24–26.

Hamilton, M., & Matson, J. L. (1992). Mental retardation. In S. M. Turner, K. S. Calhoun, & H. E. Adams (Eds.), *Handbook of clinical behavior therapy* (2nd ed., pp. 317–336). New York: Wiley.

Hamilton, S. B. (1980). Instructionally-based training in self-control: Behavior-specific and generalized outcomes resulting from student-implemented self-modification projects. *Teaching of Psychology, 7,* 140–145.

Harchik, A. E., Sherman, J. A., Sheldon, J. B., & Strouse, M. C. (1992). Ongoing consultation as a method of improving performance of staff members in a group home. *Journal of Applied Behavior Analysis, 25,* 599–610.

Haring, T. G., & Kennedy, C. H. (1990). Contextual control of problem behavior in students with severe disabilities. *Journal of Applied Behavior Analysis, 23,* 235–243.

Harris, C. L., & McReynolds, W. T. (1977). Semantic cues and response contingencies in self-instructional control. *Journal of Behavior Therapy and Experimental Psychiatry, 8,* 15–17.

Harris, F. R., Wolf, M. M., & Baer, D. M. (1964). Effects of adult social reinforcement on child behavior. *Young Children, 20,* 8–17.

Harris, V. W., & Sherman, J. A. (1973). Use and analysis of the "good behavior game" to reduce disruptive classroom behavior. *Journal of Applied Behavior Analysis, 6,* 405–417.

Hart, W. (1987). *The art of living: Vipassana meditation.* New York: HarperCollins.

Hartley, E. T., Bray, M. A., & Kehle, T. J. (1998). Self-modeling as an intervention to increase student classroom participation. *Psychology in the Schools, 35,* 363–372.

Hawkins, R. C., & Clement, P. F. (1980). Development and construct validation of a self-report measure of binge eating tendencies. *Addictive Behaviors, 5,* 219–226.

Hawkins, R. P., & Dotson, V. A. (1975). Reliability scores that delude: An Alice in Wonderland trip through the misleading characteristics of interobserver agreement scores in interval recording. In E. Ramp & G. Semb (Eds.), *Behavior analysis: Areas of research application* (pp. 359–376). Englewood Cliffs, NJ: Prentice-Hall.

Hayes, S. C., Brownell, K. D., & Barlow, D. H. (1978). The use of self-administered covert sensitization in the treatment of exhibitionism and sadism. *Behavior Therapy, 9,* 283–289.

Hayes, S. C., Brownstein, A. J., Zettle, R. D., Rosenfarb, I., & Korn, Z. (1986). Rule-governed behavior and sensitivity to changing consequences of responding. *Journal of Applied Behavior Analysis, 45,* 237–256.

Hayes, S. C., Rosenfarb, I., Wulfert, E., Munt, E. D., Korn, Z., & Zettle, R. D. (1985). Self-reinforcement effects: Artifact of social standard setting? *Journal of Applied Behavior Analysis, 18,* 201–214.

Heaton, R. C., & Safer, D. J. (1982). Secondary school outcome following a junior high school behavioral program. *Behavior Therapy, 13,* 226–231.

Heffernan, T., & Richards, C. S. (1981). Self-control of study behavior: Identification and evaluation of natural methods. *Journal of Counseling Psychology, 28,* 361–364.

Hegel, M. T., Ayllon, T., VanderPlate, C., & Spiro-Hawkins, H. (1986). A behavioral procedure for increasing compliance with self-exercise regimens in severely burn-injured patients. *Behaviour Research and Therapy, 24,* 521–528.

Heimberg, R. G. (1990). Cognitive behavior therapy. In A. S. Bellack & M. Hersen (Eds.), *Handbook of comparative treatments for adult disorders* (pp. 203–218). New York: Wiley.

Herbert, B. (1997, December 14). The success taboo. *New York Times,* p. WK13.

Hermann, J. A., de Montes, A. I., Domínguez, B., Montes, F., & Hopkins, B. L. (1973). Effects of bonuses for punctuality on the tardiness of industrial workers. *Journal of Applied Behavior Analysis, 6,* 563–570.

Herrnstein, R. J. (1969). Method and theory in the study of avoidance. *Psychological Review, 76,* 49–69.

Hersen, M., Eisler, R. M., & Miller, P. M. (1974). An experimental analysis of generalization in assertive training. *Behaviour Research and Therapy, 12,* 295–310.

Hersen, M., Kazdin, A. E., Bellack, A. S., & Turner, S. M. (1979). Effects of live modeling, covert modeling, and rehearsal on assertiveness in psychiatric patients. *Behaviour Research and Therapy, 17,* 369–377.

Hildebrand, R. G., Martin, G. L., Furer, P., & Hazen, A. (1990). A recruitment-of-praise package to increase pro-ductivity levels of developmentally handicapped workers. *Behavior Modification, 14,* 97–113.

Hilliard, R. B. (1993). Single-case methodology in psychotherapy process and outcome research. *Journal of Consulting and Clinical Psychology, 61,* 373–380.

Hinson, R. E., Poulos, C. X., & Cappell, H. (1982). Effects of pentobarbital and cocaine in rats expecting pentobarbital. *Pharmacology Biochemistry and Behavior, 16,* 661–666.

Hollis, K. L. (1997). Contemporary research on Pavlovian conditioning: A "new" functional analysis. *American Psychologist, 52,* 956–965.

Hollon, S. D., Shelton, R. C., & Davis, D. D. (1993). Cognitive therapy for depression: Conceptual issues and clinical efficacy. *Journal of Consulting and Clinical Psychology, 61,* 270–275.

Holmes, D. L. (1977). *Troubleshooting Checklist and Procedure.* (Materials produced by Eden Institute, Princeton, NJ).

Holmes, D. S. (1984). Meditation and somatic arousal reduction. *American Psychologist, 39,* 1–10.

Holroyd, K. A., & Penzien, D. B. (1985). Client variables and the behavioral treatment of recurrent tension headache: A meta-analytic review. *Journal of Behavioral Medicine, 9,* 515–536.

Homme, L. E. (1965). Perspectives in psychology: XXIV. Control of coverants, the operants of the mind. *Psychological Record, 15,* 501–511.

Homme, L. E. (1971). *How to use contingency contracting in the classroom.* Champaign, IL: Research Press.

Honeybourne, C., Matchett, G., & Davey, G. C. L. (1993). Expectancy models of laboratory preparedness effects: A UCS-expectancy bias in phylogenetic and ontogenetic fear-relevant stimuli. *Behavior Therapy, 24,* 253–264.

Hopkins, B. L., Conrad, R. J., Dangel, R. F., Fitch, H. G., Smith, M. J., & Anger, W. K. (1986). Behavioral technology for reducing occupational exposures to styrene. *Journal of Applied Behavior Analysis, 19,* 3–11.

Horan, J. J., & Johnson, R. G. (1971). Covert conditioning through a self-management application of the Premack principle: Its effect on weight reduction. *Journal of Behavior Therapy and Experimental Psychiatry, 2,* 243–249.

Horner, R. H., Eberhard, J. M., & Sheenan, M. R. (1986). Teaching generalized table bussing: The importance of negative teaching examples. *Behavior Modification, 10,* 457–471.

Horner, R. A., Williams, J. A., & Knobbe, C. A. (1985). The effect of "opportunity to perform" on the maintenance of skills learned by high school students with severe handicaps. *Journal of the Association for Persons with Severe Handicaps, 10,* 172–175.

Houts, A. C., Berman, J. S., & Abramson, H. (1994). Effectiveness of psychological and pharmacological treatments for nocturnal enuresis. *Journal of Consulting and Clinical Psychology, 62*, 737–745.

Hugdahl, K., & Öhman, A. (1977). Effects of instruction on acquisition and extinction of electrodermal responses to fear-relevant stimuli. *Journal of Experimental Psychology: Human Learning and Memory, 3*, 608–618.

Hull, C. L. (1943). *Principles of behavior.* New York: Appleton-Century-Crofts.

Hundert, J., & Batstone, D. (1978). A practical procedure to maintain pupil's accurate self-rating in a classroom token program. *Behavior Modification, 2*, 93–112.

Hunt, G. M., & Azrin, N. H. (1973). A community-reinforcement approach to alcoholism. *Behaviour Research and Therapy, 11*, 91–104.

Hutchinson, R. R. (1977). By-products of aversive control. In W. K. Honig & J. E. R. Staddon (Eds.), *Handbook of operant behavior* (pp. 415–431). Englewood Cliffs, NJ: Prentice-Hall.

Irvin, J. E., Bowers, C. A., Dunn, M. E., & Wang, M. C. (1999). Efficacy of relapse prevention: A meta-analytic review. *Journal of Consulting and Clinical Psychology, 67*, 563–570.

Isaacs, W., Thomas, J., & Goldiamond, I. (1960). Application of operant conditioning to reinstate verbal behavior in psychotics. *Journal of Speech and Hearing Disorders, 25*, 8–12.

Iwata, B. A., Dorsey, M. F., Slifer, K. J., Bauman, K. E., & Richman, G. S. (1982). Toward a functional analysis of self-injury. *Analysis and Intervention of Developmental Disabilities, 2*, 3–20.

Iwata, B. A., Pace, G. M., Cowdery, G. E., & Miltenberger, R. G. (1994). What makes extinction work: An analysis of procedural form and function. *Journal of Applied Behavior Analysis, 27*, 131–144.

Iwata, B. A., Pace, G. M., Kalsher, M. J., Cowdery, G. E., & Cataldo, M. F. (1990). Experimental analysis and extinction of self-injurious escape behavior. *Journal of Applied Behavior Analysis, 23*, 11–27.

Jackson, D. A., & Wallace, R. F. (1974). The modification and generalization of voice loudness in a fifteen-year-old retarded girl. *Journal of Applied Behavior Analysis, 7*, 461–471.

Jacobson, E. (1938). *Progressive relaxation* (2nd ed.). Chicago: University of Chicago Press.

Jacobson, N. S., Follette, W. C., & Revenstorf, D. (1984). Psychotherapy outcome research: Methods for reporting variability and evaluating clinical significance. *Behavior Therapy, 15*, 336–352.

Jacobson, N. S., Roberts, L. J., Berns, S. B., & McGlinchey, J. B. (1999). Methods for defining and determining the clinical significance of treatment effects: Description, application, and alternatives. *Journal of Consulting and Clinical Psychology, 67*, 300–307.

James, J. E. (1981). Behavioral self-control of stuttering using time-out from speaking. *Journal of Applied Behavior Analysis, 14*, 25–37.

James, J. E. (1986). Review of the relative efficacy of imaginal and *in vivo* flooding in the treatment of clinical fear. *Behavioural Psychotherapy, 14*, 183–191.

Jason, L. A. (1985). Using a token-actuated timer to reduce television viewing. *Journal of Applied Behavior Analysis, 18*, 269–272.

Jason, L. A., Neal, A. M., & Marinakis, G. (1985). Altering contingencies to facilitate compliance with traffic light systems. *Journal of Applied Behavior Analysis, 18*, 95–100.

Jensen, B. J., & Haynes, S. N. (1986). Self-report questionnaires and inventories. In A. R. Ciminero, K. S. Calhoun, & H. E. Adams (Eds.), *Handbook of behavioral assessment* (2nd ed., pp. 150–175). New York: Wiley.

Johnson, M. D., & Fawcett, S. B. (1994). Courteous service: Its assessment and modification in a human service organization. *Journal of Applied Behavior Analysis, 27*, 145–152.

Johnson, S. P., Welsh, T. M., Miller, L. K., & Altus, D. E. (1991). Participatory management: Maintaining staff performance in a university housing cooperative. *Journal of Applied Behavior Analysis, 24*, 119–127.

Johnson, W. G., Schlundt, D. G., Barclay, D. R., Carr-Nangle, R. E., & Engler, L. B. (1995). A naturalistic functional analysis of binge eating. *Behavior Therapy, 26*, 101–118.

Jones, L. J., Singh, N. N., & Kendall, K. A. (1990). Effects of gentle teaching and alternative treatments on self-injury. In A. C. Repp & N. N. Singh (Eds.), *Perspectives on the use of nonaversive and aversive interventions for persons with developmental disabilities* (pp. 215–230). Sycamore, IL: Sycamore.

Jones, M. C. (1924). The elimination of children's fears. *Journal of Experimental Psychology, 7*, 382–390.

Jones, M. L., Eyberg, S. M., Adams, S. D., & Boggs, S. R. (1998). Treatment acceptability of behavioral interventions for children: An assessment of mothers of children with disruptive behavior disorders. *Child and Family Behavior Therapy, 20*, 15–26.

Jones, R. T., Nelson, R. E., & Kazdin, A. E. (1977). The role of external variables in self-reinforcement. *Behavior Modification, 1*, 147–178.

Jordan, J., Singh, N. N., & Repp, A. C. (1989). An evaluation of gentle teaching and visual screening in the reduction of stereotypy. *Journal of Applied Behavior Analysis, 22*, 9–22.

Jospe, M., Shueman, S. A., & Troy, W. G. (1991). Quality assurance and the clinical health psychologist: A programmatic approach. In J. J. Sweet, R. H. Rozensky, & S. M. Tovian (Eds.), *Handbook of clinical psychology in medical settings* (pp. 95–112). New York: Plenum.

Kabat-Zinn, J. (1982). An outpatient program in behavioral medicine for chronic pain patients based on the practice of mindfulness meditation: Theoretical considerations and preliminary results. *General Hospital Psychiatry, 4,* 33–47.

Kabat-Zinn, J., Lipworth, L., & Burney, R. (1985). The clinical use of mindfulness meditaiton for the self-regulation of chronic pain. *Journal of Behavioral Medicine, 8,* 163–190.

Kahng, S. W., & Iwata, B. A. (1999). Correspondence between outcomes of brief and extended functional analyses. *Journal of Applied Behavior Analysis, 32,* 149–159.

Kallman, W. M., & Feuerstein, M. J. (1986). Psychophysiological procedures. In A. R. Ciminero, K. S. Calhoun, & K. E. Adams (Eds.), *Handbook of behavioral assessment* (2nd ed., pp. 325–352). New York: Wiley.

Kallman, W. M., Hersen, M., & O'Toole, D. H. (1975). The use of social reinforcement in a case of conversion reaction. *Behavior Therapy, 6,* 411–413.

Kamarck, T. W., & Lichtenstein, E. (1985). Current trends in clinic-based smoking control. *Annals of Behavioral Medicine, 7*(2), 19–23.

Kamin, L. J. (1969). Predictability, surprise, attention, and conditioning. In B. A. Campbell & R. M. Church (Eds.), *Punishment and aversive behavior* (pp. 279–296). New York: Appleton-Century-Crofts.

Kanfer, F. H., & Grimm, L. G. (1980). Managing clinical change: A process model of therapy. *Behavior Modification, 4,* 419–444.

Kanfer, F. H., Karoly, P., & Newman, A. (1975). Reduction of children's fear of the dark by competence-related and situational treat-related verbal cues. *Journal of Consulting and Clinical Psychology, 43,* 251–258.

Kaplan, R. M. (1989). Health outcome models for policy analysis. *Health Psychology, 8,* 723–735.

Kaplan, R. M., Atkins, C. J., & Reinsch, S. (1984). Specific efficacy expectations mediate exercise compliance in patients with COPD. *Health Psychology, 3,* 223–242.

Karlsson, T., & Chase, P. N. (1996). A comparison of three prompting methods for training software use. *Journal of Organizational Behavior Management, 16,* 27–44.

Karraker, R. J. (1977). Self versus teacher selected reinforcers in a token economy. *Exceptional Children, 43,* 454–455.

Kau, M. L., & Fischer, J. (1974). Self-modification of exercise behavior. *Journal of Behavior Therapy and Experimental Psychiatry, 5,* 213–214.

Kayser, J. E., Billingsley, F. F., & Neel, R. S. (1986). A comparison of in-context and traditional instruction approaches: Total task, single trial versus backward chaining, multiple trials. *Journal of the Association for the Severely Handicapped, 11,* 28–38.

Kazdin, A. E. (1971). The effect of response cost in suppressing behavior in a pre-psychotic retardate. *Journal of Behavior Therapy and Experimental Psychiatry, 2,* 137–140.

Kazdin, A. E. (1972). Response cost: The removal of conditioned reinforcers for therapeutic change. *Behavior Therapy, 3,* 533–546.

Kazdin, A. E. (1973). The effect of vicarious reinforcement on attentive behavior in the classroom. *Journal of Applied Behavior Analysis, 6,* 71–78.

Kazdin, A. E. (1978). *History of behavior modification: Experimental foundations of contemporary research.* Baltimore: University Park Press.

Kazdin, A. E. (1985). The token economy. In R. Turner & L. M. Asher (Eds.), *Evaluating behavior therapy outcome.* New York: Springer.

Kazdin, A. E., & Erickson, L. M. (1975). Developing responsiveness to instructions in severely and profoundly retarded residents. *Journal of Behavior Therapy and Experimental Psychiatry, 6,* 17–21.

Kazdin, A. E., French, N. H., & Sherick, R. B. (1981). Acceptability of alternative treatments for children: Evaluations by inpatient children, parents, and staff. *Journal of Consulting and Clinical Psychology, 49,* 900–907.

Kazdin, A. E., French, N. H., Unis, A. S., Esveldt-Dawson, K., & Sherick, R. B. (1983). Hopelessness, depression, and suicidal intent among psychiatrically disturbed inpatient children. *Journal of Consulting and Clinical Psychology, 51,* 504–510.

Kazdin, A. E., & Geesey, S. (1977). Simultaneous-treatment design comparisons of the effects of earning reinforcers for one's peers versus oneself. *Behavior Therapy, 8,* 682–693.

Kazdin, A. E., & Polster, R. (1973). Intermittent token reinforcement and response maintenance in extinction. *Behavior Therapy, 4,* 386–391.

Kazdin, A. E., Siegel, T. C., & Bass, D. (1992). Cognitive problem-solving skills training and parent management training in the treatment of antisocial behavior in children. *Journal of Consulting and Clinical Psychology, 60,* 733–747.

Kazdin, A. E., & Wilcoxon, L. A. (1976). Systematic desensitization and nonspecific treatment effects: A methodological evaluation. *Psychological Bulletin, 83,* 729–758.

Kehoe, E. J., & Macrae, M. (1998). Classical conditioning. In W. O'Donohue (Ed.), *Learning and behavior therapy* (pp. 36–58). Boston: Allyn & Bacon.

Keller, F. S. (1968). "Good-bye teacher . . ." *Journal of Applied Behavior Analysis, 1,* 79–89.

Kelly, J. F., & Hake, D. F. (1970). An extinction-induced increase in an aggressive response in humans. *Journal of the Experimental Analysis of Behavior, 14,* 153–164.

Kelly, J. A., & Drabman, R. S. (1977). Overcorrection: An effective procedure that failed. *Journal of Clinical Child Psychology, 6,* 38–40.

Kelly, J. A., St. Lawrence, J. S., Hood, H. V., & Brasfield, T. L. (1989). Behavioral intervention to reduce AIDS risk activities. *Journal of Consulting and Clinical Psychology, 57,* 60–67.

Kempe, C. H. (1976). Child abuse and neglect. In N. B. Talbot (Ed.), *Raising children in modern America: Problems and prospective solutions* (pp. 173–188). Boston: Little, Brown.

Kendall, P. C., Marrs-Garcia, A., Nath, S. R., & Sheldrick, R. C. (1999). Normative comparisons for the evaluation of clinical significance. *Journal of Consulting and Clinical Psychology, 67,* 285–299.

Kent, G. (1985). Memory of dental pain. *Pain,* 187–194.

Killen, J. D. et al. (1994). Pursuit of thinness and onset of eating disorder symptoms in a community sample of adolescent girls: A three-year prospective analysis. *International Journal of Eating Disorders, 16,* 227–238.

Kimble, G. A. (1961). *Hilgard and Marquis' conditioning and learning* (2nd ed.). New York: Appleton-Century-Crofts.

Kimble, G. A. (1993). A modest proposal for a minor revolution in the language of psychology. *Psychological Science, 4,* 253–255.

Kirby, F. D., & Shields, F. (1972). Modification of arithmetic response rate and attending behavior in a seventh-grade student. *Journal of Applied Behavior Analysis, 5,* 79–84.

Kirigin, K. A., Braukmann, C. J., Atwater, J. D., & Wolf, M. M. (1982). An evaluation of teaching-family (Achievement Place) group homes for juvenile offenders. *Journal of Applied Behavior Analysis, 15,* 1–16.

Kleinknecht, R. A. (1994). Acquisition of blood, injury, and needle fears and phobias. *Behaviour Research and Therapy, 32,* 817–823.

Klingman, A., Melamed, B. G., Cuthbert, M. I., & Hermecz, D. A. (1984). Effects of participant modeling on information acquisition and skill utilization. *Journal of Consulting and Clinical Psychology, 52,* 414–422.

Koegel, R. L., & Rincover, A. (1974). Treatment of psychotic children in a classroom environment: 1. Learning in a large group. *Journal of Applied Behavior Analysis, 7,* 45–59.

Kohler, F. W., & Greenwood, C. R. (1986). Toward a technology of generalization: The identification of natural contingencies of reinforcement. *Behavior Analyst, 9,* 19–26.

Kohler, F. W., & Greenwood, C. R. (1990). Effects of collateral peer supportive behaviors within the classwide peer tutoring program. *Journal of Applied Behavior Analysis, 23,* 307–322.

Kohler, F. W., & Strain, P. S. (1990). Peer assisted interventions: Early promises, notable achievements, and future aspirations. *Clinical Psychology Review, 10,* 441–452.

Komaki, J., Barwick, K. D., & Scott, L. R. (1978). A behavioral approach to occupational safety: Pinpointing and reinforcing safe performance in a food manufacturing plant. *Journal of Applied Psychology, 63,* 435–445.

Konarski, E. A., Johnson, M. R., Crowell, C. R., & Whitman, T. L. (1981). An alternative approach to reinforcement for applied researchers: Response deprivation. *Behavior Therapy, 12,* 653–666.

Kortick, S. A., & O'Brien, R. M. (1996). The World Series of quality control: A case study in the package delivery industry. *Journal of Organizational Behavior Management, 16,* 77–93.

Krantz, P. J., & McClannahan, L. E. (1998). Social interaction skills for children with autism: A script-fading procedure for beginning readers. *Journal of Applied Behavior Analysis, 31,* 191–202.

Krantz, P. J., & Risley, T. R. (1977). Behavioral ecology in the classroom. In K. D. O'Leary & S. G. O'Leary (Eds.), *Classroom management: The successful use of behavior modification* (2nd ed., pp. 349–366). New York: Pergamon.

Krebs, D. E. (1987). Biofeedback in neuromuscular re-education and gait training. In M. S. Schwartz (Ed.), *Biofeedback: A practitioner's guide* (pp. 343–376). New York: Guilford.

Kristof, N. D. (1996, May 19). In Japan, nothing to fear but fear itself. *New York Times,* p. E4.

Kritch, K. M., & Bostow, D. E. (1998). Degree of constricted-response interaction in computer-based programmed instruction. *Journal of Applied Behavior Analysis, 31,* 387–398.

Krop, H., & Burgess, D. (1993). Use of covert conditioning to treat excessive masturbation. In J. R. Cautela & A. J. Kearney (Eds.), *Covert conditioning handbook* (pp. 208–216). Pacific Grove, CA: Brooks/Cole.

Krumboltz, J. D., & Krumboltz, H. B. (1972). *Changing children's behavior.* Englewood Cliffs, NJ: Prentice-Hall.

Kulik, J. A., & Carlino, P. (1987). The effect of verbal commitment and treatment choice on medication compliance in a pediatric setting. *Journal of Behavioral Medicine, 10,* 367–376.

Kvale, G., Hugdahl, K., Asbjørnsen, A., Rosengren, B., & Lote, K. (1991). Anticipatory nausea and vomiting in cancer patients. *Journal of Consulting and Clinical Psychology, 59,* 894–898.

Lalli, J. S., & Kates, K. (1998). The effect of reinforcer preference on functional analysis outcomes. *Journal of Applied Behavior Analysis, 31,* 79–90.

Lancioni, G. E. (1982). Normal children as tutors to teach social responses to withdrawn mentally retarded schoolmates: Training, maintenance, and generalization. *Journal of Applied Behavior Analysis, 15,* 17–40.

Landrum, T. J., & Lloyd, J. W. (1992). Generalization in social behavior research with children and youth who have emotional or behavioral disorders. *Behavior Modification, 16,* 593–616.

Lange, A. J., & Jakubowski, P. (1976). *Responsible assertive behavior.* Champaign, IL: Research Press.

Laszlo, J. (1987). *Understanding cancer.* New York: Harper & Row.

Laties, V. G., & Weiss, B. (1963). Effects of a concurrent task on fixed-interval responding in humans. *Journal of the Experimental Analysis of Behavior, 6,* 431–436.

Latimer, P. R., & Sweet, A. A. (1984). Cognitive versus behavioral procedures in cognitive-behavior therapy: A critical review of the evidence. *Journal of Behavior Therapy and Experimental Psychiatry, 15,* 9–22.

Lattal, K. A. (1969). Contingency management of toothbrushing behavior in a summer camp for children. *Journal of Applied Behavior Analysis, 2,* 195–198.

Lazarus, A. A. (1981). *Multimodal therapy.* New York: Guilford.

Lazarus, A. A., Davison, G. C., & Polefka, D. A. (1965). Classical and operant factors in the treatment of a school phobia. *Journal of Abnormal Psychology, 70,* 225–229.

Learn Free. (2000, March 24). *Adult CPR* [On-line]. Available: http://www.learn-cpr.com

LeDoux, J. E. (1994). Emotion, memory and the brain. *Scientific American, 270*(6), 50–57.

Lee, C. (1992). On cognitive theories and causation in human behavior. *Journal of Behavior Therapy and Experimental Psychiatry, 23,* 257–268.

Lehrer, P. M. (1982). How to relax and how not to relax: A reevaluation of the work of Edmund Jacobson—I. *Behaviour Research and Therapy, 20,* 417–428.

Leitenberg, H., Burchard, J. D., Burchard, S. N., Fuller, E. J., & Lysaght, T. V. (1977). Using positive reinforcement to suppress behavior: Some experimental comparisons with sibling conflict. *Behavior Therapy, 8,* 168–182.

Lennox, D. B., Miltenberger, R. G., & Donnelly, D. R. (1987). Response interruption and DRL for the reduction of rapid eating. *Journal of Applied Behavior Analysis, 20,* 279–284.

Lennox, D. B., Miltenberger, R. G., Spengler, P., & Erfanian, N. (1988). Decelerative treatment practices with persons who have mental retardation: A review of five years of the literature. *American Journal of Mental Retardation, 1988,* 492–501.

Lepper, M. R., Greene, D., & Nisbett, R. E. (1973). Undermining children's intrinsic interest with extrinsic reward: A test of the "overjustification hypothesis." *Journal of Personality and Social Psychology, 28,* 129–137.

Lerman, D. C., Iwata, B. A., & Wallace, M. D. (1999). Side effects of extinction: Prevalence of bursting and aggression during the treatment of self-injurious behavior. *Journal of Applied Behavior Analysis, 32,* 1–8.

Lerman, D. C., Kelley, M. E., Van Camp, C. M., & Roane, H. S. (1999). Effects of reinforcement magnitude on spontaneous recovery. *Journal of Applied Behavior Analysis, 32,* 197–200.

LeVay, S., & Hamer, D. H. (1994). Evidence for a biological influence in male homosexuals. *Scientific American, 270*(5), 44–49.

Lewis, D. J. (1960). Partial reinforcement: A selective review of the literature since 1950. *Psychological Bulletin, 57,* 1–28.

Lewis, D. J., & Duncan, D. P. (1956). Effect of different percentages of money reward on extinction of a lever-pulling response. *Journal of Experimental Psychology, 52,* 23–27.

Lewis, D. J., & Duncan, D. P. (1957). Expectation and resistance to extinction of a lever-pulling response as functions of percentage of reinforcement and amount of reward. *Journal of Experimental Psychology, 54,* 115–120.

Lichstein, K. L. (1988). *Clinical relaxation strategies.* New York: Wiley.

Lichtenstein, E., & Mermelstein, R. J. (1984). Review of approaches to smoking treatment: Behavior modification strategies. In J. D. Matarazzo, S. M. Weiss, J. A. Herd, N. E. Miller, & S. M. Weiss (Eds.), *Behavioral health: A handbook of health enhancement and disease prevention* (pp. 695–712). New York: Wiley.

Liddel, A., Locker, D., & Burman, D. (1991). Self-reported fears (FSS-II) of subjects aged 50 years and over. *Behaviour Research and Therapy, 29,* 105–112.

Linden, M., & Pasatu, J. (1998). The integration of cognitive and behavioral interventions in routine behavior therapy. *Journal of Cognitive Psychotherapy: An International Quarterly, 12,* 27–38.

Linscheid, T. R., Iwata, B. A., Ricketts, R. W., Williams, D. E., & Griffen, J. C. (1990). Clinical evaluation of the self-injurious behavior inhibiting system (SIBIS). *Journal of Applied Behavior Analysis, 23,* 53–78.

Linscheid, T. R., & Meinhold, P. (1990). The controversy over aversives: Basic operant research and the side effects of punishment. In A. C. Repp & N. N. Singh (Eds.), *Perspectives on the use of nonaversive and aversive interventions for persons with developmental disabilities* (pp. 435–450). Sycamore, IL: Sycamore.

Logan, D. L. (1970). A "paper money" token system as a recording aid in institutional settings. *Journal of Applied Behavior Analysis, 3,* 183–184.

Long, P., Forehand, R., Wierson, M., & Morgan, A. (1993). Does parent training with young noncompliant children have long term effects? *Behaviour Research and Therapy, 32,* 101–107.

Lovaas, O. I. (1977). *The autistic child: Language development through behavior modification.* New York: Irvington.

Lovaas, O. I., Koegel, R., Simmons, J. Q., & Long, J. S. (1973). Some generalization and follow-up measures on autistic children in behavior therapy. *Journal of Applied Behavior Analysis, 6,* 131–166.

Lovaas, O. I., Newsom, C., & Hickman, C. (1987). Self-stimulatory behavior and perceptual reinforcement. *Journal of Applied Behavior Analysis, 20,* 45–68.

Lovaas, O. I., Schaeffer, B., & Simmons, J. Q. (1965). Building social behavior in autistic children by using electric shock. *Journal of Experimental Research in Personality, 1,* 99–109.

Lovaas, O. I., & Simmons, J. Q. (1969). Manipulation of self-destruction in three retarded children. *Journal of Applied Behavior Analysis, 2,* 143–157.

Lovitt, T. C., & Curtiss, K. A. (1969). Academic response rate as a function of teacher- and self-imposed contingencies. *Journal of Applied Behavior Analysis, 2,* 49–53.

Lowe, C. F. (1979). Determinants of human operant behaviour. In M. D. Zeiler & P. Harzem (Eds.), *Advances in analysis of behaviour: Vol. 1. Reinforcement and the organization of behaviour* (pp. 159–192). Chichester, UK: Wiley.

Lowe, C. F., Beasty, A., & Bentall, R. P. (1983). The role of verbal behavior in human learning: Infant performance on fixed-interval schedules. *Journal of Applied Behavior Analysis, 39,* 157–164.

Lowe, C. F., & Chadwick, P. D. J. (1990). Verbal control of delusions. *Behavior Therapy, 21,* 461–479.

Lowe, K., & Lutzker, J. R. (1979). Increasing compliance to a medical regimen with a juvenile diabetic. *Behavior Therapy, 10,* 57–64.

Lubow, R. E. (1998). Latent inhibition and behavior pathology: Prophylactic and other possible effects of stimulus preexposure. In W. O'Donohue (Ed.), *Learning and behavior therapy* (pp. 107–121). Boston: Allyn & Bacon.

Luce, S. C., Delquadri, J., & Hall, R. V. (1980). Contingent exercise: A mild but powerful procedure for suppressing inappropriate verbal and aggressive behavior. *Journal of Applied Behavior Analysis, 13,* 583–594.

Lucic, K. S., Steffen, J. J., Harrigan, J. A., & Stuebing, R. C. (1991). Progressive relaxation training: Muscle contraction before relaxation? *Behavior Therapy, 22,* 249–256.

Ludwig, T. D., & Geller, E. S. (1991). Improving the driving practices of pizza deliverers: Response generalization and moderating effects of driving history. *Journal of Applied Behavior Analysis, 24,* 31–44.

Luiselli, J. K. (1990). Recent developments in nonaversive treatment: A review of rationale, methods, and recommendations. In A. C. Repp & N. N. Singh (Eds.), *Perspectives on the use of nonaversive and aversive interventions for persons with developmental disabilities* (pp. 73–86). Sycamore, IL: Sycamore.

Luria, A. R. (1961). *The role of speech in the regulation of normal and abnormal behaviors.* New York: Liveright.

Luthans, F., & Kreitner, R. (1985). *Organizational behavior modification and beyond: An operant and social learning approach.* Glenview, IL: Scott, Foresman.

Lutz, J. (1994). *Introduction to learning and memory.* Pacific Grove: Brooks/Cole.

Lyons, L. C., & Woods, P. J. (1991). The efficacy of rational-emotive therapy: A quantitative review of the outcome research. *Clinical Psychology Review, 11,* 357–369.

MacKenzie-Keating, S. E., & McDonald, L. (1990). Overcorrection: Reviewed, revisited and revised. *Behavior Analyst, 13,* 39–48.

Madsen, C. H., Becker, W. C., & Thomas, D. R. (1968). Rules, praise, and ignoring: Elements of elementary classroom control. *Journal of Applied Behavior Analysis, 1,* 139–150.

Madsen, C. H., Becker, W. C., Thomas, D. R., Koser, L., & Plager, E. (1970). An analysis of the reinforcing function of "sit down" commands. In R. K. Parker (Ed.), *Readings in educational psychology* (pp. 265–278). Boston: Allyn & Bacon.

Mahoney, K., Van Wagenen, R. K., & Meyerson, L. (1971). Toilet training of normal and retarded children. *Journal of Applied Behavior Analysis, 4,* 173–181.

Mahoney, M. J. (1977). Reflections on the cognitive-learning trend in psychotherapy. *American Psychologist, 32,* 5–13.

Mahoney, M. J. (1993). Introduction to special section: Theoretical developments in the cognitive psychotherapies. *Journal of Consulting and Clinical Psychology, 61,* 187–193.

Main, M., & George, C. (1985). Responses of abused and disadvantaged toddlers to distress in age-mates: A study in the day care setting. *Developmental Psychology, 21,* 407–412.

Malatesta, V. J., & Adams, H. E. (1986). Assessment of sexual behavior. In A. R. Ciminero, K. S. Calhoun, & K. E. Adams (Eds.), *Handbook of behavioral assessment* (2nd ed., pp. 496–525). New York: Wiley.

Maletzky, B. M. (1974). Behavior recording as treatment: A brief note. *Behavior Therapy, 5,* 107–111.

Marholin, D., & Gray, D. (1976). Effects of group response-cost procedures on cash shortages in a small business. *Journal of Applied Behavior Analysis, 9,* 25–30.

Marholin, D., & Townsend, N. M. (1978). An experimental analysis of side effects and response maintenance of a modified overcorrection procedure: The case of the persistent twiddler. *Behavior Therapy, 9,* 383–390.

Marlatt, G. A., & Gordon, J. R. (1980). Determinants of relapse: Implications for the maintenance of behavior change. In P. O. Davidson & S. M. Davidson (Eds.), *Behavioral medicine: Changing health lifestyles* (pp. 410–452). New York: Brunner/Mazel.

Marlatt, G. A., & Parks, G. A. (1982). Self-management of addictive behaviors. In P. Karoly & F. H. Kanfer (Eds.), *Self-management and behavior change: From theory to practice* (pp. 443–488). New York: Pergamon.

Marshall, W. L., Gauthier, J., Christie, M. M., Currie, D. W., & Gordon, A. (1977). Flooding therapy: Effectiveness, stimulus characteristics, and the value of brief *in vivo* expossure. *Behaviour Research and Therapy, 15,* 79–87.

Marshall, W. L., Presse, L., & Andrews, W. R. (1976). A self-administered program for public speaking anxiety. *Behaviour Research and Therapy, 14,* 33–39.

Martin, G. (1982). Thought-stopping and stimulus control to decrease persistent disturbing thoughts. *Journal of Behavior Therapy and Experimental Psychiatry, 13,* 215–220.

Martin, I., & Levey, A. (1994). The evaluative response: Primitive but necessary. *Behaviour Research and Therapy, 32,* 301–305.

Mathews, A. M., Johnston, D. W., Lancashire, M., Munby, M., Shaw, P. M., & Gelder, M. G. (1976). Imaginal flooding and exposure to real phobic situations: Treatment outcome with agoraphobic patients. *British Journal of Psychiatry, 129,* 362–371.

Mathews, R. M., & Dix, M. (1992). Behavior change in the funny papers: Feedback to cartoonists on safety belt use. *Journal of Applied Behavior Analysis, 25,* 769–775.

Matson, J. L. (1983). Exploration of phobic behavior in a small child. *Journal of Behavior Therapy and Experimental Psychiatry, 14,* 257–259.

Matson, J. L., & Taras, M. E. (1989). A 20 year review of punishment and alternative methods to treat problem behaviors in developmentally delayed persons. *Research in Developmental Disabilities, 10,* 85–104.

Mayhew, G. L., & Harris, F. (1978). Some negative side effects of a punishment procedure for stereotyped behavior. *Journal of Behavior Therapy and Experimental Psychiatry, 9,* 245–251.

Mayo, L. L., & Norton, G. R. (1980). The use of problem solving to reduce examination and interpersonal anxiety. *Journal of Behavior Therapy and Experimental Psychiatry, 11,* 287–289.

McAlister, W. R., & McAlister, D. E. (1995). Two factor theory: Implications for understanding anxiety based clinical phenomena. In W. O'Donohue & L. Krasner (Eds.), *Theories of behavior therapy: Exploring behavior change* (pp. 145–171). Washington, DC: American Psychological Association.

McCaffrey, R. J., & Blanchard, E. B. (1985). Stress management approaches to the treatment of essential hypertension. *Annals of Behavioral Medicine, 7*(1), 5–12.

McCaul, K. D., & Malott, J. M. (1984). Distraction and coping with pain. *Psychological Bulletin, 95,* 516–533.

McClannahan, L. E., McGee, G. G., MacDuff, G. S., & Krantz, P. J. (1990). Assessing and improving child care: A personal appearance index for children with autism. *Journal of Applied Behavior Analysis, 23,* 469–482.

McClannahan, L. E., & Risley, T. R. (1975). Design of living environments for nursing-home residents: Increasing participation in recreational activities. *Journal of Applied Behavior Analysis, 8,* 261–268.

McClintic, J. R. (1985). *Physiology of the human body* (3rd ed.). New York: Wiley.

McConnell, J. V. (1990). Negative reinforcement and positive punishment. *Teaching of Psychology, 17,* 247–249.

McCracken, L. M., & Larkin, K. T. (1991). Treatment of paruresis with *in vivo* desensitization: A case report. *Journal of Behavior Therapy and Experimental Psychiatry, 22,* 57–62.

McFall, R. M., & Lillesand, D. B. (1970). *Conflict Resolution Inventory.* Unpublished manuscript.

McFall, R. M., & Lillesand, D. B. (1971). Behavior rehearsal with modeling and coaching in assertion training. *Journal of Abnormal Psychology, 77,* 313–323.

McFall, R. M., & Twentyman, C. T. (1973). Four experiments on the relative contributions of rehearsal, modeling, and coaching to assertion training. *Journal of Abnormal Psychology, 81,* 199–218.

McGee, G. G., Almeida, M. C., Sulzer-Azaroff, B., & Feldman, R. S. (1992). Promoting reciprocal interactions via peer incidental teaching. *Journal of Applied Behavior Analysis, 25,* 117–126.

McGee, J. J., & Gonzalez, L. (1990). Gentle teaching and the practice of human interdependence: A preliminary group study of 15 persons with severe behavioral disorders and their caregivers. In A. C. Repp & N. N. Singh (Eds.), *Per-spectives on the use of nonaversive and aversive interventions for persons with developmental disabilities* (pp. 237–254). Sycamore, IL: Sycamore.

McGee, J. J., Menolascino, F. J., Hobbs, D. C., & Menousek, P. E. (1987). *Gentle teaching: A nonaversive approach for helping persons with mental retardation.* New York: Human Sciences Press.

McKenzie, T. L., & Rushall, B. S. (1974). Effects of self-recording on attendance and performance in a competitive swimming training environment. *Journal of Applied Behavior Analysis, 7,* 199–206.

McLaughlin, T. F., Burgess, N., & Sackville-West, L. (1982). Effects of self-recording and self-recording + matching on academic performance. *Child Behavior Therapy, 3,* 17–27.

McMahon, R. J. (1984). Behavioral checklists and ratings scales. In T. H. Ollendick & M. Hersen (Eds.), *Child behavioral assessment: Principles and procedures* (pp. 80–105). New York: Pergamon.

McNeil, C. B., Eyberg, S., Eisenstadt, T. H., Newcomb, K., & Funderburk, B. (1991). Parent-child interaction therapy with behavior problem children: Generalization of treatment effects to the school setting. *Journal of Clinical Child Psychology, 20,* 140–151.

McReynolds, W. T., & Church, A. (1973). Self-control, study skills development and counseling approaches to the improvement of study behavior. *Behaviour Research and Therapy, 11,* 233–235.

Mealiea, W. L., & Nawas, M. M. (1971). The comparative effectiveness of systematic desensitization and implosive therapy in the treatment of snake phobia. *Journal of Behavior Therapy and Experimental Psychiatry, 2,* 85–94.

Meichenbaum, D. (1977). *Cognitive-behavior modification: An integrative approach.* New York: Plenum.

Meichenbaum, D. (1986). Cognitive-behavior modification. In F. H. Kanfer & A. P. Goldstein (Eds.), *Helping people change: A textbook of methods* (3rd ed., pp. 346–380). New York: Pergamon.

Meichenbaum, D., & Cameron, R. (1983). Stress inoculation training: Toward a general paradigm for training coping skills. In D. Meichenbaum & M. E. Jaremko (Eds.), *Stress reduction and prevention* (pp. 115–154). New York: Plenum.

Meichenbaum, D., & Deffenbacher, J. L. (1988). Stress inoculation training. *Counseling Psychologist, 16,* 69–90.

Meichenbaum, D. H., & Goodman, J. (1971). Training impulsive children to talk to themselves: A means of developing self-control. *Journal of Abnormal Psychology, 77,* 115–126.

Melamed, B. G., & Siegel, L. J. (1975). Reduction of anxiety in children facing hospitalization and surgery by use of filmed modeling. *Journal of Consulting and Clinical Psychology, 43,* 511–521.

Melin, L., & Götestam, K. G. (1981). The effects of rearranging ward routines on communication and eating behaviors of psychogeriatric patients. *Journal of Applied Behavior Analysis, 14,* 47–51.

Menzies, R. G., & Clarke, J. C. (1993). A comparison of *in vivo* and vicarious exposure in the treatment of childhood water phobia. *Behaviour Research and Therapy, 31,* 9–15.

Merckelbach, H., Arntz, A., Arrindell, W. A., & de Jong, P. J. (1992). Pathways to spider phobia. *Behaviour Research and Therapy, 30,* 543–546.

Merckelbach, H., Muris, P., & Schouten, E. (1996). Pathways to fear in spider phobic children. *Behaviour Research and Therapy, 34,* 935–938.

Mermelstein, R., Lichtenstein, E., & McIntyre, K. (1983). Partner support and relapse in smoking-cessation programs. *Journal of Consulting and Clinical Psychology, 51,* 465–466.

Meyer, R. G. (1975). A behavioral treatment of sleepwalking associated with test anxiety. *Journal of Behavior Therapy and Experimental Psychiatry, 6,* 167–168.

Meyer, V., Robertson, J., & Tatlow, A. (1975). Home treatment of an obsessive-compulsive disorder by response prevention. *Journal of Behavior Therapy and Experimental Psychiatry, 6,* 37–38.

Michael, J. (1975). Positive and negative reinforcement, a distinction that is no longer necessary; or a better way to talk about bad things. *Behaviorism, 3,* 33–44.

Michael, J. (1982). Distinguishing between discriminative and motivational functions of stimuli. *Journal of the Experimental Analysis of Behavior, 37,* 149–155.

Michael, J. (1986). Repertoire-altering effects of remote contingencies. *Analysis of Verbal Behavior, 4,* 10–18.

Michael, J. (1987). Experimental analysis of human behavior symposium: Comments by the discussant. *Psychological Record, 37,* 37–42.

Milgrom, P., Mancl, L., King, B., & Weinstein, P. (1995). Origins of childhood dental fear. *Behaviour Research and Therapy, 33,* 313–319.

Miller, D. L., & Kelley, M. L. (1994). The use of goal setting and contingency contracting for improving children's homework performance. *Journal of Applied Behavior Analysis, 27,* 73–84.

Miller, L. K. (1980). *Principles of everyday behavior analysis* (2nd ed.). Pacific Grove, CA: Brooks/Cole.

Miller, P. W. (1972). The use of behavioral contracting in the treatment of alcoholism: A case report. *Behavior Therapy, 3,* 593–596.

Miller, W. R., & Hester, R. K. (1980). Treating the problem drinker: Modern approaches. In W. R. Miller (Ed.), *The addictive behaviors: Treatment of alcoholism, drug abuse, smoking, and obesity* (pp. 11–141). New York: Pergamon.

Mischel, W. (1981). Metacognition and the rules of delay. In J. H. Flavell & L. Ross (Eds.), *Social cognitive development: Frontiers and possible futures* (pp. 240–271). Cambridge: Cambridge University Press.

Miltenberger, R. G., Fuqua, R. W., & Woods, D. W. (1998). Applying behavior analysis to clinical problems: Review and analysis of habit reversal. *Journal of Applied Behavior Analysis, 31,* 447–469.

Minton, L. (1999, April 25). Who controls your money? Our teen survey results. *Parade Magazine,* p. 10.

Monette, D. R., Sullivan, T. .J., & DeJong, C. R. (1990). *Applied social research: Tool for the human services* (2nd ed.). Fort Worth, TX: Holt, Rinehart & Winston.

Monti, P. M., Rohsenow, D. J., Rubonis, A. V., Naiura, R. S., Sirota, A. D., Colby, S. M., Goddard, P., & Abrams, D. B. (1994). Cue exposure with coping skills treatment for male alcoholics: A preliminary investigation. *Journal of Consulting and Clinical Psychology, 61,* 1011–1019.

Moore, S. (1987). Relaxation training. In R. J. Corsini (Ed.), *Concise encyclopedia of psychology* (pp. 969–970). New York: Wiley.

Moos, R. H., & Schaefer, J. A. (1986). Life transitions and crises: A conceptual overview. In R. H. Moos (Ed.), *Coping with life crises: An integrated approach* (pp. 3–28). New York: Plenum.

Morganstern, K. P. (1973). Implosive therapy and flooding procedures. *Psychological Bulletin, 79,* 318–334.

Morin, C. M., Culbert, J. P., & Schwartz, S. M. (1994). Nonpharmacological interventions for insomnia: A meta-analysis of treatment efficacy. *American Journal of Psychiatry, 151,* 1172–1180.

Morris, E. K., & Redd, W. H. (1975). Children's performance and social preference for positive, negative, and mixed adult-child interactions. *Child Development, 46,* 525–531.

Morris, J., & Ellis, J. (1997). The effect of verbal and graphic feedback on the data-recording of direct care trainers. *Behavioral Interventions, 12,* 77–104.

Morris, R. J., & Kratochwill, T. R. (1983). *Treating children's fears and phobias: A behavioral approach.* New York: Pergamon.

Mosley, T. H., Eisen, A. R., Bruce, B. K., Brantley, P. J., & Cocke, T. B. (1993). Contingent reinforcement for fluid compliance in a hemodialysis patient. *Journal of Behavior Therapy and Experimental Psychiatry, 24,* 77–81.

Mowrer, O. H. (1938). Apparatus for the study and treatment of enuresis. *American Journal of Psychology, 51,* 163–165.

Mowrer, O. H. (1947). On the dual nature of learning—a reinterpretation of "conditioning" and "problem solving." *Harvard Educational Review, 17,* 102–148.

Muehlenhard, C. L., Koralewski, M. A., Andrews, C. A., & Burdick, C. A. (1986). Verbal and nonverbal cues that convey interest in dating: Two studies. *Behavior Therapy, 17,* 404–419.

Murphy, H. A., Hutchison, J. M., & Bailey, J. S. (1983). Behavioral school psychology goes outdoors: The effects of organized games on playground aggression. *Journal of Applied Behavior Analysis, 16*, 29–35.

Murray, D. M., Pirie, P., Leupker, R. V., & Pallonen, U. (1989). Five- and six-year follow-up results from four seventh-grade smoking prevention strategies. *Journal of Behavioral Medicine, 12*, 207–218.

Murrell, M., Hardy, M., & Martin, G. L. (1974). Danny learns to match digits with the number of objects. *Special Education in Canada, 49*, 20–22.

Nakano, K. (1990). Operant self-control procedure in modifying Type A behavior. *Journal of Behavior Therapy and Experimental Psychiatry, 21*, 249–255.

Neef, N. A., Lensbower, J., Hockersmith, I., DePalma, V., & Gray, K. (1990). In vivo versus simulation training: An interactional analysis of range and type of training exemplars. *Journal of Applied Behavior Analysis, 23*, 447–458.

Neef, N. A., Mace, F. C., Shea, M. C., & Shade, D. (1992). Effects of reinforcer rate and reinforcer quality on time allocation: Extensions of matching theory to educational settings. *Journal of Applied Behavior Analysis, 25*, 691–699.

Nelson, G., & Carson, P. (1988). Evaluation of a social problem-solving skills program for third- and fourth-grade students. *American Journal of Community Psychology, 16*, 79–99.

Nelton, S. (1988, March). Motivating for success. *Nation's Business*, pp. 18–26.

Nesbitt, E. B. (1973). An escalator phobia overcome in one session of flooding *in vivo*. *Journal of Behavior Therapy and Experimental Psychiatry, 4*, 405–406.

Nevin, J. A. (1988). Behavioral momentum and the partial reinforcement effect. *Psychological Bulletin, 103*, 44–56.

Nezu, A. M., Nezu, C. M., & Perri, M. G. (1989). *Problem-solving therapy for depression: Theory, research, and clinical guidelines*. New York: Wiley.

Niaura, R. S., Rohsenow, D. J., Binkoff, J. A., Monti, P. M., Pedraza, M., & Abrams, D. B. (1988). Relevance of cue reactivity to understanding alcohol and smoking relapse. *Journal of Abnormal Psychology, 97*, 133–152.

Ninness, H. A. C., Fuerst, J., Rutherford, R. D., & Glenn, S. S. (1991). Effects of self-management training and reinforcement on the transfer of improved conduct in the absence of supervision. *Journal of Applied Behavior Analysis, 24*, 499–508.

NJNPI (New Jersey Neuro-Psychiatric Institute). (1972). *Behavior modification training program: Drug staff*. Princeton, NJ: Author.

Nomellini, S., & Katz, R. C. (1983). Effects of anger control training on abusive parents. *Cognitive Therapy and Research, 7*, 57–68.

Nordquist, V. M. (1971). The modification of a child's enuresis: Some response-response relationships. *Journal of Applied Behavior Analysis, 4*, 241–247.

Nordyke, N. S., Baer, D. M., Etzel, B. C., & LeBlanc, J. M. (1977). Implications of the stereotyping and modification of sex role. *Journal of Applied Behavior Analysis, 10*, 553–557.

North, M. M., North, S. M., & Coble, J. R. (1997). Virtual reality therapy for fear of flying. *American Journal of Psychiatry, 154*, 130.

Novaco, R. W. (1976). The functions and regulation of the arousal of anger. *American Journal of Psychiatry, 133*, 1124–1128.

Novaco, R. W. (1977). A stress inoculation approach to anger management in the training of law enforcement officers. *American Journal of Community Psychology, 5*, 327–346.

O'Banion, D. R., & Whaley, D. L. (1981). *Behavior contracting: Arranging contingencies of reinforcement*. New York: Springer.

O'Brien, F., Bugle, C., & Azrin, N. H. (1972). Training and maintaining a retarded child's proper eating. *Journal of Applied Behavior Analysis, 5*, 67–72.

O'Brien, S., & Karsh, K. G. (1990). Treatment acceptability: Consumer, therapist, and society. In A. C. Repp & N. N. Singh (Eds.), *Perspectives on the use of nonaversive and aversive interventions for persons with developmental disabilities* (pp. 503–516). Sycamore, IL: Sycamore.

O'Brien, T. P., Riner, L. S., & Budd, K. S. (1983). The effects of a child's self-evaluation program on compliance with parental instructions in the home. *Journal of Applied Behavior Analysis, 16*, 69–79.

O'Donohue, W., & Plaud, J. J. (1994). The conditioning of human sexual arousal. *Archives of Sexual Behavior, 23*, 321–344.

Okifuji, A., & Friedman, A. G. (1992). Experimentally induced taste aversions in humans: Effects of overshadowing on acquisition. *Behaviour Research and Therapy, 30*, 23–32.

Olds, J., & Milner, P. (1954). Positive reinforcement produced by electrical stimulation of the septal area and other regions of the rat brain. *Journal of Comparative and Physiological Psychology, 47*, 419–427.

O'Leary, K. D. (1984). The image of behavior therapy: It is time to take a stand. *Behavior Therapy, 15*, 219–233.

O'Leary, K. D., Becker, W. C., Evans, M. B., & Saudargas, R. A. (1969). A token reinforcement program in a public school: A replication and systematic analysis. *Journal of Applied Behavior Analysis, 2*, 3–13.

Oliver, S. D., West, R. C., & Sloane, H. N. (1974). Some effects on human behavior of aversive events. *Behavior Therapy, 5*, 481–493.

Ollendick, T. H. (1983). Reliability and validity of the Revised Fear Survey Schedule for Children (FSSC-R). *Behaviour Research and Therapy, 21*, 685–692.

Ollendick, T. H., Hagopian, L. P., & Huntzinger, R. M. (1991). Cognitive-behavioral therapy with nighttime fearful children. *Journal of Behavior Therapy and Experimental Psychiatry, 22,* 113–121.

Ollendick, T. H., & Hersen, M. (1984). An overview of child behavioral assessment. In T. H. Ollendick & M. Hersen (Eds.), *Child behavioral assessment: Principles and procedures* (pp. 3–19). New York: Pergamon.

Ollendick, T. H., & Matson, J. L. (1978). Overcorrection: An overview. *Behavior Therapy, 9,* 830–842.

Olson, R. P. (1987). Definitions of biofeedback. In M. S. Schwartz (Ed.), *Biofeedback: A practitioner's guide* (pp. 33–38). New York: Guilford.

Olson, R. P., & Kroon, J. S. (1987). Biobehavioral treatments of essential hypertension. In M. S. Schwartz (Ed.), *Biofeedback: A practitioner's guide* (pp. 316–339). New York: Guilford.

Olson, R. P., & Schwartz, M. S. (1987). An historical perspective on the biofeedback field. In M. S. Schwartz (Ed.), *Biofeedback: A practitioner's guide* (pp. 3–16). New York: Guilford.

Oltmanns, T. F., Neale, J. M., & Davison, G. C. (1991). *Case studies in abnormal psychology* (3rd ed.). New York: Wiley.

O'Neill, R. E., Horner, R. H., Albin, R. W., Storey, K., & Sprague, J. R. (1990). *Functional analysis of problem behavior: A practical assessment guide.* Sycamore, IL: Sycamore.

O'Reilly, M. F., Green, G., & Braunling-McMorrow, D. (1990). Self-administered written prompts to teach home accident prevention skills to adults with brain injuries. *Journal of Applied Behavior Analysis, 23,* 431–446.

Ormrod, J. E. (1990). *Human learning: Theories, principles, and educational applications.* New York: Macmillan.

Ost, L. G. (1987). Age of onset in different phobias. *Journal of Abnormal Psychology, 96,* 223–229.

Ost, L. G., & Hugdahl, K. (1981). Acquisition of phobias and anxiety response patterns in clinical patients. *Behaviour Research and Therapy, 19,* 439–447.

Overholser, J. C. (1991). Prompting and fading in the exposure treatment of compulsive checking. *Journal of Behavior Therapy and Experimental Psychiatry, 22,* 271–279.

Pace, G. M., Ivancic, M. T., Edwards, G. L., Iwata, B. A., & Page, T. J. (1985). Assessment of stimulus preference and reinforcer value with profoundly retarded individuals. *Journal of Applied Behavior Analysis, 18,* 249–255.

Paine, S. C., Hops, H., Walker, H. M., Greenwood, C. R., Fleischman, D. H., & Guild, J. J. (1982). Repeated treatment effects: A study of maintaining behavior change in socially withdrawn children. *Behavior Modification, 6,* 171–199.

Papini, M. R., & Bitterman, M. E. (1990). The role of contingency in classical conditioning. *Psychological Review, 97,* 396–403.

Paquin, M. J. (1977). The treatment of a nail-biting compulsion by covert sensitization in a poorly motivated client.

Journal of Behavior Therapy and Experimental Psychiatry, 8, 181–183.

Parrish, J. M., & Babbitt, R. L. (1991). Video-mediated instruction in medical settings. In P. W. Dowrick (Ed.), *Practical guide to using video in the behavioral sciences* (pp. 166–185). New York: Wiley.

Parrish, J. M., Cataldo, M. F., Kolko, D. J., Neef, N. A., & Egel, A. L. (1986). Experimental analysis of response covariation among compliant and inappropriate behaviors. *Journal of Applied Behavior Analysis, 19,* 241–254.

Passman, R. H. (1977). The reduction of procrastinative behaviors in a college student despite the "contingency fulfillment problem": The use of external control in self-management techniques. *Behavior Therapy, 8,* 95–97.

Patterson, C. J., & Mischel, W. (1975). Plans to resist temptation. *Developmental Psychology, 11,* 369–378.

Patterson, G. R. (1982). *Coercive family processes.* Eugene, OR: Castalia Press.

Paul, G. L. (1967). Insight versus desensitization in psychotherapy two years after termination. *Journal of Consulting Psychology, 31,* 333–348.

Paul, G. L., & Lentz, R. J. (1977). *Psychosocial treatment of chronic mental patients: Milieu vs. social-learning programs.* Cambridge, MA: Harvard University Press.

Pavlov, I. P. (1927). *Conditioned reflexes.* (G. V. Anrep, trans.). New York: Oxford University Press.

Pawlicki, R. E., & Galotti, N. (1978). A tic-like behavior case study emanating from a self-directed behavior modification course. *Behavior Therapy, 9,* 671–672.

Pear, J. J., & Eldridge, G. D. (1984). The operant-respondent distinction: Future directions. *Journal of the Experimental Analysis of Behavior, 42,* 453–467.

Pedalino, E., & Gamboa, V. U. (1974). Behavior modification and absenteeism: Intervention in one industrial setting. *Journal of Applied Psychology, 59,* 694–698.

Peek, C. J. (1987). A primer of biofeedback instrumentation. In M. S. Schwartz (Ed.), *Biofeedback: A practitioner's guide* (pp. 73–127). New York: Guilford.

Perri, M. G., & Richards, C. S. (1977). An investigation of naturally occurring episodes of self-controlled behaviors. *Journal of Counseling Psychology, 24,* 178–183.

Petri, H. L., & Mishkin, M. (1994). Behaviorism, cognitivism and the neuropsychology of memory. *American Scientist, 82,* 30–37.

Phillips, E. L. (1968). Achievement Place: Token reinforcement procedures in a home-style rehabilitation setting for "pre-delinquent" boys. *Journal of Applied Behavior Analysis, 1,* 213–223.

Phillips, E. L., Phillips, E. A., Fixsen, D. L., & Wolf, M. M. (1971). Achievement Place: Modification of the behaviors of pre-delinquent boys within a token economy. *Journal of Applied Behavior Analysis, 4,* 45–59.

Phillips, E. L., Phillips, E. A., Fixsen, D. L., & Wolf, M. M. (1973, June). Achievement Place: Behavior shaping works for delinquents. *Psychology Today*, 75–79.

Phillips, E. L., Phillips, E. A., Wolf, M. M., & Fixsen, D. L. (1973). Achievement Place: Development of the elected manager system. *Journal of Applied Behavior Analysis, 6,* 541–561.

Piaget, J. (1929). *The child's conception of the world.* London: Routledge & Kegan Paul.

Piaget, J. (1952). *The origins of intelligence* (M. Cook, trans.). New York: International Universities Press. (Originally published 1936)

Piaget, J. (1970). Piaget's theory. In P. H. Mussen (Ed.), *Charmichael's manual of child psychology* (3rd ed., Vol. 1, pp. 703–732). New York: Wiley.

Piazza, C. C., Fisher, W. W., Hanley, G. P., LeBlanc, L. A., Worsdell, A. S., Lindauer, S. E., & Keeney, K. M. (1998). Treatment of pica through multiple analyses of its reinforcing functions. *Journal of Applied Behavior Analysis, 31,* 165–189.

Piazza, C. C., Fisher, W. W., Hanley, G. P., Remick, M. L., Contrucci, S. A., & Aitken, T. L. (1997). The use of positive and negative reinforcement in the treatment of escape-maintained destructive behavior. *Journal of Applied Behavior Analysis, 30,* 279–298.

Pigott, H. E., Fantuzzo, J. W., & Clement, P. W. (1986). The effects of reciprocal peer tutoring and group contingencies on the academic performance of elementary school children. *Journal of Applied Behavior Analysis, 19,* 93–98.

Piliavin, J. A., Dovidio. J. F., Gaertner, S. L., & Clark, R. D. (1981). Responsive bystanders: The process on intervention. In J. Grzelak & V. Derlega (Eds.), *Living with other people: Theory and research on cooperation and helping.* New York: Academic Press.

Pinkston, E. M., Reese, N. M., LeBlanc, J. M., & Baer, D. M. (1973). Independent control of a preschool child's aggression and peer interaction by contingent teacher attention. *Journal of Applied Behavior Analysis, 6,* 115–124.

Pinto, R. P., & Hollandsworth, J. G. (1989). Using videotaped modeling to prepare children psychologically for surgery: Influence of parents and costs versus benefits of providing preparation services. *Health Psychology, 8,* 79–95.

Pitts, C. E. (1976). Behavior modification—1787. *Journal of Applied Behavior Analysis, 9,* 146.

Plimpton, G. (1963). Ernest Hemingway. In G. Plimpton (Ed.), *Writers at work: The Paris Review interviews* (Second series, pp. 217–239). New York: Viking.

Plotkin, W. B. (1976). On the self-regulation of the occipital alpha rhythm: Control strategies, states of consciousness, and the role of physiological feedback. *Journal of Experimental Psychology, 105,* 66–99.

Poche, C., Brouwer, R., & Swearingen, M. (1981). Teaching self-protection to young children. *Journal of Applied Behavior Analysis, 14,* 169–176.

Polivy, J., & Thomsen, L. (1988). Dieting and other eating disorders. In E. A. Blechman & K. D. Brownell (Eds.), *Handbook of behavioral medicine for women.* New York: Pergamon.

Pomerleau, O. F., & Pomerleau, C. S. (1989). A biobehavioral perspective on smoking. In T. Ney & A. Gale (Eds.), *Smoking and human behavior* (pp. 69–90). New York: Wiley.

Poppen, R. (1998). *Behavioral relaxation training and assessment* (2nd ed.). Thousand Oaks, CA: Sage.

Porterfield, J. K., Herbert-Jackson, E., & Risley, T. R. (1976). Contingent observation: An effective and acceptable procedure for reducing disruptive behavior of young children in a group setting. *Journal of Applied Behavior Analysis, 9,* 55–64.

Poulton, R., Davies, S., Menzies, R. G., Langley, J. D., & Silva, P. A. (1998). Evidence for a non-associative model of the acquisition of a fear of heights. *Behaviour Research and Therapy, 36,* 537–544.

Powell, J., Martindale, A., & Kulp, S. (1975). An evaluation of time-sampled measures of behavior. *Journal of Applied Behavior Analysis, 8,* 463–469.

Premack, D. (1959). Toward empirical behavior laws: I. Positive reinforcement. *Psychological Review, 66,* 219–233.

Premack, D. (1965). Reinforcement theory. In D. Levine (Ed.), *Nebraska symposium on motivation* (pp. 123–180). Lincoln: University of Nebraska Press.

Prochaska, J. O., & DiClemente, C. C. (1984). *The transtheoretical approach: Crossing traditional boundaries of therapy.* Homewood, IL: Dow Jones/Irwin.

Prochaska, J. O., DiClemente, C. C., & Norcross, J. C. (1992). In search of how people change: Applications to addictive behaviors. *American Psychologist, 47,* 1102–1114.

Prue, D. M., Krapfl, J. E., Noah, J. C., Cannon, S., & Maley, R. F. (1980). Managing the treatment activities of state hospital staff. *Journal of Organizational Behavior Management, 2,* 165–181.

Puder, R., Lacks, P., Bertelson, A. D., & Storandt, M. (1983). Short-term stimulus control treatment of insomnia in older adults. *Behavior Therapy, 14,* 424–429.

Rachman, S. (1991). Neo-conditioning and the classical theory of fear acquisition. *Clinical Psychological Review, 11,* 155–173.

Rachman, S. (1994). The overprediction of fear: A review. *Behaviour Research and Therapy, 32,* 683–690.

Rachman, S., & Cuk, M. (1992). Fearful distortions. *Behaviour Research and Therapy, 30,* 583–589.

Rapport, M. D., Murphy, H. A., & Bailey, J. S. (1982). Ritalin vs. response cost in the control of hyperactive children: A within-subject comparison. *Journal of Applied Behavior Analysis, 15,* 205–216.

Rasing, E. J., & Duker, P. C. (1992). Effects of a multifaceted training procedure on the acquisition and generalization of social behaviors in language-disabled deaf children. *Journal of Applied Behavior Analysis, 25,* 723–734.

Rathus, S. A. (1973). A 30-item schedule for assessing assertive behavior. *Behavior Therapy, 4,* 398–406.

Redd, W. H., & Birnbrauer, J. S. (1969). Adults as discriminative stimuli for different reinforcement contingencies with retarded children. *Journal of Experimental Child Psychology, 7,* 440–447.

Reitman, D. (1998). The real and imagined harmful effects of rewards: Implications for clinical practice. *Journal of Behavior Therapy and Experimental Psychiatry, 29,* 101–113.

Rekers, G. A., & Lovaas, O. I. (1974). Behavioral treatment of deviant sex-role behaviors in a male child. *Journal of Applied Behavior Analysis, 7,* 173–190.

Renne, C. M., & Creer, T. L. (1976). Training children with asthma to use inhalation therapy equipment. *Journal of Applied Behavior Analysis, 9,* 1–11.

Repp, A. C., Deitz, S. M., & Deitz, D. E. D. (1976). Reducing inappropriate behaviors in classrooms and in individual sessions through DRO schedules of reinforcement. *Mental Retardation, 14,* 11–15.

Repp, A. C., Felce, D., & Barton, L. E. (1988). Basing the treatment of stereotypic and self-injurious behaviors on hypotheses of their causes. *Journal of Applied Behavior Analysis, 21,* 281–289.

Rescorla, R. A. (1988). Pavlovian conditioning: It's not what you think it is. *American Psychologist, 43,* 151–160.

Rescorla, R. A., & Wagner, A. R. (1972). A theory of Pavlovian conditioning: Variations in the effectiveness of reinforcement and nonreinforcement. In A. H. Black & W. F. Prokasy (Eds.), *Classical conditioning II: Current research and theory* (pp. 64–99). New York: Appleton-Century-Crofts.

Richardson, F. C., & Suinn, R. M. (1973). A comparison of traditional systematic desensitization, accelerated massed desensitization, and anxiety management training in the treatment of mathematics anxiety. *Behavior Therapy, 4,* 212–218.

Rilling, M. (1977). Stimulus control and inhibitory processes. In W. K. Honig & J. E. R. Staddon (Eds.), *Handbook of operant behavior* (pp. 432–480). Englewood Cliffs, NJ: Prentice-Hall.

Rincover, A., & Devany, J. (1982). The application of sensory extinction procedures to self-injury. *Analysis and Intervention in Developmental Disabilities, 2,* 67–81.

Riordan, M. M., Iwata, B. A., Finney, J. W., Wohl, M. K., & Stanley, A. E. (1984). Behavioral assessment and treatment of chronic food refusal in handicapped children. *Journal of Applied Behavior Analysis, 17,* 327–341.

Rizley, R. C., & Rescorla, R. A. (1972). Associations in second-order conditioning and sensory preconditioning. *Journal of Comparative and Physiological Psychology, 81,* 1–11.

Roberts, M. W., Hatzenbuehler, L. C., & Bean, A. W. (1981). The effects of differential attention and time out on child noncompliance. *Behavior Therapy, 12,* 93–99.

Roberts, R. N., Nelson, R. O., & Olson, T. W. (1987). Self-instruction: An analysis of the differential effects of instruction and reinforcement. *Journal of Applied Behavior Analysis, 20,* 235–242.

Roberts, R. N., & Tharp, R. G. (1980). A naturalistic study of school children's private speech in an academic problem-solving task. *Cognitive Therapy and Research, 4,* 341–352.

Robins, C. J., & Hayes, A. M. (1993). An appraisal of cognitive therapy. *Journal of Consulting and Clinical Psychology, 61,* 205–214.

Rohsenow, D. J., Monti, P. M., Rubonis, A. V., Sirota, A. D., Niaura, R. S., Colby, S. M., Winschel, S. M., & Abrams, D. B. (1994). Cue reactivity as a predictor of drinking among male alcoholics. *Journal of Consulting and Clinical Psychology, 62,* 620–626.

Rohter, L. (1989, November 7). Isolated desert community lives by Skinner's precepts. *New York Times,* pp. C1, 8.

Rolider, A., Cummings, A., & Van Houten, R. (1991). Side effects of therapeutic punishment on academic performance and eye contact. *Journal of Applied Behavior Analysis, 24,* 763–773.

Rolider, A., & Van Houten, R. (1990). The role of reinforcement in reducing inappropriate behavior: Some myths and misconceptions. In A. C. Repp & N. N. Singh (Eds.), *Perspectives on the use of nonaversive and aversive interventions for persons with developmental disabilities* (pp. 119–128). Sycamore, IL: Sycamore.

Rollins, H. A., McCandless, B. R., Thompson, M., & Brassell, W. R. (1974). Project Success Environment: An extended application of contingency management in inner-city schools. *Journal of Educational Psychology, 66,* 167–178.

Romeo, F. F. (1998). The negative effects of using a group contingency system of classroom management. *Journal of Instructional Psychology, 25,* 130–133.

Ronen, T. (1991). Intervention package for treating sleep disorders in a four-year-old girl. *Journal of Behavior Therapy and Experimental Psychiatry, 22,* 141–148.

Rosen, G. M., Glasgow, R. E., & Barrera, M. (1977). A two-year follow-up on systematic desensitization with data pertaining to the external validity of laboratory fear assessment. *Journal of Consulting and Clinical Psychology, 45,* 1188–1189.

Rosen, H. S., & Rosen, L. A. (1983). Eliminating stealing: Use of stimulus control with an elementary student. *Behavior Modification, 7,* 56–63.

Rosenhan, D. L., & Seligman, M. E. P. (1984). *Abnormal psychology*. New York: Norton.

Roth, D., Bielski, R., Jones, M., Parker, W., & Osborn, G. (1982). A comparison of self-control therapy and combined self-control therapy and antidepressant medication in the treatment of depression. *Behavior Therapy, 13*, 133–144.

Rusch, F. R., & Kazdin, A. E. (1981). Toward a methodology of withdrawal designs for the assessment of response maintenance. *Journal of Applied Behavior Analysis, 14*, 131–140.

Rushall, B. S. (1993). The restoration of performance capacity by cognitive restructuring and covert positive reinforcement in an elite athlete. In J. R. Cautela & A. J. Kearney (Eds.), *Covert conditioning handbook* (pp. 47–57). Pacific Grove, CA: Brooks/Cole.

Rutter, M. (1975). *Helping troubled children*. New York: Plenum.

Safer, D. J., Heaton, R. C., & Parker, F. C. (1981). A behavioral program for disruptive junior high school students: Results and follow-up. *Journal of Abnormal Child Psychology, 9*, 483–494.

Saigh, P. A. (1986). *In vitro* flooding in the treatment of a 6-year-old boy's posttraumatic stress disorder. *Behaviour Research and Therapy, 6*, 685–688.

Sajwaj, T., Libet, J., & Agras, S. (1974). Lemon-juice therapy: The control of life-threatening rumination in a six-month old infant. *Journal of Applied Behavior Analysis, 7*, 557–563.

Sajwaj, T., Twardosz, S., & Burke, M. (1972). Side effects of extinction procedures in a remedial preschool. *Journal of Applied Behavior Analysis, 5*, 163–175.

Sanders, M. R., & Glynn, T. (1977). Functional analysis of a program for training high and low preference peers to modify disruptive classroom behavior. *Journal of Applied Behavior Analysis, 10*, 503.

Sanders, M. R., & Glynn, T. (1981). Training parents in behavioral self-management: An analysis of generalization and maintenance. *Journal of Applied Behavior Analysis, 14*, 223–227.

Santogrossi, D. A., O'Leary, K. D., Romanczyk, R. G., & Kaufman, K. F. (1973). Self-evaluation by adolescents in a psychiatric hospital school token program. *Journal of Applied Behavior Analysis, 6*, 277–287.

Sarafino, E. P. (1977). LotPACA: A lottery procedure for administering competitive awards. *Journal of Behavior Therapy and Experimental Psychiatry, 8*, 449–450.

Sarafino, E. P. (1984). Rewards and intrinsic interest. In R. J. Corsini (Ed.), *Encyclopedia of psychology* (Vol. 3, pp. 238–239). New York: Wiley.

Sarafino, E. P. (1985). Peer-peer interaction among infants and toddlers with extensive daycare experience. *Journal of Applied Developmental Psychology, 6*, 17–29.

Sarafino, E. P. (1986). *The fears of childhood: A guide to recognizing and reducing fearful states in children*. New York: Human Sciences Press.

Sarafino, E. P. (1995). *The Preferred Items and Experiences Questionnaire (PIEQ) for Adolescents and Adults*. Unpublished manuscript.

Sarafino, E. P. (1997). *Behavioral treatments for asthma: Biofeedback-, respondent-, and relaxation-based approaches*. Lewiston, NY: Edwin Mellen Press.

Sarafino, E. P. (1998). *Health psychology: Biopsychosocial interactions* (3rd ed.). New York: Wiley.

Sarafino, E. P., & Armstrong, J. W. (1986). *Child and adolescent development* (2nd ed.). St. Paul, MN: West.

Sarafino, E. P., & Goehring, P. (2000). Age comparisons in acquiring biofeedback control and success in reducing headache pain. *Annals of Behavioral Medicine, 22*, 10–16.

Sasso, G. M., Reimers, T. M., Cooper, L. J., Wacker, D., Berg, W., Steege, M., Kelly, L., & Allaire, A. (1992). Use of descriptive and experimental analyses to identify the functional properties of aberrant behavior in school settings. *Journal of Applied Behavior Analysis, 25*, 809–821.

Satterfield, J. H., Satterfield, B. T., & Cantwell, D. P. (1981). Three-year multimodality treatment study of 100 hyperactive boys. *Journal of Pediatrics, 98*, 650–655.

Scarr, S., & Kidd, K. K. (1983). Developmental behavior genetics. In P. H. Mussen (Ed.), *Handbook of child psychology* (4th ed., Vol. 2, pp. 345–434). New York: Wiley.

Schacter, D. L. (1992). Understanding implicit memory: A cognitive neuroscience approach. *American Psychologist, 47*, 559–569.

Schepis, M. M., Reid, D. H., & Fitzgerald, J. R. (1987). Group instruction with profoundly retarded persons: Acquisition, generalization, and maintenance of a remunerative work skill. *Journal of Applied Behavior Analysis, 20*, 97–105.

Schnelle, J. F. (1974). A brief report on invalidity of parent evaluations of behavior change. *Journal of Applied Behavior Analysis, 7*, 341–343.

Schreibman, L., Charlop, M. H., & Kurtz, P. F. (1992). Behavioral treatment for children with autism. In S. M. Turner, K. S. Calhoun, & H. E. Adams (Eds.), *Handbook of clinical behavior therapy* (2nd ed., pp. 337–351). New York: Wiley.

Schroeder, S. R. (1972). Parametric effects of reinforcement frequency, amount of reinforcement, and required response force on sheltered workshop behavior. *Journal of Applied Behavior Analysis, 5*, 431–441.

Schultz, D. D. (1965). *Sensory restriction: Effects on behavior*. New York: Academic Press.

Schultz, J. H. (1957). Autogenous training. In J. H. Masserman & J. L. Moreno (Eds.), *Progress in psychotherapy* (Vol. 2, pp. 173–176). New York: Grune & Stratton.

Schultz, J. H., & Luthe, W. (1969). *Autogenic therapy: 1. Autogenic methods*. New York: Grune & Stratton.

Schwartz, I. S., & Baer, D. M. (1991). Social validity assessments: Is current practice state of the art? *Journal of Applied Behavior Analysis, 24*, 189–204.

Scott, D., Scott, L. M., & Howe, B. L. (1998). Training anticipation for intermediate tennis players. *Behavior Modification, 22*, 243–261.

Scott, R. W., Peters, R. D., Gillespie, W. J., Blanchard, E. B., Edmunson, E. D., & Young, L. D. (1973). The use of shaping and reinforcement in the operant acceleration and deceleration of heart rate. *Behaviour Research and Therapy, 11*, 179–185.

Scruggs, T. E., & Mastropieri, M. A. (1998). Summarizing single-subject research: Issues and applications. *Behavior Modification, 22*, 221–242.

Seaman, J. E., Greene, B. F., & Watson-Perczel, M. (1986). A behavioral system for assessing and training cardiopulmonary resuscitation skills among emergency medical technicians. *Journal of Applied Behavior Analysis, 19*, 125–135.

Seaver, W. B., & Patterson, A. H. (1976). Decreasing fuel-oil consumption through feedback and social commendation. *Journal of Applied Behavior Analysis, 9*, 147–152.

Seligman, M. E. P. (1971). Phobias and preparedness. *Behavior Therapy, 2*, 307–320.

Seligman, M. E. P., & Johnston, J. C. (1973). A cognitive theory of avoidance learning. In F. J. McGuigan & D. B. Lumsden (Eds.), *Contemporary approaches to conditioning and learning* (pp. 69–110). Washington, DC: Winston.

Seligmann, J., Namuth, T., & Miller, M. (1994, May 23). Drowning on dry land. *Newsweek*, pp. 64–66.

Serna, L. A., Schumacker, J. B., Sherman, J. A., & Sheldon, J. B. (1991). In-home generalization of social interactions in families of adolescents with behavior problems. *Journal of Applied Behavior Analysis, 24*, 733–746.

Shaffer, D., Vieland, V., Garland, A., Rojas, M., Underwood, M., & Busner, C. (1990). Adolescent suicide attempters: Response to suicide-prevention programs. *Journal of the American Medical Association, 264*, 3151–3155.

Shaw, R. A. (1987). Reinforcement schedules. In R. J. Corsini (Ed.), *Concise encyclopedia of psychology* (p. 968). New York: Wiley.

Sheffield, F. D., Roby, T. B., & Campbell, B. A. (1954). Drive reduction versus consummatory behavior as determinants of reinforcement. *Journal of Comparative and Physiological Psychology, 47*, 349–354.

Sheffield, F. D., Wulff, J. J., & Backer, R. (1951). Reward value of copulation without sex drive reduction. *Journal of Comparative and Physiological Psychology, 44*, 3–8.

Sherman, A. R. (1972). Real-life exposure as a primary therapeutic factor in the desensitization treatment of fear. *Journal of Abnormal Psychology, 79*, 19–28.

Shiffman, S. (1984). Coping with temptations to smoke. *Journal of Consulting and Clinical Psychology, 52*, 261–267.

Shiffman, S. (1986). A cluster-analytic classification of smoking relapse episodes. *Addictive Behaviors, 11*, 295–307.

Shipley, R. H., & Boudewyns, P. A. (1980). Flooding and implosive therapy: Are they harmful? *Behavior Therapy, 11*, 503–508.

Shipley, R.. H., Butt, J. H., Horwitz, B., & Farbry, J. E. (1978). Preparation for a stressful medical procedure: Effect of amount of stimulus preexposure and coping style. *Journal of Consulting and Clinical Psychology, 46*, 499–507.

Sidman, M., & Tailby, W. (1982). Conditional discrimination vs. matching to sample: An expansion of the testing paradigm. *Journal of the Experimental Analysis of Behavior, 37*, 5–22.

Siegel, L. J., & Peterson, L. (1980). Stress reduction in young dental patients through coping skills and sensory information. *Journal of Consulting and Clinical Psychology, 48*, 785–787.

Siegel, P. S., & Foshee, J. G. (1953). The law of primary reinforcement in children. *Journal of Experimental Psychology, 45*, 12–14.

Siegel, S., Hinson, R. E., Krank, M. D., & McCully, J. (1982). Heroin "overdose" death: The contribution of drug-associated environmental cues. *Science, 216*, 436–437.

Simons, A. D., Murphy, G. E., Levine, J. L., & Wetzel, R. D. (1986). Cognitive therapy and pharmacotherapy for depression: Sustained improvement over one year. *Archives of General Psychiatry, 43*, 43–48.

Singh, N. N., Lloyd, J. W., & Kendall, K. A. (1990). Nonaversive and aversive interventions: Issues. In A. C. Repp & N. N. Singh (Eds.), *Perspectives on the use of nonaversive and aversive interventions for persons with developmental disabilities* (pp. 3–16). Sycamore, IL: Sycamore.

Singh, N. N., Watson, J. E., & Winton, A. S. W. (1986). Treating self-injury: Water mist spray versus facial screening or forced arm exercise. *Journal of Applied Behavior Analysis, 19*, 403–410.

Sisson, R. W., & Azrin, N. H. (1989). The community reinforcement approach. In R. K. Hester & W. R. Miller (Eds.), *Handbook of alcoholism treatment approaches: Effective alternatives* (pp. 242–259). New York: Pergamon.

Sitharthan, T., Sitharthan, G., Hough, M. J., & Kavanagh, D. J. (1997). Cue exposure in moderation drinking: A comparison with cognitive-behavior therapy. *Journal of Consulting and Clinical Psychology, 65*, 878–882.

Skinner, B. F. (1938). *The behavior of organisms*. New York: Appleton-Century-Crofts.

Skinner, B. F. (1948). *Walden Two*. New York: Macmillan.

Skinner, B. F. (1953). *Science and human behavior*. New York: Macmillan.

Skinner, B. F. (1954). The science of learning and the art of teaching. *Harvard Educational Review, 24*, 86–97.

Skinner, B. F. (1969). *Contingencies of reinforcement: A theoretical analysis.* New York: Appleton-Century Crofts.

Smith, B. M., Schumaker, J. B., Schaeffer, J., & Sherman, J. A. (1982). Increasing participation and improving the quality of discussions in seventh-grade social studies classes. *Journal of Applied Behavior Analysis, 15,* 97–110.

Smith, J. E., Meyers, R. J., & Delaney, H. D. (1998). The community reinforcement approach with homeless alcohol-dependent individuals. *Journal of Consulting and Clinical Psychology, 66,* 541–548.

Smith, L. K. C., & Fowler, S. A. (1984). Positive peer pressure: The effects of peer monitoring on children's disruptive behavior. *Journal of Applied Behavior Analysis, 17,* 213–227.

Smith, M. L., & Glass, G. V. (1977). Meta-analysis of psychotherapy outcome studies. *American Psychologist, 32,* 752–760.

Smith, R. E. (1973). The use of humor in the counterconditioning of anger responses: A case study. *Behavior Therapy, 4,* 576–580.

Smith, T. (1990). When and when not to consider the use of aversive interventions in the behavioral treatment of autistic children. In A. C. Repp & N. N. Singh (Eds.), *Perspectives on the use of nonaversive and aversive interventions for persons with developmental disabilities* (pp. 287–297). Sycamore, IL: Sycamore.

Sobell, L. C., Toneatto, A., & Sobell, M. B. (1990). Behavior therapy. In A. S. Bellack & M. Hersen (Eds.), *Handbook of comparative treatments for adult disorders* (pp. 479–505). New York: Wiley.

Solé-Leris, A. (1986). *Tranquility and insight.* Boston: Shambhala.

Solnick, J. V., Rincover, A., & Peterson, C. R. (1977). Some determinants of the reinforcing and punishing effects of timeout. *Journal of Applied Behavior Analysis, 10,* 415–424.

Solomon, R. L., Kamin, L. J., & Wynne, L. C. (1953). Traumatic avoidance learning: The outcomes of several extinction procedures with dogs. *Journal of Abnormal and Social Psychology, 48,* 291–302.

Speer, D. C. (1992). Clinically significant change: Jacobson and Truax (1991) revisited. *Journal of Consulting and Clinical Psychology, 60,* 402–408.

Spiegel, T. A., Wadden, T. A., & Foster, G. D. (1991). Objective measurement of eating rate during behavioral treatment of obesity. *Behavior Therapy, 22,* 61–67.

Spivack, G., & Shure, M. B. (1974). *Social adjustment of young children: A cognitive approach to solving real-life problems.* San Francisco: Jossey-Bass.

Spivack, G., & Shure, M. B. (1982). The cognition of social adjustment: Interpersonal cognitive problem-solving thinking. In B. B. Lahey & A. E. Kazdin (Eds.), *Advances in clinical child psychology* (Vol. 5, pp. 323–372). New York: Plenum.

Spooner, F. (1984). Comparisons of backward chaining and total task presentation in training severely handicapped persons. *Education and Training of the Mentally Retarded, 19,* 15–22.

Squire, L. R. (1987). *Memory and the brain.* New York: Oxford University Press.

Stainback, W. C., Payne, J. S., Stainback, S. B., & Payne, R. A. (1973). *Establishing a token economy in the classroom.* Columbus, OH: Charles E. Merrill.

Stampfl, T. G., & Levis, D. J. (1967). Essentials of implosive therapy: A learning-theory-based psychodynamic behavioral therapy. *Journal of Abnormal Psychology, 72,* 496–503.

Stanley, M. A. (1992). Obsessive-compulsive disorder. In S. M. Turner, K. S. Calhoun, & H. E. Adams (Eds.), *Handbook of clinical behavior therapy* (2nd ed., pp. 67–86). New York: Wiley.

Stark, L. J., Collins, F. L., Osnes, P. G., & Stokes, T. F. (1986). Using reinforcement and cueing to increase healthy snack food choices in preschoolers. *Journal of Applied Behavior Analysis, 19,* 367–379.

Stasiewicz, P. R., & Maisto, S. A. (1993). Two-factor avoidance theory: The role of negative affect in the maintenance of substance use and substance use disorder. *Behavior Therapy, 24,* 337–356.

Steege, M. W., Wacker, D. P., Cigrand, K. C., Berg, W. K., Novak, C. G., Reimers, T. M., Sasso, G. M., & DeRaad, A. (1990). Use of negative reinforcement in the treatment of self-injurious behavior. *Journal of Applied Behavior Analysis, 23,* 459–467.

Stein, D. J., & Young, J. E. (Eds.). (1992). *Cognitive science and clinical disorders.* San Diego: Academic Press.

Stephens, C. E., Pear, J. J., Wray, L. D., & Jackson, G. C. (1975). Some effects of reinforcement schedules in teaching picture names to retarded children. *Journal of Applied Behavior Analysis, 8,* 435–447.

Sterman, M. B. (1986). Epilepsy and its treatment with EEG feedback therapy. *Annals of Behavioral Medicine, 8*(1), 21–25.

Stern, R. M., & Ray, W. J. (1980). *Biofeedback: Potential and limits.* Lincoln: University of Nebraska Press.

Stern, R. S., Lipsedge, M. S., & Marks, I. M. (1973). Obsessive ruminations: A controlled trial of thought-stopping techniques. *Behaviour Research and Therapy, 11,* 659–662.

Stokes, T. F., & Baer, D. M. (1976). Preschool peers as mutual generalization-facilitating agents. *Behavior Therapy, 7,* 549–556.

Stokes, T. F., & Baer, D. M. (1977). An implicit technology of generalization. *Journal of Applied Behavior Analysis, 10,* 349–367.

Stokes, T. F., Baer, D. M., & Jackson, R. L. (1974). Programming the generalization of a greeting response in four retarded children. *Journal of Applied Behavior Analysis, 7,* 599–610.

Stokes, T. F., & Osnes, P. G. (1988). The developing applied technology of generalization and maintenance. In R. H. Horner, G. Dunlap, & R. L. Koegel (Eds.), *Generalization and maintenance: Life-style changes in applied settings* (pp. 5–20). Baltimore: Paul H. Brookes.

Stokes, T. F., & Osnes, P. G. (1989). An operant pursuit of generalization. *Behavior Therapy, 20,* 337–355.

Stolz, S. B., & Associates (1978). *Ethical issues in behavior modification.* San Francisco: Jossey-Bass.

Storms, M. D. (1983). *Development of sexual orientation.* Washington, DC: American Psychological Association.

Strain, P. S., Shores, R. E., & Kerr, M. M. (1976). An experimental analysis of "spillover" effects on the social interaction of behaviorally handicapped preschool children. *Journal of Applied Behavior Analysis, 9,* 31–40.

Strain, P. S., Shores, R. E., & Timm, M. A. (1977). Effects of peer social initiations on the behavior of withdrawn preschool children. *Journal of Applied Behavior Analysis, 10,* 289–298.

Stuart, R. B. (1971). Behavioral contracting within the families of delinquents. *Journal of Behavior Therapy and Experimental Psychiatry, 2,* 1–11.

Sturges, J. W., & Sturges, L. V. (1998). *In vivo* systematic desensitization in a single-session treatment of an 11-year-old girl's elevator phobia. *Child and Family Behavior Therapy, 20,* 55–62.

Sullivan, M. A., & O'Leary, S. G. (1990). Maintenance following reward and cost token programs. *Behavior Therapy, 21,* 139–149.

Suls, J., Sanders, G. S., & Labrecque, M. S. (1986). Attempting to control blood pressure without systematic instruction: When advice is counterproductive. *Journal of Behavioral Medicine, 9,* 567–576.

Sulzer, B., & Mayer, G. R. (1972). *Behavior modification procedures for school personnel.* Hinsdale, IL: Dryden.

Surwit, R. S., & Keefe, F. J. (1978). Frontalis EMG feedback training: An electronic panacea? *Behavior Therapy, 9,* 779–792.

Swain, J. C., & McLaughlin, T. F. (1998). The effects of bonus contingencies in a classwide token program on math accuracy with middle-school students with behavioral disorders. *Behavioral Interventions, 13,* 11–19.

Swain, J. J., Allard, G. B., & Holborn, S. W. (1982). The Good Toothbrushing Game: A school-based dental hygiene program for increasing the toothbrushing effectiveness of children. *Journal of Applied Behavior Analysis, 15,* 171–176.

Swan, G. E., & MacDonald, M. L. (1978). Behavior therapy in practice: A national survey of behavior therapists. *Behavior Therapy, 9,* 799–807.

Sweet, A. A., & Loizeaux, A. L. (1991). Behavioral and cognitive treatment methods: A critical comparative review. *Journal of Behavior Therapy and Experimental Psychiatry, 22,* 159–185.

Swizer, E. B., Deal, T. E., & Bailey, J. S. (1977). The reduction of stealing in second graders using a group contingency. *Journal of Applied Behavior Analysis, 10,* 267–272.

Tasto, D. L. (1969). Systematic desensitization, muscle relaxation and visual imagery in the counterconditioning of four-year-old phobic child. *Behaviour Research and Therapy, 7,* 409–411.

Taylor, C. B. (1978). Relaxation training and related techniques. In W. S. Agras (Ed.), *Behavior modification: Principles and clinical applications* (2nd ed., pp. 134–162). Boston: Little, Brown.

Taylor, C. B., Agras, W. S., Schneider, J. A., & Allen, R. A. (1983). Adherence to instructions to practice relaxation exercises. *Journal of Consulting and Clinical Psychology, 51,* 952–953.

Taylor, K. L., Bovbjerg, D. H., Jacobsen, P. B., Redd, W. H., & Manne, S. L. (1992, March). *An experimental model of classically conditioned nausea during cancer chemotherapy.* Paper presented at the meeting of the Society of Behavioral Medicine, New York.

Taylor, S. (1996). Meta-analysis of cognitive-behavioral treatments for social phobia. *Journal of Behavior Therapy and Experimental Psychiatry, 27,* 1–9.

Taylor, S. E. (1983). Adjustment to threatening events: A theory of cognitive adaptation. *American Psychologist, 38,* 1161–1173.

TFPDPP (Task Force on Promotion and Dissemination of Psychological Procedures). (1993). *A report to the Division 12 Board, October 1993.* Washington, DC: American Psychological Association Division of Clinical Psychology.

Thase, M. E., & Wright, J. H. (1991). Cognitive behavior therapy manual for depressed inpatients: A treatment protocol outline. *Behavior Therapy, 22,* 579–595.

Thera, P. (1979). *Buddhist meditation: The way to inner calm and clarity.* Kandy, Sri Lanka: Buddhist Publication Society.

Thomas, J. D., Presland, I. E., Grant, M. D., & Glynn, T. L. (1978). Natural rates of teacher approval and disapproval in grade-7 classrooms. *Journal of Applied Behavior Analysis, 11,* 91–94.

Thorndike, E. L. (1898). Animal intelligence: An experimental study of the associative processes in animals. *Psychological Review Monograph Supplements, 2,* No. 8.

Thorndike, E. L. (1931). *Human learning.* New York: Century.

Tierney, K. J., & Bracken, M. (1998). Stimulus equivalence and behavior therapy. In W. O'Donohue (Ed.), *Learning and behavior therapy* (pp. 392–402). Boston: Allyn & Bacon.

Tiffany, S. T., Martin, E. M., & Baker, T. B. (1986). Treatments for cigarette smoking: An evaluation of the contributions of aversion and counseling procedures. *Behaviour Research and Therapy, 24*, 437–452.

Timberlake, W., & Allison, J. (1974). Response deprivation: An empirical approach to instrumental performance. *Psychological Review, 81*, 146–164.

Todd, J. T., Morris, E. K., & Fenza, K. M. (1989). Temporal organization of extinction-induced responding in preschool children. *Psychological Record, 39*, 117–130.

Torgersen, S. (1983). Genetic factors in anxiety disorders. *Archives of General Psychiatry, 40*, 1085–1089.

Touchette, P. E., & Howard, J. S. (1984). Errorless learning: Reinforcement contingencies and stimulus control transfer in delayed prompting. *Journal of Applied Behavior Analysis, 17*, 175–188.

Tough, P. (1993, November 7). Into the pit. *New York Times Magazine*, pp. 52–54.

Trollope, A. (1946). *An autobiography*. London: Williams & Norgate.

Truchlicka, M., McLaughlin, T. F., & Swain, J. C. (1998). Effects of token reinforcement and response cost on the accuracy of spelling performance with middle-school special education students with behavior disorders. *Behavioral Interventions, 13*, 1–10.

Trull, T. J., Nietzel, M. T., & Main, A. (1988). The use of meta-analysis to assess the clinical significance of behavior therapy for agoraphobia. *Behavior Therapy, 19*, 527–538.

Tryon, G. S. (1979). A review and critique of thought stopping research. *Journal of Behavior Therapy and Experimental Psychiatry, 10*, 189–192.

Tucker, J. A., Vuchinich, R. E., & Downey, K. K. (1992). Substance abuse. In S. M. Turner, K. S. Calhoun, & H. E. Adams (Eds.), *Handbook of clinical behavior therapy* (2nd ed., pp. 203–223). New York: Wiley.

Turkat, I. D. (1986). The behavioral interview. In A. R. Ciminero, K. S. Calhoun, & H. E. Adams (Eds.), *Handbook of behavioral assessment* (2nd ed., pp. 109–149). New York: Wiley.

Turner, S. M., Beidel, D. C., & Jacob, R. G. (1994). Social phobia: A comparison of behavior therapy and atenolol. *Journal of Consulting and Clinical Psychology, 62*, 350–358.

Turner, S. M., Beidel. D. C., Long, P. J., & Greenhouse, J. (1992). Reduction of fear in social phobics: An examination of extinction patterns. *Behavior Therapy, 23*, 389–403.

Upper, D. (1973). A "ticket" system for reducing ward rules violations on a token economy program. *Journal of Behavior Therapy and Experimental Psychiatry, 4*, 137–140.

Upper, D. (1993). The use of covert reinforcement and thought stopping in treating a young woman's sexual anxiety. In J. R. Cautela & A. J. Kearney (Eds.), *Covert conditioning handbook* (pp. 235–244). Pacific Grove, CA: Brooks/Cole.

Van Houten, R. (1983). Punishment: From the animal laboratory to the applied setting. In S. Axelrod & J. Apsche (Eds.), *The effects of punishment on human behavior* (pp. 13–44). New York: Academic Press.

Van Houten, R., Nau, P. A., MacKenzie-Keating, S. E., Sameoto, D., & Colavecchia, B. (1982). An analysis of some variables influencing the effectiveness of reprimands. *Journal of Applied Behavior Analysis, 15*, 65–83.

Van Houten, R., Nau, P., & Marini, Z. (1980). An analysis of public posting in reducing speeding behavior on an urban highway. *Journal of Applied Behavior Analysis, 13*, 383–395.

Vargas, J. M., & Adesso, V. J. (1976). A comparison of aversion therapies for nailbiting behavior. *Behavior Therapy, 7*, 322–329.

Venn, J. R., & Short, J. G. (1973). Vicarious classical conditioning of emotional responses in nursery school children. *Journal of Personality and Social Psychology, 28*, 249–255.

Ventis, W. L. (1973). Case history: The use of laughter as an alternative response in systematic desensitization. *Behavior Therapy, 4*, 120–122.

Vygotsky, L. (1962). *Thought and language*. Cambridge, MA: MIT Press.

Wacker, D., Steege, M., Northup, J., Reimers, T., Berg, W., & Sasso, G. (1990). Use of functional analysis and acceptability measures to assess and treat severe behavior problems: An outpatient clinic model. In A. C. Repp & N. N. Singh (Eds.), *Perspectives on the use of nonaversive and aversive interventions for persons with developmental disabilities* (pp. 349–360). Sycamore, IL: Sycamore.

Wahler, R. G. (1975). Some structural aspects of deviant child behavior. *Journal of Applied Behavior Analysis, 8*, 27–42.

Wahler, R. G., & Dumas, J. E. (1984). Changing the observational coding styles of insular and noninsular mothers: A step toward maintenance of parent training effects. In R. F. Dangel & R. A. Polster (Eds.), *Parent training: Foundations of research and practice* (pp. 379–416). New York: Guilford.

Wahler, R. G., & Fox, J. J. (1980). Solitary toy play and time out: A family treatment package for children with aggressive and oppositional behavior. *Journal of Applied Behavior Analysis, 13*, 23–39.

Wahler, R. G., & Fox, J. J. (1981). Setting events in applied behavior analysis: Toward a conceptual and methodological expansion. *Journal of Applied Behavior Analysis, 14*, 327–338.

Wahler, R. G., Winkel, G. H., Peterson, R. F., & Morrison, D. C. (1965). Mothers as behavior therapists for their own children. *Behaviour Research and Therapy, 3*, 113–124.

Walker, H. M., & Buckley, N. K. (1972). Programming generalization and maintenance of treatment effects across time and across settings. *Journal of Applied Behavior Analysis, 5,* 209–224.

Walker, H. M., Hops, H., & Johnson, S. M. (1975). Generalization and maintenance of classroom treatment effects. *Behavior Therapy, 6,* 188–200.

Wallace, I., & Pear, J. J. (1977). Self-control techniques of famous novelists. *Journal of Applied Behavior Analysis, 10,* 515–525.

Wallin, J. A., & Johnson, R. D. (1976, August). The positive reinforcement approach to controlling employee absenteeism. *Personnel Journal,* pp. 390–392.

Walters, G. C., & Grusec, J. E. (1977). *Punishment.* San Francisco: W. H. Freeman.

Ward, W. D., & Stare, S. W. (1990). The role of subject verbalization in generalized correspondence. *Journal of Applied Behavior Analysis, 23,* 129–136.

Wasik, B. H. (1970). The application of Premack's generalization on reinforcement to the management of classroom behavior. *Journal of Experimental Child Psychology, 10,* 33–43.

Watson, J. B. (1913). Psychology as the behaviorist views it. *Psychological Review, 20,* 158–177.

Watson, J. B. (1930). *Behaviorism.* New York: Norton.

Watson, J. B., & Rayner, R. (1920). Conditioned emotional reactions. *Journal of Experimental Psychology, 3,* 1–14.

Watson, T. S., & Sterling, H. E. (1998). Brief functional analysis and treatment of a vocal tic. *Journal of Applied Behavioral Analysis, 31,* 471–474.

Webster-Stratton, C. (1982a). The long-term effects of a videotape modeling parent-training program: Comparison of immediate and 1-year follow-up results. *Behavior Therapy, 13,* 702–714.

Webster-Stratton, C. (1982b). Teaching mothers through videotape modeling to change their children's behavior. *Journal of Pediatric Psychology, 7,* 279–294.

Weems, C. F. (1998). The evaluation of heart rate biofeedback using a multi-element design. *Journal of Behavior Therapy and Experimental Psychiatry, 29,* 157–162.

Weiner, H. (1970). Instructional control of human operant responding during extinction following fixed-ratio conditioning. *Journal of the Experimental Analysis of Behavior, 13,* 391–394.

Weiss, R. F., Cecil, J. S., & Frank, M. J. (1973). Steep delay of reinforcement gradient in escape conditioning with altruistic reinforcement. *Bulletin of the Psychonomic Society, 2,* 372–374.

Welch, M. W., & Gist, J. W. (1974). *The open token economy system: A handbook for a behavioral approach to rehabilitation.* Springfield, IL: Charles C. Thomas.

Weld, E. M., & Evans, I. M. (1990). Effects of part versus whole instructional strategies on skill acquisition and excess behavior. *American Journal of Mental Retardation, 94,* 377–386.

Whelan, J. P., Mahoney, M. J., & Meyers, A. W. (1991). Performance enhancement in sport: A cognitive behavioral domain. *Behavior Therapy, 22,* 307–327.

Whitaker, S. (1996). A review of DRO: The influence of the degree of intellectual disability and the frequency of the target behavior. *Journal of Applied Research in Intellectual Disabilities, 9,* 61–79.

White, G. D., Nielsen, G., & Johnson, S. M. (1972). Timeout duration and the suppression of deviant behavior in children. *Journal of Applied Behavior Analysis, 5,* 111–120.

White, L., & Tursky, B. (1982). Stress and anxiety. In L. White & B. Tursky (Eds.), *Clinical biofeedback: Efficacy and mechanisms* (pp. 335–337). New York: Guilford.

White, M. A. (1975). Natural rates of teacher approval and disapproval in the classroom. *Journal of Applied Behavior Analysis, 8,* 367–372.

White, N. M., & Milner, P. M. (1992). The psychobiology of reinforcers. In M. R. Rosenzweig & L. W. Porter (Eds.), *Annual review of psychology* (Vol. 43, pp. 443–471). Palo Alto, CA: Annual Reviews.

Whitman, T. L., Mercurio, J. R., & Caponigri, V. (1970). Development of social responses in two severely retarded children. *Journal of Applied Behavior Analysis, 3,* 133–138.

Wiens, A. N., & Menustik, C. E. (1983). Treatment outcome and patient characteristics in an aversion therapy program for alcoholism. *American Psychologist, 38,* 1089–1096.

Wilcoxin, H. C., Dragoin, W. B., & Kral, P. A. (1971). Illness-induced aversions in rat and quail: Relative salience of visual and gustatory cues. *Science, 171,* 826–828.

Williams, C. D. (1959). The elimination of tantrum behavior by extinction procedures. *Journal of Abnormal and Social Psychology, 59,* 269.

Williams, C. J. (1990). *Cancer biology and management: An introduction.* New York: Wiley.

Williams, J. M. G., Watts, F. N., MacLeod, C., & Mathews, A. (1988). *Cognitive psychology and emotional disorders.* New York: Wiley.

Williamson, D. A., Williamson, S. H., Watkins, P. C., & Hughes. H. H. (1992). Increasing cooperation among children using dependent group-oriented reinforcement contingencies. *Behavior Modification, 16,* 414–425.

Wilson, C. C., Robertson, S. J., Herlong, L. H., & Haynes, S. N. (1979). Vicarious effects of time-out in the modification of aggression in the classroom. *Behavior Modification, 3,* 97–111.

Wilson, G. T. (1982). Adult disorders. In G. T. Wilson & C. M. Franks (Eds.), *Contemporary behavior therapy: Conceptual and empirical foundations* (pp. 505–562). New York: Guilford.

Wilson, G. T. (1990). Clinical issues and strategies in the practice of behavior therapy. In C. M. Franks, G. T. Wilson,

P. C. Kendall, & J. P. Foreyt (Eds.), *Review of behavior therapy: Theory and practice* (Vol. 2, pp. 271–301). New York: Guilford.

Wilson, G. T. (1991). Chemical aversion conditioning in the treatment of alcoholism: Further comments. *Behaviour Research and Therapy, 29*, 415–419.

Wilson, G. T., & Fairburn, C. G. (1993). Cognitive treatments for eating disorders. *Journal of Consulting and Clinical Psychology, 61*, 261–269.

Wilson, G. T., Leaf, R. C., & Nathan, P. E. (1975). The aversive control of excessive alcohol consumption by chronic alcoholics in the laboratory setting. *Journal of Applied Behavior Analysis, 8*, 13–26.

Wilson, G. T., & Tracey, D. A. (1976). An experimental analysis of aversive imagery versus electrical aversive conditioning in the treatment of chronic alcoholics. *Behaviour Research and Therapy, 14*, 41–51.

Wilson, K. G., Hayes, S. C., & Gifford, E. V. (1997). Cognition in behavior therapy: Agreements and differences. *Journal of Behavior Therapy and Experimental Psychiatry*, 53–63.

Wilson, W. H., & Simpson, G. M. (1990). Pharmacotherapy. In A. S. Bellack & M. Hersen (Eds.), *Handbook of comparative treatments for adult disorders* (pp. 34–47). New York: Wiley.

Wincze, J. P. (1977). Sexual deviance and dysfunction. In D. C. Rimm & J. W. Somervill (Eds.), *Abnormal psychology* (pp. 343–379). New York: Academic Press.

Winkler, R. C. (1977). What types of sex-role behavior should behavior modifiers promote? *Journal of Applied Behavior Analysis, 10*, 549–552.

Witryol, S. L. (1971). Incentives and learning in children. In H. W. Reese (Ed.), *Advances in child development and behavior* (Vol. 6, pp. 2–61). New York: Academic Press.

Wixted, J. T., Bellack, A. S., & Hersen, M. (1990). Behavior therapy. In A. S. Bellack & M. Hersen (Eds.), *Handbook of comparative treatments for adult disorders* (pp. 17–33). New York: Wiley.

Wolf, M. M. (1978). Social validity: The case for subjective measurement *or* how applied behavior analysis is finding its heart. *Journal of Applied Behavior Analysis, 11*, 203–214.

Wolf, M. M., Braukmann, C. J., & Ramp, K. A. (1987). Serious delinquent behavior as part of a significantly handicapping condition: Cures and supportive environments. *Journal of Applied Behavior Analysis, 20*, 347–359.

Wolf, M. M., Hanley, E. L., King, L. A., Lachowicz, J., & Giles, D. K. (1970). The timer-game: A variable interval contingency for the management of out-of-seat behavior. *Exceptional Children, 37*, 113–117.

Wolfe, D. A., Mendes, M. G., & Factor, D. (1984). A parent-administered program to reduce children's television viewing. *Journal of Applied Behavior Analysis, 17*, 267–272.

Wolpe, J. (1958). *Psychotherapy by reciprocal inhibition*. Stanford, CA: Stanford University Press.

Wolpe, J. (1973). *The practice of behavior therapy*. New York: Pergamon.

Wolpe, J. (1981). The dichotomy between directly conditioned and cognitively learned anxiety. *Journal of Behavior Therapy and Experimental Psychiatry, 12*, 35–42.

Wolpe, J. (1993). Commentary: The cognitivist oversell and comments on symposium contributions. *Journal of Behavior Therapy and Experimental Psychiatry, 24*, 141–147.

Wong, S. E., Terranova, M. D., Bowen, L., Zarate, R., Massel, H. K., & Liberman, R. P. (1987). Providing independent recreational activities to reduce stereotypic vocalizations in chronic schizophrenics. *Journal of Applied Behavior Analysis, 20*, 77–81.

Wood, S. J., Murdock, J. Y., Cronin, M. E., Dawson, N. M., & Kirby, P. C. (1998). Effects of self-monitoring on on-task behaviors of at-risk middle school students. *Journal of Behavioral Education, 8*, 263–279.

Woolfolk, A. E., Woolfolk, R. L., & Wilson, G. T. (1977). A rose by any other name . . . : Labeling bias and attitudes toward behavior modification. *Journal of Consulting and Clinical Psychology, 45*, 184–191.

Wysocki, T., Hall, G., Iwata, B., & Riordan, M. (1979). Behavioral management of exercise: Contracting for aerobic points. *Journal of Applied Behavior Analysis, 12*, 55–64.

Yates, B. T. (1994). Toward the incorporation of costs, cost-effectiveness analysis, and cost-benefit analysis into clinical research. *Journal of Consulting and Clinical Psychology, 62*, 729–736.

Yu, D., Martin, G. L., Suthons, E., Koop, S., & Pallotta-Cornick, A. (1980). Comparisons of forward chaining and total task presentation formats to teach vocational skills to the retarded. *International Journal of Rehabilitation Research, 3*, 77–79.

Yu, P., Harris, G. E., Solovitz, B. L., & Franklin, J. L. (1986). A social problem-solving intervention for children at high risk for later psychopathology. *Journal of Clinical Child Psychology, 13*, 30–40.

Zeiss, R. I. (1978). Self-directed treatment for premature ejaculation. *Journal of Consulting and Clinical Psychology, 46*, 1234–1241.

Ziegler, S. G. (1987). Effects of stimulus cueing on the acquisition of groundstrokes by beginning tennis players. *Journal of Applied Behavior Analysis, 20*, 405–411.

Zifferblatt, S. M., Wilbur, C. S., & Pinsky, J. L. (1980). Changing cafeteria eating habits. *Journal of the American Dietetic Association, 76*, 15–20.

Zimmerman, E. H., & Zimmerman, J. (1962). The alteration of behavior in a special classroom situation. *Journal of the Experimental Analysis of Behavior, 5*, 59–60.

Zohn, C. J., & Bornstein, P. H. (1980). Self-monitoring of work performance with mentally retarded adults: Effects upon work productivity, work quality, and on-task behavior. *Mental Retardation, 18*, 19–25.

Credits

Fig. 12.1   From D. K. Fox, B. L. Hopkins and W. K. Anger (1987). "The Long-Term Effects of a Token Economy on Safety Performance in Open-Pit Mining," *Journal of Applied Behavior Analysis*, 20, 215–224. Copyright © 1987 by the Journal of Applied Behavior Analysis. Reprinted by permission of the publisher.

Fig. 14.1   From T. H. Ollendick, L. P. Hagopian and R. M. Huntzinger (1991). "Cognitive-Behavioral Therapy with Nighttime Fearful Children," *Journal of Behavior Therapy and Experimental Psychiatry*, 22, 113–121. Copyright © 1991 Elsevier Science Ltd. Reprinted with permission from Elsevier Science Ltd.

Name Index

463

Subject Index